THE SUPPLEMENT TO
THE ELEVENTH MENTAL
MEASUREMENTS YEARBOOK

EARLIER PUBLICATIONS IN THIS SERIES

THE SUPPLEMENT TO THE ELEVENTH MENTAL MEASUREMENTS YEARBOOK

JANE CLOSE CONOLEY and JAMES C. IMPARA

Editors

LINDA L. MURPHY
Managing Editor

The Buros Institute of Mental Measurements
The University of Nebraska-Lincoln
Lincoln, Nebraska

1994
Distributed by The University of Nebraska Press

LC 39-3422
ISBN 910674-34-5

Manufactured in the United States of America.

The paper used in this publication meets the minimum requirements of American National Standard for Information Sciences—Permanence of Paper for Printed Library Materials, ANSI Z39.48-1984.

Note to Users

TABLE OF CONTENTS

INTRODUCTION

This volume, *The Supplement to the Eleventh Mental Measurements Yearbook* (*11MMY-S*), is third in our *Supplement* series. Feedback from readers suggests the *Supplements* are accomplishing their intended purpose of making evaluative information on key psychological and educational tests available in a timely manner.

The *11MMY-S* contains reviews of tests newly revised since the publication of the *Eleventh Mental Measurements Yearbook* (*11MMY*). These same reviews will also comprise about a third of the *Twelfth MMY* (projected publication in 1995). The *11MMY-S* is a bridge between the *Eleventh* and *Twelfth Yearbooks* and is useful to professionals whose work and scholarship demands rapid access to critical test reviews written by distinguished measurement experts. The increased numbers of new and revised tests being published makes essential our efforts to publish descriptions and reviews in a timely manner.

The Buros Institute of Mental Measurements serves the psychological and educational measurement communities. Our frequent publication schedule is consistent with the proud tradition of our founder, Oscar K. Buros, continuing innovative attempts to improve the quality of testing products made available to consumers.

THE SUPPLEMENT TO THE ELEVENTH MENTAL MEASUREMENTS YEARBOOK

The *11MMY-S* contains reviews of tests that are new or significantly revised since the publication of the *Eleventh MMY* in 1992. We have included reviews of tests that were available before our production deadline of May 1, 1994. These reviews plus reviews of additional new or revised tests since 1992 will appear in the *Twelfth MMY*. Reviews, descriptions, and references associates with older tests can be located in other Buros publications such as previous *MMY*s and *Tests in Print IV*.

The contents of the *11MMY-S* include: (*a*) a bibliography of 101 commercially available tests, new or revised, published as separates for use with English-speaking subjects; (*b*) 197 critical test reviews by well-qualified professional people who were selected by the editors on the basis of their expertise in measurement and, often, the content of the test being reviewed; (*c*) a test title index with appropriate cross references; (*d*) a classified subject index; (*e*) a publishers directory and index, including addresses and test listings by publisher; (*f*) a name index including the names of all authors of tests, reviews, or references; (*g*) an index of acronyms for easy reference when a test acronym, not the full title, is known; and (*h*) a score index to refer readers to tests featuring particular kinds of scores that are of interest to them.

A list of the names and affiliation of all reviewers contributing to the *11MMY-S* is also included. Typically the *Yearbooks* and *Supplements* also include bibliographies of references for specific tests related to the construction, validity, or use of the tests in various settings. This time these references are all included in the recently published *Tests in Print IV*. Reviewer's references are included in the *11MMY-S* as well as cross references to previous reviews and reference lists.

The volume is organized like an encyclopedia, with tests being ordered alphabetically by title. If the title of a test is known, the reader can locate the test immediately without having to consult the Index of Titles.

The page headings reflect the encyclopedic organization. The page heading of the left-hand page cites the number and title of the first test listed on that page, and the page heading of the right-hand page cites the number and title of the last test listed on that page. All numbers presented in the various indexes are test numbers, not page numbers. Page numbers are important only for the Table of Contents and are indicated at the bottom of each page.

INDEXES

As mentioned earlier, the *11MMY-S* includes six indexes invaluable as aids to effective use: (*a*) Index of Titles, (*b*) Index of Acronyms, (*c*) Classified Subject Index, (*d*) Publishers Directory and Index, (*e*) Index of Names, and (*f*) Score Index. Additional comment on these indexes is presented below.

Index of Titles. Because the organization of the *11MMY-S* is encyclopedic in nature, with the tests ordered alphabetically by title throughout the volume, the test title index does not have to be consulted to find a test for which the title is known. However, the title index has some features that make it useful beyond its function as a complete title listing. It includes cross-reference information useful for tests with superseded or alternative titles or tests commonly (and sometimes inaccurately) known by multiple titles. It is important to keep in mind that the numbers in this index, like those for all *TIP* and *MMY* indexes, are test numbers and not page numbers.

Index of Acronyms. Some tests seem to be better known by their acronyms than by their full titles. The Index of Acronyms can help in these instances; it refers the reader to the full title of the test and to the relevant descriptive information and reviews.

Classified Subject Index. The Classified Subject Index classifies all tests listed in the *11MMY-S* into 16 major categories: Achievement, Behavior Assessment, Developmental, Education, English, Fine Arts, Foreign Languages, Intelligence and Scholastic Aptitude, Miscellaneous, Neuropsychological, Personality, Reading, Sensory-Motor, Social Studies, Speech and Hearing, and Vocations. Each test entry includes test title, population for which the test is intended, and test number. The Classified Subject Index is of great help to readers who seek a listing of tests in given subject areas. The Classified Subject Index represents a starting point for readers who know their area of interest but do not know how to

further focus that interest in order to identify the best test(s) for their particular purposes.

Publishers Directory and Index. The Publishers Directory and Index includes the names and addresses of the publishers of all tests included in the *11MMY-S* plus a listing of test numbers for each individual publisher. This index can be particularly useful in obtaining addresses for specimen sets or catalogs after the test reviews have been read and evaluated. It can also be useful when a reader knows the publisher of a certain test but is uncertain about the test title, or when a reader is interested in the range of tests published by a given publisher.

Index of Names. The Index of Names provides a comprehensive list of names, indicating authorship of a test, test review, or reference.

Score Index. The Score Index is an index to all scores generated by the tests in the *11MMY-S*. Test titles are sometimes misleading or ambiguous, and test content may be difficult to define with precision. But test scores represent operational definitions of the variables the test author is trying to measure, and as such they often define test purpose and content more adequately than other descriptive information. A search for a particular test is most often a search for a test that measures some specific variables. Test scores and their associated labels can often be the best definitions of the variables of interest. It is, in fact, a detailed subject index based on the most critical operational features of any test—the scores and their associated labels.

HOW TO USE THIS SUPPLEMENT

A reference work like the *11MMY-S* can be of far greater benefit to a reader if a little time is taken to become familiar with what it has to offer and how one might use it most effectively to obtain the information wanted. The first step in this process is to read the Introduction to the *11MMY-S* in its entirety. The second step is to become familiar with the six indexes and particularly with the instructions preceding each index listing. The third step is to make actual use of the book by looking up needed information. This third step is simple if one keeps in mind the following possibilities:

1. If you know the title of the test, use the alphabetical page headings to go directly to the test entry.

2. If you do not know, cannot find, or are unsure of the title of a test, consult the Index of Titles for possible variants of the title or consult the appropriate subject area of the Classified Subject Index for other possible leads or for similar or related tests in the same area. (Other uses for both of these indexes were described earlier.)

3. If you know the author of a test but not the title or publisher, consult the Index of Names and look up the author's titles until you find the test you want.

4. If you know the test publisher but not the title or author, consult the Publishers Directory and Index and look up the publisher's titles until you find the test you want.

5. If you are looking for a test that yields a particular kind of score, but have no knowledge of which test that might be, look up the score in the Score Index and locate the test or tests that include the score variable of interest.

6. Once you have found the test or tests you are looking for, read the descriptive entries for these tests carefully so that you can take advantage of the information provided. A description of the information provided in these test entries will be presented later in this section.

7. Read the test reviews carefully and analytically, as described earlier in this Introduction. The information and evaluation contained in these reviews are meant to assist test consumers in making well-informed decisions about the choice and applications of tests.

8. Once you have read the descriptive information, you may want to order a specimen set for a particular test so that you can examine it firsthand. The Publishers Directory and Index has the address information needed to obtain specimen sets or catalogs.

Making Effective Use of the Test Entries. The test entries include extensive information. For each test, descriptive information is presented in the following order:

a) TITLES. Test titles are printed in boldface type. Secondary or series titles are set off from main titles by a colon.

b) PURPOSE. For each test we have included a brief, clear statement describing the purpose of the test. Often these statements are quotations from the test manual.

c) POPULATION. This is a description of the groups for which the test is intended. The grade, chronological age, semester range, or employment category is usually given. "Grades 1.5–2.5, 2–3, 4–12, 13–17" means that there are four test booklets: a booklet for the middle of first grade through the middle of the second grade, a booklet for the beginning of the second grade through the end of third grade, a booklet for grades 4 through 12 inclusive, and a booklet for undergraduate and graduate students in colleges and universities.

d) PUBLICATION DATE. The inclusive range of publication dates for the various forms, accessories, and editions of a test is reported.

e) ACRONYM. When a test is often referred to by an acronym, the acronym is given in the test entry immediately following the publication date.

f) SCORES. The number of part scores is presented along with their titles or descriptions of what they are intended to represent or measure.

g) ADMINISTRATION. Individual or group administration is indicated. A test is considered a group test unless it may be administered *only* individually.

h) FORMS, PARTS, AND LEVELS. All available forms, parts, and levels are listed.

i) MANUAL. Notation is made if no manual is available. All other manual information is included under Price Data.

j) RESTRICTED DISTRIBUTION. This is noted only for tests that are put on a special market by the publisher. Educational and psychological restrictions are not noted (unless a special training course is required for use).

k) PRICE DATA. Price information is reported for test packages (usually 20 to 35 tests), answer sheets, all other accessories, and specimen sets. The statement "$17.50 per 35 tests" means that all accessories are included unless otherwise indicated by the reporting of separate prices for accessories. The statement also means 35 tests of one level, one edition, or one part unless stated otherwise. Because test prices can change very quickly, the year that the listed test prices were obtained is also given. Foreign currency is assigned the appropriate symbol. When prices are given in foreign dollars, a qualifying symbol is added (e.g., A$16.50 refers to 16 dollars and 50 cents in Australian currency). Along with cost, the publication date and number of pages on which print occurs is reported for manuals and technical reports (e.g., '85, 102 pages). All types of machine-scorable answer sheets available for use with a specific test are also reported in the descriptive entry. Scoring and reporting services provided by publishers are reported along with information on costs. In a few cases, special computerized scoring and interpretation services are given in separate entries immediately following the test.

l) FOREIGN LANGUAGE AND OTHER SPECIAL EDITIONS. This section concerns foreign language editions published by the same publisher who sells the English edition. It also indicates special editions (e.g., Braille, large type) available from the same or a different publisher.

m) TIME. The number of minutes of actual working time allowed examinees and the approximate length of time needed for administering a test are reported whenever obtainable. The latter figure is always enclosed in parentheses. Thus, "50(60) minutes" indicates that the examinees are allowed 50 minutes of working time and that a total of 60 minutes is needed to administer the test. A time of

"40–50 minutes" indicates an untimed test that takes approximately 45 minutes to administer, or—in a few instances—a test so timed that working time and administration time are very difficult to disentangle. When the time necessary to administer a test is not reported or suggested in the test materials but has been obtained through correspondence with the test publisher or author, the time is enclosed in brackets.

n) COMMENTS. Some entries contain special notations, such as: "for research use only"; "revision of the ABC Test"; "tests administered monthly at centers throughout the United States"; "subtests available as separates"; and "verbal creativity." A statement such as "verbal creativity" is intended to further describe what the test claims to measure. Some of the test entries include factual statements that imply criticism of the test, such as "1990 test identical with test copyrighted 1980."

o) AUTHOR. For most tests, all authors are reported. In the case of tests that appear in a new form each year, only authors of the most recent forms are listed. Names are reported exactly as printed on test booklets. Names of editors generally are not reported.

p) PUBLISHER. The name of the publisher or distributor is reported for each test. Foreign publishers are identified by listing the country in brackets immediately following the name of the publisher. The Publishers Directory and Index must be consulted for a publisher's address.

q) FOREIGN ADAPTATIONS. Revisions and adaptations of tests for foreign use are listed in a separate paragraph following the original edition.

r) SUBLISTINGS. Levels, editions, subtests, or parts of a test available in separate booklets are sometimes presented as sublistings with titles set in small capitals. Sub-sublistings are indented and titles are set in italic type.

s) CROSS REFERENCES. For tests that have been listed previously in a Buros Institute publication, a test entry includes—if relevant—a final paragraph containing a cross reference to the reviews, excerpts, and references for that test in those volumes. In the cross references, "T4:467" refers to test 467 in *Tests in Print IV*, "9:1023" refers to test 1023 in *The Ninth Mental Measurements Yearbook*, "T3:144" refers to test 144 in *Tests in Print III*, "7:637" refers to test 637 in *The Seventh Mental Measurements Yearbook*, "P:262" refers to test 262 in *Personality Tests and Reviews I*, "2:1427" refers to test 1427 in *The 1940 Yearbook*, and "1:1110" refers to test 1110 in *The 1938 Yearbook*. Test numbers not preceded by a colon refer to tests in this *Supplement*; for example, "See 45" refers to test 45 in this volume. In the case of batteries and programs, the paragraph also

includes cross references—from the battery to the separately listed subtests and vice versa—to entries in this volume and to entries and reviews in earlier editions of *TIP* and the *MMY*.

If a reader finds something in a test description that is not understood, the descriptive material presented above can be referred to again and can often help to clarify the matter.

ACKNOWLEDGEMENTS

The publication of any book is always cause to thank the team that made it happen. In the case of the Buros Institute, an exceptional team deserves thanks. Linda Murphy is our Managing Editor. She makes all of our publications happen. The *11MMY-S* is the most recent example of her expertise and energy.

We also rely on Gary Anderson, editorial assistant, for his attention to making our final product as polished as it is accurate. Rosemary Sieck is our word processor; Jane Gustafson our marketing coordinator; and Janice Nelson our secretary. Each of these people play indispensable roles in creating and disseminating the Buros reference works.

During this publication effort we were fortunate to have the gifted support of both Barbara S. Plake, Director, and Ellen M. Weissinger, Associate Director of the Institute. Their leadership was responsible for keeping our focus on producing the *11MMY-S*.

Our gratitude is also extended to the many reviewers who have prepared test reviews for the Buros Institute. Their willingness to take time from busy professional schedules to share their expertise in the form of thoughtful test reviews is appreciated. The *Mental Measurements Yearbook* and *Supplement* would not exist were it not for their efforts.

The Buros Institute is part of the Department of Educational Psychology of the University of Nebraska-Lincoln and many students from the department and the university have contributed to the publication of this volume. We thank the following graduate research assistants who helped with the preparation of the *11MMY-S*: Janet Allison, Robert Bergman, Carol Berigan, Dennison Bhola, Molly Geil, Haeok Kim, Kwong-Liem Kwan, Maria Potenza, Michelle Schicke, Mark Shriver, Robert Spies, Tracy Thorndike-Christ, Paul Turner, Lori Wennstedt, and Kris Yates.

Appreciation is also extended to our past and present National and Departmental Advisory Committees for their willingness to assist in the operation of the Buros Institute. The current members of the National Advisory Committee are Richard M. Jaeger, Timothy Keith, Barbara Kerr, Frank Schmidt, and Linda Wightman. The current members of the Departmental Advisory Committee (in addition to the Buros Professional Staff) are Deborah Bandalos, Terry Gutkin, Ellen McWhirter, and Gregg Schraw.

We extend our thanks to several individuals at the UNL Computing Resource Center, especially Dave Spanel and Tim Myers, for their advice and technical support through the years. We are also grateful for the contribution of the University of Nebraska Press, which serves as distributor of the *MMY* and *TIP* series.

With each passing year and accomplishment of the Buros Institute, the support of our primary benefactor, Luella Buros, grows. She is both an instrumental and inspirational force for the Institute staff.

Her unshakable belief in the importance of our work makes a difference in all of our efforts.

SUMMARY

The *MMY* series is a valuable resource for people interested in studying or using testing. Once the process of using the series is understood, a reader can gain rapid access to a wealth of information. Our hope is that with the publication of the *11MMY-S*, test authors and publishers will consider carefully the comments made by the reviewers and continue to refine and perfect their assessment products.

Jane Close Conoley
James C. Impara
August 1994

Tests and Reviews

ACER Advanced Test B90: New Zealand Edition.
Purpose: "Designed to measure general intellectual ability."
Population: College students and adults.
Publication Date: 1991.
Scores: Total score only.
Administration: Group.
Price Data: Price information available from publisher for test materials including administrator's manual (5 pages).
Time: 50(55) minutes.
Comments: "Selected items from the ACER Advanced Test B40 and the ACER Test of Cognitive Ability."
Authors: Australian Council for Educational Research and manual by Neil Reid and Cedric Croft.
Publisher: New Zealand Council for Educational Research [New Zealand].
Cross References: For a review of ACER Advanced Test B40 by Harriet C. Cobb, see 9:4; see also T2:323 (6 references) and 7:328 (4 references); for a review of ACER Advanced Test B40 by C. Sanders, see 5:296 (3 references).

Review of the ACER Advanced Test B90: New Zealand Edition by JOHN RUST, Senior Lecturer in Psychometrics, Goldsmith's College, University of London, London, ENGLAND:

The 70-item ACER Advanced Test B90: New Zealand Edition is a new instrument that has been specifically developed for New Zealand but borrows items from the Australian ACER Advanced Test B40 (1983; 9:4) and the ACER Test of Cognitive Ability (1983; 9:23). Items were modified or rewritten, as appropriate, for the New Zealand market. The revisions involved item substitutions and repositioning, as well as changes in both question stems and options to provide a local flavour. The test consists of verbal and quantitative items, but does not include tasks involving nonverbal or perceptual material which, the authors say, would have been included if the test had been intended to give a balanced measure of general cognitive ability. The test is reported as "utilizing a number of types of item which are judged to contribute to an assessment of the general ability factor (g), as described by Spearman" (manual, p. 1). It is aimed at the higher ranges of ability. Its intended use is with "students already taking or planning to undertake tertiary courses, and with adults in a selection/training context where emphasis is likely to be placed on relatively superior intellectual abilities" (p. 1).

Item analysis was carried out within the New Zealand Ministry of Defense with recruits and trainees of suitable age and experience in training establishments throughout the country. Further minor revisions were made as a result. Standardization, however, is based on 251 male and 625 female students who were taking courses on testing, measurement, and evaluation within five university psychology departments and two university education departments. There is no explanation of why this atypical sample was used in preference to the military recruits used in the pilot study. Standardization is to a stanine score, which is appropriate for the circumstances. No information on ethnic or linguistic origin was reported. In the light of this they make the apt comment that the test is "inappropriate for use with individuals whose cultural or linguistic backgrounds are such that they could be regarded as disadvantaged in taking tests of this nature" (p. 1). The implications of this in the light of the publisher's suggestion that the test can be used with adults in a selection context does, however, warrant more attention. Sex differences were found which replicated the gender bias that exists in the parent Test of Cognitive Ability, with men obtaining higher scores than women.

No new evidence is given of reliability and validity. The user is referred to the manuals of the two ACER tests from which the items were derived. This obviously fails to meet any reasonable standard for the production of a test manual. Although it might make sense to report an adaptation and restandardization of one of the source tests alone on this basis, no indication is given of the relative contribution of each source test to the new edition. It is clear that, in the absence of any direct data, some estimate of reliability and validity might be obtained from the source tests. However, this should have been reported together with some rationale for the estimation procedure.

In some ways, the authors of this test fail to do themselves justice. The items contain a certain face validity; some strategy must have led to the original test specification which clearly could have been reported. The similarity of the content to tests in use in other countries suggests the test is potentially reliable and valid, at least for assessing the level of reasoning among college students. As it is, the manual provided fails to meet the minimum standards of reporting expected by today's psychology professionals. In the absence of proper reliability and validity data as well as of appropriate norms, it is of some concern that the test should be recommended for use with adults within a selection/training context.

[2]
ACER Test of Reasoning Ability.
Purpose: "Designed to measure general intellectual ability."
Population: Educational years 9–11 in Australian school system.
Publication Dates: 1986–90.
Scores: Total score only.
Administration: Group.
Price Data: Not available.

Time: 45(60) minutes.
Author: Marion M. de Lemos.
Publisher: Australian Council for Educational Research Ltd. [Australia].
[The publisher advised in January 1994 that this test is now out of print—Ed.]

Review of the ACER Test of Reasoning Ability by PHILIP NAGY, Associate Professor of Measurement, Evaluation, and Computer Applications, The Ontario Institute for Studies in Education, Toronto, Ontario, CANADA:

The ACER Test of Reasoning Ability is a 70-item test of "general intellectual ability" for students in years 9, 10, and 11 of Australian schools. Adult norms are provided as well. The test was developed as a multiple-choice version of the ACER Test of Cognitive Ability, an open-ended test normed in 1978 using students in years 10, 11, and 12. The change in age range is not explained. Although the test is described as suitable for use in large-scale testing programs, the author emphasizes interpretation of individual rather than group scores, for purposes related to educational guidance and vocational counselling. The manual advises appropriate cautions concerning the qualifications of test administrators and score interpreters. Respondents are advised to answer even if not absolutely sure, but not to guess wildly.

In the norming sample, there are inevitable anomalies between the actual and expected proportions of students by several variables: geography, type of school, sex, language background, and socioeconomic background. Thoughtful explanations and discussions on the potential impact of most of these are provided, including a calculation that the overrepresentation of independent schools distorts the tables by only .5 to 1.0 points.

A more serious, though far from fatal distortion is not handled satisfactorily: The norming sample has almost twice the expected proportions of students from managerial and professional homes, and only half the expected from semiskilled and unskilled homes. These discrepancies make the conversions from raw to derived scores about 2.3 points too low, but these values are not calculated for the test user as are those for the school-type discrepancies. This problem could be easily remedied in a future edition.

The adult norming sample is inadequate. It consists of 741 people who were applying for positions as police: 69% male, 82% under 25, and only 6% with more than high school education. Scores vary as expected depending on education, and remain relatively constant as a function of age (except for a drastic drop at age 35, based on only 12 people). Although these data are reported with many caveats on their use, it would have been better to omit them entirely from the manual, treat them as developmental work in progress, and market the test for use with school students only.

The administration directions are clear, but there are some problems with the practice questions that exemplify the difficulties of multiple-choice items. Practice Item 2 (there are 10 like it in the test) presents six mammals and asks which two are different. My first choice, not offered, was the pair of herbivores, sheep and giraffe; the keyed response was the pair of domesticated animals, sheep and dog. Such dubious questions should not be included, particularly as a practice exercise.

Practice Item 5 presents a 3-by-3 matrix, and asks the respondent to provide one of three missing numbers. My initial magic square strategy, in which all rows and columns have the same total, did not work. The route to the keyed response is that a simple operation (e.g., add 3, add 2) is required to go from one row or column to the next. I presented this problem to two colleagues; one used the nonproductive magic square route, whereas the other got the right answer using a holistic strategy that he described as "balance." It seems that a respondent is expected to learn the method for the three similar questions of this type from the practice exercise. However, the scripted explanation of some 230+ words is followed, as in all the examples, with "Answer any questions. Explain further if necessary." In this particular case, such open-ended directions, although common, might lead to some serious lack of standardization in administration.

The test was normed on about 400 students in each of the three years, along with two other tests, in a balanced order to examine practice effects; these were negligible. KR-21 reliability values are high, between .84 and .89, but a confidence interval for a derived score of 100 would still be 90–109. This calculation is not done for readers of the manual, who might not be aware of the wide confidence range of individual scores on such tests. In fairness, this is a problem with most such test manuals.

As validity evidence, the author cites correlations with the Standard Progressive Matrices of .63 for the timed version and .56 for the untimed. This difference might reflect a speed factor, as the test requires 70 items in 45 minutes. Correlations with teacher ratings of English, mathematics, and scholastic ability are in the same range, but if teacher ratings are a validating yardstick, then development of standardized tests seems like a lot of trouble. Correlations with the ACER Word Knowledge Test are around .75, indicating this test might be more verbal than quantitative in what it is measuring. However, the items may be roughly categorized as 31 verbal, 28 numerical, 7 logic, and 4 spatial, which seems a reasonable balance for a general measure.

No individual item or subscore information is provided in the manual. This is an unfortunate but understandable precaution against misinterpretation, for much can be learned from item difficulties, discrimination indices, and percentage omissions.

In summary, educators and psychologists in smaller countries such as Australia and Canada should not have to rely on generic tests marketed by multinational corporations. The ACER is an adequate test for use with Australian students in years 9, 10, and 11. It should not be given to adults with the present norming data. It has adequate reliability and validity evidence, and some excellent advice on interpreting scores in their context. It could be improved by some emphasis on the confidence intervals for individual scores, and by the provision, for those qualified and interested, of some item data.

Review of the ACER Test of Reasoning Ability by JOHN RUST, Senior Lecturer in Psychometrics, Goldsmith's College, University of London, London, ENGLAND:

The 70-item ACER Test of Reasoning Ability is a multiple-choice version of the earlier ACER Test of Cognitive Ability (1983; 9:23) and is designed principally for the Australian market. The ACER Test of Cognitive Ability had been developed in 1976–77 as a replacement for the Otis Higher Test on the basis of an item analysis of responses to approximately 200 pilot items by students in Australian school years 10, 11, and 12, and by first year college students. The main modifications for the new test are the elimination of five items considered unsuitable for a multiple-choice version, the provision of machine-readable scoring sheets, and a restandardization on over 1,200 subjects.

The authors argue the test is a measure of Spearman's "g." No particular consideration is given in the manual to the switch from "intelligence" through "cognitive ability" and now to "reasoning" as the underlying trait of interest. However, the authors are not alone in this and they do state their assumption that the test is measuring "a 'general factor' underlying performance on a wide range of cognitive tasks which involve the ability to see relationships and to solve problems" (manual, p. 1). Inspection of the items does suggest a slant towards verbal intelligence, and it would be helpful to have more details of the test specification on which the original construction of items was based. The renaming exercise is somewhat undermined by the use of the classical IQ format of mean = 100, s.d. = 15 for standardization that invites the user to interpret scores in terms of classical IQ. As it stands, the test is open to the traditional abuses of IQ tests and the caveats the manual provides underplay the issue and offer little alleviation.

The new standardization was carried out on a stratified random sample of Australian school children in years 9, 10, and 11. The manual gives helpful details of the various subgroups involved, and describes in some detail the analysis of data from the approximately 10% of subjects for whom English was not the first language. Ethnic minority data are also described, although for a non-Australian the failure to mention the indigenous ethnic minority is striking. One problem encountered seems to be the existence of gender bias in the test, with men scoring higher than women. Although this does receive some consideration it warrants more, particularly as the test is specifically recommended for selection purposes in occupational settings.

Kuder-Richardson internal consistency is given as reliability and is .85 for year 9 ($N = 450$), .89 for year 10 ($N = 394$), and .89 for year 11 ($N = 369$). Validity is based on concurrent validation with the Standard Progressive Matrices (T4:2544). The matrices were administered in either timed or untimed format, and correlations, calculated separately for each year group, ranged between .53 and .67 (samples sizes were between 167 and 221). These are high given the differing nature of the instruments involved. Correlations between test scores and teachers' ratings of school ability were also examined and ranged between .58 ($N = 360$) and .61 ($N = 310$). These results demonstrate that the test is a reasonably reliable and valid instrument for assessment related to educational and vocational guidance in educational settings, as is suggested in the manual.

Validity within an occupational environment has not been demonstrated, and this issue does need to be addressed, particularly in the light of the aforementioned gender bias. The school student norms are recommended for use with adults so long as the appropriate Australian school year is used for the "minimum level of education required" for the educational level of the employment category in question. Some data are supplied from a sample of 741 applicants for entry to the Victoria Police Force, some of which is described helpfully. However, the provision of an IQ transformation based on this sample is again a reversion to previous bad practice so far as the use of IQ scores are concerned. T score and

stanine are more appropriate and are also provided, although these unfortunately appear alongside the "IQs."

In summary, the ACER Test of Reasoning Ability is a group test of intelligence which has been shown to be reliable for use in years 9 to 11 of the Australian school system. Validity within an educational environment is also evident to some degree. However, the authors fail to take account of recent conceptions of "g" as a culturally dependent measure of the ability to thrive within the formal education system of a modern industrialized society. The use of the IQ format for the norms is certain to encourage the continuation of bad practice in the field. Of greater concern is the encouragement to use the IQ format within adult occupational settings, particularly when it is so evidently not based on a representative sample of the Australian population. The sampling and detailed analyses of the standardization study with school students appears to have been well thought out and could have formed the basis of recommendations for good practice in the development of valid and fair selection and assessment policies. The authors seem to have lacked the courage of their good intentions and have all too readily retreated along the well-trodden but blighted path of the classical IQ test.

[3]

AGS Early Screening Profiles.

Purpose: Constructed to screen children for possible developmental problems or giftedness.

Population: Ages 2-0 to 6-11.

Publication Date: 1990.

Scores: 3 Profile Scores: Cognitive/Language, Motor, Self-Help/Social (Parent or Teacher), and 4 Survey Scores: Articulation, Home, Behavior (Cognitive/Language, Motor).

Administration: Individual.

Price Data, 1993: $249.95 per complete kit including test plates in easel, 25 test records, 25 Self-Help/Social Profile questionnaires, Sample Home/Health History survey, 25 score summaries, tape measure, beads and string, Motor Profile administration manual (19 pages), and manual (311 pages, including reproducible Report to Parents and blackline masters "Guide for Training Examiners"); $24.95 per 25 test records; $14.95 per 25 Self-Help/Social Profile questionnaires; $14.95 per 25 Home/Health History surveys; $8.95 per 25 score summaries; $34.95 per manual.

Time: [15–40] minutes.

Comments: Two levels of scoring: Level I scores are 6 "screening indexes" and 3 descriptive categories; Level II scores are standard scores, percentile ranks, and age equivalents; ecological assessment with ratings by parents and teachers as well as direct assessment of the child.

Authors: Patti L. Harrison (coordinating author and manual author), Alan S. Kaufman (Cognitive/Language Profile), Nadeen L. Kaufman (Cognitive/Language Profile), Robert H. Bruininks (Motor Profile), John Rynders (Motor Profile), Steven Ilmer (Motor Profile), Sara S. Sparrow (Self-Help/Social Profile), and Domenic V. Cicchetti (Self-Help/Social Profile)

Publisher: American Guidance Service.

Cross References: See T4:134 (2 references).

Review of the AGS Early Screening Profiles by DAVID W. BARNETT, Professor of School Psychology, University of Cincinnati, Cincinnati, OH:

The AGS Early Screening Profiles (ESP) represents an effort by distinguished researchers to create an instrument to help meet the needs of at-risk children. Readers of this review are probably most interested in two questions. Given the many criticisms of early screening efforts, "Does this screening instrument overcome shortcomings of other screening devices?" or if not, "How should young children be screened?"

The criteria applied by the test authors, that the instrument "meets *accepted* psychometric standards" (p. v, emphasis added), is not the only framework applied in this review. The critique that follows draws on existing standards, but also *emerging* and needed standards for technical adequacy based on an analysis of research with prototypic screening instruments, research on decision making, and principles of intervention design. These deal primarily with reliability and validity of *decision outcomes* and expected intervention utility.

DESCRIPTION OF THE EARLY SCREENING PROFILES. The Early Screening Profiles are designed to evaluate the "major areas of functioning of children and their families" (p. v). The ESP consists of seven different "profiles" generated through child testing or caregiver questionnaires that may be used separately or in various combinations. The Developmental Profiles include: Cognitive/Language, Motor, and Self-Help/Social. In addition, other profiles include Articulation, Home, Health History, and Behavior "surveys." The ESP may be administered by paraprofessionals.

Like other screening instruments, children are asked to point to or name objects, select matching objects, and demonstrate knowledge of numbers and concepts. Similarly, Motor skills include imitating movements, walking on a line, and stringing beads.

The Self-Help and Socialization domains and the Articulation survey also are predictable from other scales (i.e., adaptive behavior measures, naming objects) purporting to measure these constructs. The Home survey asks questions about types of play material, content and frequency of parent-child interactions (i.e., reading), and responsibilities given to the child. The Health History also is straightforward. However, the Behavior survey is far less than what most professionals would expect. Ratings include activity level, attention span, cooperativeness, and independence based on observations over the course of testing.

The ESP generates a sea of numbers. Two scoring levels are available for the analysis of individual performances. For Level I, scores are available for the Cognitive/Language, Motor, and Self-Help/Social profiles and for total screening. Other possibilities include combining various subtests, or separating subtests such as cognitive and language subscales for ethnic minorities or children with hearing and language problems. The Level I scoring system yields "screening indexes" (six broad categories of performance based on normal curve deviations) to help identify at-risk (or gifted) children. Level II scoring provides an array of interpretive options for broad subscales and total scale (i.e., NCEs, stanines, age equivalents, etc.), and for more detailed analysis of patterns (e.g., expressive and receptive language). Age equivalents are score options from the ESP. These appear in examples, despite the wide criticism they have received. Similarly, the ESP authors state that professional judgment is required, but this quality of an instrument should be no great source of confidence for users or consumers.

PURPOSES. The "major use of the AGS Early Screening Profiles is to provide an ecologically valid, early, developmental screening of young children" (p. 6). The description of the ESP as ecologically valid is questionable. Although there are several definitions of ecological validity, perhaps the most widely accepted is an extension of classical validity: "The extent to which the environment experienced by the subjects in a scientific investigation has the properties it is supposed or assumed to have by the investigator" (Bronfenbrenner, 1977, p. 516). Neisser (1976) described ecological validity in the following ways: "if the theory has something to say about what people do in real, culturally significant situations" (p. 2), and "[H]ow people act in or interact with the ordinary world" (p. 7). Martens and Witt (1988) characterized ecological validity by the extent that interventions lead to desired outcomes without disrupting significant and desirable patterns of behaviors present in the environment. Thus, based on existing definitions of ecological validity, the ESP falls short or, at best, ecological validity remains unexamined.

Other purported uses of the ESP include screening for readiness programs (a widely criticized practice), and use of the Home survey "for a home intervention program" (p. 6) (unlikely, based on principles of intervention design). The scale is also described as useful for program evaluation efforts.

The scale authors suggest follow-up assessments for screening outcomes are necessary but recommend various assessment devices that have been criticized for their inability to yield meaningful developmental profiles and for their lack of treatment utility (Barnett, Macmann, & Carey, 1992). Furthermore, based on other analyses, the results of following screening with other similar assessment techniques will not improve overall outcomes for children. In fact, there is likely to be indefinite triangulation regarding which children need services, and the qualities of effective services will not be addressed (Barnett, Macmann, & Carey, 1992).

TECHNICAL ADEQUACY. Norms were built on a representative sample of 1,149 children from ages 2 years to 6 years and 11 months. Like other test instruments, however, the age levels samples actually used for interpretive purposes are much smaller and vary by age and scale (i.e., for Self-Help/Social: Teacher at age 5-0 to 5-5 ($n = 65$). The well-established tradition of setting the mean at 100 with a standard deviation of 15 is maintained.

Although many of the coefficient alpha reliabilities are in the .90s, others do not meet accepted standards of technical adequacy (Motor, Behavior), and others are quite low (Home). Test-retest (5 to 21 days) reliabilities range from .66 to .91. The stability of test-retest screening indexes ranged from .56 to .82, which connotes potentially significant variability in *decisions* (that would be noted by children who change screening categories based on different test occasions).

Validity evidence is mustered in many standard ways: through demonstrating a developmental progression in scores, by correlations between subparts and total scores, and by patterns of intercorrelations between scales. Correlations with other measures (such as Kaufman Assessment Battery for Children [K-ABC], Stanford-Binet Intelligence Scale [S-B], etc.) are similar to many other studies (e.g., coefficients range from .40s to .80s). However, the evidence presented also shows inconsistent patterns of divergence and convergence that may translate to remarkably variable interpretations and child outcomes (se Table 8.14, manual, p. 104).

Agreement with other screening instruments (i.e., DIAL-R, BATTELLE) is quite problematic (Table 8.18 and 8.19, pp. 107–108). The specific agreement in Table 8.24 (p. 116) with regard to categories and services also is quite low (i.e., calculations show that specific agreement is .16 for LD). Taken together, these data demonstrate insufficient evidence of concurrent and predictive validity.

On the positive side, information in the manual demonstrates a serious effort at scale development. Beyond the usual content, the authors include discussions related to such important factors as the analysis of errors around cut scores and the effects of base rates. Also, although not developed fully as a sequential decision strategy, the authors mention that a logical step between initial screening and referral for a comprehensive assessment is to simply rescreen. In sum, however, the ESP does not overcome the significant shortcomings of prototypic screening instruments. New directions are necessary.

Conclusions: Toward Robust Screening Efforts.

ECOLOGICAL VALIDITY. The *absence* of evidence that the ESP has ecological validity is a central criticism. In describing the instrument as ecologically valid, the authors are confusing the use of parent and teacher reports (multimethod assessment) about the child's functioning with significant ecological principles. The first steps in screening that stem from an ecologically valid approach are systems analysis and organizational development (e.g., Adelman, 1982). Ecobehavioral (e.g., Rogers-Warren, 1984) screening seeks to identify problem situations and factors related to problem maintenance and change (Barnett, Macmann, & Carey, 1992). Another potential benefit of ecologically valid screening efforts is that of supporting children with special needs in natural environments.

REGARDING SCREENING EXPERTISE AND INTERVENTION DESIGN. The authors of the manual state that "screening coordinators should have a good understanding of theory and research in areas such as child development, education, psychology, tests and measurement, assessment, and childhood exceptionality" (p. 9). In contrast, screening coordinators should be well founded in *intervention design*, which has to do with altering developmental trajectories, and the basics of parent and teacher consultation. In being guided in this way, professional actions and child, parent, and teacher outcomes are likely to be very different from the comprehensive assessment outcomes suggested by the ESP manual (Barnett & Carey, 1992).

TECHNICAL ADEQUACY. Criteria for at-risk status are based on the normal curve. No other criteria are applied, and agencies set their own (i.e., 1 standard deviation below the mean versus 2). However, young children move in and out of risk situations. Interpretations based on score deviations are frail with respect to changes in items, test occasions, and other factors. An appropriate estimate of error would address the robustness and usefulness of decisions and other inferences over time.

The ESP authors note the interdependence of developmental skills. However, the nature of inter-correlated skills results in a practical impasse regarding individual profile interpretations. For example, the reliability of differences between Cognitive/Language and Motor for a child at age 4 (for illustration purposes) would not meet interpretative standards. Given a Cognitive/Language x Motor correlation of .63, a reliability estimate for Cognitive/Language of .93, a reliability estimate for Motor of .78, the reliability of the *difference* would be about .61. Overall interpretations of developmental patterns would be extremely unstable. Furthermore, the extensive number of comparisons that could be made is likely to lead to a high rate of chance-related conclusions.

In response to the questions raised at the beginning of the review, differences between relatively similar screening measures simply may not matter that much. The ESP may be state of the art but it may not necessarily lead to reliable and beneficial outcomes for children. New approaches are necessary based on ecobehavioral theory, principles of intervention design, the analysis of innovative decision strategies such as multiple gating, and the analysis of decision outcomes (Barnett, Macmann, & Carey, 1992).

REVIEWER'S REFERENCES

Neisser, U. (1976). *Cognition and reality: Principles and implications of cognitive psychology.* San Francisco: Freeman.

Bronfenbrenner, U. (1977). Toward an experimental ecology of human development. *American Psychologist, 32,* 513-531.

Adelman, H. S. (1982). Identifying learning problems at an early age: A critical appraisal. *Journal of Clinical Child Psychology, 11,* 255-261.

Rogers-Warren, A. K. (1984). Ecobehavioral analysis. *Education and Treatment of Children, 7,* 283-303.

Martens, B. K., & Witt, J. C. (1988). On the ecological validity of behavior modification. In J. C. Witt, S. N. Elliott, & F. M. Gresham (Eds.), *Handbook of behavior therapy in education* (pp. 325-341). New York: Plenum.

Barnett, D. W., & Carey, K. T. (1992). *Designing interventions for preschool learning and behavior problems.* San Francisco: Jossey-Bass.

Barnett, D. W., Macmann, G. M., & Carey, K. T. (1992). Early intervention and the assessment of developmental skills: Challenges and directions. *Topics in Early Childhood Special Education, 12,* 21-43.

Review of the AGS Early Screening Profiles by CATHY TELZROW, *Psychologist and Director, Educational Assessment Project, Cuyahoga Special Education Service Center, Cleveland, OH:*

The AGS Early Screening Profiles offer a multisource, multimethod scale for identifying children who may require further assessment to determine the presence of either deficits or excellence in performance. The measure provides maximum flexibility in selection among its seven components. Examiners may administer one or all of three direct testing scales (Cognitive/Language profile, Motor profile, and Articulation survey), two parent questionnaires (Home survey and Health survey), a parent or teacher questionnaire (Self-Help/Social profile), and a Behavior survey (Examiner Questionnaire). Selection of the Early Screening Profiles components may be guided by an agency's screening purposes, such as speech/language screening, health screening, or screening for school readiness or accelerated programs.

Development of the Early Screening Profiles was guided by professional theory and practice in early childhood identification. In addition to general principles of screening related to cost, efficiency, and ease of administration, the author was committed to an ecological approach, identified as one which incorporates "multiple settings, multiple individuals within settings, and multiple behavioral domains" (p. 63). The foundations for three of these behavioral domains were provided by other AGS-published instruments and authors: the Kaufman Assessment Battery for Children (K-ABC; Kaufman & Kaufman, 1983; 9:562), and the Vineland Adaptive Behavior Scale (VABS; Sparrow, Balla, & Cicchetti, 1984; 10:381). In some instances, item types and administrative formats were borrowed from these earlier measures; for example, the Cognitive/Language profile shares many common features with the K-ABC. In the case of the Self-Help/Social profile, the link with the VABS is even more direct, in that the VABS interview edition items were modified to an abbreviated, self-report format for the Early Screening Profiles. Incorporation of the most salient elements of these technically superior instruments into an early childhood screening measure is one of the most noteworthy strengths of the Early Screening Profiles.

Although not derived so directly from other published measures, development of the remaining four components of the Early Screening Profiles also was guided by previous research. The Articulation survey, for example, masterfully reduces the sound production of 2–6-year-olds to a 20-word sample using developmentally appropriate vocabulary. The original pool of items for the Home survey was derived from the research (including the Home Observation for Measurement of the Environment [HOME; Caldwell & Bradley, 1984; 9:481]) and the author's clinical experiences. Final item selection occurred through a stepwise multiple regression procedure, with priority given to those items producing a significant increase in multiple correlations with the three Profile or Total Screening scores. Health History and Behavior surveys were constructed through a review of other similar scales and professional critiques.

Organization of the Early Screening Profiles is generally clear and concise. The easel format facilitates administration of the Cognitive/Language profile and the Articulation survey. Directions for administering and scoring the Motor profile are in a separate, self-contained book; although these are precise, they are somewhat long and complex, and will require considerable familiarity and practice on the part of examiners. Scores for these three direct test measures (Cognitive/Language profile, Articulation survey, Motor profile), as well as examiner ratings on the Behavior survey, are all recorded on a single test record. The Home survey and Health survey are incorporated into a single questionnaire, as is the Self-Help/Social profile. Results of the Early Screening Profiles are summarized on a one-page Score Summary. Expanded scoring and parent report forms, which can be duplicated for use, are included in the manual.

The Early Screening Profiles provides for two types of scoring. Level I scoring produces screening index scores for each of the profiles individually, subscales of the Cognitive/Language profile, and a total screening score, which is composed of the three profiles (parent version of Self-Help/Social profile must be used). Screening index scores, which range from 1 to 6, describe the range of performance from -3 to +3 standard deviations. Level II scores include such normative data as standard scores with bands of error, percentile ranks, normal curve equivalents, and age equivalents. Raw score performance on the Articulation survey, the Home survey, and the Behavior survey is reported in descriptive categories only (e.g., below average, average, above average). The Health survey is not scored, but is to be reviewed for recommendations regarding followup.

The technical properties of the Early Screening Profiles are thoroughly reported in the manual. Normative data are based on a representative, national sample of 1,149 children stratified according to 1990 census estimates by sex, ethnic group, geographic region, and parents' education level. Median internal consistency reliability coefficients for the profiles ranged from .68 to .95, and for the surveys from .41 to .89. The lowest internal consistency score occurred for the Home survey; the author hypothesizes that because of the "heterogeneous and diverse

items" on this survey "perhaps high internal consistency should not be expected" (p. 87). Test-retest reliability coefficients for the Screening indexes ranged from .56 to .82 (immediate) and from .31 to .87 (delayed intervals of 22 to 75 days). Interrater reliability coefficients for the Motor profile ranged from .80 to .99.

The Early Screening Profiles manual includes a table summarizing samples and measures employed in 10 concurrent and predictive validity studies. Correlations between the Cognitive/Language Profile and other measures of cognitive ability (K-ABC; Stanford-Binet Intelligence Scale, Fourth Edition [Thorndike, Hagen, & Sattler, 1985; 10:342]) were moderate to high (.48–.84). As would be expected given the origin of the Motor profile and the Self-Help/Social profile, correlations with their foundation scales (Bruininks-Oseretsky, VABS) were generally in the range of .50 and .60. Correlations with other screening tests (Battelle Developmental Inventory [BDI; Newborg, Stock, Wnek, Guidubaldi, & Svinicki, 1984], Bracken Basic Concepts Test [Bracken, 1985], Denver Developmental Screening Test [Frankenburg, Dodds, & Fandal, 1970], Developmental Indicators for the Assessment of Learning—Revised [DIAL-R; Mardel-Czudnowski, & Goldberg, 1983]) varied widely from study to study, from some negligible and even negative correlations (with the BDI in one study) to moderate rs with the DIAL-R. Predictive validity studies reported moderate to high correlations with group aptitude and achievement measures.

The comprehensive manual for the Early Screening Profiles incorporates several excellent features. In addition to thorough information regarding the development, standardization, and technical merits of the scale, there are additional features which help distinguish this from other early childhood screening measures. The manual includes a detailed description of both Level I and Level II scores, including an excellent discussion of the limitations of age equivalent scores. In addition, the manual incorporates a discussion of decision theory as related to selecting "cut-off" scores for reaching screening decisions. Finally, excellent training materials, which can be used for introducing professionals and nonprofessionals to screening young children in general and in the use of the Early Screening Profiles in particular, are provided. These features, together with its high technical quality, make the Early Screening Profiles a scholarly, comprehensive addition to a total program in early childhood identification and service delivery.

REVIEWER'S REFERENCES

Frankenburg, W. K., Dodds, J. B., & Fandal, A. W. (1970). Denver Developmental Screening Test. Denver: LADOCA.

Bruininks, R. H. (1978). Bruininks-Oseretsky Test of Motor Proficiency. Circle Pines, MN: American Guidance Service.

Kaufman, A. S., & Kaufman, N. L. (1983). Kaufman Assessment Battery for Children. Circle Pines, MN: American Guidance Service.

Mardell-Czudnowski, C. D., & Goldenberg, D. S. (1983). Developmental Indicators for the Assessment of Learning—Revised. Edison, NJ: Childcraft.

Caldwell, B. M., & Bradley, R. H. (1984). Home Observation for Measurement of the Environment. Little Rock: University of Arkansas at Little Rock.

Newborg, J., Stock, J. R., Wnek, L., Guidubaldi, J., & Svinicki, J. (1984). Battelle Developmental Inventory. Allen, TX: DLM Teaching Resources.

Sparrow, S. S., Balla, D. A., & Cicchetti, D. V. (1984). Vineland Adaptive Behavior Scales. Circle Pines, MN: American Guidance Service.

Bracken, B. A. (1985). Bracken Basic Concepts Scale. San Antonio, TX: The Psychological Corporation.

Thorndike, R. L., Hagen, E. P., & Sattler, J. M. (1985). Stanford-Binet Intelligence Scale (4th ed.). Chicago: The Riverside Publishing Co.

[4]

Alcohol Use Inventory.

Purpose: "To assess the nature of an individual's alcohol use pattern, and problems associated with that pattern."

Population: Adults and adolescents 16 years of age and over.

Publication Date: 1986–90.

Acronym: AUI.

Scores, 24: Social Improvement, Mental Improvement, Manage Moods, Marital Coping, Gregarious, Compulsive, Sustained, Loss of Control, Role Maladaptation, Delirium, Hangover, Marital Problems, Quantity, Guilt and Worry, Help Before, Receptivity, Awareness, Enhanced, Obsessed, Disruption 1, Disruption 2, Anxious Concern, Receptive Awareness, Alcohol Involvement.

Administration: Group.

Price Data, 1994: $20.75 per 10 reusable test booklets; $24 per hand-scoring key; $4.25–$5 per Profile Report; $9.20–$11.50 per Interpretive Report; $24 per 50 hand-scoring answer sheets and 50 profile forms; $70 per hand-scoring starter kit including manual, 10 test booklets, 50 answer sheets, 50 profile forms, and answer keys; $13.50 per manual ('90, 85 pages); $9.50 per Interpretive Report User's Guide.

Time: (35–60) minutes.

Comments: Reports are available via immediate on-site microcomputer scoring as well as through a mail-in scoring service or teleprocessing service.

Authors: John L. Horn, Kenneth W. Wanberg, and F. Mark Foster.

Publisher: NCS Assessments.

Cross References: See T4:146 (6 references).

Review of the Alcohol Use Inventory by ROBERT J. DRUMMOND, Professor of Counselor Education, University of North Florida, Jacksonville, FL:

The Alcohol Use Inventory (AUI) is a self-report inventory designed to assess patterns of behavior, attitudes, and symptoms pertaining to the use of alcohol of individuals 16 years of age or older who drink to some extent. It was developed for use with individuals admitted to an alcoholism treatment program. The AUI is not appropriate for use with individuals who do not drink. The AUI reflects the multiple condition theory about drinking problems and has evolved from numerous research studies originally begun in the 1960s and from previous instruments such as the Alcohol Use Questionnaire (Horn, J. L., Skinner, H. A., Wanberg, K. W., & Foster, F. M., 1984) and the Alcohol Use Inventory (Horn, 1974) known as the Drinking History Quetionnaire.

The current (1987) edition of the AUI has several new features. There are three new scales: RECEPTIV, AWARENESS, and RECPAWAR. The scale concerning the use of nonalcohol drugs was deleted. The arrangements of the scales have been altered and some of the scales renamed. Some experimental items that have been added for research purposes are not utilized in the scoring of any of the scales. Different norms are also mentioned as a new feature. Overall, there are 24 scales that assess dimensions of behavior at three different levels: primary, second-level, and third-level.

The scales appear to be reasonably associated with problem drinking. The Primary Scales focus on the "benefits," "styles," "consequences," and "concerns and acknowledgments" of drinking; for example, SOCIALIM (drink to improve sociability), MENTALIM (drink to improve mental functioning), MANGMOOD (drink to manage mood), MARICOPE (drink to deal with marital problems), GREGARUS (drink in bars, parties, with friends) and the like. There are six second-level scales derived from factor analysis of the relationships among the primary scales; for example, OBSESSED (obsessive, compulsive, sustained drinking).

Factor analysis was used to construct the scales of the AUI. The authors, however, do not present the results of the factor analysis in the manual or provide a matrix of the intercorrelations among the items or primary scales.

The AUI presents internal consistency reliabilities and test-retest information on the scales from a number of different years and groups. The third-level scale and second-level scales have higher coefficients than the primary scales as expected. Of the Primary

Scales, QUANTITY has the lowest coefficient. Most of the reliability coefficients range from .65 to .80 for the scales.

Point-biserial correlations are presented to report gender and age differences rather than the more traditional T or F comparisons. A review of the data suggests there should be separate sex norms and norms by age levels. Comparisons are presented among Native Americans, White, African Americans, and Hispanic groups with F ratios given but no multiple comparison results presented to show between which groups the differences were found. There is not a good demographic description of the makeup of the norming group. No standard errors of measurement are given for the scales. The manual authors provide the user with salient information on interpreting the scale and on the BSCS approach (Benefits, Styles, Consequences, and Concerns) associated with the use and abuse of alcohol. A sample computerized report is also presented. The manual is not especially user friendly. There are a number of gaps in the information presented in the manual as previously indicated. The information in the manual is a justification of the approaches used rather than a translation of the information in a way counselors and psychologists could use to better understand the concepts.

Overall, the AUI has as its aim "to obtain measurements that are useful with different kinds of people (are hardy), have satisfactory breadth (bandwidth), adequate internal consistency (fidelity), genuine independence and appropriate stability over time" (manual, p. 22). The AUI appears to have made good progress in meeting these goals and is based on sound research and development. Counselors will find this a useful assessment tool when working with individuals with alcohol problems.

REVIEWERS REFERENCES

Horn, J. L. (1974). Alcohol Use Inventory. Washington, DC: U.S. Patent Office.

Horn, J. L., Skinner, H. A., Wanberg, K. W., & Foster, F. M. (1984). Alcohol Use Questionnaire (AUQ). Toronto, Canada: Addiction Research Foundation.

Review of the Alcohol Use Inventory by SHARON McNEELY, Associate Professor of Educational Foundations, Northeastern Illinois University, Chicago, IL:

The Alcohol Use Inventory (AUI) evolved out of research that sought to provide a multiple-condition assessment of alcohol-related problems. The AUI is designed to provide operational indicators to describe patterns of alcohol use, allowing mental health workers to identify and understand different kinds of alcoholics.

The AUI has 24 scales, three new to this edition. Sixteen of the 17 primary scales rely on responses to less than 10 items (range 3–9) for analysis. The six second-level scales have 11 to 21 items each. The third (broad) scale relies on responses to 40 items. In all, there are 228 self-report items which are answered "Yes" or "No" or with selected frequencies of behaviors.

The primary scales provide four separate domains related to drinking behaviors. The benefits domain provides explanations as to why the respondent drinks. The styles domain shows where and when drinking occurs. The consequences domain presents results the drinker faces. The concerns and acknowledgements domain allows the respondent to admit to feelings associated with the drinking and ways help has been sought and is currently desired.

The second-level scales are not merely combinations of the primary scales, but are derived from factor analysis of the primary scales' relationships. The ENHANCED scale represents benefits of using alcohol. The OBSESSED scale presents the general drinking style of the respondent. The DISRUPT1 scale presents the consequences of drinking in terms of disruptions. Most of the items in this scale are frequently measured indicators of signs of alcoholism. The respondent may recognize and lie about these items so to not seem alcoholic. The DISRUPT2 scale also indicates uncontrolled life disruption. It provides less typical indicators of alcoholism and thus may provide more honest responses. The ANXCONCN scale measures fears and other feelings about drinking. The RECPAWAR scale shows self-awareness of drinking problems.

The third-level factor measures broad involvement with alcohol on the ALCINVOL scale. This may be used as a general indicator of alcohol-related problems.

The manual authors state that most people 16 years of age or older can read and understand the language of the test. Ideally the respondent should be alcohol-free for 8 hours or more before test administration. The respondent should be able to complete the items in 35–60 minutes. With careful reading, the instruction page may take a couple of minutes to read. Although most of the items may be readable for those 16 years and older, they require absolute honesty and a good memory for completion. If the respondent ponders items or has difficulty in reading, completion may take longer than one hour.

Because so many of the items clearly define alcohol as a problem in the item stem, the respondent may be hesitant to answer honestly for fear of being portrayed as a chronic alcoholic. Some of the items also have problems in that the possible responses do not agree with the stems, (e.g., some items should begin with "How often" instead of "Have you").

The AUI is clearly labeled as a test in bold on the cover and title pages, which may lead some respondents to believe there is a best or correct answer. The title page descriptor does not clarify this, for those who may, having taken other tests, skip the instructions page.

The internal consistency reliabilities and test-retest reliabilities are both good across all but two scales (QUANTITY—amount consumed, and MARI-PROB—marital problems resulting from drinking). In addition to the scales being fairly stable as long as the respondent's circumstances remain relatively the same, the scales also have good operational independence.

The authors suggest the AUI has strong content validity because only content relevant for decision making in treatment programs was included. The lack of further clarification as to types of treatment programs and types of decisions that relate to the content raise questions about the appropriateness of this validity for decision making. The criterion validity (criterion of alcohol dependence) is also supported. Correlates with the Michigan Alcoholism Screening Test (Selzer, 1971) vary considerably by scale, as would be expected. The manual author provides information for hand scoring and guidelines for interpretation and clinical use. The interpretations are provided in general only for high scale scores, thereby limiting other interpretations and clinical uses. Most of the norming and supportive studies have involved primarily Caucasians, possibly limiting applicability to other groups.

In summary, the AUI is one way for a clinician to obtain information about the multiple dimensions of alcoholism in clients who are fairly capable, honest, and cooperative. The AUI seems to have good reliability and validity, and to be appropriate for use with Caucasian populations. Lack of information about use with other populations should encourage cautious use and interpretation until further studies are undertaken.

REVIEWER'S REFERENCE

Selzer, M. L. (1971). The Michigan Alcoholism Screening Test: The quest for a new diagnostic instrument. *American Journal of Psychiatry, 127*, 1653-1658.

[5]
Assessment of Conceptual Organization (ACO): Improving Writing, Thinking, and Reading Skills.
Purpose: Developed to assess "understanding of conceptual organization in written language."

Population: Grades 4–6, 7–12, 10–adult.
Publication Date: 1991.
Acronym: ACO.
Scores: 3 criteria: Correct Superordinate Word Chosen, Appropriateness of Topic Sentence, Relatedness of Topic Sentence and Three Other Sentences.
Administration: Group.
Price Data, 1991: $24.95 per set of 20 assessment and 20 scoring forms (select level); $29.95 per manual (57 pages).
Time: (15–20) minutes.
Comments: Optional administration and scoring procedures available for "reluctant" writers.
Author: Christian Gerhard.
Publisher: Research for Better Schools.

Review of the Assessment of Conceptual Organization (ACO): Improving Writing, Thinking, and Reading Skills by DEBORAH L. BANDALOS, Assistant Professor of Educational Psychology, University of Nebraska-Lincoln, Lincoln, NE:

The Assessment of Conceptual Organization (ACO) was developed to provide "classroom teachers, resource personnel, and tutors with a practical way of determining whether students have a usable understanding of how ideas are organized" (p. 1). Three lists of related words are provided from which the examinee is required to choose one to use in composing a paragraph. In each list of words, one word is designated as the organizing or "superordinate" word. Examinees are instructed to determine which of the words fits this role, and to use it in forming the first sentence of a paragraph. The other words are to be used in separate sentences which make up the remainder of the paragraph. An example of a typical set of words is "table, chair, bed, furniture," where "furniture" would be the superordinate word. There are three form levels: basic, for grades 4 through 6; intermediate, for middle or high school range; and advanced, for more advanced high school students or adults. The forms differ only in the number and difficulty of the words given.

Development of the ACO was based on the theory that categorization skills are fundamental to the ability to organize one's perceptions as well as to process and convey information. Extensive work with teachers and students in formulating ways of teaching and measuring these skills led to the development of the instrument.

The ACO is intended for use as a classroom assessment device and all scoring is done by the classroom teacher. Students are assessed on three criteria: correct selection of the superordinate word, writing an appropriate topic sentence, and writing three (or more) related sentences. Each criterion is rated as either met or not met. Instructions including examples of unsatisfactory sentences are provided for this assessment, followed by a very useful section on using the results in class. However, because assessment depends entirely on the judgement of the teacher, the consistency of these ratings is questionable. The possibility of halo and leniency effects in particular is a concern, particularly as no information on reliability or any other psychometric information is provided in the manual. Although interrater reliability is of primary importance in an instrument of this type, test-retest reliability estimates would also be of interest.

The lack of psychometric information mentioned previously also extends to area of validity. This subject is not addressed specifically in the manual, although two studies are alluded to in describing the development of the instrument. In one study done by the test author, chi-square tests were used to show that ACO scores were not related to age, race, gender, reading comprehension, or vocabulary scores on a standardized test, or with the similarities, block design, or performance scales of the Wechsler Intelligence Scale for Children. Aside from the fact that the chi-square test would not appear to be appropriate for some of these analyses, it is not clear how these relationships, or the lack of them, bears on the usefulness of the ACO.

The ACO appears to be a well thought out instrument based on a great deal of practical experience. However, it cannot be recommended for general use at this time because of the lack of norms or of any form of reliability or validity evidence.

Review of the Assessment of Conceptual Organization (ACO): Improving Writing, Thinking, and Reading Skills by DALE P. SCANNELL, Professor of Education, University of Maryland at College Park, College Park, MD:

The Assessment of Conceptual Organization (ACO): Improving Writing, Thinking, and Reading Skills is a very good example of the current emphasis on trying to relate assessments more closely to the activities of classroom teachers and others who work directly with students. The scores produced by this assessment are a set of judgments made by the person who administers the instrument. In some cases, the accuracy of the judgment is quite apparent (e.g., the correct word was identified). In other cases, the judgments are more subjective (e.g., the sentence written by the examinee was appropriate).

Each test is a single page; examinees enter identifying information at the top. The directions tell examinees they will be writing a paragraph using words in one of three groups presented below. Examinees choose the group, identify the word in the list that is the organizing concept for the other words, and then write a paragraph of a specified number of sentences using all of the words in the list. Space is provided for examinees to write the title word and to write the paragraph.

Scoring includes a yes/no decision about the superordinate word, the topic sentence, and whether the sentences are appropriately related to each other. Examiners are to record how many hints they had to give and are to assess behaviors of the examinees during the test.

The quality of instruments such as this can be judged in terms of the research and theory that provide the foundation for the assessment and the appropriateness of the suggestions made for the use of the information produced by the test. These topics are covered in a well-written, comprehensive, and persuasive manual for the ACO.

The manual includes a section on categorization. The importance of this skill in learning and using knowledge and how the skill can be assessed are covered. The research background is described briefly and includes attention to the theoretical background and research conducted by the author and others.

The manual also includes a section in which the instrument is described and instructions for administration are provided. These are quite adequate and well written. The section of the manual describing how the results of the assessment can be used in class is also well done.

Some might classify this instrument as an instructional device rather than as a test. Regardless, this instrument is presented as a means of collecting information to assist teachers in targeting instruction more appropriately for students who most likely will be at different levels of skill in categorizing and presenting ideas in writing. It fulfills its purported purpose admirably.

[6]
Athletic Motivation Inventory.
Purpose: Constructed to measure the personality and motivation of athletes participating in competitive sports.
Population: Male and female athletes ages 13 and older and coaches.
Publication Dates: 1969–87.
Acronym: AMI.

Scores, 14: Drive, Aggressiveness, Determination, Responsibility, Leadership, Self-Confidence, Emotional Control, Mental Toughness, Coachability, Conscientiousness, Trust, Validity Scales (Accuracy, Desirability, Completion Rate).

Administration: Group or individual.

Price Data, 1991: $40 per athlete for non-profit teams (scoring and reports by publisher included in price); $85 per questionnaire for professional and recreational athletes (scoring and reports by publisher included in price).

Foreign Language Editions: French and Spanish editions available.

Time: (40–50) minutes.

Authors: Thomas A. Tutko, Leland P. Lyon, and Bruce C. Oglive.

Publisher: Institute of Athletic Motivation.

Comments: May be used for individual self-assessment.

Cross References: For a review by Andrew L. Comrey, see 8:409 (19 references).

Review of the Athletic Motivation Inventory by JOHN W. SHEPARD, Associate Professor of Counselor Education, The University of Toledo, Toledo, OH:

The authors of the Athletic Motivation Inventory (AMI) appear to have designed an instrument that meets its stated purpose of measuring the attitudes of athletes. The format of the AMI addresses 11 key attitudinal components necessary to develop and perform successfully as an athlete. Responses are based on participant self-appraisals. Questionnaire items appear relevant to athletics and understandable for readers functioning at or above a fifth to sixth grade level. Interpretive reports are generated to coaches and/or their potential players. These reports, though written in somewhat definitive terms, are readable, comprehensive, and personally constructive in nature. The AMI's technical manual is well organized, descriptive, and generally complete. All materials associated with the Inventory's use are visually attractive and easy to access. This group-administered measure is time effective but it is relatively expensive to use. All major sports are represented in the AMI's norming and interpretive information.

The AMI's Preliminary Technical manual is generally user friendly. The index is well laid out with helpful descriptions of the Inventory's format, purpose, history, and design. With few exception, technical information is complete and portrayed via numerous tables strategically placed throughout the manual. Cautionary statements regarding the instrument's use, applicability, and interpretation are stated in a realistic and useful manner.

Statistical analysis of the AMI reveals positive results in most areas. Test items were generated through a polling of coaches in a variety of sports. A pool of questions were field tested on approximately 500 athletes and an item analysis was conducted. A final inventory item count of 190 was utilized. Internal reliability is good and test-retest reliability fair to poor. Test-retest coefficients ranged from .46–.80 with most scores falling in the .60s. The number of subjects used in the above studies were limited to 100 and 56, respectively. Data were collected in 1972. The test-retest interval was 9 weeks.

As previously indicated, the AMI's content validity appears good in terms of items selected for inclusion. The construction of the test, however, probably occurred more than 20 years ago. It is not known whether test items are still appropriately current. No descriptions of item revisions/changes were given. Concurrent validity information was based on numerous, but again dated, studies comparing the scale with other proven measures of personality traits relevant to athletics. Cited study findings were supportive but by no means conclusive in validating the AMI's usefulness. No efforts to establish predictive validity were cited.

The manual's shortcoming involves its description of normative data. One table provides a breakdown of reference group participants by type and level of sport. No information regarding the dates or locality of the data collection was identified. Group size by sport and level of competition ranged from 100 to 5,364 with most group sizes falling below an N of 500. The authors state that group sizes will eventually be upgraded until a minimum of 1,000 for each sport/level is achieved. Progress toward this goal is not mentioned in the manual (copyright 1977). Parts of the interpretative reports appear to have been updated in 1989, but no explanation is given.

In summary, the AMI looks to be soundly constructed and useful in carrying out its stated purposes of recruiting, understanding, and preparing athletes to compete in sports. AMI materials are expensive but well laid out and practical to employ. The Inventory's normative data, however, are speciously dated. A revision/update of the manual's statistical contents appears to be in order.

[7]

The Auditory Discrimination and Attention Test.

Purpose: Designed to assess "auditory discrimination and attention for speech."

Population: Children ages 3.5–12 years referred for speech therapy.

Publication Date: 1988.
Scores: Total error score only.
Administration: Individual.
Price Data, 1992: £69 per complete set; £10.10 per 25 score sheets.
Time: (20) minutes.
Author: Rosemarie MorganBarry.
Publisher: NFER-Nelson Publishing Co., Ltd. [England].
Cross References: See T4:230 (1 reference).

Review of The Auditory Discrimination and Attention Test by KAREN T. CAREY, Associate Professor of Psychology, California State University, Fresno, Fresno, CA:

The Auditory Discrimination and Attention Test assesses a child's ability to discriminate and attend to differences between 17 pairs of words. Presented in a picture-book format the pairs have one "broad" feature, consisting of a voicing group (i.e., pear/bear), place group (i.e., key/tea), manner group (i.e., mat/bat), and a cluster group (i.e., crown/clown). Twelve colored counters are provided and the child responds to the stimulus word by placing one of the counters in slots provided on the book frame beneath the appropriate picture.

The first item presented is a demonstration item and scoring of this item is not included as a part of the 17-item test. The test is not recommended for children who fail to understand the test instructions or the demonstration procedures, nor for children who have poor concentration.

Each pair of pictures is presented to the child and the child is asked to name each word. The child is then told to place a counter in the slot underneath the picture of the word said by the examiner. The examiner gives three repetitions of each word in the pair to children $3\frac{1}{2}$ to 5 years old and six repetitions of each word in the pair to children 5 to 12 years of age. As each item is presented to the child, the examiner is to make certain the child cannot see his/her face (although how this is to be accomplished is not described). Repetitions of words at the request of the child are scored as errors, fluctuations in the child's ability to attend should result in test termination, and for children who are unable to place counters in the appropriate slots, eye-point responses may be made and the examiner inserts the counter into the slot indicated by the child.

Raw scores are obtained based on the total error score and standard scores, expressed as standard deviations from the mean, are obtained based on the child's age. In order to interpret the test, a score of -2 standard deviations from the mean indicates the child is functioning in the "danger" zone. Unfortunately, according to the author, it is difficult to ascertain whether such deviations occur because of a child's auditory discrimination difficulties or due to attentional problems. The author states that a score in the danger range would indicate the child to be in need of "auditory attention-to-discrimination tasks."

The test was standardized on children in England ranging in age from 3 years 6 months to 12 years. The actual number of subjects included in the sample cannot be deciphered from the information presented in the manual. A serious limitation of the tool is the minimal technical information provided. Sample sizes of groups on whom validity and reliability studies were conducted are not included in the manual. For example, no correlation was found between hearing loss (between 20 and 50 decibels) and error rates on the test. The number of children included in this study is not reported. Another study investigating the correlation between attention and auditory discrimination was conducted ($r = .8$). According to the test author, the 23 children included in this study were identified as having attention problems based on descriptions by Cooper, Moodley, and Reynell (1978). These descriptions are not included, however, in the manual. Internal consistency studies cannot be analyzed because descriptions of the samples and sample sizes are not included in the manual. Furthermore the same information is lacking in the section describing two reliability studies.

A correlation study of The Auditory Discrimination and Attention Test and the Auditory Discrimination Test (ADT, Wepman, 1973) with 13 subjects (mean age = 5.8 years) revealed a correlation of .328. The author describes the low correlation as a result of differences between the content of the two tests and that each test requires additional skills beyond auditory discrimination. The reason for selecting the ADT for this study rather than Wepman's more recent Auditory Discrimination Test, Second Edition (Wepman & Reynolds, 1987; 11:467) is not described.

The use of The Auditory Discrimination and Attention Test must be questioned at this time. There is not enough technical information included in the manual, the number of test items is small (i.e., 17), and the actual sample sizes upon which psychometric data are based are not described. No information is given related to socioeconomic status of the students, parents' level of education, number of years the children had been attending school, and whether or not the children included in the standardization sample had other difficulties beyond speech impairments. Finally, it seems the information that can be obtained from this instrument could be gathered in natural environments through the use of structured observations.

REVIEWER'S REFERENCES

Wepman, J. (1973). The Auditory Discrimination Test. Chicago: Language Research Association, Inc.

Cooper, J., Moodley, M., & Reynell, J. (1978). *Helping language development*. London: Edward Arnold.

Wepman, J., & Reynolds, M. (1987). Wepman's Auditory Discrimination Test, Second Edition. Los Angeles: Western Psychological Services.

Review of The Auditory Discrimination and Attention Test by GERALD TINDAL, Associate Professor of Special Education, University of Oregon, Eugene, OR:

This test by MorganBarry (1988) is designed to ascertain whether children (ages 3.5 to 12 years old) can/do discriminate between the initial and final sounds of word pairs that are very similar (entitled a "minimal pairs paradigm" by the author). A series of pictures are presented on cards (two pictures per card and 17 pairs of words in total) and the student is asked to imitate and produce the word each picture represents. For each pair, the student is given 3–6 trials. The test "was designed for use with all children who have been referred for speech therapy, and whose perceptual abilities are thought to need investigation" (manual, p. 2). As the author notes, the name of the test implies that failure to make auditory discriminations may be due to perception problems (can complete the behavior) or attention problems (do complete the behavior).

The manual author provides a very complete description of the domain from which the words were sampled, emphasizing those features that are consistent with the purpose of the test. The pictures are all well displayed on the cards and represent words of high frequency in the everyday speech of children. Administration directions are clear and unambiguous; the total testing time is brief (less than 20 minutes). The administration protocol emphasizes first the child's production of the word with presentation of each picture, and then if incorrect (appropriately matched word but articulated incorrectly or use of the wrong word to depict the picture), the tester's teaching of the word with subsequent student imitations. Finally, the student's "auditory discrimination" is tested by having the child post a chip under the picture representing the word stated by the tester; each word is presented more than once (three times for children ages 3.6–4.11 and six times for children ages 5–11.11). The directions emphasize the need for uniformity of verbalization on the part of the tester.

The child's score comprises a count of the number of errors and is then converted to a standard score.

Normative charts are presented for calculating the student's score with a z-score of -2.2 highlighted as the "danger point" (manual, p. 7). These normative tables provide deviation scores in three age groups: preschool (3.6–4.11 years old), primary (5–6.11 years old), and junior (7–11.11 years old). The data from these normative tables were generated by testing 300 children between the ages of 3–12 throughout England. Within this group, subsets of children thought to have speech, language, and attention problems were identified and analyzed separately. Although the geographic regions are presented where children were sampled, no specific sampling plan is further explicated (e.g., the number per area or use of any other blocking factor such as race or SES).

Reliability data are presented comparing "experimental" (speech-impaired) and normal students; the data are based on an unknown number of students. Differences between these groups are found only in the school-age students. No further information is presented about the methods of this pilot study which was conducted in 1984. Interrater reliability (.80) and test-retest (.90) data are reported (based on separate samples). However, no information is provided about this study (either describing the subjects or the methods of research).

There are significant differences in item difficulty across the word pairs. The most difficult pairs for all groups are "sum–sun," "fan–van," and "mouth–mouse." Further validity data are reported that reflect low correlation between hearing loss and performance on this test (for a "small group of children with hearing losses of between 20 and 50 decibels"); however, for a group of children found to have attention difficulties, a reasonably high correlation was found between their scores on this test and their attention levels. No information is provided about either of these studies (i.e., who was tested, how many, what measures were used, or what assessment procedures were followed).

Finally, concurrent validity information is provided by correlating performance on this test and the Auditory Discrimination Test (Wepman, 1973). A small sample study ($N = 13$) suggested a rather low correlation between the two measures (.33). The rationale for choosing the Auditory Discrimination Test is not well stated.

In summary, The Auditory Discrimination and Attention Test is a clear and easy to use test that may provide some information on a child's perception of sound discriminations. The behavior sampled is of questionable educational value, but it may provide low level (medically relevant) perception information. The normative values must be interpreted with great caution, particularly given the exclusively British composition of the group, a problem which may occur because of differences in accents that inherently recalibrate the error rates in U.S. English speaking populations. The reliability data reported are marginal and are not used in establishing standard errors of measurement. Validity data are likewise weak and fail to provide any convincing data that the decisions made from this instrument can help students educationally. The instrument should be used solely to obtain clinical samples of behavior.

REVIEWER'S REFERENCE

Wepman, J. (1973). The Auditory Discrimination Test. Chicago: Language Research Association, Inc.

[8]
Bankson-Bernthal Test of Phonology.
Purpose: "Designed for use by speech-language clinicians to assess the phonology of preschool and school-age children."
Population: Ages 3–9.
Publication Dates: 1989–90.
Acronym: BBTOP.
Scores, 3: Word Inventory, Consonants Composite, Phonological Processes Composite.
Administration: Individual.
Price Data, 1991: $88.98 per complete kit; $34.98 per picture book; $18 per 24 record forms; $19.98 per easel and carrying case; $24.99 per manual ('90, 111 pages).
Time: (10–15) minutes.
Authors: Nicholas W. Bankson and John E. Bernthal.
Publisher: The Riverside Publishing Co.

Review of the Bankson-Bernthal Test of Phonology by LYNN S. BLISS, Professor of Communication Disorders and Sciences, Wayne State University, Detroit, MI:

The Bankson-Bernthal Test of Phonology (BBTOP) was designed to describe consonant production and phonological error patterns and to compare a child's phonological ability with other children of comparable age.

The BBTOP includes a picture book consisting of 80 illustrations depicting objects within the vocabulary of young children. A portable easel is also available. The record form includes sections for transcription and scoring, interpretation, standardization, and design information.

The BBTOP is designed for speech-language clinicians. It is quickly and easily administered. The clinician asks the child to name the picture and scores each response. Descriptions of scoring procedures and practice protocols are presented in the manual.

Three scores are obtained. The Word Inventory score is derived by totaling the words in which all consonants were produced accurately. This measure represents an overall index of a child's phonological performance. The score is converted into a percentile rank and standard score. Consonant errors are recorded in initial and final positions. A scale score is derived for each position. The Consonants Composite score represents the sum of the two scale scores and is transformed into a percentile rank and a standard score. A phonological process analysis is included that yields a Phonological Process Composite score, percentile rank, and standard score. The following processes are evaluated: assimilation, fronting, final consonant deletion, weak syllable deletion, stopping, gliding, cluster simplification, depalatization, deaffrication, and vocalization. Interpretation of the scores is described in the manual.

The BBTOP was standardized at 61 sites within the United States on a sample of 1,070 nonimpaired children between the ages of 3 and 9. There was an approximately even ratio of males to females. The percentage of Caucasian children tested is similar to the percentage in the U.S. population. African-American and Hispanic children are somewhat underrepresented in the standardization pool. Scores for the age groups of 3 to 6 were used to derive the normative data. Percentile ranks were converted into standard scores and a stanine ($M = 5$, $SD = 2$) was selected for the standard metric.

Internal consistency coefficients are presented to estimate test reliability. The split-half reliability coefficients are all above .92. The stability of test performance was investigated with a subgroup of 34 4-year-old children. They were retested approximately 8 weeks after the initial test. Significant correlations were obtained between the test scores and significant differences were found for many of the scores. High interrater agreement was obtained on 4- and 8-year-old children.

Content validity was addressed by demonstrating the theore tical and research basis for target selection and scoring procedures. Construct validity was evident in age-related sequencing of test data and in relationships among the subcomponents of the test. The data show the BBTOP evaluates a variety of dimensions of phonological performance.

The strengths of the BBTOP are in its ease of administration, clear illustrations, numerous examples presented in the manual, adequate age range of a normative population, and appropriate reliability and validity information. This test will be very useful to practicing speech-language clinicians. Two disadvantages are evident. The first is the description of the derivation of the scale scores is difficult to follow both in the manual and on the response forms. The examples in the manual are useful and help to offset this limitation. However, a clinician must spend time learning how to obtain these scores. The second disadvantage is the reduced number of African-American and Hispanic children included in the normative scores. Clinicians working with children from diverse ethnic backgrounds may wish to collect additional normative data. In summary, the BBTOP is a well-constructed phonological assessment measure that will be useful for speech-language clinicians.

Review of the Bankson-Bernthal Test of Phonology by LAWRENCE J. TURTON, Professor of Speech-Language Pathology, Indiana University of Pennsylvania, Indiana, PA:

As they accepted the mantle of the leading experts in phonological (nee articulation) disorders, Nicholas Bankson and John Bernthal brought new standards of scholarship and clinical leadership to the forefront of the topic. Their text (1988) is now a standard for the student interested in the field of speech sound problems. With the publication of this test, the Bankson-Bernthal Test of Phonology (BBTOP), they have made two additional significant contributions to the profession. First and foremost, they have provided convincing evidence that articulation tests can be subjected to the rigors of psychometric analysis. A perusal of the previous editions of the Buros *Mental Measurements Yearbook* series provides numerous examples of "articulation" tests for which the authors have disregarded the standards of tests and measurement or have paid only lip service to them. If nothing else, this test will become the standard against which all future articulation tests can be compared for psychometric quality. No longer will a test developer be able to claim face validity or self-judgements of reliability as being sufficient.

Their second contribution rests in the availability of an instrument for developing data sets on phonological processes that can be used by the practicing clinician. The procedures are an efficient compromise between the hybrid attempt of the Khan-Lewis system (1986; 10:164) and the rigorous detail demanded by the research methodology of Shriberg and Kwiatkowski (1980) or Ingram (1981). Bankson and Bernthal chose seven processes that their analysis of the literature suggested were used beyond 3 years of age and three that are common to other analytical systems. Unfortunately, they did not provide references or data to suggest that these 10 processes are most common in the speech of children enrolled in articulation therapy, a significant factor for decision making.

The manual is explicitly clear both for an experienced clinician who is versed in phonological theory and for the young graduate student who is acquiring basic skills in phonological assessment. It allows the user to move easily through each step from testing through interpretation of the results. The picture stimuli are age-appropriate in terms of vocabulary difficulty and quality of the color drawings. On page 6, the authors do make the time-honored error in the profession of requiring "phonetic transcription" when their examples are only phonemically transcribed. Ironically, allophonic variation, the heart of phonology of spoken language, is ignored in this test of phonology.

Three values are derived from the data set: a word inventory score, a consonant score, and a phonological process inventory. The word inventory is a clever procedure to insure that the child actually knows the word and that phonological variations in a child's speech are independent of lexical difficulties. The authors are to be commended for this scoring procedure and future test developers would be wise to adopt this strategy.

Consonants are scored only in the initial and final word positions and in clusters. Thus, unless the tester pays close attention to the productions in the relatively few multisyllabic words, intervocalic allophones are eliminated from consideration in determining the status of a child's system. Bankson and Bernthal do not provide a viable explanation for this decision; a serious omission in light of the fact that Final Consonant Deletion, Weak Syllable Deletion, and Cluster Simplification have their roots in the early stages of phonological acquisition when the syllable structures and word relationships are tenuous. The nature of the pattern of the word structure in a child's speech may be predictive of the persistence of a process.

All of the scores are easily converted to standard psychometric and/or linguistic values by an experienced clinician. The tables are easily followed and evidence of a statistical linkage among the values is readily available in the manual. The tables of special interest are those found on pages 15, 76, and 78 because they provide data on age-related scores for the words and sounds tested, a data set of some comfort for those who are still attuned to making decisions on the basis of age of acquisition. Bankson and Bernthal graciously created a new set of developmental norms for their test, a unique event in the history of articulation testing. Unlike some of their predecessors (Fisher & Logemann, 1971; Goldman & Fristoe, 1969), they did not resort to using the traditional Templin (1957) norms, which may not be applicable to a different set of lexical items.

Once again, they are to be commended for this change in professional practice. More importantly, the test can be used as a consonant articulation test separate from the phonological processing concepts.

Consistent with the pattern established by Bankson in his other test (Bankson Language Test-2 [1990; 11:26]), the BBTOP has a plethora of data on reliability and validity. Using a sample of 1,070 children drawn from across the nation through a network of quality colleagues, the authors present psychometric analyses that more than vindicate their decision to publish this test. The correlations for temporal reliability ranged from .74 for Consonants Composite to .89 for the Word Inventory. The values are based on only 34 children with an 8-week spread of time and could use data from a larger sample to substantiate the claims for stability. However, we do have a base from which future research can be built.

Split-half reliability coefficients for all three measures are extremely high across all age groups (3-0 years to 9-0 years) covered by this test. The coefficients ranged from, for example, .92 for phonological processes at age 8-0 years to .98 for all three measures at 9-0 years. Standard Errors of Measurement are well within acceptable limits for all age groups. The amount of variability of an obtained score is small, suggesting the scores do reflect some consistent pattern of behavior by the child. Unfortunately, the authors report only correlational type data for interobserver reliability, albeit, very high coefficients (.85 to .99). A data set on percentages of agreement is necessary for this kind of test because the analysis is not based on total number of errors but the specific error per item. Data on the consistency of phonemic transcription per item per tester would greatly strengthen the claims for reliable scoring and valid analyses. Furthermore, the data base for all reliability measures must be extended to children who are in therapy so that the profession will be able to judge the adequacy of the test for the children who are the real target population for these inventories.

As with reliability, Bankson and Bernthal made the effort to present the user with a logical, coherent body of evidence for content and construct validity, eliminating the need to justify the test on the basis of face validity. On the other hand, they omitted an analysis of concurrent validity, which should have been easy to obtain, assuming they determined the normality of their standardization population with the same tests. Furthermore, the lack of data sets to allow for comparisons relative to the standard systems developed by Weiner (1979), Shriberg and Kwiatkowski (1980), and Ingram (1981) leaves another gap that needs to be filled by subsequent research.

These analyses would have told the reader how well the scores from the BBTOP correlate with natural speech productions, the essence of phonological development.

Construct validity values were obtained from correlational studies of score patterns and were followed up by detailed factor analyses. The data indicated that the ability to name the items was independent from the ability to produce the sounds. A tester can be confident that phonology and not the lexicon is the major focus of the test. The factor analyses also suggest a predictable pattern of independence for the phonemic units and the phonological processes. The data suggest that children do utilize the processes as separate sets and not as a single, unitary skill.

There is, however, a critical component of phonological theory that is not addressed in the manual by the authors. If phonological processes are supposed to be strategies employed by children to learn adult forms (Stampe, 1979), and if they tend to disappear at about age 4-0 years, what is actually being tested by the BBTOP? Are we attempting to identify developmental strategies for the language learner or phonological rules that control the child's developed, adult system? In Tables 4.2 and 9.5 of the manual strong evidence is presented that the developmental process for the standardization group ended at age 6-0 years. All consonants and clusters items were produced above the 90% level or higher (except for final clusters); all processes appear to have disappeared except in a few children as can be noted by the size of the standard deviation at age 6-0 years as compared to the mean score. The children in the standardization group followed the predicted pattern of phasing out processes early in life.

An understanding of phonological processes within the system of a child or a group of children requires knowledge of their level of language development because we cannot determine if a phonological variation is a process or a phonological rule unless we know what the relationship of these patterns is to lexical, morphological, and syntactic development. As a profession, we would be suspect were we to engage children in a treatment program for *normal* developmental strategies as opposed to aberrant phonological rules.

Utilization of this test and any other process measure demands the use of supportive data on language acquisition; samples of conversational speech; and detailed, in-depth, follow-up testing of the processes (rules) identified by the test results. The authors report the BBTOP can be administered in 10 to 15 minutes. Any good clinician dealing with young children will do language testing; they need only spend 20 to 30 additional minutes to obtain evidence in the way of a sample to determine whether the child is using rules or processes. Phonological processes could turn out to be the coarticulation phenomenon of the '90s. McDonald (1964) presented the profession with a partial concept and created a test and therapy model before adequate research was done to substantiate the model. We are at risk now with phonological concepts unless we clearly distinguish between developmental phenomena and adult rules.

A final problem with the concept of phonological processes as used in the profession is that we have failed to generate new therapy principles and techniques to match the developmental model (other than minimal pairs [Weiner, 1981]). We can make decisions differently; but, we have not freed ourselves from the restrictions of traditional or sensory-motor therapies. (See Hodson & Paden [1990] for an example of phonological decision making but traditional therapy techniques.) Phonological information will be of its greatest significance when it can generate treatment programs that simulate normal developmental sequences that can be justified by modern concepts of phonology and biology.

These issues are not unique to the BBTOP, but they do permeate this test as well as other writings in this developmental domain. However, Bankson and Bernthal have made a valiant effort to upgrade the quality of testing in the area of articulation. They are to be complimented for advancing the state of the art for all of us who work with children. Whether one uses this test as a general test for articulation or as a "phonological" test, it is simply the best on the market today. The other commercial instruments that failed to follow psychometric procedures for test development can be retired and replaced by the BBTOP because with this procedure one will know what is being tested and what the scores actually mean. The other concerns about reliability and validity raised in this review are easily dealt with in traditional psychometric research and will, no doubt, be available in the professional journals in the future.

REVIEWER'S REFERENCES

Templin, M. C. (1957). *Certain language skills in children*. Minneapolis, MN: The University of Minnesota Press.
McDonald, E. T. (1964). *Articulation testing and treatment: A sensory-motor approach*. Pittsburgh, PA: Stanwix House, Inc.
Goldman, R., & Fristoe, M. (1969). Goldman-Fristoe Test of Articulation. Circle Pines, MN: American Guidance Service.
Fisher, H. B., & Logemann, J. A. (1971). The Fisher-Logemann Test of Articulation Competence. Chicago: The Riverside Publishing Co.
Stampe, D. (1979). *A dissertation on natural phonology*. New York: Garland Publishing, Inc.
Weiner, F. F. (1979). *Phonological process analysis*. Baltimore, MD: University Park Press.

Shriberg, L. D., & Kwiatkowski, J. (1980). *Natural process analysis (NPA): A procedure for phonological analysis of continuous speech samples*. New York: John Wiley & Sons.
Ingram, D. (1981). *Procedures for the phonological analysis of children's language*. Baltimore, MD: University Park Press.
Weiner, F. F. (1981). Treatment of phonological disability using the method of meaningful minimal contrast: Two case studies. *Journal of Speech and Hearing Disorders, 46*, 97-103.
Khan, L. M., & Lewis, N. P. (1986). Khan-Lewis Phonological Analysis. Circle Pines, MN: American Guidance Service.
Bernthal, J. E., & Bankson, N. W. (1988). *Articulation and phonological disorders* (2nd ed.). Englewood Cliffs, NJ: Prentice-Hall, Inc.
Bankson, N. W. (1990). Bankson Language Test-2. Austin, TX: PRO-ED, Inc.
Hodson, B. W., & Paden, E. P. (1991). Targeting Intelligible Speech: A Phonological Approach to Remediation. Austin, TX: PRO-ED, Inc.

[9]

Basic Personality Inventory.

Purpose: Constructed to be a "measure of personality and psychopathology."

Population: Ages 12 and over.

Publication Dates: 1984–89.

Acronym: BPI.

Scores, 12: Hypochondriasis, Depression, Denial, Interpersonal Problems, Alienation, Persecutory Ideas, Anxiety, Thinking Disorder, Impulse Expression, Social Introversion, Self Depreciation, Deviation.

Administration: Individual or group.

Price Data, 1991: $44 per examination kit including 10 reusable test booklets, 25 answer sheets, scoring template, 25 profile sheets, answer sheet and coupon for BPI report, and manual ('89, 87 pages); $22.75 per 25 test booklets; $5.50–$9 (depending on volume) per 25 answer sheets; $8 per scoring template; $5.50–$9 (depending on volume) per 25 profile sheets (select adult or adolescent norms); $22 per manual; scoring service offered by publisher.

Time: [35] minutes.

Author: Douglas N. Jackson.

Publisher: Sigma Assessment Systems, Inc., Research Psychologists Press Division.

Cross References See T4:254 (16 references).

Review of the Basic Personality Inventory by SUSANA URBINA, *Associate Professor of Psychology, University of North Florida, Jacksonville, FL:*

The Basic Personality Inventory (BPI) is a test designed to meet two clear goals: (*a*) to identify and measure a set of constructs broadly spanning the domain of psychopathology, and (*b*) to do so in a manner that incorporates modern methods and stringent standards of test construction. Jackson, the test author, chose to accomplish the first goal by trying to isolate the constructs that underlie the empirically derived diagnostic efficiency of the Minnesota Multiphasic Personality Inventory (MMPI).

Then, he attempted to reconstitute them in the context of a set of "purer" (i.e., more homogeneous), more meaningful (i.e., bipolar rather than unipolar), more widely useful (i.e., with both normal and dysfunctional individuals), and nonoverlapping dimensional scales.

The BPI was also designed to correct or minimize undesirable features, such as objectionable item content and the use of pejorative terms in scale names, that have plagued the MMPI and other older inventories such as the Millon Clinical Multiaxial Inventory (MCMI). With a total of 240 items, the BPI is a fairly short test that can be completed in about a half hour by persons with reading comprehension as low as the 5th grade level. The paper-and-pencil version can be easily scored by hand with a single template. The test is also available in formats suitable for computer administration, scoring, and interpretation; unfortunately, some scales for assessing response style are available only through computer scoring.

DEVELOPMENT. Although the BPI was published in the late 1980s, Jackson and his collaborators have been working on it since the mid 1970s and have accumulated a fair amount of research on the test. The construction of the BPI started with factor analyses of the MMPI and the Differential Personality Inventory (DPI), which is a comprehensive but still unpublished measure of 28 major and distinct dimensions of psychopathology that Douglas Jackson and Samuel Messick are developing. Eleven of the factors that emerged from these analyses were common to both tests and showed a good deal of convergence; these dimensions provided the conceptual basis for the 11 content scales of the BPI. A 12th scale, composed of critical items dealing with deviant tendencies and behaviors, was added later to assess distortion of responses in the negative direction; this Deviation scale is the only one in the BPI that does no t measure a homogeneous psychological trait.

Once the traits to be assessed by the BPI scales had been defined and conceptualized, original items were prepared. Item preparation took into account the need for homogeneity of the scales and for suppression of evaluative response biases. The selection of the 20 items for each scale (half keyed in the "True" direction and half in the "False" direction) was based on all the previously specified editorial criteria. In addition, a number of statistical indices, such as an item's variance and its correlations with its own scale, with irrelevant scales, and with a desirability scale, were used to select items.

NORMS. The BPI provides separate norms for adults and for adolescents and, because of consistent sex differences, for males and females as well. The adult norms are based on the responses of 709 men and 710 women selected randomly from telephone directories in the United States and voters records in Canada. In order to obtain high response rates to the mailed inventories, each adult in the sample was sent only a subset of one third of the BPI or 4 out of the 12 scales. The United States adults, who made up the vast majority of the sample, were almost all white (95.6%) and had more education and higher occupational levels than the general population. The adolescent norms were gathered on 880 males and 1,380 females from two Canadian provinces who did take the entire BPI and did so in person rather than by mail (D. N. Jackson, personal communication, February 25, 1993).

The profile sheets for adolescents and adults, separated by sex, show clear differences in the ranges of the scale scores for the two age groups. The distributions of the adults' scores show far less variability than those of the adolescents, possibly as a result of the restricted demographic composition of the adult sample. On the Self Depreciation scale, for example, the lowest tabled raw score (0) yields a T score equivalent of 43 and the highest raw score (15) yields a T score of 110 for adult males, whereas for adolescent males the lowest and highest raw scores (0 and 20) yield T scores of 38 and 104 respectively. At any rate, it appears the normative samples of the BPI, at the adult level, may not be representative of the general population. The author himself suggests that accumulation of separate norms for nonwhite subgroups is indispensable in order to use the test with ethnic minorities and promises this is being planned for the future.

PSYCHOMETRIC PROPERTIES. The extraordinary care devoted to the conceptual aspects of the BPI is evident in the quality and variety of investigations of its psychometric properties. On the issue of reliability, for instance, the manual presents data on internal consistency (KR 20) reliabilities for 9 samples and test-retest reliabilities for two groups; these coefficients range from .49 to .90, with central values in the .70s. Moreover, the reliability of the BPI is also described from the standpoints of factor structure at the item level and of congruence among desirability ratings and frequencies of endorsement across items. Although the reliability indices presented are not uniformly high, the patterns in their fluctuations are largely consonant with what would be expected given the premises that underlie the scales.

Jackson's commitment to a construct-based approach to personality testing is also evident in the data he and his collaborators have gathered to examine the validity of the BPI scales. Evidence of convergent and discriminant validity has been collected using the multitrait-multimethod framework and includes several factor analytic studies and studies of criterion-related validity, including a multiple discriminant analysis of delinquent and nondelinquent groups. Attention to proper procedure in the gathering of these data extends to highly desirable yet seldom seen practices such as establishing the reliability of *criterion* data by more than one method.

Because the BPI was designed to tap the constructs underlying the MMPI clinical scales, data comparing results on the two inventories are particularly relevant. A factor analytic study using 235 male alcoholics suggests the two inventories share a substantial amount of common variance that can be accounted for almost completely by five factors whose loadings are conceptually consistent across both measures. Comparisons of the BPI scales with the Wiggins MMPI content scales fare rather well for the most part. Correlations between the BPI and the Millon Clinical Multiaxial Inventory, the State-Trait Anxiety Inventory, and the Adjective Check List are also presented but, not surprisingly, they are not as good as those between the BPI and the MMPI.

SUMMARY. At this point in its development, the BPI is still far from establishing diagnostic utility on a par with that of the MMPI (11:244). However, it has already achieved its primary goal of providing a shorter and psychometrically purer alternative for the study of personality and psychopathology. The BPI also shows promise as a tool for individual assessment of delinquent and nondelinquent adolescents. In order to enhance its potential usefulness in the assessment of adult psychopathology, the BPI must have a more representative set of adult norms as well as norms for ethnic subgroups and more studies of clinical populations.

Review of the Basic Personality Inventory by TAMELA YELLAND, Psychologist, Veterans Administration, Anaheim Vet Center, Anaheim, CA:

The Basic Personality Inventory (BPI) was designed to tap similar personality dimensions as the Minnesota Multiphasic Personality Inventory (MMPI), but with fewer items, more construct-oriented scale development, and less item overlap between scales. The BPI has 240 true-false questions rated to the 5th grade reading level. It has 12 scales, including one measure of overall psychopathology, one measure of the test taker's approach to the test, and 10 constructs of psychopathology.

The test has been targeted for psychiatric adult and deviant adolescent populations. It is self-administered, using paper-and-pencil or computer administration and scoring. The raw scores are easily plotted on a profile setup like the MMPI with standard *T* scores and a mean of 50. Unlike the MMPI, however, there is no cutoff score for clinical significance, because the scales were designed to distinguish between polar opposites. The author suggests that the lower (below 50) scores may be used to infer areas of personality strength and normal personality functioning. It is important to caution against utilizing these scores for anything more than inferences. Interpretation of the lower scores for normal populations has not been established as a valid use of this test.

Norms for male and female adults (age 19 and over), and adolescents (ages 12–18) have been established. Adult norms were based on U.S. and Canadian samples, which were well stratified except for race. Because 95.6% of the sample was white, the generalizability of the test is severely limited. It is not recommended for use with nonwhite populations until further norming data are added. The adolescent norms were derived from both normal and delinquent populations.

Scale definitions and expanded interpretations are provided, and are based on professional opinions. The manual author states the expanded interpretations are for use with delinquent adolescent populations. Unfortunately, no expanded interpretations are provided for any other population. The scale definitions are generally descriptive of behavior but are difficult to translate into diagnoses. This is one of the weaknesses of the test. Information necessary for the interpretation of the profiles and the translation of results into diagnoses, treatment plans, and insight into functioning is sorely lacking for adults and nondelinquent adolescents.

Profile validity is also difficult to differentiate. The "Denial" scale was created to tap the test taker's approach to the test and tendencies to suppress or exaggerate symptomatology. This particular scale was not developed through careful factoring as were the other scales, and does not appear to differentiate the motives of the test taker adequately.

The strengths of the BPI center on its design and psychometric quality. The author based the BPI on an earlier measure that had 28 scales, and through a series of factor analyses and modifications of the constructs, identified 10 scales. Items were edited to limit social desirability, reduce intercorrelations between scales, and to maximize content validity and internal consistency reliability for each scale. Internal consistency was established with adult and adolescent populations, and test-retest stability was demonstrated with young adults. Attempts were made to establish convergent and discriminant validity for the test, which the author admits is a difficult undertaking for a general personality measure. The results of these attempts and the solid construct and content analyses provide confidence in the validity of the measure for its intended use as a measure of psychopathology.

In conclusion then, the BPI is well designed, short, and easy to administer and score, and provides promising insights into the psychopathological functioning of adults and adolescents. It is not recommended for use with nonwhite populations, for interpretation of normal functioning solely, or for interpretation of psychopathological functioning without corollary measures. When further norms and interpretive data have been gathered, this instrument will no doubt be a valuable asset.

[10]
Basic Reading Inventory, Fifth Edition.
Purpose: Designed to assess the student's performance level in reading by a series of graded word lists and graded passages.
Population: Grades Pre-primer–8.
Publication Dates: 1978–91.
Acronym: BRI.
Scores, 3: 3 reading level scores (Independent, Instructional, Frustration) for each of 3 subtests (Word Recognition in Isolation, Word Recognition in Context, Comprehension).
Administration: Individual.
Forms, 5: A, B, C, LN, LE (suggested that A be used for an oral reading measure, B for a silent reading measure, C for a listening measure or posttest, LN for a narrative passages measure, and LE for an expository passages measure; Forms A, B, and C contain word lists and passages ranging from the beginning reader level (pre-primer) through the 8th grade; Forms LN and LE for third to eighth grade in difficulty).
Price Data: Price data for test materials including manual ('91, 284 pages) available from publisher.
Time: Administration time not reported.
Author: Jerry L. Johns.
Publisher: Kendall/Hunt Publishing Company.
Cross References: See T4:255 (4 references); for a review by Gus P. Plessas of the second edition, see 9:119.

Review of the Basic Reading Inventory, Fifth Edition by JERRILYN V. ANDREWS, Assistant for Assessment and Data Collection, Office of School Administration, Montgomery County Public Schools, Rockville, MD:

The Basic Reading Inventory (BRI), an individually administered, informal reading inventory (IRI), is intended for use by classroom teachers, reading specialists, special educators, and students taking courses in reading and diagnosis. The BRI is designed to help a teacher ascertain a student's Independent, Instructional, and Frustration reading levels as well as identify strategies the student uses for word identification, the student's strengths and weaknesses in answering various types of comprehension questions, and listening level.

The 284-page manual includes all five forms of the BRI, instructions for administering and scoring, sample strategies to help students overcome some reading difficulties, a good brief review of the literature on IRIs, and a description of the procedures used in revising the BRI. Although this seems relatively complete, the organization of the manual renders it less useful and user friendly than it could have been. There are two distinct sets of instructions for administering and scoring the BRI; the manual presents the timesaving procedures, intended for people who already understand administering and scoring reading inventories and who want to shorten testing time, in Section 2 and the regular procedures in Section 3. There are some substantial differences between the two sets of instructions and no data are presented to indicate how well the results of different testing procedures correlate. For new users, who are likely to read a manual from front to back, confusion is likely as they go from a general introduction to timesaving administration, which assumes they know quite a bit, followed by regular administration.

To illustrate this problem, the timesaving instructions for scoring Word Recognition in Isolation direct the user to total the correct responses in the "timed" and "untimed" columns. The column headings in the example and the terms used elsewhere in the manual are "sight" and "analysis." An experienced IRI user might quickly understand this change, but a novice probably will not. In addition, in Section 2 the user is told to decide whether to count total miscues or significant miscues before these terms have been introduced or defined. Both sets of instructions for administering and scoring the tests allow a great deal of flexibility and various alternatives are suggested. This flexibility may seriously reduce the likelihood that two testers would come to the same conclusions about a student.

In the review of the IRI literature (Section 7), the manual notes that questions of reliability and validity of IRIs continue to be raised. The BRI certainly illustrates this problem. This fifth edition of the BRI still contains no reliability, validity, or normative data.

The manual authors say that for this edition components were refined that "warranted revision, clarification, expansion, and updating" (p. ix) but give no idea of what was changed or why. It explains how the graded word lists were created and field tested on 309 students in grades 1–8 in the U.S. and Canada, but no data are presented to show that there are appropriate differences in difficulty between each level. The authors explain the forms of the BRI were equated in difficulty and generally how that was done; however, the only data presented to support this claim of equivalence are the number of 1-, 2-, and 3-syllable words on each form. In describing the process of revising the reading passages and the comprehension questions, several clearly appropriate steps are listed but again no data are provided regarding the outcome of the procedures. The field testing of this edition is also described, but the only data are the number of students who read each passage on Forms LN and LE. If technical data are available, they should be reported so potential users can make informed judgments about the quality of the test. If basic technical data have not been gathered on a test that is in its fifth edition, then clearly users are being expected to take far too much on faith.

For diagnostic use the authors suggest dividing the comprehension questions into five types: fact, topic, evaluation, inference, and vocabulary. A caution is offered that "these categories of comprehension questions, while widely used in basic reading programs and reading comprehension tests, have little or no empirical support" (p. 59). It is particularly notable that for a given form and grade level the BRI contains five fact, one topic, one evaluation, one vocabulary, and two inference questions. A student might be given four levels of the BRI but four items may not make a very reliable scale. Further, the user is told it is permissible to omit some questions.

A second suggested strategy involves dividing the comprehension questions into lower level (fact) and higher level (the other four) ones. Using this strategy students' relative strengths in lower and higher order skills can be calculated (see p. 63 for an example). A difference of proportions test done by this reviewer, however, found no significant difference between the proportion of correct answers on lower and higher level questions. No clear idea of how to decide if a difference is educationally significant is provided.

In summary, although this is clearly labeled an IRI, the lack of any basic technical information makes it impossible for this reviewer to recommend the use of the BRI for placing and diagnosing students. Graded passages and word lists from a reading program would serve the purpose just as well. Further,

the organization of the manual does not make the BRI a good choice for teaching preservice and inservice teachers how to use an IRI.

Review of the Basic Reading Inventory, Fifth Edition by ROBERT T. WILLIAMS, Professor of Occupational and Educational Studies, Colorado State University, Fort Collins, CO:

This inventory is intended for the individual informal assessment of oral reading, silent reading, and listening comprehension in the classroom or clinic. A series of graded word lists and 100 word passages make up the assessment material. There are also longer graded passages (approximately 250 words) of both narrative and expository text. The manual includes guidelines for the quantitative and qualitative evaluation of reading performance and the evaluation of comprehension through comprehension questions, reader retelling, or a combination of the two.

The Basic Reading Inventory seems confused about whether it wants to be a quantitative tool to categorize a reader's performance in traditional terms or a qualitative tool to describe a reader's interaction with written language. The Basic Reading Inventory lacks a consistent philosophy of the reading process, therefore, the use and interpretation of the results seems inconsistent. Although instructions allow one to "count miscues in two different ways so different philosophies or perspectives in scoring can be accommodated" (p. 31), the Inventory would have been more clear and more useful if the assumptions of the various philosophies or perspectives had been summarized and the procedures for each philosophy or perspective had been identified. The various philosophies or perspectives are suggested by statements sprinkled throughout the manual. They are not formally presented so that a user may select a philosophy or perspective and consistently employ it.

The Basic Reading Inventory has no statistically established validity or reliability. This lack might be acceptable in an informal inventory where the purpose was to evaluate or estimate an individual reader's ability to read and comprehend material to be used for instructional and/or recreational reading. If this were the purpose, the evaluator would want to use the material from which the reader would read or learn. The Basic Reading Inventory does not serve well for placement in instructional or recreational reading material because it does not use appropriate material. The use of informal assessment to guide instructional decisions in the classroom or clinic is laudable. The use of material other than that which will be used for instruction is questionable.

The Basic Reading Inventory and its accompanying materials do not help teachers or others involved in the evaluation process develop a background in psycholinguistics, learning theory, or the nature of the reading process. Use of the Basic Reading Inventory may lead preservice or beginning teachers, diagnosticians, or clinicians to assume there is no consistent foundation of reading and that one is left to interpret reading performance as one chooses. Educators, reading diagnosticians, and therapists with strong academic, experiential, professional, and personal foundations in the interactive, psycholinguistic nature of the reading/thinking process would probably not use the Basic Reading Inventory. They would most likely "build" their own reading experiences based upon the expectations they have of the language users with whom they are interacting.

In summary, the use of graded passages for evaluating reading performance in the clinic and for practice by preservice and inservice professionals is valuable. Procedures and practices that recognize and evaluate the dynamic, interactive nature of the reading process are preferred by this reviewer. For the classroom teacher who understands and appreciates this dynamic, interactive aspect of reading, material used for classroom instruction or recreational reading is more effective than the Basic Reading Inventory to evaluate a reader's competencies.

[11]

Behavior Disorders Identification Scale.

Purpose: "Developed to contribute to the early identification and service delivery for students with behavior disorders/emotional disturbance" through direct observations by educators and parents.

Population: Ages 4.5–21.

Publication Date: 1988.

Acronym: BDIS.

Scores, 5: Learning, Interpersonal Relations, Inappropriate Behavior Under Normal Circumstances, Unhappiness/Depression, Physical Symptoms/Fears.

Administration: Individual.

Price Data, 1993: $147 per complete kit including 50 pre-referral behavior checklist forms, 50 pre-referral intervention strategies documentations, School Version technical manual (34 pages), 50 School Version rating forms, Home Version technical manual (34 pages), 25 Home Version rating forms, and Teacher's Guide to Behavioral Interventions (291 pages); $25 per 50 pre-referral behavior checklist forms; $25 per 50 pre-referral intervention strategies documentations; $12 per School Version technical manual; $32 per 50 School Version rating forms;

$12 per Home Version technical manual; $15 per 25 Home Version rating forms; $26 per Teacher's Guide to Behavioral Interventions; $12 per computerized School Version quick score (IBM or Apple II); $190 per computerized Teacher's Guide to Behavioral Interventions (IBM, Macintosh, or Apple II).

Time: [20] minutes for School Version; [15] minutes for Home Version.

Comments: "Includes both a school and home version to provide an ecological perception of student behavior problems"; "used to measure the student's improvement as a result of the intervention program developed with the intervention manual."

Authors: Fred Wright and Kathy Cummins Wunderlich (Teacher's Guide to Behavioral Interventions).

Publisher: Hawthorne Educational Services, Inc.

Review of the Behavior Disorders Identification Scale by DOREEN WARD FAIRBANK, Adjunct Assistant Professor of Psychology, Meredith College, Raleigh, NC:

The Behavior Disorders Identification Scale (BDIS) is an individually administered instrument designed to measure emotional disturbance/behavior disorders in the school and home environment for the purposes of early identification and educational service delivery. The authors base the BDIS on the definition of emotional disturbance/behavior disorders contained in PL 94-142. Specifically, the five subareas of the BDIS were designed to correspond to the five dimensions of emotional disturbance/behavior disorders included in the PL 94-142 definition: Learning, Interpersonal Relations, Inappropriate Behavior, Unhappiness/Depression, and Physical Symptoms/Fears. The second part of the PL 94-142 criteria involves the frequency, intensity, and context of the behavior. The BDIS addresses this aspect of the federal mandate in the response categories to items: "Not in my Presence" (score of 1), "One time in several months" (2), "Several Times, up to one time a month" (3), "More than one time a month, up to one time a week" (4), "More than one time a week, up to once a day" (5), "More than once a day, up to once an hour" (6), and "More than once an hour" (7).

The BDIS goes a step further than most tests in helping teachers to comply with the legal requirements of PL 94-142 by providing a manual for developing the student's Individual Educational Plan (IEP) goals and objectives. This manual (titled *Teacher's Guide to Behavioral Intervention*) is a very thorough reference manual that should be especially helpful to the new special education teacher or the regular education teacher who may have a student with emotional disturbance/behavior disorders in her/his classroom. This manual may also prove beneficial for establishing goals for regular classroom students who exhibit minor behavior problems.

The complete BDIS kit consists of a prereferral behavior checklist and a form for documenting prereferral intervention strategies, a School Version technical manual and rating forms, a Home Version technical manual and rating forms, and a Teacher's Guide to Behavioral Intervention. Therefore, a clear strength of the complete BDIS kit is that it provides the examiner with all the materials necessary to comply with the PL 94-142 requirements (the prereferral documentation, the assessment, and the IEP goals and objectives) of serving a student with emotional disturbance/behavioral disorders.

The BDIS, considered ecological in nature, relies both on the school and home environment for the behavioral observations and documentation. The BDIS Home Version rating form is completed by a parent/guardian who has knowledge of the student at home, whereas the School Version rating form is more likely to be completed by a teacher. Administration of each version of the BDIS can be completed in about 20 minutes without the student being present. Scoring the BDIS is completed by converting raw scores to subscale standard scores and the overall percentile score using the technical manual for either the school or home version.

In the norming of this instrument, careful attention was paid to sample size and geographic distribution to acquire a sample that is likely to be representative of the U.S. population of children and youth. The developers of the BDIS appear to have done an excellent job in this regard, especially with respect to stratifying the normative sample by sex and by age. The generalizability of the BDIS could have been enhanced further, however, by enrolling in the normative sample adequate numbers of racial/ethnic minority youth to permit assessment of the psychometric characteristics of the instrument by ethnicity. The authors of the School Version manual indicate that 95% of the 3,188 students in the normative sample were white, and as a result it is unlikely there are sufficient numbers of minority youth in the sample to assess the reliability, validity, and utility of the BDIS for African-American, Latino, and other minority youth by age groupings and sex. Further work examining the sensitivity and specificity of this instrument for detecting behavior disorders in minority children and youth is warranted.

Another clear strength of the BDIS is the care paid to examining the psychometric properties of this instrument. The five factors of the BDIS appear robust. Test-retest and interrater reliabilities are within acceptable ranges. The authors describe the work done to examine statistically the underlying dimensions of the BDIS and its factors using principal components analysis. Concurrent validity was investigated by correlating this instrument with another measure of emotional disturbance and behavior disorder in youth, the Behavior Evaluation Scale (BES; McCarney, Leigh, & Cornbleet, 1983, 9:128). Overall, the findings from these analyses appear supportive of the construct and criterion-related validity of the BDIS. A potential limitation, however, is that the principal components analyses were conducted without breaking down the total sample by important characteristics related to the prevalence of emotional disturbance/behavior disorders (e.g., sex, SES, ethnicity). Future efforts might examine whether underlying dimensions of the BDIS vary by sex by employing confirmatory factor analytic techniques to examine specifically the factor structure of the BDIS separately for males and females.

In summary, the BDIS was developed to assess the existence of behaviors that meet the PL 94-142 criteria for identifying students with emotional disturbance/behavioral disorders, target areas of need for behavioral intervention/improvements, identify IEP goals and objectives, measure behavior change over time due to program implementation, and help identify areas of need for home intervention. Overall, the BDIS is a comprehensive, reliable, and valid instrument that is a welcome addition to the assessment of students with emotional disturbance/behavior disorders.

REVIEWER'S REFERENCE

McCarney, S. B., Leigh, J. E., & Cornbleet, J. E. (1983). Behavior Evaluation Scale. Columbia, MO: Educational Services.

Review of the Behavior Disorders Identification Scale by HARLAN J. STIENTJES, School Psychologist, Grant Wood Area Education Agency, Cedar Rapids, IA:

The Behavior Disorders Identification Scale (BDIS) was developed to assist in the early identification of students (age $4\frac{1}{2}$ to 21 years) with behavior disorders and emotional disturbance. The BDIS includes both a School Version and a Home Version, in an attempt to gather information from knowledgeable individuals in several environments. Both scales are divided into five subscales: Learning Problems, Interpersonal Problems, Inappropriate Behavior or Feeling, Unhappiness/Depression, and Physical Symptoms or Fears. A Teachers' Guide to Behavior Intervention includes a listing of generic behavioral objectives and intervention strategies for 110 behavior problems.

The BDIS manual author outlines many of the faults of other behavior checklists. Claims are made that these faults are remedied in the BDIS. For the most part this is not true. The BDIS is based upon a theoretical construct utilized in the definition of behavior disorders/emotional disturbance that appears in PL 94-142. Throughout the manual unsubstantiated claims are presented without reference to research (e.g., the claim that fears are a more important component to troublesome behavior now than when the definition of behavior disorders was written and therefore, now need to be included). This assumption is not supported by reported data from principal component analysis; nevertheless, a separate subscale combining physical symptoms and fears is included.

In addition, several questionable practices are advocated. The BDIS author encourages interpretation of subscales as individual measures, but does not suggest limits of statistically meaningful variation. The implication is that the subscale profile can lead to appropriate selection of behaviors for programming and intervention. This claim would not appear to be educationally sound or practical. Variation of one standard deviation below the mean on any of the five subscales is said to represent extreme behavior significant enough to qualify the student for special program services. This would seem to be advocating that fully 15% of the student population is behaviorally disordered.

Furthermore, the scaling system, in an attempt to be precise, leaves the rater with an onerous task. For example, some of the 83 items on the school version are 35 to 40 words long. These items must be given a rating between "7 (more than once an hour)" and "1 (not in my presence)." As a result, teacher and parent judgment of acceptability may be quite poor.

The Teachers' Guide to Behavioral Intervention is also of questionable value. Generic goals and objectives are listed for 110 behaviors. Strategies are then listed for each of the behaviors. For the most part, the strategies are vague without enough specifics to make them useable.

Although the idea behind the BDIS has some value, the instrument and intervention guide appear to be of little practical value and cannot be recommended for use in this format.

[12]

Behavior Evaluation Scale—2.

Purpose: To provide information about student behavior.
Population: Grades K–12.
Publication Dates: 1983–90.
Acronym: BES-2.
Scores, 6: Learning Problems, Interpersonal Difficulties, Inappropriate Behaviors, Unhappiness/Depression, Physical Symptoms/Fears, Total.
Administration: Individual.
Price Data, 1993: $111 per complete kit including 50 pre-referral behavior checklist forms, 25 data collection forms, technical manual ('90, 34 pages), 50 student record forms, and BES-2 intervention manual ('93, 244 pages); $20 per 50 pre-referral behavior checklist forms; $25 per 25 data collection forms; $12 per technical manual; $30 per student record form; $24 per intervention manual; $12 per computerized quick score (IBM or Apple II).
Time: (15–20) minutes.
Comments: "Criterion referenced"; ratings by teachers or other school personnel.
Authors: Stephen B. McCarney, Michele T. Jackson, and James E. Leigh.
Publisher: Hawthorne Educational Services, Inc.
Cross References: For reviews by J. Jeffrey Grill, Lester Mann and Leonard Kenowitz of the earlier edition, see 9:128.

Review of the Behavior Evaluation Scale—2 by BERT A. GOLDMAN, Professor of Education, University of North Carolina at Greensboro, Greensboro, NC:

The Behavior Evaluation Scale—2 (BES-2) by Stephen McCarney and James Leigh has six primary purposes: (*a*) screen for behavior problems; (*b*) assess the behavior of referred students; (*c*) assist in the diagnosis of behavior disorders/emotional disturbance; (*d*) contribute to the development of individual education programs for students in need of special education services; (*e*) document progress resulting from behavioral interventions; and (*f*) collect data for research purposes. The scale can be used with most students from kindergarten through 12th grade who exhibit behavioral or emotional problems. In approximately 15 to 20 minutes classroom teachers and other school personnel who have the opportunity to observe students' behavior over time in a variety of contexts can screen students to identify those who may have problems that warrant further diagnostic evaluation and possible special services.

Each of the 76 items representing a specific behavior is associated with one of five subscales which include: Learning Problems, Interpersonal Difficulties, Inappropriate Behaviors, Unhappiness/Depression, and Physical Symptoms/Fears. Users of the scale rate each behavior item for frequency of occurrence on a 7-point scale as follows: 1—*never or not observed*; 2—*less than once a month*; 3—*approximately once a month*; 4–*approximately once a week*; 5–*more than once a week*; 6–*daily at various times*; and 7–*continuously throughout the day.*

After the items are rated by the user they are multiplied by a designated weight of either 1, 3, or 5 based upon the seriousness of each behavior item. Seriousness was determined by 276 regular and special education teachers. These item scores are then added to determine the five subscale raw scores. Next, by use of a table, the raw scores are converted into standard scores and percentile ranks. Further, the sum of the five subscale standard scores, by using a table, is converted to a behavior quotient and a percentile rank. Also, a standard error of measurement for each subscale standard score and for the behavior quotient is provided in a table. Finally, the behavior quotient and the five subscale standard scores can be plotted on a profile indicating at a glance whether a student's behavior is average or atypical relative to normative data for each characteristic.

A supplemental form, the Data Collection Form, may be used optionally by school personnel to procure daily documentation of the occurrence of any or all of the behaviors on the scale.

Development of the BES-2, as described in the manual, appears to have been accomplished through a series of carefully planned and executed procedures dating back to the preparation of the original 1983 BES. The test authors collaborated with many Missouri teachers of behaviorally disordered students to compile the 47 items of the 1983 BES. The list of 47 items was given to 80 Missouri special education teachers and related professionals for revision resulting in a 50-item scale. Each item was assigned by the authors to one of the five characteristics in the federal definition of behavior disorders/emotional disturbance included in PL 94-142. Next, 104 elementary and secondary level teachers from eight Missouri school districts representing metropolitan, suburban, and rural areas ranging in size from 400 to 10,000 students each conducted two evaluations with the BES, one on a student who exhibited serious classroom behavior problems and one on a student considered to be typical or average in the teacher's class. Suggestions from these 104 teachers and from statistical item analyses formed the basis for the final version of the 1983 scale containing 52 items.

In 1988 a revised 83-item pool was prepared by adding 31 new items to the existing 52 items of the 1983 scale. The new items were suggested by a large number of diagnosticians, teachers, and other school personnel, and two nationally recognized experts in behavior disorders/emotional disturbance. A new set of weightings for each item was established by 276 regular and special education teachers of grades K–12 from 16 states. Following a preliminary item analysis of the 83 items developed from a small sample of Missouri students, another item analysis was conducted from input by 675 teachers from 31 states using over 2,700 students. This work resulted in the elimination of seven items with discriminating power outside a range of .30 to .80, leaving 76 items in the final scale which were judged to be appropriate by at least 95% of the teachers and by a final item analysis.

BES-2 norms are based upon 2,272 students from 31 states representative of the four major United States geographical regions and other demographic characteristics of gender, residence, race, ethnicity, physical/emotional condition, grade level, and parents' educational status. Grade level, gender, race, ethnicity, geographic region, residence, and parents' education all seem to reflect representative proportions of the United States population. Although the authors of the manual indicate the normative sample included 31 states, the acknowledgment section of the manual identifies only 28 states plus the District of Columbia. Whereas the scale is intended for working with behavior problem students, only 2.4% (about 54) of the normative sample consisted of such youngsters.

Item weightings on the original BES items were 1, 2, or 3. Weightings for the BES-2 were determined first by having 276 regular and special education teachers evaluate each item on a 1–9 scale according to its perceived severity. Those items ranking within one standard deviation of the mean weighting for all items received a weighting of 3; those ranking more than one standard deviation below the mean received a 1; and those ranking more than one standard deviation above the mean received a weighting of 5. No further explanation is given for the weighting system except to say it enables measurement of a broad range of severity of behaviors in a more sensitive manner.

The scale appears to be relatively easy for classroom teachers to administer, score, and interpret results. Clear, step-by-step directions are presented in the manual so that classroom teachers should have little or no difficulty in using the scale. There are, however, two minor errors in the manual. The first error probably goes undetected by most classroom teachers who may not be aware of the subtle difference between percentile and percentile rank. Thus, where the directions instruct the user to record numbers on the Student Record Form in the spaces designated percentile rank, those spaces are actually labeled %ile which stands for percentile not percentile rank. The manual authors' second error is in the example presented to demonstrate how to determine each item's weighted score. In the example, Item 8 was assigned a rating of 4 (approximately once a week) and Item 8 has a weighting of 5. However, in the last sentence of the example, these two numbers, 4 and 5, have been reversed so that the example indicates that the rating of 5 (which should be 4) is to be multiplied by its weighting of 4 (which should be 5). Because the correct result is 20 in either case, this error should cause little if any confusion. However, what may be confusing is that for raw scores, *higher* raw scores indicate greater concern; but when the raw scores are converted to standard scores, *lower* standard scores indicate greater concern.

The sum of the five subscale standard scores is converted to a total scale quotient with a mean of 100 and a standard deviation of 15. Why introduce the concept "quotient" when there is no quotient involved? Further, the manual authors point out the similarity between this procedure and the one introduced by Wechsler for use with his intelligence scale. The use of a scale quotient and its similarity to an intelligence quotient may very well lead some users of the BES-2 to think the BES-2 quotient is an IQ.

Data regarding reliability generally appear satisfactory. In the case of internal consistency, all alpha coefficients for BES-2 scales 1, 2, and 3 were .90 or higher and for Scale 4, the alpha coefficients ranged from .87 to .89. Alpha coefficients for grades K–3 and 4–6, although acceptable, were .78 and .75 respectively for Scale 5. The remaining Scale 5 alpha coefficients for grades 7–9 and 10–12 were better (i.e., .81 and .82 respectively). Total scale alpha coefficients were all .97 except for one .98.

Test-retest reliability (10 to 14 days) coefficients for the five subscales were in the .90s with one .89. The total scale test-retest reliability coefficients were .97 (normal group) and .94 (behaviorally disordered group).

Even though, as the manual authors point out, a student may appear to be withdrawn in one class while exhibiting the opposite behavior in another class, it would be helpful to have some indication of interrater reliability, given that the BES-2 scores are based upon the rater's judgment of the student's behavior.

Three types of validity are presented and although some of the findings are questionable, overall there is convincing evidence of the scale's validity. Evidence of content validity was determined from the combination of statistical item analyses and the professional judgment of 675 professional educators.

Criterion-related validity was based upon two studies. One of the studies involved correlations of the five subscales of BES-2 with the Teacher Rating Scale of the Behavior Rating Profile (BRP). BES-2 Subscales 2, 3, and 5 produced correlations of .73, .81, and .62 respectively with the BRP Teacher Rating Scale that were significant at the .01 level of confidence. BES-2 Subscale 4 produced a .44 correlation significant at the .05 level. BES-2 Subscale 1 (Learning Problems) produced virtually zero correlation (.01) with the BRP scale. The only explanation given for this lack of correlation was that BES-2 Subscale 1 contains items primarily related to academically related problems rather than the social or emotional problems contained in the other BES-2 subscales. However, no description of the content of the BRP scale is given. Also, the reader is not told anything about the validity of the BRP scale.

The second criterion-related validity study was based on 190 regular and special education teachers' overall rating of student's classroom behavior on a 9-point scale and their BES-2 ratings of the student. Each teacher rated one student. Although 9 of the 10 correlations were significant at least at the .01 level, they are based upon the ratings of the same teachers using both the 9-point scale of classroom behavior and the BES-2. It would be more convincing to see the correlation between the ratings on each student from independent evaluators (i.e., one group of teachers using the 9-point scale of classroom behavior and the other group of teachers using the BES-2).

Construct validity was investigated by three studies. The first study compared the BES-2 scores of 108 students (K–12) who had been diagnosed as behaviorally disordered with 102 regular class students randomly selected from the standardization sample. Mean differences between the two groups were statistically significant (.001 level) for each of the five subscales indicating significantly more behavior/emotional problems for the behaviorally disordered students on the five subscales. In a second study the BES-2 subscale and total scale scores of a sample of students were compared with the mean subscale and mean total scale scores of the standardization sample. All mean differences between the two groups were statistically significant beyond the .001 level which supports the diagnostic validity of the scale. Further, all but one subscale intercorrelation ranged between .57 and .75 and all subscale correlations with the total score ranged between .77 and .95 providing evidence that the subscales measure different aspects of the behavioral construct. The one intercorrelation of .90 between Subscales 2 and 3 suggests that these subscales are measuring very similar domains. Finally, 69 of the 76 items (91%) correlated highly enough with their subscales to indicate the items within subscales are measuring the same constructs.

In summary, authors McCarney and Leigh appear to have done a thorough job in developing the Behavior Evaluation Scale—2. The manual is written clearly with only a few minor errors. Classroom teachers should find the directions for administering, scoring, and interpreting the results well explained and easy to follow.

Information concerning the instrument's reliability and validity are given in considerable detail and present strong evidence, with only a few questionable aspects, supporting acceptable reliability and validity. Also, in general, the standardization process appears to be based upon representative samples of students, teachers, and other professional personnel.

The BES-2 appears to be a good instrument to assist teachers and other school personnel to identify students who have serious behavioral and emotional problems.

Review of the Behavior Evaluation Scale—2 by D. JOE OLMI, Assistant Professor of School Psychology, Department of Psychology, University of Southern Mississippi, Hattiesburg, MS:

The Behavior Evaluation Scale—2 (BES-2) is a norm-referenced child behavior rating scale designed to aid in the identification of children in grades K–12 who may be at risk for behavioral disorders/emotional disturbance. It comprises 76 items that encompass five subscales (Learning Problems, Interpersonal Difficulties, Inappropriate Behavior, Unhappiness/Depression, Physical Symptoms/Fears) specific to the five characteristics of behavior disorders/emotional disturbance included in P.L. 94-142. The BES-2 is a revision of its 1983 predecessor, the Behavior Evaluation Scale (BES). As stated by the authors, it has six primary purposes: (*a*) screen for behavior problems; (*b*) assess the behavior of referred students; (*c*) assist in the diagnosis of behavior disorders/emotional disturbance; (*d*) contribute to the development of individual education programs for students in need of special education services; (*e*) document progress resulting from behavioral interventions; and (*f*) collect data for research purposes (p. 2).

The instrument includes a manual, the Student Record Form, and the Data Collection Form. The manual is brief, concise, well organized, and easily understood. It includes an overview of the instrument, information about its development, its statistical properties, the administration guidelines, and interpretation information. The tables and appendices facilitate easy scoring. The Student Record Form is the actual behavior rating protocol, with the Data Collection Form serving as an ongoing assessment device for documenting the observed frequency of the behaviors contained in the scale.

The Student Record Form includes sections detailing demographic data, a behavior profile with shaded regions denoting clinical significance, the 76 items for rating, the Data Summary Section, guidelines for administration, and space for comments. Each item of the BES-2 is to be rated by the teacher(s) of the referred child, after several opportunities for contact or observation, on a Likert scale ranging from 1 (*never or Not Observed*) to 7 (*Continuously Throughout the Day*). Items particular to the five subscales are placed randomly to prevent response bias. The amount of time needed to respond to the items is approximately 15–20 minutes as indicated in the manual. Transferring the ratings to the Data Summary Section and scoring took this reviewer approximately 25 additional minutes.

The rating of behaviors on the BES-2 yields total scale and subscale standard scores with a mean of 10 and standard deviation of 3, percentiles and standard errors of measurement associated with the total scale and subscale scores, and a total scale quotient with a mean of 100 and standard deviation of 15. Subscale standard scores below 8 (25th percentile) are considered behaviorally deviant, as are total scale quotients below 90. The authors point out that scores for the scale tend to "truncate" at the upper end. Because scores at the lower end suggest behavioral deviance this is not a significant problem.

Items selected for inclusion on the BES-2 were derived from the original items of the BES with 31 additional items that were selected based on suggestions by "diagnosticians, teachers, and other school personnel who had used the original BES" (p. 8). Item suggestions were also provided by experts in the field of behavior disorders/emotional disturbance. Item weightings were established by 276 general and special education teachers (K–12) from 16 states who ranked the "perceived severity of the behavior represented by each item" (p. 8) on a scale from 1 to 9 with 9 being the most severe. Three final weighting categories (1, 3, 5) were established by the authors. How that decision was made was not fully discussed by the authors.

Correlations of each item with the total scale and subscale were computed with a .30 to .80 coefficient range generally accepted as the standard for inclusion. In the final analysis, some items with correlations below and above the range were accepted for inclusion due to being considered important behaviors by a significant number of teachers who rated the items. Of the 76 items selected for inclusion, 89% of them satisfied the inclusion criteria. Five items fell below .30 and four items fell above .80, but were retained. These standards for inclusion are acceptable for an instrument of this nature.

The standardization sample of the BES-2 was composed of 2,272 students across K–12 grade levels from 31 states representing the four geographical regions of the United States. Five hundred sixty-eight teachers administered the instrument to randomly selected students in their classes with the numbers ranging from a low of 137 eleventh graders to a high of 207 fifth graders. The demographic breakdown of students in the sample closely compared to U.S. statistical information compiled in 1980 for gender, race, geographic region, residence, and parents' education level for the general population and school-age population. Children with emotional disturbance/behavior disorders composed 2.4% of the standardization sample.

Normative conversion tables are included in the manual for four grade groupings (K–3, 4–6, 7–9, 10–12) representing lower elementary, upper elementary, middle school, and upper secondary. The authors acknowledge "a statistical justification for developing different normative tables based upon differences in certain subscale mean scores at different grade intervals" (p. 11), but favored the less precise method of grade grouping. One might consider this decision to be a psychometric defect.

Another flaw related to these broad grade-based norms is the assumption that the student referred for evaluation has not been retained due to academic deficits. For example, the referred student might currently be placed in the 5th grade, when in fact he/she would be in the 7th grade had there been no retentions. In this case the student would be compared to a normative sample comprising much younger children.

Coefficients of internal consistency (coefficients alpha) for the subscales and total scale across the four grade groupings ranged from .75 to .98. With a time interval between first and second ratings of behaviors by teachers of 10 to 14 days, test-retest coefficients for subscales and the total scale exceeded or were rounded to .90. These coefficients are acceptable. Criterion-related validity was suggested in comparisons of the BES-2 with the Behavior Rating profile (BRP) Teacher Rating Scale. The correlation

between the total scale BES-2 and the BRP was .76, which was significant at the .01 level. Correlations of the subscales were significant at the .05 level (Unhappiness/Depression) and .01 level (Interpersonal Difficulties, Inappropriate Behaviors, Physical Symptoms/Fears). The Learning Problems subscale did not correlate significantly with the BRP. Construct validity coefficients were acceptable.

In summary, the BES-2 is an improvement over its predecessor. When used in conjunction with other assessment procedures, it can be a useful instrument. The manual is brief and easily followed. Forms are well organized, but the user may be less inclined to use the Data Collection Form for follow-up. As part of a more comprehensive battery, the psychologist, school psychologist, school social worker, special education teacher, or diagnostician can be adequately served by the Behavior Evaluation Scale—2.

[13]
Behavior Rating Profile, Second Edition.

Purpose: "To evaluate students' behaviors at home, in school, and in interpersonal relationships."
Population: Ages 6-6 to 18-6.
Publication Dates: 1978–90.
Acronym: BRP-2.
Scores: 5 checklists: Student Rating Scales (Home, School, Peers), Teacher Rating Scale, Parent Rating Scale, plus Sociogram score.
Administration: Group.
Price Data, 1994: $139 per complete kit; $25 per 50 rating scale booklets (specify student, parent, or teacher form); $21 per 50 profile forms; $28 per manual ('90, 75 pages).
Foreign Language Edition: Spanish edition available.
Time: (15–30) minutes per scale.
Authors: Linda Brown and Donald D. Hammill.
Publisher: PRO-ED, Inc.
Cross References: See T4:281 (1 reference); for reviews by Thomas R. Kratochwill and Joseph C. Witt of an earlier edition, see 9:130 (1 reference); see also T3:273 (1 reference).

Review of the Behavior Rating Profile, Second Edition by SARAH J. ALLEN, Assistant Professor of School Psychology and Counseling, University of Cincinnati, Cincinnati, OH:

The Behavior Rating Profile, Second Edition (BRP-2) is a norm-referenced ecological battery of indirect assessment measures designed to evaluate the perceived behavior of children 6-6 through 18-6 years of age in a variety of settings and from several different perspectives. There are six instruments in the BRP-2 battery including: the three Student Rating Scales, the Parent Rating Scale, the Teacher Rating Scale, and the Sociogram. Each scale or sociogram is an independent measure that may be administered individually or in combination with any of the other instruments. The instruments may be administered in any order.

The Student Rating Scales include three self-rating scales that describe behavior in the areas of Home, School, and Peers. Each scale contains 20 items that combine into a single 60-item instrument. Administered in either an individual or group format, students identified for assessment are asked to describe their own behavior by responding "True" or "False" to each item.

The Parent Rating Scale is completed by the child's primary caregivers, usually one or both parents. Composed of 30 items, each item is a sentence stem describing behaviors that may be observed at home. Respondents are asked to classify each behavior using the following rating scale: "Very Much Like My Child," "Like My Child," "Not Much Like My Child," or "Not At All Like My Child."

There also are 30 items on the Teacher Rating Scale. Each item is a sentence stem describing behaviors that may be observed at school. Intended to be completed by one or more of the student's teachers, respondents are asked to rate problem behaviors using four categories similar to those found on the Parent scale (e.g., "Very Much Like the Student" to "Not At All Like the Student").

The final instrument contained in the BRP-2 battery is the Sociogram which is intended to provide peers' perceptions of the target student. Unlike the other instruments in this battery, the Sociogram is not a rating scale but rather a peer nomination procedure. Specifically, pairs of stimulus questions (e.g., "Which of the students in your class would you most like to work with on a project in school?" and "Which of the students in your classroom would you least like to work with on a project in school?") are proposed to the target student's entire class. Each student is then asked to list three classmates whose names would answer the questions.

The BRP-2 (1990) is the most recent edition of an indirect assessment instrument that may be familiar to some readers; earlier editions of the Behavior Rating Profile were published in 1978 and 1983. Although the size of the normative sample has been increased and its demographic characteristics strengthened, the BRP-2 is remarkably similar to its predecessors. In fact, there have been no changes in the items, nor in the way that BRP instruments are administered and scored throughout the life of the battery. As a result, the authors contend the research results pertaining to earlier versions of the instrument can be applied with confidence to the current BRP-2. Unfortunately, however, some of the limitations associated with previous versions of the BRP battery are applicable to this edition as well.

For example, one of the limitations of the BRP-2 is that all of the items on the Student, Parent, and Teacher Rating Scales are worded negatively. An instrument that examines only weaknesses or deficits without any consideration of relative strengths provides an incomplete assessment of a child and increases the respondent's vulnerability to a negative response set and search for pathology.

A second criticism related to item content is that a number of items on the BRP-2 do not operationally define terms or describe specific behaviors. For example, the meaning of descriptions such as "is lazy" (Item 5, Teacher Rating Scale; Item 11, Parent Rating Scale) and "has too rich a fantasy life" (Item 17, Parent Rating Scale) may vary depending upon the interpretation of respondents. The lack of behavioral specificity in item content will impede the use of results derived from these rating scales in identifying target goals, as well as planning and evaluating intervention programs.

With regard to item format, it is important to note that undesirable behavior is indicated by "True" and "Very Much Like" the child on every item. As a result, the Rating Scales are vulnerable to the effects of response bias.

A final concern with the format is that the BRP-2 Rating Scales do not provide specific information about the recency, frequency, duration, or intensity of particular behaviors. Follow-up questioning will be necessary in order to clarify responses such as "True" on the Student Rating Scales and "Very Much Like" the child on both the Teacher and Parent Rating Scales.

A number of positive features identified in the BRP-2 also deserve mention. For example, the BRP-2 was designed to take an ecological approach to behavioral assessment. That is, the battery was constructed so that patterns of behavior across settings could be examined by eliciting the perceptions of at least two different individuals within several settings. The authors caution, however, that these instruments are not intended to be used as a complete appraisal system. Rather the information derived from the BRP-2 should be supplemented by information derived from measures of other domains (e.g., aptitude, achievement) and other assessment methods (e.g., direct observation, testing).

Secondly, the instruments comprising this battery are easy and inexpensive to use, in terms of both time and cost. The rating scales, in particular, are not difficult to learn, nor to implement, and scoring procedures are easy to follow. The Sociogram probably is the most time-consuming portion of the battery to administer and score. In the interest of both efficiency and efficacy, it is noted that each of the instruments comprising the BRP-2 may be used individually or in combination with any of the other instruments depending upon the nature of the problem and/or scope of the assessment without jeopardizing its integrity.

The manual for the BRP-2 is well written and comprehensive. Instructions for administration, scoring, and interpretation of the instruments are clear and can be easily understood. Unlike those accompanying most rating scales, the BRP-2 manual includes a comprehensive description of its construction and statistical characteristics. The psychometric characteristics of these instruments are reported in the manual, thereby allowing the reader an opportunity to evaluate their merits (information that should be, but is not always, readily available to consumers).

Lastly, the psychometric qualities of the BRP-2 exceed those of many other behavior rating scales. Specifically, each of the instruments in the BRP-2 battery is norm-referenced. Expanded with each edition, the normative sample presently includes 2,682 students, 1,948 parents, and 1,452 classroom teachers from 26 states. The demographic characteristics of the sample closely parallel those of the most recent census. Apparently, a Spanish-language version of the BRP-2 (*Perfil de Evaluacion del Comportamiento*, Brown & Hammill, 1982) is available, standardized on a normative sample of students, parents, and teachers in various states of Mexico. Caution should be exercised when attempting to apply those norms to a Spanish-speaking student from the United States.

With regard to reliability, internal consistency and test-retest data were presented, but interrater reliability was not addressed. Coefficient alphas were reported for each BRP-2 rating scale across five grade level ranges. There are discrepancies between text and table (manual, pp. 44 and 45) regarding these coefficients. Internal reliability appears adequate but the manual should be corrected.

Studies of the instrument's test-retest and alternate forms reliability are limited. However, the results of one published study (Ellers, Ellers, & Bradley-Johnson, 1989) examining the test-retest stability of the BRP found the Teacher Rating Scale was sufficiently reliable across grade Levels 1–12 (coefficients all in .90s). The results of the Parent Rating Scale were sufficiently reliable for grades 3–12 (all coefficients in .80s and .90s). The Student Rating Scales were least reliable; only 10 of the 18 correlation coefficients were .80 or above. With the exception of the Teacher Rating Scale, none of the scales held up well at the first and second grade level.

In terms of validity, a number of studies representing both the authors' own and independent research were reported in the manual. Substantial preliminary evidence is provided to demonstrate construct validity.

In summary, the BRP-2 is the most recent edition of a battery of indirect assessment measures designed to evaluate the perceived behavior of children 6-6 through 18-6 years of age. The BRP-2 battery includes three Student Rating Scales (Home, School, and Peer), a Parent Rating Scale, a Teacher Rating Scale, and a Sociogram.

The BRP-2 is distinguished from other behavior rating scales by its reliance on an ecological approach to behavioral assessment. Specifically, the battery was constructed so that patterns of behavior across settings could be examined by eliciting the perceptions of at least two different individuals within several settings. However, the BRP-2 should not be regarded as a comprehensive appraisal system; at best, it is one ecologically founded assessment tool that may be used in conjunction with other assessment procedures.

Unlike many other behavior rating scales, the BRP-2 is norm-referenced. A comprehensive description of instrument development and psychometric characteristics of the BRP-2 accompany the instructions for administration in a well-written manual. The potential utility of the BRP-2 Rating Scales is limited by both item content and an item format that increase respondents' vulnerability to response set bias, emphasize undesirable or inappropriate behaviors, and lack behavioral specificity.

REVIEWER'S REFERENCE

Ellers, R. A., Ellers, S. L., & Bradley-Johnson, S. (1989). Stability reliability of the Behavior Rating Profile. *Journal of School Psychology*, 27, 257-263.

Review of the Behavior Rating Profile, Second Edition by LISA A. BLOOM, Assistant Professor of Special Education, Western Carolina University, Cullowhee, NC:

The Behavior Rating Profile-2 (BRP-2) was designed to assess children's behavior from the perspectives of the teacher, parents, target student, and his/her peers. This instrument includes five behavior rating scales and a sociometric technique. The Student Rating Scale represents three scales to be completed by the child and includes 60 true-false items covering behavior at home, school, and with peers. A Parent Rating Scale to be completed by primary care givers includes 30 items. The Teacher Rating Scale includes 30 items related to school problem behavior. The final component of the BRP-2 is a sociogram based on a peer-nominating technique. The sociogram requires at least 20 of the student's classmates to respond to 1–2 pairs of questions such as "Which of the students in your class would you most like to have as your friend" and "Which of the students in your class would you least like to have as your friend?"

ADMINISTRATION AND SCORING. The BRP-2 is easy to use and score. The examiner is encouraged to obtain completed rating scales from several sources including both parents, several teachers, and several classmates. These ratings are converted to percentile ranks and standard scores and charted on a student profile. The Sociogram is scored by computing a rank of the target student in the class out of the total number of students in the class. This score is also converted to a standard score and percentile rank.

The items, procedures, and scoring of the BRP-2 have remained unchanged since the first edition. Several reviews of the BRP-2 are available elsewhere (see Posey, 1989; Bacon, 1989; Broughton, 1985). This review will focus on the new technical information included with the BRP-2 manual.

ITEM SELECTION. Item selection involved the following. First, similar assessment instruments were reviewed. Second, parents and teachers of students with learning disabilities and emotional disturbances were asked to describe behaviors characteristic of their children. Finally, these pools were used to generate experimental versions of the Rating Scales which consisted of 299 items. The BRP-2 manual authors describe the item selection criteria in much greater detail than in the first edition. To select the best items, two internal criteria were imposed. Item discrimination coefficients had to be statistically significant at .05 or beyond and the magnitude of the coefficients had to be between .30 and .80. Second, items which were indicated in more than half of the subjects in the item analysis group were eliminated. The authors considerably increased the number of protocols for item analysis in the revised edition although only the previously selected 120 items were subjected to the analysis. The authors report a final confirmatory analysis of protocols using the Guilford method from 700 student rating scales, 270 parent rating scales, and 530 teacher rating scales. Median item discrimination coefficients ranged from .43 to .83, which is well within acceptable limits.

In the first edition, raw score conversions to scaled scores were based upon normative data from 1,966 students ages 6-6 to 18-6, 955 teachers, and 1,232 parents in 15 states. In the second edition, 718 students from 11 additional states, 716 parents from 4 additional states, and 497 teachers from 11 additional states were added to the normative sample and resulted in slight changes in the normative tables for converting raw scores to standard scores and percentile ranks. The authors of the new manual present demographic characteristics of the normative samples in tabular form. Sample characteristics are comparable to the U.S. population.

Adequate reliability and internal consistency data are reported. Internal consistency was studied using coefficient alpha. Coefficients ranged from .74 to .98 and were highest for the Teacher Rating Scale.

Test-retest reliability is based on two studies. The first was reported in the original edition. Although the results were favorable, they were based on a small sample of 36 normal high school students. The second study conducted by Ellers, Ellers, and Bradley-Johnson (1989) involved 198 students from grades 1–2, 212 parents, and 176 teachers in central Michigan. These authors report the results for the Teacher Rating Scale were sufficiently reliable for all grade levels. The coefficients were all in the .90s. The Parent Rating Scale was sufficiently reliable for screening purposes for grades 3–12 and for eligibility for grades 3–6 and 11–12. For grades 3–12, coefficients ranged from .80 to .96. However, results suggested the scale was less reliable for grades 1–2 with a coefficient of .69. For the student scales, only 4 of the 18 coefficients were in the .90s and 5 in the .80s with a range of .43 to .92. Like the Parent Rating Scale, the results for grades 1 and 2 were the least reliable. Thus, the parent and student scales must be used with caution for these ages.

Concurrent and construct validity are reported in terms of the intercorrelation of the BRP-2 instruments and the BRP-2's relation to other measures of child behavior. In one study adequate correlations between the BRP and the Walker Problem Behavior Identification Checklist, the Quay-Peterson Behavior Problem Checklist, and the Vineland Social Maturity Scale are reported. However, these correlations are based on only four groups of 27 children each. In the new edition, studies of correlation between the BRP and the Test of Early Socioemotional Development, the Index of Children's Personality Characteristics, the Behavior Evaluation Scale, the Devereux Elementary School Behavior Rating Scale II, and the Children's Manifest Anxiety Scale are reported. The results of these studies suggest that the BRP demonstrates sufficient relationship to other similar instruments to consider it to have concurrent validity. However, the best evidence of concurrent validity would be obtained by relating the BRP to direct observation of behavior. This type of endeavor is not described. Technical information in terms of reliability and validity are not provided for the sociogram component of the BRP.

STRENGTHS AND WEAKNESSES. The BRP-2 represents an attempt to provide new and more detailed information about the technical adequacy of the test. The user should be more confident with the BRP-2 based on this information. The strength of the BRP-2 is that it can provide the user with data from several sources and is flexible enough so that information on school or home behavior alone could be obtained. A weakness of the BRP-2 is that the items describe negative behaviors exclusively. They do not afford the opportunity to identify student strengths. Additionally, the items do not describe observable behaviors, making it difficult to use the BRP for identifying appropriate goals and objectives. Other weaknesses include the lack of technical information on the sociogram and the limited reliability of the student scales. As long as these limitations are considered, the BRP-2 could provide the user with useful ecological information.

REVIEWER'S REFERENCES

Broughton, S. F. (1985). [Critique of the Behavior Rating Profile]. In D. J. Keyser & R. C. Sweetland (Eds.), *Test critiques: Vol. IV* (pp. 92-102). Kansas City, MO: Test Corporation of America.

Bacon, E. H. (1989). [Review of the Behavior Rating Profile]. In J. C. Conoley & J. J. Kramer (Eds.), *The tenth mental measurements yearbook* (pp. 84-86). Lincoln, NE: Buros Institute of Mental Measurements.

Ellers, R. A., Ellers, S. L., & Bradley-Johnson, S. (1989). Stability reliability of the Behavior Rating Profile. *Journal of School Psychology, 27*, 257-263.

Posey, C. D. (1989). [Review of the Behavior Rating Profile]. In J. C. Conoley & J. J. Kramer (Eds.), $The tenth mental measurements yearbook (pp. 86-87). Lincoln, NE: Buros Institute of Mental Measurements.

[14]

BRIGANCE™ K & 1 Screen for Kindergarten and First Grade Children [Revised].

Purpose: Designed to screen for readiness for kindergarten or first grade.

Population: Grades K, 1.

Publication Dates: 1982–92.

Administration: Individual.

Price Data, 1993: $59.50 per manual ('92, 88 pages).

Time: [15–20] minutes per child.

Comments: "Criterion-referenced"; 1987 edition still available.

Author: Albert H. Brigance.

Publisher: Curriculum Associates, Inc.

a) KINDERGARTEN.

Scores, 13: Personal Data Response, Color Recognition, Picture Vocabulary, Visual Discrimination-Forms and Uppercase Letters, Visual-Motor Skills, Gross-Motor Skills, Rote Counting, Identifies Body Parts, Follows Verbal Directions, Numeral Comprehension, Prints Personal Data, Syntax and Fluency, Total.

Price Data: $16.85 per 30 data sheets; $16.85 per 10 class summary folders; $49.85 per 120 3-year data sheets.

b) FIRST GRADE.

Scores, 14: Personal Data Response, Color Recognition, Picture Vocabulary, Visual Discrimination-Lowercase Letters and Words, Visual-Motor Skills, Rote Counting, Recites Alphabet, Numeral Comprehension, Recognition of Lowercase Letters, Auditory Discrimination, Draw A Person, Prints Personal Data, Numerals in Sequence, Total.

Price Data: $17.15 per 30 data sheets; $17.15 per 10 class summary folders; $50.15 per 120 4-year data sheets.

Cross References: See T4:331 (3 references); for reviews of an earlier edition by Ann E. Boehm and Dan Wright, see 9:166.

Review of the BRIGANCE™ K & 1 Screen for Kindergarten and First Grade Children [Revised] by RONALD A. BERK, Professor, School of Nursing, The Johns Hopkins University, Baltimore, MD:

The BRIGANCE K & 1 Screen is the third edition of this popular screening instrument (earlier editions were published in 1982 and 1987). It was designed originally as a criterion-referenced test to assess the basic skills of kindergarten and first grade children. Twelve skill areas are covered on the kindergarten screen and 13 on the first grade screen.

The entire assessment consists of four components: (*a*) basic skills tests, (*b*) a screening observation form, (*c*) teacher's rating form, and (*d*) parent's rating form. With the exception of the observation form to be completed by the test user, the other components are prepared in both kindergarten and first grade versions. Inasmuch as the assessment is labeled as "criterion-referenced" and "curriculum-referenced," the user would expect to find the items keyed to a set of objectives or content specifications. No content domain specifications are presented from which the items on any of the component measures were generated. This certainly precludes the interpretation of student performance in terms of specific skills or instructional objectives. The author notes only that the "assessments provide data that can be translated into instructional objectives" (p. iii).

Because this is a revised edition, the changes made must be identified. The author notes four changes: (a) The basic assessments for kindergarten and first grade were separated for the convenience of test users (previously, both levels were integrated into one section); (b) "do and do not" recommendations were added to specify the limitations of the test and purposes for which the results should be used (this was prompted by reports that the earlier editions were being misused for diagnosing learning difficulties, placement in special education programs, and developing individualized education plans); (c) the reference list was updated; and (d) the sequence of some items was changed, such as the consonant sounds in the Auditory Discrimination (first grade) area (this was done based on a review of developmental age data and the updated normative data for the BRIGANCE Inventory of Early Development—Revised).

The justification for these four changes appears to be based on some type of data collection from the earlier editions. However, no empirical evidence or specific research is cited to furnish a sound foundation for the changes. Although convenience, score misuse, out-of-date references, and updated norms may be appropriate reasons for the changes, substantial documentation is required to justify the need for a test revision. Clearly the reasons given do not support this 1991 "revision." Other than reordering "some items," no structural or content changes in the items for the 27 skill areas were undertaken. The 1991 edition is essentially the same as the 1982 edition.

The previous edition of the BRIGANCE Screen was reviewed in the MMY (9:166). Unfortunately, none of the criticisms noted in those reviews were addressed in the latest edition. In particular, there is no evidence of the technical adequacy of the tests, observation form, and rating forms.

The appropriateness of reliability and validity evidence for any instrument hinges on the specific use of the scores and the inferences drawn from those scores. The purpose of the BRIGANCE K & 1 Screen is "to obtain a broad sampling of a students's skills and behaviors . . . (1) to identify any student who should be referred for a more comprehensive evaluation . . . (2) to help determine the most appropriate initial placement or grouping of students . . . (3) to assist the teacher in planning a more appropriate program for the student" (p. v). These score uses should be viewed in the context of the author's recommendations: "Don't make any decisions based solely on the score obtained from the screening . . . [and] Don't use screening data for making decisions such as exclusion from a program or placement in a special program" (p. xiii).

These statements by the author suggest the scores on the Screen be used primarily to classify students into the appropriate grade level (K or 1) and instructional groups, particularly those students who may have disabilities requiring special placement. This classification decision should be made by a screening team who should use the scores on this Screen in conjunction with other data before formulating a recommendation.

The fact that the author recommends the Screen as a "quick means of sampling the skills of a student" and "the score should be evaluated in light of . . . other data" (p. xiii) does not relieve the author of the responsibility for furnishing evidence on the psychometric soundness of the instrument. If the scores are used to classify students, evidence on the accuracy of those classifications is essential to evaluate the effectiveness of the tool. Discriminant validity evidence in the form of correct classification probabilities and false positives/false negatives would be very helpful. This could be computed based on recommended "cutoff scores" for referral decisions (p. xvi). Evidence of decision reliability should also be reported along with classification accuracy.

Beyond these types of technical information to justify the use of the scores, additional evidence is needed related to (a) the match of the items to any domain specifications; (b) the representativeness of the items in relation to their respective domains; (c) the qualifications of the subject-matter experts who judged content-related validity; (d) the appropriateness of the instruments for students who do not speak English and how the assessment should be conducted with such students; (e) studies of test design, content, or format that might bias test scores for particular ethnic, cultural, and gender groups; (f) the method and rationale for selecting the cutoff scores, including technical analyses; and (g) item analysis results and criteria for item selection based on the numerous field tests.

In summary, similar to the 1982 edition, this edition of the Screen remains unproven. It does not satisfy the criteria for a "revised edition." The scores cannot be criterion referenced or norm referenced without the proper content specifications and psychometric analyses to support the intended uses and inferences. The BRIGANCE K & 1 Screen is a screening device of unknown characteristics according to the purposes for which it was developed. Potential users should consider alternative measures that satisfy the requisite standards for instrument construction and supportive technical information.

Review of the BRIGANCE™ K & 1 Screen for Kindergarten and First Grade Children [Revised] by T. STEUART WATSON, Assistant Professor of Educational Psychology, Mississippi State University, Starkville, MS:

This test is a revision of the popular 1987 edition. Despite criticisms regarding potential misuses of the test and lack of technical information, the author correctly notes that the previous version of this instrument has enjoyed widespread use.

PURPOSE. Generally, the BRIGANCE K & 1 Screen is a criterion-referenced instrument that was designed to tap several broad key skill areas: language, motor ability, number skills, body awareness, and auditory and visual discrimination. The author contends that assessment of skill development in these areas allows for a better prediction of who will or will not be academically successful, although no predictive or discriminant validity data are presented to support this contention. In addition, the Screen is intended to identify students who may require comprehensive evaluations, place and group students in terms of ability, assist the teacher in designing curriculum objectives, and to comply with federal and state screening mandates.

TEST CONTENT. The basic assessment includes 12 skill tests for kindergartners and 13 for first graders. Although the test seems to have content validity for both groups, there is no specific explanation for the criteria used to select new items or the criteria used to retain items for this version of the test. Only cursory explanations are given as to how the 1991 edition was developed.

A major difficulty with this test is that each stimulus page contains numerous stimulus items. For example, the Visual Discrimination skill test for first graders contains 10 rectangular boxes of four words or letters per box. It would have been preferable to have fewer stimulus items per page, particularly when attempting to assess young children whose attention and/or visual acuity are suspect.

The supplemental assessment battery contains some useful tests designed to sample vocabulary and sight word recognition at the preprimer/primer level, basic number skills, articulation, and verbal expression. The first two tests in the supplemental battery (Responses to Pictures), however, present a cluttered stimulus picture that is confusing and unwieldy. Having to sort through the pictures to access the appropriate information is an unnecessary and interfering task for the examinee.

Screening information forms are provided that allow the examiner to make checklist observations of problematic behaviors during screening. Separate forms for kindergartners and first graders are also included for teachers and parents to note whether certain behaviors are within the child's repertoire of skills. Items on the parent and teacher forms closely resemble those on most measures of adaptive behavior. It is highly unlikely, given the expedient nature of the screening process, that these forms will be used in any meaningful way.

ADMINISTRATION AND SCORING. The manual begins with helpful information regarding screening procedures and directions, assessing functional vision and hearing, general recommendations for screening, and possible explanations for low scores. The information contained in these pages is probably more beneficial to the novice, rather than experienced, examiner. The author also provides sample layouts to expedite the screening process, an orientation to the materials, specific recommendations on the effective use of the screen, and directions for completing the data sheets (with completed models provided). Again, these portions of the test manual are more applicable to someone without a great deal of testing experience.

Although it is stated that teachers and other professionals may administer the screen without specialized training in test administration, there are no data to validate this assertion. Interrater reliability studies should be performed to show that those with and without specialized training administer the test and score items similarly. When assessing children of this age, it is often difficult to elicit responses, especially when the responses are one-word, right or wrong answers. Examiners with test administration training may have an edge in prompting responding in children who are hesitant to complete the tasks, thus obtaining a more valid sample of behavior. Despite its deceptively simple-to-administer format, care must be taken to ensure that tests such as this are administered and scored properly, especially when educational and programming decisions are made that are highly dependent on the results of this test.

Scoring is straightforward and easy. Answers to the stimulus items are generally unambiguous and require little interpretation or queuing. The data sheets, or record forms, are in triplicate and seem too small for the amount of information contained on them. There is not enough room for the examiner to quickly record responses and note behavioral observations within a skill area during testing.

An area of particular concern is the section for placement recommendations on the bottom of the data sheet. This seems to imply that educational placement decisions can be made based on the results of this single instrument, regardless of the author's cautionary statements about such a practice. This information is better left off a data sheet.

TECHNICAL INFORMATION. No reliability or validity data are available for this test. This is surprising given the wide use of the test and the applications for which it is intended. More troubling is the fact the author does not mention technical data, either to explain why none are available for this test or why any are excluded. Does the author assume that because this test is criterion referenced, technical data are superfluous? Or that because the test has gained widespread use and acceptance there is obviously no need for reliability and validity data? The omission of such data is the test's most serious flaw.

RECOMMENDATIONS. Without validity data, it is inappropriate and unethical to recommend this test for something other than as an informal screening measure that may be of minor assistance to teachers in planning some curriculum objectives. There are no data to support its use in making placement or class grouping decisions. Unfortunately, most who use this test will do so for the purpose for which it is least suited.

[15]
California Critical Thinking Skills Test.

Purpose: Designed to be "a standardized assessment instrument targeting core critical thinking skills at the post-secondary level."
Population: College and adult.
Publication Dates: 1990-92.
Acronym: CCTST.
Scores, 6: Analysis, Evaluation, Inference, Inductive Reasoning, Deductive Reasoning, Total.
Administration: Group.
Forms, 2: A, B (alternate).
Price Data, 1992: $60 per specimen kit including Form A, Form B, and manual ('92, 20 pages); $35 per 20 copies of test (volume discounts available); $10 per Delphi Report (22 pages).
Time: 45 minutes.
Author: Peter A. Facione.
Publisher: The California Academic Press.

Review of the California Critical Thinking Skills Test by ROBERT F. McMORRIS, Professor of Educational Psychology and Statistics, State University of New York at Albany, Albany, NY:

In the new Roget's Thesaurus (Chapman, 1992, p. 842), a synonym given for "critical" is "crucial." Certainly critical thinking skills are crucial for individuals and society, and developing an appropriate

test to assess critical thinking is no trivial task. The California Critical Thinking Skills Test (CCTST) contains 34 multiple-choice items with a 45-minute time limit. The items cover a variety of topics: Some items are realistic, providing high face validity, but they potentially confound reasoning with content; and some are "nonsense," content-free items for those who prefer a more abstract approach. The items seem reasonably interesting, but occasionally it seems the four or five options do not contain the best answer possible. Was the key independently verified by experts? What criteria were used for item retention? What criteria were used to place an item on a subscale? How speeded is the test?

A Delphi panel developed a consensus definition of critical thinking (CT), core CT skills with examples, and dispositions crucial to becoming a critical thinker. The test contains three subscores based on the panel's work: Analysis, Evaluation, and Inference. The developer, Facione, also apologetically offers two other subscores, Deductive Reasoning and Inductive Reasoning, based on 30 of the 34 items, to meet a California State University objective. (Given the double use of most items, we will refer to subscores rather than subtests.)

The developer conducted several studies using the CCTST at California State in Fullerton involving 1,196 undergraduates, 20 instructors, five different courses, and three academic departments. These data are bases for validity, reliability, and norm information.

VALIDITY. Test users are urged to study the items to judge validity, especially to estimate whether the test meets their conceptualizations of critical thinking.

According to the CCTST Fact Sheet, "The CCTST measures the growth in CT skills which is an intended outcome of completing a college level general education CT course." Facione has collected considerable pre and post data, some quite cleverly by measuring post at the end of the first semester and pre with similar students at the beginning of the second semester. Gain runs between .04 and 1.45 in mean scores on a 34-item test, statistically significant with large samples but hardly fantastic as a descriptive index of learning. Perhaps the test is not instructionally sensitive, perhaps the instruction was insufficiently potent, or perhaps other noise (e.g., more student motivation pre, or instructor present post) did not balance/cancel. This issue and the data are discussed by Facione (Technical Report #1; 1991).

Pretest scores correlate with college GPA (.20), SAT-V (.55), SAT-M (.44), most Nelson-Denny Reading scores (.40s), and posttest scores (.70). In general, these correlations with tests and with grades seem reasonable and supportive. Given, however, this correlation of .70 between pre- and posttest scores, Technical Report #2 contains a questionable section on Effectiveness of Particular Courses, with posttest means compared to four decimal places with no notion of whether the input for different courses was comparable.

Facione may emphasize statistics instead of meaningfulness in examining gender differences. He notes the male/female difference in posttest means is significant although the pre difference is nonsignificant, and he tries to justify differential gain by an elaborate rationale using SATs and grades. Yet the mean differences pre and post are almost equal and hardly impressive (about $^3/_4$ point). The difference in sample size—479 for pre and 710 post—helps in estimating why the posttest means differ statistically by gender.

Students responded to four questions after the 34 items were presented. Eighty percent of the students answered the item "Critical thinking and being logical are quite easy for me" positively on pretest and 84% answered positively on posttest, yet, as noted by the developer, mean item difficulty on the test was only 49.5. Perhaps on another study, a question could be added such as "How well did this test measure your critical thinking ability?"

Another question, "My GPA is an accurate reflection of how logical my thinking is," drew the author's comment: "It is not clear to this investigator why students perceive their GPA and their CT abilities not to be strongly correlated when in fact they are" (Technical Report #3, p. 13). Although the correlation between GPA and CCTST was statistically significant, the term "strongly correlated" may imply a higher relationship than $r = .20$ supports.

We applaud Facione's considering the question of differential functioning according to ethnicity/race for native English speakers. He was hampered by three tiny sample sizes out of the six groups. We recommend that with additional data he consult a methodologist experienced in conducting bias studies.

Another way to consider validity is through multitrait-multimethod matrices (Campbell & Fiske, 1959). The author sets the stage: "Three [subscores] ... 'Analysis,' 'Evaluation,' and 'Inference,' correlate strongly with each other and with the overall CCTST ... same is true of the two CCTST [subscores], 'Deductive Reasoning' and 'Inductive Reasoning,' which divide CCTST items along that more traditional matrix" (Technical Manual #4, p. 2). Treating pre and post as methods and the five subscores as traits, the validity diagonal contained one correlation

coefficient in the .30s, two in the .40s, and two in the .50s. The heterotrait-monomethod triangles contained two correlations in the .20s, three in the .30s, and three in the .40s. Three estimates of reliability were provided for the total score: KR20s for pretest (.69) and posttest (.68), and a pre-post correlation (.70). Subscore reliability might be estimated using Spearman-Brown; starting from .70 for the total score, reliability for a half-length test would be approximately .54. Given this estimate of reliability, the validity coefficients among subscores appear to this reviewer as reasonably supportive. I hope the developer will use the multitrait-multimethod matrix approach, for example, to estimate whether results of this measure converge with other measures of critical thinking and yet retain some uniqueness when related to measures of general intellectual ability.

RELIABILITY. To summarize the information given above, total-score internal consistency appears to be close to .70. Subscore reliability, although not provided, might be in the .50s. No standard errors of measurement are provided; for the total score, the standard error is about 2.5 based on either the typical formula or Lord's approximation.

The reliability information does not support interpretation of differences for individuals, either for a profile or for gain. Subscore reliability is too low and intercorrelations too high to allow a profile to be dependable. Assessment of gain appears impossible: With total-score KR20s of .68 and .69, and pre-post correlation of .70, the reliability of the difference is estimated to be 0.

NORMS. As noted above, the norm group is composed of undergraduates from one of the California State colleges. To what extent does this group represent the national college student population? The groups contain both native and nonnative English speakers; subgroup norms could easily have been provided. Percentiles are provided for both pretest and posttest groups and for both total score and the five subscores. Subscores are particularly tricky to interpret: A one-point difference in number of correct items can change the percentile rank by up to 27%.

How might such percentile ranks be used? The developer specifies in the directions for test administrators, "If you plan to furnish students their individual percentile scores, indicate when and how that will be accomplished." What an invitation for mischief! There is little mention of limitations for interpretation, no provision of standard errors of measurement, no information on difference scores, no urging to have counselors or other interpreters available, and so on.

SUMMARY. The Delphi panel's characterization of the ideal critical thinker (Technical Report #1, p. 5; Facione, 1991, p. 2) could also be considered descriptive of those selecting, interpreting, and even reviewing tests. (Indeed, considering either the test or this review, you may join me in feeling like you have encountered an extensive reading passage with a multitude of critical-thinking questions at the end.) Some of the critical thinker's characteristics may even help summarize the developer's traits, for example, "habitually inquisitive, . . . flexible, . . . diligent in seeking relevant information, . . . persistent in seeking results which are as precise as the subject and the circumstances of inquiry permit" (Technical Report #1, p. 5). For such a new test, there is considerable information available with replies for many questions of interpretation. Further, responses to some of the questions raised in the Technical Reports are extended in Facione's 1991 paper, a combination thought provoker, information summarizer, and soft seller.

This test does not have the history, the reliability, or the variety of norm groups of a test like the Watson-Glaser Critical Thinking Appraisal (9:1347). The CCTST is a bit shorter, however, and already has a creative, developing, and somewhat supportive program for validation. Perhaps a systematic study of structural relationships among subsets of items for this test and other measures of critical thinking would help the developer deal with his desire to seek causation and components of interpretation in spite of the interrelatedness of the variables. Such a suggestion is offered hesitatingly, however, given that he may already have overinterpreted tests of hypotheses and underattended to descriptive information. To revisit Thesaurus synonyms for "critical," the developer has sought to be "explanatory," and the user needs to be "judicial."

Test users are urged to remain cautious in interpreting results of this measure, especially for individuals, to avoid interpreting profiles or gain scores, especially for individuals, and to supplement the information on validity, reliability, and norms provided by the developer and summarized here.

REVIEWER'S REFERENCES

Campbell, D. T., & Fiske, D. W. (1959). Convergent and discriminant validation by the multitrait-multimethod matrix. *Psychological Bulletin, 56,* 81-105.

Facione, P. A. (1991). *Using the California Critical Thinking Skills Test in research, evaluation, and assessment.* Millbrae, CA: California Academic Press. (ERIC Document Reproduction Service No. ED 337498)

Chapman, R. L. (Ed.). (1992). *Roget's international thesaurus* (5th ed.). New York: Harper Collins.

Review of the California Critical Thinking Skills Test by WILLIAM B. MICHAEL, Professor of Education and Psychology, University of Southern California, Los Angeles, CA:

Based on more than a decade of research and extensive validation efforts involving 1,196 college students, 20 instructors, and five courses in critical thinking given by three departments at a comprehensive urban state university in California, The California Critical Thinking Skills Test (CCTST) consists of 34 multiple-choice items. The test, which is administered within a period of 45 minutes, affords scores on three subtests intended to represent critical thinking (CT) constructs of Analysis (9 items), Evaluation (14 items), and Inference (11 items). In addition, scores are furnished on two conventional or traditional categories of Deductive Reasoning (16 items—four from Analysis, four from Evaluation, and eight from Inference) and Inductive Reasoning (14 items—one from Analysis, ten from Evaluation, and three from Inference).

A Delphi panel comprising 46 nationally visible scholars in CT from several different academic disciplines labored 2 years to achieve a consensus concerning the definition of CT for general education at the lower division college level. Besides making several recommendations concerning CT instruction and assessment, the panel members created a list of core CT skills and subskills along with illustrations as well as a compilation of those personal dispositions thought to be crucial to one's becoming a competent and effective critical thinker. Their work culminated in a monograph entitled *Critical Thinking: A Statement of Expert Consensus for Purposes of Educational Assessment and Instruction* (ERIC TM 014423). The monograph may be obtained from ERIC, the American Philosophical Association, and the Institute for Critical Thinking at Montclair (New Jersey).

At the present time, there is no manual to accompany the CCTST. However, four technical reports are available that furnish statistical data, research findings, and percentile norms for the previously mentioned sample of college students. One can gain a reasonably accurate notion of the coverage in these documents from their titles: Technical Report No. 1, *CCTST Experimental Validation and Content Validity,* (ERIC TM 015818); Technical Report No. 2, *Factors Predictive of CT Skills,* (ERIC TM 015819); Technical Report No. 3, *Gender, Ethnicity, Major, CT Self-Esteem, and the CCTST;* and Technical Report No. 4, *Interpreting the CCTST, Group Norms and Sub-Scores.*

During the academic year starting in 1989 and terminating in 1990, pretests were administered prior to students taking one of five possible general education courses in critical thinking (a requirement in the university at which the research was conducted) followed by the administration of posttests to ascertain whether improvement in these skills had occurred. Typically, pretest differences in average performance were not associated with gender, ethnicity, college major, or self-confidence in CT skills. On posttests, males seemed to gain slightly more than females, and significant differences appeared relative to college major and membership in an ethnic group. Substantial correlations were noted between scores on the CCTST and those in verbal and mathematics portions of a scholastic aptitude test as well as those in an English placement measure and an entry level mathematics test. When aptitude test scores and native language were controlled, self-confidence in CT was not a significant factor in accounting for pretest or posttest results. A careful study of the technical reports will provide the potential user of the CCTST a substantial body of information regarding not only the definitions of the constructs of CT but also the complexity of the interrelationships of pretest and posttest scores with demographic, intellectual, and affective variables.

The CCTST would appear to possess substantial content validity—perhaps more than any other competing instrument in light of the collective wisdom of the eminent scholars who contributed to its development. The resulting score distributions, which are normal in form, provide a basis for differentiating quite adequately among the examinees. The 34 items are not easy. On the pretest the highest score for the sample of students studied was 29, and on the posttest 31 with respective means of 15.89 and 17.27. This reviewer has serious reservations concerning the scoring of three of the items and moderate reservations regarding the scoring of four others. There may be some concern relative to the 45-minute time limit. Perhaps one hour would be somewhat less threatening and conducive to a higher level of performance, especially for those students for whom English is not the first language. With a longer period of test administration, systematic empirical investigations relating performance on the CCTST to the host of variables that already have been studied might lead to somewhat different outcomes from those obtained with a shorter time limit.

Data pertaining to the reliability of the total scale as well as to the three subtests are meager. In Technical Report No. 1 internal-consistency estimates (KR-20) of only .69 and .68 occurred for total scores on a pretest and posttest administration. Normative information in the form of percentiles on both the pretest and posttest for the college sample studied is quite helpful, although corresponding data for subtests did not appear in the technical reports.

Although one can have considerable confidence that the content of the test represents a strong consensus among experts, additional research regarding the construct validity of the test would be very much in order. It would appear from the preliminary correlational data that both verbal and quantitative intelligence constitute a significant component of CT. It would be interesting to carry out both exploratory and confirmatory factor analyses of the CCTST with other well-known measures of CT and with tests of verbal and mathematical abilities to ascertain whether the hypothesized constructs can be empirically verified. It would also be rewarding to determine what the relationship of the hypothesized dimensions of the CCTST would be to a number of problem-solving abilities such as those identified by Guilford and his coworkers within the context of the structure-of-intellect model. One can anticipate that CT might conceivably be represented by a hierarchy of factor dimensions comprising both higher-order and first-order constructs.

In summary, preliminary evidence indicates the CCTST possesses considerable content validity. A manual is very much needed to synthesize existing information from the four technical reports. Additional efforts should be directed to obtain evidence regarding the empirical validity of the constructs, to provide reliability estimates of scores on the total scale and subscales, and to present more comprehensive normative data. The potential of the CCTST is great. One can hope that the author will be able to obtain the very much deserved necessary support to expend the additional effort needed to generate the required psychometric information that will permit the widespread use of this instrument in both undergraduate and graduate programs in colleges and universities.

[16]

Campbell Leadership Index.

Purpose: "An adjective checklist designed to be used in the assessment of leadership characteristics."

Population: Leaders.

Publication Date: 1991.

Acronym: CLI.

Scores, 22: Ambitious, Daring, Dynamic, Enterprising, Experienced, Farsighted, Original, Persuasive, Energy, Affectionate, Considerate, Empowering, Entertaining, Friendly, Credible, Organized, Productive, Thrifty, Calm, Flexible, Optimistic, Trusting.

Administration: Group or individual.

Price Data: Available from publisher.

Time: (25–30) minutes.
Comments: Self-ratings plus 3–5 observer ratings.
Author: David Campbell.
Publisher: NCS Assessments.
Cross References: See T4:369 (1 reference).

Review of the Campbell Leadership Index by GEORGE DOMINO, Professor of Psychology, University of Arizona, Tucson, AZ:

The Campbell Leadership Index (CLI) is a 100-item adjective check list designed to assess leadership characteristics. Respondents rate each adjective and the accompanying definition on a 6-point scale ranging from *always* to *never*. Three to five observers are then also required to rate the respondent using the same items and scale responses.

These ratings yield a total of 22 scores encompassing five "orientations" or areas: *L*eadership (8 scales), *E*nergy (1 scale), *A*ffability (5), *D*ependability (4), and *R*esilience (4). (Note the italicized initials spell LEADER.) In addition to the 22 scores, the resulting profile also yields two summary scores, one for self and one for observers.

The CLI is a component of the Campbell Work Orientations (CWO) which is a collection of surveys focusing on the psychological aspects of the working environment. Campbell proposes that leadership can be defined as "actions which focus resources to create desirable opportunities" (p. 3), and that leadership can occur in the carrying out of seven tasks: vision, management, empowerment, politics, feedback, entrepreneurship, and personal style. One of the unique aspects of the CLI is that it is both a self-report measure and a method of gathering descriptive information from others. The CLI is intended to be used primarily with people in leadership positions. Typical participants are people attending leadership training programs.

The initial item pool for the CLI consisted of 300 adjectives. This pool underwent a number of revisions primarily in response to respondents' complaints about the length, to the current version of 100 items, of which only 96 are scored. Other considerations in the item reduction such as "eliminating items that proved to be unrelated to leadership effectiveness" (p. 123) are mentioned but no evidence is presented regarding the process.

The 22 scales were developed by using an iterative approach whereby clusters of adjectives were grouped into preliminary scoring scales, then samples of convenience were assessed, and modifications made on the basis of both correlational and logical analyses. For each of the 22 scales a table of item intercorrelations based on $N = 235$ are presented. Some of the coefficients are quite high (e.g., adventurous and daring, $r = .61$), most are in the middle ranges (e.g., hardy and sedentary, $r = .35$), and some are quite low (e.g., naive and well-connected, $r = -.11$). It should be noted that all of the scales are quite brief ranging from three to a maximum of seven items.

Once the 22 scales were developed, their intercorrelations were examined, and the five orientations (LEADeR) were constructed by gathering together the scoring scales with the highest intercorrelations. A subsequent factor analysis supports this five-dimension solution. Scores on the CLI ar e expressed as *T* scores and are based on some 30 normative groups ranging from college student leaders and nonleaders, to various types of business executives, industrial psychologists, municipal fire chiefs, and military officers. Most of these groups appear to be primarily male, but some female groups were also assessed.

The manual author states that "formulating a simple, general statement about the validity of the CLI has proved to be a difficult task" (p. 129). That indeed seems to be the case, although there is an extensive discussion of various types of validity. Content validity is said to be one of the CLI's strongest points, yet a perusal of the adjectives indicates that "competent" is not included, and that a number of adjectives included in Gough's ACL "military leadership" scale, for example, are missing from the CLI. Several concurrent validity studies are presented indicating that self-ratings on the CLI may not accurately reflect current status, but composite observer ratings do. Both construct and discriminant validities are discussed, with findings supportive of the CLI. Extensive reliability data, including alpha coefficients, interrater reliability coefficients, and test-retest coefficients are presented, generally suggesting adequate to excellent reliability.

Appendix A of the manual gives personological descriptions of high and low scorers on each of the 22 scales, although it is not indicated how these psychodynamic portraits were derived.

The respondent apparently receives a rather detailed computerized feedback in the form of a profile, made up primarily of tables, running some 21 pages in length. There is also a CLI Developmental Planning Guide, apparently written for the individual respondent (however, in this Guide the CLI is described as being composed of 21 scales, yet Table 1 lists 22). The Guide also defines a "consistency check" as showing how often responses were inconsistent, such as checking ALWAYS to both "sensitive" and "insensitive"; yet the manual gives no information on the makeup of this consistency check.

The manual has three goals: (*a*) to describe the background that led to the CLI, (*b*) to serve as an administrative manual, and (*c*) to serve as a technical resource manual. The first two goals are well met. The manual is clearly written, quite detailed, and considers the use of the CLI for self-development, team building, and selection and placement procedures. No extravagant promises are made and potential applications of the CLI to individual cases are well tempered with cautionary comments. The manual is professionally printed and gives an outer appearance of professionalism with just the right touch of erudition. The CLI is a "slick" package, not in a pejorative sense, and shows thoughtful preparation for a specific target audience—business executives who utilize the talents of psychological firms. But the price is steep—$160 is the unit price. This is clearly a measure to be used in an applied setting, and not for research purposes.

Several criticisms of the CLI can be made. First, no published studies are cited. Given that the CLI "has been under development for the better part of a decade" (Preface) and that its author is a most prolific and competent psychologist, the lack of references to peer-reviewed papers is particularly disturbing. Secondly, self-reports are susceptible to faking, social desirability, and other response styles. Any self-respecting manual should address these issues— the CLI does not. A third criticism is that although considerable validity data are presented, there is no evidence to show the relation ship of the CLI to any other test measuring dimensions of leadership, nor to any of the standard personality inventories such as the CPI (California Psychological Inventory), that might be relevant to further establish the construct validity of the CLI. Furthermore, no evidence is presented against real life criteria of leadership either in a concurrent or predictive fashion.

In summary, there are many psychological testing programs on the marketplace that have been designed for use in the business environment. It is my impression that most lack the kind of reliability and validity evidence that can be found with the CLI. Thus, the CLI seems to be a real contribution, though more evidence needs to be presented to satisfy academic and professional users.

Review of the Campbell Leadership Index by CHARLES HOUSTON, Director of Planning and Research, Virginia Western Community College, Roanoke, VA:

Dr. David Campbell, co-author of the well-known Strong-Campbell Interest Inventory, has provided the leadership for the development of the Campbell Leadership Index (CLI). The CLI provides a 100-adjective checklist designed to identify leadership characteristics. Comparisons are made between an individual's self-reported leadership characteristics and three to five observers. A quantifiable profile that compares self and observers' perceptions on 22 scales within five orientations is developed in order to help an individual understand specific leadership characteristics. A sample description of CLI Orientations, Scales, Typical Adjectives, and Psychological Interpretation would be as follows: An orientation toward farsighted leadership would be described with adjectives such as insightful or forward-looking and suggests a psychological interpretation such as looks ahead, plans, is a visionary. The implications of these orientations and scales are that effective leaders are rated higher on most, if not all, of these dimensions than are ineffective leaders.

SELF VERSUS OBSERVER DIFFERENCES. Although there are usually some differences between self and observers' ratings, a 10-point difference is suggested as a red flag for discerning discrepancies between self versus observers' ratings. Higher observers' ratings than individual's ratings imply that an individual is too modest, whereas lower observers' ratings imply that observers do not give you as much credit as you give yourself on CLI dimensions. Broad agreements between self and observers' ratings are a "healthy finding" and usually indicate that individuals are seen favorably by most of the people with whom they interact.

Selecting areas needing improvements and capitalizing on areas of strength can improve effectiveness as a leader. Action-planning worksheets are provided because good intentions for improving leadership characteristics are best translated into meaningful deeds when action plans are written down and formulated into goals. In summary, the CLI is proposed as an aid in understanding the characteristics and behaviors which influence potential for leadership. The processes and results of the CLI give a set of self versus observers' views from which individuals can develop action plans for improving leadership potential.

CLI'S STRENGTHS AND WEAKNESSES. The CLI is an outstanding attempt to develop and understand the construct of leadership. The CLI's manual is very comprehensive including overviews, applications, uses, norms, planning guides, validity/reliability considerations, etc. The CLI is also a component of the Campbell Work Orientations (CWO), a collection of surveys focusing on the psychological aspects of the working environment. Both the CLI and the CWO can be used in any setting where well-established, quantifiable psychological measures are useful. Excellent individual and group profiles, which compare self and observers' ratings, are available. The CLI also includes a Development Planning Guide that effectively and efficiently presents the concepts and constructs related to this leadership index. The Development Planning Guide can provide executives and other organizational members with a concise summary of the CLI's objectives, organization, and implications in discerning leadership characteristics.

There are several major limitations in using the CLI. First, the CLI is very complex and certainly requires professionals to explain its uses and interpret its results. Major efforts in workshops, training sessions, educational seminars, and briefing sessions will be needed in order to insure that employees understand the goals and objectives of the CLI inventory. Without these training sessions, it is highly unlikely that desirable organizational outcomes will be achieved. Second, the measures of personal characteristics, the privacy and dignity of the individual respondent, and confidentiality at both the data-collecting and results-reporting stages are critical areas that must be addressed in using the CLI. The potential for negative consequences of observers taking advantage to berate and unfairly criticize an individual can happen even in a healthy organization. Because of these limitations, many small businesses, companies, educational institutions, etc. should consider potential problems in using the CLI with serious caution.

In summary, the CLI is a major development in identifying the underlying factors of leadership. It can certainly assist an organization in identifying leadership characteristics and the complex processes necessary to define this construct; however, the specific uses of the CLI must be considered carefully in terms of "cost-benefits" (not financial cost of the CLI, which is very reasonable) within the organization. Finally, the CLI certainly requires significantly more planning than other standard psychological inventories and may be more appropriate for leadership training or development programs rather than assessing current leadership practices within the organization.

[17]

Canadian Cognitive Abilities Test, Form 7.
Purpose: "Designed to assess the development of cognitive abilities related to verbal, quantitative, and nonverbal reasoning and problem solving."
Population: Grades K–2, 3–12.

Publication Dates: 1970–90.
Acronym: CCAT.
Scores, 3: Verbal, Quantitative, Non-Verbal.
Administration: Group.
Price Data, 1994: $7.95 per 10 class record sheets; $21.95 per technical notes ('90, 34 pages).
Comments: Canadian version of Cognitive Abilities Test, Form 4 (T4:537).
Authors: Original edition by Robert L. Thorndike and Elizabeth P. Hagen; Canadian revision by Edgar N. Wright.
Publisher: Nelson Canada [Canada].
  a) PRIMARY BATTERIES.
Population: Grades K–1, 2–3.
Levels, 2: Primary 1, 2.
Price Data: $43.95 per 35 test booklets; $5.45 per scoring key; $16.45 per examiner's manual ('89, 85 pages); $27.45 per examination kit.
Time: (90) minutes (untimed).
  b) MULTILEVEL EDITION.
Population: Grades 3–12.
Price Data: $9.45 per test booklet (Levels A–H); $3.95 per Level A test booklet; $20.45 per 35 hand/machine scorable answer sheets; $17.45 per examiner's manual ('89, 101 pages); $6.95 per supplemental manual Level A with key; $13.45 per scoring mask; $29 per examination kit.
Time: (90) minutes.
Cross References: For reviews by Giuseppe Costantino and Jack A. Cummings, see 10:42 (3 references); see also T3:361 (5 references) and 8:180 (2 references).

Review of the Canadian Cognitive Abilities Test, Form 7 by JOHN O. ANDERSON, Associate Professor, Faculty of Education, University of Victoria, Victoria, British Columbia, Canada:

The Canadian Cognitive Abilities Test (CCAT) provides measures of three cognitive skills labelled Verbal, Quantitative, and Non-Verbal for students from kindergarten through grade 12. The tests are composed of multiple-choice items that require the respondent to complete tasks of interpretation and use of symbols: words, numbers, and abstract graphics. The primary levels (1 and 2) are contained in separate test booklets in which the students enter their responses, the grades 3 to 12 levels (A to H) are contained in a single multilevel booklet that is to be used with a separate answer sheet. The CCAT is a Canadian adaptation of the Cognitive Abilities Test (T4:537); the adaptation consisted primarily of the development of Canadian norms for the test. The test is supported by two resource documents, the

Examiner's Manual and the Technical Manual, and a computerized scoring service.

The Verbal battery consists of two subtests at the primary levels: oral vocabulary and verbal classification. Students are read questions (47 for Level 1 and 56 for Level 2) by the teacher from a script in the Examiner's Manual. They then select and mark the appropriate diagram in their test booklets. In the multilevel booklet, the Verbal battery consists of three subtests: verbal classification, sentence completion, and verbal analogies. Students are required to locate the appropriate level of test they are writing, read the test item, and respond correctly on a separate answer sheet. Each student is to complete 75 items.

The Quantitative battery consists of two subtests at the Primary levels: relational concepts and quantitative concepts. Items (47 for Level 1 and 56 for Level 2) are read by the teacher and students are to select the most appropriate diagram in response. The students completing levels A to H in the multilevel booklet complete 60 items in three subtests: quantitative concepts, number series, and equation building.

The Non-Verbal battery consists of two subtests at the Primary levels: figure classification and matrices. Level 1 has a total of 46 test items and Level 2 has 53 Non-Verbal items. Students are to complete 65 items in three subtests in the multilevel Non-Verbal battery: figure classification, figure analogies, and figure analysis.

The CCAT yields scores for each of the three batteries: Verbal, Quantitative, and Non-Verbal. The types of scores produced are: Universal Scaled Scores (USS), Standard Age Scores (SAS), percentile scores at different ages and grades, and stanines for different ages and grades. The USS are standard scores derived from an equating study (linking all levels of the CCAT) and reported on a scale that is common for all levels of the CCAT. The USS scale is centered at Level D (approximately grade 6) with a mean of 125 and standard deviation of 20. The SAS is a standard score derived for each age group completing the test; it is analogous to IQ-type scores in that it has a mean of 100 and standard deviation of 16. The percentile scores and stanines are developed both for grade and age. The resource documents describe how these scores were derived and contain tables for converting one score format to another but the manuals fail to discuss the meaning and use of these different kinds of scores. All these types of scores are similar in that they inform the user about an individual's test performance in relation to that of a norm group. So a question that has to be answered is: Why have a USS, SAS, grade and age percentiles,

and stanines? A clear discussion of how to use each type of score is clearly in order.

Overall test performance appears to be typical for a test of this nature. The average subtest scores are in the 55% range for grades 3 to 12 (Level A to H) and in the 65–70% range for grades 1 and 2. Kindergarten students average around 55% of the Level 1 tests. Item difficulties range from .40 to .75, and discrimination indices (point biserial correlations) average about .40.

The reliability of the CCAT is described both in terms of internal consistency through KR20 coefficients for the three subtests at all levels, and in terms of stability of scores over time. The internal consistency estimates are in the .81 to .94 range indicating respectable performance. The stability of scores was estimated by considering the average performance within a school district over time and across different grades. The results, although not compelling, do suggest the test does generate consistent results across time at least at the aggregate level. Some indication of stability across time at the individual student level would add further credibility to the quality of the test.

The validity of the CCAT is addressed briefly in the Technical Manual. The issue of content validity is discussed in terms of what kinds of tasks the test items demand of students: "The tasks require the interpretation and use of symbols" (p 20). Test users are encouraged to examine the test in terms of what it is demanding of students and to compare these demands to the user's conception of cognitive abilities. Although this encouragement is solid advice, it does not, of itself offer evidence of test validity. The issue of criterion-related validity is addressed by presenting the correlations of CCAT scores with those of the Canadian Tests of Basic Skills (CTBS). Over 300 correlation coefficients are tabulated. They are all moderately positive (.40 to .80) but are not convincing evidence of criterion-related validity. A sound rationale as to why the CTBS is a criterion for CCAT validity should be provided. Construct validity is dealt with by correlating the scores from the Verbal battery of the CCAT with results from another general abilities test, the Henmon-Nelson Ability Test. The positive correlations (.78 to .84 at the different grades) do support concurrent and construct validity for the CCAT.

The resource documents accompanying the CCAT are the Examiner's Manual and the Technical Manual. These provide information on the administration of the test, the derivation of the various scores, description of the development of the test, and discussion of interpretation and use of CCAT results. These manuals are well structured and written, offering generally sound comment and caution about test use. The advice to evaluate test items in terms of the test user's conceptualization of cognitive skills is good practice. The caution to regard the skills being measured as developed skills, not innate characteristics, is also sound advice. The discussion and illustration of test interpretation by means of simulated case studies is also informative. The authors also point out the language competence required to successfully respond to many items has to be considered in interpreting results. These and other points are well taken. I hope they will be attended to by test users.

However, there are some areas in the manuals that could be expanded or modified to improve these documents. One such area is the description of the test itself—the nature of cognitive skills the test is designed to measure. The concept of cognitive skills is complex with no single universally accepted definition. The conceptualization used by the authors of the CCAT should be fully articulated for the test user; it is not. A related issue is the provision of reference lists to allow the user to locate research and theoretical literature relevant to CCAT use. Unfortunately, there is a complete absence of references in any of the CCAT documents.

Another area of concern in regard to the manuals relates to the use of composite scores. The authors correctly point out that three distinct cognitive skills are tested with the CCAT: Verbal, Quantitative, and Non-Verbal. They make a cogent argument for interpreting the three separately. Then, in a turnabout, they provide 10 pages of tables for obtaining composite results—one overall cognitive score for each student. The only rationale offered for the use of composite scores is that *regulations* may require them. Shifting from a 3-factor conceptualization of cognitive skills to a single factor (a unidimensional *g* model of intelligence, one might assume) on the basis of administrative regulations certainly undermines any pretensions of construct validity the CCAT has attempted to establish.

In summary, the Canadian Cognitive Abilities Test appears to be a useful instrument to provide information on students' general functioning in the three areas of verbal, quantitative, and pattern-recognition skills. As noted in the Examiner's Manual (p. 53) the test can serve to identify those students performing well above or below age and grade expectations, and in doing so provide educators with information useful in the development of sound educational intervention.

Review of the Canadian Cognitive Abilities Test, Form 7 by JOHN HATTIE, Professor of Education, The University of Western Australia, Nedlands, AUSTRALIA:

The Canadian Cognitive Abilities Test (CCAT) assesses the development of three major cognitive abilities: verbal, quantitative, and nonverbal reasoning and problem solving. There is a battery of six tests for grades K–3 and another battery of nine tests for grades 3–12.

The test has been developed from Thorndike and Hagen's Cognitive Abilities Tests (T4:537) with minor changes in spellings and systems of measurement. The author of the manual for the Canadian version states the items are based on content familiar to children, although some items (e.g., caribou, Aesop fables, lumberman, Halloween, ketchup, and nickel) would not be appropriate to non-Canadians or non-North Americans and thus care should be taken when administering to those with other than a North American cultural background. There are few changes from the earlier edition: Some new items and "new art" are included.

The test developers claim the test assesses many abilities such as comprehension of oral English, following directions, holding material in short-term memory, scanning stimuli to obtain specific or general information, assessing general information and verbal concepts, comparing stimuli, classifying familiar objects, and using quantitative and spatial relationships. There is diagnostic information at the battery level (for Verbal, Quantitative, and Non-Verbal levels) but there are no diagnostics at either the test level or item level, or related to the above abilities. The test is not speeded but would take at least 2 hours of a child's time over two or three sessions. For this time investment, the test user obtains information on three scales (Verbal, Quantitative, and Non-Verbal) and an overall score. This is far from acceptable. The test has little use for anyone but the researcher. Too much is asked of the children for so little return.

Following the trend of many recent tests, the CCAT is a thinly disguised IQ test that merely does not highlight the term "IQ." The use of an IQ is frowned upon, so instead "standard age scores" are derived. These standard age scores are scaled to a mean of 100 with a standard deviation of 16, and are interpretable irrespective of age. These standard age scores can be converted to percentile ranks (which can lead to so many problems of interpretation), and to national stanine scores, both by age and grade.

The instructions are clear, although they require good listening skills. The level of oral comprehension required to understand the instruction at the lower levels may be too high for many examinees.

The Canadian sampling is excellent and the estimates of reliability are high. There are, however, no estimates of stability (despite the fact the manual includes data from which such estimates could have been derived) and the section on validity is weak. The correlations between the scales are presented but there are no factor analyses, no multitrait-multimethod analyses, and little conceptual analysis.

I performed a factor analysis on the data provided in the manual. There was most support for a single general factor for the grade 1, 3, 7, and 11 matrices. When a second factor was requested, this general factor split into verbal and quantitative factors but the correlation between them was very high (.64, .69, .72, .68 for each grade level, respectively). There was little support for a nonverbal factor separate from the quantitative factor.

The relationship between the CCAT and the Canadian Tests of Basic Skills and the Henmon-Nelson Ability Test (Canadian version) is very high. This relationship probably reflects the general ability assessed by all three batteries. It would have been useful to be convinced that the test assesses achievement rather than a general ability.

Altogether, this test does not reflect good measurement practice in the 1990s, requires too much time relative to the return of information, needs a good dose of modern measurement procedures, and given the availability of so many alternatives it probably will be used by few. If users desire to use the battery they could use the Verbal scale and probably would derive as much information compared to using the whole battery.

The test could be improved if the developers provided a computerized version using adaptive testing as this would cut the administration time, diagnostics could be added at the item or subtest level, and more acceptable equating across levels could be achieved.

[18]
The Candidate Profile Record.

Purpose: Constructed to predict successful performance in clerical positions.
Population: Applicants for clerical positions.
Publication Dates: 1982–89.
Scores: Total score only.
Administration: Group.
Price Data: Available from publisher.
Time: (30–45) minutes.
Authors: Richardson, Bellows, Henry & Co., Inc.

Publisher: Richardson, Bellows, Henry & Co., Inc.

Review of The Candidate Profile Record by F. MARION ASCHE, Professor of Education, Virginia Polytechnic Institute and State University, Blacksburg, VA:

The Candidate Profile Record (CPR) is an "autobiographical questionnaire designed for use in the prediction of successful performance in non-exempt clerical positions" (p. 1). It has 105 items and is not timed but typically requires 30–45 minutes for individual or group administration. It is based on some 10 years of continuing validity research with participating organizations (banks) and was developed based on the observation that competencies required for success in clerical and customer contact occupations apparently exceed those measured by typical general aptitude and clerical skills tests.

An extensive Technical Report details the large-samples, multiple-replication study conducted to refine the CPR and provide evidence of criterion-related validity which would meet EEOC guidelines. This study was also used to determine if autobiographical questionnaire scores could predict job performance across secretarial and clerical classifications with significantly lower impact than that produced by the use of traditional general aptitude tests. (Impact defined as irrelevant score variation associated with race or gender.) The research included four consortium groups of banks with several hundred locations and a total of over 37,000 respondents on one or more phases of the study. Three instruments were developed: (*a*) the Job Requirements Questionnaire (JRQ), to determine the duty requirements of each specific job classification as well as to determine the extent to which the same underlying abilities were necessary to successfully perform clerical duties, regardless of differences in job tasks; (*b*) the Non-Supervisory Performance Evaluation Record (PER) based on the JRQ and designed to serve as the criterion instrument; and (*c*) The Candidate Profile Record (CPR). The JRQ was produced in three forms for Teller/Customer Service job classifications, for Processing/Verifying classifications and for Secretarial/Clerical classifications. The same 32 ability statements were included on all three forms but each had unique task statements. The PER includes only the more general ability statements, not specific job tasks.

The CPR was used, along with the RBH Test of Learning Ability, Form STR, and the Minnesota Clerical Test (MCT) as multiple predictors of ratings on the criterion measure (PER) by the employee's immediate supervisor, and when feasible, by a second supervisor having adequate knowledge of the employee's performance. The experimental CPR was administered to applicants and new hires before advising them of the hiring decision and was not scored at that time or used in the hiring decision. Those hired were rated on the PER at the end of their probationary period or their termination, whichever occurred first. A total of 37,524 incumbents in Groups 1 through 4 completed the JRQ in one of its three forms. The PER was subsequently completed by 5,869 immediate superiors and 3,309 second raters.

Item analysis and item weighting procedures were used with Group 1 data to assess item validities. The original experimental CPR was subsequently shortened. Item weights and validities were then tested across the three remaining independent samples. The final CPR and scoring system were thus the result of repeated evaluations of the relationship between item responses and the Rater 1 criterion. The final step was to sum the resulting item weights to compute a total CPR score for all cases in all samples and evaluate its score distributions and validity along with those of the other experimental predictors (the RBH Test of Learning Ability and the Minnesota Clerical Test).

The two a priori design criteria of low impact and job relatedness (criterion-related validity) were addressed by examining mean CPR score differences of subgroups, intercorrelations, and correlations of CPR scores with job performance as rated on the PER in comparison with the other instruments for the total sample and within subgroups. The CPR evidenced substantially lower score differences between gender and racial subgroups than the general aptitude measure (RBH). CPR scores were relatively independent of the MCT and had a moderate relationship to the RBH. CPR score relationships to job performance were quite consistent across subgroups, indicating robust validity across geographic locations, gender, and ethnic groups.

A fairness analysis was conducted defining unfairness as the underprediction of actual job performance. Mean regression residual scores (obtained by subtracting actual performance scores from predicted scores) for each subgroup indicated a statistically significant overprediction for African-Americans, a slight overprediction for males (NS), and a slight underprediction (NS) for females. A monotonically increasing CPR–job performance relationship was clearly demonstrated for the total sample (the higher the score on the CPR, the greater the proportion of employees being rated as average or above in performance). Regression analyses which assessed the criterion-related validity of the CPR in conjunction with the MCT, the RBH, and all three instruments indicated decreased score validities when either the MCT, RBH, or both were used.

Because the research presented was based on clerical occupations in the bank setting only, it is not clear that validity generalization may be extended to other institutional settings. There was only one statement in all materials provided that mentioned that the CPR is designed to supplement, not replace normal interview, reference checks, and other procedures. Also, the Administrators Guide may be misleading in a very important area. It is implied that an *individual's* probability of success can be directly interpreted from his or her score on the CPR. Because no confidence band is provided for such predictions, the user may be led to assume that group results apply without error to the individual. Current materials provide very little information regarding how CPR items were developed. Reliability data were provided only for the PER (mean correlations of performance ratings by Rater 1 and Rater 2 for each of the sample groups). This reviewer did not locate reliability estimates for the CPR or JRQ. The fairly consistent correlations of the CPR with the PER across samples, however, provides an indirect estimate of the reliability of the CPR.

The CPR and its related instruments designed to assess job tasks/abilities and job performance represent a unique contribution to the field of clerical testing. The underlying theory that actual job performance is a reflection of underlying abilities and personal characteristics that generalize across specific job titles and go beyond those generally measured by traditional clerical performance and general ability tests appears to be supported by the evidence provided. The availability of site or job classification task and ability analyses as a part of the overall system should be considered an advantage in terms of judging appropriateness to new settings and continuing assessment of validity generalization. The availability of site-scored answer sheets and reusable CPR booklets helps make costs of administration reasonable.

Review of The Candidate Profile Record by GEORGE C. THORNTON III, Professor of Psychology, Colorado State University, Ft. Collins, CO:

The Candidate Profile Record (CPR) is a 105-item autobiographical inventory designed to measure competencies beyond basic aptitudes to perform clerical and customer service jobs. It was developed primarily for banking positions, but a companion job analysis instrument can be used to determine if the CPR is appropriate in other settings.

The development of the CPR represents the best and the worst aspects of the empirical test construction method using criterion keying. The "best aspects" are represented by a well-run study with four consortia, job analyses in 30 organizations, pooled responses for nearly 6,000 employees, and extensive performance ratings and turnover data. Item analyses identified biographical information that showed repeated differentiation between performance levels. The unit-weighted composite of valid items was found to be related to performance in independent samples. Correlation coefficients and an easy-to-read expectancy table demonstrate criterion validity (rs are approximately .30) for ethnic and gender groups. The CPR was found to be more highly related to the criteria than tests of learning ability and clerical speed and accuracy.

The "worst aspects" are represented by the fact that no theory of constructs underlying effective job performance is offered and, although the manual authors say the CPR measures basic competencies such as ability to communicate and to get along with others, there is no description of the attributes measured by the inventory. No construct validity evidence for the CPR is presented.

The background information covers school performance, early work experiences, self-descriptions of confidence and talkativeness, saving and spending patterns, and self-evaluations of skills. Some items may be considered invasions of privacy (e.g., expulsion from school, whether you have a bank account, and how many nights you go out) and other items may be quite transparent (e.g., how self-confident are you, and would you like to work with customers). It would be helpful to know what effects dissimulation, faking, or social desirability response sets have on reports of these background variables and the predictive validity of the test.

The answer sheet can be hand scored or adapted for computer scanning and scoring. A well-written administrator's guide, a detailed technical report, and a succinct executive summary are provided.

No normative data are provided beyond the means and standard deviations for groups from the developmental samples. These data are helpful, but norms for other subgroups (e.g., geographical regions, urban/rural residence) would be informative. Furthermore, no reliability estimates are presented for the CPR.

Adverse impact, differential validity, and discrimination (fairness) were investigated, but the implications of the findings are not fully discussed. Results showed no differential validity among ethnic or gender subgroups, but whites scored approximately one-half standard deviation (SD) higher on the CPR than African and Hispanic Americans, and whites received performance ratings approximately one-third SD higher and were involuntarily terminated less frequently than blacks. Regression analyses using formulae from the total sample showed that African American performance was actually overpredicted. Thus, the manual concludes that a single expectancy table is appropriate for all applicants.

What is left unstated is the important warning that the lower means on the CPR for minorities may result in adverse impact against African and Hispanic Americans. The 5- or 6-point deficit in raw scores would typically move minorities to a lower-level converted score. Whether this difference would result in adverse impact would be a function of the cutoff score used by any individual organization.

The results also suggest the CPR was not able to achieve the most important objective of causing "substantially lower impact than that produced by the use of traditional general aptitude tests" (Technical Report, p. 1). Whereas African Americans scored .40 SD lower than whites on the CPR, they scored 1.11 SD lower on the learning ability test, .38 lower on the names test, and .18 lower on the numbers tests. Thus, it would appear the CPR will produce lower adverse impact in comparison with one test, but higher adverse impact in comparison with two other tests.

In summary, the CPR was carefully developed using a large data pool collected from diverse banks. It provides a unique instrument to gather background information found to be predictive of performance and turnover. Although differential validity was not found, and the CPR was statistically fair in predicting success for ethnic and sex subgroups, adverse impact may still exist because, on average, minorities score approximately one-third standard deviation lower than whites. Organizations should examine the content of the biographical information to determine if any questions might be objectionable to their applicants.

[19]

Career Beliefs Inventory.

Purpose: Designed to assist people to identify career beliefs that may influence their career goals.

Population: Junior high school and over.

Publication Date: 1991.

Acronym: CBI.

Scores, 26: Administrative Index, Employment Status, Career Plans, Acceptance of Uncertainty,

Openness, Achievement, College Education, Intrinsic Satisfaction, Peer Equality, Structured Work Environment, Control, Responsibility, Approval of Others, Self-Other Comparisons, Occupation/College Variation, Career Path Flexibility, Post-Training Transition, Job Experimentation, Relocation, Improving Self, Persisting While Uncertain, Taking Risks, Learning Job Skills, Negotiating/Searching, Overcoming Obstacles, Working Hard.

Administration: Group.

Price Data, 1992: $30 per 25 test booklets; $40 per 10 prepaid answer sheets (price includes scoring by publisher); $30 per manual (46 pages); $32 per specimen set.

Time: Administration time not reported.

Author: John D. Krumboltz.

Publisher: Consulting Psychologists Press, Inc.

Review of the Career Beliefs Inventory by DAVID L. BOLTON, Assistant Professor for Education, West Chester University, West Chester, PA:

The Career Beliefs Inventory (CBI) attempts to determine what beliefs may prevent individuals from reaching their career goals. It differs from other career guidance tools, which tend to look at the vocational interests of the person being counseled. An assessment of career beliefs is important when conducting career counseling. The test manual makes that point convincingly.

The Inventory covers 25 scales, divided into five categories. These categories are described as covering the beliefs that affect career choice. The 25 scales were developed based on about a thousand beliefs, reported over an 8-year period, that blocked individuals from reaching their career goals. Although the scales seem logical as possible factors related to career beliefs, there is little evidence provided by the author that the scales are distinctly different. In the manual section on validity, the author reports a factor analysis in which four factors are reported and named. The factor analysis seems to contradict the structure of the inventory and one is left wondering which to believe. Just looking at the items that comprise the scales, it appears that some scales would be highly related.

My general impression after reading the manual is the author views the Inventory as the beginning of a discussion rather than a definitive measurement of the person being counseled (and rightfully so). This is reinforced by the fact that many of the scales have very few items. Ten of the scales have only two items and only three scales have more than five items. Consequently, the reliabilities for some of the scales tend to be low. Although, as the author indicates,

the test-retest and Cronbach-alpha reliabilities for the scales are satisfactory, any interpretation of the scales would be questionable.

The issue of reliability of the scales is of most concern with regards to assessing the validity of the instrument. In attempting to establish construct validity, the author attempts to correlate Inventory scores with other measures related to vocational selection. In doing so, he is trying to show the CBI is distinct from other instruments. For example, the author correlates each of the CBI's 25 scales with the various scales of the Strong Interest Inventory. After doing so, only 2.97% of the correlations were greater than an absolute value of .26 and were significantly different than zero at the .01 level. The author concludes the measures are assessing two different things. However, the low correlations may be simply due to the low reliabilities of the 25 scales coupled with a measure of unreliability of the scales on the Strong Inventory. In fact, one might expect to find reasonable correlations between the CBI and the Strong. For example, one could expect the correlations between the CBI's Taking Risk or Negotiating/Searching scales and the Strong's Introversion-Extroversion Scale. There are other similar examples in the manual. In general, the author seems to exhibit a shotgun approach to establishing construct validity; not hypothesizing specific interrelationships between variables, but correlating all 25 scales with scales from other instruments, hoping that there are no correlations between them and explaining away the correlations that are significant. Construct validity should be attempted in a more systematic fashion with specific hypotheses.

In assessing concurrent validity, the author correlates the scales with self-ratings of job satisfaction. Most coefficients are not significant. The significant correlations tend to be low, generally in the low to mid-20s. Despite the low correlations, the author tries to draw conclusions from these data. Most of the relationships explain no more than 6% of the variance, thus making interpretations likely to be misleading.

The attempts to establish validity seem like overkill considering the purpose of the instrument. The CBI is a tool to start a discussion. As the author points out, the preliminary interpretation of the scales should be viewed as tentative. As such, the best form of validity might be the testimony of the users. The author indicates the CBI has a successful history of use. Although perhaps true, it is difficult to assess the author's assertion as evidence of validity.

The norms are based on a sample of over 7,500 people in the United States and Australia. Those in the norming group from the United States come from a variety of states. Norms are provided for eight different groups broken down by sex, employment status, and maturity level (adult, college student, school student), with varying numbers for each group. The author does not claim the norming group is representative of any particular population.

The manual is easy to read. The instructions on the use of the instrument are somewhat skimpy. Only one case study is provided and one has the impression that it was selected because it was simple. It is not clear if this is a typical case. Because the CBI is to be a starting point for a discussion, it is important that more instruction be provided to the user of the test. I would not want to use the instrument solely on the basis of this one case study. This section of the manual requires considerable work.

Another concern regards scoring. Scoring must be done by a scoring service. Because the answers provided on the CBI serve as a basis for a discussion, it makes sense to discuss the answers immediately so individuals can explain their responses. A handscoring option would be very useful.

Although the CBI may be helpful for vocational counseling, a counselor with knowledge of the 25 scales could address the same issues without using the CBI. As such, knowledge of the 25 scales may be more important than the use of the instrument itself.

Review of the Career Beliefs Inventory by ROBERT M. GUION, Distinguished University Professor Emeritus, Bowling Green State University, Bowling Green, OH:

The Career Beliefs Inventory (CBI) is more an interview aid than a measurement tool. There are 26 "scales," 10 with as few as two items and none (except an "Administrative Index" designed to identify careless or otherwise "inaccurate" responses) with more than eight. The scales are scored, but the scores are signals to help vocational counselors explore with their clients any assumptions or beliefs that may be interfering with career development. Innumerable specific beliefs might prevent appropriate career decisions, but the scales offer generalities in which the more specific beliefs might fit. Low or moderate scores suggest areas to search during an interview. For example, a low score on "Approval of Others" might stem from the client's efforts to please a parent, a spouse, or some other person—or it might be a generalized search for approval. There are only two items for the Approval scale, one a statement that approval is deemed necessary and the other a reverse statement proclaiming that it is not. In neither case does the inventory itself look to see whose approval

is or is not wanted; that, if the score is in the warning range, is left for the interview to ferret out. The CBI may serve a useful purpose, and the user (or reviewer) should not fault the CBI for not serving some other purpose.

The manual does not say which of the 96 items fit individual scales. A statement that the respondent would not move to some regions of the country, even with a "terrific" job offer, is not hard to place in the Relocation group; other items are not as certainly assigned. This may explain why answer sheets are purchased only with prepaid scoring. Sending off answer sheets for scoring elsewhere, however, seems an unnecessary interference with the counseling process. Hand scoring would be tiresome but not difficult. The response to each item uses the traditional 5-point scale from *strongly agree* to *strongly disagree*, direction of scale values depending on whether the item is positively or negatively worded. Hand scoring is feasible, could be used immediately and perhaps even in collaboration with the client, and would be much cheaper. Use of the scoring service is feasible and practical for groups in school guidance programs, but the CBI seems especially useful for counseling people who are out of school—perhaps unemployed (or about to be, as in an outplacement counseling setting) or employed but seeking a change. Waiting for scoring by the publisher seems undesirable in such cases. Further, the CBI does not provide any particular precision in measurement, thus, appears not to warrant an elaborate scoring procedure.

Habit is sometimes a terrible thing. Habit decrees that all tests and inventories be treated as devices for measuring more or less well-defined constructs with reasonable precision. Typically, that means giving the constructs names and definitions, writing items to fit, determining internal consistencies, and finding evidence of validity—preferably of construct validity. The CBI manual follows the habit. The results are not very impressive, but most of them have only limited relevance to the purpose of this particular inventory, anyway. Test-retest reliability estimates are probably relevant—a belief that inhibits effective career planning today should do so later unless something intervenes. Such reliability estimates are reported for three samples. The largest coefficient reported was for the high school sample, with a one-month interval, on the Career Plans scale, and this largest coefficient was a mere .74. Indeed, only three of the 78 coefficients reported reach .70, and nine were less than .40. If the CBI were used to make decisions about individuals, these would be appalling coefficients—but that is not its purpose.

The score on each scale is the average of the response values, multiplied by 10. If all item responses within a scale are 5s, the mean is 5 and the scale score is 50. According to the manual, a score below 40 represents uncertainty about the belief represented by high scores on the scale and a topic for probing in the interview. The appropriate use of the scores is, therefore, more like criterion-referenced than norm-referenced interpretations of test scores, yet true to psychometric habit, tables of norms are provided.

Habitual psychometric thought demands scales should be internally consistent. Coefficient alphas were reported for employed adults (male, female, and combined data), unemployed adults, and four student groups differing in age levels. For such small scales, these would not be expected to be very high—and they were not. A two-item Career Plans scale (whether decisions are firm or still open to change) had alphas ranging from .69 to .84, and alphas for three other scales were fairly consistently in the .70s; beyond these, the items defining the various scales seemed not to be remarkably internally consistent, although the manual author says the reliabilities "are deemed quite satisfactory" (p. 17). I do not deem them so, yet I do not deem the issue very important, either. If the inventory is used as a basis for a counselor's decision about the directions of needed probing, individual items may prove just as useful as the set of items, whether sets are internally consistent or not.

Similarly, several pieces of information are given that purport to be relevant to construct validity. The constructs themselves are not defined conceptually, so the question of construct validity is hard to pin down. Evidence of construct validity comes essentially in two forms: evidence that the measure can, in fact, be interpreted as reflecting the intended construct, and evidence that alternative interpretations are not plausible. In the case of the CBI, the first evidence of validity is that the inventory asks people what they believe: "Asking people to report their beliefs is the most straightforward way of discovering them" (p. 18). I happen to be predisposed to accept this, but it is not inherently persuasive for those who are not. Some concurrent validity evidence reports that some scale scores are correlated at least .20 with measures of satisfaction in some of the eight groups, although the reason for being impressed by the fact is not clear. Evidence explicitly directed to the construct validity question is mainly disconfirmatory; that is, these scales do not systematically correlate significantly with scales other than anxiety on other ability, interest, or personality measures. Some factor analytic data are presented, for reasons not entirely clear.

The point is that no case is made in the manual for evaluating any of the CBI scales as measures of important, continuous variables; to the contrary, the case made is that the scales are to be used as triggers for giving direction to the counseling process. No predictions, no irrevocable decisions, no nomothetic relationships are postulated making position on scale very important. What is important is whether counselors find the use of this inventory helpful in their efforts to help clients achieve some insight into the beliefs or assumptions that might stand in the way of sound career decisions. For this limited and individualistic purpose, the CBI can be useful, although the degree of usefulness may depend more on the skills of the counselor than on the psychometric properties of this instrument.

[20]
Children's Articulation Test.
Purpose: Designed to "assess child's ability to produce consonants, vowels and diphthongs in an in-depth relationship to other consonants and vowels."
Population: Ages 3–11.
Publication Date: 1989.
Acronym: CAT.
Scores, 7: Medial Vowels/Diphthongs, Final Consonants, Initiating Consonants, Abutting Consonants, Abutting Consonants and Vowels/Diphthongs, Connected Speech, Language Concepts.
Administration: Individual.
Price Data, 1994: $32.95 per test; $6.75 per 25 scoring sheets.
Time: [15] minutes.
Author: George S. Haspiel.
Publisher: Dragon Press.

Review of the Children's Articulation Test by KATHRYN W. KENNEY, Director, Kenney Associates, Certified Speech-Language Pathologists, Gilbert, AZ:

The Children's Articulation Test (CAT) consists of a scoring sheet and a 4-inch by 8-inch combined stimulus book/test manual. The test stimuli include 72 line drawings in a flip book format. The line drawings are cartoon like and easily recognizable for the most part. Each is accompanied by the printed form of the target word which is appropriate for older children who are proficient readers. The protocol is designed to obtain productions of consonants in initial and final position of single words with a CVC syllable shape, in abutting context across word boundaries (CVC#CVC), and in connected speech. Vowel productions are obtained in single words (CVC), across word boundaries in word initial position (CVC#VC), and in connected speech. The remaining stimuli are purported to provide information on "language concepts." The items require reading the 26 letters of the alphabet in random order, identifying the numerals 1 to 10 in random order, answering questions about the names of people in a family, the names of shapes, and discriminating between shapes and letters based upon size dimensions.

The author's stated purpose is to sample a "child's production of all consonants in all phonemic contexts and any vowel/diphthong distortion" (p. i) in order to "serve as a guide to frugal, efficient treatment" (p. i). The need for a test of this design or the population for which is was intended is never specified. The CAT cannot be used as a diagnostic or screening test of articulation because normative data are not provided. Without the necessary normative data the most appropriate use of the CAT would be as a criterion-referenced test when coupled with information provided on phoneme acquisition in normally developing children (Prather, Hedrick, & Kern, 1975). When used in this manner the CAT could be described as a protocol for obtaining a phonemic inventory. As such it adds little to our knowledge base in phonological development or disorders.

The appropriateness of appending "language concepts" tasks to a test of articulation is questionable. The selection of the tasks is never addressed nor is their validity as a measure of language development among children ranging from 3 to 11 years of age. The items do not even correspond with the author's vaguely stated purpose of the test.

The author briefly addresses critical information concerning test construction, test administration, and scoring. In the description of the protocol it was indicated that the test stimuli were controlled for syllable shape and word boundary. Syllable shape is called "test pattern" and word boundary is shown by the joining of two words in the test pattern. This is the extent of the discussion on test construction. Furthermore, the rationale for the need to control these variables is never stated. The stimuli selected include easily depicted nouns, many of which are included in lists of vocabulary suitable for preschool children. Although specifics regarding the method of test construction are lacking, the comprehensive nature of the test protocol could be regarded as a strength if additional information about the test design, validity, and reliability were available. The CAT was designed to obtain consonant and vowel productions in several speaking situations including single words, abutting word pairs, and connected speech. Other test protocols are not specifically designed to accomplish this. The Goldman-Fristoe (Goldman &

Fristoe, 1986) Sounds-in-Words and Sounds-in-Sentences Subtests assess speech productions in single words and in a story-retell format, but not in abutting contexts. A Screening Deep Test of Articulation (McDonald, 1976) samples speech in word initial, word final, and abutting contexts but not in conversation.

The manual provides the most information on test administration. Instructions are provided on how to use the flip book to elicit responses. It is a little awkward to read the instructions while practicing test administration because both instructions and stimuli are in the same book. The instructions on how to score responses are provided on the scoring sheet which indicates that errors should be recorded as substitutions, omissions, or distortions. No rationale is given for the use of this type of scoring system.

A serious shortcoming in the CAT is a lack of information on validity, reliability, and normative data. None are provided. The purchaser of the CAT is obtaining a test protocol, stimulus materials, and a scoring sheet. A clinician interested in obtaining a standardized instrument of articulation skills will need to purchase another instrument.

SUMMARY. The CAT could be useful as a protocol for obtaining information about consonant and vowel productions in a variety of speaking contexts. Little or no information is provided on test construction, validity, or reliability, making the CAT a poor selection as a diagnostic or screening test of articulation. Better choices would be the Goldman-Fristoe Test of Articulation (T4:1045) or the McDonald Screening Deep Test of Articulation (10:328), although these tests also have shortcomings.

REVIEWER'S REFERENCES

Goldman, R., & Fristoe, M. (1986). The Goldman-Fristoe Test of Articulation. Circle Pines, MN: American Guidance Service, Inc.
McDonald, E. T. (1976). A Screening Deep Test of Articulation. Tucson, AZ: Communication Skill Builders, Inc.
Prather, E., Hedrick, D., & Kern, C. (1975). Articulation development in children aged two to four years. *Journal of Speech and Hearing Disorders, 40*, 179-191.

Review of the Children's Articulation Test by LAWRENCE J. TURTON, Professor of Speech-Language Pathology, Indiana University of Pennsylvania, Indiana, PA:

The Children's Articulation Test (CAT) is one more example of the misuse of the word "test." According to the manual, it is an all-purpose instrument that will allow a clinician to assess articulation in a standard three-item approach plus coarticulation plus language, fluency, and voice. It is in reality a simplistic screening device that relies solely on the professional knowledge base of its user. The manual is devoid of any data on reliability, validity, normative data, and standards for decision making.

The stimuli are cartoon-type images that are appealing to children and have the added bonus of the printed word to help the older child label the picture. But there is no evidence these items are age-appropriate, free of cultural bias, or discriminating for phonological disorders. The author makes unsubstantiated claims about "a phonological analysis of the child's production" (p. 1) of speech sounds but never describes how it is to be done.

This reviewer finds no reason to recommend this instrument. It is weak in terms of psychoeducational standards, phonological theory, and clinical applications. Authors and publishers should refrain from marketing stimuli like the CAT. Perhaps, however, only professional discretion in the market place will deter the proliferation of similar "tests."

[21]

Children's Attention and Adjustment Survey.
Purpose: "Designed to measure the diagnostic criteria of inattention, impulsivity, hyperactivity, and aggressiveness or conduct problems."
Population: Ages 5–13.
Publication Date: 1990.
Acronym: CAAS.
Scores, 7: Inattention, Impulsivity, ADD, Hyperactivity, ADHD, Conduct Problems, DSM III-R ADHD.
Administration: Individual.
Editions, 2: School, Home.
Price Data, 1993: $31.95 per 25 self-scorable booklets (select School or Home form); $15.90 per 25 scoring profiles; $26.50 per manual (75 pages); $95.45 per starter set including manual and 25 each of Home Form, School Form, and Scoring Profile.
Time: (2–5) minutes per form.
Comments: Ratings by teacher or parent.
Authors: Nadine Lambert, Carolyn Hartsough, and Jonathan Sandoval.
Publisher: American Guidance Service, Inc.

Review of the Children's Attention and Adjustment Survey by CLAIRE B. ERNHART, Professor of Psychiatry, Case Western Reserve University and MetroHealth Medical Center, Cleveland, OH:

The Children's Attention and Adjustment Survey (CAAS), developed to document symptoms of attention deficit hyperactivity disorder (ADHD), was devised as part of the authors' longitudinal study of the contributions of biological, familial, health, and temperament characteristics to the development of hyperactive symptoms, particularly as these symptoms culminate in medical intervention. Reading the manual for this test is difficult because the psychometric work was an integral part of the longitudinal study. The authors weave some of their theoretical interpretations and the procedures of the overall study into the manual. This tends to interfere with presentation of the psychometric data.

The instrument consists of 31 items, with slightly different wording in two versions, called Home and School, for parent and teacher use, respectively. The items were derived from descriptions of hyperactivity in a number of articles, which are cited as the sources for the items. In addition to differentiating hyperactive from control children, it was expected that the identified behaviors would be sensitive to stimulant medication.

A four-level rating (*not at all, a little, quite a bit,* and *very much,* scored 1–4) was used for each item. After factor analyses, slightly different patterns of items from each of the two scales were classified into four nonoverlapping scales: Inattention, Impulsivity, Hyperactivity, and Conduct Problems. (Some items retained are not scored on any scale.) Nonindependent composites are identified as Attention Deficit Disorder (ADD), Attention Deficit Hyperactivity Disorder (ADHD), and DSM III-R Attention Deficit Hyperactivity Disorder. The ADD composite score is the sum of the Inattention and Impulsivity scores; the ADHD composite is the sum of the Inattention, Impulsivity, and Hyperactivity scores. The DSM III-R ADHD score includes only the seven items from these scales listed in the DSM III-R criteria.

Evaluation of the standardization process apparently requires knowledge of the longitudinal study. This problem is most apparent as one seeks descriptions of the children involved. There were 3,674 assessments made at grades 1 through 5 of children recruited from schools in the greater San Francisco area. This total, however, may have included repeated measures on the same children over time. Some of these children were identified as hyperactive through the use of multiple criteria; several tables provide an N for the hyperactive group of 129. Another group, called the Proportional Sample, consisted of 121 boys and 62 girls. It was stated that this sample was used for studies of the structure, reliability, and validity of the CAAS scales. The specific sample used in some analyses is not specified (nor is whether or not it included the hyperactive group). Where sample sizes are given the discrepancies are not explained.

The Inattention, Impulsivity, and Hyperactivity scales each include from three to six items. Standard score conversions were provided for each scale based on a mean of 100 and a standard deviation of 15. (The sample size in this determination is not clear.) Given the small number of items and the extreme skewness of the distributions, these standard scores should not be relied upon. For example, the Impulsivity scale, with three items in the School Form, yields a standard score of 102 for its lowest possible raw score because 54% of a "representative sample" scored at this level. Furthermore, increments in standard scores with increments in raw scores are not smooth. Because they have more items, the composite scores are more reliable.

Alpha reliabilities and intercorrelations for the School Form were based on $N = 5,020$. Alphas ranged from .78 for Impulsivity to .94 for the longer ADHD scale. Test-retest reliabilities over 3 years ($N = 139$) ranged from .32 to .44. Data for only 135 children were used for similar analyses of the Home Form. These data yielded alphas from .40 for the Impulsivity scale to .82 for the ADD scale. The correlations between corresponding subscales of the School and Home Forms ranged from .04 for the Impulsivity scale to .34 for the Inattention scale ($N = 178$.) In a 3-year follow-up dataset ($N = 135$), the correlations between corresponding subscales ranged from .17 for the Impulsivity scale to .30 for the Conduct Problems scale. Differences between parent and teacher ratings of these behaviors are not uncommon, but they pose a major problem if these instruments are to be used diagnostically.

Norms, cutoff scores, and presumably other analyses were not differentiated by age, grade, or sex. It was stated there were no age differences. It may be that sample sizes were too small to demonstrate statistical significance. (The frequencies in each grade for girls in the Proportional Sample ranged from 7 to 13.) It was also stated there were only a few small differences between boys and girls, but other tables document significant correlations of sex and scores.

The content of the items appears valid; it is certainly consistent with much of what is written about ADHD. Given uncertainties about sample sizes and definitions of some terms and categories, it is difficult to assess the validity data provided. Use of cutoff scores yields a large number of false positives when evaluated with the data provided. The authors suggest that the false positive rate could be reduced by using a second criterion, "age of onset of symptoms."

This instrument may yield interesting findings in the authors' longitudinal study. Is it useful otherwise? The individual scales are too short to be more than crudely indicative of the dimensions. The ADHD scale might be effective as a screening instrument. Administration time is brief. Teachers could evaluate entire classes to identify children for further evaluation, but it would then be necessary to eliminate the false positives. Parents waiting in a clinic could complete the Home Form along with registration forms. As a screening device, the CAAS might identify children in need of follow-up assessment.

Because the Child Behavior Checklist (Achenbach & Edelbrock, 1988; T4:433) is well known, psychometrically well documented for use by parents and teachers, and has a well-written manual, it will probably continue to be the instrument of choice for most clinicians and researchers. The CAAS is not a strong competitor.

REVIEWER'S REFERENCE

Achenbach, T. M., & Edelbrock, C. (1988). Child Behavior Checklist. Burlington, VT: T. M. Achenbach.

Review of the Children's Attention and Adjustment Survey by STEPHEN L. KOFFLER, Managing Director, Center for Occupational and Professional Assessment, Educational Testing Service, Princeton, NJ:

The Children's Attention and Adjustment Survey (CAAS) is a rating scale system designed to evaluate behaviors related to hyperactivity in children, specifically the condition referred to as attention deficit hyperactivity disorder (ADHD) in the third revision of the American Psychiatric Association's (1987) *Diagnostic and Statistical Manual of Mental Disorders* (DSM III-R).

The scores from the CAAS can be used to (*a*) obtain a profile of a child from the perspective of both parents and teachers with respect to four critical symptoms associated with ADHD (Inattention, Impulsivity, Hyperactivity, and Conduct Problems); (*b*) determine the status of a child with respect to attention deficit disorder (ADD) or attention deficit hyperactivity disorder (ADHD); and (*c*) apply criterion scores to ratings in order to screen for further medical and psychological evaluation.

The CAAS is composed of two 31-item forms—the Home Form that is completed by a parent or other adult familiar with the child's behavior at home and the School Form that is completed by a classroom teacher or teacher's aide. Each form takes about 2 to 5 minutes to complete and the items are scored on a 4-point scale (*not at all characteristic, a little characteristic, quite a bit characteristic*, and *very much characteristic*). The items were selected based on a review of the literature on behaviors associated with characteristics of hyperactive children.

OVERALL EVALUATION. The CAAS is a very thoughtfully developed instrument. The manual is very detailed and the authors provide thorough research-based rationale and support for their approaches, decisions, and conclusions, using literature reviews and especially their own studies (the CAAS has been in development since the early 1970s when the authors began a longitudinal study of hyperactive children). There is also extensive material provided about score interpretation.

SCALES. Scales were developed and standard scores are reported for the four symptoms. The number of items in each scale is small—ranging from 3–8 for the School Form and 4–6 for the Home Form. In addition, combined scores can also be calculated for ADD and ADHD and a seventh score can be obtained for DSM III-R ADHD. The four symptom scales were developed based on a factor analysis of the items in each form. Three of the four scales on the School Form and Home Form are comparable, but not identical, in terms of items. The fourth scale (Impulsivity) includes completely different sets of items for each form.

An apparent problem with the CAAS is that some of the 31 items do not contribute to any scale. Based on the factor analysis, four items did not meet the selection criteria for inclusion in any scale for either form. In addition, four other items were included in a scale only for the School Form or for the Home Form. Thus, some items in each form are not used for any scale, and it is not clear why they are included in the CAAS.

NORMS. The standardization sample for the School Form consisted of over 4,000 kindergarten to 5th grade children in public, private, and parochial elementary schools in Alameda and Contra Costa counties in California, who were involved in the authors' studies of the prevalence of hyperactivity. The standardization sample for the Home Form included children aged 6 through 14+ years who participated as control subjects in the authors' study and were never considered to be hyperactive. This latter sample was expanded to be representative of the elementary school children on whom the School Form was standardized. The standardization sample size for the Home Form was 183, far fewer than that for the School Form.

The characteristics of the standardization samples are clearly documented. There is no indication, however, that the students in the norm group are representative of a larger population. Thus, if there is something systematic about the children in the standardization samples, the generalizability of the data beyond the selected schools in California may be questionable.

Norm-referenced data are provided for each of the seven scales for the School Form and Home Form, including raw score to standard score conversions and standard scores to percentiles and stanines. The manual authors state that scaled score distributions are provided by age for the School Form. However, only one table (presumably combined across ages) is provided in the manual. For the Home Form, there were no age differences, so a single set of norms is provided (based on the 183 children in the sample). A child whose score is "not at all characteristic" for each of the three items in the Impulsivity scale would be at the 56th percentile on that scale.

The maximum raw score for each scale translates to a scaled score of 145, the highest possible scaled score. Such a translation is possible if the scale was developed with that restriction. However, the manual does not provide sufficient information about the derivation or meaning of the scaled scores and percentile ranks. In addition, the small number of items in each of the four symptom scales has an effect on the shape of the percentile distribution.

Cutoff scores are provided for both forms in order to use the scores in a criterion-referenced sense for diagnostic purposes. The cutoff score for each scale appears to have been set at the scaled score corresponding to a raw score that is one standard deviation above the raw score mean. More information is needed to describe the rationale behind the actual selection of the cutoff scores although validity related data are provided to show their appropriateness in terms of classification.

VALIDITY. Considerable construct-related and content-related evidence is provided regarding the rationale behind and process of item and scale selection. Also thorough, research-based discussions of other validity evidence are provided. The manual authors discuss a series of validity studies including: (a) the relationship of the CAAS scale scores/profile of physician-diagnosed hyperactive children to the data from the standardization samples; (b) the relationship of the CAAS scale score with external criteria, such as teacher and peer ratings of aggressiveness; teacher, parent, and psychologist ratings of hyperactivity; and cognitive test scores on measures of attentiveness, intelligence, and achievement; and (c) the proportions of each of these subject groups within the criterion range on the CAAS scales.

The intercorrelations range from .36 to .60 for the four Home Form symptom scales and from .67 to .74 for the School Form scales. As the authors note, the high correlations for the School Form question the independence of the four factors despite the care that they took to obtain the highest internal consistency and to eliminate items that shared variance with two or more factors. The authors, characteristic of the thoroughness they exhibit throughout the manual, provide the results of differential validity studies conducted to investigate this issue and to show support for maintaining the four scales.

RELIABILITY. The alpha reliabilities for the four symptom scales ranged from .78 (Impulsivity) to .92 (Conduct Problems) for the School Form and from .75 (Hyperactivity) to .81 (Inattention) for the Home Form. The manual also provides information about the relationship between the School Form and the Home Form and test-retest correlations over a 3-year period. The authors report factor analytic and alpha reliability studies of both forms. They assert their results indicate structural consistency across the scales. These findings contrast with the results of others who showed differences in the dimensions on School and Home scales.

SUMMARY. The CAAS has much to recommend it, even though there are some apparent problems/questions about certain aspects of the instrument. The CAAS was carefully and thoughtfully conceived and developed and includes a manual that is very detailed about all aspects of the instrument and provides clear information for users. As the authors note, the CAAS should not be the sole information source for a diagnosis or decision about an individual; however, it should provide considerable useful input for that diagnosis or decision.

REVIEWER'S REFERENCE

American Psychiatric Association. (1987). *Diagnostic and statistical manual of mental disorders—revised* (3rd ed.). Washington, DC: Author.

[22]

Children's Inventory of Self-Esteem.

Purpose: Constructed to measure self-esteem.
Population: Ages 5–12.
Publication Date: 1987–90.
Acronym: CISE.
Scores, 15: Passive, Aggressive, and Total scores for each of the following scales: Belonging, Exceptionality, Control, Ideals, Total.
Administration: Group or individual.
Price Data, 1994: $40 per complete kit including 10 reusable inventories, 50 answer sheets, 25 profile/strategy booklets, and manual ('90, 25 pages).
Time: (10) minutes.
Comments: Ratings by parents and teachers.
Author: Richard A. Campbell.
Publisher: Brougham Press.

Review of the Children's Inventory of Self-Esteem by KATHY E. GREEN, *Associate Professor of Education, University of Denver, Denver, CO:*

The Children's Inventory of Self-Esteem (CISE) is a relatively new test (copyright 1987–90) designed to provide information about four areas of self-esteem, their relative strength, and the child's coping mechanisms. It is intended for use by psychologists and other clinicians. Also provided are suggestions for clinicians in interviewing the child's parents and teacher, and information for parents about how to promote stronger self-esteem. The measure consists of 64 brief behavioral statements to be marked dichotomously as descriptive or not descriptive of the child. A significant adult (parent and/or teacher) completes the form. There is a version for boys, for girls, and a unisex version—which differ only in pronoun use. Administration and scoring takes 10–15 minutes and may be done individually or in groups. The CISE is not designed to be normative, thus there are no tables of average scores. Ten scales and 15 different scores can be generated assessing Belonging, Exceptionality, Control, Ideals, and Total self-esteem, and a Passive versus Aggressive subscale for each of the five components. Each behavior that is marked as true of the child is given one point, with higher scores indicating lower self-esteem. The clinician interprets test results, and can provide a booklet to parents listing suggestions to enhance self-esteem in each of the four areas. The manual is directed to clinicians, with 7 of 22 pages devoted to suggestions and descriptions of CISE use with clients.

Although the manual is written understandably, it provides very little information other than how to score the test and examples of test interpretation. No information is provided about the theoretical rationale of the measure; no information is provided regarding reliability; no information is provided regarding validity, or any technical aspect of measure development. Self-esteem and its subscales are neither defined nor differentiated. Because no norms are provided, it is difficult to use the measure diagnostically. It is suggested that children with high scores be offered counseling, but what is a "high" score? The author offers no guidelines. Because no validation information is available, it is not possible to tell the extent to which a self-esteem score would correlate with, for example, a measure of neurological impairment or other conditions that might result in some of the same behaviors.

Evaluation of behavioral descriptions on the CISE are provided by parents and teachers, rather than by the child. Self-ratings and inferred self-ratings provided by others are both conceptually and empirically distinct. In one respect, self-esteem is of a fundamentally private nature making behavioral observation insufficient as its sole reflection. And, behavior may be influenced by situational context and constraints and by developmental level as well as by self-esteem. Evaluation of self-esteem only by parents and teachers and not by the child may miss an important aspect of the construct—that is, how does the child feel about his/her coping and what is important to that child? A measure that includes *both* other- and self-perceptions may be more appropriate.

Finally, the CISE is listed as appropriate for use with children between ages 5 and 12. Each behavioral description agreed with earns one point. But at different ages, it may be developmentally appropriate to display some of the listed behaviors. The child may have low self-esteem if he/she does not behave that way. The author may have considered developmental level in instrument construction, but there is no mention of it in the manual and no accommodation for it in scoring.

In summary, the author of the CISE seems to have clear notions of the aspects of self-esteem he wants to assess and clearly wishes to have a measure easily used by clinicians with prescriptive advice attached. The measure is behaviorally oriented, and easily understood, administered, and scored. But lacking are any conceptual rationale for its development, evidence that it actually measures self-esteem or how well it does so, basis for interpretation of scores derived from its use, consideration of the child's developmental level, and consideration of the child's perspective. At this stage, the measure should be used only experimentally.

Review of the Children's Inventory of Self-Esteem by NICHOLAS A. VACC, Professor and Chairperson, Department of Counselor Education, University of North Carolina at Greensboro, Greensboro, NC:

The Children's Inventory of Self-Esteem (CISE), designed for use with children between 5 and 12 years of age, is available in three forms: one that avoids gender references and one each for boys and girls. The instrument measures a child's self-esteem by reporting scores for Belonging (B), Exceptionalities (E), Control (C), Ideals (I), and Total (T). Within each of the areas assessed there are 10 scales, resulting in a total of 15 different scores obtained for the CISE. The Belonging scale measures a child's sense of being part of something and being connected to his/her social environment. The Exceptionality scale is associated with a child's sense of uniqueness from others. The Control scale is reported to assess

a child's sense of control, power, and influence over his/her life. The Ideals scale measures a child's sense of purpose, values, and models in his/her life. The Total score is the summative evaluation of a child's self-esteem. The author of the CISE purports that, in essence, the subscales are the components of self-esteem (i.e., belonging, exceptionalities, control, and ideals) and collectively yield a total measure of self-esteem. Also, the instrument measures a child's coping mechanism (Passive or Aggressive).

The CISE is designed for use by counselors, social workers, and school and clinical psychologists. It is an objectively scored paper-and-pencil test comprising 64 items which are completed by a significant adult in the child's life (e.g., parent, teacher, or someone else closely associated with the child). Administration time is approximately 10 minutes, and scoring takes approximately 2–5 minutes. The instrument is accompanied with an interpretation sheet that provides intervention strategies for helping to change a child's level of self-esteem. The instrument also includes a profile page which affords a visual representation of the scores. If multiple assessments are conducted for a child, space is included for up to four scores (e.g., instrument completion by the mother, father, teacher, and principal).

Embedded in the instrument's development is the author's point of view that children strive to fulfill their unmet needs through passive and/or aggressive strategies. The instrument interpretation is framed with a paradigm of children who take no direct action or avoid situations versus children who take aggressive actions to accomplish their goals by not considering the needs of others. The author reports the CISE was designed primarily as a practitioner's tool for use by clinicians in working with parents, teachers, and the child. As reported in the manual, a clinician can derive inferences for causes of the child's low self-esteem based on the results of the CISE. Often clinicians find information helpful that is reported from someone who can observe a child in his/her environment; these inferred ratings of self-esteem through observed behavior, however, are not comparable to those obtained through a child's self-report.

The author warns that the instrument should not be used for labeling. Rather, it should be used for understanding children. The major focus of the manual is to provide information about administering the CISE (i.e., time requirements, age levels, and instructions); scoring the scales of Belonging, Exceptionality, Control, Ideas, Total, and Passive/Aggressive; and interpreting the results (i.e., identifying a child with low-esteem, what can be done for a child, and working with adults). Missing, however, is information supporting the validity of the instrument. Although the instrument has been available since 1987, the manual is devoid of normative data and empirical psychometric data that evaluates the CISE's validity and reliability. Norms are not included, and there is no presentation of data or literature concerning (*a*) factors that may have contributed to the selection of subscales of belonging, exceptionalities, control, and ideals or (*b*) the author's suggestions that children strive to fulfill their unmet needs through passive and/or aggressive strategies.

In summary, the major problems with the CISE seem to be (*a*) vague and incomplete information concerning its technical development and (*b*) a lack of references to support its use. Aiding clinicians with an easy-to-use, time efficient instrument for identifying and remediating problems concerning a child's self-esteem is a good idea, but the CISE needs further development before it can be recommended. More information is needed concerning the constructs (B, E, C, I, T, and passive and/or aggressive coping), norms, reliability, and validity. Until more empirical data are available, the value of the instrument is highly questionable.

The author indicated that the CISE is intended as a practitioner's tool rather than a normative instrument. However, regardless of whether an instrument is designed for clinical practitioners or other uses, the test developer has an obligation to (*a*) address issues that document an instrument's value and (*b*) provide information that will assist in the interpretation of the test's results. It is unfortunate that the manual does not document empirically the author's claim of the CISE's utility. Also, the CISE's value for counseling has not been empirically documented by the author. Without evidence to support the conclusions reported in the manual, a user of the CISE is operating on "faith."

[23]

Chronicle Career Quest™.

Purpose: Designed to "help individuals identify careers related to personal interests and preferences."

Publication Dates: 1989–93.

Acronym: CCQ.

Scores: 12 G.O.E. clusters: Artistic, Scientific, Plants and Animals, Protective, Mechanical, Industrial, Business Detail, Selling, Accommodating, Humanitarian, Leading Influencing, Physical Performing.

Administration: Group or individual.

Forms, 2: S and L.

Price Data, 1994: $3.50 per specimen set including 1 each Form S and L, Interest Inventory, Interpretation Guide ('93, 20 pages), Administrator's Guide ('92, 20 pages), and Career Paths; $8 per 100 Occupational Profiles; $5.50 per 50 summary sheets; $4 per 50 Career Paths Chart; $10 per Technical Manual ('92, 30 pages); $12 per Career Crosswalk.

Time: (10–15) minutes for Interest Inventory (Form S and Form L); (10–15) minutes for Interpretation Guide (Form S and Form L); (20–45) minutes for Career Paths (Form S); (180–240) minutes for Career Paths (Form L).

Author: Chronicle Guidance Publications, Inc.

Publisher: Chronicle Guidance Publications, Inc.

a) FORM S.)

Population: Grades 7–10.

Price Data: $40.50 per kit including 25 Interest Inventories, 25 Interpretation Guides, and Administrator's Guide; $18.75 per 25 reusable Career Paths (Form S).

b) FORM L.)

Population: Grades 9–16 and adult.

Price Data: $49.50 per kit of 25 Interest Inventories, 25 Interpretation Guides, and Administrator's Guide; $20.75 per 25 reusable Career Paths (Form L).

Review of the Chronicle Career Quest™ by LARRY G. DANIEL, Associate Professor of Educational Leadership and Research, University of Southern Mississippi, Hattiesburg, MS:

The Chronicle Career Quest™ (CCQ) is a group-administered career guidance instrument that includes three major components: an Interest Inventory, a self-scoring Interpretation Guide, and a Career Paths Occupational Profile. Both short (Form S) and long (Form L) forms of the instrument are available. The instrument presents examinees with a number of occupational "activities" (i.e., items) to which examinees indicate their degree of interest. The occupational activities are categorized across 12 broad interest areas. This categorization is consistent with a structuring of occupations used by the United States Employment Service in its *Guide for Occupational Exploration.*

Form S includes nine items across each of the 12 interest areas for a total of 108 items, Form L includes 12 items across each of the 12 interest areas for a total of 144 items. The Form S items are identical to items included in Form L, with an occasional minor wording change. Form L simply includes three additional items for each interest area not included in Form S. The response format across the two forms varies slightly. Form S uses the dichotomous response options *like* (L) and *dislike* (D). Form L uses a three-option format of *uninteresting* (U), *interesting* (I), and *very interesting* (VI).

According to the CCQ's technical manual, Form S is intended for use with students in grades 7 through 9; Form L is intended for use with students in grades 10 through 12. However, the accompanying administrator's guide suggests that Form S may be used with students as late as grade 10 if occupational awareness, motivation, and/or reading level are somewhat low. Moreover, Form L may be used with students as early as grade 9 if they have at least some occupational awareness. Form L is also recommended for use with college students and other prevocational adults.

Once the Interest Inventory is completed, students are directed to complete the Interpretation Guide. The instrument may be easily scored by the examiner or by the average student. Students then use the 12 interest area scores to determine the several interest areas that represent their major occupational interests, and are referred to a listing of job titles included in the Interpretation Guide that are consistent with their interest areas. Students now proceed to the third component of the instrument, the Career Paths Occupational Profile. In this phase, they select one or more of the jobs included in the Occupational Guide listing to research further. The completed Occupational Profile includes descriptive information about such things as duties associated with the job, training requirements, salary, hours, and opportunities for advancement. All this information may be useful in assisting the student in making a career choice.

The technical manual includes information about reliability and validity studies of the Interest Inventory component of the CCQ. These data are based on responses of 1,554 examinees for Form S and 1,329 examinees for Form L. In general, the samples for these studies included a fair representation of males and females across several different geographic regions of the United States, as well as wide diversity in ethnicity generally reflective of percentages in the actual American population. Internal consistency reliabilities for the full scale of both forms were in the mid-.90s. Interest subscale reliabilities for Form L were in the .80 range, with a few subscales as low as the mid-.70s, and a few as high as .90. Alphas for subscale scores for Form S average in the mid-.70s, and range in value from .58 to .87. Content validity of the items was addressed by comparing the selected items to occupational categories as delineated by the *Guide for Occupational Exploration*. The instrument's construct validity was addressed by examining intercorrelations among the 12 interest area subscale scores across several administrations of the instrument using different samples. In general, these correlations were consistent with models hypothesized by Holland, thus supporting the validity of the interest inventory.

On the whole, the CCQ is a defensible system for assisting students in determining career opportunities. Each occupational activity (item) is rated in isolation of all others. Hence, unlike other similar instruments (e.g., Career Directions Inventory [T4:392]; Kuder Occupational Interest Survey [T4:1375]), the CCQ yields scores that reflect *absolute* opinions about each occupational activity rather than *comparative* assessment of activities. The Career Paths Occupational Profile that ultimately results from the completion of the Interest Inventory is a logical process that allows the student to critically examine multiple facets of a given occupation. The various documents associated with the three components of the instrument are well organized and written generally at an appropriate level for middle and high school students. Another nice feature is the color coding of the three component documents across each form of the instrument (white for Form S and blue for Form L). This helps the administrator or the examinee to avoid selecting the wrong accompanying documents when moving from one phase of the CCQ process to the next.

The CCQ is not without its shortcomings, however. One questionable feature in the presentation of the Interest Inventory is the intentional grouping together of all items relative to each interest area. This procedure for ordering of the items may encourage response set. On the other hand, this procedure facilitates ease of scoring. As a solution, the authors might consider randomly arranging the items to discourage response set along with designing a computer program to sort and regroup the items into meaningful categorizations for scoring purposes.

The number of response options is also problematic. Generally, by allowing for greater response variance, a test developer increases the reliability of test items. This trend is demonstrated in the reliability data presented in the technical manual for Form S as compared to Form L. Subscale reliability coefficients for Form S, which allows for only two response options, were noticeably lower than those for Form L, which allows for three response options. The authors might even consider using additional scale steps with either of the forms to allow for even greater response variance.

An additional problem relative to reliability is the absence of studies of equivalence or stability of the Interest Inventory. Considering that the age ranges for the two forms of the instrument overlap, investigation of the equivalence of the forms across a given sample would add to the knowledge of the instrument's psychometric properties. Moreover, stability of the instrument determined by two administrations of the instrument across a relatively short interval would indicate the degree to which factors relative to a given testing occasion affect scores on the instrument.

Finally, several typographical and other related proofreading errors were noted in the text of the technical manual. Although these are by no means major flaws, they do cause some confusion in interpreting the technical information presented in the text. The authors may wish to further review and edit the technical manual to correct these errors.

Despite the aforementioned problems, the CCQ is a promising tool for educational personnel desiring to direct their students toward occupational choices. When used in conjunction with other sources of information about students, the CCQ serves well both to direct students toward appropriate interest areas and to educate students on various careers.

Review of the Chronicle Career Quest™ by DON-ALD THOMPSON, Professor of Counseling Psychology, School of Education, The University of Connecticut, Storrs, CT:

Chronicle Guidance Publications is one of America's oldest and best known publishers of career education/development materials. The Chronicle Occupational Briefs series, Career Profile Guide, and the C-LECT computer-based career guidance system represent early and respected entries in their respective areas of career development resource materials.

The Chronicle Career Quest Interest Inventory (CQII) was first published in 1987. The current version has only minor differences in content, but since 1987 the publisher has completed reliability and validity studies and has added normative data. The technical manual that now accompanies the test package indicates a 1992 publication date. There are two forms of the Inventory. Form S is for use with students in grades 7–10, and Form L is for those in grades 9 through adult.

The CQII can be considered from two different perspectives, each of which can lead to different conclusions regarding the value of this measure. From one perspective, the CQII can be viewed as a part of a larger career exploration program for which the primary purpose is "to help users explore their interests as they seem to relate to occupations" (Administrator's Guide, p. 2). In this context, there are five primary components to the program including the CQII, Interpretation Guide, Career Crosswalk, Career Paths, and Reports to Parents. From a second perspective, the CQII can be examined strictly as a vocational interest inventory. This review will examine both roles.

The Interest Inventory is structured around the 12 interest areas that are used in the U.S. Department of Labor publication, *Guide for Occupational Exploration (G.O.E.).* For each interest area, the respondent indicates whether they *Like* or *Dislike* (Form S), or find *Very Interesting, Interesting,* or *Uninteresting* (Form L), a series of job-related activities (e.g., Grow crops or raise farm animals). On Form S, there are nine activities for each area, whereas Form L provides 12 activities for each interest area. The inventory can be administered individually or in groups and takes about 15 minutes. The instructions and the administration and scoring processes are simple and quickly accomplished. However, there are discrepancies in the instructions for taking and scoring the inventory. Although they may appear to be minor, I believe that inconsistent terminology could cause confusion for some test takers. An example of the problem is found on Form S, where the instructions for completing the inventory state "2. If you would not like to do this activity, put an X in the D (Dislike) box. If you would like this activity, put an L (Like) in the L (Like) box." Scoring instructions in the CQ Interpretation Guide instruct the user to count the number of checkmarks in the L boxes for each scale. Because the earlier instructions said nothing about checkmarks, this would appear to be an error by the publisher. A similar inconsistency in terminology also appears in Form L, where the user is instructed to place an X in the boxes, and then later told to count the checkmarks.

A description of the development of the activities lists that make up the 12 scales is contained in the technical manual; however, this description does not indicate explicitly where the items came from, but it leaves the impression the initial pool of items was assembled by a group of experts using the *G.O.E.* as the principal source for the occupational activities. The initial item pool was then reduced and refined using several sophisticated statistical analyses.

In reviewing the activities listed for each scale, it is apparent that many of the activities represent specific job tasks that would be carried out by a worker in a particular occupation (e.g., test metals to learn how strong they are). Although it might seem the simplest and most direct manner to establish a person's interests is to simply ask, many empirical studies suggest that direct questioning is often an unreliable, inconsistent, and perhaps invalid method of determining occupational interests. This is a particular problem with younger test subjects because they lack the necessary experience and/or knowledge to know if they would like or dislike particular occupational tasks. Although many activities listed on the inventory are such that even younger students would have some personal experience with them (e.g., work with chemicals in a chemistry lab), many other activities are likely to be rather obscure for most students taking the inventory (e.g., use a radiation machine to treat hospital patients). I suspect very few 7th to 10th graders understand enough about the nature of this activity to determine whether they would like or dislike it. It is possible that students will respond to these items based on either inadequate or erroneous information.

The demographic data reported for the norm sample in the technical manual show good diversity in terms of geographic location, ethnicity, and sex. However, the manual authors provide very limited information about how the samples were drawn, and no information about the school sites other than the states from which samples were drawn. No indication is given whether the samples were drawn randomly from large representative groups at each site, or if intact class groups were used. The publisher supplied additional data regarding the norm samples that indicate the school sites were generally representative of American schools, but were somewhat skewed to urban schools or loosely defined "suburban" schools which have much higher minority percentages than would characterize the U.S. population as a whole. Few rural school sites were used as part of the sample. These factors seem to account for the overrepresentation of African American and Hispanic persons in the sample. No further information regarding how the samples were drawn at each site was provided except for a statement about on-site coordinators, preferably school counselors, who will be responsible for identifying an in-school sample.

The only instance of reliability data reported for the CQII is Cronbach's alpha. This form of reliability establishes only whether the individual scales are internally consistent. The alpha coefficients reported show a range of .58 to .95 for Form S, and .74 to .96 for Form L on the 12 interest areas. No test-retest reliability to determine the stability over time of the scale scores is reported.

For interest inventories, two primary techniques are used to establish validity. Empirical or criterion-related validity techniques determine whether the test can effectively predict future behavior or performance on a similar well-validated measure. The other primary type is construct validity (sometimes called homogeneous). The CQII reports only construct validity data, and the focus of the examination of the construct is on the internal consistency of each scale. To establish the construct validity, the publisher subjected scores from the 12 subscales to a factor analysis and discarded all items that did not meet a minimum factor loading requirement. In essence, this established that each item on the scale was strongly related to the other items on the scale, and therefore the items were all related to the same construct. This is a common practice in instrument development and is an empirically acceptable technique. In the absence of other data that establish exactly what the scale is measuring, it may have limited utility. The intercorrelation matrix of scale scores does show generally low to moderate correlations between the 12 scales, suggesting they are in fact measuring different dimensions.

It may seem a minor issue, but I was concerned about the fact the technical manual had two errors among the citations listed in the text. In one case, a reference was used in the text and not listed in the References, and in another, the citation had a discrepant date with the Reference page.

In summary, the Chronicle Career Quest is a good tool for initiating career exploration when it is used in conjunction with the other materials provided as part of the package, and with the direct assistance of a counselor or career development specialist. The major advantages of the CQ include tight integration with other Chronicle career resource materials, low cost, and quick and easy administration and scoring. The psychometric characteristics of this measure, although perhaps adequate for a counseling or career development tool, do not meet the more rigorous standards one should expect from a standardized interest inventory that would be used to help young people make occupational choices. The reliability data are limited, and consist of only a measure of internal consistency and there are no indications that an individual's scores would have stability over time. More importantly, there is no empirical evidence regarding the effectiveness of this measure as a predictor of occupational satisfaction or success.

[24]

Cultural Literacy Test.
Purpose: Designed to assess "general knowledge in the humanities, social sciences, and sciences."
Population: Grades 11–12.
Publication Date: 1989.

Scores, 4: Humanities, Social Sciences, Sciences, Composite; plus "criterion-referenced" scores for 23 objective areas.

Administration: Group.

Editions, 3: Machine-scorable (A, B), hand-scorable (Survey Edition B).

Price Data, 1991: $135 per complete machine-scorable test kit including 35 test booklets, 35 student report folders, administration and interpretation manual (30 pages), and materials needed for machine scoring; $42.30 per 35 Survey Edition reusable test booklets including administration and interpretation manual; $42.30 per 35 Survey Edition answer sheets including directions for administration and 35 student report folders; $6.90 per 35 student report folders; $6 per Guide to Cultural Literacy; $2.10 per administrator's summary (21 pages).

Time: 50 minutes.

Author: Cultural Literacy Foundation.

Publisher: The Riverside Publishing Co.

Cross References: See T4:698 (2 references).

Review of the Cultural Literacy Test by JERRY S. GILMER, Assistant Research Scientist, College of Medicine, The University of Iowa, Iowa City, IA:

The Cultural Literacy Test (CLT) is a test of general knowledge of subject matter in the three areas of Humanities, Social Sciences, and Sciences. The CLT was developed by the Cultural Literacy Foundation, a private, not-for-profit organization dedicated to the advancement of education, and supported by the National Endowment for the Humanities. The test is intended for high school juniors or seniors and purports to measure their level of cultural literacy as defined by Hirsch in *Cultural Literacy, What Every American Needs to Know* (Hirsch, 1987): "To be culturally literate is to possess the basic information needed to thrive in the modern world." Indeed, the entire philosophical underpinnings of the CLT are based on *Cultural Literacy, What Every American Needs to Know* and *The Dictionary of Cultural Literacy* (Hirsch, Kett, & Trefil, 1988).

The CLT is a test of factual information with the important qualifier that the facts tested have been rigorously selected to relate to cultural literacy, as defined in the supporting materials. According to the Manual for Administration and Interpretation, "A literate reader, writer, or speaker has knowledge of a large body of specific information—the same information that other literate people in the culture know. This body of shared information is 'cultural literacy'" (p. 3), and schools must "provide students with this body of shared cultural information" (p.

3). Much of this body of "shared cultural information" was originally listed in the appendix to *Cultural Literacy, What Every American Needs to Know* as "What Literate Americans Know" and was subsequently expanded and published with extensive discussion in *The Dictionary of Cultural Literacy*.

This body of knowledge has been categorized by the Cultural Literacy Foundation into the three areas of Humanities, Social Sciences, and Sciences which are further divided into 23 subcontent areas. The CLT corresponds directly to these 23 areas with five items covering each area for a total of 115 items. Parallel Forms A and B have been developed in machine-scorable booklets for administration in grades 11 and 12. Actual testing time is 50 minutes. In addition to the books *Cultural Literacy* and *The Dictionary*, the two machine-scorable forms, and the Manual for Administration and Interpretation, other available material includes individual report folders for each student, an Administrator's Summary containing general information about the test and a sample test, and a Guide to Cultural Literacy containing references for students to increase their knowledge in the relevant subject areas. Also available is a version of Form B in a nonscorable booklet with a separate Easy-Score Answer Sheet.

Local percentile ranks and national percentile ranks based on a national standardization sample of students in grades 11 and 12 in 1988, are reported to school teachers and students for the composite and each of the three areas of Humanities, Social Sciences, and Sciences. In addition, individual students' raw scores and national and local raw score averages are reported to teachers for each of the 23 subcontent areas.

The Manual for Administration and Interpretation contains technical data and other information related to each of the test forms, the standardization and sampling procedures, and reliability and validity. In general, Forms A and B appear to be reasonably parallel, but a 4.54 difference in the Social Sciences means between A and B is unexplained and, perhaps, not of practical importance because scores and norms are reported *by form*. The KR-20 reliability indices for the Humanities, Social Sciences, Sciences, and Composite scores are all greater than .82, with the Composite reliabilities being .95 and .94 for Form A and B, respectively.

The discussion of validity of the CLT is weak in the manual and the supporting tables comparing the CLT to four well-known standardized tests of achievement and ability tend to raise questions concerning the intended comparisons rather than answer questions. For example, why were these specific tests selected for validity comparisons and what do the results really show? The correlations between the CLT and the other tests are generally between .40 and .70 and could be interpreted to suggest that either the CLT measures something different than the other tests, or it does not, or both! Also, some of the Form A correlations with other tests are sufficiently different from some of the Form B correlations with the same tests to warrant additional questions concerning the parallelism of the two forms.

Prospective users of the CLT may wish to consider at least three basic issues during their decision-making process. All of these issues directly pertain to the validity of the CLT. The first of these relates to the proposed construct. Is there actually a construct of cultural literacy and is it reasonable and meaningful to try to define it? Is the proposed definition of cultural literacy—being in possession of basic information—reasonable? Strong arguments in support of the construct and its definition, as well as the philosophical foundations, are presented in *Cultural Literacy* and *The Dictionary*. Prospective users will want to be familiar with these discussions. In the absence of direct scientific evidence relating to construct validity, the test developers state in the Administrator's Summary: "The primary evidence for the validity of the *Cultural Literacy Test* comes from its close relationship to the construct of cultural literacy, as defined by the authors, and from the acceptance of this construct by various reviewers, educators, and the general public" (p. 8).

The second basic issue prospective users should consider relates to the alignment of the CLT with the construct of cultural literacy. Does the test actually measure cultural literacy as defined? Do test scores directly reflect students' levels of cultural literacy? Evidence in support of these issues does exist in the very direct alignment of the test with the 23 subcontent categories and also in the discussions of test development procedures in the Manual for Administration and Interpretation. One of the obvious concerns, however, is the degree to which five fact-based test items represent very broad content domains like The Bible and Physical Sciences and Mathematics. When a student correctly answers only one out of five specific questions about World Geography, for example, can a reliable and valid interpretation be made about the overall level of knowledge this student possesses in the broad area of World Geography? Based on the reliabilities reported in the Manual for Administration and Interpretation and the Spearman/Brown formula for estimating the reliability of a modified-length test, the reliabilities of the scores for the 23 five-item clusters would be between .40 and .50. These reliability estimates would necessarily limit generalizations to the broad content domains.

The third issue of concern for prospective users relates to the predictive ability of the CLT. What is the relationship between test performance and thriving in the modern world? At present, there appears to be no psychometric evidence either supporting or refuting a relationship between performance on the CLT and functioning in the world. The correlations between the CLT and other achievement and ability measures reported in the manual suggest a slight to moderate relationship between the CLT and functioning in the world to the extent these other measures relate to functioning in the world, but this evidence is indirect, at best.

In addition to these general but important concerns about the CLT, there are specific points regarding the actual use of the test that need additional clarification. For example, the Manual for Administration and Interpretation indicates that the "questions students miss can serve to point them toward learning about the subject matter of the test question" (p. 16). Although this is obviously true, it is unclear if either students or the teachers receive any information about exactly which items each student missed. In any event, even if students do some research in the areas of the missed items, they would not necessarily significantly increase their knowledge in the particular subcontent area beyond the specific content of the missed items.

Another point regarding test use pertains to the proposition in the manual that the "test will monitor students' progress in attaining essential knowledge" (p. 5). Exactly how this monitoring function will be fulfilled is unclear, however, when the test is for administration to high school juniors and seniors; the time available for remediation and additional follow-up is so limited as to render such activities virtually ineffective, particularly when such activities must compete with all the other demands on the educational system.

The principles underlying the CLT are laudable and the test aims toward fulfilling lofty goals. The issues and concerns discussed here, particularly regarding validity, may, however, limit the application and potential effectiveness of the test in the schools and ultimately, in society.

REVIEWER'S REFERENCES

Hirsch, E. D., Jr. (1987). *Cultural literacy, what every American needs to know*. Boston: Houghton Mifflin Company.

Hirsch, E. D., Jr., Kett, J. F., & Trefil, J. (1988). *The dictionary of cultural literacy*. Boston: Houghton Mifflin Company.

Review of the Cultural Literacy Test by ARLEN R. GULLICKSON, Professor, Western Michigan University, Kalamazoo, MI:

The publishers of the Cultural Literacy Test present cultural literacy as general knowledge of subject matter in three topic areas: Humanities, Social Science, and Sciences (including mathematics). This test apparently is intended as a stimulus to increase the cultural literacy of students. Although the test may serve that purpose, it is at best a crude measure of cultural literacy. Disappointingly, the test's supporting literature strongly advocates improving student literacy and communication skills; yet close study suggests the quality of the test is overstated, and the test development process has failed to meet reasonable standards for measuring such literacy. Five specific areas of concern are addressed.

VALIDITY. Both test content and supporting research are inadequate. The test is a vocabulary measure in 3 main content areas (Humanities, Social Science, and Sciences) and 23 subcontent (or objectives) areas, with five items representing each objective. For example, all of the content for the disciplines of physical science and mathematics is addressed through five items. Similarly, all of fine arts is assessed through five items. Although the criteria used in selecting vocabulary items seem appropriate, the limited number of terms used in each area makes the test prone to large sampling errors in measurement of any student's knowledge of an objective. Thus, the test provides only the crudest of measures for individual objectives. Those same concerns carry over to the three main content areas. For example, cultural literacy in the sciences is measured by a total of 25 items covering physical science, mathematics, earth sciences, life sciences, medicine and health, and technology.

The primary-research-based argument for the test's validity is built around correlations with aptitude measures. The importance of these correlations is not clear, especially given the argument that cultural literacy is a requisite for all students. Additionally, the correlations between the cultural literacy test and aptitude measures are as high as the test's correlations with achievement measures. This suggests the test is as much a measure of aptitude as a measure of achievement in cultural literacy.

CRITERION REFERENCED. The test is purveyed as a criterion-referenced test. A student who takes this test is presented with normed scores for the three topic areas and a composite across the three areas. Additionally, raw scores are presented for each of the 23 objectives that comprise the topic areas. These scores are represented as being criterion referenced

though no criterion, aside from norms, is provided. This representation gives credibility to the importance of the raw scores and may well mislead teachers and students regarding the actual literacy of the student in any targeted area.

TEST RELIABILITY. The test provides two forms that are reported to be parallel (equivalent). Yet, no correlative evidence is provided to support this argument. Instead, the author argues for equivalence based on commonality of scores for the two tests. The means across forms for the three main subareas do suggest comparability. However, this comparability is more a matter of perception than reality. Scores on the sets of five-item objectives, which make up the test, vary substantially for the two forms. Those differences across objectives tend to average out, giving the appearance that the tests are the same. The best measure of equivalence across forms, correlation between Form A and Form B, is not provided.

Equivalence across forms probably is not a problem if the teacher administers only one form to all students. However, if Form A is administered to some students and Form B to others, and then the teacher tries to interpret objectives scores, substantial differences due to test differences are likely to be viewed as differences in cultural literacy.

Cultural literacy as described must be a stable trait at least across a brief span of time. Thus, the two primary measures of reliability that should be provided are (*a*) equivalence across forms noted previously and (*b*) test-retest. Neither measure is provided to the user. Instead, only internal consistency (KR 20) is reported for the respective forms.

Internal consistency gives an inflated perspective of the test's capabilities and should be viewed as an upper bound on test reliability. Those coefficients show that only composite scores can possibly meet minimum requirements for individual interpretation. On this basis alone, then, it can be argued that subtest and objective scores should be interpreted only for groups such as a class of students.

NORMS. The "national" norms are based on the testing of students in 33 high schools or school districts across 18 states, with fewer than 3,000 students used in the norming of each form. Thus, results of the test are *not* representative of broad reaches of the U.S. For example, no students were included from the northern tier of states stretching from Wisconsin to Idaho. As such, the norms do not provide a strong reference group for score interpretation.

SECURITY. Substantial rhetoric is given to the importance of test security, and test security is given as the reason the test is administered in machine-scorable booklets. Yet, except for minimal precautions in the way the test is scored, no special security is given to the test. Given the nature of the test, it seems likely that the teacher could learn the test and, if he or she so desired, could quickly and easily teach to the test. Such cheating probably is not a serious problem, but certainly test security falls far short of optimum.

CONCLUSION. The test may serve as a reasonable measure in addressing the issue of cultural literacy for research purposes. However, much remains to be done to improve its capabilities and to firmly establish present claims about the test. As such, it should *not* be used in its present form to direct individual student improvement in cultural literacy.

[25]
Dental Admission Test.
Purpose: "Designed to measure general academic achievement, comprehension of scientific information, and perceptual ability."
Population: Dental school applicants.
Publication Dates: 1946–93.
Acronym: DAT.
Scores, 8: Natural Sciences (Biology, General Chemistry, Organic Chemistry, Total), Reading Comprehension, Quantitative Reasoning, Perceptual Ability, Academic Average.
Administration: Group.
Price Data: Available from publisher.
Time: 235(330) minutes in 2 sessions.
Comments: Formerly called Dental Aptitude Testing Program; test administered 2 times annually (April, October) at centers established by publisher.
Author: Department of Testing Services.
Publisher: American Dental Association.
Cross References: For reviews by Henry M. Cherrick and Linda M. DuBois, see 9:308; see also T3:673 (2 references); for reviews by Robert L. Linn and Christine H. McGuire of an earlier edition, see 8:1085 (7 references); see also T2:2337 (8 references), 7:1091 (28 references), 5:916 (6 references), and 4:788 (2 references).

Review of the Dental Admission Test by JANET BALDWIN, Assistant Director, GED Testing Program, Washington, DC:

The Dental Admission Test (DAT), conducted by the American Dental Association, is required of all applicants for admission to dental schools. Dental schools consider DAT test scores along with other information such as collegiate records and references in making admission decisions. Successful participation in the DAT program requires completion of at least one year of college, which should include courses in biology and in general and organic chemistry. The DAT is administered two times a year

(April/October) and consists of four tests which take about 4 and a half hours to complete.

The format of the DAT includes a series of multiple-choice tests that include a Survey of the Natural Sciences (SNS), which measures undergraduate-level achievement in biology (40 items), general chemistry (30 items), and organic chemistry (30 items); a 50-item Quantitative Reasoning Test (QRT), which measures knowledge of basic mathematics and algebra; a 50-item Reading Comprehension Test (RCT), based on reading passages in dental, basic, or clinical science not covered in an undergraduate curriculum; and a 75-item Perceptual Ability Test (PAT), which includes five sets of perceptual tasks that measure ability to recognize two- and three-dimensional visual patterns.

The 1989–1990 user's manual noted several changes from previous versions of the DAT. In 1988, the standard score scale used to report the results of the test was changed from the -1 to 9 scale that was used since the test began to the new 1 to 30 scale. This change represents a major revision in the standard score scale from one based on a norm-referenced, true-score psychometric model, to an ability-referenced scale based on the Rasch psychometric model (Rasch, 1960, 1980; Wright, 1977; Wright & Stone, 1979). As noted in supporting documentation provided by the publisher (Smith, Kramer, & Kubiak, 1988), this model provides a way to compare the abilities of different applicant cohorts over time and over test forms, thereby improving the measurement properties and utility of the test scores. For example, the new scale permits both norm-referenced and criterion-referenced interpretations.

Also introduced in 1988 was the DAT Supplemental Score Report (SSR), which was designed to help admissions committees evaluate the quality of the standard scores relative to various examinee response patterns. Studies (Smith, Kramer, & Kubiak, 1990) conducted by the test developers indicated that there are examinees for whom the standard scores on the DAT may misrepresent their abilities due to the presence of measurement disturbances such as guessing, test anxiety, excessive cautiousness, cheating, or language skills unrelated to ability. As some of these disturbances may be due to the speeded nature of the tests, it is useful to ask whether the tests are too speeded for valid measurement of the abilities of some examinees or, more fundamentally, whether the ability to work quickly is an important criterion for dental school admission. To address such concerns, the test developers provide a useful description of how to interpret various score patterns on the DAT's Quantitative Reasoning Test. However, the format of these SSRs is numerically dense. Therefore, some training may be required to make effective use of these reports.

Other changes noted in the manual include increasing the number of reading passages on the RCT from one passage with 50 items to three passages, each with 16 to 17 items. In 1990, the QRT was to have been reduced in length from 50 to 40 items, containing 10 fewer applied mathematics items. Validation studies of the PAT (Kramer, Kubiak, & Smith, 1989) found multidimensionality in the data. This finding led to the appropriate suggestion that DAT transcripts should no longer include a single PAT score but rather separate scores for each of the five subtests—Angles, Apertures, Cubes, Orthographic Projections, and Form Development. This change was planned for the Spring 1990 tests, although no mention is made of the change in the 1991–1992 manual.

RELIABILITY. The only type of reliability information reported in the user's manual is internal consistency reliability coefficients (KR20). The reliability coefficients of the four tests used in the October 1989 administration ranged from .79 to .92. Reliability coefficients for the Survey of the Natural Sciences subtest scores were provided only for tests administered in 1988, not in 1989. A more notable omission is the absence of reliability coefficients for the Perceptual Ability Test subtest scores, as these are not reported for 1988 or 1989. No alternate form reliabilities or estimates of stability over time are provided for any of these scores.

VALIDITY. The DAT Program provides substantial documentation of the validity of the tests. In addition, the user's manual describes the content of the DAT, test construction and scoring procedures, and summaries of research studies on the tests. Both predictive and content validity evidence is included in support of the DAT. DAT Academic Average scores (the arithmetic mean of the QRT, RCT, Biology, General Chemistry, and Organic Chemistry standard scores) were found to be significantly and positively correlated with freshman dental grades by 100% of dental schools. However, correlations of these scores with dental first-year grades ranged between a l01 of .146 (Technic) and a high of .457 (Freshman GPA). A multiple regression using the individual DAT test scores—QRT, RCT, Biology, General Chemistry, Organic Chemistry, and PAT—resulted in better prediction of freshman GPA (Multiple $R = .575$) than did the Academic Average scores (Multiple $R = .457$). Multiple regression using individual DAT scores, predental GPA, and

predental science GPA result in the best combination of predictors for first-year GPA (Multiple $R = .700$). PAT scores had the strongest relationship to techn ic course and preclinical operative technic performance (.346 and .315, respectively).

In summary, the test developers provide evidence of good internal consistency and considerable information in support of the predictive value of the DAT scores. Moreover, previous shortcomings—such as the absence of procedures for equating scores across cohorts and test forms—have been addressed with the new ability-referenced standard score scale. In light of the test developers' concerns about the influence of measurement disturbances on test scores, the introduction of the SSRs and the considerable amount of technical documentation on the DAT should facilitate the interpretation of scores.

REVIEWER'S REFERENCES

Rasch, G. (1960, 1980). *Probabilistic models for some intelligence and attainment tests.* Chicago: University of Chicago Press.
Wright, B. D. (1977). Solving measurement problems with the Rasch model. *Journal of Educational Measurement, 14,* 97-116.
Wright, B. D., & Stone, M. H. (1979). *Best test design.* Chicago: MESA Press.
Smith, R. M., Kramer, G. A., & Kubiak, A. T. (1988). Revision of Dental Admission Test standard score scale. *Journal of Dental Education, 52*(10), 548-553.
Kramer, G. A., Kubiak, A. T., & Smith, R. M. (1989). Construct and predictive validities of the Perceptual Ability Test. *Journal of Dental Education, 53*(2), 119-125.
Smith, R. M., Kramer, G. A., & Kubiak, A. T. (1990). Incidence of measurement disturbances in the Dental Admissions Quantitative Reasoning Test. *Journal of Dental Education, 54*(6), 314-318.

Review of the Dental Admission Test by JERRY S. GILMER, Assistant Research Scientist, College of Medicine, The University of Iowa, Iowa City, IA:

The Dental Admission Test (DAT) is sponsored and developed by the Council on Dental Education of the American Dental Association (ADA) and has been administered on a national basis since 1950. The test is administered in April and October each year at numerous testing sites in the U.S. and foreign countries. Much of the DAT is designed to measure academic achievement, with one subtest designed to measure perceptual ability. The test is used by dental schools to assist with admissions. Support materials related to the DAT appropriately point out that, along with test scores, other factors such as previous academic performance should be considered when making admissions decisions. The support materials also indicate that successful performance on the DAT is generally related to completion of college courses in biology and general and organic chemistry. The four subtests of the DAT, along with a fifth section containing pretest items, require one-half day for administration. Each of the five test sections is separately timed and there is a mandatory 15-minute rest period after the first 2 hours and 20 minutes of testing.

The Survey of Natural Sciences Test contains 100 items with 40 covering basic first-year biology, 30 items in general chemistry, and 30 items in organic chemistry. The Quantitative Reasoning Test contains 30 mathematical problems and 10 items (reduced from 20) in applied mathematics. The Reading Comprehension Test consists of three reading passages with 16 or 17 items related to each passage. The Perceptual Ability Test (PAT) contains 90 items (75 scored and 15 experimental) and is not designed to measure any of the traditional achievement areas such as verbal, scientific, or quantitative reasoning. The PAT covers two-dimensional and three-dimensional problems in angle discrimination, block counting, form development, and object visualization—areas which the ADA believes are important in measuring one's ability to perceive small differences, which is, in turn, related to the development of fine manual dexterity, an attribute important to the practice of dentistry.

Eight scores are reported for the DAT: one for each of the Quantitative Reasoning, Reading Comprehension, and Perceptual Ability tests, and four for the Survey of Natural Sciences—biology, general chemistry, organic chemistry, and total science. The eighth score is an Academic Average which is the average of the quantitative reasoning, reading comprehension, perceptual ability, biology, and the general and organic chemistry tests.

The DAT preparation materials available to candidates include a small information booklet that contains a content description of each test along with application procedures and an application form. The preparation materials also include a booklet of sample items from the four tests along with answers. The Manual for Administration is written clearly and should be effective in establishing uniform administration procedures across all testing sites.

Of several changes in the DAT program in recent years, one of the most significant is the use of test score equating techniques. Test equating provides for scale comparability across testing dates. For example, with appropriate test equating it is safe to assume that a person with a score of 20 on a test has more of the trait tested than a person with a score of 15, regardless of which version of the test each person took and provided the test content specifications have not changed dramatically. In conjunction with test equating, the ADA also instituted a totally different score scale for the DAT; the new scale ranges from 1 to 30 and is based on the Rasch testing model primarily as it is presented in *Best Test Design*

(Wright & Stone, 1979). Test equating and the use of an interval-type scale are major improvements in the DAT program over the purely norm-based -1 to 9 scale used previously. Because of the Rasch common-item equating used for the DAT, the structure of the tests required some changes; all tests now contain a small set of items (an anchor test) which was used in previous versions of the DAT. In addition, the Reading Comprehension Test was changed from one reading passage to three passages to allow for the reuse of items. This anchor test is the key to linking the score scales in the equating process.

The extensive series of reports prepared each year present a large amount of psychometric data and other information regarding the tests. These reports present acceptable reliability indices, correlations, and other additional evidence of test validation and contain no evidence of any major problems resulting from the conversion to the new score scale. Data appear to be comparable to similar data obtained prior to the scale conversion. Validity evidence is presented based on correlations between the DAT and dental school grades and performance on national boards.

The DAT is supported by an effective research program. Some recent or ongoing projects include an examination of gender-related differential item functioning in the quantitative reasoning test (which resulted in a reduction of the number of applied mathematics items), a study of the dimensionality of the perceptual ability test, an investigation of the cognitive behaviors assessed by the test items and consideration of pretesting problem-solving and higher-order-thinking items and examining how these thinking items are related to predictive validity.

One type of information that does not appear to be included in all of these reports, however, is data related to the issue of the fit of the Rasch model to the data. Fit indices are routinely included as output from the commonly used computer scaling and calibration programs and such information would be a valuable contribution to a DAT technical manual, which is also not available at this time. In addition to the issue of model fit, the technical manual should also present additional information on scale homogeneity, details of equating, and other psychometric concerns. The DAT would also benefit from a broader research program related to gender and minority issues; minority concerns, specifically, do not appear to be well documented. Despite these issues, however, the DAT is a well-developed, extensively researched, and strongly supported program. The transition to an equated score scale represents a major and significant improvement over the previous, norm-based, scale. The DAT remains a worthy predictor of dental school performance and an appropriate factor in dental school admissions decisions.

REVIEWER'S REFERENCE

Wright, B. D., & Stone, M. H. (1979). *Best test design*. Chicago: MESA Press.

[26]
Detroit Tests of Learning Aptitude—Adult.

Purpose: Designed to identify strengths and weaknesses in mental abilities and to identify examinees who are markedly deficient in general mental ability.

Population: Ages 16-0 and over.

Publication Date: 1991.

Acronym: DTLA-A.

Scores, 20: 12 subtest scores: Word Opposites, Story Sequences, Sentence Imitation, Reversed Letters, Mathematical Problems, Design Sequences, Basic Information, Quantitative Relations, Word Sequences, Design Reproduction, Symbolic Relations, Form Assembly and 8 composite scores (Linguistic Verbal, Linguistic Nonverbal, Attention-Enhanced, Attention-Reduced, Motor-Enhanced, Motor-Reduced, General Mental Ability, Optimal).

Administration: Individual.

Price Data, 1994: $209 per complete kit including picture book 1, picture book 2, 25 response forms, 25 examiner record booklets, 25 profile/summary forms, and manual (120 pages); $44 per picture book 1; $19 per picture book 2; $18 per 25 response forms; $39 per 25 examiner record booklets; $18 per 25 profile/summary forms; $32 per manual; $98 per microcomputer scoring and report system software (Apple or IBM).

Time: (90–150) minutes.

Comments: Upward extension of the Detroit Tests of Learning Aptitude (Second Edition) (10:85) and (Third Edition) (T4:752).

Authors: Donald D. Hammill and Bryan R. Bryant.

Publisher: PRO-ED, Inc.

Review of the Detroit Tests of Learning Aptitude—Adult by THOMAS E. DINERO, Associate Professor of Evaluation and Measurement, Kent State University, Kent, OH:

The Detroit Tests of Learning Aptitude—Adult (DTLA-A) is a battery of 12 tests intended to measure developed mental abilities in adults ranging in age from 16 to 79 years. According to the manual, "results can be used to estimate general cognitive functioning (intelligence), predict future success (aptitude), or show mastery of particular content and skills (achievement)" (p. 6). The tests overlap in intention and content with those of the Detroit Tests

of Learning Aptitude (T4:752) which has a 50-year history. The subtests are: Word Opposites (WO), Story Sequences (SS), Sentence Imitation (SI), Reversed Letters (RL), Mathematical Problems (MP), Design Sequences (DS), Basic Information (BI), Quantitative Relations (QR), Word Sequences (WS), Design Reproduction (DR), Symbolic Relations (SR), and Form Assembly (FA).

In the manual the authors present an elaborate history and description of intelligence as a tested construct, presenting both sides of the unifactorial versus multifactorial issue. They finally settle on a compromise for their instrument that is rather consistent with Wechsler, Cattell, and Horn's fluid and crystallized intelligences, Das's simultaneous and successive processing, and Jensen's associative and cognitive levels. This conceptualization allows the formation and interpretation of a variety of composite scores simultaneously with individual scaled subtest scores and a total General Mental Ability Quotient.

The test materials include a manual, two booklets, manipulatives, and six dice with rune-like patterns. The package is well produced. The tests are designed for individual administration by trained examiners and can take up to $2\frac{1}{2}$ hours over two administrations. The timing is flexible because not all subtests are timed. Although scoring of some subtests is straightforward, scoring for others involves examiner judgment or coding of rank order responses.

A wide variety of normalized and standardized subtest scales is available ranging from those for the 12 subtests to composites intended to reflect the linguistic domain (Verbal Quotient and Nonverbal Quotient), an attentional domain (Attention-Enhanced Quotient and an Attention-Reduced Quotient), a motoric domain (Motor-Enhanced Quotient and Motor-Reduced Quotient), and a variety of theoretical composites.

The tests were normed on 1,254 adults residing in 31 states. The norming group reflects the racial, ethnic, gender, residence, and geography of the United States very well.

There is a discussion of internal consistency and temporal reliability (called time sampling) in the manual. Although Cronbach's alpha coefficients are as low as .66 for one of the subtests, all the composites had internal consistency alphas above .89 on samples of 50 subjects within each of six age ranges. Test-retest reliabilities over a 2-week interval determined from a sample of 28 White and 2 Black examinees ranged from .67 on the Story Sequence to .88 on the Mathematical Problems. Because of their length, the reliabilities of the composites were correspondingly higher.

The discussion of the tests' validities is a more complex, and less clear-cut, issue. The authors present lengthy rationales for the inclusion of each of the subtests (usually based on historical and contemporary precedent and logical argument) under the guise of content validity. There is little or no justification for the actual content of the tests themselves. This is the weakest aspect of the battery. The Story Sequences, for example, contain pictures involving taking out garbage (where one of the frames includes what appears to be a garage full of tied plastic garbage bags), television repair, an excursion to a laundromat, and a visit by a male to a barbershop. The pictures contain simple line drawings with minimal detail. The sequences do not appear to be organized in any logical cause-and-effect pattern but instead in a pattern that might be clear only to people who have actually had the experiences depicted.

Other content issues may be more serious. "Mathematical Problems," for instance, includes knowledge of algebra, number series (same as in Quantitative Relations), recollection of the Pythagorean Theorem, and knowledge of Roman numerals. "Basic Information" ranges from "What dairy product would you buy in a grocery store?" and "What are Zeus, Apollo, and Mercury?" to "'La Cucaracha' was the marching song of what famous Mexican revolutionary?" This latter item may be an attempt at multiculturalism, but, if so, it would certainly be clearer to a bilingual person if it were rephrased. To the authors' credit, in the numerical sequences where more than one answer is possible, all are given (with the exception of one the reviewer found). Most of the other tests are content free. This reviewer is not arguing with the concept of "basic information" but with the idea that anyone has yet determined what basic *means* within our complex culture.

Also under the rubric of content validity the authors discuss item analysis, including the typical true score theory, item difficulties, and discrimination indices. This reviewer does not want to debate this approach, but does want to point out several weaknesses in the data. First, they use Anastasi's criteria for acceptable (statistically significant point biserial correlations of .2 or .3 for discrimination coefficients and, for item difficulties, percentages correct ranging from 15 to 85 and centering on 50). Although all of their point biserial correlations exceed .2, none of them exceeds .71, and many are in the .30s and .40s. They describe the coefficients as meeting the criterion, which they do, but the examiner who avoids the actual data may be using a series which does not meet his or her own criteria. The item difficulties

range from the .30s to the .90s (with 12 of them exceeding 1.00!).

To establish criterion-related validity, two studies were done, resulting in correlations ranging from nonsignificant to .92 corrected for attenuation with subscales of the Scholastic Abilities Test for Adults (SATA), the Wechsler Adult Intelligence Scale—Revised (WAIS-R), and the Woodcock-Johnson Psycho-Educational Battery (WJ-R).

The authors' arguments for construct validity are tenuous. First, they refer to the same item discriminations used for defending content validity when they discuss construct validity. Although information on item discriminations could be useful in both contexts, within the same test such discussion blurs the distinction between the two test criteria. Such a blur may be appropriate if one assumes that construct validity subsumes all other types, but should be explained by the authors.

In addition, the authors report a confusing study of the factor structure. A first analysis revealed one factor with eigenvalue greater than one (no value recorded) and an unexplained subsequent analysis using Promax rotation of four factors. The authors recommend a one factor interpretation, quite inconsistent with the profusion of subtests described elsewhere in the manual.

The authors state that the "DTLA-A was built to minimize cultural and social bias" (p. 80), but that the battery does have "a decided bias regarding the English language" (p. 80). The authors could certainly have reduced this bias by simplifying some of the instructions (eliminating the words "cue" and "quantitative problems," for instance), which tend to seem stilted. However, reducing language bias in a vocabulary test seems paradoxical even if the inclusion of such a test is not.

The test manual is quite long with some organizational problems. The authors present a complex and internally inconsistent style, at one point discussing a Promax rotation and at another giving detailed instructions on how to calculate an examinee's exact (to the day) age. Their inconsistency also appears in the theoretical rationale for the tests and the wide variety of content included. For example, sometimes an aptitude is a "capacity" as in musical aptitude. In other contexts aptitude seems to mean intelligence and/or achievement (as in "many people consider a good vocabulary to be one of the many aptitudes necessary for success in life in general,") (p. 3). One gets the impression the authors have adopted Anastasi's term "developed ability" both to avoid any genetic-environmental debate and to allow a wide variety of content into their battery. They also show inconsistency in their use of "prorated" composite quotients (if a subtest is missing, calculate the quotient anyway but don't interpret it clinically).

In conclusion, the DTLA-A appears to rely greatly on its association with the DTLA which has credibility because of its longevity. The authors have done a massive job in organizing materials and research. The manual deserves study by anyone hoping to use the tests for clinical or research purposes. At this writing, it is recommended the tests be used only as the authors recommended in their discussion of discrepancy scores or in much needed validation studies. Readers requiring a strong measure of intelligence are urged to consider the Wechsler Intelligence Scale for Children, Third Edition (WISC-III; T4:2939). Questions concerning the construct validity will have to be answered with further analyses such as structural equation modeling and/or some variation of hierarchical factor analysis, a methodology which would have been consistent with the authors' theoretical discussion.

Review of the Detroit Tests of Learning Aptitude— Adult by CYNTHIA ANN DRUVA-ROUSH, Assistant Director, Evaluation and Examination Service, The University of Iowa, Iowa City, IA:

The Detroit Tests of Learning Aptitude—Adult (DTLA-A) is a series of 12 subtests designed to assess the mental abilities of individuals 16 years of age and over. Eight composite scores are provided.

A number of theoretically based indices are reported as well: (*a*) Cattell and Horn's Model of Fluid and Crystallized Intelligence, (*b*) Jensen's Model composed of the Associative Level and Cognitive Level of processing, (*c*) Das's Model of Simultaneous and Successive Processing, and (*d*) Wechsler's Model defining a Verbal Scale and a Performance Scale.

The stated purpose of the DTLA-A is to: (*a*) determine strengths and weakness among developed mental abilities, (*b*) "identify older adolescents and adults who are significantly below their peers in important abilities," (*c*) "make predictions about future performance," and (*d*) "serve as a measurement device in research studies investigating aptitude, intelligence, and cognitive behavior" (p. 14).

The 12 DTLA-A subtests are administered on an individual basis within a $1\frac{1}{2}$- to $2\frac{1}{2}$-hour testing period. The manual provides explicit standardized administration procedures. Items within a subtest are to be presented until the individual fails a predetermined number of consecutive items. Detailed scoring procedures are provided complete with well-developed examples. Raw scores for each test are converted

to standard scores which are then converted into several composite quotients. An interpretation is provided for each subtest and composite. Subtests are grouped into four contrasting "intra-ability" (p. 44) quotients (e.g., verbal and nonverbal, attention-enhanced and attention-reduced). A discrepancy analysis is proposed to examine whether pairs of contrasting test scores are statistically different, indicating to an educational psychologist the need to examine a possible source for the discrepancy in an individual's scores. Sufficient caution in interpreting and presenting test results is provided.

The battery of tests was normed using a group of 1,254 persons residing in 31 states. The sampling procedures involved a two-stage sampling scheme. A random sample of test administrators was chosen who then chose a purposive, nonrandom sample of 10 to 30 individuals whose demographic makeup matched that of their community. Raw score means and standard deviations were developed at 1-year intervals from ages 16 to 29, and at decade intervals thereafter. Both standard scores and percentiles were developed. Reliability was examined by sampling 500 protocols from the normative sample. The subtest coefficient alphas across the various ages range from .66 to .97. All but one of the composite coefficient alphas is above .90. Test-retest reliability was measured by administering the test to 30 individuals and then administering it again after 2 weeks. (It was assumed the same form was used as no mention is made of multiple forms.) The test-retest reliability coefficients range from .67 (Story Sequences) to .88 for the subtests and .72 to .95 for the composites. (Tables 6.2 and 6.3 in the manual are reversed in order.)

Evidence for content validity is established essentially through comparison of each subtest's content in comparison to a listing of behaviors usually measured by tests of aptitude and intelligence. No detailed table of specifications for the various aspects of intelligence is ever provided. Only a comparison of their content with other measures of intelligence is made. In the comparison with Salvia and Ysseldyke's classification system (1981), the higher processing of generalization and induction are missing. A detailed discussion of the rationale for the items and the format for each subscale is provided.

In the construction of the subtests, the pool of items was first administered to 100 people. A point biserial correlation discrimination index of .3 was arbitrarily selected to serve as the minimum level of acceptability for items to be retained on the experimental version of the subtest. Items distributed between 15% and 85% in difficulty were considered acceptable. Based upon the results of the administration of the first experimental version, a second experimental version was created and administered to 120 individuals. Items meeting the above criteria were used in the final version of the DTLA-A. Based upon samples of 50 from each group in the normative sample, median discrimination indices range from .30 to .71 and item difficulties from .24 to .95. (Table 7.4 in the manual has DR and FA subtest difficulty values greater than 1.00.)

Evidence for criterion validity was established by correlating results of the DTLA-A with the Wechsler Adult Intelligence Scale—Revised (WAIS-R) and Part 1 of the revised Woodcock-Johnson Psycho-Educational Battery (WJ-R) for 28 individuals. A second group of 40 individuals was administered the DTLA-A, the Scholastic Abilities Test for Adults (SATA), and the vocabulary and picture completion portion of the WAIS-R. A median correlation of .52 is reported. More helpful than a table of these correlations between the DTLA-A and other intelligence tests would have been a breakdown into a multitrait-multimethod matrix (Campbell & Fiske, 1959). A discussion as to how the various subscales related to other subscales assessing the same construct on other tests would seem essential. The authors of the battery fail to state or show why the DTLA-A is a better measure of intelligent behavior than other batteries (e.g., WAIS).

Evidence for construct validity was provided through examination of several research questions that pertain to the constructs presumed to be measured by the test battery. A weak argument is provided that because the intelligence scales fail to increase significantly with age, there is age differentiation. In their discussion of interrelationships among DTLA-A values, only 140 individuals from the normative sample were chosen. No explanation is given for not studying the entire normative group. Some discussion is provided as to the range of correlation values of subscales with the overall index (.40–.73). Again, a better discussion would have used a multitrait-multimethod matrix to lend evidence for convergent and divergent validity. A median correlation of .49 (rather low) was reported for a sample of 28 individuals between the DTLA-A and various measures of the Woodcock Johnson Achievement Test (Part 2 of the WJPB), the Nelson-Denny Reading Test, the Diagnostic Spelling Potential Test, the Wide Range Achievement Test—Revised (WRAT-R), and the SATA Achievement Test. Why these specific achievement tests are chosen is not explained. Why not American College Testing Assessment scores? A principal components factor analysis was performed. A single factor was found. A second analysis using Promax rotation was performed. Four factors emerged with eigenvalues greater than one. The interpretation of the four factors defined by the second analysis is not adequate. The manual simply summarizes that the test has a general factor only.

REVIEWER'S REFERENCES

Campbell, D. T., & Fiske, D. W. (1959). Convergent and discriminant validation by the multitrait-multimethod matrix. *Psychological Bulletin, 56*, 81–105.
Salvia, J., & Ysseldyke, J. E. (1991). *Assessment* (5th ed.). Boston: Houghton Mifflin.

[27]

Developing Skills Checklist.
Purpose: Designed to measure skills and behaviors that children typically develop between prekindergarten and the end of kindergarten.
Population: Ages 4–6.8.
Publication Date: 1990.
Acronym: DSC.
Scores: 9 scales: Mathematical Concepts and Operations, Language, Memory, Auditory, Print Concepts, Motor, Visual, Writing and Drawing Concepts, Social-Emotional.
Administration: Individual.
Price Data: Price information available from publisher for test materials including Norms Book and Technical Bulletin (90 pages).
Time: Administration time not reported.
Authors: CTB Macmillan/McGraw-Hill.
Publisher: CTB Macmillan/McGraw-Hill.

Review of the Developing Skills Checklist by ELAINE CLARK, Associate Professor of Educational Psychology, University of Utah, Salt Lake City, UT:

The Developing Skills Checklist (DSC) is a component of the CTB Early Childhood System that was developed to assist in instructional planning for young children. Specifically, the DSC is an individually administered test of prereading and mathematic skill, fine and gross motor development, printing and writing, and social and emotional development. Like similar tests of early child learning, the DSC places more emphasis on direct testing; however, unlike many others, input from teachers and parents is sought by way of classroom observations and a home behavior checklist.

The DSC can be administered by teachers or trained aides in less than an hour. Stations can be set up to facilitate the testing of several children by more than one examiner, or a single examiner can administer the test to a particular child. The test can be scored by machine, or easily by hand. Norms for the Mathematical Concepts and Operations, Language, Memory, auditory function, printing and writing, and prereading scales can be found in the Norms Book and Technical Bulletin, but not easily. The test user must scan through numerous table listings, 61 to be exact, to locate this information. Once the norms are found, the test user will be pleased to find norms for both age (from 4 years, 0 months to 6 years, 8 months, reported at 2-month increments) and time of year (spring prekindergarten, fall kindergarten, winter kindergarten, and spring kindergarten). In addition to these normative data, descriptive statistics are given for each scale, and item difficulties, based on the national norming sample, are provided for each item. There are no normative data, however, for the Visual and Motor scales (not even descriptive statistics were provided for the Home Inventory, but then, other than a sample of the Home Inventory in the administration manual, the inventory was never found).

The procedures used for test development appear adequate, and include efforts to reduce content bias and sample widely across a full range of skills and behaviors that typically develop between prekindergarten and the end of the kindergarten year. The standardization and norming studies for the DSC took place during the fall of 1988 and the winter and spring of 1989. The normative sample is large ($N = 3,985$) and seems to be fairly representative of the U.S. population. The sample consists of almost equal numbers of males and females, and the expected proportion of whites and nonwhites. The DSC was stratified on the basis of school size, type of community, socioeconomic status, and geographic region. Percentages of the sample enrolled in special education programs are provided.

Reliability data, in the form of standard error of measurement and internal consistency (KR20), are adequate for most scales (i.e., KR20s ranged between .81 and .95 for all scales except Visual, the mean of which was .69). Unfortunately no information can be found on test-retest reliability. This is unfortunate because stability data may help with the interpretation of other test data (e.g., changes in interitem correlation coefficients across time, such as a .48 correlation between Language scale and prereading total during prekindergarten and .70 during fall kindergarten).

Given the fact the primary purpose of the DSC is instructional planning, not screening and diagnosis, information about content validity is critical. Adequate attention was paid to the content validity of the DSC, consequently, the tasks measure basic skills and behaviors that children in the early years of school typically display. Construct validity of the DSC was examined by comparing the DSC with the Early School Assessment (ESA), another component of the CTB Early Childhood System. Evidence of construct validity was weak. Considerable variance was unaccounted for, and correlations between the DSC and ESA scales showed little discrimination. Until further comparative data are available, it will remain unclear as to whether the lack of discriminant validity is a function of the test itself or lack of skill differentiation at this age. No data on predictive validity were included in the technical manual; however, the author indicated that predictive validity studies were planned for spring of 1990 and 1991. It will be interesting to see what the nature of the predictions are, and how well the DSC can predict future performance. There is some question, however, as to whether the DSC has an adequate ceiling for this. A rather sizeable group of the normative sample approximate the maximum score on a number of the DSC scales. A low ceiling also poses a threat to the test's use in instructional design. It is unclear what the curriculum would look like for children who get all the answers correct, which appears to be the case for most of the sample.

The testing materials are adequate, however, not terribly engaging for a young child. Most of the manipulative materials are red or blue, but a marked improvement over the colorless pictures in the testing booklets. The DSC Administration and Score Interpretation Manual provides sufficient information about standard test procedures and specific test instructions; however, this information is not easily found due to the manual's poor organization. The same can be said of the Norms Book and Technical Bulletin; that is, most of the expected technical information is present, but test users will be frustrated by trying to find it. Inconsistencies in the technical manual are also a problem (e.g., sample numbers for various demographic characteristics do not match). Two supplemental manuals are provided, one for administering the Social-Emotional Observational Record, and the other for the Print and Writing Concepts Scale. When these manuals are located, which by the way will not be easy because they are printed on the same paper as the test protocols and in the same blue and black ink, users will discover that much of the information is redundant. It would have been more convenient to include any information found exclusively in these manuals (e.g., directions for administering and scoring the Print and Writing Concept scale) in the DSC Administration and Score Interpretation Manual. Similarly, the hard-to-find Writing and Drawing Book, which is nothing more than two blank pieces of paper with space for examiner notes, could also have been included in the main recording protocol. The separate recording forms for the Social-Emotional observations and home report, however, are needed because teachers must retain the observation protocol for recording behaviors and parents are given the Home Inventory to complete.

In conclusion, the DSC shares many of the strengths and weaknesses of other developmental tests. On the positive side is its practical application. The DSC, though an individually administered test, can be given by a classroom teacher in a reasonable period of time. However, given the poor organization of the manuals and look-alike protocols (both annoying aspects of the test), administering and scoring the DSC may take more time initially than do other measures. Another plus for the DSC is the breadth of item content and inclusion of data from the child, teacher, and parents. One of the more negative aspects of the DSC, however, is its low ceiling. A test with broader difficulty range would be preferred, and is critical if used for any purpose other than instructional planning.

Review of the Developing Skills Checklist by CLAIRE B. ERNHART, Professor of Psychiatry, Case Western Reserve University and MetroHealth Medical Center, Cleveland, OH:

The Developing Skills Checklist (DSC) is primarily a criterion-referenced test designed to assist preschool and kindergarten teachers as they plan programs to aid individual children in meeting curriculum requirements. The areas covered are prereading and mathematics skills, social and emotional skills, fine and gross motor development, and print and writing concepts. The content of the items is closely related to the classroom activities through which children master kindergarten skills. The coverage is comprehensive. The activities and materials are attractive.

Although details of the standardization are not provided in the Preliminary Edition of the Norms Book and Technical Bulletin, the psychometric procedures that are described reflect knowledge of sampling methods and pretesting of items. A national probability sample of about 6,000 children of ages 48 to 80 months enrolled in prekindergarten and kindergarten provided the normative data. Data are classified by 3-month age groupings and by four time-of-year categories. Time-of-year refers to spring of a prekindergarten year and fall, winter, and spring of kindergarten. Criterion-related scoring methods are useful in evaluating the progress of a child through these stages of early education.

Examiner training is limited to administering the DSC to an adult before working with children; the DSC is designed to be used by teachers. The scoring materials, spread through several manuals, lack detailed instructions about further questioning or the scoring of unusual responses. Scoring and transferring scores to record sheets is tedious. Mastery of the scoring and coding system takes considerable effort. For example, both the manual and the Norms Book and Technical Bulletin refer to a scale called "Prereading Total." It is, however, only by referral to the score sheet that one learns this is the sum of the Language, Memory, Visual, Auditory, and Print Concepts scales. No guidance regarding the use of this norm-referenced score is given. This score is not part of the criterion-referenced cutoff procedures.

Time for administration is not given, but it would probably be about 1 hour per child. The manual authors suggest that four portions of the test might be given at round robin stations, with children rotating across stations with 10 minutes per station in an area such as a gym. Additional writing and drawing work may be administered to an entire class in one sitting. Information used for the Social-Emotional Record results from a limited number of behaviorally recorded observations at other times. The merits of the round robin method, as opposed to individual administration, were not assessed. It may present problems both in terms of developing rapport with some children and because of the distractions associated with the moving about of other children.

Very little information about the construction of the scales in terms of assignment of items to scales or scales to the Prereading Total, mentioned above, is given. The Mathematical Concepts and Operations scale is not included in the Prereading Total, yet this scale correlates more highly with the Prereading Total than does the Language scale, which is a component.

Also, little information is provided regarding the collection of reliability and validity data. KR20 coefficients for seven scales consisting of 16 to 116 items are reasonable (range from .64 to .95). Associated standard errors of measurement are also provided.

Because this is primarily a criterion-referenced test, content validity is emphasized. A reasonable level of construct validity is demonstrated through intercorrelations of the scales within the DSC. Correlations between DSC scales and similarly labeled scales of the Early School Assessment (standardized for the end of kindergarten or beginning of first grade) are not usually higher than the correlations for differently named scales. The Bulletin states that follow-through studies are being conducted to assess predictive validity.

Criterion-referenced proficiency criteria were established through an unspecified combination of judgment and statistical analysis. For each of 34 objectives in six scales, cut scores are provided to indicate whether or not performance is consistently observed and, hence, whether further instruction toward the objective is indicated or whether the child is ready to undertake more difficult activities in the domain. Scoring and evaluation of the Writing and Drawing Concepts and Social-Emotional scales require more interpretation in order to judge a child's progress.

Normative scores are provided in percentiles for age and time of year, stanines, and a normal curve equivalent. (The mean of the normal curve equivalent is apparently 50, the standard deviation is not given.) Even for the youngest children, most distributions are negatively skewed. The instrument is thus more suitable for describing the needs of children requiring further instruction than for identifying children who might benefit from an enrichment program.

The DSC is a professionally constructed instrument that should prove useful in assisting teachers to plan instruction for individual children. Users must be willing to cope, however, with the various manuals and to relate the scales to actual classroom activities. Although it is not a diagnostic test, norms provided by the DSC can be used to identify children to be referred for detailed assessments. The normative data might also be used in global manner for the evaluation of educational programs for this age range. it is not designed as a school readiness test.

[28]

Developmental Indicators for the Assessment of Learning—Revised/AGS Edition.

Purpose: Constructed as a screening instrument to identify children with potential developmental problems and children who appear to be developing in an advanced manner.
Population: Ages 2-0 to 5-11.
Publication Dates: 1983–90.
Acronym: DIAL-R.
Scores, 4: Motor, Concepts, Language, Total.
Subtests, 3: Motor, Concepts, Language.
Administration: Individual.
Price Data, 1993: $249.95 per complete kit including area subtests for motor, concepts, and language areas, set of administrative forms (100 cutting cards, 50 record booklets), 50 parent information forms, training packet, and manual ('90, 148 pages); $119.95 per upgrade packet including set of administrative forms, 50 parent information forms, training

packet, and manual; $34.40 per set of administrative forms; $17.45 per 50 Parent-Child Activity forms; $8.95 per set of 3 operator's handbooks.
Time: (20–30) minutes.
Comments: Updated edition of the 1983 revision of the Developmental Indicators for the Assessment of Learning.
Authors: Carol Mardell-Czudnowski and Dorothea S. Goldenberg.
Publisher: American Guidance Service.
Cross References: See T4:762 (6 references); for reviews by David W. Barnett and G. Michael Poteat of an earlier version, see 10:89 (6 references); see also 9:326 (1 reference) and T3:696 (2 references); for reviews by J. Jeffrey Grill and James J. McCarthy of an earlier edition, see 8:428 (3 references).

Review of the Developmental Indicators for the Assessment of Learning—Revised/AGS Edition by DARRELL L. SABERS, Professor of Educational Psychology, University of Arizona, Tucson, AZ:

The Developmental Indicators for the Assessment of Learning—Revised/AGS Edition (DIAL-R) differs only slightly from the original DIAL-R. First, the norms are new, although the newness comes from the analysis of previous data rather than from a different sample of respondents. Second, these new norms result in different cutoff levels for the three descriptions that can be made about a child as a result of DIAL-R screening: (*a*) Potential Problem, (*b*) OK, or (*c*) Potential Advanced. A new manual was developed to report these changes. The other components remain the same as in the previous DIAL-R except for materials for training examiners. The authors' attempt to respond to earlier reviewers of the DIAL-R seems indicated by the statement, "DIAL-R users should keep in mind that all previous reviews of the DIAL-R must be tempered by the information presented in this manual" (p. 1). However, the descriptions of the DIAL-R in previous *MMY* reviews are still relevant.

The cutoff levels are changed, so the validity studies reported in the manual may not be valid for judging the use of the AGS edition. Validity studies may have included decisions based on previous cutoff levels. The manual includes many cautions about interpreting the validity data because of this change.

The original DIAL was inadequately normed because the sample was obtained only in the state of Illinois. The DIAL-R was standardized on a more widespread sample, although there is still a limitation: Only two sites from each of four regions of the country were used. Minorities were deliberately oversampled for the purpose of providing minority norms as well as Caucasian norms. The initial DIAL-R norms were based on a subsample of 1,861 students adjusted to match the 1980 U.S. Census. The effect of the AGS analysis was to weight these minority data and the Caucasian data in proper proportion to the U.S. Census data. In the AGS edition, the Angoff and Robertson procedure for developing norms was used for the three samples for which norms are presented: Minority, Caucasian, and Census.

Because there were no alterations to the DIAL-R test in the AGS edition, only the data resulting from the scoring will be different from the previous edition of the DIAL-R. Thus, any previously known advantages or disadvantages of the DIAL-R that do not pertain to norms and cutoff levels remain relevant. Poteat (1989) cautioned, "It is recommended the norms be used with caution because of the lack of information on the recruitment of subjects, the possible effects of the truncation procedure, the small number of standardization sites, and the failure to stratify by socioeconomic status" (p. 248). Only the second of these four points could be corrected in the AGS analysis.

There are a few remaining concerns over the original standardization of the DIAL-R that the reanalysis of the data could not correct. The term "minority" is not defined beyond indicating that these students were not classified as Caucasian. Hispanics were classified according to indication of race; that is, whether they indicated that they were Caucasian or minority. There was an attempt to stratify sites by urban and rural, but that was not very successful. Some additional data were obtained to increase the numbers of children in rural sites. Both the urban-rural and the Caucasian-minority stratifications are problems whether the minority norms or total norms are used.

The manual includes many cautions about misinterpretation of data and misuse of the test. However, although standard errors of measurement are reported, the issue of error of measurement is almost ignored. All cutoff points are exact for each of the three indicator areas (Language, Concepts, and Motor) and for the total score with no suggestion that the error of measurement in each area should be considered. For example, for the earliest age a total score of 3 indicates a Potential Problem whereas a score of 4 means OK.

The authors emphasize the importance of "ecological validity"; that is, an "authentic" setting for preschool assessment is required for the DIAL-R. This authenticity is achieved by having the child tested by three operators at different places in a large open room. The desired authenticity of the setting may be achieved for a child with some preschool experience, but could introduce fear for the child who has had no previous experience in such a setting. The examiner may want assurance that such a setting is realistic for the child who has had few experiences with a group of children, or a potential user may wonder why there are no provisions or norms for the DIAL-R when used in a regular one-on-one testing situation. No evidence is found in the manual to address these concerns. This reviewer suggests caution when using the DIAL-R with children with differing degrees of familiarity with preschool experiences.

The predictive validity evidence for the DIAL-R consists of studies where the criterion measures were tests. One expects predictive validity to be measured with criteria other than test scores. Another oversight is that one operator must measure a distance of 5 feet to set the conditions for testing, but is not provided with a string or tape of that length.

There are obvious strengths of the DIAL-R which deserve mention. Training materials are available for providing instruction to the operators who will cooperate in the testing situation (the DIAL-R must be administered by a team for the norms to be valid, but many reviewers question the validity of the norms anyway). Separate written tests (two parallel forms) over each area and overall are included so that the examiners can check their progress in learning how to administer the DIAL-R prior to conducting the assessment of children.

The dials used to present some of the stimuli in each area are attractive to children. One child tested enjoyed turning the dial herself, and said later, "Let's play the game again."

One small child (age 3) had difficulty manipulating the large sorting chips. Her mother commented that, "You could see what her preschool emphasizes by her performance on the test." If one agrees that the DIAL-R has content validity for a preschool curriculum, it may be easy to recommend the DIAL-R as an achievement test for preschoolers.

The use of the test to assess children locally does not require national norms. The serious reservations of this reviewer about the norms, the use of cutoff scores, and the restricted definition of authentic setting should not be seen as serious limitations when the test is used for preschool assessment. The important concern is the degree to which the content of the DIAL-R is considered relevant to the preschool curriculum. With apologies to the late Will Rogers, "I never showed the DIAL-R to anyone who didn't like it."

REVIEWER'S REFERENCE

Poteat, G. M. (1989). [Review of The Developmental Indicators for the Assessment of Learning—Revised.] In J. C. Conoley & J. J. Kramer (Eds.), *The tenth mental measurements yearbook* (pp. 246-248). Lincoln, NE: Buros Institute of Mental Measurements.

Review of the Developmental Indicators for the Assessment of Learning—Revised/AGS Edition by SCOTT SPREAT, Administrator of Clinical Services, The Woods Schools, Langhorne, PA:

The DIAL-R (Developmental Indicators for the Assessment of Learning) is an individually administered screening test. It is designed to identify youngsters who may need more intensive diagnostic assessment of their learning abilities. The manual identifies four clinical applications of the DIAL-R. They are the identification of (*a*) children with potential problems, (*b*) potentially advanced children, (*c*) children who may be "at risk," and (*d*) individual strengths and weaknesses in order to plan instruction. The DIAL-R is an untimed assessment of conceptual, motor, and language abilities of children from the ages of 2-0 to 5-11 years.

The DIAL-R is a revision of the earlier Diagnostic Indicators for the Assessment of Learning (1975). The initial version was revised in 1983; the current version was produced in 1990 and primarily represents an effort at renorming the instrument. Other changes included providing a wider range of cutoff points, a more complete explanation of the norm sample, and expanded psychometric support data.

ADMINISTRATION. The DIAL-R consists of three separate screening areas (Language, Motor, and Concepts). Each area has a total of eight items, and these items are divided into tasks that sample typical developmental behaviors of preschool children.

The DIAL-R is administered by a team of three adults, each of whom is responsible for one of the areas. In addition, each team has a coordinator. Children progress from one area to the next, so at any given time three children may be under evaluation. The manual did not explain the rationale for the use of three or four persons to administer this test. With appropriate training, I can see no reason why a single person could not administer the entire test. It would appear the administration procedures complicate a relatively straightforward assessment process. Administration instructions are clear and easy to follow.

NORM GROUP. The DIAL-R was normed in 1983, and these norming data were reanalyzed for this 1990 version of the DIAL-R. The norm group was 2,227 children selected from eight representative metropolitan areas across the country. The Caucasian norm group included 1,220 children, and the minority norm group included 1,007 children. These two groups were combined and weighted according to the 1980 U.S. Census to create a census-based norm group. Thus, three norm tables are presented in the manual: Caucasian, Minority, and Census Group. Each norm table is divided in 3-month intervals from 2 years through 5 years 11 months. Cutoff scores are defined in terms of various standard deviations in the performance of the norm group.

Considerable information is provided about the various properties of the norm groups. These include sex, age, geographic region, father's age and education, mother's age and education, race, and primary language. In contrast, little information is presented on the actual recruitment process. For a test for school-age children, this issue might be of less significance because recruiting would probably be done in schools where there is an equal probability of selection. It would have been instructive for the authors to present information that explained how representativeness of the sample was ensured. The manual suggests a possible overrepresentation of children whose parents suspect some sort of problem.

RELIABILITY. Data are presented on both test-retest and internal consistency data. Test-retest data were collected on 65 individuals with about one month between administrations. The obtained correlation coefficients would be considered acceptable for the Concept area and the Total DIAL-R score (.90 and .87 respectively); however, the coefficients for both Motor and Language failed to exceed a barely minimal threshold of .80. Only the DIAL-R Total Score achieved an acceptable level of internal consistency. A Cronbach's alpha of .86 was obtained. Internal consistency estimates for the three subscales did not exceed .80. No data are provided on interrater reliability, even though rater judgement would seem to be a possible source of bias for this test. No reliability data are presented on the behavioral observations.

Related to the modest reliability for subscales, the standard errors of measurement are relatively large. Consider the situation of a 4-year, 4-month-old child who achieves the mean score on the Motor subscale. According to the reported standard error of measurement, the 68% confidence interval for this score of 20.1 would vary from 17.4 to 22.8. Thus, we know that the average score is somewhere between the 25th and 69th percentile.

Given the above findings on reliability, only the Total Score of the DIAL-R can be recommended for use with individual students. Subscale scores are adequate for research purposes, but are likely to introduce too much error into any screening process.

VALIDITY. The authors appropriately caution that the reported validity studies were done using previous versions of the norms rather than the reanalyzed 1990 norms. Studies that were based on the correlation of DIAL-R total scores or subscale scores are unaffected by the reanalysis; however, studies reporting sensitivity or overall agreement would not apply to the new version.

A number of validity studies are reported in the manual. In many cases, insufficient information is presented about the study to enable a consumer to evaluate it, but the authors have included the full references for these studies allowing interested consumers to obtain the original source.

Construct validity was reported in terms of the correlation of the DIAL-R Total score with age and with the Learning Accomplishment Profile. As noted in the manual, scores on a developmental scale should correlate with age, and the reported correlation of .98 between age and DIAL-R Total score confirms this. This high correlation also suggests the reliability of the scale may actually be higher than reported. Correlations with various subscales of the Learning Accomplishment Profile suggest that in common areas, the two scales are measuring the same basic constructs. Earlier factor analytic work is no longer reported in the manual.

Although the DIAL-R is not considered an intelligence test, concurrent validity was demonstrated via a comparison of the DIAL-R and the Stanford-Binet Intelligence Scale (Form L–M) for identifying children at extreme ends of the skill development continuum. This comparison was done using the 1990 norms and it revealed the DIAL-R was fairly efficient in identifying children with potential problems; however, it was less satisfactory in identifying children in the potential advanced category.

Concurrent validity was also assessed by correlating the DIAL-R scores with conceptually similar scores on the Kaufman Assessment Battery for Children (K-ABC). Total Score, Motor, and Concepts all achieved moderate correlations with various K-ABC subscales. It is probable the reliabilities of the two instruments limited the obtained correlations.

A variety of information was presented on predictive validity, or the extent to which scores on the DIAL-R are related to some subsequent measure of performance. The DIAL-R was strongly related to subsequent scores on the Metropolitan Readiness Test and a variety of teacher ratings. Less strong, but still significant correlations were reported with the Clymer-Barrett Readiness test and the Stanford

Reading Test. The DIAL-R was also reported to predict kindergarten performance with high accuracy, but actual data were not presented.

In addition to the above information, the manual presented validity data on criterion validity, ecological validity, cross-cultural studies, and face validity. The manual also invites continuing research on the psychometric properties of the scale.

There are some concerns with the reliability of the instrument, and it is probably reasonable to limit the use of the subscale scores to research purposes. Only the Total score has sufficient reliability to justify its use with individual children. The validity data suggest the scale is adequate for the purpose for which it was designed. Additional information on the recruitment of the norm sample would be appreciated, and the administration procedure could probably be simplified. Neither of these latter issues are of great significance.

[29]

Developmental Test of Visual-Motor Integration [Third Revision].

Purpose: Constructed to screen for visual-motor problems.
Publication Dates: 1967–89.
Acronym: VMI.
Scores: Total score only.
Administration: Group.
Price Data, 1994: $20.42 per manual ('89, 112 pages).
Time: Administration time not reported.
Authors: Keith E. Beery and Norman A. Buktenica (tests).
Publisher: Modern Curriculum Press.
a) SHORT FORM.
Population: Ages 3–8.
Price Data: $41.12 per 25 test booklets.
b) LONG FORM.
Population: Ages 3–18.
Price Data: $57.13 per 25 test booklets.
Cross References: See T4:768 (42 references), 9:329 (15 references), and T3:701 (57 references); for reviews of an earlier version by Donald A. Leton and James A. Rice, see 8:870 (24 references); see also T2:1875 (6 references); for a review by Brad S. Chissom, see 7:867 (5 references).

Review of the Developmental Test of Visual-Motor Integration [Third Edition] by DARRELL L. SABERS, Professor of Educational Psychology, University of Arizona, Tucson, AZ:

The "third revision" of the Developmental Test of Visual-Motor Integration (VMI) is not a revision in the usual use of the term. Only the scoring system, manual, and norms have been changed from previous editions. The same 24 items have been used since 1964 when the test was known as the Developmental Form Sequence. Because the VMI has remained essentially the same test through the ensuing years, the comments in previous *Mental Measurement Yearbook* reviews remain relevant to this revision.

There are two reasons why a user might prefer the latest VMI to a previous edition: A different scoring system and new norms. However, this revision is questionable in both aspects.

The scoring system retains the dichotomous nature of scoring items used in previous editions, but instead of awarding 1 point per item, weights of 2, 3, and 4 points are awarded for correct responses to more difficult items. Abundant examples of scored responses demonstrate some arbitrary decisions regarding the application of the scoring criteria. A very sloppy line approximating a vertical line is acceptable as a substitute for a straight vertical line in Item 1 (worth 1 point), but a missed intersection on Item 22 results in a score of 0 rather and 4. Thus, because the items are scored dichotomously, a slight drawing error may result in a loss of 4 points, whereas the inability to draw a straight line was previously ignored. A lack of a "good corner" on Item 20 results in a score of 0 but a score of 4 was assigned on Item 22 to a response with nearly the same error.

Because "weighted scores and scores based on the original scoring guidelines correlate almost perfectly at .98" (p. 25) there is little justification for applying weighted scoring. In addition, it is psychometrically unsound to assign different weights to highly intercorrelated dichotomously scored items. If dichotomous scoring were not used, it might be defensible to assign item scores ranging from 1 to 4. Beery indicates that partial scoring is not allowed because "such scoring would make inappropriate use of the VMI norms" (p. 25). The current norms are, however, already questionable.

It is not clear how the norm tables for the third revision were developed. The norm group appears to consist of the original 1,030 records from a 1964 sample from Illinois (which appear to be called the 1967 U.S. norms), 2,060 from California in 1981 (which, combined with the original data, were considered to be the 1982 norms), and 2,734 from several eastern, northern, and southern states in 1988. Because the 1988 results were not significantly different from earlier samples, all three groups were combined to form the 1989 VMI norms. The merging of the three groups casts doubts about these norms.

The similarity of the three data sets is surprising for several reasons. Bracken (1992) suggests that it is well known that a gradual increase in intelligence results in differences in test scores as a result of standardization dates. How can the VMI be so unrelated to intelligence that it does not show growth? The reason for no growth could easily be that one of the groups included in these norms fails to represent the U.S. norms at the date tested. If that is the reason, which group and what effect there is on the total norms should be known before credibility can be given to the norms presented in this manual.

Another problem is that there is one set of norms to be used for three types of administration: individual, stopping after three consecutive errors; individual, complete test; and group. The manual does not present the examiner with the necessary information for valid use of the VMI scores.

There is nothing in the manual describing how the data based on number-correct scoring were combined with the weighted scores to produce the norms included in this edition. The user should not have to guess how these data were combined or how the performances of the three groups were compared prior to the creation of the present norms. Because the scoring criteria are more explicit in the third revision than in previous editions, why would a user expect that the earlier scores are now valid?

Previous *MMY* reviewers have questioned the lack of evidence regarding validity for the VMI. There remains inadequate description of the construct that is being measured by the test. However, because the "primary purpose of the VMI is to help prevent learning and behavioral problems through early screening identification" (p. 8), predictive validity might appear to be the type of evidence most needed. Some evidence is cited regarding the prediction of achievement; none is cited regarding behavioral problems.

The VMI might be viewed as an achievement test measuring how well the child can draw geometric figures. Achievement tests often are not justified on the basis of construct validity, and there is reason to remediate weaknesses found on achievement tests if the content is judged important. Beery does present some suggestions on remediation, and asks, "Would these children achieve more fully and easily if their visual-motor weaknesses were remediated? And the related question remains: How can such weaknesses best be remediated?" (p. 18). Beery's position on remediation is more reasonably taken when using an achievement test than an IQ test, and his questions are especially appropriate when the test covers skills considered to be prerequisite for future learning.

The VMI cannot be recommended as a measure of intelligence, and the present norms are suspect for the purpose of deriving normative scores for the construct of visual-motor integration. As a test of achievement in copying geometric figures, the lack of adequate description for the norms is a minor problem. For use as an achievement test, the relevancy of the VMI's content needs to be judged according to the user's purpose. Regardless of the testing purpose, there is no obvious advantage in using the third revision over previous editions.

REVIEWER'S REFERENCE

Bracken, B. A. (1992). The interpretation of tests. In M. Zeidner & R. Most (Eds.), *Psychological testing: An inside view* (pp. 119-156). Palo Alto: Consulting Psychologists Press.

Review of the Developmental Test of Visual-Motor Integration [Third Edition] by JAMES E. YSSEL-DYKE, Director, National Center on Educational Outcomes, University of Minnesota, Minneapolis, MN:

The Developmental Test of Visual-Motor Integration (VMI) is designed to assess the extent to which children can integrate visual and motor skills as evidenced by copying a set of 24 geometric designs. The author indicates the "primary purpose of the VMI is to help prevent learning and behavioral problems through early screening identification" (p. 8). The test is rooted in the assumptions that adequate visual-motor integration is a necessary prerequisite to school success, that when it is absent it should be remediated, and that successful remediation of difficulties will enable students to be successful in school and/or overcome learning and behavior problems. There is no evidence in the manual that such assumptions are firmly grounded, nor is such evidence present in the professional literature. The VMI is best viewed as a 24-item measure of children's skill in copying geometric designs. Children are asked to copy the designs, and their efforts are scored pass-fail.

The 1989 version of the test is an update on earlier versions. The items have remained the same throughout revisions of the test, but scoring procedures have changed. Scoring range was expanded from 1–24 to 1–50, and items were weighted in terms of their developmental difficulty. The author argues that in spite of the changes, technical data for earlier versions of the test still apply to the 1989 edition.

The VMI was originally standardized on 1,030 children in Illinois. In 1981 the test was cross-validated with groups of children from California. Then, in 1988 the test was again cross-validated with students from several eastern, northern, and southern states. There are minimal data on the make-up of the norm group, and no description of the cross-tabulations for the standardization samples, so those who use the test to make norm-referenced interpretations are comparing those they assess to an unknown group. The test should be used with caution in making norm-referenced comparisons.

Reliability of the VMI is based on a set of investigations of interscorer, internal consistency, and test-retest reliability of the measure by others who have used the scale since its inception. Interscorer reliabilities ranged from .58 to .99 with a median of .93. Test-retest reliabilities ranged from .63 to .92, whereas split-half reliabilities ranged from .66 to .93. The samples on whom the reliabilities were obtained are not described.

Beery reports correlations of performance on the VMI with measures of handwriting, readiness, chronological age, and performance on other tests like the Bender Visual Motor Gestalt Test. These relationships do not establish evidence the test measures what the author says it measures. Evidence for predictive validity is mixed, with some investigators finding moderately strong correlations between performance on this test and later achievement, others reporting little relationship.

SUMMARY. The VMI can be used to provide assessors with information on how well students copy geometric designs. It provides a larger behavior sample than tests like the Bender Visual Motor Gestalt Test (T4:291) and the Memory-for-Designs Test (T4:1606). It has better reliability than those measures, though indices of reliability are on unspecified samples. The standardization sample is not described, so norm-referenced use of the test should be avoided.

[30]

Diagnostic Achievement Battery, Second Edition.

Purpose: "To assess children's abilities in listening, speaking, reading, writing, and mathematics."

Population: Ages 6-0 to 14-11.

Publication Dates: 1984–90.

Acronym: DAB-2.

Scores, 20: Spoken Language (Listening [Sentence Completion, Characteristics], Speaking [Synonyms, Grammatic Completion]), Written Language (Reading [Reading Comprehension, Alphabet/Word Knowledge], Writing [Punctuation, Spelling, Capitalization, Writing Composition]), Mathematics (Math Calculation, Math Reasoning), Total Achievement.

Administration: Individual.

Price Data, 1994: $119 per complete kit; $29 per student booklet; $34 per 25 profile/answer sheets;

$29 per 25 student worksheets; $31 per manual ('90, 99 pages); $79 per computer scoring system (specify IBM or Apple).
Time: (60–120) minutes.
Authors: Phyllis L. Newcomer and Dolores Curtis (student booklet).
Publisher: PRO-ED, Inc.
Cross References: See T4:774 (1 reference); for a review by William J. Webster of the original edition, see 9:333.

Review of the Diagnostic Achievement Battery, Second Edition by JEAN-JACQUES BERNIER, Full Professor, and MARTINE HÉBERT, Assistant Professor, Department of Measurement and Evaluation, University Laval, Quebec, Canada:

The Diagnostic Achievement Battery, Second Edition (DAB-2) is a standardized individual test used to assess children's abilities in listening, speaking, reading, writing and mathematics. The DAB-2 is designed for use with children between the ages of 6-0 and 14-11 and provides 3 construct scores (Spoken Language, Written Language, and Mathematics), 5 component scores (Listening, Speaking, Reading, Writing, and Mathematics) and 12 subtest scores. The Second Edition retains eight subtests of the first DAB published in 1984 (Sentence Completion, Characteristics, Synonyms, Grammatic Completion, Alphabet/Word Knowledge, Spelling, Math Calculation, and Math Reasoning). Two subtests were changed in administration as well as in scoring format (Capitalization and Punctuation). One subtest (Reading Comprehension) was altered slightly by changing a few items. One new subtest (Writing Composition) provides a score based on writing vocabulary and content maturity and replaces the Written Vocabulary subtest in the original edition.

According to the author, the DAB-2 is intended to accomplish four goals: (*a*) identify those pupils who are significantly below their peers in the area of spoken language (listening and speaking), written language (reading and writing), and mathematics; (*b*) determine a child's strengths and weaknesses; (*c*) document pupils' progress in achievement areas as a consequence of specific intervention programs; and (*d*) serve as a measurement instrument in research in the area of academic achievement.

The test development model reflects principles such as reviewing commonly used curricula and teaching programs, the representativeness of the skills measured on the basis of achievement areas delimited by P.L. 94-192, as well as empirical validation of items by using item difficulty and discrimination indices.

The DAB-2 is a standardized norm-referenced test. The standardization sample included 2,623 students from 40 different states tested in 1988–89. The sample was representative of the national population in terms of sex, residence, race, and ethnicity variables as well as geographic distribution. The administration and scoring instructions presented in the examiner's manual are clearly written and make it easy to use this instrument and interpret the different scores obtained. Raw scores may be converted into percentiles, standard scores ($M = 10$, $SD = 3$), grade equivalents, and composite scores ($M = 100$, $SD = 15$). Tables providing minimal differences between subtest scores and composite scores to achieve a significant difference (.05 level) are included, permitting a discrepancy analysis by contrasting test scores within and across domains. Also, the examiner who wishes to engage in further assessment can find additional references in the manual.

Testing time may vary from 1 to 2 hours. Although the subtests have no time limits, entry, basal, and ceiling points are offered for most subtests. The individual format of the DAB-2 permits a greater variety of item and response format than what is available in group-administered tests. The instructions provided on the profile/answer form and the student worksheet are easy to follow and respond to the suggestions of test users of the first edition.

DAB-2 subtests and composite scores present acceptable reliabilities. Internal consistency measures based on alpha coefficients range from the .70s to the .90s for the subtests scores with the great majority reaching or exceeding .80 and from .83 to .99 for the composite scores. The author reports acceptable stability coefficients. However, one must specify that these coefficients were based on the first edition of the DAB and were obtained from a sample of only 34 children with a 2-week interval. For the DAB-2, only subtests that were changed dramatically (Capitalization and Punctuation) and the new Writing Composition were submitted to test-retest reliability analysis. The coefficient obtained with a sample of 52 students and a 1-week interval suggests that scores are stable over time.

With regards to the criterion validity, DAB-2 subtests and composite scores were correlated with the Wide Range Achievement Test—Revised (WRAT-R) and the Detroit Tests of Learning Aptitude—School Edition (DTLA-SE) in a sample of 45 students from grades 1 through 6. Analysis of the correlation coefficients obtained does not provide strong evidence of criterion validity for every type of scores. In some cases, it appears that different subtests measure different aspects of the same skill.

Substantial evidence for construct validity is presented and supports the author's pretention for this hypothesis. Indeed, performance on the DAB-2 subtests is significantly related to chronological age and grade level, the subtests intercorrelation coefficients as well as the correlation with scholastic aptitude tests are sufficiently high, and the test has been shown to discriminate between "regular" and learning-disabled pupils.

One criticism is the author does not provide sufficient information concerning the new Writing Composition subtest. Although the data from this subtest are not amenable to standard analysis, it would be of interest to provide some information (for example, mean across different age groups).

In summary, the DAB-2 is a well-designed individual diagnostic test. The addition of information concerning the administration instructions and the new studies improving norms, reliability, and validity make this instrument an excellent tool.

Review of the Diagnostic Achievement Battery, Second Edition by RIC BROWN, Acting Director, University Grants and Research Office, California State University, Fresno, Fresno, CA:

The author describes the Diagnostic Achievement Battery, Second Edition (DAB-2) as a standardized achievement test to assess abilities in listening, speaking, reading, writing, and mathematics. The need expressed for this individual test stemmed from the reported problems with group tests and their inability to diagnose effectively specific weaknesses in children. The author contends that although other individual tests (e.g., Woodcock Reading Mastery Test, KeyMath Diagnostic Arithmetic Test—Revised) are more specific and others (Peabody Individual Achievement Test—Revised, Test of Adolescent Language-2) are more comprehensive, no other test examines the variety of skills related to P.L. 94-192 as does the DAB-2.

The purposes of the DAB-2 as described by the author are to (*a*) identify students who are below their peers in areas of spoken language (listening and speaking), written language (reading and writing), and mathematics who may benefit from remedial assistance; (*b*) determine specific area strengths and weaknesses; (*c*) document progress in specific areas as a result of intervention; and, (*d*) serve as a measurement device of academic achievement.

The DAB-2 was developed around three major constructs, subsuming five major components composed from 12 subtests. The test manual provides a detailed description of each of the following constructs listed with its respective components and tests:

Spoken Language (Listening—Story Comprehension, Characteristics; Speaking—Synonyms, Grammatical Completion); Written Language (Reading—Comprehension, Alphabet/Word Knowledge; Writing—Punctuation, Spelling, Capitalization, Writing Composition); Mathematics (Mathematics—Calculation, Reasoning). A score for each subtest can be calculated and various subtests can be combined to produce composite scores and construct scores.

For those familiar with the 1983 version of the DAB, the author indicates that eight subtests remain unchanged. Reading Comprehension was altered by changing a few questions and Writing Composition replaced Written Vocabulary. Two subtests (Capitalization and Punctuation) were noted to be significantly altered.

Many tables are presented to support the reliability and validity of the test, although most of the data are from very small, convenience samples. Although the author reports 2,623 children tested between the ages of 6 and 14 are included for norming of the DAB-2, data reported for validity and reliability are based upon small samples as well as from a 1982–83 testing. For example, for item selection, 100 students from (apparently) one city were used for item difficulty and item discrimination statistics.

In terms of reliability, 50 tests for each 1-year age interval yielded alpha coefficients (internal consistency) of .70 to .98 for all subtests. Test-retest (2 weeks) reliability is reported for 34 Delaware children in 1981 for the DAB and 52 students in Los Angeles (for three subtests) with 1-week time interval for the DAB-2. Acceptable coefficients, all greater than .80, were found. For validity support, small samples of 46 students from Pennsylvania in 1982 and 45 students in Texas in 1989 were given the DAB and DAB-2 respectively, with a variety of similar tests (e.g., Wide Range Achievement Test, Woodcock Reading Mastery Test). Subtest correlations ranged from .36 to .81. Although what is presented in terms of reliability and validity is encouraging, the data are on very small, convenience samples and must be interpreted with caution.

Norms (means) for each subtest are presented for each age from 6 to 14 based on the selected sample of 2,623 children from 40 states. The subjects were obtained by asking previous users of the original DAB and other users of the publisher's tests to give 20 to 30 DAB-2 tests. Although clearly not a random sample, the demographics of the selected sample do match the 1985 Statistical Abstracts for the general population of the U.S.

Specific instructions for administration using a student booklet and a profile/answer form are provided in the examiner's manual. Although there are no set time limits, a range from 1 to 2 hours is recommended. For each age, an entry point on each subtest is specified (to avoid easier items as older children are tested) and five consecutive incorrect answers stop the testing session for a subtest. Specific examples are given for each subtest in terms of the entry point and the ceiling.

The profile/answer form provided makes determining the subtest and composite scores very simple by providing a workspace and computation grid. Space is also provided for some examinee information including results of other similar tests the child may have taken. The conversion of raw scores (number of items correct) on each subtest forms the basis for developing what the author refers to as standard scores (each subtest distribution has 20 points and is normed by age with a mean of 10 and a standard deviation of 3). These scores are then combined to form a total score which is then converted (by use of a table) to what the author calls quotients. Although not specifically stated, these quotient scores give the appearance of an IQ test distribution. A variety of tables are provided to produce these scores as well as provide percentiles and the ubiquitous grade equivalents (with the appropriate caveat that they not be used).

SUMMARY. Although the test is called a diagnostic battery, very little text is devoted to interpretation. Some cautions are given regarding test use as well as a 3-point process to discuss the results with others.

It is not clear what the unique contribution of this test is relative to other group or individual academic achievement tests. The subtests seem to measure common constructs and the questions are fairly standard (e.g., read a sentence or two and answer questions regarding theme, sentence completion items, synonym word lists, verbal spelling and verbal math problems). Additionally, the DAB-2 has a problem in terms of the adequacy and representativeness of the norm group. This test has norms that are now 4 years old and are based on a nonrandom group of children. Further, for a user to know that a particular child in a particular state is below the mean of some selected norm group belies the concept of diagnostic assessment.

[31]

Diagnostic Assessments of Reading.

Purpose: Constructed to assess skills in reading and language.
Population: Grades 1–12.
Publication Date: 1992.
Acronym: DAR.
Scores: Mastery level scores in 6 areas: Word Recognition, Word Analysis, Oral Reading, Silent Reading Comprehension, Spelling, Word Meaning.
Administration: Individual.
Price Data, 1992: $150 per complete kit including testing materials listed below plus teaching strategies materials; $12 per student book; $15 per 15 student record booklets; $30 per response record with directions for administration; $6 per manual (33 pages).
Time: (20–30) minutes.
Authors: Florence G. Roswell and Jeanne S. Chall.
Publisher: The Riverside Publishing Co.

Review of the Diagnostic Assessments of Reading by KEVIN D. CREHAN, *Associate Professor of Educational Psychology, University of Nevada, Las Vegas, Las Vegas, NV:*

DESCRIPTION. The Diagnostic Assessments of Reading (DAR) is an individually administered multilevel-multiscale system for determining areas of reading and language proficiency and weakness. The DAR is the assessment part of a package designed to diagnose reading difficulties and assist in the development of remedial instructional programs. The six areas of reading and language assessed are Word Recognition (WR), Word Analysis (WA), Oral Reading (OR), Silent Reading Comprehension (SRC), Spelling (SP), and Word Meaning (WM). Mastery tests within each of these areas, except SR, are provided for Beginning Levels 1-1 and 1-2 and Primary Levels 2 and 3. The Word Analysis mastery tests are skipped if the examinee scores at Level 4 or higher on the Word Recognition test. The Word Analysis mastery tests include scales measuring Consonant Sounds, Consonant Blends, Short Vowel Sounds, Rule of Silent E, Vowel Digraphs, Diphthongs, Vowels with R, and Polysyllabic Words. Prereading measures of Naming Capital Letters, Naming Lower Case Letters, Matching Letters, and Matching Words are also included. Mastery tests for all areas except WA are provided as follows: Intermediate, Levels 4 through 8; and Advanced, Levels 9/10 and 11/12. Directions for administration and scoring are clear and should lead to efficient use (administration time is 20–30 minutes) and acceptable objectivity in scoring by the classroom teacher.

Results of testing an individual student are summarized on the DAR Interpretive Profile which displays mastery level attained for WR, WA, OR, SRC, SP, and WM. A mastery check list is provided for the sub-areas of WA if used. Performance on the

DAR is evaluated for strengths and weaknesses leading to selection of appropriate Trial Teaching Strategies (TTS) which are part of the total package accompanying the DAR. Case studies for prototypical DAR profiles are provided to aid in using the TTS. Ultimately, a program of remedial instruction is developed based on the student's DAR profile and teacher judgment of performance on the TTS exercises.

BACKGROUND. The rationale for the development of the DAR instruments is based on Carroll's (1977) theory of three components underlying reading comprehension: language, cognition, and reading skills. Reading comprehension is explained by the development and relative strengths in these areas. An additional basis for the DAR is a state developmental theory, presented by DAR coauthor Jeanne S. Chall in 1979 and as subsequently elaborated (Chall, 1983). The authors believe that assessment of the components of reading and language skills and direct instruction in deficit areas are more useful than attempting to identify and remedy the supposed underlying causes of reading difficulty.

RELIABILITY AND VALIDITY. An unpublished preliminary technical note provided by the publisher presents some results of a pilot testing in 1989 and a validation study in 1990–1991. The pilot, or tryout, study observed 1,664 students in grades 1 through 8 with sample sizes ranging from 90 to 318 per grade. Students who were judged by teachers to be reading at grade level were selected to participate in the study. The vocabulary subtest of the Gates-MacGinitie Reading Tests (GMRT) was used as an anchor for two preliminary forms of the DAR. Students were tested at and out of grade level on one of two pilot forms of the DAR. The results of this pilot were used to develop the final form of the test, using reading passages and test items with the "best statistical characteristics" from the two pilot tests. The actual item selection process was not described. Means scores of the pilot sample were generally comparable to the GMRT standardization sample scores, but were somewhat less variable. Correlations among DAR subtest scores and GMRT vocabulary scores were moderate and varied over grade. The highest correspondence between DAR subtests and the GMRT vocabulary score was for the WR subtests, with an average correlation of .61 over grade levels 2 through 8 (range .24 to .80). Correlations could be attenuated due to the relatively lower variability of the tryout sample compared to the national standardization sample to the GMRT.

A nominal validation study was conducted during the 1990–91 school year in grades 1 through 12,

with a sample of 1,216 students judged by their teachers as achieving below potential in reading. Sample sizes ranged from 10 to 185 per grade. Smaller sample sizes at grades 9/10 and 11/12 were combined in the data summarization. Again, the GMRT was used for comparison. Students were first tested on the GMRT, then administered the DAR and given the TTS exercises. Two subsequent administrations of the GMRT were conducted but the results of these testings were omitted from the report. Not surprisingly, the validation sample, selected as underachieving, had lower scores on the GMRT than the national standardization sample for this test. Correlations among the GMRT vocabulary and comprehension subtests and the highest mastery level attained on the DAR subscores were moderate in aggregate. A pattern of higher correlations between highest DAR mastery level and GMRT Vocabulary as compared to GMRT Comprehension was evidenced over grades. Surprisingly, this was true even for correlations between DAR mastery level in SRC and the GMRT Vocabulary. Seven of the nine levels had higher correlations between GMRT Vocabulary and DAR SRC than for GMRT Comprehension and DAR SRC.

Several tables of item statistics and descriptive statistics were provided for the validation sample. These tables, especially those reporting percentile ranks, need careful interpretation, given the nature (nominal underachievers) and sizes of the samples involved in the study.

SUMMARY. The DAR and TTS assessment and teaching materials demonstrate considerable thought and effort in preparation and production. It is likely the materials will be valuable to teachers attempting to develop remedial reading programs for individuals and small groups. However, more evidence must be developed and reported to support the psychometric quality and instructional utility of the package. The preliminary technical report does not report the reliability of results for either the pilot study or the validation study. Reliability of results might be inferred from correlations of DAR subtests with GMRT scores but more direct evidence is desired. Evidence related to concurrent/construct validity of the DAR and the GMRT does not fit consistently what would be expected. One would expect that two nominal measures of reading comprehension would correlate higher than would a measure of vocabulary and a measure of comprehension. Perhaps this apparent anomaly is attributable to the nature of the two score distributions involved in the correlation. The DAR SCR score is a relatively gross measure of mastery with a change in one level (one point) conceivably equivalent to a year's growth in reading comprehension, whereas the GMRT Comprehension normative score is on a more refined scale.

Additional studies of DAR score reliability should be conducted to determine the stability and consistency of the mastery level decisions as well as to establish further evidence of validity.

REVIEWER'S REFERENCES

Carroll, J. B. (1977). Developmental parameters of reading comprehension. In J. T. Guthrie (Ed.), *Cognition, curriculum, and comprehension* (pp. 1-15). Newark, DE: International Reading Association.
Chall, J. S. (1983). *Stages of reading development*. New York: McGraw-Hill Book Company.

Review of the Diagnostic Assessments of Reading by GENE SCHWARTING, *Project Director of Early Childhood Special Education, Omaha Public Schools, Omaha, NE:*

For a number of years, attempts have been made to develop assessment tools with related educational programs to work towards remediation of those specific areas of relative weakness as noted in the obtained test profile for each individual. The Diagnostic Assessments of Reading with Trial Teaching Strategies (DARTTS) package is yet another effort, focusing on the area of reading. The goal is ambitious, as the instrument purports to serve this purpose for grades 1 through 12.

The Diagnostic Assessment of Reading (DAR) measures skills in six areas of reading: Word Recognition (used to determine student placement into all but one of the other scales), Word Analysis (containing eight regular and four prereading subtests), Oral Reading, Silent Reading Comprehension, Spelling, and Word Meaning. Objectives indicated by the authors include the assessment of relative strengths in reading and language, determination of the areas in which further instruction is needed, and the provision of feedback to students regarding skills and needs. Materials include a teacher's manual, a student book, student record booklets, and response records with directions for administration.

Trial Teaching Strategies (TTS) consists of a series of short lessons that may be utilized to follow up on the DAR through a diagnostic teaching approach. Materials include a teacher's manual, record booklets, 10 envelopes with stimulus cards, and six storybooks.

All materials are well designed, although they are not sufficiently colorful to appeal to younger children. Directions are clear, but do require study prior to administration due to complexity with regards to sequence and variability of the levels of mastery from one task to another.

A concern is the manual's lack of psychometric information regarding the DAR—nowhere in the manual is there information on background or development of the instrument, the credentials of the authors, norming, reliability, validity, or relationships with other assessment instruments or reading curricula. A request to the publisher for such information elicited a response which noted the authors have substantial experience in the diagnosis and treatment of reading disorders as well as in administration of programs for such purposes. Norming was conducted in 1990–91 on 1,216 students, grades 1 through 12, who were also administered the 1989 Gates-MacGinitie Reading Tests. Unfortunately, information as to the geographical location, sex, race, socioeconomic status, and selection process for the subjects was not provided.

Correlations among the DAR and Gates subtests vary widely, with some comparisons (such as Word Recognition with Vocabulary and Silent Reading Comprehension with Comprehension) being significantly lower than anticipated (in the .50 to .70 range). Intercorrelations of the various DAR subtests are sometimes quite high, raising the question of whether they actually measure different skills. Measures of reliability were not provided.

In summary, the Diagnostic Assessments of Reading with Trial Teaching Strategies (DARTTS) package appears to be an adequate tool for assessing and teaching reading skills. However, prospective users should be provided additional information in the manual. Without normative data, concern exists as to the applicability of the instrument for a school population.

[32]
Digital Finger Tapping Test.
Purpose: Constructed to measure "psychomotor performance as an element in neuropsychological functioning."
Population: Individuals with potential cortical damage or impairment.
Publication Date: 1985.
Acronym: DFTT.
Scores, 2: Right Hand, Left Hand.
Administration: Individual.
Price Data: Not available.
Time: (10) minutes for administration, scoring, and interpretation; 10 seconds per trial.
Authors: Allen D. Brandon and Thomas L. Bennett.
Publisher: Western Psychological Services.
[NOTE: The publisher advised us January 1994 that this test is now out of print.]

Review of the Digital Finger Tapping Test by KEVIN J. McCARTHY, Louisiana State University, School of Medicine, and PENELOPE W. DRALLE, Associate Professor of Psychiatry, Louisiana State University School of Medicine, Department of Psychiatry and Psychology, New Orleans, LA:

The Digital Finger Tapping Test (DFTT) is available from Western Psychological Services (WPS) and consists of an administration manual and an electronic tapping device incorporating "a tapping-key and a self-contained timer, which automatically begins timing with the first depression of the tapping key" (manual, p. 2). The device is a lightweight, black box and is powered by a 9-volt battery. Its appearance is similar to a remote control unit for a TV or garage door opener. The display window for the tapper is visible both to the subject and the examiner and remains blank until the end of 10 seconds. It then indicates the number of taps for that interval and does not record any additional taps after the 10-second period. The DFTT is portable and adaptable for testing in a number of situations. The self-contained timer is a feature designed to reduce examiner error and thereby increase the accuracy in measuring individual performance.

The manual provides an adequate description of standardized instructions to be used with each client. Further, record forms are provided for recording individual performance scores. The manual contains specific instructions to the subject and directs the examiner in a clear, unambiguous fashion.

The normative data collected on the digital finger tapper (PY-2) and on the manual key-driven device included in the standard Halstead-Reitan Neuropsychological Test Battery (T4:1119) are on 80 introductory psychology students at Colorado State University between the ages of 18 and 20. Subjects were screened for non-righthandedness and previous brain injury.

The manual notes that "both males and females showed significantly faster rates of tapping regardless of whether their dominant or nondominant hand was used" (manual, p. 7) on the DFTT. Furthermore, males obtained significantly faster rates than females within an average increment in rate for the DFTT of 5.76 taps per 10 seconds faster than the standard manual tapper. In conjunction with the differences, the authors acknowledge that the "norms typically used for the manual apparatus (e.g., Russell, Neuringer, & Goldstein 1970) cannot be used" (manual, p. 7). The manual does note that "the average standard deviations of rates obtained between these instruments were comparable (DFTT = 5.33, manual = 5.10)" (manual, p. 6). Further, they noted that "observed differences in tapping rate by instrument and sex were significant ($p<.05$)" (manual, pp. 6–7). The manual also notes that "finger tapping scores are significantly affected by several factors including the sex of the individual, educational level, emotional state, and prior test experience" (manual, p. 9). The factors addressed in the normative study are gender and dominance. Because the data provided by the normative sample represent a narrow range, the DFTT should be used with caution. The manual notes,

> Based on the fact that standard deviations are similar across both instruments, and, on the average, there is more than a 5-point advantage using the DFTT, we recommend the widely used Russell et al. (1970) norms be increased 5 points when using the DFTT to evaluate level of impairment in adults. Using a 5-point increment would be analogous to data-smoothing techniques frequently used in the development of test norms to prevent an overreliance on the uniqueness of a given data sample. (manual, p. 8)

The authors suggest that use of such technique is justified on the basis of statistical propriety.

Certainly, the electronic version of the test presents an instrument worth consideration if only for the enhanced accuracy of measurement. Its introduction at this time seems premature based upon the limited normative data available to evaluate its effectiveness as a neuropsychological test instrument. In a research setting, the DFTT may enhance the clinician's evaluation of fine-motor speed. Its use in a clinical setting using the Halstead-Reitan established norms and cutoffs even with the adjustment for speed is questionable at this time.

As indicated in the manual, a difference of just several taps can have a significant impact on the tapping score. When standardized cutting scores are used, these differences can lead to misinterpretation of the clinical data. Also, as noted in the manual, co-factors including gender, age, educational level, emotional state, and prior test experience variably impact performance.

The DFTT manual (WPS Catalog #W-206B) seems to be consistent since its publication in 1985, but the actual tapping test/timer/stop watch has changed significantly over the same period of time. The tapping device sent for review is WPS W-277 and is different from the DFTT apparatuses listed in the 1988–89 catalog, the 1991–92 catalog, and the device WPS PY-2 used in the normative study. None of the instruments involved have the same dimensions, the same configurations, nor the same standard functions. When inquiry was made regarding this discrepancy to Western Psychological Services we were assured by the company spokesperson that the manual was appropriate for use with the W-277 instrument.

It would appear the authors of this instrument have sought to develop an electronic version of the finger tapper using existing reliability and validity data. The manual notes, "A review of the reliability and validity of this standard instrument would go beyond the scope of this brief administration manual" (manual, p. 10). By incorporating general references to Reitan's work and referring the reader to standard neuropsychological literature on the Halstead-Reitan Neuropsychological Test Battery, it would appear the publishers are attempting to enhance the credibility and clinical usefulness of their device by utilizing statistical evaluations of a different instrument. Evaluation of the DFTT as a distinct instrument should include reliability and validity data in light of its inherent differences from the standard finger tapper. Additionally, it should be noted the tappers may have different levels of tension and are obviously postured at different angles, suggesting substantial difference in function. As the authors noted, "The developmental use of the digital finger tapping test (DFTT) as a clinical and research instrument was based on the knowledge that even minimal error . . . can have a major influence on the resulting finger tapping score" (manual, pp. 2–3). Certainly, variations in basic function contribute to the standard error of measurement. As the authors note, "Misinterpretation of several finger taps in a 10-second interval can have critical implications" (manual, p. 2). Additional normative studies incorporating age and organic factors in addition to instrument and sex would enhance the clinical usefulness of this instrument.

Although the DFTT is likely to be an effective and valuable research instrument, deficiencies in reliability, validity, and normative studies curtail its current clinical usefulness. Neuropsychological assessment incorporating the manual Halstead-Reitan tapper, when used in conjunction with appropriate norms, is likely to provide the most relevant data for clinical evaluation.

REVIEWER'S REFERENCE

Russell, E. W., Neuringer, C., & Goldstein, G. (1970). *Assessment of brain damage: A neuropsychological key approach.* New York: Wiley.

Review of the Digital Finger Tapping Test by AGNES E. SHINE, Assistant Professor of Educational Psychology, Mississippi State University, Mississippi State, MS:
The Digital Finger Tapping Test (DFTT) is an individually administered test of psychomotor speed.

The manual states the DFTT was "developed to minimize examiner error in timing" (manual, p. 2). The DFTT is similar to other finger tapping tests in administration and scoring. The major procedural difference is the inclusion of an electronic test/counter/timer device. This is an advantage since accurate timing is, obviously, a key measure in the assessment of psychomotor speed. The DFTT requires the examinee to tap with the index finger of the dominant hand for five 10-second trials. After a brief rest, the same procedures are followed for the nondominant hand. If the range of scores for each hand across the trials is within 5 points, the test is terminated for the hand and scored. If the range of scores is larger than 5 points, additional trials are administered with a maximum of 10 trials per hand. Scoring the test is very simple. The test protocol is clearly written and easy to use.

The manual of the DFTT is quite brief and information usually found in test manuals is incomplete or missing. The manual does not indicate who can administer the test or what type of professional preparation is needed to administer and interpret the test. Noticeably missing from the manual is a clear indication for whom the test is appropriate and for what age levels. The standardization sample is restricted to 80 (40 males and 40 females) subjects enrolled in an introductory psychology course at Colorado State University. Because the manual states that the test can be used in the prediction of cerebral dysfunction, a wider random stratified sample including different age ranges and subjects with known impairment should have been included in the sample. The limited sample used in the standardization of the DFTT severely limits the utility of the test.

Specific validity and reliability data for the DFTT were not reported in the manual. Instead, the authors discussed the psychometric properties of other finger tapping tests (e.g., Halstead Finger Oscillation Test).

The test authors made a point of describing the procedures used during the standardization of the test. Each subject was administered the DFTT using the electric apparatus and a manual apparatus used in other similar tests. The authors found the subjects were significantly faster on the electronic apparatus and that males outperformed females. Based on this finding the test authors cautioned using traditional finger tapping norms. Instead, the authors recommended using their own norms. These norms consisted of adding 5 points to the widely used Russell impairment norms (Russell, Neuringer, & Goldstein, 1970). Although the authors indicated the norms could be used when making an estimate of the level of impairment, it was suggested that more research was needed.

The authors discussed several factors that may affect finger tapping scores such as gender differences, educational level, and prior test experience. One important aspect the authors failed to mention was the difference in scores may have been due to the physical structure of the apparatus used. For example, on the electric apparatus the tapping key must be depressed .13 inches. On the manual apparatus the tapping key must be depressed .50 inches. It should also be noted that for the electric apparatus 80 grams of pressure was needed to change the counter whereas 400 grams of pressure was needed to change the counter on the manual apparatus. Given the difference in the physical requirements of the task, it is unclear whether or not the tasks are equivalent. Therefore, fatigue may be a greater factor on the manual apparatus trials whereas less energy may be needed to complete the finger tapping trials on the DFTT, thus resulting in higher finger tapping scores.

The authors should be applauded for their introduction of an electric apparatus in measuring finger tapping speed, ease of scoring, and test protocol. Although the DFTT is appealing to those in clinical practice, a number of issues must be addressed in the manual before recommending the DFTT for wide use in the prediction of cerebral dysfunction. Specifically, a larger standardization sample is indicated. The sample should include normal as well as neuropsychologically impaired individuals. Validity and reliability studies should be included in the test manual. Norms and cutoff scores should be generated for impaired and nonimpaired performance. Adherence to test development standards would most certainly allow the DFTT to contribute to the improvement of practice in the area of measuring finger tapping speed. At present, based on the information provided in the test manual, the DFTT should be used with extreme caution.

REVIEWER'S REFERENCE

Russell, E. W., Neuringer, C., & Goldstein, G. (1970). *Assessment of brain damage: A neuropsychological key approach.* New York: Wiley.

[33]

Draw A Person: Screening Procedure for Emotional Disturbance.

Purpose: Designed to screen for children who may have emotional disorders.

Population: Ages 6–17.

Publication Date: 1991.

Acronym: DAP:SPED.

Scores: Total score only.

Administration: Group.

Price Data, 1994: $64 per complete kit including 25 record forms and manual (77 pages); $29 per 25 record forms; $29 per manual.

Time: 15(20) minutes.

Author: Jack A. Naglieri, Timothy J. McNeish, and Achilles N. Bardos.

Publisher: PRO-ED, Inc.

Cross References: See T4:816 (1 reference).

Review of the Draw A Person: Screening Procedure for Emotional Disturbance by MERITH COSDEN, Associate Professor, Counseling/Clinical/School Psychology, Department of Education, University of California, Santa Barbara, CA:

The Draw A Person: Screening Procedure for Emotional Disturbance (DAP:SPED) is a formal system of administering and scoring human figure drawings to screen children for emotional problems. Practitioners can detect children who are "at risk" of having an emotional disturbance by comparing the scores obtained on their figure drawings with the scores from the normative sample.

The DAP:SPED was developed by the same author of the Draw A Person: A Quantitative Scoring System (Naglieri, 1988; T4:814) which is designed to screen for cognitive deficits. The same basic protocol is used in each assessment system, with different scoring criteria used to provide the information needed in each domain.

The test relies on a pattern of administering human figure drawings that was first used by Harris (1963) called the Goodenough-Harris Draw A Person test. A child is asked to create three drawings: a woman, a man, and a picture of themselves. The use of three pictures, and, in particular, the use of the self-drawing, was considered experimental in the Goodenough-Harris system. The three drawings are used in both the DAP:SPED and the Draw A Person: A Quantitative Scoring System, although little support has been provided for use of the three figures.

The criteria used for scoring the DAP:SPED were developed systematically. A standardization sample of 2,260, 5–17-year-old students was drawn to be representative of U.S. geographic regions, gender, ethnicity, and socioeconomic status. This is part of the same sample used to standardize the Draw A Person: A Quantitative Scoring System. Preliminary scoring criteria were generated from prior studies of the use of figure drawings to expose emotional disturbance. These scoring criteria were tested on a small sample of subjects and modified several times to assure that the descriptors could be coded reliably.

The modified criteria were then applied to the drawings of the larger standardization sample. The system is designed to detect behavior that occurs infrequently in the normative population; only items that occurred in less than 16% of the standardization sample were kept in the final coding system. Emotional disturbance is not detected from any one type of response in this system; rather, it is screened through observation of a large number of unusual responses thought to reflect emotional problems.

Through the standardization procedure it was found that subjects did not vary in their responses to the three types of figures. Thus, each picture is scored by the same criteria, and scores are summed to provide an indication of the client's needs. This suggests the three different types of pictures may not be needed for the protocol. Little variation in scores was found as a function of age. Scores are clustered by ages 6–8, 9–12, and 13–17. Significant sex differences were obtained, however. As a result, norms are presented separately by sex for each of the age groups. Raw scores, summed across the three pictures, are converted to T scores with a mean of 50 and a standard deviation of 10. T scores of 55 and over are considered appropriate for further evaluation, whereas scores of 65 and above are considered strong indicators of the need for additional assessment.

Reliability of the DAP:SPED is relatively high. The two studies in the manual on intrarater reliability (the same rater scoring each drawing twice) and interrater reliability (different raters scoring the same drawings) found reliability correlations in the .8 to .9 range. One study on the stability of test scores over a 1-week period found slightly lower correlations between scores, $r = .67$; students' scores were not significantly different across test periods, however, indicating that the scores were relatively stable.

Four studies on the validity of the DAP:SPED, none independently published at the time of this review, are presented in the manual. In each study, the scores of a group of children who have been diagnosed with a range of emotional problems are compared with the scores of a group of individuals without known diagnoses but who are otherwise matched to the clinical group by age and sex. In each instance, the diagnosed group had significantly higher scores on the DAP:SPED than did the control group. Using a cutoff score of 55 or more the studies were able to accurately classify children at conventional levels of statistical significance; however, the numbers of children accurately classified, as well as those who would be misclassified under this system, were not reported.

Although the DAP:SPED appears straightforward in its conception and purpose, I have several concerns about its utility. The test makes certain assumptions about the nature of emotional disturbance. Among them, that emotional problems can be generically assessed, that all types of emotional problems will be screened through the items on the test, and that emotional disturbance is more effectively screened through the presence of a number of unusual items rather than one or two specific criteria. The manual does not provide strong support for these assumptions.

In determining whether the DAP:SPED is a useful screening device one has to justify the time expended in administering and scoring the test with the benefits obtained. To what extent is this screening tool able to accurately capture emotional disturbance? And is it more effective and less intrusive than other screening tools? The available research on this instrument does not adequately address the number of false positives or false negatives likely to occur from use of this tool. This concern aside, the context in which the DAP:SPED is used is seen as critical to its utility. If the DAP:SPED is administered to a broad group of children who have not been identified with special needs, it may be useful in detecting some students who are at risk for or experiencing emotional problems. On the other hand, if the DAP:SPED is part of a screening battery for a child who teachers or counselors have already identified as needing some help, it appears less likely that it would provide significant additional information.

In sum, children's drawings are easily administered and clinically interesting, thus tempting to use for screening and assessment. However, the actual contribution of these procedures to the screening process remains unclear. The DAP:SPED does not provide specific information with regard to the type of emotional disturbance children are experiencing, nor is it clear that it is sensitive to all types of emotional disturbance. For children already identified by teachers or parents as experiencing some emotional problems, this instrument may not add substantively to their understanding of the child. For broad screening purposes, however, the DAP:SPED may yield useful information not otherwise available.

REVIEWER'S REFERENCES

Harris, D. B. (1963). *Children's drawings as measures of intellectual maturity*. New York: Harcourt, Brace & World.
Naglieri, J. A. (1988). Draw A Person: A Quantitative Scoring System. San Antonio, TX: The Psychological Corporation.

Review of the Draw A Person: Screening Procedure for Emotional Disturbance by GALE M. MORRISON,

Associate Professor of Education, Graduate School of Education, University of California, Santa Barbara, CA:

The stated goal of the Draw A Person: Screening Procedure for Emotional Disturbance (DAP:SPED) is to "provide a screening measure to aid in the identification of children and adolescents who may have emotional or, as termed by some, behavioral disorders" (p. 3). The rationale for their approach to measurement is based on what the authors consider shortcomings of existing projective human figure drawing systems. Thus, their emphasis is on easy and objective scoring, recent national norms, differentiation between disturbed and normal populations, reliability, and provision of the ability to score for cognitive functioning (as measured by a separate system, not included in this review).

The test development procedures were clearly described. The initial pool of items was chosen for previously documented clinical significance; the final set of items was chosen for item contributions to the reliability (item-total correlations) and validity (infrequency of occurrence in a normal sample). The clinical and substantive significance of projective tests is not emphasized beyond the initial selection of items. The authors deliberately chose the number of emotional indicators in drawings as their sole index of emotional disturbance. Interpretations of the meaning of the drawings are *not* included. Although this approach perhaps gives less interesting information, it facilitates the creation of an instrument that is psychometrically sound as well as easily and objectively quantified.

The manual authors provide a clear description of the scoring system. Templates are provided for the scoring of figure size and placement on the page. Sample drawings and a delineation of corresponding scores for training purposes are provided. The record form is clear and efficient.

Standardization procedures included the selection of a large sample that represented factors of age, gender, geographic region, ethnicity, and household income. A weakness in the description of the standardization procedures is that the authors failed to describe how these subjects were chosen. Also, in terms of representativeness, no information was given on the inclusion or exclusion of children with handicaps. Test users are left uninformed about the extent to which the standardization sample is representative of a range of abilities. Therefore, norms are provided for what is assumed to be a normal sample. Because the DAP:SPED is a screening instrument for emotional disturbance, it would be interesting to be able to compare scores to a sample of children and adolescents with emotional disturbances as well. Such norms are not provided.

The scoring that resulted in the normative data was completed by "approximately 20 raters" (p. 7) of undisclosed background. Test authors should be more exact in their description of this aspect of the standardization procedures.

Documentation of validity relies primarily on four studies (done by the test authors) that document the ability of this instrument to discriminate between emotionally disturbed and normal populations. These studies lend support to the fact that scores on the DAP:SPED can discriminate between disturbed and nondisturbed children and adolescents. The screening function of the instrument would be more convincingly validated by comparing the scores on the DAP:SPED with other screening instruments such as teacher, parent, or child behavior and/or emotional adjustment rating scales or behavioral observations by teachers and other school support personnel. These other measures are more closely aligned with the function of screening at the prereferral stage (rather than post-identification) for children and adolescents experiencing emotional and behavioral difficulties.

The authors also note the lack of correlation of the DAP:SPED scores with a measure of intelligence as evidence of validity. Because one of the intended purposes of this instrument was to provide an instrument that lends itself to assessment of cognitive functioning (specifically, the Draw A Person: A Quantitative Scoring System or the DAP:QSS) and because the same standardization sample was used, information concerning validity also could have been easily gleaned by comparing the DAP:QSS and the DAP:SPED. The test user is left wondering why such information was not presented.

Information about internal consistency, test-retest stability, and inter- and intrarater reliability was presented. Although the case for inter- and intrarater reliability was based on a limited number of raters, the reliability indices, in general, were acceptable considering the screening function of the instrument. The authors appropriately emphasized the importance of using standard error of measurement (*SEM*) in developing confidence intervals and provided detailed information for determining these confidence intervals.

Cutoff scores are provided. The description of the process of determining these scores is vague. However, the authors do urge that appropriate caution be used in the use of these cutoff scores.

The test authors provide the appropriate cautions about the function and scope of the instrument as a screening instrument, emphasizing the importance of gathering additional information about children or adolescents who get scores that indicate further evaluation is needed. However, the authors could have discussed the implications of the widespread use of this instrument in a school setting, where children or adolescents potentially could be identified when they might not otherwise be having significant difficulties with school. The consequences for the individual students, as well as the school system, of referring false positives for further evaluation should be discussed.

In summary, the DAP:SPED has been constructed for the purpose of screening children and adolescents for emotional disturbance. Appropriate cautions were given by the authors about using the instrument beyond its screening function. Administration and scoring procedures are objective, easy, and clear. The DAP:SPED manual includes recent national norms for age and sex groups of a "normal" sample. Addition of norms for a sample of emotionally disturbed children and adolescents would add an additional perspective for test users. Although somewhat limited in scope and size, studies completed by the authors have established initial validity and reliability. Their validity argument would be improved by comparisons with other instruments that are known indicators of emotional and behavioral disturbance.

[34]
Dropout Prediction & Prevention.
Purpose: Developed to identify students at risk for dropping out of school.
Population: Grades 9–12.
Publication Date: 1990.
Acronym: DPP.
Scores: Total score only.
Administration: Individual.
Price Data, 1991: $4 per 25 scales (select High School Form or Experimental Form for 8th Grade); $15 per manual (93 pages); $15.50 per specimen set.
Time: [5] minutes.
Comments: Scale information obtained from student cumulative records.
Authors: Clarence E. Nichols and Rochelle E. Nichols.
Publisher: Clinical Psychology Publishing Co., Inc.

Review of the Dropout Prediction & Prevention by IRVIN J. LEHMANN, Professor of Measurement, Michigan State University, East Lansing, MI:

To predict school dropouts and develop a program of remediation would, without a doubt, be a major boon to American education. This was the intent of the Dropout Prediction & Prevention (DPP) instrument.

After undertaking a careful review of the literature on school dropouts, instrument authors Nichols and Nichols concluded that available instruments were unsuitable for a variety of reasons: "they were too cumbersome, had a low predictor value, did not include enough predictor factors, were too expensive and time-consuming to administer, or because the necessary information was too difficult to obtain or was not available" (manual, p. 15). I am sympathetic to the difficulties associated with instrument development, but the above assertions create concern regarding how the DPP has been validated.

The DPP does not appear to be based on a particular theory; rather, the instrument builds on some previous research in the area. The test authors suggest that an acceptable prediction instrument has to satisfy the following criteria: (a) easy to administer and score; (b) based on data already collected (that is, no interviews or tests); (c) short; and, (d) accurate. No doubt, by accurate, the authors meant valid. The DPP is short, can gather the data needed from existing files, and is relatively simple to administer and score. But, is it valid?

Nichols and Nichols describe the feasibility study they undertook to identify potential dropout factors. The sample consisted of only 50 students (25 dropouts and 25 graduates). The composite instrument was developed on only 20 students (10 dropouts and 10 graduates). Although identifying the perfect number needed to support instrument development is difficult, this sample appears grossly inadequate.

Insufficient information is provided regarding the representativeness of the sample. The authors suggest their sample was drawn from a pool comparable to the U.S. Census with some exceptions. Regrettably, the exceptions were not described.

From an original pool of 20 items, the final instrument consists of five items: (1) days absent, (2) years repeated, (3) G.P.A., (4) alternative school, and (5) number of parents in the home. A weight was assigned to the type of response for each variable and the total weighted score (each weighted score is called a scaled score which is *not* correct or conventional usage of the term). Those students having a total scaled score of 5 or more are identified as potential dropouts.

Although Nichols and Nichols used regression analysis to identify the five variables making up the scale (there were actually six, but parental education was deleted because of the availability or reliability of this information in the students' files), they do not provide a regression equation. This is an oversight.

One might also raise the question why regression analysis appears to have been used to identify those factors/items that make up the scale. Why wasn't discriminant function analysis used to identify those items that differentiate between students who graduate and those who drop out? Computing a multiple R will only provide information as to the contribution particular variables make in predicting a criterion.

Finally, I do not understand why z-scores were computed for five predictor variables. There might be a good reason but the reader is left in the dark as to their purpose.

The essential type of validity evidence needed for an instrument such as the DPP is *predictive* validity, which for the DPP, are data that show (*a*) the instrument permits users to make better decisions with the data than the best decision one could make without DPP data, and (*b*) the cost of testing and faulty decisions.

The value of any test, and especially those claiming predictive power, is dependent upon the difference between the cost of testing and how much is saved in the cost of errors (for the DPP, it would be either predicting a dropout when one would not have occurred but *more* damaging would be the error where the potential dropout would *not* be identified, that is, a false negative). Because the DPP's major purpose is not only identifying potential dropouts but also the program developed to identify and counsel such students, it is essential that false negatives be minimized. Again, the question to be answered is whether or not the DPP has a smaller number of false negatives than would be made without using the data it provides. Only careful long-term research will supply information about incremental validity gains through use of the DPP.

Any instrument claiming predictive validity must be cross validated. Although I am not completely satisfied with the cross-validation sample, primarily because of its small size and lack of representativeness, the authors used proper procedures to attempt a cross validation.

In summary, the DPP *may* be a promising instrument but more research is needed with larger and more representative samples. Until then, potential users should be very careful in making decisions about who should and should not enter a dropout prevention program based on results of this approach. The program, per se, seems quite reasonable but its success in preventing dropouts is not well documented.

Review of the Dropout Prediction & Prevention by BERT W. WESTBROOK, *Professor of Psychology,*

North Carolina State University, Raleigh, NC and SUZANNE MARKEL-FOX, *Post Doctoral Fellow, Center for Mental Health Policies and Services Research, University of Pennsylvania, Philadelphia, PA:*

The Dropout Prediction & Prevention (DPP) was developed to facilitate the school counselor's task in identifying and tracking students who are at risk for dropout but who may fall between the extremes of those with very poor attendance and behavior, and those who are successful in school. The DPP, which purports to measure the risk of student dropout from elementary (8th grade) or secondary school, was designed to be part of a global dropout prevention program. The accompanying booklet describes model preventive programs in detail.

The DPP has two forms, a Dropout Prediction Profile for High School Students, and experimental Dropout Prediction Profile for 8th-graders. The factors to be entered on the high school form include attendance (days absent last full year), years repeated (number of years not promoted), grade-point average, alternative school (any behavior placement), and parents in home (one- or two-parent home). On the 8th-grade experimental form, the items are the same except for alternative school, for which behavior problems (causes classroom disturbance) is substituted. Data are entered on the DPP from existing school records. This can be accomplished by the school counselor or a reliable office assistant who is not a student, because some of the information may be sensitive (e.g., number of parents in the home, previous placements for behavior problems). The booklet authors suggest that some of these data are already computerized in many school districts and that a minor modification of the school system software would allow for automatic data entry.

DEVELOPMENT OF THE INSTRUMENT. The authors generated the items on the DPP based on their experience with students who had performed poorly in school or who had dropped out. Then, randomly selected records of 25 each of graduates and dropouts were used in a feasibility study of the instrument. The variables included "attendance, years repeated, over age, grades, suspensions, behavior placements, standardized test scores, sibling dropout, and delinquency" (manual, p. 23). The rationale for the item choice and the scoring and weights attributed to scores was not described, and the data from this administration are not reported. There was no mention of any theoretical basis for the item choice or the structure of the DPP.

Results from the study of 50 individuals were reportedly analyzed (no details of this analysis were provided) and 20 items which included "all sources of student information that had any potential for influencing dropout behavior" (manual, p. 23) were tested on another set of records, from 10 graduates and 10 dropouts. Lack of detail makes it impossible for the reader to understand what constituted a "successful trial" of the initial instrument, nor why items were expanded from 9 to 20. Again, no results for the 20 subjects are reported, so it is impossible to evaluate the goodness of the predictors which were eventually selected.

Validation and cross validation of the items judged to be the best predictors of dropping out was reportedly performed on a sample of 400 student records, 200 of which represented graduates and 200 dropouts. Stepwise regression procedures identified the six most discriminating items ($R^2 > .68$), five of which were chosen for inclusion on the instrument. The sixth variable, parent education, although adequately productive, was not included because of inconsistent availability of the information. However, the authors report a fair degree of overlap in predictions based on the use of the DPP (Figure 2, manual, p. 26); the rejection of the parent education variable because of inconsistency of results with a small sample might have been a premature decision.

ADMINISTRATION AND SCORING. Raw scores are entered in the appropriate column and then scaled by means of a weighting scale which is conveniently placed in the right-most column on the same single sheet used for all data entry. Each item is weighted separately and then all weights are summed to yield a cumulative total score. This weighting process appears rather arbitrary. For example, a student who has repeated three grades, missed more than 80 days, maintains a grade point average of 1, has been placed in an alternative setting, and who has only one parent in the home, would receive a weighted score of 11. Yet another student with less than 21 absences, a grade point average of 2, no history of alternative placements and both parents in the home, but who has repeated twice, would receive a score of 4, which would not meet the criteria for dropout risk.

Scaled scores are derived from weighted raw scores and the cumulative total renders a single arbitrary cutting score: either graduate (scaled score of 0 to 4) or not graduate (any score over 5). The DPP authors discuss the incremental validity of modified cutting scores, and recommend that administrators with particular budgetary or personnel limitations may wish to use that flexibility. "As the horizontal axis moves toward the top of the chart, the school administrator will improve his or her prediction of graduates; however, error in predicting dropouts will increase. In terms of saving education dollars, the higher the axis the greater the savings, because fewer dropouts are identified for prevention programs" (manual, p. 32).

TECHNICAL CONSIDERATIONS. The sample of student records used for developing the normative scores for the DPP came from one high school in a medium-sized city in south-central Pennsylvania. The high school served 1,297 students, 75.8% of whom were African-American, 18.2% Euro-American, and 6% Hispanic and "other." The 200 graduates came from the graduating class of 1982. The 200 dropouts came from the same school, but had dropped out over a period of 4 years. The authors do not describe the racial composition of the groups nor how the 200 students from each group were selected.

Stepwise regression analysis was used to select the final five items, after which one-half of the sample was cross validated. Dropout prediction scores were correlated with the dichotomous criterion (graduated or dropped out). The authors described the findings from their multiple regression as discriminative but did not report convergent and discriminant validity studies. The items on the DPP were tested using records from students who graduated in 1982 or who had dropped out of school over a 4-year period including 1982. The authors did not repeat the analyses performed on the first group, which makes it difficult to determine whether the five variables retained are indeed the best predictors. Records were randomized and data obtained from them were analyzed using stepwise multiple regression.

Means, standard deviations, and range of variables are not reported. This is an egregious oversight; variability can determine whether the variable is likely to be rejected based on regression analysis. This is particularly important in the present example, because the population upon which this instrument was tested is very unusual. Minority groups are overrepresented, students were absent frequently (mean = 37 days), had a mean retention record of nearly one year of school, and a mean of one parent in the home.

OVERALL CRITIQUE. The DPP is easy to complete and the booklet offers many helpful recommendations for local development and implementation of dropout prevention programs, as well as problems to avoid. Used in conjunction with a Student Information Management System, the DPP could generate risk profiles at a relatively low cost. The DPP could also be used as part of a training program for future counselors, special education teachers, and dropout prevention coordinators.

The DPP uses information readily available in most school systems, and should significantly reduce the time involved in identifying students potentially at risk for school dropout. The authors include detailed recommendations for developing aggressive dropout prevention programs, based on their own experience. Some of the resources they identified include academic skills improvement programs, alternative school programs, school and community recreation programs, counseling, employment, and programs that address the students' special interests and needs. The booklet includes a practical guide for establishing and maintaining a prevention program. Successful prevention programs from across the United States are also reviewed, and the elements of a good prevention program are covered in some detail. For this reason, the DPP may be a good tool for a school board or planning committee which is preparing to develop and budget for a dropout prevention program.

Unfortunately, however, the development and presentation of this instrument do not meet the requirements of the *Standards for Educational and Psychological Testing* (AERA, APA, & NCME, 1985). There was no technical manual provided; in its place was a booklet that included practical application considerations and incomplete information about the test's statistical properties. The authors offered no validity or reliability information aside from the inadequately reported validity studies conducted in the development of the instrument. The sample of student records used for development and validation of the final instrument may not be representative of the high school population at large. In addition, because the school district where these students were served offered a variety of alternatives to standard high school education, including a vocational-technical facility, the district may not be representative of school districts in general across the United States. This instrument was developed and tested exclusively from school records, without any student contact.

The 25% dropout rate reported by various governmental and educational agencies underscores the need for a dropout prediction instrument. However, because two items alone (years repeated, grade point average) accounted for 61% of the variance in rates of graduation reported by the test developers, further carefully designed validity studies should be conducted for this instrument to be a worthwhile investment for school districts and social agencies.

Care should be taken to use the DPP in conjunction with personal student/family contact. The Dropout Prediction Profile (DPP) appears to be a concise and easy-to-use instrument that can draw upon data already available to the school counselor. Used as part of an overall prediction and prevention program,

as proposed by the developers of the instrument, this profile may be a practical screening tool. In its current form, however, it should not be considered a measuring instrument.

Overall, the development procedures for this instrument were atheoretical and lacking in sound methodological analysis. The DPP may be a good starting point for development of a dropout prevention counseling program, but its validity and reliability remain to be demonstrated. It would not be wise to base placement decisions on scores generated by this checklist.

REVIEWER'S REFERENCE

American Educational Research Association, American Psychological Association, & National Council on Measurement in Education. (1985). *Standards for educational and psychological testing.* Washington, DC: American Psychological Association, Inc.

[*35*]
Early School Assessment.
Purpose: Designed to measure prereading and mathematics skills.
Population: End of prekindergarten to middle of kindergarten, middle of kindergarten to beginning of grade 1.
Publication Date: 1990.
Acronym: ESA.
Scores, 7: Prereading (Language, Visual [also used in Mathematics total], Auditory, Memory, Total), Mathematics Concepts and Operations (Visual [also used in Prereading total], Total).
Administration: Group.
Levels, 2: 1, 2.
Price Data: Price data available from publisher for test materials including: complete testing kit including 35 machine- or hand-scorable test booklets (select level), 35 practice books, scoring key, class record sheet for hand scoring, and examiner's manual (81 pages, select level); 35 parent conference forms (select level); teacher's guide (51 pages, select level); preliminary norms book; preliminary technical bulletin; test organizer; scoring service available from publisher.
Time: 229 (Level 2) to 239 (Level 1) minutes over 8 sessions.
Authors: CTB MacMillan/McGraw-Hill.
Publisher: CTB MacMillan/McGraw-Hill.

Review of the Early School Assessment by SONYA BLIXT, Professor of Evaluation and Measurement, and CHRISTINE F. STRAUSS, Graduate Assistant in Evaluation and Measurement, Kent State University, Kent, OH:
The Early School Assessment (ESA) measures prereading and math skills as an aid in determining

the formal training needs for children in the early years of school. The ESA is group administered and is presented to children as an enjoyable game in story format. Although the main purpose of the ESA is to guide instructional planning, the authors indicate that it can also be used to identify children who qualify for federally funded programs.

Objective Performance Indexes (OPI) serve as criterion-referenced scores in determining each child's level of proficiency in a specific area. Based on the number of correct responses for each scale, children are categorized as proficient, in need of continuing instruction, or in need of introduction to the topic. Suggestions for at-home activities matched to the OPI are provided to aid parents in helping their children develop these skills. Furthermore, the distracters for each item were chosen based upon common errors made in answering the item. Thus, incorrect answers further aid the teacher in diagnosing the type of instruction needed for the child. Although the three diagnostic categories are helpful in determining the level of instruction necessary for each student, there is no rationale provided in the test manuals that justifies the criteria used for determining these specific cut scores.

Scoring can be done either by hand or machine. The test booklet provides norm-referenced scale scores, national percentile ranks, stanines, and normal curve equivalents by grade level and time of year (fall, winter, spring). The norming group is a sample of approximately 23,000 prekindergarten, kindergarten, and first-grade children from diverse school districts, geographic areas, socioeconomic levels, and ethnic backgrounds. The norms tables are easy to read and understand, although several readings of the description of the sampling methods left the reviewers unclear about the procedures used.

The manual provides the theoretical rationale for the development of the objectives of the instrument, as well as the instructions for use of the test. The instructions booklet, though clearly written, permits the teacher to determine the time of the test, the number of breaks to give to the children, and the duration of these breaks. Such lack of standardization in the administration of the test causes reservation regarding the interpretation of the norm-referenced scores. Comparisons to other children's performance are not meaningful if standard procedures are not implemented in the instructions given to each group of children.

ITEM SELECTION. A pilot study was conducted using 1,200 items. Items were selected based upon established content criteria, and were tested for gender and cultural bias, using both item reviewers and empirical tests. Biased items were revised or eliminated, according to the requirements of McGraw-Hill's *Guidelines for Bias-Free Publishing* (1983).

Scaling was based on a three-parameter IRT model using items from the California Achievement Test (CAT) Form E to ensure adequate ability ranges in the items. It is not clear why the three-parameter IRT model was used. This is the least stable of the IRT models and difficulty and discrimination indices may interact causing a scale score to be difficult to interpret.

VALIDITY. It is important to establish the predictive validity of the ESA in estimating achievement, that is, does, in fact, proficiency on the Prereading Total scale predict reading achievement in the early grades? The technical manual authors state that predictive validity studies are in progress and the results will be supplied in the final technical report.

In an attempt to establish concurrent validity, the ESA was correlated with the Developing Skills Checklist (DSC). The DSC measures a fuller range of skills than does the ESA, though no reliability or validity information on this instrument is available. The Prereading Total scale on both instruments correlated between .67 and .76. The Total Mathematics scale of the ESA correlated between .59 and .73 with the Mathematical Concepts and Operations scale of the DSC. However, the ESA Total Mathematics scale had similar correlations with the Memory scale of the DSC (.57 to .71), and even *higher* correlations with the DSC Prereading Total (.62 to .74). It is therefore difficult to know what the Total Mathematics scale of the ESA is measuring. The correlations between the other scales of the ESA (e.g., Visual, Memory, Language) and their DSC analogues ranged from .32 to .70. The intercorrelations among all subscales of the ESA range from .52 to .94. Despite these moderate to high correlations, the use of an established instrument, rather than the DSC, would have been preferable in demonstrating concurrent validity. It would then be clearer what constructs are being measured by the ESA scales.

RELIABILITY. Internal consistency reliability (KR20) is reported for each scale of the ESA. In Level 1, the Prereading and Mathematics Totals have reliabilities ranging from .90 to .93. The other scales range from .69 (Language) to .87 (Mathematical Concepts and Operations). The lower reliability for the Language scale seems reasonable when considering that it is based on only 21 items, as opposed to the larger pool of items composing the Prereading (86 items) and Mathematics (54 items) Totals. The Prereading Total scale and the Mathematics Total scale have internal consistency reliabilities ranging from .89 to .93 in Level 2 of the ESA. The reliabilities of the shorter scales range from .73 (Memory) to .90 (Auditory; Mathematical Concepts and Operations).

Test-retest reliability was established using a 2-week interval between the pre- and posttests. The reliability for Level 1 ranges from .67 (Language) to .91 (Prereading Total and Mathematics Total). Level 2 reliabilities ranged from .76 (Visual) to .91 (Prereading Total). Overall, the internal consistency and temporal stability of the scales were acceptable for this type of instrument.

SUMMARY. Two positive features of the test materials are the clear instructions for use of the norms tables and the suggestion of at-home activities that correspond to the proficiency level of each child. However, the timing of the test is under the discretion of the examiner. This lack of standardization weakens the comparisons to other groups of children.

It is apparent that much time and effort went into the item selection process. Items were tested for bias and calibrated using an established instrument (CAT). However, the interpretation of the scale scores may be ambiguous because of the scaling method used. Although the reliabilities are adequate, the concurrent validity was estimated using an instrument (DSC) that has not been established as measuring what it purports to measure. In summary, the ESA may be useful in guiding classroom instruction, but one should hesitate using it for diagnostic purposes without further evidence of cut-score criteria and predictive validity information.

REVIEWER'S REFERENCE

McGraw-Hill Book Co. (1983). *Guidelines for bias-free publishing.* New York: the author.

Review of the Early School Assessment by HERBERT C. RUDMAN, Professor of Measurement and Quantitative Methods, Department of Counseling, Educational Psychology and Special Education, Michigan State University, East Lansing, MI:

The Early School Assessment series (ESA) is one part of a multi-faceted assessment program that attempts to meet the varying perceptions of what is important in early childhood education. Views of preschool and kindergarten programs differ among preschool educators. Some would emphasize developing a child's social, emotional, cognitive, and psychomotor skills. Others would advocate a narrower view of preparing children for formal instruction in reading, mathematics, and language. The CTB Early Childhood System presents a four-component program that attempts to encompass the scope of views of what is important in the earliest years of education.

The system includes the ESA (a two-level series of group-administered tests of prereading and mathematics skills), the Developing Skills Checklist (which includes assessments of social and emotional skills, fine and gross motor development, and print and writing concepts; 12), a Primary Test of Cognitive Skills (a group administered scholastic aptitude test that measures memory, verbal, spatial, and conceptual abilities; 67), and *Play, Learn and Grow! Instructional Activities for Kindergarten and First Grade* (a set of software and literature-based instructional activities linked to the objectives reflected by the ESA and Developing Skills Checklist). Only the first of these, The Early School Assessment (ESA), is reviewed here.

TEST CONTENT. The content measured by the ESA is similar to that measured by other standardized tests given at similar grade levels (the end of the prekindergarten through the beginning of first grade). There are some interesting approaches to the testing of some of the concepts (notably listening comprehension and following directions), but on the whole the ESA is a good though not remarkable measure of early school achievement. In a questionable attempt to personalize the characters used in the test items, children who will be taking the test are introduced to the characters a few days before the test is administered. A story is read to the children entitled, "Meet Our Friends." After the story is read, the children are given a picture to color that includes five children, two rabbits, and a puppy. When the test is given a few days later, the examiner begins by naming the eight characters. Presumably the children will remember those names. However, as one gets into the tests themselves, these names and character recognition play almost no role in the testing process. Although a laudable attempt to reduce test anxiety, no evidence is presented to indicate that it does.

Unlike the Stanford Early School Achievement Test (SESAT; T4:2556), its closest multi-subject competitor, the Early School Assessment does not reflect an important part of the early school curriculum: the environment. Although the ESA will satisfy those who view early childhood curriculums as preparation for the structured academic programs that follow in grades 1–12, it falls short by not dealing with the social and natural environments that are part of kindergarten programs: community, the family, transportation, plants, animals, weather. On the other hand, it does offer a more balanced set of materials which meet the needs of those varying views of what should comprise an early childhood curriculum.

The Teacher's Guides for both levels of the ESA are very well written and should be helpful, especially, for new teachers. The guides include the theoretical basis for the Early School Assessment (a succinct and clear discussion), a section on test interpretation (which unfortunately does not clearly explain the guessing parameter, which results in varying derived scores from a given raw score), and sections dealing with the instructional objectives sampled and examples of the items that reflect those objectives. On the whole, the Teacher's Guide is an important part of the ESA and should not be ignored by those who will administer and use the tests. Ancillary materials also include the Norms Book, Technical Bulletin, and the Examiner's Manual.

TECHNICAL ASPECTS. The norms booklet is clearly written for teachers as are other components accompanying the ESA. The scores used include raw scores and such criterion-referenced scores as percent correct and proficiency criteria labeled: "+" (continue instruction at the same level), and "-" (reteach material). Norm-referenced scores used include scale scores (equal interval scales which serve as the basis for translating raw scores into percentile ranks, stanines, and normal curve equivalents). Demographic data appear to be comprehensive in terms of the variables one would normally consider (school type, system size, geographic region, ethnic group membership, SES, gender, and program followed). However, one cannot tell from these descriptions how representative they actually are when compared to U.S. Census data. This is a significant omission that will, perhaps, be addressed in subsequent editions. If these national norms are to have external validity they need more than descriptive categories and percents in each category. The user making judgments about the validity of conclusions to be applied to the local sample needs to know how well this "national" sample fits the national population parameters.

The Technical Bulletin accompanying the ESA needs the most modification of all of the ancillary materials provided. It suffers from brevity and leaves this reviewer with a feeling of tentativeness of the topics covered and the data presented. The opening paragraph speaks of a nationally representative sample of private and public schools surveyed for data on curricular trends and the like but no evidence is presented in the bulletin of the basis of that representativeness. "Popular basal text series" were analyzed, but given the early school nature of the material reviewed, what text books are to be found at the prekindergarten and kindergarten levels? None of these are noted in any of the accompanying ancillary materials.

Important facets of test construction are handled well in the Technical Bulletin with some exceptions. The three-parameter Item Response Theory model is fairly well explained although the notation for equations is sparse. The paragraphs dealing with bias review need considerable elaboration. Differential item functioning between ethnic and racial groups ought not to be treated globally. There is considerable variance within these groups as well as between groups. To state that items were deleted from a test because of differential functioning without an explanation of whether the deleted items affected the validity of the test is a mistake that should be addressed. A statement is made in the text of the Technical Bulletin (p. 7) that "one simply cannot conclude that Spanish-speaking children are illiterate if they fail an English test, *since it is probable that they are literate in Spanish*" (italics added). No evidence is given for this assumption. Of course, if one does not speak a second language they can hardly be judged illiterate, but it does not follow that they are literate in the language they do speak. This kind of an observation does not belong in a technical bulletin without supporting data.

The validity statements within the Technical Bulletin appear to be weak. Content validity is supported by lists of curricular objectives without detailed explanations of sources for these objectives. Predictive validity is acknowledged to be tentative until longitudinal studies can be completed, and evidence for construct validity is given as intercorrelations between two components of the same Early Childhood System (i.e., ESA scales and the Developing Skills Checklist). Because both tests were published and developed within the same publishing company, it is not surprising that intercorrelations are moderately high. The presentation of evidence for construct validity would better be served by correlating results with an established test or tests from a different source such as the Stanford Early School Achievement Test.

Reliabilities are moderately high, given the age level of the standardization population, but when compared to the SESAT they are somewhat lower in comparable subtests. Test-retest reliability coefficients for separate scales range from a low of .67 (Language) to a high of .86 (Mathematical Concepts and Operations; Visual) for ESA Level 1, and .76 (Visual) to .86 (Auditory) for ESA Level 2. Total Prereading and Mathematics coefficients were .91 (Level 1). For Level 2, the Prereading Total coefficient was .91, and for Mathematics Total, the coefficient was .88.

Intercorrelations between scales should be relatively low if diagnostic-like decisions are going to be made about relative proficiencies in various content areas. The intercorrelations for ESA Levels 1 and 2 were consistently higher than for SESAT Levels 1 and 2. Caution should be exercised when drawing differences between subscale results.

SUMMARY. The Early School Assessment component of CTB's Early Childhood System incorporates a multidimensional approach to assessing children in prekindergarten through the beginning of first grade. It incorporates tests, checklists, and instructional components into one assessment system. In that sense it provides teachers a comprehensive tool for working with children ages 4 and 5.

The one component, the Early School Assessment, under review here is a good test featuring some imaginative approaches to listening skills, math concepts, and language. The coverage of a preschool and kindergarten curriculum is limited by the exclusion of social and natural environment. Although pictures of animals and social situations abound, the concepts measured have little to do with the pictured situations and dwell on distinctions between large and small, most and least, thin and thick, and the like. The social concept of "family" is not addressed even though a picture may show such a grouping.

Despite limitations, the ESA deserves consideration by early childhood educators who are attempting to wed the contrasting views of early childhood education as furthering the development of children, and those who view this period as one preparing them for more formal instruction.

[36]
Eating Disorder Inventory-2.
Purpose: Constructed as a self-report measure of psychological features commonly associated with anorexia nervosa and bulimia nervosa.
Population: Ages 12 and over.
Publication Dates: 1984–91.
Acronym: EDI.
Scores, 11: Drive for Thinness, Bulimia, Body Dissatisfaction, Ineffectiveness, Perfectionism, Interpersonal Distrust, Interoceptive Awareness, Maturity Fears, Asceticism (provisional), Impulse Regulation (provisional), Social Insecurity (provisional).
Administration: Group or individual.
Price Data, 1994: $73 per complete kit including 25 item booklets, 25 symptom checklists, 25 answer sheets, 25 profile forms, and manual ('91, 74 pages); $16 per 25 item booklets; $16 per 25 symptom checklists; $16 per 25 answer sheets; $10 per 25 profile forms; $20 per manual.

Time: (20) minutes.
Comments: Computer version available.
Author: David M. Garner.
Publisher: Psychological Assessment Resources, Inc.
Cross References: See T4:847 (38 references); for a review of an earlier edition by Cabrini S. Swassing, see 10:100 (16 references).

Review of the Eating Disorder Inventory-2 by PHILIP ASH, Director, Ash, Blackstone and Cates, Blacksburg, VA:

The Eating Disorder Inventory-2 (EDI-2) is an expanded version of the Eating Disorder Inventory (EDI) introduced in 1983. It is a self-report measure of symptoms usually associated with anorexia nervosa (AN) and bulimia nervosa (BN). The EDI-2 retains the 64 items (grouped into eight scales) of the EDI and adds 27 new items in three provisional scales: Asceticism, Impulse Regulation, and Social Insecurity. The Inventory takes about 20 minutes to complete.

The EDI-2 package also includes the EDI Symptom Checklist (EDI-SC), a structured self-report inventory soliciting current and historical information about the client's eating-related and menstrual history. Users are advised to administer the EDI-SC along with the EDI-2 in clinical settings and other circumstances where detailed specific symptom occurrence and frequency are required. The EDI-SC takes about 10 minutes to complete.

The EDI-2 is supported by a very good manual that includes a 250+ items reference list, reflecting the growing volume of EDI and eating disorders research. Most of the data reported, however, derive from research limited to the original EDI scales.

Descriptive age and weight data are reported for groups of patients ($N = 782$) who took the original scales, later patient groups that took all 11 scales ($N = 107$), and a female college comparison group ($N = 205$). Eating disorder patients are divided into three subgroups: Anorexia Nervosa Restrictors (AN-R; $N = 129$); Anorexia Nervosa Bulimics (AN-B; $N = 103$); and Bulimia Nervosa (BN; $N = 657$). The 205-person Female College Comparison group mean age was 19.9 years. The eating disorder groups were somewhat older (AN-R, 23.5 yrs; AN-B, 24.4 yrs; BN, 24.6 yrs). Although the age differences were statistically significant, their implications for assessing the scale scores are not clear. Bulimia patients weighed (present weight as percent of average) as much as female college students (99.6% of average); anorexic patients weighed about a third less.

Percentile rank norms are provided for the 11 scales for the eating disorder patients combined, for each of the three eating disorder diagnostic groups, and a sample of nonpatient college females, for nonpatient college males, high school boys, high school girls, 11- to 18-year-old females (broken down into age subgroups) and, for the new scales, for a mixed male-female college student group.

Two sets of internal consistency reliability estimates for the original eight scales for the eating disorder samples yielded coefficients of .8 or higher. Estimates for nonpatient female comparison groups also yielded high coefficients, with about a third of the coefficients scattering below .80. The internal consistency of the scales is further demonstrated by item-total correlations for each of the 11 scales for the eating disorder group, ANs, and a female college sample. Item-total correlations are uniformly high, as is to be expected from the fairly high internal consistency reliability estimates. The item-total correlations are included, incorrectly I believe, in the discussion of validity. Neither test reliability estimates nor item-total coefficients speak to item or test validity.

Three test-retest studies for nonpatient (students, staff nurses) samples over intervals of 1 week, 3 weeks, and 1 year showed, for the 1 or 3-week interval, coefficients generally of .8 or higher. For the 1-year interval, over the eight scales the median was .57. Such shrinkage is to be expected. Test-retest data on eating disorder patients would also be desirable.

Three factor analyses substantially confirm the eight-scale structure of the original EDI for eating abuse patient samples; another study, however, on three nonpatient samples, yielded a three-factor solution into which most of the original scales collapsed. Apparently the meanings of the traits and constructs measured differ for eating disorder patients and for normals.

Data on the original eight-scale Inventory's validity for a variety of purposes is fairly extensive. The original development of the EDI involved item selection on the basis of a contrasted group's (patients versus female college student normals) design, which was followed by comparing clinicians' judgments with self-report patient profiles. For the provisional scales, mean differences between the eating disorders patients and the nonpatient college females were significant. Correlations between clinician ratings or other independent criteria and scores for these scales do not yet appear to be available. A degree of convergent validity is demonstrated by correlations between the original EDI scales and two other eating disorder

scales—EAT-26 (Garner, Olmsted, Bohr, & Garfinkel, 1982) and the Restraint scale (Herman & Polivy, 1975). Scores on the EDI correlated substantially with the scores yielded by both. Correlations between EDI scales and other personality instruments also yielded many positive correlations (from about -.08 to .76) indicating that the constructs measured by the EDI involve to some degree other personality characteristics not unique to eating disorders. Finally, a number of treatment outcome studies have shown that, particularly for those with good posttreatment outcomes, there tend to be significant intraindividual score changes in the favorable direction.

The manual author distinguishes between the formal diagnosis of an eating disorder and assessment of the severity of the symptomology that is frequently associated with it. The EDI should not be used alone, but as a first step in symptom-severity assessment. To establish the diagnosis, a clinical interview to determine if the client meets criteria for an eating disorder diagnosis as set forth in the *Diagnostic and Statistical Manual of Mental Disorders-III—Revised* (American Psychiatric Association, 1987), or the *International Classification of Diseases* (World Health Organization, 1987) should be undertaken.

Overall, the EDI-2 is a significant contribution to the assessment of eating disorders. The growing volume of research bespeaks its perceived usefulness. Although external validity is limited primarily to comparisons with college-age females, the EDI-2 can help expand clinical knowledge about eating disorders and associated personality attributes. Its use is recommended in that context.

REVIEWER'S REFERENCES

Herman, C. P., & Polivy, J. (1975). Anxiety, restraint and eating behavior. *Journal of Abnormal Psychology, 84,* 666-672.

Garner, D. M., Olmsted, M. P., Bohr, Y., & Garfinkel, P. E. (1982). The Eating Attitudes Test: Psychometric features and clinical correlates. *Psychological Medicine, 12,* 871-878.

American Psychiatric Association. (1987). *Diagnostic and statistical manual of mental disorders* (revised 3rd ed.). Washington, DC: American Psychiatric Association.

World Health Organization (WHO), Division of Mental Health. (1987). *International classification of diseases-10 (ICD-10).* Geneva, Switzerland: WHO.

Review of the Eating Disorder Inventory-2 by STEVEN SCHINKE, Professor, Columbia University School of Social Work, New York, NY:

The Eating Disorder Inventory (EDI-2) is a self-report measure of symptoms frequently related to anorexia nervosa or bulimia nervosa. As such, the EDI-2 was designed as an aid to forming a diagnosis and not as the exclusive basis for making a diagnosis. The original inventory consisted of three subscales assessing attitudes and behaviors concerning eating, weight, and shape (Drive for Thinness, Bulimia, Body Dissatisfaction), and five subscales tapping more generalized organizing constructs or psychological traits clinically relevant to eating disorders (Ineffectiveness, Perfection, Interpersonal Distrust, Interoceptive Awareness, Maturity Fears). The latest version of the EDI includes 27 more items tapping three new constructs: Asceticism, Impulse Regulation, and Social Insecurity.

The EDI-2 provides clinical information regarding the psychological and behavioral dimensions of eating disorders. The original subscales show appropriate content, criterion, convergent, and discriminant validity. Further, many of the findings from these earlier validation studies have been replicated by new research. The psychometric properties of the instrument are sound and the constructs measure symptom domains that have clinical utility.

The authors of the measure have evidence the EDI-2 is sensitive to clinical change and that it can play a valuable role in clinical evaluations of eating disorder patients. More research is needed to determine the clinical utility and predictive validity of the new subscales measuring Impulse Regulation and Social Insecurity.

Reliability coefficients for the EDI-2 scales are between .44 and .93. Test-retest reliability for EDIs administered one week apart to 70 student and staff nurses revealed coefficients of .79 to .95 for all subscales except Interoceptive Awareness. After 3 weeks, test-retest reliabilities for 70 nonpatient university undergraduates were all above .80, excluding Maturity Fears.

Psychiatrists, psychologists, and social workers who work with young women or men who are suspected or known to have eating disorders would benefit from using the EDI-2. For suspected eating disorders cases, the measure is useful for gathering information with current and historical diagnostic relevance. For known eating disorders cases, the measure can monitor constructs over treatment and deliver outcome data. Reliability and validity scores for the EDI-2 are good. The authors are careful to point out the limitations of the EDI-2. These limitations are mainly due to the instrument's reliance on self-report. Overall, the EDI-2 is an excellent clinical tool for assessing eating disorders.

[37]

Eby Gifted Behavior Index.

Purpose: Designed to identify students for gifted programming based on the use of gifted behaviors.

Population: Elementary and high school and college students.
Publication Date: 1989.
Scores, 8: General, Verbal, Math/Science/Problem-Solving, Musical, Visual/Spatial, Social/Leadership, Mechanical/Technical/Inventiveness, Product Rating.
Administration: Individual.
Price Data, 1991: $24.95 per complete kit including manual (16 pages).
Time: Administration time not reported.
Comments: Ratings by teachers; checklists may be used separately.
Author: Judy W. Eby.
Publisher: United/DOK Publishers.

Review of the Eby Gifted Behavior Index by LISA A. BLOOM, Assistant Professor of Special Education, Western Carolina University, Cullowhee, NC:

The Eby Gifted Behavior Index (EGBI) was developed by the author "to allow classroom teachers to observe and evaluate the extent to which [gifted] behaviors are used and demonstrated by students in six different content and talent areas" (manual, p. 1). It consists of a product rating scale that provides criteria for the evaluation of original works produced by students and seven gifted behavior checklists designed to identify gifted behavioral processes in general and in six talent fields: Verbal, Math/Science/Problem-Solving, Musical, Visual/Spatial, Social/Leadership, and Mechanical/Technical/Inventiveness.

The Product Rating Scale consists of 10 criteria for rating a target student product such as a written work or piece of artwork. Each criterion is to be rated on a scale from 1 to 5. The manual suggests that items be rated by examining a student product and observing the student in the process of creating the product or questioning the student about the process used to create the product. No sample questions are offered. Specific guidelines for completing the scale are not provided and rating criteria are subject to user judgment. The items for the Product Rating Scale are vague and intentionally generic so that any type of product can be evaluated. For example, the first criteria, perceptiveness, is defined as "Distinction between the important and unimportant elements of the topic or issue; Perception and use of subtle and mature patterns, connections and relationships" (Product Rating Scale, p. 1).

The gifted behavior checklists for the talent areas each consist of 10 gifted behavior descriptors. The general checklist consists of 20 items. Like the Product Rating Scale, the user is asked to rate student behavior on items in the seven checklists on a scale from 1–5. Ratings are based on observations of students. Again, detailed directions for completing the scale are not provided. Some of the descriptors such as "States mechanical goal and plans for reaching it" are more observable than others, for example "Understands the relationships of parts to the whole" (Mechanical/Technical/Inventiveness Checklist).

The product checklist and behavior checklists are scored by totaling the ratings from each criteria. Each behavior checklist also has a space for describing recent products seen by the rater. A sample student matrix for summarizing results is provided. The matrix is, however, confusing. The directions for completing the matrix allude to weighting scores and combining them with scores on other measures but no instructions for doing so are provided. Ranges of scores to use in considering students for gifted programs are recommended but are not empirically based.

Information on the reliability of the EGBI is not provided. Because of the subjective nature of the scoring procedures and the items, reliability may be a problem.

Albeit limited, the author does provide information on content and criterion-related validity. First, the author reports that content validity was established by having teachers with 5 or more years of experience teaching gifted students review the instruments. Revisions were made on each form until the teachers reached consensus. Second, criterion-related validity was established via a study with a small sample of 20 students from elementary school, high school, and college. Products from these students were rated by independent judges. These ratings were compared with the process and product ratings made by teachers using the EGBI. The teachers' ratings had an average correlation of +.46 with the independent judges' ratings. This study involved only two of the six talent areas, art and writing.

The author's rationale for developing this instrument is included in the manual. The author cites literature to support her view of gifted behavior as developmental and observable rather than unchanging. Although this notion can be supported by current literature, this instrument fails to provide a psychometrically sound instrument for identifying giftedness.

The EGBI is easy to administer despite the number of subjective judgments required. It also appears to be easy to score with the exception of the matrix. Because it is relatively easy to use, this instrument may be useful as a way to encourage teachers to look for signs of giftedness other than high grades.

However, because of its weak psychometric properties, the EGBI would be an inappropriate tool for screening, eligibility decisions, or evaluation of gifted students.

Review of the Eby Gifted Behavior Index by JEFFREY K. SMITH, Professor of Educational Psychology, Graduate School of Education, Rutgers, the State University, New Brunswick, NJ:

The Eby Gifted Behavior Index is a set of rating scales designed for classroom teachers to use in the assessment of student selection to gifted programs. No lower or upper bounds are given for age or grade level, but a validity study suggests the scales may be used from elementary school through college. The same set of scales is used for all students. There are seven scales for rating what the author calls gifted behavior. Six concern subject areas and a seventh is an overall rating (listed above). An eighth scale can be used for rating a product generated by a student. The seven behavior rating scales consist of 20 five-point Likert-type items. Two items are written for each of 10 behavioral variables that are argued to serve as the basis for the operational definition of gifted behavior. The 10 behavioral variables are: Perceptiveness, Active interaction with the environment, Reflectiveness, Persistence, Independence, Goal orientation, Originality, Productivity, Self-evaluation, and Communication of findings. Each of the six subject matter scales ask roughly the same set of questions, but slant them toward the content of interest, and the general scale poses the same statements fairly broadly. The Product Rating Scale uses just 10 Likert-type items. These items are basically summaries of the items in the general rating scale.

The strength of the materials reviewed for this assessment probably lies in the items themselves. They seem a fairly thorough delineation of a mainstream view of the desirable gifted child. That is, giftedness is portrayed here as the ability to find an important problem; work on it diligently, enthusiastically, and independently; generate new ideas for the problem and evaluate them; see the project through to a timely and high quality solution; and communicate one's ideas effectively. This conceptualization probably represents what many if not most educators want in gifted children and thereby meets a certain demand. Because the scales are summated and total scores are used, the whole package is necessary to be considered gifted. The student who daydreams, has trouble completing work, or does not communicate well may be out of luck no matter how creative or original his or her ideas are. This is a problem endemic to programs and identifying procedures; we want our gems polished, not in the rough. The child who consistently produces 3s and 4s on the scales will do better than a child producing 1s and 5s. The administration manual provides ranges for children's performance and suggests who should and should not be in special programming. No data are presented to substantiate these claims. The administration manual also argues that the approach taken here is different from others in part because it views gifted behavior as developmental and the current view is that giftedness is static. This is not an accurate depiction of the field nor is there anything about this measure that is inherently more developmental than other measures.

No reliability data of any type are presented for the scales. This is a particular problem for a measure that relies heavily upon teachers' impressions of students. There is a small validity section that presents generally positive results from a criterion-related study in the areas of art and writing at the elementary, high school, and college levels. Means and standard deviations are not presented for the study; only correlations can be evaluated.

The Eby Gifted Behavior Index contains a reasonable set of Likert-type items for quantifying behaviors associated with giftedness. The technical data provided are quite inadequate and the writing in the administration manual substantially oversells the measure. In the absence of more substantial documentation it is not possible to recommend this measure for use in schools.

[38]

ECOScales.

Purpose: Designed "for assessing the interactive and communicative skills of preconversational children and their adult caregivers."
Population: Delayed child-significant adult dyads.
Publication Date: 1989.
Scores: Ratings on behaviors in 5 areas of competencies: Becoming Play Partners, Becoming Turntaking Partners, Becoming Communicating Partners, Becoming Language Partners, Becoming Conversation Partners.
Administration: Individual.
Price Data, 1991: $48.99 per complete kit including 24 ECOScales forms, 24 practice plans and records, and manual (141 pages); $15.93 per 24 ECOScales forms; $14.94 per 24 practice plans and records; $19.95 per manual.
Time: [10–30] minutes.
Comments: Ratings by professional based on observations and interview.

Authors: James D. MacDonald, Yvonne Gillette, and Thomas A. Hutchinson (manual).
Publisher: The Riverside Publishing Co.

Review of the ECOScales by ALLEN JACK EDWARDS, Professor of Psychology, Southwest Missouri State University, Springfield, MO:

The Ecological Communication (ECO) Scales are based on a model that proposes assessment of interaction and conversation between children and adults (in dyadic relationships). The data recorded from observation of the dyad may be used for describing the child's performance level. This result permits program planning where performance shows deficiencies and subsequent monitoring of progress. The Scales may be used on a single instance or multiple occasions. If communication training is needed, additional volumes may be purchased to assist in the effort. Because the purpose of this review is to judge the qualities of the test alone, only the ECOScales will be considered.

As the authors point out (p. 93 of the manual), the ECOScales are not, strictly speaking, a test. Indeed, they also state the manual is not a test manual (p. v). These statements are valid because the intent is much more than to measure the degree (or presence) of a behavior at a point in time. The "score" attained is to serve as a guide to develop means of helping adults and children (who are "delayed" in communication) become more functional both as social interacters and in communication. The authors are to be commended for their forthright description of purposes and rationale at the same time they employ standard reliability and validity criteria within the limits to which they apply to the scales. These "limits" deal principally with situations where inferences are made about dyadic interactions, and decisions arrived at based on those inferences (p. 93).

The scale evolved through several channels. There was the usual literature review, several parent-child interaction studies, and longitudinal programs developed for clinical intervention with parent and child. There are 40 behaviors rated on a scale of 1 (low) to 9 (high) by the observer. These are classified into five categories (Play, Turntaking, Communicating, Language, and Conversation). The result represents what is called the Competencies Profile. Within each category, there is one (or more) behavior used to plot an Interaction Profile (Interactive Goals, Child Goals, Adult Strategies, and Problems). Thus, the 40 items serve both for assessment and for potential intervention. A Practice Plan and Record is provided both for recording parent interactions and objectives.

The ECOScales form may be used to record multiple observations for the same dyad.

VALIDITY. One evidence of validity for the scales involved videotape samples made at different times in the process, yielding five observations. There was no significant change between the two observations before treatment, significant change during treatment, with maintenance of gains in the post-treatment phase of one month. The authors state that these results testify to the effectiveness of ECO intervention as well as the validity of the Scales in measuring both status and change. Although one might wish a longer period than one month post-treatment, the data are supportive of the claims.

Concurrent validity was computed by comparison to an index of a child's language development based on an interview with the parent or other significant person in the life of the child (Receptive-Expressive Emergent Language Scale: For the Measurement of Language Skills in Infancy [REEL], Bzoch & League, 1979; reviewed in 8:956 and revision to be reviewed in the *12th MMY*). The REEL was administered before treatment, with the mean indices correlated with means from "selected" (not specified) Interaction ratings and Competency ratings during the pretreatment, treatment, and post conditions. Thirty of 40 coefficients met the minimum criterion ($r = .40$ or greater) on the Interaction scales; 34 of 40 on the Competencies scales.

The authors also have presented data about intercorrelations on both Competencies and Interactions. The results indicate that relationships for the same scale on two occasions are lower than between different scales on a single occasion. Thus, the correlation for Language at Time 1 and Language at Time 2 is lower, for example, than between Language at Time 1 and Conversation at Time 1. This would indicate, where the divergence is large enough, that changes are occurring in Language competence that influence the degree of relationship. The authors table these values and imply that the results are pertinent to demonstrating validity for the *treatment* (i.e., intervention directed at Language competence, in this example). However, they do not present analyses which would justify that other than chance variables are responsible.

Overall, the evidence for validity—though explicitly presented—is marginal.

RELIABILITY. Four sources are presented to indicate reliability of the Scales. First is interjudge agreement, using two raters trained specifically to rate behaviors to a criterion developed for the program. Videotape segments of dyadic relationships were used in the experimental condition, with the raters compared for percent agreement between ratings. Unfortunately, details of the results are published in a separate volume, not available to this reviewer.

A second expression of reliability is described by the authors as "stability." They follow the procedures usually employed: correlation of performance over time when change is not expected (test-retest). The larger the coefficient under these circumstances, the greater the probability the test has adequate consistency to warrant its use. Comparing pretreatment conditions, during which change would not be expected, they report coefficients (rs) that support the position of stability. Of the nine rs, eight are statistically significant, but range in magnitude only from .47 to .86. Although test-retest coefficients may be attenuated by various factors (depending in part upon time interval between testings), the values reported are not very impressive.

Of greater concern is the interpretation of results for the one-month period between the end of treatment and follow-up. Here, rs were statistically significant in seven of nine comparisons, with a range from .31 to .72. Generally, these values were lower than the pretreatment coefficients. The point may be made that there was apparently less stability for this latter period than for the former. Without stating so explicitly, the authors leave the impression this suggests that the treatment effects continue to exert positive effects. Such may be the case, but there are other possible reasons, and any conclusion should be guarded considering that four of the nine comparisons favor pretreatment "low" stability over post-treatment.

Cronbach's alpha (a method of estimating the average of all possible split-half comparisons within a test) was used to compute internal consistency. The values are reported for the pretreatment and post-treatment evaluations separately, and in most cases are in the .80s and .90s, signifying good to excellent reliability.

Finally, the standard error of measurement (an estimate of the limits around an obtained score within which repeated measurements would yield scores) was computed using the results of Cronbach's alpha. These values are tabled, with the authors suggesting that any obtained score be considered in terms of a 95% probability level (about 2 *SEm*s generally).

Overall, reliability would seem to be fair to good.

EVALUATION. From a conventional measurement viewpoint, the ECOScales must be considered marginal in meeting criteria of adequacy. Whether it should be considered a "test" at all, and consequently whether the accepted measurement principles are appropriate, is debatable.

REVIEWER'S REFERENCE

Bzoch, K. R., & League, R. (1970). The Receptive-Expressive Emergent Language Scale: For the Measurement of Language Skills in Infancy. Gainesville, FL: The Tree of Life Press.

Review of the ECOScales by CATHY TELZROW, Psychologist and Director, Educational Assessment Project, Cuyahoga Special Education Service Center, Cleveland, OH:

The ECOScales incorporates an ecological approach to the assessment of children's social communication. Designed primarily for use with populations of young children who are nonverbal or who have significant disorders in interactive communication, the ECOScales results in a description of the behavior of both the target child and the adult communication partner. Unlike traditional, norm-referenced tests that provide a measure of a child's relative performance but typically offer few insights regarding remediation, the ECOScales is designed as an intervention planning tool. Thus, the instrument not only identifies the competencies and deficits of the target child's communication, but also analyzes the interactive ecology of the dyadic relationship.

The ECOScales is the assessment component of a comprehensive model of communication enhancement for persons with developmental disabilities. Other components mentioned in the ECOScales manual include a developmental guide that describes the author's model; a case book, designed to illustrate application of the models in intervention settings; and video resources illustrating the effects of these interventions in a pre-post treatment format.

The ECOScales employs structured observation and interview to assess five broad competencies: social play, turn taking, communication, language, and conversation. The ECOScales manual describes each of these competencies in detail, offering important distinctions among the apparently similar dimensions of communication, language, and conversation. As is clearly evident from this list of competencies, the authors emphasize the social interactive and pragmatic aspects of communication rather than the phonological, syntactical, or semantic characteristics common to traditional language-based assessments.

The ECOScales manual provides cursory guidelines for structuring assessment observations. These guidelines include a brief description of the context (e.g., play with people only, play with people and objects/toys), sample instructions, and possible objects/toys to be used during observations. In addition, the manual provides guidelines about conducting a "post observation validity check" (querying the adult regarding the generalizability of the behaviors observed) and an interview to further assess the communication dyad. In the judgment of this reviewer, these guidelines are vague and incomplete, particularly for practitioners without a strong foundation in both social-interactive communication and ecological assessment. Although sample interview questions are included in the manual's appendix, the authors caution that these are offered "as guides to discovering what the adult knows and feels about the child's social and communicative skills" (p. 124), and should be used only to supplement observations. Finally, the ECOScales incorporates a "trainability" assessment, perhaps best conceptualized as assessment for intervention planning. Once again, the authors offer general guidelines for conducting this portion of the assessment, but note, "because your success in assessing trainability will depend on your skills in interacting and communicating with children, there is no set regimen for this process" (p. 15).

The ECOScales scoring employs clinician ratings determined from the observations and interviews described above. True to their ecological philosophy, ratings are assigned to adult communicative strategies and the interactive process as well as to specific child characteristics. The instructions direct the observer to assign ratings from 1 to 9 to each of the ECOScale behaviors. General guidelines for assigning numerical ratings are offered, but these require interpretation of evaluative terms such as "poor," "inappropriate," "fair," and "almost appropriate." Furthermore, these descriptors are assigned to pairs of ratings, thus offering observers no means of differentiating between a rating of 1 or 2, 3 or 4, etc. Scores can be summarized on two profiles, one organized by the five communicative competencies, and one according to the interactive element (i.e., interactive goals, child goals, adult strategies, and problems). The latter profile, in particular, is helpful in directing ecologically based interventions. Finally, total ratings from each of the four interaction scales and each of the five competencies can be recorded on a summary table to facilitate repeated measurements as part of a treatment program.

Evaluating the technical properties of a non-normative assessment measure, particularly one that utilizes an ecological approach, is extraordinarily complex. The ECOScales manual includes a chapter that provides a thorough, scholarly discussion of this topic. Item selection was directed by the literature, by the authors' work in clinical and research settings, and by peer reviews in teaching and clinical contexts. Conclusions regarding the validity of the ECOScales are derived from a single study involving 25 parent-child dyads in which a 34-item version of the instrument was used before, during, and following intervention. Results of this treatment-effects study offer support for the construct validity of the instrument (i.e., sensitive to treatment effects). Concurrent validity is indicated by moderately high correlations with the Receptive-Expressive Emergent Language Scale (REEL; Bzoch & League, 1970) for this population across several administrations. Interrater agreement figures are reported as one measure of reliability; when compared with criterion ratings performed by one of the ECOScales developers, average percentage agreements ranged from approximately 81 to 93. Internal consistency reliability coefficients ranged from the low 70s to the high 90s.

In summary, the ECOScales offers a systematic means of conducting ecological assessments of the communication of persons who are nonverbal or who have significant interactive deficits. The measure has a strong foundation in both research and clinical practice. The manual is not sufficiently explicit regarding the conditions for structuring and recording observations for the novice clinician; thus, use of this procedure is best reserved for individuals who have training and experience in social-interactive communication, in clinical interviewing, and in ecological assessment. When employed by such individuals, the ECOScales offers a unique system for describing the present context of interaction, for helping to target and structure ecological interventions, and for monitoring progress over time.

REVIEWER'S REFERENCE

Bzoch, K. R., & League, R. (1970). The Receptive-Expressive Emergent Language Scale: For the Measurement of Language Skills in Infancy. Gainesville, FL: The Tree of Life Press.

[39]
Evaluating Movement and Posture Disorganization in Dyspraxic Children.

Purpose: Designed to determine and analyze the normal and disorganized components of movement and posture.
Population: Learning disabled children ages 5 and above.
Publication Date: 1989.
Scores, 2: Quality Performance List, Problem Performance List.
Subtests, 10: Supine to Stand, Supine to Flexion Hold, Prone Reach, Alternating Prone Reach, Kneel-Walk Forward and Back, Alternating One Foot Kneel, Alternating Half Kneel-Stand, One-Foot Balance, Squat Pick-up, Unilateral/Bilateral Toss.

Administration: Individual.
Price Data, 1993: $89 per 5 manuals (52 pages) and analysis of movement and posture disorganization (VHS videotape); $16.95 per 5 manuals.
Time: (45) minutes for subtests; (30) minutes for videotape.
Comments: "Criteria-referenced" test; full-color videotape shows examples of normal and disorganized movement responses for each subtest.
Author: W. Michael Magrun.
Publisher: Therapy Skill Builders.

Review of Evaluating Movement and Posture Disorganization in Dyspraxic Children by RANDY W. KAMPHAUS, Associate Professor of Educational Psychology, University of Georgia, Athens, GA:

A few sentences from the preface of the manual sum up well the strengths and weaknesses of the instrument. According to the manual, this is a "criteria-based referenced test for the evaluation of quality movement components and disorganized compensations. The test is designed to be used for evaluating incoordination or dyspraxia in learning disabled children who demonstrate soft neurological signs of motor clumsiness. The test criteria are based on subjective analysis of normal movement and postural components" (p. ii).

The first stated objective to develop a criteria-referenced test of motor movements seems to be the most clearly met of the test development objectives. The authors seemingly expended considerable effort in developing subtests and scoring criteria. The videotape is extremely helpful in this regard allowing examiners to develop a detailed understanding of a child's motor behavior.

The second objective regarding the assessment of dyspraxia in learning-disabled children is not supported by any information in the test manual. The manual does not include any validity evidence demonstrating the ability of this measure to differentiate learning-disabled children from other populations of exceptional children or among subtypes of learning disabilities. Most importantly, epidemiological data on the frequency of motor difficulties among learning disabled children are not presented in the manual. Hence, there is no compelling reason given for why children with learning disabilities should be the intended audience. This statement leads to many questions. Why not use this test with dyspraxic children with other etiologies such as traumatic injuries? According to the *Standards for Educational and Psychological Testing* (AERA, APA, & NCME, 1985), validity evidence should be presented for various interpretations of an assessment device. No validity evidence supporting use of the measure with learning-disabled children is given. This central premise regarding the utility of the measure with learning-disabled children is therefore highly questionable.

A similarly questionable test development practice is the development of test criteria that are based on subjective analysis. Subjective analysis or the use of content experts to define content domains and design item blueprints is a common and wise practice for many test development activities. There is no information in this manual, however, to suggest that any content input was provided by individuals other than the test author. Although the advantages of criteria referencing are extolled in the manual, the specific methods for devising this referencing are not provided. Most importantly, the degree to which the items, subtests, and scoring criteria are supported by experts in the field is not known.

Several aspects of the scale are laudable. The differentiation between level and quality of performance is an important distinction that is often not available in assessment instruments. Although the administration of the scoring instrument at first appears difficult to master, the videotape is extremely helpful. In fact, it is absolutely crucial for proper examiner training.

Although not pretending to be a norm-referenced measure, the instrument should show some evidence of reliability. At the very least, an estimate of interrater or interscorer reliability would be appropriate.

The manual, at times, is difficult to comprehend, and often seems to use "technobabble" that hinders direct communication with the reader. Language in the manual could also be identified as sexist as is indicated in the following quote: "Movement and posture are man's demonstrative tools" (p. 1).

In summary, in many ways the concept of this scale is a good one. One can see how the subtests are designed to assess qualitative aspects of motor behavior. The execution, however, of the test development goals is so suspect as to make the test unusable without some evidence of reliability and validity. The notion that this test is applicable to learning-disabled children above and beyond other populations is not supported in any way in the test manual. This test is in conflict with the *Test Standards* in that sufficient validation is not provided for even the most basic interpretation(s) of the measure. The test cannot be used with confidence until such evidence becomes available.

REVIEWER'S REFERENCE

American Educational Research Association, American Psychological Association, & National Council on Measurement in Education.

(1985). *Standards for educational and psychological testing.* Washington, DC: American Psychological Association, Inc.

Review of Evaluating Movement and Posture Disorganization in Dyspraxic Children by BARBARA A. ROTHLISBERG, Associate Professor of Psychology in Educational Psychology and School Psychology I Program Director, Ball State University, Muncie, IN:

Dyspraxia, or impairment in the production of voluntary movement, is a less comprehensive dysfunction than its "parent" disorder, apraxia. The term apraxia evolved from the concept that certain voluntary motor acts had associated with them higher mental functions. Thus, voluntary motor behaviors are the result of a mental representation of the behavior and the consequent observed motor sequence the representation evokes (Luria, 1980). Given the complexity and variety of motor functions, different forms of apraxia have been proposed, ranging from those focusing on gross to fine motor sequences of movement. Typically, evaluations of apraxic behavior concentrate on the individual's ability to reproduce or imitate a series of learned movements of the face and limbs, including gestures and the use of common tools (Lezak, 1983). In situations of equivocal neurological involvement, dyspraxic behavior has been defined by the impairment, but not total loss, of motor fluency.

Evaluating Movement and Posture Disorganization in Dyspraxic Children presents itself as a criteria-based format from which teachers, psychologists, and other health professionals can gather insights into the movement patterns of dyspraxic children (including the learning disabled) and thereby provide a more integrated therapy program. The 10 subtests (e.g., Supine to Stand, Supine to Flexion Hold, etc.), developed based on subjective analysis of motor clumsiness, are designed to provide the observer with the "parameters necessary for skilled performance" (manual, p. 4). Normal 6-year-old children are claimed to be able to easily perform each of the developmental movement sequences. An accompanying videotape (*Analysis of Movement and Posture Disorganization*) offers examples of both skilled and disorganized motor performances.

The administrative procedure for each of the subtests is probably the easiest part of the evaluative process. The clinician or therapist simply demonstrates the motor sequence for the child and then asks the child to imitate the movements. Three attempts may be made by the examinee to determine whether performance improves or declines with practice. The therapist has the option of computing subtest scores based on the average of all trials or of counting only one of the attempts. Given the nature of the subtests (i.e., the analysis of motor sequences), it is suggested in the manual that the child's performance be videotaped for more careful analysis.

To score each subtest, the therapist must evaluate the quality of the child's reproduction based on the subjective evaluation of his/her starting position, movement initiation, transitional phase, and final position. This will be a difficult process for those individuals unfamiliar both with movement disorders and with the terminology common to occupational or physiological therapists (e.g., flexion, hyperextension, anterior, etc.). Movements are to be separated and quantified for each subtest into two lists: quality of performance and problem performance. The checklists consist of sets of movement criteria which the test author suggests are standards of adequate performance. Quality performance criteria are intended to allow the clinician to determine which components of the movement sequence the child has successfully completed. Successes are noted by placing a "Y" (yes) next to the appropriate criterion listed. An "N" (no) indicates that all or some portion of that criterion is immature. If an "N" appears on the quality checklist, the clinician then refers to the problem performance list, where movement components or criterion are further subdivided into subcomponents. The presence of difficulty, as detailed on the problem performance list, suggests what aspect of the given subtest will demand remediation.

Components of movement on the quality performance list are awarded up to one point for successful production; partial credit is awarded if only selected subcomponents have been mastered. For example, on Subtest 1: Supine to Stand, Criterion 6 on the quality performance list is "Are child's arms relaxed and hands open?" If "no" is answered, the therapist refers to the problem performance list which breaks down Criterion 6 into 6a "Are elbows flexed?" and 6b "Are hands fisted?" If the child shows only one of the problems, he/she is awarded ".5" for partial difficulty on the problem list); if both problem criterion are presented, "0" points are awarded on the quality performance list with the "1" point appearing on the problem performance list. Each criterion can have assigned to it a different number of subcomponents and each subcomponent is worth a fraction of one point based on the number of subcomponents present. Likewise, subtests vary in the number of quality performance criteria involved. For instance, Unilateral/Bilateral Ball Toss lists only 3 quality performance criteria whereas Alternating Prone Reach offers 16 criteria. In addition, therapists are encouraged to modify the criteria for the subtests to meet their particular needs. A scoring example for Subtest 1 is given in the manual to help clarify the complicated scoring procedure.

Although the evaluation system supposedly is appropriate for a wide audience, it appeared to this reviewer to be specialized for therapists well versed in movement disorders. The quality and performance lists employ terms that would have little meaning to nonprofessionals. For example, "Does R foot show dorsiflex or toes used for push off?" (Problem list-5e for Subtest 7: Alternating Half Kneel-Stand) or "Does child lean over L and abduct R leg?" (Problem list-5a for Subtest 8: One Foot Balance) obviously include specialized vocabulary. Use of the video to clarify understanding of movement sequences is limited by the marginal quality of the filming and the lack of explanation of scoring procedures.

The intent of the convoluted scoring system is to make it possible for the clinician to obtain a total quality score (TQS)—the sum of all points and partial points earned for performance—and a total problem score (TPS)—the sum of all total and partial points given on the problem performance list. A "percent of disorganization for each subtest" can then be computed by dividing the TPS for each subtest by the maximum possible score (MS) for that subtest. A cumulative percentage of disorganization can also be determined by dividing the cumulative TPS by the cumulative MS. Such a scoring procedure is claimed to offer the clinician a mechanism through which improvements in performance can be documented and reviewed, but may only confuse the teacher or therapist uninitiated to this type of assessment. Even those individuals who may believe they understand the scoring may be at a loss as to the benefits such movement information provides.

Unfortunately, the lack of evident rationale for Evaluating Movement and Posture Disorganization in Dyspraxic Children creates difficulties for the user in his/her attempts to determine if the evaluation system is set on a strong theoretical or experiential base. No background information on the construct of dyspraxia is provided nor is it explained how the 10 subtests were derived as key areas for evaluation and treatment. A brief introductory narrative on the evaluation system makes only oblique references to quality of movement and the "postural control and a delicate balance of dissociated integration" (manual, p. 1) needed for each motor sequence. Although neuropsychology texts may stress the fine motor aspects of apraxia in evaluation of motor skill (see, for example, Lezak, 1983 or Luria, 1980) the subtests included in this measure seemed to focus only upon gross motor incoordination and balance and did not even acknowledge fine motor activities! Thus, the association of dyspraxic behavior to specific learning disabilities was never explored—leaving the reviewer to wonder about the long term utility of such a system.

Without a knowledge base from which to judge the components of the evaluation system, the user must take on faith the claims of the system's author. No norms or references established the claim that average 6-year-olds can complete the motor sequences; no checks on the reliability or the validity for the subtests were offered. In addition, no direction was given to aid in planning any remedial strategy. Given the fact the measure suggests itself as appropriate for and benefiting teachers and psychologists in their understanding of dyspraxic children, such oversights severely curtail the type of information this instrument can provide to someone not specifically trained in the evaluation of movement disorders. Indeed, it is questionable what purpose would be served by using the scoring criteria unless one had an extensive occupational therapy background.

In summary, Evaluating Movement and Posture Disorganization in Dyspraxic Children may be a reasonable scoring system for occupational therapists who are well versed in the terminology and knowledge base of their discipline, but of extremely restricted benefit to teachers, psychologists, and other health care workers who have limited experience with gross motor skill development. Lack of both a conceptual knowledge base and the documented utility of the evaluation criteria make the instrument of questionable value to the clinical community at-large in rehabilitating dyspraxic children.

REVIEWER'S REFERENCES

Luria, A. R. (1980). *Higher cortical functions in man* (2nd ed.). New York: Basic Books.
Lezak, M. D. (1983). *Neuropsychological assessment* (2nd ed.). New York: Oxford University Press.

[40]

Executive Profile Survey.

Purpose: Constructed to assess "self-attitudes, self-beliefs, and value patterns" needed for executive-level jobs.
Population: Prospective executives.
Publication Dates: 1947–83.
Scores, 11 dimensions: Ambitious, Assertive, Enthusiastic, Creative, Spontaneous, Self-Focused, Considerate, Open-Minded, Relaxed, Practical, Systematic.
Administration: Group or individual.

Price Data, 1994: $25 per 25 reusable test booklets; $18 per manual ('83, 82 pages); $36.75 per introductory kit.
Time: (60) minutes.
Comments: Self-administered; manual title is Perspectives on the Executive Personality.
Authors: Virgil R. Lang and Samuel E. Krug (manual).
Publisher: Institute for Personality and Ability Testing, Inc.
Cross References: For a review by William I. Sauser, Jr., see 9:401.

Review of the Executive Profile Survey by S. DAVID KRISKA, Personnel Psychologist, City of Columbus, Columbus, OH:

The Executive Profile Survey (EPS) measures 11 dimensions related to the occupational self-concept of top-level executives. The EPS is theoretically based on David Riesman's (*The Lonely Crowd*) inner/other-directed orientations, Erich Fromm's (*Man for Himself*) descriptions of marketing, hoarding, receptive, and exploitive orientations, and Charles Morris's (*Varieties of Human Values*) identification of 13 distinctive life styles.

The 11 profile dimensions on which the EPS is scored are entitled: Ambitious, Assertive, Enthusiastic, Creative, Spontaneous, Self-Focused, Considerate, Open-Minded, Relaxed, Practical, and Systematic. In addition, there are two validity scales to identify faking good and responding randomly. The 94 items on the EPS are usually answered within a hour and with minimal supervision.

The first section includes 13 paragraphs test takers must read and judge whether they like or dislike the lifestyle described in the passage. The second section includes 33 statements and test takers decide how well each describes themselves. The last section includes 48 adjectives test takers judge as either true or false about themselves.

The response forms are scored by the publisher and the results report, including percentile scores and descriptions of high scores for each dimension, is quickly returned to the user. The user must establish his or her credentials with IPAT (the publisher) prior to obtaining the EPS. The development of the EPS spanned more than 10 years and included the testing of approximately 2,000 executives from a variety of businesses. The current form was published in 1978.

Factor analytic results support the development of the 11 dimensions and provide construct validity evidence. A comparison involving the 1,768 executives surveyed in 1966 and again in 1972 resulted in factor congruence statistics ranging from .61 to .88. The users' manual also includes scale reliabilities that range from .81 to .90. The validity evidence presented in the users' manual also includes several pages of correlations with scales of the 16PF, California Psychological Inventory (CPI), Edwards Personal Preference Schedule, and the Adjective Checklist. In general, the correlations are as expected in terms of signs of correlations, pattern of significant correlations, and magnitude of correlations. Many of the correlations between scales of the EPS and scales of other instruments are greater than .40 and range up to .71 for the EPS Systematic dimension with the Self-Description Inventory Orderly dimension. Further validity evidence is provided by a multiple discriminant function analysis of almost 2,000 executives. This analysis shows that the EPS differentiated executives from 29 different occupations. For example, an executive from a giant advertising agency has a profile different from that of a president of a large bank. The users' manual also includes correlations of EPS scales with job performance of bank presidents. The performance indicators include measures of responsibility, income, and tenure. All of the EPS scales, except the Relaxed dimension, correlate significantly with at least one of the performance indicators.

The data base for the EPS is based on 1,992 male executives surveyed between 1966 and 1976. The sampling plan itself was carefully executed and includes individuals from all 50 states. Although carefully conducted, the sampling is cause for concern. The data base for score reporting norms includes information that is over 20 years old, and is lacking in race and sex information. A user concerned about glass ceilings needs to obtain more information about this instrument than is contained in the manual. Moreover, because only executives are included in the sample, evidence of how well the EPS distinguishes executives from other professionals is lacking. The manual does include results showing executives respond differently than college students, but the obvious confounding with age makes these results less useful than a comparison of similarly aged people.

In summary, the EPS is a useful instrument for examining an individual's personality. The construct validity evidence regarding the 11 dimensions is sound. However, although the EPS promotional literature claims it can be used to select an individual with executive abilities, the users' manual does not present the results to support the claim.

Review of the Executive Profile Survey by GREGORY J. MARCHANT, Associate Professor of Educational Psychology, Ball State University, Muncie, IN:

The Executive Profile Survey is a well-developed instrument designed to yield scores on 11 dimensions relative to successful executives. The instrument is composed of three parts. The first part contains 13 short paragraphs describing life styles, which the respondent must rate on a 1 to 7 scale of desirability. The second part of the instrument requires basically a yes, no, or uncertain response to 33 statements. In the third part, the respondent must decide how applicable 48 adjectives are on a 7-point scale. The 94-item questionnaire usually takes less than one hour to complete, and the results are computer scored and a computer-generated report is processed by the company.

The social psychological basis for the instrument rests in the 1950s. The original 69-item questionnaire was designed and pilot tested in 1961, and in 1966 the responses from 666 executives were factor analyzed. Eleven of the 17 factors produced by the 1966 study and a 1972 analysis demonstrated clear matches and were used as dimensions. The dimensions for the instrument are factor scores obtained by multiplying each item by its factor weight for each factor. For the latest version of the instrument (1983) the names of the 11 dimensions were changed from the 1978 version, but the scales and their scoring remain the same. The 11 dimensions are: Ambitious, Assertive, Enthusiastic, Creative, Spontaneous, Self-Focused, Considerate, Open-Minded, Relaxed, Practical, and Systematic. The dimensions have demonstrated good reliability (consistency estimates > .81).

A major study using the instrument was conducted in 1972. This study included Fortune 500 chief executive officers ($n = 90$), newspaper editors ($n = 145$), executives with a Harvard MBA ($n = 114$), college and university presidents ($n = 173$), and business school deans ($n = 42$). Some small studies were conducted between 1972 and 1974, and the instrument was revised again for a study conducted in 1978. For the 1978 study, 25 items were added to provide two validity and verification scales. A computer program was created to conduct a sophisticated analysis of each individual's responses relative to the 2,000 executives accumulated in the data base. The validity scales allow for a test of faking perceived good characteristics and the computer analysis adjusts for this.

Some validity estimates such as correlations with other instruments are presented in the manual; however, the ultimate validity of the instrument would rest in its ability to discern the characteristics of successful executives from unsuccessful ones or even from a nonexecutive sample. Although some relations between the dimensions and income and number of exployees were reported, no study using the instrument was identified in the manual or by a computer literature search that clearly distinguished "successful" executives.

The way in which the respondents' results are interpreted is unclear and problematic. The respondent's raw score on each dimension is converted to a percentile rank based on the total executive sample. For example, an individual could score at the 69th percentile on the Considerate dimension. The score is above "average," but is it high enough or too high? The computer report would probably describe the individual as "high" on the dimension, but how high is too high? Can an executive be too considerate? (See Kaplan, 1990 for a discussion of taking ambition to extremes to the point of being counterproductive.) One would need to consult the manual for assistance. There one could find tables of information for comparison based on subsamples. For instance, based on the 1966 data from presidents of banks with deposits between $100,000,000 and $500,000,000 the respondent would be too considerate compared to the 26th percentile rank of the sample ($n = 129$). However, the individual would be just considerate enough based on the 1972 data from presidents of banks with deposits between $9,000,000 and $10,000,000 ($n = 129$). Percentile ranks on dimensions changed by as much as 25 from the 1966 data to the 1972 data for the same sample category. This suggests that interpretation of an individual's score represents an effort to hit a moving target based on occupational setting, company, sex, time, and perhaps many other variables.

The change in the previously mentioned scores points to another problem in using the current version of the instrument. If a percentile rank on a dimension can change by as much as 25 over a 6-year period, what could have happened after more than 20 years? Ross and Unwalla (1988) found that characteristics associated with upward mobility have changed in recent years based on a comparison of 1952 and 1982 survey data on corporate executives. It is quite likely that the characteristics of successful executives have changed over the last 20 years and this change has not been reflected in the instrument.

In summary, the personality of an executive can play a major role in the success or failure of a business (McCarthy, 1992). The Executive Profile Survey is a well-documented instrument designed to assess characteristics of executives along 11 dimensions. However, the instrument uses constructs established over 20 years ago and compares individuals to a sample of successful executives most of whom were surveyed over 20 years ago. There appear to be many variables influencing the desirability of a particular score on a dimension such that it would be difficult to make personnel judgements based on the information from the instrument. Further research using the instrument on an updated data set is recommended.

REVIEWER'S REFERENCES

Ross, J. E., & Unwalla, D. (1988). Making it to the top: A 30-year perspective. *Personnel, 65*(4), 70-78.

Kaplan, R. E. (1990). The expansive executive: How the drive to mastery helps and hinders organizations. *Human Resource Management, 29*(3), 307-326.

McCarthy, J. L. (1992, January). Special skills needed to spearhead a turnaround. *American Banker, 157*(11), 6.

[41]
Family Environment Scale, Second Edition.

Purpose: Developed to "measure the social-environmental characteristics of all types of families."

Population: Family members.

Publication Dates: 1974–86.

Acronym: FES.

Scores, 10: Cohesion, Expressiveness, Conflict, Independence, Achievement Orientation, Intellectual-Cultural Orientation, Active-Recreational Orientation, Moral-Religious Emphasis, Organization, Control.

Administration: Group.

Editions, 3: Real (R), Ideal (I), Expectations (E).

Price Data, 1992: $15 per 25 Form R test booklets; $16 per 25 test booklets (select Form I or Form E); $10 per 50 answer sheets; $15 per 25 self-scorable answer sheets; $7 per set of scoring stencils; $8 per 50 profiles; $80 per prepaid narrative; $15 per 25 interpretive report forms; $13 per manual ('86, 68 pages); $19 per specimen set.

Time: [15–20] minutes.

Comments: A part of the Social Climate Scales (T4:2495).

Authors: Rudolf H. Moos and Bernice S. Moos (manual).

Publisher: Consulting Psychologists Press, Inc.

Cross References: See T4:961 (136 references); for reviews by Nancy A. Busch-Rossnagel and Nadine M. Lambert of an earlier edition, see 9:408 (18 references); see also T3:872 (14 references); for a review by Philip H. Dreyer, see 8:557 (4 references). For a review of the Social Climate Series, see 8:681.

Review of the Family Environment Scale, Second Edition by JULIE A. ALLISON, Assistant Professor of Psychology, Pittsburg State University, Pittsburg, KS:

The Family Environment Scale, Second Edition (FES) was developed to measure social and environmental characteristics of families. The scale is based on a three-dimensional conceptualization of families. Each dimension includes related subscales. The Relationship dimension includes measurements of Cohesion, Expressiveness, and Conflict. The Personal Growth dimension involves assessments of Independence, Achievement Orientation, Intellectual-Cultural Orientation, Active-Recreational Orientation, and Moral-Religious Emphasis. The System Maintenance dimension includes Organization and Control measures. Scores for each of these 10 subscales are derived to create an overall profile of family environment. Based on these scores, families are then grouped into one of three family environment typologies (which generally reflect the three underlying dimensions of the scale), based on their most salient characteristics. A measure of Family Incongruence may also be derived in order to examine the extent to which family members may agree or disagree about their family climate. Additionally, three separate forms of the FES are available that correspondingly measure different aspects of these dimensions. The Real Form (Form R) measures people's perceptions of their actual family environments. In contrast, the Ideal Form (Form I) rewords items to assess individuals' perceptions of their ideal family environment, whereas the Expectations Form (Form E) instructs respondents to indicate what they expect a family environment will be like under, for example, anticipated family changes.

Each of the subscales is represented by nine brief statements concerning family climate. Respondents are asked to make a dichotomous judgement about whether the statement is true or false about their family, resulting in 90-item scales. Inclusion of items into the FES was based on five psychometric criteria: "The overall item split should be as close to 50–50 as possible to avoid items characteristic only of unusual families" (p. 19), items should correlate more highly with their own subscale than any other, "each of the subscales should have an approximately equal number of items scored true and scored false" (p. 19), "the subscales should have low to moderate intercorrelations" (p. 19), and "each item (and each subscale) should discriminate among families" (p. 19). Each of these criteria was met in subsamples of a variety of different families. Internal consistency for each of the subscales ranged from moderately low (.61) to moderately high (.78). Additionally, acceptable evidence for test-retest reliability, and construct and discriminant validity has been found. Normative data on the Form R subscales are available

from a total of 1,625 different families (1,125 normal, 500 distressed), each of which came from a variety of sources. Normative data for Form I are available, but based on only 281 families, and should therefore be considered tentative.

Research applications of the FES are many and varied. The FES has been used to describe and compare different types of families (e.g., variations in family profile in abusive families), and to aid in the understanding of how different family social climates may develop (e.g., the effects of parental occupations, child-rearing attitudes and practices). The FES has also succeeded in aiding the understanding of how family environment may influence a family's successful adaptation to life transitions and crises. It has been included in studies investigating how family climate may affect children and their personal and social growth, as well as the psychosocial and health-related impact of family climate on adults. Finally, researchers have used the FES to help predict and measure treatment outcomes of psychiatric and alcoholic patients.

The FES is a viable approach to the study of family systems. Although the instrument should not be considered a comprehensive approach because of its primarily social nature, it would be a valuable complementary tool to researchers and practitioners alike.

Review of the Family Environment Scale, Second Edition by BRENDA H. LOYD, Professor of Education, University of Virginia, Charlottesville, VA:

The Family Environment Scale, Second Edition (FES) is a 90-item paper and pencil instrument that measures perceptions of family structure, orientation, and interactions. The 90 items are used to produce 10 subscales, representative of three domains of family environment. The three subscales of Cohesion, Expressiveness, and Conflict represent the Relationship domain. The six subscales of Independence, Achievement Orientation, Intellectual-Cultural Orientation, Active-Recreational Orientation, and Moral-Religious Emphasis represent the Personal Growth domain. The two subscales of Organization and Control represent the System Maintenance domain.

There are three different forms of the scale. Form R, the Real Form, is the form on which the normative data were gathered; this form receives the greatest emphasis and fullest interpretation in the test manual. Directions for the Real Form ask an individual to decide which of the statements are true of his or her family and which statements are false. Form I, the Ideal Form, presents the same statements as Form

R but uses future tense instead of present tense verbs. For the Ideal Form, individuals are asked to decide which statements are true of an ideal family and which are false. Form E, the Expectations form, presents the same statements as Form I, but asks an individual to decide what his or her family will be like and to determine which statements are true or false for this future family.

The administration and scoring of the instrument are, in general, clear and simple. The raw scores on the 10 subscales are computed in an efficient, straightforward manner. Calculating standard scores from raw scores is accomplished through a conversion table for Form R subscale scores. However, the mathematical derivation of the standard scores from raw scores is not clearly described in the manual and conversion tables are not provided for Form E and Form I. A Family Incongruence Score, derived from administration of the scale to more than one member of a family, is more difficult to compute, and a detailed example is provided in the manual. Standard scores corresponding to the Family Incongruence Scores are also presented in a conversion table; however, the derivation of these standard scores is not presented in the test manual.

RELIABILITY. Internal consistency reliability estimates for the Form R subscales range from .61 to .78. Intercorrelations among these 10 subscales range from -.53 to .45. These data suggest that the scales are measuring relatively distinct characteristics of family environment and with reasonable consistency. Although the internal consistency estimates are reasonable and the subscales could be used for determining differences between groups, for an individual's score the standard error of measurement should be taken into account. Scores for two individuals would need to differ by approximately 3 raw score points on most subscales to be sure that the difference was not due to measurement error. Similarly, when evaluating a profile, small differences should not be overinterpreted.

Estimates of Form R subscale stability across time are provided. Test-retest reliabilities for 2-month, 3-month, and 12-month intervals range from .52 to .91. These estimates suggest that the scale is reasonably stable across these time intervals. These stability estimates are based on samples of 47, 35, and 241 respectively. Within these samples, multiple members of a family are measured suggesting that the stability estimates, which are larger than the estimates of internal consistency, may be inflated due to dependence of individuals within the samples.

Estimates of reliability, stability, and intercorrelations for Form E subscales, Form R subscales, and for the Family Incongruence Score are not provided in the test manual.

VALIDITY. The face and content validity of the instrument are supported by clear statements about family situations that relate to subscale domains. Most statements refer to "family members"; this could refer to traditional or nontraditional family situations. In a few items, references to the Bible, bowling, Little League, lectures, plays, and concerts may suggest a middle-class orientation.

Evidence of construct validity is presented in the manual through comparative descriptions of distressed and normal family samples; comparisons of parent responses with those of their adolescent children; descriptions of responses by families with two members, three members, four members, five members, and six or more members; and descriptions of families with a single parent, of minority families, and of older families.

Additional validity evidence is provided in the manual through summaries or references to approximately 150 additional research studies. These studies help delineate the strengths and weaknesses of the scale. For example, the factor structure of the domains and subscales has been examined in 14 studies and the results of those studies have suggested considerable variation in the number and nature of the underlying dimensions.

SUMMARY. The Family Environment Scale is a well-constructed measure of family social structure that allows for multiple perspectives and for consideration of multiple aspects of the family system. The psychometric properties are sufficient to make this a valid instrument for group research. The FES is reasonable for clinical use with an individual or family if attention is restricted to interpretation of differences that are larger than the standard error of measurement. Caution is suggested in interpreting profiles without additional evidence to support the interpretation. Additional caution is suggested when families are nontraditional or from non-majority cultures.

[42]

The Gifted Program Evaluation Survey.

Purpose: Constructed to evaluate the effectiveness of a gifted program as perceived by parents, teachers, students, and administrators.

Population: Gifted and talented programs.

Publication Date: 1991.

Scores: Item scores only.

Administration: Individual.

Forms, 4: Parent, Teacher, Student, Administrator.

Price Data, 1991: $24.95 per evaluation kit consisting of manual/forms (42 pages).

Time: Administration time not reported.
Author: Richard Lahey.
Publisher: United/DOK Publishers.

Review of the Gifted Program Evaluation Survey by DAVID W. BARNETT, Professor of School Psychology, University of Cincinnati, and RITA M. BARNETT, Teacher, and LOIS NICHOLS, Teacher of Gifted and Talented, Oak Hills Local School District, Cincinnati, OH:

The Gifted Program Evaluation Survey is an assessment instrument that was developed to help determine the strengths and weaknesses of gifted and talented programs in the schools. Survey questions were based on a 7-year longitudinal evaluation of a school district's gifted and talented program. The survey is designed to gather information from parents of gifted children, students in the gifted program, teachers who have identified gifted and talented children in their classrooms, and administrators involved directly with program implementation.

The instrument consists of three parts. Part I is an anonymous questionnaire (33 items for parents, 37 for students, 40 for teachers, and 41 for administrators) with five possible responses (ranging from *Strongly Agree* to *Strongly Disagree*). Items include global ratings of the overall program and policy (i.e., grading, "pull out" characteristics, etc.), interactions between the gifted program and regular classrooms, reactions associated with factors such as self-esteem, relationships with peers, and specific ratings pertaining to a number of dimensions such as critical skills, creativity, problem solving, and leadership. Part II is a narrative form used to ascertain suggestions, problems, and benefits. Part III is optional and allows for open-ended individual or small-group consultation or discussion. Strategies for implementation are suggested for each part of the evaluation.

After survey responses are collected, the author suggests that responses to Part I for each category be converted to percentages, and that bar graphs be used to show the information. However, the format may be unwieldy (the number of graphs would be 151). Furthermore, the content of questions and item numbers between teacher, parent, and child questionnaires do not correspond, making the identification of patterns labor intensive. (However, teacher and administration forms are similar.) In order to compare and contrast responses among parents, teachers, and students, questions that are similar in content should be grouped, but recommendations to equate questions are not given.

For Part II, the narrative, the author recommends that a summarizing paragraph for each question should be written (seven for parents, eight for students, four for teachers, and four for administrators) to include the issues and concerns repeated most often. From the summarizing paragraphs, strengths and weaknesses of the program are identified and recommendations are made that include strategies for implementation.

For the submission of results, a booklet format is suggested with graphic representation on the left side of a page and the evaluator's summary of data and recommendations on the right side. Sessions should be held to share information and recommendations with stakeholders. The author also stresses the importance of follow-up sessions to insure that desired changes have been implemented and that evaluation occurs as an ongoing process.

Overall, the Evaluation Survey requires further development. Educational programs need strong evaluation procedures either to justify or expand programs. Only some of the basics of program evaluation are addressed (i.e., multiple raters, synthesis, and reporting) by this survey. It would be helpful to include sections on the basics of evaluation design from planning programs and initiating programs (i.e., goals, models of service delivery) to the challenges of evaluating existing or mature programs (i.e., the differences between formative and summative evaluation). Using principles of evaluation design, the author could communicate where the Survey fits into an overall plan. Basic to the integrity of a program evaluation is assessing whether the desired program is actually carried out in practice in a manner consistent with stated program philosophy, theory, and goals. This crucial factor is not addressed by the present evaluation system. In many cases, programs deviate greatly from plans and intentions.

The Survey is based on ratings that frequently have low to modest correlations with observed behavior. A concern is the potential biases of gifted and talented personnel conducting evaluations. Many questions are framed in ways that would lead to socially desirable responses. Some questions may lead to conclusions that would be difficult to validate even through rigorous experimental design (i.e., "High ability students seem to be better problem solvers and critical thinkers because of the TAG [talented and gifted] experience"). Furthermore, many districts would be interested in cost-outcome procedures not addressed by this evaluation process.

Documentation for technical adequacy is not addressed. Information pertaining to background review and strategies for item selection (an issue of content validity) are not included. Evaluation strategies should include an analysis of instruments and selection procedures for TAG programs. These facets of design may result in considerable problems resulting from basic decision reliability and validity issues. Also, the author does not provide details concerning the number of surveys distributed and the number returned. Methods to determine the representativeness and adequacy of survey results would be critical before considering the need for program changes.

Despite these concerns, the content and process of the evaluation procedures will be of great interest to districts. The most useful function may be to provide a look into a district's significant local efforts related to program evaluation. The criticisms relate not so much to the Survey itself, but to the need for more attention to the basics of evaluation design as a context.

Review of the Gifted Program Evaluation Survey by STEPHEN H. IVENS, Executive Director, DRP Services, Touchstone Applied Science Associates, Brewster, NY:

Questionnaires to be completed by various parties at interest can be an important component of a program evaluation. The Gifted Program Evaluation Survey is a handbook that consists of a series of such questionnaires designed to be administered to parents, students, teachers, and administrators to assess their perceptions of a school district's program for gifted and talented students. In addition to the questionnaires, the handbook contains chapters that discuss strategies for implementation, and for compiling, organizing, categorizing, and analyzing the data. Each questionnaire consists of approximately 40 items with 5-point, *strongly agree* to *strongly disagree*, Likert-response options. In addition, each questionnaire contains a section with free response items. The items are consistently well-written and integrated across the four questionnaires.

Although the publishers state these questionnaires are "a generic version" of a longitudinal evaluation conducted at a specific school district in New York, the term "generic" appears to be a misnomer. All items in the questionnaires refer specifically to the "TAG" program, an acronym for "Talented and Gifted Program." As a result, the items may not be applicable for talented and gifted programs, in general. For example, items such as "I would have liked TAG to have started in the lower grades," "I would have liked TAG classes in the high school," and "My regular classroom teachers did not like me leaving class for TAG" are not consistent with the "generic version" claim of the publisher.

Although it is not likely that many schools could use the questionnaires in The Gifted Program Evaluation Survey as published, this handbook does serve as a useful model for those who wish to design their own program evaluation instruments. Although helpful suggestions are provided for analyzing and presenting the results from the questionnaires, no technical information is provided.

In summary, The Gifted Program Evaluation Survey is a pretentious title for what is, at best, a useful model for school personnel who want to develop their own instruments to assess the perceptions of parents, students, teachers, and administrators as part of a program evaluation.

[43]
Hay Aptitude Test Battery.
Purpose: "Helps select applicants with the ability to deal accurately with numerical and alphabetical detail and the ability to work with numbers."
Population: Applicants for clerical and plant positions.
Publication Dates: 1947–88.
Scores, 3: Number Perception, Name Finding, Number Series Completion.
Administration: Group.
Price Data, 1991: $100 per 25 complete batteries; $30 per 25 warm-up tests; $40 per 25 of any other test.
Time: 13(30) minutes.
Comments: Cassette tape available for administration.
Author: Edward N. Hay.
Publisher: E. F. Wonderlic Personnel Test, Inc.
a) THE WARM-UP TEST I.
Time: 1(3) minutes.
b) NUMBER PERCEPTION TEST.
Forms, 2: A, B.
Time: 4(9) minutes.
c) NAME FINDING TEST.
Time: 4(9) minutes.
d) NUMBER SERIES COMPLETION TEST.
Time: 4(9) minutes.
Cross References: For a review by Robert P. Vecchio of an earlier edition, see 9:470; see also T2:2132 (2 references) and 5:849 (2 references); for reviews by Reign H. Bittner and Edward E. Cureton, see 4:725 (8 references).

Review of the Hay Aptitude Test Battery by SUE M. LEGG, Associate Director, Office of Instructional Resources, University of Florida, Gainesville, FL:

The Hay Aptitude Test Battery is designed as a selection instrument for clerical job applicants "with the ability to deal accurately with numerical and alphabetical detail and the ability to work with numbers," according to the test manual (p. 3). These skills are deemed vital for a range of occupations from bookkeepers to stockroom clerks. The tests consist of a 1-minute low-level general knowledge test and three 4-minute tests that require applicants to recognize distinctions among similar names, rearranged numbers, and to recognize patterns in number series.

The structure of the test limits its usefulness. The general knowledge test is offered as a practice test, but this test gives practice only in taking a timed test. It does not prepare the examinee for the scanning skills required in the alphabetic and numerical recognition tests. A scoring key is provided for the practice test, and evidence of predictive validity based on 21 employees' supervisor ratings was presented. Correlations of the scores of the practice test are included in a table of intercorrelations with the other three tests and the Wonderlic Personnel Test. Yet, the practice test is the only one which has no score interpretation section in the manual. This ambiguity in purpose could lead to inappropriate use of the test score.

Another limitation of the test design is its low level of difficulty. The manual cautions that test score differences are important between applicants scoring between the 35th and 50th percentiles but not between applicants at the high end of the range. It is likely that these tests are best used to screen out incompetent applicants rather than to differentiate between applicants with varying degrees of competence in clerical skills. This is an important point because the median scores tend to represent slightly more than one-half of the items, but improvement in scores beyond this level may be more a function of speed than of accuracy. The degree to which high levels of speed in name or number recognition are important clerical skills is not clear.

The degree to which these tests are valid indicators of general clerical skills is uncertain. The manual states the tests represent skills in many jobs; indeed accuracy is important. Whether or not number and letter recognition are adequate indicators of accuracy is not documented. The validity evidence provided includes chi-square analyses and correlations of scores and salary, performance ratings, and typing volume. No details of these studies are given beyond the number of cases for each position. The sample sizes ranged from 39 for bookkeepers to 140 for clerical-bank. Moreover, the rationale for including salary as a criterion implies that higher paid clerks are more accurate. This assumption may not be true.

Higher paid workers may be better organizers or supervisors or may only have been employed longer.

The extent to which these tests represent a "job sample" as stated in the manual is not explicated. No task analyses data are provided. Nor are there any instructions to the test administrator about the possible limitations of these tests for selecting applicants beyond a discussion of possible disparities between test scores and applicants' prior experience.

The Hay Aptitude Test Battery may be a useful screening device to identify applicants with problems in discriminating among letters or numbers. It may also help identify applicants who can do clerical tasks accurately. The test does not give direct evidence that it predicts spelling or typing skills or the many other skills that are required to be an effective clerical employee. If it is used, it should be done with a clear understanding of the requirements of the job and the degree to which these particular measures of speed and accuracy are related to success in particular positions.

Review of the Hay Aptitude Test Battery by M. DAVID MILLER, Associate Professor of Foundations of Education, University of Florida, Gainesville, FL:

The Hay Aptitude Test Battery is designed to help in the selection of job applicants into positions (particularly clerical workers) requiring the ability to work accurately with numerical and alphabetical detail. The manual claims the tests have been proven valid for plant jobs and operating positions as well.

The test battery consists of four tests with high face validity for measuring detail aptitude. The tests are speeded tests composed of simple activities.

The Warm-Up Test 1 consists of 20 simple information items with a 1-minute time limit. The purpose of the test is to familiarize applicants with the testing procedures and to reduce anxiety. The other tests are each timed for 4 minutes and are more focused on detail rather than information. The Number Perception Test consists of 200 pairs of numbers which the applicant identifies as the same or different. The Number Series Completion Test consists of 30 number sequences for which the applicant must complete the last two numbers. The Name Finding Test consists of 32 names which need to be identified from a list of 128 names. Each test includes clear and simple directions, as well as practice exercises to familiarize applicants with the tasks. In addition, the Name Finding Test, which has 32 names on one side of the sheet and the list of 128 names on the reverse side, is available for both right-handed and left-handed applicants.

Although the test battery appears reasonable for job selection of clerical workers and others, the psychometric evidence does not support the inferences made with the test. Many of the problems identified in a review of an earlier edition of the test battery by Vecchio (1985) continue to plague the exam. Psychometric evidence is lacking, or weak, in the areas of reliability, validity, norms, and standards.

RELIABILITY. No reliabilities are reported for the Warm-Up Test 1 nor the Number Perception Test. Given the intended purpose of the Warm-Up Test 1, not reporting the reliability is not as serious of a limitation as for the Number Perception Test. High split-half reliabilities are reported for the Name Finding Test (.94) and the Number Series Completion Test (.94). However, as pointed out by Vecchio (1985) and the measurement literature (e.g., Anastasi, 1988), split-half reliabilities are spuriously high for speeded tests. A more appropriate form of reliability with a speeded test would be alternate form or test-retest.

VALIDITY. Several pieces of evidence in support of the validity of the tests are reported. However, problems with these data limit their usefulness. First, a study of the Warm-Up Test 1 as a predictor of overall job performance is reported. Besides the ethical issues in using tests in a way unknown to the applicant (see Vecchio, 1985), the study can be faulted in two ways: The expected values for the chi-square are too small with the small sample size ($N = 21$), and the test was given under nonstandardized conditions (i.e., as an untimed "power test").

Second, several studies are reported as providing evidence of criterion-related validity. Although these studies could provide a reasonable basis for the use of the test battery, not enough information is provided to assess the adequacy of the criteria used or the specific procedures of the studies. In addition, no references are provided for the studies. According to Standard 10.3 of the Standards for Educational and Psychological Testing (AERA, APA, & NCME, 1985), "the rationale for criterion relevance should be made explicit. It should include a description of the job in question and of the judgements used to determine relevance" (p. 60). Vecchio (1985) also points to a published account of the failure of the Number Perception Test to correlate with supervisor ratings, raising the question of the representativeness of the reported results (all reported studies show reasonable levels of criterion-related validity).

The correlations of the tests with each other and the Wonderlic Personnel Test are also reported. No interpretations of these correlations are given. Only three correlations were of moderate size with two of them involving the Warm-Up Test 1 (a test ostensibly used to reduce anxiety). The three correlations were between the Warm-Up Test 1 and the Wonderlic Personnel Test (.55), the Warm-Up Test 1 and the Number Series Test (.55), and the Wonderlic Personnel Test and the Number Series Test (.54).

Subpopulation differences on the test battery are reported for gender and education level. Not surprisingly, higher education is related to higher scores. The relationship with gender, which should be seen as problematic when hiring applicants, is found only on the Number Series Test with males scoring higher. Ethnic differences, which should be examined, are not.

Finally, each of the tests is reported as being "job related" and the tasks are being "similar to those required in a 'job sample.'" No evidence is provided for these claims nor is the "job sample" described. Again, providing no evidence for these claims clearly violates Standards 10.5 and 10.6 of the Standards for Educational and Psychological Testing (AERA, APA, & NCME, 1985) dealing with the content-related validity of the exam.

NORMS AND STANDARDS. Norms and suggested cutoffs are provided. The norms appear to be based on a convenience sample (past users of the test battery who have returned the results) with potentially mixed occupations. In violation of Standard 4.4 of the Standards for Educational and Psychological Testing (AERA, APA, & NCME, 1985), insufficient detail is provided to judge the appropriateness of the norms.

Similarly, the basis for the cutoffs suggested is not clearly explained (Standard 10.9). It is unclear who set the cutoffs, how they were set, and for what job classifications. On the other hand, the test manual emphasizes that the cutoffs are only "suggested" and companies may need to set their own standards.

In summary, the Hay Aptitude Test Battery is a series of tests that show good face validity in measuring detail aptitude. However, the psychometric information available may not justify its use. On the other hand, the Standards for Educational and Psychological Testing (AERA, APA, & NCME, 1985) emphasize the role of the test user in examining the particular uses and interpretations of the test. The Hay Aptitude Test Battery may be psychometrically sound, but insufficient evidence (or inadequate documentation of the evidence) leads to the need for further study to justify its use in personnel selection.

REVIEWER'S REFERENCES

American Educational Research Association, American Psychological Association, & National Council on Measurement in Education. (1985). Standards for educational and psychological testing. Washington, DC: American Psychological Association, Inc.

Vecchio, R. P. (1985). [Review of the Hay Aptitude Test Battery]. In J. V. Mitchell, Jr. (Ed.), *The ninth mental measurements yearbook* (pp. 651-652). Lincoln, NE: Buros Institute of Mental Measurements.

Anastasi, A. (1988). *Psychological testing* (6th ed.). New York: Macmillan Publishing.

[44]
Henmon-Nelson Ability Test, Canadian Edition.

Purpose: "Designed to measure those aspects of cognitive ability which are important for success in academic work and in similar endeavors outside the classroom."

Population: Grades 3–6, 6–9, 9–12.

Publication Dates: 1957–1990.

Scores: Total score only.

Administration: Group.

Price Data, 1994: $49.45 per 35 reusable or consumable test booklets (specify level); $37.45 per 100 answer sheets (hand/machine scorable); $10.45 per scoring mask (all levels); $10 per examiner's manual ('90, 44 pages); $8.95 per 10 class record sheets; $12.45 per examination kit.

Time: (30) minutes.

Comments: Adapted from the 1973 U.S. edition of the test (The Henmon-Nelson Tests of Mental Ability, 3:1073).

Authors: Tom A. Lamke, M. J. Nelson, and Joseph L. French.

Publisher: Nelson Canada [Canada].

Cross References: See T3:1073 (13 references); for a review by Eric F. Gardner, see 8:190 (14 references); see also T2:391 (52 references); for a review by Norman E. Wallen and an excerpted review by John O. Crites of an earlier edition, see 6:462 (11 references); for reviews by D. Welty Lefever and Leona E. Tyler and an excerpted review by Laurance F. Shaffer, see 5:342 (14 references); for a review by H. M. Fowler, see 4:299 (25 references); for reviews by Anne Anastasi, August Dvorak, Howard Easley, and J. P. Guilford and an excerpted review by Francis N. Maxfield, see 2:1398.

Review of the Henmon-Nelson Ability Test, Canadian Edition by JOHN O. ANDERSON, Associate Professor, Faculty of Education, University of Victoria, Victoria, British Columbia, CANADA:

The Henmon-Nelson Ability Test is intended to measure cognitive ability related to academic success for Canadian students in grades 3 to 12. As such it is not an index of academic achievement but is an index of academic aptitude or potential. The test is essentially the U.S. version with norms tables based on a sample of Canadian students and minor modifications to the items.

The Henmon-Nelson Ability Test consists of three levels: grades 3 to 6, 6 to 9, and 9 to 12. Each level consists of 90 multiple-choice items measuring student ability in tasks associated with problems with numbers, graphical representations, and words (e.g., synonyms and sentence completion). The items are ordered by difficulty (*p*-values presumably) so that the student will be required to respond to an eclectic ordering of item types: for example, a number problem then identification of a synonym and then perhaps a graphic relations-type task. The Henmon-Nelson yields a single score for the student based upon summing the number of correct responses. An interesting characteristic of the test is that each of the three levels of the test has exactly the same scoring key.

The tests can be obtained as either reusable booklets for use with a separate answer sheet or as *consumable* booklets. In both formats, the 90 items are printed in a horizontal format which gives the booklets a very crowded, text-dense appearance. Given that the students, regardless of level, are given 30 minutes to complete the test it would seem that speed would be a major factor in determining overall performance particularly with younger children. This concern about test speededness is reinforced by the low completion rates of the norm group reported in the examiner's manual (Table 6.2).

The norms are based on the responses of English-speaking students from 48 schools from across Canada. On average there were 772 students per grade administered the test, the number of students per grade varied from 457 in grade 3 to 1,410 in grade 7. It appears that test administration was conducted sometime during the 1988–89 school year but it is unclear exactly when, and if all schools completed the test in the same time interval. This can have some influence on the interpretation of grade-related scores. Tables are provided to transform raw scores into both grade- and age-based stanines and percentiles and into standard age scores (mean = 100, *sd* = 16). The examiner's manual explains the scoring of the test and the use of the norms tables clearly with appropriate cautions. The score conversion tables are straightforward and well laid out for each level of the test.

The issue of validity is discussed briefly in terms of content, construct, and criterion-related validity largely on the basis of work done on early versions (U.S.) of the test but no references to this work are provided. These studies suggest the test is valid in terms of relevant content, correlation to other respected tests of cognitive ability, and correlation to academic performance. In addition, a study was conducted as part of the development of this Canadian Edition by correlating Henmon-Nelson scores to those of the Verbal component of the Canadian Cognitive Abilities Test (CCAT) for samples of students in grades 4, 7, and 10. The correlations ranged from .78 to .84, suggesting concurrent validity to the Verbal component of the CCAT.

The examiner's manual does not offer any references to relevant research literature and is rather light on details about test and item characteristics. It would be informative and an aid to score interpretation to provide test score distributions and item statistics, particularly item difficulty and omission rates. Further, in order to engender confidence in using scores from the Henmon-Nelson Ability Test to make judgements about students, the manual should provide information regarding differences in test performance based on gender and cultural background of respondent, and on the format of the test booklet used (separate answer sheet versus consumable booklet).

In conclusion, the Henmon-Nelson Ability Test provides a quick, easily administered and scored test of student performance related to aspects of language usage, spatial relations, and numeracy. However, the single score derived from responses to this diverse item set is not easily interpretable in relation to academic performance. Academic performance is generally considered in terms of specific abilities and skills such as numerical problem solving, word knowledge, pictorial analogies, and the like. A score derived from responses to an amalgam of item types, which the Henmon-Nelson provides, does not seem well suited for informing instructionally related decisions. A test which provides more task specific information, such as the aforementioned CCAT would likely be more informative.

Review of the Henmon-Nelson Ability Test, Canadian Edition by DAVID J. BATESON, Associate Professor of Mathematics and Science Education and the Educational Measurement Research Group, University of B.C., Vancouver, B.C., CANADA:

The items for all three levels (grades 3–6, grades 6–9, and grades 9–12) of the Canadian edition of the Henmon-Nelson Ability Test are derived directly from the 1973 U.S. edition. They have been "Canadianized" by metricating and changing contexts (state/province, governor/premier), and have also been updated so that money questions reflect more modern prices. The 90 items in each of the levels lead to a single general cognitive ability or academic aptitude score that can be reported as a Standard Age Score (SAS, mean of 100, standard deviation of 16) along with percentile rank and stanine of the

SAS, or percentile rank (or stanine) of the raw score by grade within the level.

From a psychometric point of view, the tests appear to more than meet presently acceptable standards. The examiner's manual is a well-written document that provides accurate, understandable, and, therefore, useful discussions and cautions for the user. Administration and "hand" scoring are fast and simple, and there appears to be little chance for examiner transcription or addition errors to occur. The reported KR20 reliability coefficients are quite acceptable for a test of this kind, ranging from .90 to .96, depending on the level and grade. The authors recognize the potential problem of speededness, with 90 items to be completed in 30 minutes, and present arguments and evidence regarding the issue. The problem is temporized by having the items ordered in increasing difficulty. Correlation coefficients between the same grades using different levels of the test, although satisfactory, are not as high as one might expect. The fact that content between the levels is, at times, considerably different may explain this situation. For example, there are 15 symbolic analogies at Level 3–6, eight at Level 6–9, and none at Level 9–12. Validity evidence provided shows appropriately high correlations with the Canadian Cognitive Abilities Test, Form 7.

There may be two potential problems with these instruments. First, the tests come in two formats, the consumable Clapp-Young self-marking forms, which have been successfully used in the U.S. editions for many years, and reusable forms with accompanying machine-scorable answer sheets. The manual provides different administration and scoring instructions for the two formats, but then ceases to differentiate between the formats. Unfortunately, the authors provide no evidence that results would be equivalent regardless of format. Based on experience, I would predict that results from the different formats would not be equivalent, particularly at the lower grade levels. This is particularly cause for concern because the format used for the reliability, validity, and norming studies is not reported.

The second problem is connected with sampling. Although the document does an excellent job in presenting the sampling framework and schools used for the norming study, this presentation draws attention to a possible bias in the sample. At all three levels of the test, approximately two-thirds of the items depend on English language verbal abilities. Performance on these items can be greatly influenced by a student having English as a second language, a situation applying to a growing number of Canadian students. Because "English as a Second Language" students were not appropriately represented in the sample, the norms may not be appropriate.

In summary, the Henmon-Nelson provides a quick, inexpensive, and usable result for those wishing an undifferentiated gross score of academic aptitude or general cognitive ability. Caution with respect to the test utility and normative interpretations should be used in the case of students for whom English is a second language.

[45]

JOB-O.

Purpose: "To facilitate self-awareness, career-awareness, and career exploration."

Publication Dates: 1981–92.

Administration: Group.

Price Data, 1992: $1.65 per test booklet; $.30 per answer folder; $4.95 per administration (Professional) manual ('85, 20 pages).

Comments: Also known as Judgement of Occupational Behavior-Orientation.

Authors: Arthur Cutler, Francis Ferry, Robert Kauk, and Robert Robinett.

Publisher: CFKR Career Materials, Inc.

a) JOB-O E (ELEMENTARY).

Population: Grades 4–7.

Scores: 6 ratings: Mechanical/Construction/Agriculture, Scientific/Technical, Creative/Artistic, Social/Legal/Educational, Managers/Sales, Administrative Support.

Time: Administration time not reported.

b) JOB-O.

Population: Junior high school through adult.

Scores, 9: Education, Interest, Inclusion, Control, Affection, Physical Activity, Hands/Tools/Machinery, Problem-Solving, Creative-Ideas.

Foreign Language Editions: Spanish and Vietnamese test booklets and answer sheets available.

Time: (60–65) minutes.

Price Data: $89.95 per Apple or IBM software.

c) JOB-O A (ADVANCED).

Population: Grades 10–12 and adult.

Scores, 16: Occupational Interest, Training Time, Reasoning Skills, Mathematical Skills, Language Skills, Working with Data, Working with People, Working with Things, Working Conditions, Physical Demands, Leadership, Helping People, Problem-Solving, Initiative, Team Work, Public Contact.

Price Data: $99.95 per IBM software.

Time: [50–55] minutes.

Comments: May be self-administered.

Cross References: For a review by James W. Pinkney of an earlier edition, see 10:160; for a review by Bruce J. Eberhardt of an earlier edition, see 9:560.

Review of the JOB-O by MARION F. ASCHE, Professor of Education, Virginia Polytechnic Institute and State University, Blacksburg, VA:

The original Judgement of Occupational Behavior-Orientation (JOB-O) was designed as a career interest inventory in 1970. Since that time, it has undergone several minor revisions and two additional versions have been added. The JOB-O A (Advanced Version, Career Decision Making) was first copyrighted in 1988 and is designed to be used with adults and persons who have previously taken the JOB-O. The JOB-O E (Elementary, Career Awareness) was introduced in 1989 and is designed for use with students in grades 4–6. The revised JOB-O (Career Exploration) is recommended for students in grades 7 through 10. The format of all three instruments is similar, consisting of a reusable booklet and a consumable answer folder. This review focuses on the JOB-O but includes descriptions of how basic features are modified in the other two versions.

The JOB-O is presented as a career assessment inventory in which the user is asked to make self-assessments about nine career-relevant variables and then to compare these estimates with the "requirements" of 120 selected jobs. Because the labor market is enormously complex, the 120 occupations selected for inclusion are those which account for a large percentage of employment in this society and which show promise of being in demand over the next decade. Other criteria for inclusion of particular job titles were that jobs requiring all levels of education are included and that each of the eight broad career clusters covered by the JOB-O are represented.

The JOB-O first asks the respondent to estimate how long he or she wants to go to school (go to work right out of high school, attend community college or special school, go through a 4-year or more college program). The second variable asks respondents to select, from the eight job clusters provided, the one or two in which they have the greatest interest. For each grouping, the cluster is named (e.g., Performing Arts, Design, Communications Occupations) and several specific job titles are listed. Variables 3 through 5 are based on the FIRO-B (inclusion, control, and affection). Variable 6 deals with desired level of physical demands (based on the *Dictionary of Occupational Titles* estimates of physical demands of jobs). Variables 7 through 9 deal with the extent to which the respondent wishes to work with hands-tools-machinery, problem solving, and creativity-ideas. Variables 3 through 9 are estimated on a 3-point scale (*usually or often, sometimes or occasionally,* and *seldom or rarely*).

After completing the self-estimates on each of the nine variables, the respondent is asked to compare responses with those provided for the 120 job titles, writing the number of matches for each job title in the space provided. The respondent is asked to consider all job titles for which there are five or more matches, then to choose the three that are most interesting and to enter basic information (from the response folder) for these three including number employed, percent of growth, job outlook, average earnings (high, medium, low), kind of training, years of training, and related jobs. The respondent is finally asked to pick the one job title he or she likes best for further research using such resources as the *Occupational Outlook Handbook*, visiting a career resource center, talking to a counselor, etc.

The JOB-O A differs from the JOB-O in a number of ways although the basic approach of self-estimates and matching is the same. Eighteen variables are self-appraised including interests (direct estimate rather than picking job clusters); training time; reasoning skills; mathematical skills and language skills; desire to work with data, people, and things; working conditions (inside, outside, or both); physical demands of job (light, medium, heavy); and eight areas of personal skills including leadership, helping people, problem-solving, initiative, team work, public contact, manual dexterity, and physical stamina. Responses are not direct self-assessments but rather statements of preference for jobs having or requiring varying levels of each of the variables. Matching is a bit different with the JOB-O A in that the respondent matches his or her responses with 24 job clusters rather than with 120 specific job titles (with a listing of several examples of specific jobs within each cluster provided for reference). The job research section is similar but with greater emphasis on making a specific career decision.

The JOB-O E is a much simplified version of the basic JOB-O which focuses on interests only. Six broad job clusters which parallel Holland's typology and the *Guide for Occupational Exploration* interest areas are included for investigation. The respondent is asked to rate his or her degree of interest in each as high, some, or low after reading a limited amount of information about jobs in each cluster. The stated purpose of the JOB-O E is to increase the student's self awareness and career awareness.

The JOB-O instruments have a number of desirable characteristics. They are straightforward, have

"face validity," should be relatively easy for most individuals to complete and score, and appear to be useful for individual and group career exploration. A Spanish version of the JOB-O is available as is a computer version of the JOB-O A. The information provided on the included occupations is concise and useful.

There are also, however, a number of shortcomings and potential problems with the JOB-O series. Although the authors claim that almost five million persons have taken the JOB-O, there are no data reported on characteristics of this sample such as gender, ethnicity, age, etc. There is no way to tell whether the instrument responses relate to such variables in a way that might promote continued occupational stereotyping. The "Professional Manual" is severely lacking in technical detail. There are essentially no reliability data provided (one 1973 test-retest correlation of selected occupations) and only one study related to concurrent validity is cited. The validity study was also conducted in 1973 and compared responses with those on the Kuder Occupational Interest Survey (Form DD) using a Chi-square test to determine there was no significant difference in responses. No information on sample size or characteristics is provided for either study and neither study appears to have been published. Evidence of content validity consists of the rather usual statements regarding rational judgement by experts but no detail as to how items were selected or sampled is provided.

Although the authors state that "no claim is made for predictive validity" they go on to state that data are available for a 10-year study and that it is "hoped that a study will be completed in the future" (p. 7). It would seem that if the primary purpose of the JOB-O is to assist students in matching their interests (and to a limited extent, abilities) to potential future careers, evidence of predictive validity is absolutely essential. How else can one judge whether or not taking the JOB-O is helpful or misleading to individuals in their career exploration? Unfortunately, although the authors include cautions in the JOB-O booklet itself that the instrument does not measure ability and that it is an exploratory instrument to "help you compare your interests with the 120 major job titles in the world of work" (p. 2), the manual authors suggest that for high-school, college, and adult levels, it can be used for making job decisions. In fact, the final page of the answer insert is labeled "It's Decision-Making Time."

Consider the following from the Users Guide, "Any teacher, counselor, teacher aide, or career technician with the usual degree of professional competence can administer JOB-O without specific professional training" (p. 3). The important difference between administering the JOB-O and assisting students in interpreting the results is not explained. Inadequate attention is paid to the problems of self-assessment and to the lack of information on measured aptitudes or abilities of respondents. These problems are similar to those cited by both Eberhardt (1985) and Pinkney (1989) in earlier reviews of the JOB-O. It is particularly disturbing that earlier criticisms and the obvious weaknesses of the test manual have not been addressed.

On a more philosophical level, there is one additional area of concern that deserves mention. The theoretical rationale for the JOB-O and other instruments of this type lies in the "matching model" originally proposed by Frank Parsons in the early 1900s, an approach that still is a mainstay of much vocational guidance practice. The basic premise is the probability of career success and satisfaction is maximized when the individual chooses a career in which his or her interests and abilities most nearly match the modal interests and abilities of incumbents. The user must be the judge of the viability of this model but should be aware that there is a great deal of variability in the interests and abilities of individuals who are successful and satisfied within any broad cluster of occupations. Because there is substantial within-group variability, there is necessarily a great deal of overlap among occupations and gr oupings. It is therefore somewhat misleading to imply that averages of incumbents are "requirements" although they may constitute best estimates in the statistical sense.

CONCLUSION. The authors have addressed an important area of need—career awareness and exploration. The use of occupational clusters to simplify the complex world of work makes sense and the importance of interests in job success and satisfaction is widely recognized. The intuitive appeal and simplicity of the JOB-O, however, tend to mask its technical shortcomings and make its misuse by uninformed individuals more likely. Individuals who take the JOB-O should be assisted with interpretation of results by practitioners with specific career/vocational guidance preparation and should be cautioned against premature foreclosure in occupational or educational decision making based on such limited information.

REVIEWER'S REFERENCES

Eberhardt, B. J. (1985). [Review of Judgement of Occupational Behavior-Orientation]. In J. V. Mitchell, Jr. (Ed.), *The ninth mental measurements yearbook* (pp. 767-769). Lincoln, NE: Buros Institute of Mental Measurements.

Pinkney, J. W. (1989). [Review of JOB-O, 1985-1995]. In J. C. Conoley & J. J. Kramer (Eds.), *The tenth mental measurements yearbook* (pp. 409-410). Lincoln, NE: Buros Institute of Mental Measurements.

Review of the JOB-O by LAWRENCE H. CROSS, Associate Professor of Educational Research and Measurement, Virginia Polytechnic Institute and State University, Blacksburg, VA:

The original JOB-O was designed as a career interest inventory that ostensibly can provide a process for career development at three levels: career awareness, career-exploration, and career-decision making. In 1989, the authors of the JOB-O introduced an elementary version (JOB-O E) that emphasizes career awareness for students in grades 4–6 and an advanced version (JOB-O A) that emphasizes career decision making for older students and adults. Because the original JOB-O has been in use for approximately 20 years and has been the object of reviews in two previous editions of the *Mental Measurements Yearbook*, this review will focus on the two new versions.

The assessment booklet for the elementary version is devoted almost entirely to two-page descriptions of six job clusters called job groups. After reading each two-page description, students are instructed to record on a consumable answer sheet whether they have "high," "some," or "low" interest in each job group (cluster). The description of each job group lists four major occupations with single sentence descriptions of the type of work associated with each. This is followed by a list of five interests people in a job group presumably have in common. For example, users learn that "LEGAL WORKERS work in the field of LAW" and "they are interested in making friends and keeping them" (p. 10). The adjacent page lists approximately 20 job titles along with a one-sentence characterization of the associated work. For example, a "SECURITIES BROKER—sells a variety of stocks and bonds of all kinds." Students are directed to ask their teachers to help pronounce the names of jobs new to them, but one has to wonder how much understanding 4th graders will gain if their teacher pronounces securities broker. Nonetheless, after recording their level of interest in each job group, children are instructed to write the titles of three of the jobs they like best in each job group. Career exploration is then addressed by directing the students to select one job they like best in each of two job groups and respond to questions about these jobs using the descriptions contained in the JOB-O E booklet.

If not frustrated by having to make choices with limited information, students in 4th through 7th grades may find the JOB-O E an interesting career awareness activity. I fear they may find it a little laborious as a career exploration exercise. The authors appear to take career decision making at this age a bit more seriously than seems warranted, as indicated by the title of the last page in the assessment booklet: "ADDITIONAL THINGS TO THINK ABOUT WHEN MAKING *FINAL* CAREER DECISIONS" (p. 17, emphasis added).

The advanced version (JOB-O A) is much more elaborate than the elementary version. The first part of the instrument is devoted to self-assessment of user "interests and skills," which are then matched to "jobs with similar skill and job requirements." Whereas the standard JOB-O assesses "interests and skills" with 9 questions, the advanced version asks 18 questions. It should be noted that two different editions were provided for this review, and only the one with the most recent publication date (1990) is reviewed here, even though there appear to be fewer problems with the older edition. Initially, the respondents review a list of nine occupational interest areas (clusters) and select the one area they like best. The only information provided to inform this key decision is a one-sentence description of the presumed interests of people in each occupational area. It is noteworthy that interests in occupational areas are requested, rather than interests that might be related to occupational areas.

The next seven questions are poorly worded and could introduce serious problems of interpretation. For example, the second question asks, "How long do you want to prepare for a job?" (p. 5). A better phrasing might be: How many years are you willing to prepare for a job? The next three questions concern the reasoning, mathematical, and language skills the respondent will "bring to a job." Curiously, the stem of each question asks what skill level he or she would *like* to bring to the job. Because most people surely would like to bring advanced level skills to the job, what reason would there be to select the other response options? These items are followed by another three questions that ask about the "skill level that best meets your desire to work with DATA, PEOPLE, and THINGS" (p. 7). The problem with the items thus introduced is that the response options are not mutually exclusive. In one item, the descriptor "operate things" is given for both Options 1 and 2, and for another item the descriptors "teach" and "train" are used for two different options. If the items used to assess "interests and skills" are flawed, the resulting job-matches must also be flawed.

As noted in the user's guide, "The general goal of the JOB-O A is to match the user's interests and skills with the work activities and requirements that will be found on the job." To achieve this goal, respondents are directed to compare their answers to the 18 "interests and skills" questions with response profiles to the same items that presumably represent the skills and interests of workers in various jobs. The JOB-O A booklet provides profiles for 24 job groups, and for three illustrative job titles within each job group. For each job group and job title, respondents are instructed to count the number of matches they have across the 18 variables but to count 3 points for matches on the first two variables. To compare profiles with 24 job groups, and with 72 job titles, across the 18 variables, requires 1,728 comparisons! Clearly identifying job-matches is a tedious undertaking, which is further complicated by the fact that the answer sheet does not provide spaces to record the number of matches for job titles within job groups.

The last page of the answer sheet is headed: "Make a career decision!" (p. 16). Here respondents are directed to list up to seven jobs they like most, and to "choose three that you want to research further to make a good career decision." The respondent is then instructed to consult the *Occupational Outlook Handbook* and other references to find information about the jobs selected for exploration.

To the extent these instruments provide valid "job matches," they can potentially facilitate career exploration by directing attention to jobs compatible with interests. Of course, mismatches could have the unfortunate consequence of misdirecting career exploration and leading to poor career decisions. Incredibly, no empirical evidence is offered to support the validity of (a) the profiles of skills and interests "required" for the various jobs, (b) the choice of variables used to assess skills and interests, or (c) the inference that greater job satisfaction or job success will result if people pursue jobs which closely match their interests and skills as measured by the JOB-O instruments. Authors of the Professional Manual state the selection and coding of the variables was based on a "rational judgmental procedure" rather than on quantitative relationships, and "no claim is made for predictive validity." Although rational judgements may have provided a starting point for developing the JOB-O instruments, it is noteworthy that after nearly 20 years, no empirical evidence has been presented to substantiate the face validity claims made for an instrument that reportedly has been administered to almost five million people.

In light of the logical deficiencies noted above for the assessment items and in the absence of empirical evidence to support the validity of the resulting job-matches, none of these instruments should be taken seriously, except perhaps for increasing awareness of job titles. To base career decisions on any of them would be "Risky Business" at best.

[46]

Kaufman Brief Intelligence Test.
Purpose: Intended as a brief measure of verbal and nonverbal intelligence.
Population: Ages 4–90.
Publication Date: 1990.
Acronym: K-BIT.
Scores, 3: Vocabulary, Matrices, IQ Composite.
Subtests, 2: Vocabulary (including Part A, Expressive Vocabulary and Part B, Definitions) and Matrices.
Administration: Individual.
Price Data, 1993: $99.95 per complete kit including easel, manual (123 pages), and 25 individual test records; $24.95 per 25 individual test records; $26.95 per manual.
Time: (15–30) minutes.
Comments: Definitions task not administered to children ages 4–7 years; examiners are encouraged to teach individuals, using teaching items, how to solve the kinds of items included in both subtests.
Authors: Alan S. Kaufman and Nadeen L. Kaufman.
Publisher: American Guidance Service.
Cross References: See T4:1344 (4 references).

Review of the Kaufman Brief Intelligence Test by M. DAVID MILLER, Associate Professor of Foundations of Education, University of Florida, Gainesville, FL:

The Kaufman Brief Intelligence Test (K-BIT) is an individually administered measure of intelligence. The K-BIT can be administered in 15–30 minutes for ages 4 to 90. The test is composed of two subtests measuring verbal or crystallized thinking (Expressive Vocabulary and Definitions) and nonverbal or fluid thinking (Matrices). The Vocabulary subtest measures verbal knowledge through pictures (Expressive Vocabulary) and definitions. The Matrices subtest measures the ability of subjects to perceive relationships and complete analogies through pictures or abstract designs. In addition, overall IQ is measured through the K-BIT IQ Composite.

For each subtest and the composite, age-based standard scores are provided with a mean of 100 and a standard deviation of 15. In this way scores are on a common metric with other intelligence scales (e.g., the Wechsler scales) and achievement tests (e.g., Wide Range Achievement Test—Revised, Peabody Individual Achievement Test—Revised, and the Kaufman Test of Educational Achievement).

Although the K-BIT is scaled as the Wechsler instruments, the authors caution that a test user should not assume "the K-BIT may substitute for a comprehensive measure of a child's or adult's intelligence" (p. 1). Instead, the K-BIT is designed for use in situations where a complete intelligence screening is not necessary such as an initial or large scale screening for more in-depth evaluation, a screening for job placement or hiring, or for research purposes. The K-BIT is intended to be a brief intelligence measure that is reliable, valid, well normed, and can be administered by personnel without sophisticated psychometric backgrounds. Test administration and scoring directions are clear and simple to follow, but the authors caution that greater psychometrtic sophistication is needed for score interpretation.

DEVELOPMENT. The K-BIT was developed in conjunction with the Kaufman Adolescent and Adult Intelligence Test (KAIT) and the AGS Early Screening Profiles. In addition, the norms for the K-BIT and KAIT overlap making scores directly comparable. After initial screening with the K-BIT, a more complete intelligence profile with comparable results can be obtained from the KAIT for ages 11 to 90. Similarly, more information can be gained for younger subjects on the AGS Early Screening Profiles which is appropriate for ages 2 to 6.

NORMS. Norms are based on a national sample of 2,022 subjects ranging in age from 4 to 92. Although the sample is not random, subjects were tested at 60 sites representing 29 states. The actual sample size met or exceeded the target sample size at most age levels, with sample size decreasing with age level. For example, 100 subjects were targeted for each age from 4 to 10. In contrast, older subjects were combined into broader groups with similar targeted sample sizes (i.e., ages 20–34 [$N = 200$], ages 34–54 [$N = 150$], and ages 55-90 [$N = 100$]). Given the steady decline in composite IQ and performance IQ after age 20 (e.g., see pp. 194-197 in Kaufman, 1990), the adequacy of the norms for older subjects seems questionable. Sample sizes are adequate for subjects under age 20.

The sample was stratified by sex, geographic region, socioeconomic status, and race or ethnicity. The sample matched the U.S. population on gender, race, and ethnicity. However, the Northeast region of the country was slightly underrepresented. In addition, examinees or parents of examinees with some college (1–3 years) or technical school were slightly overrepresented.

Norms were developed using state-of-the-art procedures as proposed in Angoff and Robertson (1987). The smoothing and normalizing procedures led to some small differences in the standard scale across ages. As a result, caution needs to be exercised in making comparisons across ages. For example, a subject who is one standard deviation above the mean on the Matrices subtest at age 4 ($M = 99.1, s = 16.3$) would have a standard score of 115.4. A comparable subject (one standard deviation above the mean) at age 5 ($M = 96.9, s = 13.1$) would score 110.0. Thus, a mean difference between two groups might be interpreted as significant when it could be attributed to a difference in scales.

Scores are reported in six ways: standard scores ($M = 100, s = 15$), percentile rank, normal curve equivalents, stanines, or in descriptive categories. The latter scores are developed to "reflect in words the approximate distance from the group mean" (manual, p. 40). For example, the middle 50% of the scores are "average" whereas the bottom 2.2% are "lower extreme."

RELIABILITY. Split-half reliabilities are reported by age level for each subtest and the composite. The reliabilities across age level were high for the Vocabulary subtest (.89–.98) and the K-BIT IQ Composite (.88–.98). Reliabilities were lower, but acceptable for the Matrices subtest (.74–.95). On the other hand, assuming that items above (below) the last (first) item attempted are correct (incorrect) could lead to a spuriously high reliability estimate. As a result, test-retest reliabilities may give more appropriate estimates. Test-retest reliabilities, which are reported for wider age ranges, are comparable to the split-half reliabilities for the Vocabulary subtest (.86–.97), the Matrices subtest (.80–.92), and the K-BIT IQ Composite (.92–.95).

In addition to the reliability coefficients, the standard error of measurement (SEM) is reported to assist in the interpretation of individual scores on each subtest and the composite. The SEM by age level ranges from about 2 to 5 on the composite and the Vocabulary subtest. On the Matrices subtest, the SEM ranges from about 3 to 7. For each subtest and the composite, the SEM was lower for older subjects. Further simplifying features for test users are the tabled multiples of the SEM which are used in estimating "Bands of Error" in the score reports. Tabled values include 68%, 85%, 90%, 95%, and 99% confidence levels, with the manual recommending a 90% confidence level.

Finally, tabled values are also used to compare differences between subtests. Using the standard error of the difference, the magnitude of the difference between the Vocabulary subtest and the Matrices subtest can be compared against a tabled value to determine significance at the .05 or .01 level. These two features on the score report should be useful in score interpretation.

VALIDITY. Many of the suggested uses of the K-BIT (e.g., initial screening, hiring and promotion, measurement across time) are not addressed through validation studies. Studies more closely linked to particular uses of the K-BIT should be done. The construct validity of the K-BIT is examined in the test manual. The construct validity of the K-BIT is in part addressed through the initial selection of subtests that are good measures of general intelligence. The Vocabulary subtest is a typical measure of verbal intelligence, based on the Binet-Wechsler tradition whereas the Matrices subtest has a foundation in the Raven's Progressive Matrices.

Using data collected in national tryouts, classical item analysis, Rasch one-parameter latent trait analysis, and item bias analysis (see Holland & Thayer, 1988) were completed. Based on these analyses, the K-BIT seems to be psychometrically sound. Additional studies are reported to examine the construct validity of the test both internally and externally. The internal studies show a reasonable correlation of the two subtests at each age level (.38 to .75) and the expected growth patterns on tasks and subtests across ages. Externally the K-BIT is correlated with a series of measures of intelligence and achievement. The combined evidence from the correlations show that the K-BIT has moderate to high correlations with other intelligence tests and moderate correlations with the achievement tests.

SUMMARY. The K-BIT is a well-constructed brief test for measuring intelligence. State of the art procedures have been used in norming and measuring reliability and validity. The combined evidence, which is fairly extensive, points to a psychometrically sound measure of verbal, nonverbal, and composite intelligence. Caution should be exercised in interpreting standard scores for older subjects (ages 20–90) because of the use of small Ns in the norming. In addition, further validation of the K-BIT is needed for the potential uses listed in the manual.

REVIEWER'S REFERENCES

Angoff, W. H., & Robertson, G. J. (1987). A procedure for standardizing individually administered tests, normed by age or grade level. *Applied Psychological Measurement, 11*, 33-46.

Holland, P. W., & Thayer, D. T. (1988). Differential item performance and the Mantel-Haenszel procedure. In H. Wainer & H. I. Braun (Eds.), *Test validity* (pp. 129-145). Hillsdale, NJ: Lawrence Erlbaum.

Kaufman, A. S. (1990). *Assessing adolescent and adult intelligence.* Boston: Allyn and Bacon.

Review of the Kaufman Brief Intelligence Test by JOHN W. YOUNG, Assistant Professor of Educational Statistics and Measurement, Rutgers University, New Brunswick, NJ:

The Kaufman Brief Intelligence Test (K-BIT) is an individually administered measure of verbal and nonverbal intelligence appropriate for ages 4 to 90 years. The K-BIT is intended for those circumstances, such as a large-scale screening of students or patients, in which a brief measure of intelligence will suffice. The test is easy to administer and may be given by appropriately trained technicians or paraprofessionals. Total testing time is approximately 15 to 30 minutes and tends to be shortest for young children and longest for adults. The K-BIT consists of two subtests: Vocabulary (composed of Part A, Expressive Vocabulary and Part B, Definitions) and Matrices.

The K-BIT was developed to meet the needs of professionals for a brief, self-contained, and adequately normed test of both verbal and nonverbal abilities. Presently, many intelligence measures are inadequate for situations when testing time is limited. Administering only some of the subtests from a comprehensive intelligence test can yield misleading results. Research has shown that an individual will earn quite different scores on a two-subtest short form of a longer test as compared to scores earned when the subtests are embedded in the longer test battery (Thompson, Howard, & Anderson, 1986). In comparison, K-BIT norms are based on the administration of both subtests that comprise the whole test.

K-BIT SUBTESTS. Subtest 1, Vocabulary, is an 82-item measure of verbal ability that requires the examinee to respond orally. Part A, Expressive Vocabulary (45 items), administered to all examinees, requires the individual to name a pictured object such as a lamp or a calendar. Part B, Definitions (37 items), for examinees 8 years and older, requires the individual to provide the word that fits two clues: a phrase description and a partial spelling of the word. The Vocabulary subtest measures a person's language development and his or her level of verbal concept formation.

Subtest 2, Matrices, is a 48-item measure of nonverbal ability using several item types involving visual stimuli, both concrete (persons and objects) and abstract (designs and symbols). All items are multiple choice and require the examinee to either select one of five alternatives that goes best with a stimulus picture or to choose one of six or eight options to solve a 2x2 or 3x3 matrix of pictures or patterns.

The Vocabulary subtest is intended to measure crystallized intelligence, the type of learning and problem solving that derives directly from formal schooling and cultural experiences. In contrast, the Matrices subtest measures fluid intelligence, the type involved in novel problem situations and is assumed to be less culture-bound. Collectively, the two subtests yield a more complete assessment of an individual's level of intelligence than either subtest alone.

SCORES. All items are scored 0 (incorrect) or 1 (correct). Raw scores are converted to standard scores ($M = 100$, $SD = 15$) for each subtest using one of 53 age group conversion tables. The two subtest scores are also combined to yield an IQ Composite Score.

STANDARDIZATION. The K-BIT is normed on 2,022 subjects ages 4 to 90 years tested during 1988–89. The sample was stratified on the basis of age, sex, geographic region, socioeconomic status (examinee or parental education level), and race to match U.S. Census 1990 projections, if available, or 1985 estimates if projected figures were unavailable. The normative sample appears to be representative of the contiguous U.S. population on all combinations of the stratification variables.

RELIABILITY. Split-half reliability coefficients were computed for several age categories in the norming sample. For the subtests, coefficients range from .74 to .98 with means of .93 for the Vocabulary subtest and .88 for the Matrices subtest. For the IQ Composite, the split-half reliability ranges from .88 for age 5 to .98 for ages 55–90 with a mean of .94. Test-retest reliability coefficients were computed for a sample of 232 examinees, ages 5 to 89, based on a retest interval of 12 to 145 days (mean interval = 21 days). The coefficients for the four age groups in the sample have a mean of .94 for the Vocabulary subtest, .85 for the Matrices subtest, and .94 for the IQ Composite.

VALIDITY. Test validity was established in a three-stage process: selection of the subtests, item analysis, and internal and external test analysis. Use of the Vocabulary and Matrices subtests is cited as a logical choice because of the corresponding dichotomy on other measures of intelligence such as the Verbal/Performance split on the Wechsler tests and the crystallized/fluid distinction on the Stanford-Binet. Over 300 items were pretested on a sample of 1,058 examinees in 1986–87. Based on several item analysis methods, the original item pool was trimmed to the current form of the K-BIT. As evidence of construct validity, changes in raw scores on the subtests are shown to reflect growth patterns often found in developmental studies of intelligence. Mean raw scores on the Vocabulary subtest increase steadily through early adulthood, peak in middle age, and then decline gradually. In contrast, mean raw scores on the Matrices subtest peak in early adulthood and then decline steadily and rapidly through the adult years. Results from numerous concurrent validity studies are included which show the correlation of K-BIT scores with established intelligence tests and school achievement tests.

COMMENTS ON THE K-BIT. The K-BIT is a well-normed, standardized, individual intelligence test that appears to be useful when testing time is limited and only a gross measure of intellectual functioning is required. The authors of the K-BIT have developed other psychometric instruments including the Kaufman Assessment Battery for Children (K-ABC; T4:1343), the Kaufman Adolescent and Adult Intelligence Test (KAIT; T4:1342), and the Kaufman Test of Educational Achievement (K-TEA; T4:1348). Test administrators will find the K-BIT a welcomed addition to these other tests. Although the authors state the K-BIT can be administered by other than highly trained professionals, this practice should be discouraged as the probability of test misuse increases greatly. Overall, the K-BIT has many good qualities to recommend its use.

REVIEWER'S REFERENCE

Thompson, A. P., Howard, D., & Anderson, J. (1986). Two-and four-subtest short forms of the WAIS-R: Validity in a psychiatric sample. *Canadian Journal of Behavioral Science, 18*, 287-293.

[47]
Kuder General Interest Survey, Form E.
Purpose: Constructed to assess "broad interest areas" related to occupational choices.
Population: Grades 6–12.
Publication Dates: 1963–91.
Scores, 11: Outdoor, Mechanical, Computational, Scientific, Persuasive, Artistic, Literary, Musical, Social Service, Clerical, Verification.
Administration: Group.
Price Data, 1994: $49.35 per complete hand-scored kit including 25 consumable booklets, 25 interpretive leaflets, and instructions for administration; $44.85 per complete locally machine-scored kit including same materials above; $79.30 per CTB machine-scored kit including materials above plus 2 answer sheet return envelopes, 2 scoring control cards, and complete scoring; $15.25 per 25 punch pins and backboards; $22 per 100 punch pins; $40 per 100 backboards; $11.95 per Job and College Major Charts; $5.60 per manual ('88, 48 pages); $7.40 per specimen set; information regarding microcomputer administration and scoring available from publisher.

Time: [45–60] minutes.
Comments: Extension of the Kuder vocational interest inventories series.
Author: G. Frederic Kuder.
Publisher: CTB MacMillan/McGraw-Hill.
Cross References: See T4:1374 (4 references) and T3:1269 (4 references); see also 8:1009 (16 references); for reviews of an earlier edition by Barbara A. Kirk, Paul R. Lohnes, and John N. McCall, and excerpted reviews by T. R. Husek and Robert F. Stahmann, see 7:1024 (8 references).

Review of the Kuder General Interest Survey, Form E by MARK POPE, President, Career Decisions, San Francisco, CA:

The Kuder General Interest Survey (KGIS), Form E is a lower extension of Frederic Kuder's measures of vocational interests. These measures evolved from a need to measure vocational interests at the junior high school level. In order to accomplish this task, the publishers of the KGIS have made a substantial attempt to design the inventory for this population. The KGIS attempts to avoid the use of concepts about which the individual's knowledge may change considerably, such as specific occupational titles, restrict the vocabulary used in the survey to a 6th grade reading level, use a larger number of items on each scale to enhance reliability because the responses of younger people tend to be slightly less reliable, and report scores on broad interest areas rather than on specific occupations as done by the Kuder Occupational Interest Survey (T4:1375). The broad interest areas for which scores are reported include: Outdoor, Mechanical, Computational, Scientific, Persuasive, Artistic, Literary, Musical, Social Service, and Clerical.

The version reviewed here was the self-scorable version although two other versions are available, both requiring computer scoring. The materials for the self-scorable version of the KGIS include a preliminary edition (1988) of a general manual; a 42-page consumable booklet that includes the test taker instructions, question booklet, self-scorable answer sheet, profile sheet, and interpretive report form; a memorandum of instructions for the test administration; an 8½ by 11 inch sheet of white corrugated cardboard; and a stainless steel, pointed punch pin. No other materials are supplied with the KGIS.

The preliminary edition of the general manual is a 45-page booklet containing three sections (general, interpretive, and technical) along with two substantial appendices and a references list concerning the KGIS. The general section begins with a subsection on why vocational interests are measured at all followed by an overview of the KGIS, a list and description of the scales, a narrative on the development of the KGIS, and ends with a how-to subsection on its use in guidance and counseling. The interpretive section contains specific detailed information on the use and interpretation of the KGIS. The technical section consists of information on the history and construction of Kuder's inventories in general and the KGIS in particular along with the development of the 1988 norms, the raw-to-percentile-score conversion tables, scale intercorrelations, and reliability and validity data.

Two substantial appendices are also included that consist of background on the Kuder interest inventories (Appendix A) along with a sample interpretive counseling session (Appendix B). Appendix A puts the KGIS in a historical perspective with the development of the other Kuder inventories. Appendix B also is very helpful to the counselor who is preparing for an interpretive session with a student/client.

An important issue for junior high school or high school students and their parents might be the stability of vocational interests over time. If interests change substantially, the interpretation of scores received on any career interest measure would be affected. The publishers of the KGIS discuss the stability of interests in younger people, citing specific research using both the KGIS and the Kuder Preference Record.

The response format used in the KGIS is the forced-choice triad which consists of three activities. The test takers are instructed to mark the one they like most and the one they like least.

In both popular press and professional literature, interest inventories have received scrutiny for their use of separate sex norms. The publishers have responded to this in the manual with a section on the use of separate sex normative data and a disclaimer regarding innate biological sex differences versus environmentally provoked sex differences.

The current version of the KGIS was restandardized in 1987. In the technical section, the publishers note the changes from the 1963 to 1987 standardizations. They conclude the changes seen in these scores reflect the changes in sex role stereotypes that occurred over that period of time.

An issue that deserves attention is the use of the KGIS in multicultural settings. In the preliminary manual no summary demographic data were included from the 1987 restandardization other than general geographic, sex, and educational data. The publishers did state there were data for 11,550 students of the 13,007 students in the restandardization sample.

Ethnic, racial, and economic status data, however, were not included in this preliminary general manual. Such data were requested by this reviewer; however, the data could not be located. This situation is intolerable for a major psychological inventory. Data should be available and saved as historical reference if for no other reason.

The 42-page consumable, combined administration/questions/answer/profile/interpretive form contains very detailed and user-friendly instructions that enable the test taker easily to complete the administration and scoring process almost unaided by a counselor/test administrator. In this self-scorable format (as with any self-scorable format with large numbers of items) there is, however, substantial room for error, but because of the peculiar format of this inventory, errors are particularly possible.

For example, the response format requires the test taker to place the piece of white corrugated cardboard in front of page 35 and then to use the punch pin to punch holes through the answer sheet (four sheets of paper). I know people have been doing this for a long time (I took the self-scorable version of the Kuder Preference Record in 1968 using this same unique format), but much manual dexterity, detail orientation, and concentration is required to consistently push that awkward little steel needle through four sheets of paper and to consistently hit that little hole for "M" (most like) or "L" (least like). An examinee might wish for a good set of calluses on the appropriate fingers because the test taker is required to punch two holes for each of 168 items with a little steel needle. A "push pin" like those found on most bulletin boards might be a better ergonomic design.

Another example of a potential source of error is in the scoring. First, the instructions in the consumable booklet are not very explicit concerning how to open the answer sheet section to begin the scoring. The scoring is very tedious. Scorers must find the starting place for each scale and then follow the circles and lines, counting the punched holes, until they reach the end place. Four of the six pages have two different scales on the page creating possible confusion. The beginning place for scoring Scales 5 and 6 is the same item. As scoring progresses for Scales 5 and 6 it is not easy to differentiate between them. The publisher has included research that verifies the increased error rate for the self-scored version.

The profile sheet, included in the consumable booklet, has two separate sex-differentiated profiles on the same side of the sheet of paper. Although this placement is very useful for counseling (i.e., the counselor does not have to flip the page over to enable the test taker to see the other profile) the resulting profiles are too close together to read easily and accurately. Also, the boxes where raw scores are to be written are too small for double digit numbers.

In a major change, the 1987 profile sheet does have a place for test takers to calculate their Holland (RIASEC) code. This enables comparison across other career interest inventories which generate the same coding (Strong Interest Inventory, Self-Directed Search, Vocational Preference Inventory, etc.). Although the data used to justify this procedure and the mathematic calculation used to arrive at the scores are somewhat suspect, the resultant code when used cautiously as an estimate of the RIASEC model can be useful in career exploration for the individual student/client. The method, rationale, and justification for this conversion are included in the interpretive and technical sections of the general manual.

There are several reasons to recommend use of the KGIS with junior high and high school students and with adults who require a measure with a low reading level. The Kuder interest inventories have a long and respected place in the history of career interest measurement. The modest cost and availability of hand-scored results make the KGIS a good instrument to be used in financially strapped school districts. The manual contains substantial statistical data along with some interpretive information; however, an update with additional normative demographic data should be published soon. Of the major hand- or self-scorable career interest inventories (Self-Directed Search [T4:2414], Vocational Preference Inventory [T4:2910], Career Occupational Preference System [T4:399], the KGIS should be chosen for use with junior high school students who want to get a Holland (RIASEC) code to aid in career exploration. The KGIS is useful with computerized career information systems.

Review of the Kuder General Interest Survey, Form E by DONALD THOMPSON, Professor of Counseling Psychology, School of Education, The University of Connecticut, Storrs, CT:

The Kuder Interest Inventory series began in 1939. The longevity of the series in the competitive world of commercial test publishing indicates the authors and publishers have been doing something right. With over a half century of existence, the Kuder inventories have been the subject of extensive empirical study. This research base provides considerable evidence regarding the utility of these measures.

The Kuder General Interest Survey (KGIS-Form E) represents the third generation of Kuder tests, and was built on a foundation established by its predecessors. There is considerable debate among psychometrists regarding the methods used to validate the Kuder inventories and the interpretation of the meaning of the volumes of research. The KGIS was first published in 1963, with subsequent revisions in 1976 and 1988. The current version has only minor differences in content, but since 1975, the publisher and other researchers have completed additional reliability and validity studies and new normative data have been added. The general manual that accompanies the test package contains the following statement: "The basic purpose of the surveys is to stimulate career exploration and suggest career possibilities—to open up options, rather than limit them. Because the General Interest Survey suggests broad interest areas to be explored, it is better suited to the guidance of younger people" (p. 4). This statement and other information in the manual suggests the publisher views the KGIS as a tool that is appropriately used as a part of a systematic and comprehensive career exploration program rather than as a standalone measure of occupational interests.

The KGIS is available in three different scoring versions. The self-scored version uses the punch pin method for recording answers and can be self-scored by the test taker. The other two forms are computer scored (one is mailed to the publisher and the other is locally scored on a microcomputer at the user site). For the computer-scored versions, the test is taken with paper and pencil and then scanned into the computer, and both computer-scored versions provide a comprehensive narrative report. The specimen set for the self-scored version used for this review includes a consumable test booklet with the survey, an answer pad, profile sheet, and interpretive guide; a memorandum of instructions; and a general manual that includes administration, counseling, interpretation, and technical information.

The same form of the KGIS is used for grades 6 through 12; however, separate norms are provided for grades 6–8 and 9–12. The average testing time is between 45 minutes and 1 hour, and administration can be done individually or in groups. The inventory contains 168 items written at the 6th grade reading level. Each item contains three possible alternative activities and the testee is required to choose the *most liked* and *least liked* from each triad by using a punch pin to perforate a small circle adjacent to the activity. The KGIS is structured around 10 vocational interest areas (scales) and one verification scale. The verification scale provides an estimate of whether the testee has responded sincerely and correctly, whereas the vocational scales provide percentile scores for the testee in comparison to the norm group. The 10 vocational scales are Outdoor, Mechanical, Computational, Scientific, Persuasive, Artistic, Literary, Musical, Social Service, and Clerical. The instructions, administration, and scoring processes are relatively simple and quickly accomplished. Based on my experience with the scoring and interpretation, however, there can be problems for younger students and low level readers that may cause significant scoring errors. Research reported in the manual also points out this possibility. Based on the description of the development of the activities statements, it appears that item content for the KGIS has remained the same through the three revisions, and many of the items were taken directly from the Kuder Form C. The revision of Form C to the KGIS in 1964 involved simplifying the language of some activities statements, adding some new ones, and the addition of new norms in the 1988 version. A review of the activities listed for each scale indicates there has been a concerted effort to avoid using terminology that suggests specific job tasks and occupational titles. Most of the activities are ones that many youngsters (especially middle class) will have experienced and therefore should understand.

The reported norms show good diversity in terms of geographic location, grade level, and sex; however, it is troubling that no indication of ethnic or racial composition of the sample is provided. Also, there is no information regarding how the samples were drawn. The description does indicate the samples were drawn from "45 cities" (p. 23), leading to the possible conclusion that no rural areas were included as sample sites. In addition, there is no indication whether the samples were drawn randomly from large representative groups at each site, or if intact class groups were used.

The reliability data reported are test-retest over a 2-week period. Correlations range in the 70s and 80s and are acceptable for this type of measure. Generally, the higher the grade level of the respondent, the higher the test-retest reliability. Also, the KGIS manual author reports stability indices in the .40 to .60 range for scores on Kuder Form C over a 4-year period. No measures of internal consistency are reported in the manual.

For interest inventories, there are two principal types of validity. Empirical or criterion-related validity examines if the test can effectively predict future behavior or performance on a similar well-validated measure. The other principal type is construct validity (sometimes called homogeneous). The manual author indicates the KGIS vocational scales have been compared to similar scales of both the California

Occupational Preference System (COPS) and the Vocational Preference Inventory (VPI). The correlations indicate moderate concurrent validity with the scales of these measures.

The intercorrelation matrix of KGIS vocational scale scores indicates generally low to moderate relationships between and among the 10 scales, suggesting they are, in fact, measuring different constructs.

Earlier reviewers have criticized the KGIS for: (a) having a middle-class bias and a limited number of items to which persons from underrepresented groups might relate; (b) variations in both the logically expected and unexpected correlations between vocational scales; (c) the validity data regarding predictiveness with later occupational satisfaction and/or success are inadequate; and (d) test-retest reliability data do not provide confidence in the long-term stability of scores. The present examination of the KGIS indicates that criticisms a, b, and c continue to be problem areas. Criticism d appears to have been addressed adequately in the current revision.

This reviewer noted several areas where improvements could be made. First, the antiquated punch pin method for recording answers should be eliminated (other inventories such as the COPS have developed much improved methods for self-scoring). Also, the interpretation process for the self-scored version is not as simple and easy as suggested and will take considerable involvement of a professional. I would not recommend purchase of the self-scored version. The computer-scored versions will save time and money in the long run and provide more accurate scoring and a good interpretive report.

There are several improved features that make this edition of the KGIS a more useful tool for initiating career exploration. The addition of Holland's RIASEC code conversions to the interpretation sheet make the results profile easier to interpret and it is simpler to locate career resource materials that are keyed to the RIASEC system. Also, the verification scale is a particularly attractive feature of this inventory, because faking and response sets are common problems with interest and personality inventories. The 1988 norms have provided more comprehensive comparison data and provide a much needed correction regarding the changing preferences for certain career areas.

In summary, the KGIS could be a valuable tool for initiating career exploration when it is used with youngsters of middle school age and with the direct supervision of a counselor or other staff member. Major advantages of the KGIS include its unambiguous language; its long history of use; and it is inexpensive, quick, and easy to administer. Because there is no empirical evidence regarding the effectiveness of this measure as a predictor of future occupational satisfaction or success, the KGIS should not be used to help clients make specific career choices and, therefore, is not recommended as a stand-alone interest measure. Also, its use should be confined to younger students, and then primarily for initiating a broad exploration of career interests.

[48]
Language Assessment Scales, Reading and Writing.

Purpose: Designed to measure "English language skills in reading and writing necessary for functioning in a mainstream academic environment."

Population: Language-minority students in grades 2–3, 4–6, 7–11.

Publication Date: 1988.

Acronym: LAW R/W.

Scores, 3: Reading, Writing, Total.

Administration: Group.

Levels, 3: 1, 2, 3.

Forms, 2: A, B.

Price Data, 1992: $83.30 per 35 Level 1 test booklets and examiner's manual (67 pages); $35.70 per 35 Level 2 or Level 3 Reading test booklets and Reading/Writing examiner's manual (Level 2, 79 pages; Level 3, 73 pages); $27.30 per 35 Level 2 or Level 3 Writing test booklets; $21.50 per 50 CompuScan answer sheets (select Level 2 or 3); $74.50 per 9 Level 1 scoring stencils; $10.35 per set of scoring stencils (select Level 2 or 3); $7.95 per examiner's manual (select level); $11.20 per technical report (98 pages); $54 per training kit.

Time: (50–75) minutes for Level 1; (49–87) minutes for Level 2; (53–86) minutes for Level 3.

Comments: May be used in conjunction with LAS Oral (T4:1387).

Authors: Sharon E. Duncan and Edward A. DeAvila.

Publisher: CTB Macmillan/McGraw-Hill.

Cross References: See T4:1386 (5 references).

Review of the Language Assessment Scales, Reading and Writing by C. DALE CARPENTER, Professor of Special Education, Western Carolina University, Cullowhee, NC:

The Language Assessment Scales, Reading and Writing (LAS R/W) is intended to assess the functioning of language minority pupils in reading and writing. The purpose is to measure competence to succeed in a mainstream class and cutoff points are set to aid in entry and exit decisions for students in special programs for English as a Second Language (ESL). This instrument follows the introduction of Language Assessment Scales, Oral (LAS Oral; T4:1387) and is meant to be used in conjunction with the LAS Oral.

The approach used follows a probabilistic model. The aim is to predict the point at which language minority students would achieve proficiency comparable to that of students in mainstream classes succeeding at the 40th percentile rank level or better. It is not designed to measure higher level skills with accuracy. Although the LAS R/W is used with the LAS Oral to arrive at a Language Proficiency Index, the LAS R/W must be evaluated for its own qualities because it may be used alone.

Each level has two forms and contains four measures of reading—mechanics and usage, vocabulary, fluency, and reading comprehension—and two to three measures of written expression—sentence completion, sentence writing, and essay writing. All use multiple-choice items except for three writing subtests. The three writing subtests are used to elicit sentences (or endings for sentences) and a story. The content and format are appropriate. The authors are to be commended for using an open-ended format for the writing subtests as they better tap written expression than would all multiple-choice items. They should also be commended for including a passage to be read with accompanying comprehension questions for reading comprehension. Other formats included on some tests do not adequately measure comprehension.

The number of items on the LAS R/W is small. Only 10 or 15 items are used for multiple-choice items. For reading comprehension, there is one story and 10 multiple-choice items. For story writing, students write only one story. Students write five sentences in sentence writing.

TECHNICAL ADEQUACY. The small number of items may be one of the factors contributing to relatively low (about half are less than .80) reliability coefficients for internal consistency on many of the subtests. Forms A and B correlate highly with each other for adequate alternate form reliability. Although the need for interrater reliability is stressed, it is not reported based on the criteria available for the writing measures.

Validity is addressed in several ways. Form A and Form B predict three levels of proficiency with efficiency for reading, writing, and reading and writing combined. As might be expected, proficiency in writing does not predict proficiency in reading nor does proficiency in reading predict proficiency in writing. Scores on the LAS R/W correlate highly with scores on the California Test of Basic Skills (CTBS) and with teacher classifications of student proficiency. Unfortunately, solid evidence to show that the LAS R/W will predict success in mainstream classes is not strong. Nevertheless, evidence is presented in the Technical Report which supports validity of the LAS R/W.

The norm sample included almost 4,000 pupils in grades 1 through 12. Pupils came from the Southwest, Northeast, Midwest, and Hawaii. Approximately twice as many language minority as language majority students were included. The home language of participants included English, Spanish, Chinese, Vietnamese, Tagalog, Japanese, Arabic, and Native American. No information about the socioeconomic status of the pupils is provided.

SUMMARY. The LAS R/W is a valuable complement to the LAS Oral. The design appears appropriate to assist in making entry and exit decisions from ESL programs although evidence does not clearly justify using the LAS R/W alone or even in combination with the LAS Oral to make such decisions. The LAS R/W is simple to administer but scoring the non-multiple-choice portions requires training, and interscorer reliability has not been established. The LAS R/W appears to fill a need and further validity data would help to establish its place in the field. If practitioners want an instrument to predict success in mainstream classes or to decide eligibility for ESL programs, the LAS R/W in conjunction with the LAS Oral may be helpful, but users cannot feel confident that decisions based on these instruments would be better than teacher judgement or other available instruments. Both low reliability and less than adequate validity contribute to lack of confidence for this use. If the LAS R/W is to be used with any student to measure reading and writing achievement, it has problems due to the small number of items and lack of sensitivity at the upper ranges of performance. The design of the instrument makes it promising, however, as a screening measure.

Review of the Language Assessment Scales, Reading and Writing by THOMAS W. GUYETTE, Assistant Professor of Speech Pathology, University of Illinois at Chicago, Chicago, IL:

The purpose of this test is to measure "those English language skills in reading and writing necessary for functioning in a mainstream academic environment" (p. 2). The authors emphasize that this is not an achievement test but rather a test used to make decisions about placement and reclassification of language minority students. The test can be used in conjunction with the Language Assessment Scales:

Oral (T4:1387) in order to obtain a more complete picture of language skills.

The Language Assessment Scales, Reading and Writing comes with 12 different test forms. First, there are separate test forms for the two language modalities (i.e., Reading and Writing). Second, there are separate test forms for each of three educational levels (Form 1, 2, 3). Form 1 is appropriate for grades 2 and 3. Form 2 is appropriate for grades 4–6. Form 3 is appropriate for grades 7–9+. Third, there is an alternate form for each of the above domains.

Test content areas include receptive and expressive vocabulary, fluency, reading for information, mechanics and usage, finishing sentences, and short essay writing. Not all educational levels include all content areas. The Vocabulary section is composed of 10 items that measure the student's ability to match pictures to words. The Fluency section measures the student's ability to fill in a missing word in a sentence. In the Reading For Information section the student reads a paragraph and responds to 10 true-false questions regarding the content of the paragraph. The Mechanics and Usage section is composed of 15 items that test skills in areas such as punctuation and grammatical usage. The Finishing Sentences section is composed of 5 items that measure the student's ability to finish or complete a sentence correctly. In the "What's Happening?" section an action picture is used to elicit a one-sentence written response.

The documentation accompanying the test provides adequate instructions to prepare administrators, students, and proctors to give or take the exam. There is also a description of precautions to be taken during test administration. The authors suggest that the test be administered in two 45–55-minute sections.

Scoring is unambiguous for Sections 1 through 4. However, the scoring of Sections 5 and 6 involves examiner judgement using a 4-point rating scale. The manual provides descriptions of each point on the scale. To further reduce the ambiguity there are numerous sample responses and discussions of scoring for each section. The authors describe a procedure for testing reliability between raters. They suggest that raters strive for 90% agreement.

Once a raw score is obtained it is converted to a standardized score using the appropriate tables. A standardized score can be obtained for the Reading section, the Writing section, and the combined Total. The interpretation of the standardized score is facilitated by the Competency Level Tables that allow interpretation of the standardized score into one of the following categories: Non-Reader, Limited Reader, Competent Reader.

A separate manual is provided for the validity and reliability data. Reliability and validity data were collected from students in the Northeast, Midwest, Southwest, and the Pacific. There were approximately 3,969 completed tests with 2,504 fluent-English speakers, 1,221 limited-English speakers, and 36 non-English speakers. Home languages of subjects were Spanish, English, Chinese, Vietnamese, Tagalog, Arabic, Japanese, and Native American.

Several different measures of test reliability are presented. Reliability quotients are presented for each subscale. Alpha values were calculated within each subscale for Forms A and B across the three educational levels. Values ranged from $r = .6492$ to $.9064$ with the majority of values in the .7 and .8 range. These data suggest the internal consistency of the test subscales is adequate. In an attempt to increase the reliability of placement decisions, the authors provide limited information on the standard error of measurement. Confidence interval bandwidths are provided for those scores that fall near the cutoff between language competent and language limited and between language limited and nonliterate. If the student scores within the category confidence intervals then it is suggested that placement should be considered provisional. I did not find information on test-retest reliability or interrater reliability regarding the scoring of certain items.

Several different measures of alternate form validity are presented. First, the authors present correlations between the subscales on Forms A and B. The majority of correlations are greater than $r = .8$ except in those subscales involving less objective scoring. The authors also present information on the agreement of placement decisions based on Forms A and B. Presenting cross-tabulations across three categories (competent, limited, non-reader/writer) the authors demonstrate agreement of 80–90% when classifying students into the end categories (competent and non-reader/writer) but exhibit only 60–70% agreement in the "limited" category.

Two studies of concurrent validity are also presented. In the first, the classification of students based on the Language Assessment Scales (LAS) is compared with the classification of students based on the results of a standard ized test of basic skills. Correlations between the two tests are in the .8 to .9 range. Cross-tabulation data indicate 92% agreement on the classification of these students. In a second study, classification of students based on the Language Assessment Scales is compared to a classification system used by a school district to classify students learning English as a second language. Although there is a linear relationship between the two classification systems, the percent agreement between the two systems is only 65.66%.

In summary, the LAS is a screening test designed to produce placement information for language minority students. Generally the manual provides adequate information about test rationale, administration, scoring, and interpretation. Information on test reliability and validity is adequate.

[49]

Leader Behavior Analysis II.

Purpose: Developed to assess leadership style.
Population: Middle and upper level managers.
Publication Date: 1991.
Acronym: LBAII.
Scores, 6: Style Flexibility, Style Effectiveness, Directing Style, Coaching Style, Supporting Style, Delegating Style.
Administration: Group.
Editions, 2: Self, Other.
Price Data, 1990: $29.50 per complete kit including 1 LBAII-Self instrument, 8 LBAII-Other instruments, data summary sheet, and scoring instructions; $2.95 per instrument (select Self or Other).
Time: [15–20] minutes.
Comments: Ratings by employees and self-ratings.
Authors: Drea Zigarmi, Douglas Forsyth, Kenneth Blanchard, and Ronald Hambleton (tests).
Publisher: Blanchard Training & Development, Inc.

Review of the Leader Behavior Analysis II by H. JOHN BERNARDIN, University Research Professor, and DONNA K. COOKE, Assistant Professor, College of Business, Florida Atlantic University, Boca Raton, FL:

The Leader Behavior Analysis II (LBAII) instruments are designed to measure perceived leadership style from the perspective of either the leader him or herself or subordinates to the leader. Currently, there are two main versions. The LBAII Self assesses self-perceived leadership style and the LBAII Other assesses perceptions of a manager's leadership style. There are also Self and Other versions written specifically for sales force managers. The revised version of the Situational Leadership theory is the basis for the LBAII and application of its principles are expected to result in increased satisfaction and organizational effectiveness (Hersey & Blanchard, 1982; Blanchard, Zigarmi, & Zigarmi, 1985). Recent research on the original theory of situational leadership has not been favorable (Blank, Weitzel, & Green, 1990).

Two types of managerial behavior, Directive and Supportive, are dichotomized (high and low) to produce four LBAII styles. Style 1 (S1) = high Direction/low Support, Style 2 (S2) = high Direction/high Support, Style 3 (S3) = low Direction/high Support, and Style 4 (S4) = low Direction/low Support. The technical manual reports that the instruments have been edited to eliminate gender and race biases. However, for the LBAII Self there were gender differences on the S2 and S3 dimensions. Tests of racial/ethnic differences were not reported. The instruments are available in 14 translations with norms provided by the distributors.

Each LBAII version has 20 items. Each item is a description of a situation requiring the selection of one of four behavioral responses. One weakness in this methodology is that there are only four possible behavioral alternatives for each situation, none of which may resemble the actual or anticipated behavior of the manager. No options are available for selecting alternative responses. Little discussion is presented in the manual to explain either how the authors arrived at the four alternative behaviors per situation or the extent to which the situations were representative of important, leadership situations. As an alternative, Fiedler (1967) presented considerable data and research to justify the three contingency factors captured in his contingency theory of leadership.

As reported in the manual for the LBAII, most users employ only the Self version prior to a training program. Few studies have compared Self and Other scores, despite considerable research illustrating the lack of validity in self-assessments and showing discrepancies in self and significant other assessments to be moderators of several measures of unit and group effectiveness (e.g., Atwater & Yammarino, 1992).

Scoring for the LBAII is done by the respondent and is rather complicated. The derivation of the "Flexibility" score is a measure of the degree to which the four styles are selected with equal frequency. The other score, style "Effectiveness," is computed by comparing the selected style to the recommended style. Effectiveness is described as the more important of the two scores. For each item the behavioral styles are rated excellent, good, fair, and poor. The excellent style is weighted 4, the good style is weighted 3, and the fair and poor styles are weighted 1 each. The empirical justification for the magnitude of the weights of the behavioral responses and the unit-weights across items is not given in the manual.

The lengthy manual is written for the non-researcher. Although there is some redeeming value, the manual is generally not well organized and the reader must use the Table of Contents and the List of Tables in order to gather information. The manual provides a poor introduction to the LBAII and the explicit purpose for the instrument is not presented. Although the changes in the situational leadership model prompted the new instruments, a clear delineation of the differences in the old and new situational models is not presented. The authors assume familiarity with two previous works, one of which does not appear in the reference list. Although mean Flexibility and Effectiveness scores, standard deviations, and sample sizes are presented for the Self version from 13 studies, very little data are available for the Other version. Research clearly shows that follower-derived leadership scores are much more valid than self-assessments of leadership style. More normative data are needed on both instruments. Because these are instruments for use in applied settings, it is expected that there would be attention paid to helping the user to improve the Effectiveness score. The only guidance given is to review the descriptions of the prescribed behaviors in the questionnaire. There is no description of what key elements in the situation would call for a particular management style. The user appears to be none the wiser from using the instrument.

Because the manual is apparently designed for non-researchers, the authors attempt to explain technical terms such as reliability and validity. They describe their strategy of estimating concurrent criterion-related validity as "prediction." This could be very misleading, particularly to their non-researcher audience, and the footnote does not clarify the distinction. Overall, the manual is disorganized and poorly written, in spite of the summary of the computer readability analysis results.

The internal consistency reliability of the LBAII Other's dimensions were calculated in three studies. The alphas of S1 and S4 were typically in the .80s. S2 and S3 have lower reliabilities, generally in the .70s. Only one study reported alphas for the Self scale. They were .51, .45, .56, and .42 for S1, S2, S3, and S4, respectively. the alphas for the sales manager versions range from .29 to .82, with S2 tending to be the most unreliable. These estimates are low for scales of this nature, although the authors consider them to be "extremely good" (for Other) and "adequate" (for Self).

More than 60 pages are devoted to establishing the validity of the LBAII Other against Wilson's Multi-Level Management Survey (MLMS) because the MLMS measures the Directive and Supportive constructs. Considering the numerous leader behavior instruments, other more widely known and better established operationalizations of related constructs should have been included. Worth noting was an unpublished dissertation cited in the manual in which the author correlated the LBAII to Consideration and Initiating Structure from the Leader Behavior Description Questionnaire (LBDQ). The correlation coefficients, though small (e.g., .07, .12), were all in the correct direction and significant at the .05 or better level.

The LBAII's predictive validity was tested against eight MLMS subscales which served as the dependent variables. They measured, for example, the follower's satisfaction with factors such as climate and commitment. One would have reasonably expected the effectiveness criteria to include measures of output, because increased output is thought to be a benefit of using the LBAII prescriptions. The independent variables of the ANOVA with the MLMS were the four style scales, plus the Flexibility and the Effectiveness scales. Out of the eight analyses, Flexibility was never a significant variable, and Effectiveness was not a significant variable in five. This is disappointing because Effectiveness is supposed to be the most important score. The six scores failed to explain variance in work involvement and commitment. It is possible that the ipsative nature of the style scales disqualifies them from use in an ANOVA.

In summary, the authors have not demonstrated that the LBAII fulfills its purpose to measure Directive and Supportive styles. The instrument appears to be of limited use to both researchers and practitioners due to the relatively poor reliabilities and the failure to justify the situations presented. Further research to establish construct validity is needed and the authors of the instrument admirably offer free use of the instruments for research purposes. Without a clearer understanding of the relationship between instrument scores and the new situational theory, it is difficult for researchers to assess validity and virtually impossible for users to understand how to improve Effectiveness scores.

Vecchio (1987) has argued that the LBDQ-XII and the Leader Opinion Questionnaire (a self-assessment instrument) (Stogdill & Coons, 1957) are more widely accepted (and researched) measures of task (i.e., initiating structure) and relationship (i.e., consideration) leadership style. Other instruments which have more substantive research trails are the Managerial Style Questionnaire (MSQ; T4:1532) from McBer and Company, the Management Skills Profile (MSP) from Personnel Decisions Incorporated (Davis, Hellervik, & Sheard, 1989), and the Team Evaluation and Management Systems (TEAMS;

Edwards, 1990). Both self and "significant other" assessments are available for the MSQ, the MSP, and TEAMS. Normative data for the MSP are more extensive than for the LBAII of the MSQ and excellent training materials are available as an adjunct to the MSP.

REVIEWERS' REFERENCES

Stogdill, R. M., & Coons, A. E. (Eds.) (1957). *Leader behavior: Its description and measurement*. (Research Monograph No. 88). Columbus, OH: Ohio State University, Bureau of Business Research.

Fiedler, F. E. (1967). *A theory of leadership effectiveness*. New York: McGraw-Hill Book Co.

Hersey, P., & Blanchard, K. (1982). *Management of organizational behavior*. Englewood Cliffs, NJ: Prentice-Hall.

Blanchard, K., Zigarmi, P., & Zigarmi, D. (1985). *Leadership and the one minute manager*. New York: William Morrow.

Vecchio, R. P. (1987). Situational leadership theory: An examination of a prescriptive theory. *Journal of Applied Psychology, 72*, 444-451.

Davis, B. L., Hellervik, L. W., & Sheard, J. L. (Eds.) (1989). *Successful manager's handbook*. Minneapolis: Personnel Decisions, Inc.

Blank, W., Weitzel, J. R., & Green, S. G. (1990). A test of the situational leadership theory. *Personnel Psychology, 43*, 579-597.

Edwards, M. R. (1990). Assessment: Implementation strategies for multiple rater systems. *Personnel Journal, 21*(6), 130-139.

Atwater, L. E., & Yammarino, F. J. (1992). Does self-other agreement on leadership perceptions moderate the validity of leadership and performance predictions? *Personnel Psychology, 45*, 141-164.

Review of the Leader Behavior Analysis II by SHARON McNEELY, Associate Professor of Educational Foundations, Northeastern Illinois University, Chicago, IL:

The Leader Behavior Analysis II (LBAII) comes in two forms, the Self, and the Other, both designed to provide perceptions of leadership style by having the respondent choose one of four leader decisions in 20 "typical" job situations. The authors' Validity and Reliability Study booklet reports this update of the original Leadership Behavior Analysis (LBA) is supposed to present "generic" situations that try to achieve business realism while eliminating gender and race biases as much as possible.

The Self form of the test has the respondent assume that he/she is the leader and is to choose the decision that "would most closely describe your behavior in the situation presented." The Other form allows the name of the leader to be inserted, with the respondent then describing this person's behavior. According to the study, the Self form yields six different scores, two primary: the Effectiveness, and the Flexibility Scores; and four secondary style scores. The Effectiveness Score is meant to represent how effective the respondent is in certain situations, whereas the Flexibility Score indicates how often the respondent used a different style to solve the situations.

The authors present correlations showing that the LBAII is statistically and conceptually related to the

Multi-Level Management Survey (MLMS; Wilson, 1981). The MLMS is used for construct validity studies. These studies do not lend full support to the Flexibility construct. However, the authors explain these findings by arguing the managers should be able to use more than one leadership style to solve management problems. To their credit they do assert the score "may not be an important psychometric measure of the general concept of Leadership in comparison to the MLMS" (p. 27). The predictive validity studies also do not lend consistent support to the LBAII.

The four leadership styles have also been redefined from the LBA, based on two types of observable and verifiable managerial behaviors: Directive and Supportive. The definitions of these styles assume the extremes of high or low can be applied to each behavior. The lack of a middle ground for each behavior is somewhat troublesome, and may help explain why there is consistent correlation with most of the MLMS' 15 subscale scores, in that the LBAII may not be measuring anything different than the MLMS scales. In this case, the 15 scales of the MLMS may be more effective for use in labeling behaviors and providing feedback to managers concerning specific strengths, weaknesses, and desired behaviors than information gleaned from the LBAII.

Reported studies on the internal consistency of the LBAII show moderate correlations (.43–.60 for Self, .54–.86 for Other). Further, 5 of the 20 items do not fit within the Rasch model for unidimensionality, and only one test-retest reliability study has been done yielding a .72 stability coefficient on Flexibility scores.

Although an experienced manager may focus on a few key words in select orders to complete the survey in a short time, the LBAII has an untimed administration that could take well over an hour for the careful reader or new manager to complete. The choices for each item usually contain much of the same wording in different order, and severely limit the possible choices of action for the respondent. Not only are the responses very similar, but they also appear redundantly across most of the situations. This could lead to sloppy reading and haphazard responding with corresponding threats to reliability and validity.

The authors described the prompts as business-appropriate situations. The situations are, however, redundant, with recurrences of employees not doing their tasks, groups not functioning effectively, and the manager missing something important. The authors contend that the situations also are free of gender bias. Twelve of the 20 situations identify either the

male or female employee. However, the six male versions appear in the first 11 items. Four of the six female versions occur in the last 7 items. Females are presented as "new" employees in one-half of these situations, compared to only one of six for the males. Although statistical analysis may not support discrimination between male and female managers, more studies need to be done on this area.

In summary, although the LBAII may be better suited to use in today's business environment than the LBA, its use of six scales, lack of adequate reliability, inconsistent construct validity, possible gender-presentation biases, and possible unlimited time for administration lead me to rate it as only a fair instrument, at best.

The LBAII should not be used in isolation for making any decisions about respondents or their leaders. The MLMS (T4:2655) provides more varied and useful information to businesses, and may be more appropriate for use despite its age.

REVIEWER'S REFERENCE
Wilson, C. L. (1981). Survey of Management Practices (Form SMP-SE). New Canaan, CT: Clark Wilson Publishing.

[50]

Learning Efficiency Test-II (1992 Revision).
Purpose: "Yields information about a person's preferred modality for learning and provides insights about the impact of interference on memory storage and retrieval, and the kinds of metacognitive strategies used during learning."
Population: Ages 5–75.
Publication Dates: 1981–92.
Acronym: LET-II.
Scores, 15: Visual Ordered Recall (Immediate Recall, Short Term Recall, Long Term Recall) Visual Unordered Recall (Immediate Recall, Short Term Recall, Long Term Recall), Auditory Ordered Recall (Immediate Recall, Short Term Recall, Long Term Recall), Auditory Unordered Recall (Immediate Recall, Short Term Recall, Long Term Recall), Total Visual Memory, Total Auditory Memory, Global Memory.
Administration: Individual.
Price Data, 1992: $60 per test kit including manual ('92, 159 pages), stimulus cards, and 50 record forms; $25 per specimen set including manual and sample forms.
Time: (10–15) minutes.
Author: Raymond E. Webster.
Publisher: Academic Therapy Publications.
Cross References: See T4:1423 (1 reference); for a review by Robert G. Harrington of an earlier form, see 9:601.

Review of the Learning Efficiency Test-II (1992 Revision) by ALICE J. CORKILL, Assistant Professor of Counseling and Educational Psychology, University of Nevada, Las Vegas, NV:

The Learning Efficiency Test-II (LET-II), a revision of the Learning Efficiency Test (LET; 9:601), is an individually administered, diagnostic test appropriate for use with individuals from age 5 through adult who do not have mental disabilities or are not hearing impaired or deaf. It is designed to determine how efficiently one processes and retains visual and auditory input. The test was designed to identify the information processing characteristics that impede learning. The deficits are identified as auditory, visual, retention of ordered information, retention of unordered information, and perhaps, number of items retained.

The test manual provides a brief review of the literature pertaining to the relationship between information processing ability (short-term memory deficits) and learning disabilities. A brief report of research using the LET suggests that under certain circumstances it does an adequate job of identifying individuals who would benefit from special education services. Compelling evidence of the relationship between the type of information processing tasks used on the LET-II and classroom performance in reading and math is in very short supply.

The LET-II measures ordered and nonordered retention of visual and auditory input in three time frames: (*a*) immediate, no interference; (*b*) short-term memory, brief delay with an interference task (counting by ones between specified numbers 10 places apart); and (*c*) long-term memory, another brief delay with a different interference task (repeating a 6–9 word sentence). The LET-II author claims the interference tasks used approximate typical classroom interference. In addition, the test is described as identifying the student's (*a*) learning style, (*b*) immediate memory capacity, (*c*) short term memory capacity, and (*d*) transfer ability between short and long term memory.

The learning style is apparently identified as either auditory or visual. Immediate and short term memory capacity are identified by how many stimulus items are recalled immediately or after a brief delay with minimal interference. Whether transfer from short to long term memory is being measured is debatable. The time required for each interference task, whether counting 10 places or repeating a 6–9-word sentence is less than 10 seconds for an adult and 10, perhaps 15, seconds for a kindergarten student. Whether a delay as short as 20 seconds (from presentation of

stimulus materials to long term recall) actually measures transfer ability between short and long term memory is doubtful.

The input is in the form of nonrhyming consonant strings as short as two letters and as long as nine. The upper limit of nine letters was selected based on research that suggests the average adult can retain about seven items plus or minus two in short term memory. Thus, the nine-letter string should adequately assess the full range of short term memory.

Serial strings were constructed by randomly selecting from a list of 11 nonrhyming, phonetically nonconfusable consonants. Nonrhyming consonants were selected rather than digits to reduce the potential effect of guessing (i.e., only 9 digits as possible stimulus materials as opposed to 26 letters). Further, letters recalled out of order allegedly represent sequential memory problems rather than reflecting selection from a restricted response domain (i.e., digits). The stimulus materials used in the LET-II are the same as in the LET.

No new reliability studies have been conducted since the 1981 publication date of the LET. For the LET, 40 secondary students with learning and behavior problems were used in order to determine test-retest reliability. The interval between administrations ranged from 1 to 6 weeks with a mean test interval of 3.68 weeks. Test-retest reliability coefficients ranged from .81 to .97. An informal reliability study involving 55 students with learning disabilities reports test-retest reliability coefficients ranging from .71 to .86 with a median of .80. Given the time span between publication of the LET and the LET-II and that the test materials for the LET and the LET-II are identical, an in-depth study of reliability using larger samples of subjects at a variety of age levels could have been conducted.

The LET-II was standardized on a sample of 1,126 subjects between the ages of 5 years, 0 months and 85 years, 4 months (average *n* at each age group = 53.62; smallest group: 55–59 years, *n* = 25; largest group: 17–19 years, *n* = 113). Students, who were enrolled in public schools, were randomly selected for participation provided they were functioning at grade level or higher and had not been referred for special education services. Adults were recruited from community or social agencies. Adults were screened and were required to obtain a standard score higher than 85 on the Peabody Picture Vocabulary Test. Further, students with organically or physically based learning problems or with behavioral or emotional problems were excluded from the standardization sample. Adults with obvious physical or sensory impairments were also excluded. The sample was 53.73% female and reports 66.43% Caucasian and 33.57% African American. No differences in performance were found between males and females. As a result, one set of norms appropriate for both males and females is provided. The test manual author states that a "broad range of socio-economic backgrounds" (p. 29) were represented but no specific information is provided. Further, no information concerning where, geographically, the subjects came from is reported. The incomplete information made available suggests caution in using this instrument.

Directions for administering the test are clearly described. Directions for scoring are somewhat less clear but can be understood by closely examining a provided example. Scaled scores are obtained for immediate, short term, and long term recall on both the visual and auditory modality subtests and for ordered and unordered recall. This results in six scores for each modality. The scaled scores are based on the length of the longest string recalled correctly at immediate recall. One point is given for each correct letter recalled. Thus, scores can range from 0 to 9. Tables are provided for converting raw scores to standard scores. Although the test manual states the youngest examinee at age 5.0, conversion information for 5-year-old examinees is not provided. As was cited in the review of the LET (Harrington, 1985), the limited range of raw scores (0–9) results in potentially inadequate discriminating ability.

Standard scores have been added to the LET-II. These standard scores were deemed necessary in order for the LET-II to serve as a tool for qualifying a student for special education services. Standard scores are computed by summing total numbers of letters recalled correctly under immediate, short term, and long term recall—both ordered and unordered by modality. The summed raw scores are converted to standard scores using provided tables. These standard scores appear to have a mean of 100 and a standard deviation of 15 so they may be compared to intelligence test scores. The summed raw scores for visual (the Visual Modality Factor) and auditory (the Auditory Modality Factor) modality subtests are added together resulting in a Global Memory Factor. This sum is converted to a standard score using provided tables. Although no tables were available for subjects age 5.0 for scales scores, subjects age 5.0 are included in the standard score conversion tables. Standard scores may be converted to percentile ranks using provided tables. The standard error of measurement was reported as problematic for the LET but is less so for the LET-II. Whether this is due to greater precision in the conversion from raw to scaled or standard scores (which is possible, given the larger norming sample) or differences in how percentile ranks are acquired, for example, is not clear.

Assessment of content validity of the LET-II is not different from that of the LET given the use of identical stimulus materials. Construct validity was examined by comparing correlation matrices between groups of average students, students with emotional disabilities, students with learning disabilities, students with mental disabilities, and slow learners (it is unclear what qualifies someone as a "slow learner"). The manual author suggests that inconsistent patterns of intercorrelations on scores on both subtests indicate different information processing abilities between modalities. No substantiating research is cited. Further claims include that students with learning or mental disabilities and slow learners show impaired recall for each time frame and subtest when compared to students of average ability or students with emotional disabilities. Even a brief perusal of the means and standard deviations of these groups shows differences in recall ranging no greater than 2.22 items (this for auditory modality, ordered recall, short term memory). The average difference in recall scores at immediate recall was 1.04; at short term, 1.28; at long term 1.24; with an overall average difference in recall of 1.19 items. Although reported as statistically significant differences across the board, a question of practical significance arises. The differences as presented are not convincing.

Predictive validity was addressed via stepwise multiple regression using the same groups in the diagnostic validity study. The LET-II and the LET-II plus WISC-R (Wechsler Intelligence Scale for Children—Revised) scores were used to predict actual reading and math scores. For the LET-II alone, correlations with reading achievement for other than average students range from .282 to .558. When the WISC-R is included, the correlations range from .605 to .676. For mathematics achievement—LET-II only: .410 to .613; LET-II + WISC-R: .596 to .682. Correlations for average students although reported as significant ($p<.01$) are so low as to be inconsequential. Of the four groups of students with disabilities, the LET-II alone shows greatest potential predictive ability for students with mental disabilities. There is, however, no information about whether inclusion of the LET-II enhances the predictive ability of the WISC-R. It is likely that the contribution to prediction of the LET-II is insignificant when added to the WISC-R. The LET-II does appear to show some predictive ability, but just as with the LET, limited information about the sample precludes generalizability.

Evidence of construct validity was addressed via factor analysis using five age groupings from the norming sample. The factor analysis resulted in a two-factor solution. One factor was identified as Global Memory; the other as Modality. All 12 scores of the LET-II (6 scores for each modality) load at a satisfactory level on the Global Memory Factor for each age group. In addition, for each age group there are positive and negative loadings consistent with modality for each subtest. That is, on the Modality Factor, the factor loadings are consistently positive for one modality and negative for the other by appropriate modality subtest. The findings were consistent regardless of age level.

Guidelines for interpreting the test results are available in the manual. An individual's score can be interpreted in as many as four ways: (*a*) comparison to norm group, (*b*) examination of scaled scores for identifying specific modality strengths and weaknesses, (*c*) use of standard scores as a measure of cognitive functioning, and (*d*) determining the strategies used to retain the serial strings. With the exception of determining strategies, the interpretation relies on the actual test scores. In order to determine the strategies someone uses to retain the serial strings, the examiner is supposed to listen for whispered rehearsal, watch for lip movement, listen to how the stimulus materials are reported, and so on. These procedures may or may not actually aid in examining retention strategies. Suggested strategies for remediation are included. As with the LET, some of the suggestions are questionable.

SUMMARY. As it stands, it appears that little has changed since the publication of the LET. Although 12 years have passed between publication of the LET and the LET-II, insufficient reliability and validity information is available. The major strength of this instrument lies in ease of administration and time to administer (roughly 15 minutes). It could be used as a preliminary examination of information processing difficulties, but given the problems with reliability and validity it should be viewed as supplemental to other, more well-established instruments designed to identify individuals with learning or mental disabilities.

REVIEWER'S REFERENCE

Harrington, R. G. (1985). [Review of the Learning Efficiency Test]. In J. V. Mitchell, Jr. (Ed.), *The ninth mental measurements yearbook* (pp. 832-833). Lincoln, NE: Buros Institute of Mental Measurements.

Review of the Learning Efficiency Test-II (1992 Revision) by GREGORY SCHRAW, Assistant Professor of Educational Psychology, University of Nebraska-Lincoln, Lincoln, NE:

The Learning Efficiency Test-II is a norm-referenced, individually administered test of visual and auditory memory appropriate for individuals from 5 to 75 years of age. The purpose of the test is to provide diagnostic information regarding memory capacity and possible impairment. This information may be used by diagnosticians to isolate problems with retention due to modality (visual vs. auditory), type of memory (sensory vs. short-term vs. long-term), or fidelity of recall (ordered vs. nonordered).

The test consists of two main batteries, visual and auditory memory, with each battery consisting of six subtests measuring ordered and unordered recall in immediate, short term, and long term memory. Each of the 12 total subtests may be compared directly using standard scores.

A concise yet thorough description of the LET-II's theoretical underpinnings is provided in the test manual. The test is based on the two-store model of memory that proposes information is processed sequentially in discrete memory systems which include sensory, short term, and long term stores. The effects of interference on memory and how interference is assessed using the LET-II are described as well.

The LET-II can be administered and scored in 10 to 20 minutes depending upon the memory skill shown by the examinee. In both the visual and auditory tests, individuals are provided random letter strings that are repeated immediately or after completing an interference task such as counting number strings or repeating unrelated sentences. Individuals begin with two-letter strings and proceed to longer strings until two consecutive errors are committed on the test of immediate memory. Only nonrhyming consonants are included in the LET-II (e.g., F, H, P, X) because rhyming consonants (e.g., B, C, G, T) are known to interfere with reading-disabled students' recall.

Scoring and interpretation are especially easy. Raw scores may be converted to standard scores or compared to developmental norms using conversion tables included in the Appendices. The manual also includes an extensive interpretation section that discusses a variety of diagnostic errors and provides several illustrative case studies. A special section on remediation strategies has been added to the revised version as well. The remediation section provides a number of helpful suggestions and references of special usefulness to practitioners.

Norms for the LET-II are based on a combined sample of roughly 1,150 examinees at all age levels. Unfortunately, neither test-retest or split-half reliabilities are reported for the LET-II. In contrast, test-retest reliabilities for the LET (1981) ranged from .71 to .86 (median of .80). A predictive validity study found the LET-II correlated with teacher ratings of achievement between .28 and .61 across several different groups of academically disadvantaged students. Correlations with observed reading ability approached .50 in most cases. A factor-analytic study of the LET-II's construct validity reported two factors: a *global memory* factor on which all 12 subtests loaded, and a *modality* factor which distinguished between the auditory and visual subtests.

The strengths of the LET-II include (*a*) easy administration and scoring, (*b*) a high degree of face validity, (*c*) statistically significant predictive validity, and (*d*) a clearly written and informative manual. There are no substantial weaknesses that limit its use.

As noted above, additional reliability data on the LET-II would be helpful, although there was no evidence from the LET that reliability was ever a concern for this instrument. Second, a parallel form of the instrument, which currently is not available, would be helpful for follow-up testing following a lengthy intervention.

Overall, the LET-II provides a quick, reliable way (on the basis of test-retest data) to assess memory capacity and specific problems with memory storage. The main advantage of the LET-II is that it enables the test giver to isolate retention problems with respect to modality and type of memory store. The ability to identify specific problems quickly and accurately should greatly facilitate remediation. Its use for testing memory storage among all age groups is recommended without reservation.

[51]

Learning Inventory of Kindergarten Experiences.

Purpose: Developed to screen for kindergarten readiness.
Population: Beginning kindergarten.
Publication Date: 1988.
Acronym: LIKE.
Scores: Item scores only in 4 areas: Motor, Language, Preacademic, Prereading.
Administration: Individual.
Price Data, 1990: $175 per complete kit including paper supplies (50 record sheets, 50 summary sheets, 5 grid summary sheets, pads of 50 circles, squares, and geometric shapes, strips and squares of colored paper, 10 letter cards, 6 numeral cards, 18 picture cards), test manual (42 pages), and instruction manual (14 pages); $50 per set of paper supplies; $25 per 50 record sheets; $20 per set of manuals.
Time: Administration time not reported.

Authors: Nathaniel O. Owings, Paulette E. Mills, and Cynthia Best O'Dell.
Publisher: University of Washington Press.

Review of the Learning Inventory of Kindergarten Experiences by DOUGLAS A. PENFIELD, Professor of Education, Graduate School of Education, Rutgers University, New Brunswick, NJ:

The Learning Inventory of Kindergarten Experiences (LIKE) is a norm-referenced screening procedure designed to measure the skill development of kindergarten children. The authors suggest that it can also be used to "aid the teacher in curriculum planning" and "to detect potential handicapping conditions" (manual, p. 7). The LIKE is composed of a collection of items believed to be correlated with future academic success. Some items were taken from existing kindergarten screening procedures and then modified to meet current test needs. The authors have acknowledged that a number of items were selected from the Madison Public Schools Kindergarten Screening tool and the Miller-Yoder Language Comprehension Test (Clinical Edition).

The LIKE is broken into five subtests defined as (*a*) gross motor, (*b*) fine motor, (*c*) conceptual, (*d*) comprehension, and (*e*) academic/production. Test items are developmentally sequenced within each subtest. Assuming a small number of practice trials, new examiners should have little trouble in administering the instrument. The authors suggest the test can be administered in 30 minutes or less. This time estimate is heavily dependent upon the skill of the examiner in presenting the questions and the receptiveness of the child.

Materials needed to carry out the assessment are many and varied (see LIKE description above). They are packaged in ziploc type bags and assembled with other test information in a handy carrying case. Directions for administering the LIKE are very explicit and should be followed precisely. An Instruction Manual, consisting of the test questions, procedures to be followed when administering the questions, and scoring methodology, provides a detailed outline of the testing process. Other pertinent information regarding the LIKE can be found in the Interpretation Manual.

When scoring, one point is awarded for each question answered correctly. In most instances, there is more than one question associated with a test item. Points are summed within an item and then across items to produce a subtest total score. The expected total subtest score of a child "at or below the 30th percentile" and "at or above the 50th percentile" (manual, p. 15) is presented for comparative purposes. Subtest percentile rank norms are displayed in tabular form for the variables age (5, 5½, 6), school type (rural, urban), and sex (female, male). These tables tend to be somewhat difficult to comprehend, especially the ones displaying the percentile distributions for school type and sex by subtest, and they should definitely be reformatted. Simple examples in the text illustrating the use of the norms tables would also be beneficial. Please note that there is a minor error in the Interpretation Manual which should be readily apparent to an examiner. One page 15, one of the scoring categories is labeled "Scores at or below the 50th percentile" instead of "Scores at or above the 50th percentile." A display grid and screening record sheet allow the examiner to record the response of each child to each item on the test. This consolidation of test information should aid teachers when setting objectives for the purpose of remediation.

A K-R 20 reliability coefficient, computed on a sample of 364 children, was reported to be .92. The sample was composed of incoming kindergarten children drawn from both an urban and rural setting. The authors address the question of validity by discussing content, predictive, and concurrent validity. Content validity was assessed by comparing the structure of the test items with the abilities inherent in a normal kindergarten population. Expected age norms for each test item as well as an associated reference are presented. With respect to predictive and concurrent validity, there is no evidence of either at the present time. An item analysis was also performed on the test items. Question difficulty levels and biserial correlations between the question score and the total test score are reported for the sample of 364 entering kindergarten children. The authors regard biserial correlations above .2 as indicative of a useful question. Only a small number of questions fell below this benchmark.

To some, the scope of the LIKE may appear somewhat limited as a preacademic assessment tool. Regardless, the authors have attempted to focus their attention on those skills suggestive of future academic growth. Given the attention span of a child and the time allotted for testing, the LIKE represents a good cross-section of test items useful in screening kindergarten children.

Review of the Learning Inventory of Kindergarten Experiences by DONNA WITTMER, Assistant Professor of Education, University of Colorado-Denver, Denver, CO:

The Learning Inventory of Kindergarten Experiences (LIKE) covers four primary areas including Motor, Language, Preacademic, and Prereading resulting in five subtest areas: gross motor, fine motor, conceptual–aural/oral, comprehension, and academic/production. These are typical areas covered for a kindergarten readiness test. Items were selected from other procedures that have proven to be predictive of later academic skills. Process skills such as classification, conservation, and seriation are included. However, areas such as eye-hand coordination, visual-perceptual skills, recognizing rhythm patterns, visual matching skills, tactile skills, motor behavior memory skills, verbal memory skills, attending/task-order skills, and social interaction skills are not covered. Broad areas such as sensory integration, discrimination, and attending/responding are not included. This assessment taps academic knowledge acquired, such as knowledge of names of colors and shapes, alphabet recognition, and number recognition rather than focusing primarily on skills needed to learn academics and function well in school (e.g., matching, visual-perceptual, and motor behavior memory skills). Thus, this assessment seems less culturally sensitive than one would hope to find in a kindergarten readiness assessment.

The LIKE does not assess a critical area that has been found to be highly related to school success, social skills. The authors state that social skills "cannot be adequately evaluated in the manner presented here" (manual, p. 8). Because this is an assessment that is *not* designed to be given over time, the authors did not think that social skills could be assessed adequately given that the child is going to be tested only once. However, a parent questionnaire on social skills would have at least tapped into this vital area. This assessment also does not include any type of parent questionnaire or opportunity for parents to validate the findings.

The authors state they do not condone the use of the LIKE to "screen" children out of kindergarten. One large school district has used the LIKE to rule on whether children who are underage for kindergarten should be allowed to enter. In order to enter kindergarten, the underage children must be above the 50th percentile. The basic purpose of the test, then, is "(1) to identify certain key preacademic abilities in beginning kindergarten children; (2) to aid the teacher in curriculum planning . . . and (3) to detect potential handicapping conditions in beginning kindergarten children" (p. 7). The areas of children's needs and strengths are being identified so that teachers and parents can plan a more appropriate program for the kindergarten children. Given the stated purposes of the assessment, the authors would have ensured ecological validity if the assessment had been designed to be given over time, as a program assessment. Designed as it is, it invites a misuse of the test by professionals who would "screen" children out of kindergarten by saying they are not "ready" based on a one-time kindergarten "readiness" test.

This assessment is designed for teachers to administer together with help from a speech/language pathologist. The assessment is easy to administer with few materials required. The materials needed are included in a small blue case that is very easy to carry. The test is designed to be given to children individually. Professionals must exercise care in the administration of this test by making sure that children are familiar with the person administering the test and that testing conditions are as comfortable and familiar as possible. Three types of responses are recorded: right answer, wrong answer, and don't know/no response.

The statistical information on the test is scanty. Although the publication date is 1988, the normed sample was obtained in 1977. The LIKE was given to 364 children who were just entering kindergarten in the fall of 1977. Most of the children in the normed sample (285) were enrolled in the Bozeman School system, an urban setting, whereas 79 children were enrolled in the neighboring rural Gallatin Valley Schools. The normed sample, then, is not representative of race and socioeconomic groups in the United States. The children ranged in age from 5 to 6 years. Percentile ranks were determined for raw scores based on this population. Validity and reliability issues are not addressed well. Concurrent and predictive validity studies have not been completed.

In summary, I would not recommend this kindergarten "readiness" test for several reasons. The standardization sample is not adequate and the items tap academic knowledge more than processing skills. Also, although the authors advocate using the test as a curriculum-based assessment with a major purpose being to design a curriculum program for the child, testing is not done over time, social skills are not assessed, and parent input is nil.

[52]

Learning Style Profile.
Purpose: Designed to evaluate student learning style as the basis for student advisement and placement, instructional strategy, and the evaluation of learning.
Population: Grades 6–12.
Publication Dates: 1986–90.
Acronym: LSP.

Scores, 23: Cognitive Skills (Analytic, Spatial, Discrimination, Categorizing, Sequential Processing, Memory), Perceptual Responses (Visual, Auditory, Emotive), Persistence Orientation, Verbal Risk Orientation, Study and Instructional Preferences (Verbal-Spatial, Manipulative, Study Time [Early Morning, Late Morning, Afternoon, Evening], Grouping, Posture, Mobility, Sound, Lighting, Temperature).
Administration: Group.
Price Data: Price information available from publisher for materials including Technical Manual ('88, 105 pages).
Time: (50–60) minutes.
Authors: James W. Keefe (test, Handbook II), John S. Monk (test), Charles A. Letteri (test, Handbook I), Marlin Languis (test), Rita Dunn (test), John M. Jenkins (Handbook I), and Patricia Rosenlund (Handbook I).
Publisher: National Association of Secondary School Principals.
Cross References: See T4:1433 (1 reference).

Review of the Learning Style Profile by SONYA BLIXT, Professor of Evaluation and Measurement, and JAMES A. JONES, Doctoral Candidate and Graduate Assistant in Evaluation and Measurement, Kent State University, Kent, OH:

According to the examiner's manual, the Learning Style Profile (LSP) is designed to be given within a 50-minute period, but is not timed. Part of the test is printed upside down on the backs of the pages. After examinees complete 108 of the 126 multiple-choice items, they must turn the test booklet upside down to finish the remaining items. These last items differ from the previous ones in that a drawing is shown as an initial stimulus, then each subsequent page contains a drawing for which the examinee needs to determine if it is a match with the initial drawing without turning back. Printing this portion of the LSP upside down on the backs of pages was done presumedly to conserve paper, but this produces an unnecessary distraction for examinees.

Scoring the LSP can be accomplished by hand or computer. Although not difficult to hand score, it would be quite time consuming because there are several scales and for some items, responses are given different weights. The raw score is converted to a *T*-score, and then a corresponding "X" is placed in one of three categories: one standard deviation or more below the mean, within plus or minus one standard deviation of the mean, and one standard deviation or more above the mean. The LSP uses varying labels for these categories depending on the subscales (weak, average, and strong; low, average, and high; and high, neutral, and high for the bipolar subscales). In addition to subscale scores, a consistency score is also computed for the preferential questions to give an indication of the potential validity of the profile for the student. When hand scored, the norms provided by the examiner's manual are not broken down by sex, race, or grade. If computer scored, separate norms are used, but the examiner's manual indicates differences in scores generated by the two methods are not notable.

The technical manual appears well documented, but had some interesting omissions. The final version of the LSP was normed on a sample of 4,871 students enrolled in grades 6 through 12 from approximately 40 schools randomly selected by zip code. Not explained, however, was how the students were selected once the schools were identified. In comparing the numbers of students and schools, clearly not all the students from grades 6 through 12 were used from a given zip code, but no information was provided as to what additional selection procedures were used.

The coefficient alphas, test-retest (10-day), and test-retest (30-day) reliability coefficients as well as tables providing descriptive statistics for the items comprising the subscale are provided in the technical manual for most of the items. Brief summaries of some attempts to establish validity are also given. More information regarding the standard error of measurement and potential group differences between the scores for sex, race, or grade levels would be useful, however.

The internal consistency coefficients of the subscales ranged from .47 to .76 with an average coefficient alpha of .61. The examiner's manual attributed this low average reliability to the small number of items that comprise each subscale. The range of items was from 2 to 20 with 5 items comprising the typical scale. Tripling the length of the subscales from 5 items to 15 would produce a theoretical increase in the internal consistency reliability from .61 to .82 based on the Spearman-Brown Prophecy formula. The three subscales of the LSP with 20 items, however, had an average coefficient alpha of only .49, so number of items alone may not be the reason for the LSP's low internal consistency. The test-retest coefficient for a 10-day time period ranged from .36 to .82 with an average coefficient of .62. For the 30-day time period, the range increased to .21 to .76 with an average coefficient of .47.

The examiner's and technical manuals discussed the content, concurrent, and construct validity of the LSP. The content validity of the LSP was judged by a task force assembled by the test developers. The concurrent validity was assessed by correlating the subscales of the LSP with other tests that purport to measure a similar construct. For the majority of the subscales this meant correlating the LSP with the Learning Style Inventory (T4:1432), which also suffers from low reliability and questionable validity. Overall, the correlations between the subscales ranged from a low of .15 to a high of .71 with a mean of correlation of .51. The construct validity was assessed by examination of the first and second order factor structure of the LSP and did not incorporate any criteria external to the test that would enhance credibility.

The LSP handbooks describe how the test items assess the various areas and give some suggestions for incorporating a given subscale area into curriculum. The assumption communicated in these manuals is that the LSP will identify the strengths and weaknesses in learning style of an individual or classroom. The teacher could then conceivably use the suggestions in the handbooks to enhance the effectiveness of classroom instruction. Given the low reliabilities and questionable validity of many of the subscales of the LSP, this assumption seems unwarranted.

The LSP manuals describe the test as a first-level diagnostic tool that can be used to modify curriculum. The instability of the subscale scores would make this practice inadvisable. Although the manual includes warnings against overinterpretation of the subscale scores, the inclusion of the handbooks provides additional temptation. Even if the LSP were used only as a screening device, the manuals are not clear as to what follow-up testing would be appropriate. In summary, the addition of the LSP to the already full testing agenda of the typical school is not justified.

Review of the Learning Style Profile by PHILIP NAGY, Associate Professor of Measurement, Evaluation, and Computer Applications, The Ontario Institute for Studies in Education, Toronto, Ontario, CANADA:

The Learning Style Profile (LSP) attempts to use research on cognitive style and learning style, mostly from the period 1950–1975, to develop a group-administered screening test. It also incorporates scales designed to assess study preferences such as for time of day, lighting, and temperature. The test booklet, examiner's and technical manuals, and two handbooks on developing skills and accommodating preferences represent a massive undertaking, for which the authors should be commended. However, the product is not commensurate with the effort.

As the authors point out, psychologists lost interest in this field of cognitive styles just as practitioners took it up. There were reasons for this loss of interest, despite much conceptual (e.g., Messick, 1970) and empirical (e.g., Messick & French, 1975) effort. The root difficulty 20 years ago was a failure to assess cognitive style accurately enough to legitimate individual rather than group average scores. Attempts to find aptitude-treatment type interactions met with little success. This lack of evidence of educational import was attributed by some to these reliability problems, whereas others expressed more fundamental doubts about the underlying theory. Meanwhile, and since then, isolated reports of remarkable success with individuals fueled hope for useful clinical applications at the classroom level—a hope that downplayed the fact that the clinical successes were often with learning-disabled and in some cases brain-damaged populations. The problems in moving from laboratory to classroom have not been overcome in the Learning Style Profile.

The test booklet contains 126 items. Although not labelled as preliminary, the LSP bears the marks of a work-in-progress: a few errors and inconsistencies, some replacement pages, and one scale conceded to be still experimental. This is not a criticism. The profile is untimed, but aimed at requiring one class period. Most of the items (there are a few unscored distractors and experimental items) are divided, by hand or using machine-scorable answer sheets, into 23 subscale scores: 6 skills, 3 perceptual responses (Visual, Auditory, Emotive), 2 orientations (Persistence and Verbal Risk), and 12 preferences. There is also a consistency score for the preferences. My comments are mostly directed at the skills, perceptual responses, and orientations, rather than the preferences. Little can be said about preference questions that ask, for example, what time of day a student prefers to study, except to wonder if such information requires the expense of a standardized test.

Raw subscale scores are converted to T-scores (mean 50, standard deviation 10) and plotted on a one-page profile sheet. Hand scoring uses a single norming table, but computer scoring "simultaneously adjusts for sex, grade and race" (examiners manual, p. 10). Some detail on how this is done, and how much difference it makes, would improve the manual; many cells in the sex-by-grade-by-race breakdown are tiny.

There are strong points to this package. These must be stated before further criticisms.

First, the profile and its subtests are rooted in the literature and based on a theoretical framework. There is an information-processing framework for the entire package, and a literature outlining the history of each subtest. The manual provides good summaries of this literature.

Second, the development steps are outlined, and reliability and validity evidence clearly presented. Most subscales have internal consistency and test-retest evidence, and many have construct validity evidence. For example, the Analytic Skill subscale has been validated against its parent Group Embedded Figures Test.

Third, the authors present strong factor analytic evidence for the integrity and independence of the subscales. Analysis of all but two subscale scores supported four large groups, cognitive, study preference, perceptual response, and instructional preference, with only a little overlap. This evidence is probably as clear as can be expected of such elusive constructs (compare, for example, Messick & French, 1975).

Fourth, the authors offer sound advice on cautious interpretation of the profile data. Users are cautioned, and prompted by the profile form, to focus on scores more than one standard deviation from the mean; these individuals "are more likely to be governed by the element of style" (examiner's manual, p. 14).

Fifth, we are cautioned that this is only a screening device, and references are given to individual diagnostic instruments for most subscales. As well, the authors admit that some scales may be "contextually sensitive" (examiner's manual, p. 6). One quibble is that much of this information is buried in a long technical manual, and does not appear in the much simplified examiner's manual.

Sixth, the authors discuss the augmentational versus adaptational issue, that is, whether to retrain the child to cope with the existing learning environment, or to change the learning environment rather than train the child. The compromise position, practiced in the two accompanying handbooks, is that "Augmentation is more suited to cognitive style 'growth'; adaptation to affective and physiological style 'matching'" (technical manual, p. 7).

In short, this package is a major contribution to research in a difficult area. This does not make it, unfortunately, a viable standardized test, or even a useful screening instrument. What are the problems?

First, the norming is unsystematic. The authors used (in round numbers) a probability sample of 4,900 for all but one scale, but apparently added another sample of convenience (initial purchasers) of about 3,800. In addition, undescribed samples were used for other aspects of the validation: about 3,900 to validate a replacement scale, 483 for test-retest studies, and three samples of 100 for different validity studies. In fairness, data are provided to investigate how important grade, sex, and race differences might be, and the authors offer to supply a data tape for further investigation. However, better sampling and clearer definitions (e.g., geographical regions) would have helped. Failing that, a comparison between the probability sample and the large sample of convenience might have served to set this issue aside.

Second, there are reliability problems, both for internal consistency and stability over time. The Analytic Skill subscale has a Cronbach's alpha of .56, the median for the non-preference subscales. This is as good as figures from 20 years ago, but it still gives unacceptably wide confidence intervals for individual scores. For example, an observed score of 3, on a 5-item test, has a 95% confidence interval between 1 and 5 (.63 and 5.37 before rounding), from a weak to a strong rating. Even as a screening device, this is of dubious value. And this problem does not disappear for even the longest (20-item) subtests. In addition, despite claims of "relatively stable characteristics," 30-day test-retest reliabilities are largely below .50. These figures are somewhat attenuated by low internal consistency, but still raise the question of whether these variables, even accurately measured, are stable enough over time to be of practical value (see Gardner, 1973).

Third, there are problems with the underlying rationale. The profile uses an information-processing model that includes six phases and six operations. In conjunction with these operations, several cognitive style "controls" are posited: analyzing, comparing, focusing, scanning, searching, sharpening, narrowing, and categorizing. The model is global enough to be untestable, and thus speculative at best. The authors have been thorough in furnishing references on the antecedents of the subscales, but provide none supporting the relationship between cognitive controls and operations. I infer the project team hopes that use of the profile will provide data to support its theoretical foundation. This is laudable for a research program, but not for a commercially available test.

Fourth, there are difficulties linking the definitions of some subscales with their content. For example, the Categorization subscale tests how narrow or wide people perceive categories to be. The authors connect the narrow view with "intrinsic (denotative)" (technical manual, p. 29) properties, and the broad with "imputed (connotative)" (p. 29) meanings. This may be so, but the theory then goes on to link the narrow view with "greater *skill*" (p. 29, emphasis added) in categorization. This is not supportable. More on this

test will be mentioned in connection with the next problem.

Fifth, there are difficulties with some items and instructions. In the Categorization subscale, knowledge of the world impinges on validity. For example, Questions 17 and 18 give the length of the average whale, and then ask for guesses on the length of the longest whale and shortest whale respectively. Choices nearest the mean are scored best, but the biologically correct answers are far more extreme than these "best" answers. Similar problems exist for most of the items in this subscale.

As another example, the Memory skill items present a moderately complex cartoon drawing of a robot (later repeated with a bird and turtle) on a single page with the instructions "Study the picture below carefully. You will need to remember what it looks like. You will not be able to turn back to see it again" (test, p. 21). The next page shows a similar (possibly identical) picture, and asks if it is the same or different. The instructions are repeated on this second page, and another robot appears, with the same questions, on the third (and fourth, fifth, and sixth) page. The problem is that there is no opportunity to see two figures side by side, to learn the level of detail required for the observation. Nor is there any feedback for respondents to see if they are on the right wavelength. Thus, it becomes a stressful guessing game. Coupled with the two-choice nature of the response, this subscale is highly suspect.

Finally, the most serious problem with this profile is the lack of evidence that the subscales have any relationship to learning or instruction. For example, in the Analytic skills subscale, subjects have to recognize the presence or absence of moderately complex shapes in even more complex visual patterns. The handbook exercises link this skill to other analytic skills, such as the ability to write specific directions, produce a flowchart, or follow steps in a "scientific method." In the light of what is now known about the difficulty of skill transfer (Perkins & Salomon, 1989; Brown, Collins, & Duguid, 1989) even between cognitive contexts, this rationale has little currency.

In summary, this profile is an ambitious report on an intriguing research project. The documentation has established that the skills assessed by the subscales are unequivocally independent of each other. It has added to the validity evidence for many constructs from the cognitive style research of the 1950–1975 period. It has avoided the problem of treating people near the mean of a scale as if they were at the extreme, and has offered appropriate cautions about the difference between a screening device and a clinical instrument. And it has dealt with the problem of changing the child versus changing the environment. However, it has not improved the reliability difficulties of 20 years ago, and thus the scores of individuals remain suspect. There are also unsupportable inferential leaps from theory to subscale design, and a lack of evidence for the educational benefits of using this instrument. As the authors themselves state many times in the manual "no concurrent or predictive validity studies have yet been conducted" (technical manual pp. 21, 25, 30, etc.). As a research enterprise, I recommend this project; as a diagnostic kit for applied classroom use, I cannot.

REVIEWER'S REFERENCES

Messick, S. (1970). The criterion problem in the evaluation of instruction: Assessing possible, not just probable, intended outcomes. In M. C. Wittrock & D. E. Wiley (Eds.), *The evaluation of instruction: Issues and problems* (pp. 183-202). New York: Holt, Rinehart & Winston, Inc.
Gardner, R. W. (1973). Reliability of group-test scores for cognitive controls and intellectual abilities over a one-year period. *Perceptual and Motor Skills, 36,* 753-754.
Messick, S., & French, J. W. (1975). Dimensions of cognitive closure. *Multivariate Behavioral Research, 10,* 3-16.
Brown, J. S., Collins, A., & Duguid, P. (1989). Situated cognition and the culture of learning. *Educational Researcher, 18*(1), 32-42.
Perkins, D. N., & Salomon, G. (1989). Are cognitive skills context-bound? *Educational Researcher, 18*(1), 16-25.

[53]

The Leisure Diagnostic Battery.
Purpose: Developed to assess leisure functioning.
Population: Ages 9–18, adult.
Publication Date: 1987.
Administration: Group.
Levels, 2: Version A, Version B.
Price Data, 1991: $19.95 per manual ('87, 102 pages).
Time: (30–60) minutes.
Authors: Peter A. Witt and Gary D. Ellis.
Publisher: American Alliance for Health, Physical Education, Recreation, and Dance.
  a) SHORT FORM.
  Scores, 6: Perceived Leisure (Competence, Control), Leisure Needs, Depth of Involvement in Leisure Experiences, Playfulness, Total.
  b) LONG FORM.
  Scores, 6 to 9: Same as for *a* above plus 3 optional scores: Barriers to Leisure Involvement Scale, Leisure Preference Inventory, Knowledge of Leisure Opportunities Test.

Review of the Leisure Diagnostic Battery by E. THOMAS DOWD, Professor and Director of Counseling Psychology, Kent State University, Kent, OH:

INTRODUCTION. The Leisure Diagnostic Battery (LDB) was constructed by the authors to assess leisure functioning along several dimensions with a variety of handicapped and nonhandicapped individuals. It is actually a collection of tests. There are both long and short forms as well as separate forms for adolescents (ages 9 through 18) and adults and two different response formats.

The long forms consist of two sections each. Section 1 consists of 95 questions arranged in five subscales: Leisure Competence, Leisure Control, Leisure Needs, Depth of Involvement, and Playfulness, which together are considered to measure the construct of Perceived Freedom in Leisure. Section 2, given only if the score on Section 1 identifies a problem, consists of 112 items arranged in three subscales: Barriers to Leisure, Knowledge of Leisure Opportunities, and Leisure Preferences. Long Form Version A (adolescents) uses a 3-point Likert scale for most subscales; *Doesn't sound like me, Sounds a little like me,* and *Sounds like me.* Long Form Version C (adults) uses a 5-point Likert scale, ranging from *Strongly disagree* to *Strongly agree.* No reason is given for the change in response format. The last two subscales use multiple-choice and forced-choice responses, respectively. Version B Long Form was originally designed for mentally retarded individuals, but the authors were not satisfied with its psychometric properties and have not released this version.

The short forms were developed later and consist of 25 items taken from the first five scales, Perceived Freedom in Leisure. Version A is for adolescents and Version B is for adults. In both the long and short forms, the adolescent and adult versions differ only in the wording of some items.

CONCEPTUALIZATION. The LDB is based on a psychological, rather than an activities, conception of leisure. Leisure is defined as a high degree of perceived freedom to engage in activities out of intrinsic motivation, rather than external constraint. Intrinsic motivation is said to arise from a self-serving attributional pattern, in which involvement in leisure activities is attributed to internal and stable factors. In contrast, the self-degenerative pattern, leading to extrinsic motivation and learned helplessness, is said to arise from the attribution of engagement in leisure activities to external and unstable factors. Thus, the authors argue that perceived freedom and learned helplessness represent opposite ends of a continuum of "leisurability." Although attribution theory may be oversimplified in this model, this is a fairly sophisticated view of leisure and a distinct improvement over the older model that defined specific activities as leisure and others as nonleisure.

The individual items were developed over a period of time according to the theoretical domains mentioned earlier. The process appears to have been extremely thorough. Unfortunately, although the authors state the conceptual structure of the test was reviewed by over 30 people knowledgeable in the social psychology of leisure, they do not state who or how many individuals actually wrote the items. This is important because the use of few authors of test items can have a constraining effect on the range and scope of items generated. Likewise, the authors state the scales were checked for readability but do not say how this was done.

RELIABILITY. Existing reliability data, although quite good, are incomplete. The authors imply that additional data are being collected. Internal consistency reliabilities for Long Form Version A, which are much more extensive than test-retest, consistently range in the .80s and .90s. Test-retest reliabilities are mostly in the .70s and .80s, with a few in the .60s and one in the .50s. Unfortunately, no reliability data have yet been collected for Long Form Version C. The authors state they expect it to be about the same, but differences might occur because Version A uses a 3-point response scale whereas Version C uses a 5-point response scale. This means that no reliability data exist for the adult test in the long form, although strangely enough there are reliability data for adults in the short form version.

Internal consistency reliabilities of the short forms are comparable with those of the long forms, ranging from .83 to .94. No test-retest reliability data have been collected for the short forms.

VALIDITY. Convergent, predictive, and discriminant validity data are provided for Long Form Version A. All seem generally good. Predictive and discriminant validity data are provided for the Short Form Versions A and B, again generally supportive. The manual has sections on the nature of reliability and validity. Content, predictive, and construct validity are presented in the manual, but are not covered completely by scale development efforts.

NORMS. Although no national norms yet exist for this instrument, the authors present numerous data sets from specific populations on which the test has been normed. A valuable aspect of the normative samples is that some consist of individuals with a variety of handicapping conditions. The authors provide an excellent discussion of the interpretation of the test scores, and appropriately advocate that local norms be developed by users. Appendix A gives detailed directions on how to do this. Test users should have little difficulty interpreting these scores meaningfully.

FACTOR ANALYSIS. This, in my view, is the most problematic aspect of this instrument and one that implicates its construction. The authors hypothesized

that a single factor from the first five subscales would exist, which they subsequently found and labeled "Perceived Freedom." They seem, throughout the manual, to imply that the total score of the first five subscales should be used. But if this is true, why identify or use the subscales at all? In fact, the authors appear not to do so, stating in the interpretation guidelines that users might obtain some useful information from the subscale scores. This concern is exacerbated by the lack of an intercorrelation matrix indicating how the subscales correlate with each other. Thus, the user does not even know if the subscales represent discrete concepts at all.

The manual is very thorough and detailed. Not only are there extensive presentations of normative data, reliability, validity, and interpretation, but also detailed directions for administration. It would be difficult for the user to go wrong! The manual is written for the novice, which might offend some sophisticated users, but which is preferable to an overly technical manual.

In summary, this is a well-constructed instrument, with a sound theoretical rationale and impressive psychometric properties. I would encourage the authors to continue the collection of reliability and validity data for the other versions and to provide intercorrelations among the subscales. Perhaps some rationale for the difference in response format between the adolescent and adult forms might be given. I suspect the authors thought the 3-point scale might be more understandable to an adolescent population. In view, however, of the lack of reliability data on the adult long form, I am concerned about the possible impact of such a format change.

Review of the Leisure Diagnostic Battery by ELLEN WEISSINGER, Associate Professor of Educational Psychology, University of Nebraska-Lincoln, Lincoln, NE:

The Leisure Diagnostic Battery (LDB) is a collection of instruments designed to assess current level of leisure functioning and to identify constraints that may inhibit leisure functioning. The instruments were developed for use with orthopedically handicapped adolescents in rehabilitation settings, but the authors state the battery is appropriate for educable mentally retarded persons and nonhandicapped populations. A revised version with slightly modified item wording is offered for adults. Both long (95 items) and short (25 items) forms of the adolescent and adult versions are available.

The long forms of the LDB consist of two sections. The first includes five scales: Perceived Leisure Competence, Perceived Leisure Control, Leisure

Needs, Depth of Involvement in Leisure Experiences, and Playfulness. A 3-point response format (*doesn't sound like me* to *sounds a lot like me*) is provided for adolescents and a 5-point format (*strongly agree* to *strongly disagree*) for adults. Scores on these first five scales can be summed to a total score, which is referred to as "Perceived Freedom in Leisure."

If the results of the Perceived Freedom in Leisure battery suggest deficiencies in one or more areas of leisure functioning, the second section of scales is then administered. These three instruments (Barriers to Leisure Involvement Scale, Knowledge of Leisure Opportunities Test, Leisure Preference Inventory) identify specific problems with leisure functioning. For both adolescents and adults, the Barriers scale is scored on the same 3- and 5-point formats as the Perceived Freedom in Leisure scales. The Leisure Opportunities Test utilizes a multiple-choice format; the Leisure Preference Inventory, a forced-choice format. The authors estimate that the long form takes approximately 30 minutes to complete. The short form of the adolescent and adult versions of the LDB consists of 25 items from the competence, control, needs, and involvement scales of the long form. A single, total score results from the short form.

The test manual describes in detail the procedures used to define conceptually and operationally the constructs represented by each scale. Initial pools of items were written based on applicable theoretical and empirical literature. Based on pilot data from 200 adolescents (52% male, mostly white, mean age = 13.2), final items were selected using item-total and interitem correlations and factor loadings. Items for the short forms were selected from the long forms based on item-total correlation coefficients.

The test manual presents internal consistency reliability data from five datasets (total $n = 897$) for the adolescent long form. Alpha coefficients for individual scales ranged from .75 to .90 and total score alphas were from .87 to .89. Two-week test-retest correlations for the adolescent long form were .54 and .90 for two datasets (total $n = 137$). No reliability data were offered for the adult long form. Alpha coefficients for the adolescent short form ranged from .83 to .94 across eight data sets (total $n = 575$). Alphas for the adult short form ranged from .88 to .94 across six data sets (total $n = 1,405$). Temporal stability data were not offered for either version of the short form.

As evidence of convergent validity, the authors present factor analyses from seven datasets (total $n = 982$) for the adolescent long form verifying the five scales that contribute to the total score do load on a common underlying factor for six of the datasets.

This factor is presumed to be Perceived Freedom in Leisure, though no convergent validity data are offered that directly justify this presumption. As evidence of discriminant validity, the authors correlate LDB long form scale scores with age and gender. These data generally followed the hypothesized pattern of nonsignificant correlations. The authors also present several analyses of hypothesized score differences between various disabled and nondisabled groups as evidence of discriminant validity. Finally, the authors correlate scores on the Perceived Freedom scales with scores on the Barriers scale, Knowledge test, and Preferences Inventory. These correlations, which generally followed hypothesized trends, were offered as evidence the perceived freedom scales predict scores on the scales that indicate leisure constraints.

For the adolescent and adult versions of the short form, validity data similar to those presented for the long form were offered. In addition, evidence of construct validity was provided by correlating short form scores with other measures of theoretically related constructs. These correlations generally follow the predicted pattern of hypothesized relationships with such constructs as life satisfaction (.43), self-esteem (.39), self-concept (.22), and leisure satisfaction (.81).

The test manual is logically organized and clearly written. Extensive background information on scale development is offered. A brief primer on psychometric language and concepts is included. Sections that concern procedures for administering and scoring the battery are thorough and easily understood. The section that deals with normative interpretation lacks any national norms, but instructs the user in four methods for local or institutional norming. A bibliography is attached.

In general, the LDB appears to demonstrate psychometric qualities that are sufficient to justify its use as an assessment battery. Internal consistency data support the existence of unitary constructs. Temporal stability data suggest constructs that are relatively stable over a 2-week period. Validity data suggest that constructs presumed to be measured by the LDB scales generally follow hypothesized patterns of relationships. However, additional construct validation is required before the theoretical definitions of measured constructs are fully understood. It is also necessary to have additional data concerning the ability of the LDB scales to predict observable external variables related to leisure functioning. The establishment of this degree of predictive validity is essential for instruments intended as diagnostic tools in clinical settings. Finally, the establishment of more extensive normative data would seem to be necessary in order to make the LDB fully useful as a diagnostic tool. Even with these limitations, the LDB is clearly the most sophisticated and sound measurement battery available for assessing leisure behavior.

[54]

Life Experiences Checklist.

Purpose: Designed to assess a client's quality of life.

Population: Adults.

Publication Date: 1990.

Acronym: LEC.

Scores, 6: Home, Leisure, Relationships, Freedom, Opportunities, Total.

Administration: Individual.

Price Data, 1990: £28.75 per complete set; £17.25 per 25 checklists.

Time: (10) minutes.

Author: Alastair Ager.

Publisher: NFER-Nelson Publishing Co., Ltd. [England].

Review of the Life Experiences Checklist by JUDITH CONGER, Professor of Psychology and Director of Clinical Training, Purdue University, West Lafayette, IN:

DESCRIPTION AND APPLICATION. The Life Experiences Checklist (LEC) is designed to assess the "quality of life" through the endorsement (or nonendorsement) of a broad range of experiences, events, and activities. In addition, a space is provided on the answer sheets for comments that a respondent might want to make. The focus is on the range and number of activities that an individual experiences, rather than on subjective perceptions of well-being, although there is an obvious connection between them. The checklist is composed of five broad areas: Home, Leisure, Relationships, Freedom, and Opportunities, each of which contains 10 items (Total items = 50). It is an easily administered and easily scored instrument. The checklist can be completed by an individual or by a rater on the person's behalf, through either direct administration or an interview format. The author cautions relating scores obtained in different formats; however, a correlation of .80 is reported between information gleaned through a subject versus an informant interview based on a study cited in the manual.

The author sees the applications of the LEC as falling into four broad areas: quality assurance, program planning, individual therapy, and staff training. The instrument appears to be most applicable to longer term client care or monitoring where there has been resettlement from institutional to community care or resettlement within institutional or community facilities in which care givers actually have some control in planning and intervening. The LEC, however, could be used to assess quality of life of an individual, as well as to assess the quality of life provided by a particular setting or living arrangement by assessing multiple respondents. Used in this way, it could provide some estimate of quality assurance. Further, specific areas could be explored and used for client or programmatic interventions if an individual has a particularly low endorsement in a subarea thought to be important for the person's overall welfare. For example, a very low endorsement in the leisure area might suggest some modifications in the overall program or lifestyle of an individual. In that regard the instrument aids in a more holistic approach and might suggest environmental or organizational interventions influencing the individual and/or programmatic level.

PSYCHOMETRIC CHARACTERISTICS. The basic normative sampling was done on 410 individuals in the general population in Great Britain. Norms are provided on the answer sheet and are broken down into percentage of respondents who endorsed a particular item by subsamples of urban, suburban, rural, as well as the combined sample, thereby attempting to provide a more relevant comparison sample for the individual. A perusal, however, indicates very similar response patterns across these samples for many of the items, although there is some variation on a few. Thus, although this is an appealing idea, in reality there is less discrimination than one might want. Further, the respondents are described as "householders" with little other description of the sample in the manual as regards demographics such as sex, age, ethnicity, education, etc. There is no information as to how the sample was drawn from the general population further masking possible biases, although there are references to studies on the LEC where information was obtained and those studies might contain more specific details. Additional information is reported in the manual for other populations such as undergraduates, medical students, psychology students, and clients of various types, although in the latter case the *N*s are often quite meager. Finally, data are also presented in terms of centile equivalents for subscale scores; however, because the distributions are different (and skewed) for each subscale, a score of 5 on the Home scale places one at the 6th percentile, a score of 5 on the Leisure scale places one at the 48th percentile. This can be misleading and lead to misinterpretation, as the author notes.

There are several studies reported dealing with various types of reliability. A total test-retest reliability of .93 is reported with a sample of 20 students using an "agreement index" score with subsection scores ranging from .91 to .96. Further, there was an informant-rater correlation of .80 based on 10 subjects with learning difficulties, as well as an interrater correlation of .80 that appears to be based on 10 subjects, although it is not clear if this sample of 10 represents the same learning-impaired subjects or not. Expanded reliability data, particularly with the subscale scores using larger samples, including the general population, are needed. Further, internal consistency estimates on the subscale scores might be useful in ascertaining the homogeneity of each area subscore.

There are some validity data reported indicating, for example, that the LEC is positively related to staff-client ratio ($r = .36$) and negatively related to the number of clients on a ward ($r = -.36$). Further, the LEC was correlated with a list of social and demographic factors with a range of correlations between -.19 (more than three dependent children) and -.36 (social class). Although it is suggestive that social and economic variables are negatively related to Life Experiences, most of the relationships are rather modest, albeit statistically significant due to the large N. Validity coefficients are often modest and a construct such as this may gain validational strength through its modest associations with other variables. Still, data bearing directly on the relationship between the LEC with other quality of life measures would be useful. This approach could provide stronger validational evidence for this measure.

In summary, the LEC appears to be an interesting, easily administered, and potentially useful instrument which is in need of further psychometric investigation. As such, in my opinion it is still in the development phase and ought to be considered "experimental." In the future, the author may want to consider some kind of transformation which would allow conversion into a more "standard" type score for subscales so that comparisons across subareas can be made more easily. A major drawback of the LEC for U.S. users is that it appears to be entirely normed on a British population.

[55]

Memory Assessment Scales.

Purpose: Developed to assess areas of cognitive function that are involved in memory.
Population: Ages 18 and over.
Publication Date: 1991.
Acronym: MAS.

Scores: 16 scores: Short-Term Memory (Verbal Span, Visual Span, Total), List Acquisition, Delayed List Recall, Delayed Prose Recall, Global Memory Scale (Verbal Memory [List Recall, Immediate Prose Recall, Total], Visual Memory [Visual Reproduction, Immediate Visual Recognition, Total], Total), Delayed Visual Recognition, Names-Faces (Immediate, Delayed) and 7 Verbal Process scores: Total Intrusions, List Clustering (Acquisition, Recall, Delayed Recall), Cued List Recall (Recall, Delayed Recall), List Recognition.
Administration: Individual.
Price Data, 1994: $199 per complete kit including stimulus card set, 25 record forms, manual (131 pages), and attache case; $171 per kit minus attache case; $95 per stimulus card set; $38 per 25 record forms; $45 per manual.
Time: [40–45] minutes.
Author: J. Michael Williams.
Publisher: Psychological Assessment Resources, Inc.

Review of the Memory Assessment Scales by RONALD A. BERK, Professor, School of Nursing, The Johns Hopkins University, Baltimore, MD:

The Memory Assessment Scales (MAS) is an individually administered battery of tasks that are designed to measure memory functions in normal and clinical populations. Three areas of cognitive functioning are assessed: "(a) attention, concentration, and short-term memory; (b) learning and immediate memory; and (c) memory following a delay" (manual, p. 3). For each area, separate verbal and nonverbal tasks are used to measure material-specific (verbal versus visual-spatial) memory abilities. Both recall and recognition formats are used.

The MAS consists of 12 subtests based on seven memory tasks. Five of the subtests involve the repeated assessment of retention of information. These subtests yield 16 scores: 12 subtest scores plus a Short-term Memory Summary score, Verbal Memory Summary score, Visual Memory Summary score, and Global Memory score.

The research on amnesic disorder was the primary source for both the theoretical models of memory function and the tasks developed for the MAS. The assessment procedures used in these studies of memory disorder provided an item pool from which tasks on the MAS were selected or modified. Although descriptions of the content from which the tasks were generated are given for each area or subscale, no content domain specifications are presented to display the relationship between the content in each area and the task distribution or coverage. Also, no evidence of content-related validity is reported from any panel of experts. Such evidence is essential to determine the match of the tasks to their respective content and the representativeness of the task distribution. Further, the content of the tasks does not reflect the possible ethnic and cultural diversity of the intended population of test takers. This is particularly evident in the Names-Faces and Delayed Names-Faces Recall Subscales where the 10 faces (six women, four men) are all Caucasian, selected from the yearbook of a local high school, and their names were chosen from the local phone book to be "generally familiar names" (p. 44).

A major consideration in the design of the MAS was to balance the number of tasks against the realistic time constraints of the usual clinical setting. This translates into the maximum number of important tasks that can be administered within one hour. Although administration time can vary with the skills of the test taker, the author's goal seems to have been attained.

Administration and scoring of the MAS can be performed by individuals not formally trained in neuropsychology or clinical psychology. A trained person with a background in psychological testing may serve as an examiner. Training in administration and scoring should be provided by a qualified psychologist. Interpretation of the scores should not be attempted without a firm understanding of psychological theories and principles of memory functioning.

The standardized procedures for administration are clearly explained in the manual. Directions to be read to each test taker are presented in sufficient detail so the test taker can respond appropriately to the tasks. No sample materials or practice questions are provided.

The scoring procedures to be applied to the MAS Record Form are described in the manual. The step-by-step computation of scores for each subscale, conversion to standard scores, computation of summary scale scores, and plotting of the MAS subscale profile are presented in a simple straightforward manner with sample data. The standard score scale for the subscales has a mean of 10 and standard deviation of 3; the summary scores are scaled with a mean of 100 and standard deviation of 15. The scoring criteria for the drawings in the Visual Reproduction Subscale are clearly defined, with interexaminer generalizability (reliability) coefficients based on naive and experienced examiners exceeding .95. The guidelines for interpretation of all of the scores in terms of age and education norms and in comparison to WAIS-R (Wechsler Adult Intelligence Scale—Revised) Full

Scale IQ are clinically meaningful, with several illustrative case examples. The clinical evaluations interpreted from the normalized scores are intended to focus on a person's functional level of cognitive ability and the diagnosis of memory disorder resulting from brain illness or injury.

The normative sample from which 19 tables of normative scores are derived consisted of 843 adult volunteers without a history of neurological disease or chronic substance abuse. It included 361 men and 482 women who were 18 to 90 years of age. A stratified random subsample of 467 was selected from the 843 to reflect the U.S. population distribution by age and gender and by age and education. No profiles of the demographic characteristics for the total sample as well as the census-matched subsample were presented. Such information is necessary to understand the norms and to determine their appropriateness for the wide range of individuals who will take the MAS. Normative scores are presented only by age, age and gender, and age and education. Difference scores are also reported between the Global Memory Scale and WAIS-R Full Scale IQ, between all pairs of MAS subscales, and between pairs of MAS summary scores. They are based on the standard error of a difference score at the .05 level of significance.

Despite the rigor demonstrated in the computation of the normative scores, the partitioning of the sample into age subgroups of approximately 38 subjects each undermines the stability of the estimated scores. The polynomial regression analyses used in the continuous norming procedure can yield biased estimates of the scores with such small samples. Although the age-decade and age-education norms provide useful structures for interpretation, the instability of those norms due to inadequate sample sizes belies their usefulness. Aggregating the age categories differently to assure larger samples would have been more desirable.

The technical adequacy of the MAS was reported via several reliability and validity studies. As far as reliability evidence, generalizability coefficients were computed to assess score stability (test-retest) over 6 months based on a sample of 30 adults. The coefficients ranged from .70 to .95. The most unstable subscales were Verbal Span, Visual Span, List Acquisition, List Recall, and Immediate Visual Recognition. Given the small sample size used for these analyses, those estimates should be regarded as tentative. Generalizability coefficients were also reported for the Visual Reproduction task to determine interexaminer reliability, noted previously. Again, very small samples of subjects' drawings (5 to 10) were used in the analyses of variance.

Construct-related validity evidence was reported in terms of an intercorrelation matrix of subscale scores, factor analyses using normal ($n = 471$) and neurologically impaired ($n = 52$) samples, and comparisons of criterion group performance based on patients with dementia ($n = 34$), closed-head trauma ($n = 37$), left hemisphere lesion ($n = 16$), and right hemisphere lesion ($n = 23$). These types of evidence were appropriate and informative; however, the sample sizes in these studies question the importance assigned to the results in their interpretation. No caveats were given by the author to acknowledge these limitations. One type of validity evidence not studied is the concurrent validity of MAS scores with those of alternative memory scales. Such evidence would furnish insight into the measurement of the memory disorder construct.

In summary, the MAS is a systematically developed clinical tool to assess memory functions. Its design, scoring, and interpretation procedures are meaningful and clearly explained. Despite these assets, there are several technical weaknesses: (*a*) no content-related validity evidence, (*b*) norms estimated from inadequate and possibly biased samples, and (*c*) reliability and validity studies that report and interpret results beyond the scope of the limited samples used for the analyses. Although the MAS is a potentially useful instrument, clinicians should exhibit caution in interpreting the scores and should regard the results as preliminary until these technical problems can be corrected.

Review of the Memory Assessment Scales by JOHN W. YOUNG, Assistant Professor of Educational Statistics and Measurement, Rutgers University, New Brunswick, NJ:

The Memory Assessment Scales (MAS) is an individually administered battery of tasks developed to assess a variety of memory functions in normal and clinical populations. The MAS has been standardized and validated for use with adults ages 18 to 90. The major functions measured by the MAS include: verbal and nonverbal learning and immediate memory; verbal and nonverbal attention, concentration, and short-term memory; and memory for verbal and nonverbal material following delay. In addition, measures of recognition, intrusions during verbal learning recall, and retrieval strategies are also available. The MAS was designed with consideration of the constraints faced by many test administrators: the possibility of bedside administration, the need for easily transportable test materials, and the need

for simple scoring procedures. Norms that enable the comparison of an individual's results with several target groups are an important feature of the MAS.

The MAS consists of 12 subtests based on seven memory tasks. Five of the subtests assess the retention of information learned in an earlier subtest. These subtests measure memory functioning following brief or extended delay. Total testing time is approximately one hour.

MAS SUBTESTS. The 12 MAS subtests in order of presentation are as follows: (*a*) List Learning: an auditory verbal learning task that requires the subject to recall a list of 12 common words; (*b*) Prose Memory: an auditory verbal prose recall task that requires the subject to recall a short story; (*c*) List Recall: requires the subject to recall the words presented in the List Learning subtest; (*d*) Verbal Span: a short-term auditory memory task that requires the subject to repeat increasingly longer series of numbers; (*e*) Visual Span: a nonverbal analogue of the Verbal Span subtest; (*f*) Visual Recognition: measures recognition memory for geometric designs; (*g*) Visual Reproduction: requires the subject to reproduce a geometric design; (*h*) Names-Faces: measures the ability to associate names with faces; (*i*) Delayed List Recall: requires the subject to recall the words presented in the List Learning subtest; (*j*) Delayed Prose Memory: requires the subject to recall the short story from the Prose Memory subtest; (*k*) Delayed Visual Recognition: subject is presented with 20 geometric designs and required to identify those 10 which were presented earlier in the Visual Recognition subtest; (*l*) Delayed Names-Faces Recall: requires the subject to recognize the correct names of individuals in photographs from the Names-Faces subtest.

SCORES. Detailed scoring procedures for each of the subtests are provided. Subtest raw scores are converted to standard scores ($M = 10$, $SD = 3$) using one of the age group conversion tables. In addition to the 12 subtest scores, the MAS provides three Summary Scale scores: Short-Term Memory, Verbal Memory, and Visual Memory. A measure of general memory ability, the Global Memory Scale score, is computed from the Verbal and Visual Memory Summary scores. Examinee responses, subtest and summary scores, and a subtest profile can be recorded on the MAS record form.

STANDARDIZATION. The MAS is normed on 843 adults, ranging in age from 18 to 90 years, who do not have a history of neurological disease. A stratified sample of 467 subjects, a subset of the original sample of 843, was selected to match the distribution of the U.S. population based on Census Bureau projections for 1995, classified by age and gender and by age and educational level. The normative sample closely matches the projected population values when compared on the stratification variables.

RELIABILITY. Test-retest reliability for the MAS was estimated using generalizability theory because traditional reliability coefficients are not appropriate for repeated administrations of the same task. A complete discussion of generalizability theory can be found in Cronbach, Gleser, Nanda, and Rajaratnam (1972). Generalizability coefficients can be interpreted in a similar fashion as traditional reliability coefficients. Generalizability coefficients for the subtests range from .70 to .95 with a mean of .85; for the Summary Scales, coefficients ranged from .86 to .92 with a mean of .90; for the Global Memory Scale, coefficients ranged from .94 to .95 with a mean of .95. These coefficients fall within the range of acceptable values.

VALIDITY. The validity of the MAS was established using three types of studies: convergent and discriminant validity, factorial validity, and group differentiation. The convergent and discriminant validity of the MAS was examined by correlating subtest scores from 677 normative subjects. Tests of short-term memory are predicted to correlate highly with each other but only low to moderately with tests of either verbal or visual memory. The same would be expected of verbal or visual memory tests and their relation to the two other categories of tests. The pattern of correlation results reported generally support these predictions. Factor analyses were performed on MAS subtest scores for two samples of adults: 471 normals and 52 neurologically impaired. Construct validity of the MAS was tested using marker variables computed from combinations of WAIS-R (Wechsler Adult Intelligence Scale—Revised) subtest scores. MAS subtests were expected to load on the same factor as the marker variable that theoretically measured similar constructs. Factor analytic results reported appear to support the use of three separate Summary Scale scores. Validity of the MAS was also examined by comparing the scores of the 843 normal subjects in the normative sample with the scores of 110 impaired individuals. Impaired subjects were one of four types: dementia, left-hemisphere lesion, right-hemisphere lesion, and closed-head trauma. The pattern of scores for these groups on the Summary Scales and the Global Memory Scale are reported to be consistent with studies of these disorders.

COMMENTS ON THE MAS. The MAS appears to be a valid, reliable, and comprehensive measure of memory functioning appropriate for normal and impaired populations. Although standardization of the

test appears adequate, further norming with a larger sample and conducting additional validity studies would strengthen the applicability of this instrument. The test manual is detailed but clearly written and is suitable for both novice and experienced administrators. The section on the interpretation of scores and subtest profiles can provide highly useful information when developing clinical diagnoses.

REVIEWER'S REFERENCE

Cronbach, L. J., Gleser, G. C., Nanda, H., & Rajaratnam, N. (1972). *The dependability of behavioral measurements: Theory of generalizability for scores and profiles.* New York: Wiley.

[56]
Menstrual Distress Questionnaire.

Purpose: Designed as "a self-report inventory for use in the diagnosis and treatment of premenstrual and menstrual distress."

Population: Women who experience strong to severe premenstrual or menstrual distress.

Publication Dates: 1968–91.

Acronym: MDQ.

Scores, 8: Pain, Water Retention, Autonomic Reactions, Negative Affect, Impaired Concentration, Behavior Change, Arousal, Control.

Administration: Group or individual.

Forms, 3: Form C, Form T, Short Form T.

Price Data, 1993: $110 per complete kit; $25 per 10 Form C questionnaires; $80 per 50 Form T questionnaires; $17.50 per Form C prepaid test report answer sheet; $99.50 per 50 Form T prepaid test report answer sheets; $57.50 per manual ('91, 124 pages); $220 per IBM microcomputer edition for Form C.

Time: (15) minutes for Form C; (5) minutes for Form T or Short Form T.

Author: Rudolph H. Moos.

Publisher: Western Psychological Services.

Cross References: See T4:1608 (7 references), 9:695 (6 references), and T3:1466 (4 references).

Review of the Menstrual Distress Questionnaire by JENNIFER J. FAGER, Assistant Professor of Education, College of Education and Counseling, South Dakota State University, Brookings, SD:

The Menstrual Distress Questionnaire (MDQ) "is a 47-item self-report inventory for use in the diagnosis and treatment of premenstrual and menstrual symptoms" (p. 1). The questionnaire developer designed the instrument to "distinguish cyclical from noncyclical changes in physical symptoms, mood and behavior, and arousal" (p. 1). These changes in symptoms are examined during three phases of the menstrual cycle: four days before menstrual flow, during menstrual flow, and the remainder of the cycle. The questionnaire is also designed to identify the type and intensity of symptoms experienced during each phase of the menstrual cycle, and as an aid in identifying the effect of specific interventions administered by clinicians and researchers.

The Menstrual Distress Questionnaire includes three forms. Form C (Cycle), which includes the 47 self-report items, was designed to measure symptoms experienced during each of the three stages of the menstrual cycle. Women completing Form C use a rating scale of zero (*No experience or symptom*) to four (*Present, Severe*) to rate the severity of symptoms listed on the form based upon their menstrual cycles in general. Form T (Today), using the same 47 items and rating scales as Form C, examines symptoms experienced during the menstrual cycle. In addition, Short Form T consists of the first 22 items and the first four scales of Form T.

The MDQ includes statements representing eight scales; these eight scales include three somatic scales: Pain, Water Retention, and Autonomic Reactions. The three scales that tap mood and behavioral changes include Negative Affect, Impaired Concentration, and Behavior Change. Of the two remaining scales, one measures arousal and the other is a control scale or a scale measuring symptoms not traditionally associated with menstrual cycles. The scales are used on all forms to examine symptoms before, during, and between menstrual cycles.

The results provided by the forms are designed for different uses. Form C is designed for use in the screening process of menstrual symptoms and is used to identify actual menstrual problems. Form T is to be used for diagnosis, treatment, and research applications and provides a detailed, concurrent record of cyclical changes in symptom severity when used every other day for one or two cycles. The Short Form T is used if one is not interested in monitoring changes in the Impaired Concentration, Behavior Change, Arousal, and Control scales.

Each of three forms of the MDQ have three options in scoring. The forms can be hand scored from results on the AutoScore Form. Other scoring options include a computer-scannable mail-in answer sheet or a microcomputer program. Each patient who takes the MDQ is provided with a report from each form. Form C provides patients with a score profile, an analysis of symptom significance, charted results, and a display of item responses. In addition to the information provided from the scoring of Form C, Form T provides the patient with an overview of treatment options. These results allow the patient

and clinician to determine the best procedures for treating the identified menstrual problems.

In order to establish content validity the instrument developer conducted a review of the research and assessment procedures to examine menstrual cycle symptoms. The 47 symptoms that appear on the MDQ were the result of the gathering of information from several sources. The procedure included collecting information via an open-ended questionnaire given to women, symptoms identified in the review of research, and a list from the Blatt Menopausal Index. The instrument developer also included symptoms to tap feelings of excitement and well-being as well as control symptoms or symptoms not usually associated with menstrual cycles. The questionnaire developer did not provide complete data on the women involved in the instrument development procedures nor did he identify the source of the items not found in the literature but included on the questionnaire.

The MDQ was piloted on 839 women to establish reliability and validity criteria. A factor analysis provided the author with the eight scales mentioned earlier. Internal consistencies for the initial sample varied from .89 to .53 using the Kuder-Richardson Formula 20. Additional data on the internal consistencies are provided based on previous research in the field completed by researchers other than the author.

The questionnaire developer suggests in the preface to the manual that the MDQ has been used for over 20 years in research of menstrual cycles and symptoms. Difficulties arise in analyzing the reliability of the instrument, however, due to the lack of information provided on the standardization sample. Although the author provides basic demographic information on the sample such as age, education, and marital status, it is unclear from the manual where and when the sample was obtained. It is also unclear from the information provided in the manual whether or not the psychometric data were completed for the current publication data or for the initial conceptualization of the instrument used over two decades ago.

The manual that accompanies the MDQ is a complete review of the research that incorporates research data into the description of the questionnaire. This information, although useful to researchers, is cumbersome for clinicians. This is particularly true in the sections of the manual related to test development and use. I would recommend a separation of the research from the initial instrument development information of clarification of how the research has aided in the instrument development for the MDQ user.

The reference list and annotated bibliography included in the manual provide researchers interested in menstrual symptom research with many resources for further investigation. Chapter 6 of the manual reviews the literature in treatment of perimenstrual distress providing ample opportunity for researchers and clinicians to seek additional information in treating patients. As a resource manual it is invaluable.

The MDQ provides the patient, the clinician, and the researcher with extensive information on menstrual symptoms. The reports provided from an analysis of results from both Form C and Form T are thorough in their examination when scored by computer. Hand scoring is laborious and may be complicated for clinicians working under time constraints. The printouts provided from the computer-scored forms are easy to read and interpret. Sample reports are included in the manual to aid in interpreting results.

If the problems associated with clarification of the manual are rectified, the Menstrual Distress Questionnaire will be a useful tool for clinicians working with patients experiencing menstrual difficulties. As it now stands the MDQ is helpful to researchers in menstrual distress; however, additional information should be provided regarding the development of the instrument.

Review of the Menstrual Distress Questionnaire by DONNA L. SUNDRE, *Associate Assessment Specialist/ Assistant Professor of Psychology, James Madison University, Harrisonburg, VA:*

GENERAL INFORMATION. The Menstrual Distress Questionnaire (MDQ) and its manual represent over 25 years of research and instrument development focusing on understanding the physical and psychological fluctuations associated with the menstrual cycle. An expanding base of literature has indicated a renewed interest in women's health issues and evidence for the linkage of perimenstrual symptoms to a variety of health risks (Logue & Moos, 1986). Designed to provide clinicians with a standard method for diagnosing and treating premenstrual and menstrual symptoms and researchers with measures for exploring perimenstrual symptoms, treatments, and etiological theories, the MDQ is a 47-item self-report inventory, which can be group or individually administered. The 47 items provide a listing of common symptoms and feelings associated with menstruation. Subjects are requested to indicate the presence and severity of the symptoms and feelings using a 5-point scale (0 = *No experience of symptom*; 4 = *Present, severe*). The MDQ is composed of eight scales; three measure somatic symptoms: Pain, Water Retention, and Autonomic Reactions. Three scales assess mood and behavioral changes: Negative Affect, Impaired Concentration, and Behavior Change. One of the two remaining scales measures Arousal, and the other is a Control scale designed to assess the extent to which symptoms not typically associated with the menstrual cycle are reported.

Three forms are available. Form C (Cycle) is administered once and intended to estimate severity of symptoms at the three stages of the most recent menstrual cycle: most recent flow, four days before flow, and the remainder of the cycle. Form T (Today) assesses the presence and severity of the 47 symptoms on the day of administration. Short Form T consists of the first 22 symptoms of Form T comprising the first four scales.

PRACTICAL EVALUATION. The self-report instruments, although not attractive or particularly durable, are straightforward, and the directions easy to understand. All three forms can be administered in any of three ways: with computer-scannable mail-in answer sheets, via microcomputer, or using a carboned answer sheet (AutoScore Form). Administration should be relatively uncomplicated and require no more than 15 minutes with literate subjects. Scoring procedures are, of course, related to the administration method selected, and should meet most needs with immediate results available using microcomputer administration or the carboned answer sheets. Users can hand score the AutoScore Forms and individual profiles can be generated by carefully following the instructions provided. The scannable answer sheets can be mailed to the publisher where they will be scanned, scored, and interpreted. The computer report is promised to be mailed out within one working day. Although many individuals would be qualified to administer this instrument, the author is careful to advise that users should be familiar with the MDQ interpretation guidelines, psychometric properties, and limitations included in the manual.

The manual is well written, fairly well organized, and includes a very helpful annotated bibliography of 1985–1989 related research. It provides clear instructions for the administration of the instruments and care is taken to mention the importance of completing all items, building rapport with the respondent, and ensuring the confidentiality of responses. Hand-scoring procedures are also carefully described, including how to handle missing data and how much missing data can be reasonably tolerated. *Technical Evaluation.*

NORMS. The original norming sample of 839 women is in one paragraph of the manual described as "representative" and in the next as "homogeneous." This is puzzling because the intended target population with whom potential users of the inventory would wish to compare scores would not necessarily be limited to a homogeneous sample of younger (Mean = 25.2 years), highly educated (Mean = 15.2 years), recently married (Mean = 2.7 years) women with over half (56%) having no children. More disturbing is the lack of description of the sampling design and participation rates to evaluate the nature, adequacy, and appropriateness of the intended norming group. The tables included in Appendix A have combined data from the original sample of 839 with 1,542 observations from a multitude of undescribed samples obtained by other investigators to form means and standard deviations for Form C scales. Appendix A also presents a sample of 399 responses used to form means and standard deviations for Form T scales. No subgroup norms are reported; this is unfortunate because the characteristics of the menstrual cycle are known to vary with factors such as age (Logue & Moos, 1986).

A number of additional and potentially important limitations to the original norms must be mentioned. The original norming group was not presented a current version of the MDQ. The norming sample was asked to respond to Form A, a questionnaire similar to the current Form C (Cycle), which has been modified in the following ways: The items have been reordered; the rating scale has been changed from 1 to 6 to the current 0- to 4-point scale; and the premenstrual phase duration has been reduced from the week prior to menstrual flow to 4 days prior to menstrual onset. The impact of such contextual effects is unknown; however, Appendix B in the manual presents raw score to T-score conversions for the 0–4-point scale with exactly the same ns reported in Appendix A using the original Form A 1–6-point scale and other modifications described above. More information concerning the creation of the norms is required.

It would also appear that scores generated from pencil-and-paper instruments are to be considered parallel with microcomputer presented scores. Considerable effort was spent exploring and describing the lack of differences resulting in questionnaire versus interview responses; however, similar attention has not been addressed to questionnaire versus microcomputer administration of the inventory. No data providing evidence of comparability have been provided. Without assurance that the two modes of score generation are equated, the reliability and validity of the scores may also be variant. Thus, generalizing reliability and validity evidence from the original sample to data collected using computer administration is not advisable at this time.

RELIABILITY. All MDQ scales were developed through factor analysis, therefore measures of internal consistency should be adequate. For the most part, the scales comprise homogeneous items, and the factor structure seems to be stable across varied samples and menstrual cycle stages. Of further interest, preliminary studies addressing symptom reports across menstrual cycles for premenstrual, menstrual, and intermenstrual phases resulted in moderate to high positive correlations. These results suggest good intercycle reliability in subject reports for each of the three cycle phases and are encouraging. However, the sample was very small ($n = 15$) and not described. A curiosity relates to the presentation of KR-20 internal consistencies, a common method for estimating the consistency of responses that can be scored as right or wrong, for scales comprising items measured on the 0- to 4-point metric. An additional puzzle relates to the rather high correlations of the subscale factors derived using varimax rotation, which generally results in orthogonal or independent factors. The subscale factors appear to be related to one another. The manual also includes data from a variety of research studies, some using adaptations of the MDQ, to demonstrate internal consistency with less information than that provided regarding the original norming sample.

VALIDITY. The most crucial psychometric property of any measurement is validity, and this reviewer was disappointed in the implicit rather than explicit treatment given to the validity of measurement throughout the manual. A section devoted to all aspects of validity was expected in the first chapter, which included a section on psychometric properties. Immediately following the descriptions of evidence for scale internal consistency and intercycle consistency, some validity evidence was expected. It is not that such evidence does not exist; it is spread throughout the manual without explicit referral to it as such. The author may contend that much of the following chapters describe validity evidence; this is true, but for the sake of the reader it should have been summarized briefly in the psychometric properties section with referrals to other chapters of the manual. The stability of the factor structure is prerequisite to validity evidence, and the correlations between factors suggest that although the scales are related, unique variance is accounted for by each. This is the critical issue: What is the variance attributable to? Although the author suggests the variance is not due to memory or order effects, the truly critical issue remains unanswered in this section and potential readers must search several additional chapters to locate and evaluate the potential validity of the instrument for intended purposes.

SUMMARY EVALUATION. Despite the criticisms mentioned above, the MDQ has much to offer. The MDQ and various adaptations have been widely used in the published research. Now that the instrument is commercially distributed, the research published using the MDQ may be easier to interpret because adaptations will be allowed only by the publisher. The development of a truly representative norming group and subgroup norms may be forthcoming.

The MDQ compares favorably to other available instruments. For example, the Premenstrual Assessment Form (PAF) (Halbreich & Endicott, 1982), which examines only premenstrual physical, mood, and behavior changes, has two forms which allow retrospective (previous three cycles) and concurrent (daily) symptom assessments. Comparisons of MDQ and PAF prevalence rates are discrepant, with about twice as many women reporting premenstrual symptoms with the PAF; however, severe symptom reports (about 3%) are similar for both inventories. The conclusion drawn by Logue and Moos (1986) was that research indicates that women tend to report greater symptomology on retrospective assessments and the greater prevalence rates generated by the PAF are a function of retrospective reports across *three* cycles. The same authors point out fairly consistent results from the two MDQ forms, although the retrospective Form C (Cycle) version, consistent with other research findings, does result in slightly higher reports of mild symptomology than the concurrent Form T (Today). Moos does suggest the use of Form C for screening and repeated administrations across cycles of Form T for more accurate and detailed profiles.

Although the MDQ materials, and particularly the computerized reports, are expensive, the information provided is elaborate. For women experiencing severe perimenstrual distress, the research generated from this instrument represents both a source for understanding the phenomenon and a means to assist their clinicians in arriving at appropriate diagnoses and prescribing effective treatments.

REVIEWER'S REFERENCE

Halbreich, U., & Endicott, J. (1982). Classification of premenstrual syndromes. In R. Friedman (Ed.), *Behavior and the menstrual cycle*. New York: Marcel Dekker.

Logue, C. M., & Moos, R. H. (1986). Perimenstrual symptoms: Prevalence and risk factors. *Psychosomatic Medicine, 48*, 388-414.

Meyer-Kendall Assessment Survey.

Purpose: Constructed to assess work-related personality style.

Population: Business employees and job applicants.

Publication Dates: 1986–91.

Acronym: MKAS.

Scores, 12: Objectivity, Social Desirability Bias, Dominance, Extraversion, People Concerns, Attention to Detail, Anxiety, Stability, Psychosomatic Tendencies, Determination, Achievement Motivation, Independence.

Administration: Group or individual.

Price Data, 1993: $99.50 per complete kit including 2 assessment sheets, 2 pre-assessment sheets, and manual ('91, 72 pages); $35 per assessment sheet (price includes scoring and report by publisher); $7.50 per pre-assessment sheet; $50 per manual.

Time: (15–20) minutes.

Authors: Henry D. Meyer and Edward L. Kendall.

Publisher: Western Psychological Services.

Review of the Meyer-Kendall Assessment Survey by MARK H. DANIEL, Senior Scientist, American Guidance Service, Circle Pines, MN:

The Meyer-Kendall Assessment Survey (MKAS) is a self-report measure of 10 personal attributes thought to be important for success in business management. According to its authors (one a corporate psychologist and the other the president of a management consulting firm), the MKAS "was designed to fill the need for a business-oriented personality inventory" (p. 47). Thus, it is a normal-range instrument for adults that is intended for use in career and out-placement counseling, personnel work, and research.

Despite its 1991 copyright date, the MKAS is not a new instrument. It evolved from the Employee Questionnaire (EQ) of World War II, and it is almost identical to the EQ-C developed by Meyer in 1958. The present version was created in 1980 by rephrasing the brief "yes/no" items of the EQ-C from first-person to second-person (e.g., "You are inclined to put off making decisions"). Although it may take some time to get used to this second-person format, the authors report no difference in score levels between the two versions. It appears the norms as well as all statistical analyses reported in the manual are based on data from the EQ-C, that is, the version written in the first person.

The MKAS may be scored only be sending completed forms to the publisher. The resulting computer-generated report provides T scores and percentiles on the 10 personal attributes and on two response tendencies (Objectivity and Social Desirability Bias), each of which reflects the person's tendency to give a favorable self-report.

There are no higher-order composite scores, but the 10 attribute scales are clustered into four groups: Interpersonal Style (Dominance, Extraversion, and People Concerns); Detail Interest (Attention to Detail); Psychological Characteristics (Anxiety, Stability, and Psychosomatic Tendencies); and Motivational Levels (Determination, Achievement Motivation, and Independence). These groupings seem reasonable on content grounds, although without knowing the item composition of each scale it is difficult to judge. Factor analyses reported in the manual show the Psychological Characteristics scales belong to a common factor but the other groupings consist of scales drawn from several factors.

TECHNICAL CHARACTERISTICS. Norms are based on 187 applicants for managerial positions, of whom 91% were males; no data are provided on age, race/ethnicity, region, or type of industry. In view of the large amount of data collected over the years for the EQ-C and the MKAS, it is puzzling that this relatively small group is the only norm group available. The rationale presented in the manual for using this norm group is not very persuasive. Data purporting to show that this group's scores are close to those of a group of 2,300 miscellaneous employees are presented, although if one does some calculations one finds that on 6 of the 10 personal attribute scales the means differ by one-third to almost one-half of a standard deviation; furthermore, several of the standard deviations differ markedly. A third group of 644 corporate managers differs from the norm group on several of the scales (higher on Determination, Achievement Motivation, and Psychosomatic Tendencies and lower on Anxiety). These data do not explain why the sample of 187 applicants should be the sole norm group. No rational bias for selecting this group is offered in the manual. One or more larger or better-defined groups might provide more valuable information to the user.

The ancestor of the MKAS, the Employee Questionnaire, developed its scales by empirical keying. That is, each scale was made up of items that differentiated between people known to be high or low on the target attribute. In the course of several revisions new scales were added and others were dropped, and items were subjected to additional types of statistical analysis. Nevertheless, the low internal-consistency reliabilities of the MKAS show that these scales have not been developed to have homogeneous content. In the norm sample, coefficient alpha for the 10 personal-attribute scales ranges from .18 to .63 with

a median of .45. These results raise concern about whether the scales measure distinct constructs. In particular, three of the scales—People Concerns, Anxiety, and Stability—each have three or four correlations with other scales that are near the theoretical maximum, given their reliabilities. More generally, the low level of internal consistency precludes high scale specificity and calls into question the meaningfulness of profile analysis. The high test-retest reliabilities, averaging .78 for a sample of 39 business students (2-week interval), unfortunately do not provide evidence of scale distinctiveness.

Validation data provide some support for scale interpretability. Correlations with the Guilford-Zimmerman Temperament Survey (GZTS) in the norm sample provide convergent validity for the Extraversion scale ($r = .79$ with GZTS Sociability) and the Dominance scale ($r = .70$ with Ascendance). These are the two MKAS scales with internal-consistency reliabilities above .6. The three Psychological Characteristics scales (Anxiety, Stability, and Psychosomatic Tendencies) each have their highest correlation with the GZTS Emotional Stability scale, and although the correlations are only in the .50s, these are respectable given the low reliabilities of these MKAS scales.

Other criterion-related validation comes from several studies that compared the score patterns of individuals at varying levels of management, correlated scale scores with job ratings or sales success, or examined the scores of rapidly promoted managers. Only brief narrative summaries of these studies are provided in the manual. Results suggest that upper-level managers score relatively high in Dominance, Stability, and Independence and relatively low in Attention to Detail and Anxiety. The consistency of these findings with prior research supports these scales' construct validity. Interestingly, Attention to Detail correlates positively with rated job performance, as do Dominance, Objectivity, Extraversion, and Achievement Motivation.

SCORE REPORT. The computer-generated report provides extensive analyses in addition to the profile of scale T scores and percentiles. There are two validity indexes, one based on a combination of the number of highly frequent and highly infrequent responses, and the other sensitive to patterned responding. Two graphs depict the probability that the individual belongs to one of four empirically derived occupational groups (from a cluster analysis of the norm sample) and to one of five hypothetical, "prototypical" groups (executive, supervisor, technical, staff, and sales professional). These probabilities are sophisticated and require some study to be interpreted properly; the manual appropriately cautions users who are unfamiliar with the underlying technical concepts to ignore these graphs, although the report itself does not contain this warning.

An unusual feature of the MKAS is the optional Pre-Assessment Worksheet (PAW) on which the test user may describe the ideal score range on each MKAS scale for the position of interest. The user may submit one or more PAWs along with completed MKAS forms for scoring. The resulting report for each examinee gives a numerical index of similarity to the ideal profile and indicates which scales contributed most to dissimilarity, enabling the user to judge the importance of these discrepancies. This system appears to give the user control over the influence that each scale will have on the similarity index: By specifying a wide score range, the user can make it unlikely for individuals to fall outside the range, thereby minimizing the scale's influence.

Both the several forms of profile analysis described above and the verbal narrative included in the report place considerable weight on the individual scales. In light of the scales' low reliabilities, this may be inappropriate. The narrative discusses individual T scores without reference to their (often sizable) standard errors. One portion of the report alludes to this problem by saying that "the Determination scale should be interpreted in relation to the other scales, since by itself it has relatively low reliability" (p. 24). However, how information from the other scales can help interpret a scale whose alpha coefficient is .18 is not obvious.

SUMMARY. The MKAS score report offers a number of useful aids to interpretation, but the technical properties of the scales are a weak foundation for this sophisticated structure. Some of the scales appear to be valid measures of dimensions that are known to be relevant to business management, but for others there are few data to support interpretation; and the very low reliabilities of some scales undermine their use in pattern analysis. Several other instruments, such as the GZTS (T4:1115) and the Gordon Personal Profile and Inventory (T4:1053), assess similar sets of dimensions more reliably and with greater evidence of validity.

Review of the Meyer-Kendall Assessment Survey by GREGORY H. DOBBINS, *Associate Professor of Management, The University of Tennessee at Knoxville, Knoxville, TN:*

The Meyer-Kendall Assessment Survey (MKAS) is an omnibus personality instrument designed to assess constructs predictive of work performance. It differs from other personality measures (e.g., California Psychological Inventory [CPI], Gough, 1987) in that the items were specifically designed for a work context.

The 12 constructs assessed by the MKAS are consistent with those assessed with other personality instruments, although there are three scales (Determination, Achievement Motivation, and Independence) that are particularly relevant for work settings. Each of the constructs is clearly defined, although several of the scales are multidimensional. For example, the People Concerns scale assesses tact, empathy, and tolerance for others. Although empathy and tolerance for others are conceptually similar, an individual may be empathic, but not tolerant. Indeed the CPI contains separate scales to assess empathy and tolerance. Similarly, Attention to Detail is purported to measure preference for involvement with details and the ability to delegate responsibility. Although these two areas are conceptually related, there are differences between them (e.g., an individual with low preference for details may still not delegate).

ADMINISTRATION PROCEDURES. The MKAS is very short by personality test standards. Applicants are asked to indicate whether each of the 105 statements describes them or does not describe them. The statements are clearly written and unambiguous. Although the reading level of the instrument is not presented in the technical manual, the vocabulary and content of the scale items should be readable by most applicants.

The MKAS contains a pre-assessment worksheet that asks the organization to indicate the range of values that would be acceptable on each of the 12 scales. This serves as a formal mechanism to insure that the organization considers the temperament needed for the position. In addition, completing the pre-assessment worksheet should focus attention on the extent to which the applicant matches the organization's definition of an acceptable candidate.

The MKAS is scored by sending completed answer sheets to Western Psychological Services. The computer-generated interpretations are very thorough and clear. An overview of the instrument and its limitations are described. T-scores and a paragraph interpretation are presented for each scale. However, all scale interpretations appear to be independent (i.e., interpretations on one scale are not affected by performance levels on the other scales). Configural interpretations are not presented.

The computer-generated reports also indicate the extent to which the applicant matches one of four personality groups (Type I–sociable and people-oriented; Type II–typical; Type III–dependent and distressed, and Type IV–introverted) and five occupational groups (executives, supervisors, technical, staff, and sales professionals). Finally, the report provides a probability estimate that the person matches the prototype specified by the organization in the preassessment worksheet.

PSYCHOMETRIC CHARACTERISTICS OF THE MKAS. The technical manual indicates that "The most compelling evidence for the validity of the MKAS comes from its successful use in assessing more than 3,000 supervisors, salespeople, managers, professionals, and job applicants" (p. 47). However, close scrutiny of the reliability and validity of the MKAS raises some serious concerns. First, the scales generally have poor reliability. Test-retest reliabilities for the various scales averaged .78 over 2 weeks and .51 over 2 years. Coefficient alphas range from .18 to .67 for the 12 scales. These findings suggest that either the individual items are unreliable, there are too few items per scale, or that the constructs assessed with each MKAS scale are multidimensional. As was noted earlier, the MKAS is remarkably short for a comprehensive personality inventory and some of the scales do appear to be multidimensional.

Some validation work has been conducted with the MKAS. Several studies (e.g., Meyer & Fredian, 1959; Meyer & Pressel, 1954) have compared employees at different levels (e.g., factory and office workers, corporate officers, and general managers) and have shown that the groups score differently on some of the MKAS scales (e.g., stability, dominance, attention to detail, anxiety). Other research has evaluated the construct validity of the MKAS. Some of this work has focused on the discriminant validity of the MKAS scales. The scales show remarkably low levels of intercorrelations, especially for a self-report personality instrument. These small correlations may be a function of the low reliabilities for some of the MKAS scales.

The relationship between the MKAS and other personality instruments has also been examined. When the MKAS was correlated with the Guilford-Zimmerman Temperament Survey (GZTS; Guilford & Zimmerman, 1949), a large number of statistically significant relationships were revealed. Some of these relationships were supportive of the construct validity of MKAS scales. For example, Ascendance on the GZTS is correlated .70 with Dominance on the MKAS. However, there are also a large number of uninterpretable correlations between the GZTS and MKAS. Once again, this may reflect the low reliabilities of some of the MKAS scales.

There has been limited investigation of the criterion-related validity of the MKAS. Attention to detail and objectivity were significantly related to sales success in a study described in the technical manual. Other criterion-related validity studies are alluded to in the technical manual, but are not clearly presented. Furthermore, the validity of the scoring procedure and the inferences generated by the computerized scoring procedure have not been examined. Thus, it is not clear that an applicant who is identified as having a 90% chance of matching the manager prototype will actually be more effective as a manager than an applicant who is identified as having a 40% chance of matching the manager prototype. Clearly, such investigations are critical and must be examined in future research.

There have also been few studies examining the test fairness of the MKAS. In fact, two of the three normative groups referenced in the technical manual are almost all male (91%) and the sex composition of the third group is not presented. Similarly, little research has examined the use, reliability, and validity of the MKAS with women and minorities.

In summary, the psychometric characteristics of the MKAS must be considered questionable at best. The scales do not appear to be reliable and there has been limited work examining the constructs being assessed. Perhaps most distressing is the lack of evidence concerning the effectiveness of predictions made with the MKAS. The predictive validity of the inventory is the most essential ingredient for organizations that are using it. Unfortunately, data relevant for this issue are missing at the present time.

SUMMARY. There are two potential advantages associated with the MKAS. First, it was designed to assess work-related aspects of personality. Hence, it was not imported from clinical or counseling psychology. Second, the pre-assessment worksheet of the MKAS asks the organization to describe the characteristics of an acceptable applicant and an algorithm determines how well each candidate matches the profile. This should insure that the organization thinks about the temperament that is needed for the job prior to selecting a candidate.

Unfortunately, there are serious psychometric limitations with the MKAS. The reliabilities of the scales are very low. In addition, limited construct and criterion-related validation research has been conducted on the MKAS. Furthermore, given the reliabilities of the MKAS scales, I am not very optimistic that the MKAS can do a good job predicting job performance.

The MKAS may turn out to be a very effective instrument for selecting employees in work settings. However, given the lack of evidence to support its use and its current psychometric characteristics, I would not recommend that it be used by organizations at the present time. There are more rigorously developed personality instruments (such as the CPI [T4:361]) that can be easily adopted to work-related settings. Given the rejuvenation of personality as a predictor of job performance in work settings, perhaps the MKAS and other personality inventories will be investigated more carefully in the future.

REVIEWER'S REFERENCES

Guilford, J. P., & Zimmerman, W. S. (1949). Guilford-Zimmerman Temperament Survey. Orange, CA: Sheridan Psychological Services.
Meyer, H. D., & Pressel, G. L. (1954). Personality test scores in the management hierarchy. *Journal of Applied Psychology, 38*, 73-80.
Meyer, H. D., & Fredian, A. J. (1959). Personality test scores in the management hierarchy: Revisited. *Journal of Applied Psychology, 43*, 212-220.
Gough, H. G. (1987). California Psychological Inventory. Palo Alto, CA: Consulting Psychologists Press.

[58]
The Mother-Child Relationship Evaluation, 1980 Edition.

Purpose: Designed to measure "attitudes by which mothers relate to their children."
Population: Mothers.
Publication Dates: 1961–80.
Acronym: MCRE.
Scores, 4: Acceptance, Overprotection, Overindulgence, Rejection.
Administration: Group.
Price Data, 1993: $35 per complete kit; $16.50 per 25 test forms; $19.50 per manual ('80, 16 pages).
Time: [25–30] minutes.
Comments: Experimental form.
Author: Robert M. Roth.
Publisher: Western Psychological Services.
Cross References: See T4:1671 (2 references); for information regarding an earlier edition, see P:174; for reviews by John Elderkin Bell and Dale B. Harris of an earlier edition, see 6:146.
[Note: The following reviews are based on materials available in 1992. In February 1994 the publisher advised that this instrument is being replaced by the Parent-Child Relationship Inventory.—Ed.]

Review of the Mother-Child Relationship Evaluation, 1980 Edition by BETH DOLL, Assistant Professor of School Psychology, University of Colorado at Denver, Denver, CO:

Despite its title, the Mother-Child Relationship Evaluation (MCRE) does not assess a relationship. Instead, it is a questionnaire sampling a mother's attitudes towards children and the role of parent. Items have been written to form four scales representing maternal attitudes of Acceptance, Overprotection, Overindulgence, and Rejection. Only one of these scales, Acceptance, assesses positive parent beliefs. The majority of the questions describe inappropriate maternal attitudes, diminishing the utility of the scales for identifying strong parenting skills that could provide the foundation for intervention.

The questionnaire is outdated in several respects. It presumes the mother is the caretaking parent and uses the words "mother" and "parents" interchangeably; fathers are never mentioned in the scale or the manual. Items frequently refer to the child as "it" as in "A child is not at fault when it does something wrong" (p. 3, test form). In some instances, items describe parenting behaviors that were discouraged in the past, but have since come to be accepted parenting practices. For example, an item assessing maternal overindulgence describes the practice of lying next to one's child to settle him or her to sleep. Although several decades ago child therapists considered this to be inappropriate parenting, the practice might be seen today as evidence of a nurturing parent-child relationship. Finally, the format of the mother's response sheet is confusing, requiring that letters be circled in one of 20 columns on the page.

The MCRE manual does not provide the psychometric data necessary to justify its use in any applied setting. Estimates of the scales' internal consistency range from .41 to.57, insufficient for a clinical instrument. No information is available on the stability of the scores over time. Description of the MCRE's validity is scanty. A single short paragraph reports that scores on the three negative scales (Overprotection, Overindulgence, and Rejection) show negative correlations with the one positive scale (Acceptance). Additional validity analyses are required to establish that scores from the four scales relate in a meaningful way to independent measures of mother attitude. Factor analytic studies are necessary to establish that items on the four scales do, in fact, assess distinct dimensions of parental attitudes, and that each item has been assigned to the appropriate scale.

Tables that provide users with percentiles and *t*-scores for each scale are deceptive because this is not, in fact, a standardized measure. Instead, these descriptive statistics are based on an experimental population of 80 middle-class mothers. Insufficient information is provided about the family composition of these mothers; and, major changes have occurred in families with children since the scales were first published. The norms are not likely to reflect the differing home environments of single-parents, teenage mothers, mothers from social/ethnic minorities, or low-income mothers. Although the manual states that the MCRE is not a refined clinical measure, it still encourages clinical interpretation of the scales by providing a graphic score profile and sample case interpretations. Scale descriptions and sample interpretations utilize provocative language such as "hostility" and "lack of ego strength" in referring to the mother, and "psychopathic reactions" and "counter hostility" in referring to the child. This level of interpretation is unjustified given the limited reliability and validity information provided about the scores.

Better measures exist for evaluating parent-child relationships. The Parenting Stress Index (PSI; Abidin, 1986; T4:1933) is a research instrument that assesses dysfunctional parent-child relationships. The PSI has adequate reliability and strong validity, although, like the MCRE, it lacks representative norms (Doll, 1989). Alternatively, observations of mother-child behavior during problem-solving situations have provided useful research measures of parent-child relationships and are currently being evaluated as a clinical tool (Pianta, Smith, & Reeve, 1991).

The MCRE is not recommended for use in applied settings. Its reliability and validity are insufficient to justify its use in making important decisions about parents and children, and the normative information provided is not adequate for use with present day families. As a research instrument, the questionnaire would require considerable revision in order to recognize the diversity of families and cultures, the role of fathers in childrearing, and revised knowledge about child-parent relationships. Users are advised to consider alternative measures of parental attitudes.

REVIEWER'S REFERENCES

Abidin, R. R. (1986). Parenting Stress Index. Charlottesville, VA: Pediatric Psychology Press.
Doll, E. J. (1989). [Review of Parenting Stress Index, 2nd ed.]. *Professional School Psychology, 4*, 307-312.
Pianta, R. C., Smith, N., & Reeve, R. E. (1991). Observing mother and child behavior in a problem-solving situation at school entry: Relations with classroom adjustment. *School Psychology Quarterly, 6*, 1-15.

Review of the Mother-Child Relationship Evaluation, 1980 Edition by NORMAN FREDMAN, Professor and Coordinator, Counselor Education Program, Queens College, City University of New York, Flushing, NY:

The Mother-Child Relationship Evaluation, 1980 Edition, is virtually identical to the 1961 experimental form. Criticisms by John Elderkin Bell (1965) and Dale B. Harris (1965) in *The Sixth Mental Measurements Yearbook* are still applicable.

About a third of a century ago, Robert Roth gathered 80 volunteer PTA mothers, 25 to 35 years of age, who resided in the same middle-class community. That remains the norm group. No fathers, no minorities, no sample representative of the nation's parents. Would even the same PTA mothers, or

their daughters, give the same responses today when ideas of childrearing have so radically changed?

The conceptual framework remains the work of P. M. Symonds and Marian Fitz-Simons from the 1940s. There are four 12-item subscales for the inventory, one of Acceptance and three specific expressions of nonacceptance: Overprotection, Overindulgence, and Rejection. Mothers are asked to record the strength of their agreement with each of the 48 items using a 5-point Likert scale. The raw scores can be converted into T-scores or percentile equivalents and then plotted on a separate profile sheet. The manual states, "If three or four scales are relatively high and of similar magnitude (i.e., in the same quartile) the mother's attitudes towards her child can be considered as confused" (p. 4).

Barbara Whitman and Robert Zachary (1986) evaluated the factor structure of the inventory. They found that eight of the 48 items failed to correlate uniquely with the a priori scales. They discovered four different factors: Factor I corresponded to Acceptance; Factor II reflected a need to exert firm parental control; Factor III related to the original scales of Overindulgence and Overprotection; Factor IV concerned a willingness to seek outside help with problems in childrearing. These four factors, however, accounted for only 33% of the total variance.

Intercorrelations of the scales remained similar to the original findings. The Acceptance scale correlated negatively (-.38 to -.53) with each of the other three, which intercorrelated positively (.43 to .54) among themselves. Whitman and Zachary found no significant response differences between fathers and mothers.

Many items may measure different constructs than the a priori subscales indicate. Some items ("Children cannot choose the proper food for themselves"; "A child needs more than two medical examinations each year") might depend on the age of the child. Six times the item is phrased, "My child"; the remaining times it is phrased "children" or "child." Thus, the attitude elicited is not consistent across items. The results of Whitman and Zachary's research suggest the need for both revision and renorming of the instrument.

The directions to the mother who responds to the items state: "Keep in mind the child for whom you are seeking help" (p. 1, test form). This seems to indicate that the inventory is intended for clinical use. Robert Roth's italicized warning is at the beginning of the manual: "It is emphasized that the MCRE is primarily exploratory and experimental, rather than a refined clinical measurement" (p. 1). Perhaps, like the Surgeon General's warning, this caveat can be placed on each profile sheet to warn judges and mental health personnel.

REVIEWER'S REFERENCES

Bell, J. E. (1965). [Review of The Mother-Child Relationship Evaluation.] In O. K. Buros (Ed.), *The sixth mental measurements yearbook* (pp. 319-320). Highland Park, NJ: Gryphon Press.
Harris, D. B. (1965). [Review of The Mother-Child Relationship Evaluation.] In O. K. Buros (Ed.), *The sixth mental measurements yearbook* (p. 320). Highland Park, NJ: Gryphon Press.
Whitman, B., & Zachary, R. A. (1986). Factor structure of the Mother-Child Relationship Evaluation. *Educational and Psychological Measurement*, 46(1), 135-141.

[59]
Music Achievement Tests 1, 2, 3, and 4.

Purpose: Constructed to measure musical achievement.
Publication Dates: 1968–86.
Acronym: MAT.
Administration: Group.
Price Data, 1987: $7.50 per record (select test); $22 per set of 4 records; $2 per administrative and scoring manual (select test); $5.50 per interpretive manual (select Tests 1 and 2 ['69, 143 pages] or Tests 3 and 4 ['70, 254 pages]).
Comments: Record player necessary for administration.
Author: Richard Colwell.
Publisher: MAT.

a) TEST 1.
Population: Grades 3–12.
Scores, 4: Pitch Discrimination, Interval Discrimination, Meter Discrimination, Total.
Price Data: $5.75 per 35 answer sheets including hand-scoring template and class record sheet; $25 per 250 answer sheets including administrative and scoring manual ('68, 32 pages), hand-scoring template, and class record sheet.
Time: (18) minutes.
a) TEST 2.
Population: Grades 4–12.
Scores, 6: Major-Minor Mode Discrimination, Feeling for Tonal Center, Auditory-Visual Discrimination (Pitch, Rhythm, Total), Total.
Price Data: $7 per 35 answer sheets including same materials as *a* above; $31.50 per 250 answer sheets including administrative and scoring manual ('68, 36 pages), hand-scoring template, and class record sheet.
Time: (28) minutes.
a) TEST 3.
Population: Grades 4–12.
Scores, 5: Tonal Memory, Melody Recognition, Pitch Recognition, Instrument Recognition, Total.

Price Data: $6.50 per 35 answer sheets including same materials as *a* above; $28.50 per 250 answer sheets including administrative and scoring manual ('70, 32 pages), hand-scoring template, and class record sheet.
Time: (32) minutes.
a) TEST 4.
Population: Grades 5–12.
Scores, 7: Musical Style (Composers, Texture, Total), Auditory-Visual Discrimination, Chord Recognition, Cadence Recognition, Total.
Price Data: $6.50 per 35 answer sheets including same materials as *a* above; $28.50 per 250 answer sheets including administrative and scoring manual ('70, 32 pages), hand-scoring template, and class record sheet.
Time: (38) minutes.
Cross References: See T2:207 (5 references); for a review by Paul R. Lehman, see 7:248 (5 references).

Review of the Music Achievement Tests 1, 2, 3, and 4 by J. DAVID BOYLE, Professor and Chairman, Department of Music Education and Music Therapy, School of Music, University of Miami, Coral Gables, FL:

DESCRIPTION OF TESTS. The Music Achievement Tests (MAT) include four tests, each of which has several subtests. All parts of the tests require responses to recorded tonal or musical stimuli and essentially involve one of three types of tasks: (*a*) aural discrimination, (*b*) aural recognition, or (*c*) aural-visual discrimination. Test 1 provides measures of (*a*) Pitch Discrimination in two contexts, one asking which of two successive tones is higher and the other asking which of three successive tones is lowest; (*b*) Interval Discrimination, also in two contexts, one asking whether a three-tone pattern moves scalewise or in leaps and the other asking whether the melody of a musical phrase generally moves scalewise or in leaps; and (*c*) Meter Discrimination, which asks whether a musical phrase moves in duple or triple meter. Test 2 provides measures of (*a*) Major-Minor Mode Discrimination in two contexts, chords only and musical phrases; (*b*) Feeling for Tonal Center, also in chords only and musical phrase contexts; and (*c*) Auditory-Visual Discrimination, part of which assesses auditory-visual Pitch discrimination and part of which assesses auditory-visual Rhythm discrimination.

Test 3 provides measures of (*a*) Tonal Memory, which involves identifying the tone of an arpeggiated chord that differs from the tones of a previously played block chord; (*b*) Melody Recognition, which first presents a melody alone and asks respondents to identify the voice (high, middle, or low) in which that melody occurs in a subsequent three-voice harmonization of that melody; (c) Pitch Recognition, which presents two notated pitches, the sound of the first pitch, and the sounds of three subsequent pitches, one of which respondents must designate as the second notated pitch; and (d) Instrument Recognition, which involves selecting the name of an orchestral instrument heard, some unaccompanied and some with orchestral accompaniment. Test 4 provides measures of (a) Musical Style, the first subtest of which asks respondents to select the names of probable composers for given recorded excerpts and the second subtest of which requires recognition of monophonic, homophonic, or polyphonic textures; (b) Auditory-Visual Discrimination, but with more difficult rhythms than were assessed in Test 1; (c) Chord Recognition, which requires matching one of three chords heard with a previously heard chord; and (d) Cadence Recognition, which requires determination of cadence type (full, half, or deceptive) for given musical phrases.

NORMATIVE AND TECHNICAL DATA. Responses of some 20,000 students ranging from grade 3 through high school provided the data for standardization of Tests 1 and 2; standardization data for Tests 3 and 4 were based on responses of some 9,000 students from grade 4 through high school. Both normative samples were selected to reflect representation of four geographic areas of the U.S. and a balance of students from three broad classifications of city size. Total test and subtest percentiles and standard scores for Tests 1 and 2 are provided for grades 3 through 8, for high school, and for combined grades 4 through 12. Total test and subtest percentiles and standard scores for Tests 3 and 4 are provided for grade level (4 through 12 for Test 3 and 5 through 12 for Test 4). Additional norms for combined grades 4–6, 7–9, and 10–12 and for students with piano experience and instrumental experience are available for tests 3 and 4.

Kuder-Richardson Formula 21 reliability coefficients are the only reliability data available for all parts of all tests. Ranges of the coefficients for the various grade levels for each of the four tests are as follows: Test 1—.84 to .92; Test 2—.80 to .97; Test 3—.46 to .90; Test 4—.81 to .88. Subtest ranges generally are much lower, and the subtests reliabilities for Tests 3 and 4 are lower than those for Tests 1 and 2. Notably low reliabilities are reported for the Composer and Cadence subtests of Test 4; their grade level reliability coefficients range respectively from .36 to .64 and from .25 to .46. The manual for Tests 3 and 4 contains reliability data for several other breakdowns of the norming group: (a) sex, (b)

geographic area, (c) size of school system, and (d) musical participation (instrumental, choral, and general) and experience (piano and instrumental).

The manuals contain information on three types of validity data—content, criterion-related, and predictive. Data for the predictive validity, however, are too limited to be useful. Claims for content validity are based on the extent to which the tests' contents are believed to reflect certain basic instructional objectives common to nine basal music series and one MENC (Music Educators National Conference) curriculum guide that were published during the 1960s. Subsequent conferences between the test author and noted "elementary school music authorities" (p. 22, Test 1 and 2 manual) regarding the types of items being developed for the MAT substantiated the view the test content indeed reflected the content of those basic objectives. (Objectives related to performance and creativity, which did not lend themselves to groups measurement, were not considered for the MAT.) Tests 1 and 2 are based on objectives for grades 1 through 5; Tests 3 and 4 are based on objectives for grades 4 through 8.

Criterion-related validity claims are based on correlations between music teachers' selections of their "best five and poorest five" (p. 23, Test 1 and 2 manual) students and test scores for several of the trial versions of the MAT; correlations between teachers' selections and selected students' scores on the final form of the MAT were .92 ($N = 1,893$).

The manuals include item difficulty and item discrimination indices for every item in the MAT. Also, standard error of measurement data are provided. In all, the technical data provided in the manuals suggest that much care was taken in the development and standardization of the MAT. Further, the technical aspects of the recorded items, answer sheets, and administrative procedures reflect similar care and professionalism.

USES AND USABILITY OF THE MAT. The reviewer and his students have used various parts of the MAT on a number of occasions over the past 20 years, and it has proven to be easily administered, easily understood by students taking the tests, and useful for a variety of research and evaluation purposes. In this reviewer's opinion, the MAT is by far the most useful standardized music test on the market today. It provides measures of many achievement tasks that are relevant to music instruction in today's schools.

The fact that the MAT's content validity is based on its reflections of instructional objectives of elementary basal music series of the 1960s may be a concern to some test users; however, this reviewer examined the objectives of several basal music series published in the late 1980s (Silver Burdett's *World of Music*, 1988; Macmillan's *Music and You*, 1988; University of Hawaii's *Music, Comprehensive Musicianship Program*, 1986; and the Music Educators National Conference's *The School Music Program: Description and Standards*, 2nd ed., 1986) and found that, with a couple of exceptions, most aural recognition, aural discrimination, and aural-visual discrimination tasks measured by the MAT are still relevant to the instructional objectives of these series. In essence, curriculum in elementary music basal series has changed little since the development of the MAT, and the claim of content validity made at the time of test development is still warranted.

This is not to imply that this reviewer holds every aspect of the MAT in equally high regard. Some of the subtests appear much more useful than others, and at least two subtests of Test 3 seem less relevant than other subtests. Even though the technical data do not necessarily suggest it, the Tonal Memory subtest, which is different from all other tonal memory tasks on other music tests, and the Pitch Recognition subtest seem to be the least useful. Regardless, the MAT remains an important measurement tool for music teachers and researchers.

REVIEWER'S REFERENCES

Curriculum Research and Development Group. (1986). *Music: Comprehensive musicianship program* (K-8). Honolulu: University of Hawaii.
Music Educators National Conference. (1986). *The school music program: Description and standards*. Reston, VA: Music Educators National Conference.
Music and you (K-8). (1988). New York: Macmillan Publishing Company.
World of music (K-8). (1988). New York: Silver Burdett & Ginn, Inc.

Review of the Music Achievement Tests 1, 2, 3, and 4 by RUDOLF E. RADOCY, Professor of Music Education and Music Therapy, University of Kansas, Lawrence, KS:

PURPOSE. The Music Achievement Tests (MAT) measure auditory skills that Richard Colwell, employing the advice of nine other individuals active in music education during the 1960s, including professors, music supervisors, and publishers' representatives, believed to be important components of music achievement. The battery's content was based also on examination of the then most recent versions of elementary/junior high school general music series texts in use during MAT development; copyright dates ranged from 1963 through 1970. The manual for Tests 1 and 2 indicates a sixfold purpose: Evaluating mastery of basic auditory objectives, discovering students who might profit from instrumental instruction, yielding information with which to counsel students, providing data for use in program evaluation, showing students where they stand in relation to program objectives, and providing information for curriculum researchers.

TEST CONTENT. MAT Test 1 includes three parts. Pitch Discrimination includes two sections: In the first section, the student indicates whether a second tone sounds higher than, lower than, or the same as a first tone for 15 pairs. In the second section, the student hears 10 groups of three tones and indicates which one of the three sounds is the lowest in each group. The Interval Discrimination subtest includes 10 three-tone patterns in the first section and 18 phrases in the second section. In each case, the student indicates whether each tonal sequence moves in steps or skips ("leaps"), or if he or she is unsure. The Meter Discrimination subtest asks the student to classify 15 excerpts as duple or triple meter, or indicate uncertainty.

The second MAT test includes three parts, each of which has two subtests. In Major-Minor Mode Discrimination, the student classifies 15 chords as major or minor, and indicates whether each of 13 phrases is in major or minor, or changes within the phrase. The second part, Feeling for Tonal Center, includes subtests of cadences and phrases. In the cadences section, the student hears four-chord sequences and then indicates whether the first, second, third, or none of a set of three following tones was the tonic for each of 10 items. Similarly, in the phrases section the student notes which of three, if any, tones following each of 10 accompanied phrases was the tonic tone. In Auditory-Visual Discrimination, discrepancies exist between what the student sees in notation and what he or she hears. In the pitch section, the 12 items include measures where the discrepancy is in pitch; the 12-item rhythm section features measures discrepant in rhythm. In each case, the student indicates the measures that contain a discrepancy.

Test 3 includes four parts. Tonal Memory presents 20 block four-tone chords, each followed by the arpeggiated version. The student indicates whether any change occurs between the simultaneous and successive tone versions, and if it does, the number of altered tone. In Melody Recognition, the student indicates whether the melody in 20 items is in the highest, middle, or lowest voice, or if he or she is unsure. In Pitch Recognition, the student sees two printed notes for each of 20 items. He or she hears the first tone and then hears three more tones, from which he or she must identify which one, if any, is the notated second tone. The Instrument Recognition part includes two subtests: In a solo section, the student indicates what instrument of a choice of four plus "none" is playing each of 10 unaccompanied solo passages. In an accompanied section, the student makes a similar indication for each of five accompanied passages.

Four parts comprise Test 4. Musical Style includes two sections, the first of which requires the student to choose from four possibilities the likely composer of each of 20 excerpts. The second 20-item section requires indicating whether the musical texture is monophonic, homophonic, or polyphonic. The Auditory-Visual Discrimination part presents 14 four-measure phrases; the student follows notation and indicates each measure in which the notation is different from what he or she hears. (Discrepancy is always due to rhythm.) Chord Recognition includes 15 single chords, each followed by four others. The student indicates whether the first, second, third, or no chord is the same as the original, or if he or she is unsure. The final part, Cadence Recognition, includes 15 phrases; the student indicates whether each phrase ending comprises a full, half, or deceptive cadence.

NORMS. The four tests comprising the MAT were normed with national samples ranging from approximately 9,000 to 20,000 students. Percentile ranks and standard scores (mean = 500, standard deviation = 100) for different grade levels and combinations thereof are provided. For Tests 1 and 2, norms are presented for grade 3 through 8 individually, for high school, and for a 4–12 grade combination. The norms presented for Tests 3 and 4 are for individual grades 4 or 5 through 12 and for combinations of grades 4–6, 7–9, and 10–12. In addition, separate Tests 3 and 4 norms appear for students with experience in piano and in band and orchestra instruments for the various grade combinations. The manuals present detailed descriptions of the who, where, and when of the standardization groups.

RELIABILITY AND VALIDITY. For MAT Test 1, a reliability estimate for the total test across all grade levels of .88 by the KR21 method and .94 by the split-halves method is reported. For Test 2, a KR21 estimate of .92 is reported. Similar reliability estimates for Tests 3 and 4 based on all grade levels combined are not reported. KR21 estimates for total test scores and section scores for separate grade levels are provided. For Test 1, these figures range from a low of .557 (5th grade, Meter Discrimination) to a high of .921 (high school, total test). The reliability extremes for Test 2 range from .425 (4th grade, Feeling for Tonal Center) to .965 (high school, total test). The Test 3 range is from .427 (4th grade, Pitch Recognition) to .907 (12th grade, total test). Test 4 reliability estimates range from .254 (5th

grade, Cadence Recognition) to .883 (12th grade, total test).

Content validity is based on the judgments of the experts with whom Colwell conferred and the content of the music series texts and several music education textbooks. Several studies are cited to show evidence of predictive validity regarding other evaluations of musical achievement.

OVERALL EVALUATION. The MATs have been available since 1970. The version inspected by this reviewer is identical to that of over 20 years ago. The only apparent difference, other than cost, is that the test is now available from a firm in Urbana, Illinois (home of the University of Illinois, Richard Colwell's former employer) rather than the Follett Educational Corporation. Many contemporary comments regarding the MAT could have been made 20 years ago, and vice versa.

The MATs are carefully constructed and normed. The manuals provide a wealth of information about development, administration, scoring, and interpretation. Colwell is careful to describe what the test is not (e.g., a measure of musical performance or aptitude) as well as what it purportedly is. The four tests are easy to administer and score; one would not have to be a musician to administer the tests and obtain scores.

The necessity for consulting two manuals may be annoying. In the interest of efficiency and eliminating redundancy, a manual encompassing all four tests could be assembled.

Although phonograph recordings remain an important component of most schools' musical resources, they are technologically obsolete. Cassette recordings, easier to manage and store, and compact discs, superior in quality and durability, might be more useful. (In fairness, the quality of the phonograph recordings is quite satisfactory.)

The decision to use the MAT is a matter of relevance to the curriculum in the school contemplating its use. The auditory skills which the battery tests are important musical skills, and they are all relevant in comprehensive music education. Students should be learning to listen analytically so that they may identify chord changes, modalities, cadences, meters, and textures. They should be sensitive to differences in pitch and timbre and to discrepancies between what is written and what is heard. Although some of the materials that inspired the test items may be outdated, the items themselves and the skills the items require remain contemporary. Of course, if a particular curriculum does not include the skills, or presents them in a substantively different way, the MAT may lack validity for that curriculum.

The MATs remain the best known standardized measure of musical achievement. They provide a basis for norm-referenced comparisons, among schools and school systems as well as with a large reference group. The passage of time inevitably calls into question the continuing representativeness of the norming groups.

In summary, although the MATs are not new, they may continue to be useful as a diagnostic measure and an individual achievement measure in school settings where the measured skills are deemed important. They also may be useful for comparing particular achievements of music programs that agree regarding the curricular relevance of the tested auditory skills.

[60]
Occupational Aptitude Survey and Interest Schedule, Second Edition—Aptitude Survey.

Purpose: Designed to measure career development of students.
Population: Grades 8–12.
Publication Dates: 1983–91.
Acronym: OASIS-2 AS.
Scores, 6: General Ability, Verbal Aptitude, Numerical Aptitude, Spatial Aptitude, Perceptual Aptitude, Manual Dexterity.
Administration: Group.
Price Data, 1994: $98 per complete kit including 10 test booklets, 50 answer sheets, 50 profile sheets, and manual ('91, 38 pages); $29 per 10 test booklets; $28 per 50 answer sheets; $19 per 50 profile sheets; $26 per manual.
Time: 35(45) minutes.
Comments: May be used in conjunction with the OASIS-2 Interest Schedule (T4:1863).
Author: Randall M. Parker.
Publisher: PRO-ED, Inc.
Cross References: See T4:1862 (2 references); for reviews by Rodney L. Lowman and Kevin W. Mossholder of an earlier edition, see 10:243.

Review of the Occupational Aptitude Survey and Interest Schedule, Second Edition—Aptitude Survey by LAURA L. B. BARNES, Assistant Professor of Educational Research, Department of Applied Behavioral Studies, Oklahoma State University, Stillwater, OK:

The Occupational Aptitude Survey and Interest Schedule, Second Edition—Aptitude Survey (OASIS-2AS) is intended to provide students with information "regarding their relative strengths in several aptitude areas related to the world of work" (p. 1). The Aptitude Survey was developed basically as a shorter version of the U.S. Department of Labor

General Aptitude Test Battery (GATB). Through factor analytic studies of the 12 GATB subtests, five factors were deemed to be responsible for a significant portion of test score variance. These five factors became the basis for developing the five subtests of the OASIS-2AS. The OASIS-2AS yields six scores: a General Ability score derived by summing raw scores from the Vocabulary and Computation subtests and five scores corresponding to each of the five subtests. Briefly, the subtests are: Vocabulary, which requires students to find two words that have the same or opposite meaning; Computation, which is composed of arithmetic problems; Spatial Relations, which requires students to visualize and compare objects; Word Comparison, which requires students to compare two names, letters, or numbers to see if they are the same or different; and Making Marks, which measures how quickly students can make marks in a square.

Test materials are easy to use and administration is straightforward. Hand scoring is easily accomplished and computer scoring is available. Separate answer sheets with somewhat different instructions are required for machine and hand scoring. Hand scoring takes about 3 to 5 minutes per examinee. Raw scores on each test are converted to percentiles and stanines by referring to the norms table in the Examiner's Manual. No formal training is required for administering and scoring the tests beyond that required to ensure that standardized conditions are maintained; however, the manual appropriately cautions that test interpretation should be done only by trained professionals. Score interpretation is facilitated by the inclusion of a table containing job titles organized according to the "minimum level of aptitude estimated to be needed to perform the work" (p. 30) and containing the *Dictionary of Occupational Titles* (DOT) and *Guide for Occupational Exploration* (GOE) codes for those jobs. The section in the manual on Interpreting Test Results provides guidelines and two case-study illustrations for interpreting test results to students.

According to the Examiner's Manual, the standardization sample of 1,505 cases from grades 8 through 12 was obtained from 13 states and reflects regional, gender, racial, and urban-suburban/rural characteristics similar to U.S. Census data. Presumably this refers to the 1980 Census, although the manual does not specifically state this, nor does the manual provide the dates for normative data collection. It must be inferred that the bulk of the standardization data were collected before 1983 (the date of the first edition of the OASIS), because the author states that the original norm group was retained and increased by 107 cases. Separate norms by grade are not provided based on statistical analyses indicating no significant differences among the grade levels. In fact, there was no pattern indicating that older students performed any better than younger students. Likewise, separate sex norms were eliminated; although females as a group scored significantly higher than males on the Computation subtest ($p<.05$), the 2.0 difference was within a 95% confidence band based on the standard error of measurement.

Internal consistency reliabilities are reported for Vocabulary, Computation, General Ability, and Spatial Relations (the latter as split-half coefficients) and alternate forms reliabilities are given for the two speeded tests: Making Marks and Word Comparison. These are reported separately by grade, and except for the General Ability composite, also by sex. Median reliabilities (adjusted for range restriction) across grades range from .78 to .90 and no difference between males and females is apparent in terms of measurement consistency. Two-week test-retest coefficients are reported for a combined group of junior and senior high students with coefficients ranging from .76 to .94. Generally, the highest reliabilities are reported for General Ability, Word Comparison, and Making Marks, and the lowest for Spatial Relations. The author states that these tests do not have high enough reliability to be used as a sole predictor of specific job performance but are sufficiently high for use within the context of vocational exploration. This reviewer agrees, but would point out further the lack of long-term stability data also severely limits the usefulness of these tests for predictive purposes. It should be noted also that characteristics of the examinee groups from which reliability estimates were obtained are not reported in the manual. Because reliability estimates are known to be population specific, potential users should be aware that reported reliabilities may not be obtained in all cases. Instructions for completing student profile sheets encourage appropriate consideration of measurement error in interpreting scores and score differences. Standard errors of measurement and standard errors of score differences are reported.

With respect to validity, the OASIS-2AS subtests have high correlations, mostly in the .80 range (with the lowest being .61), with their respective GATB factors. Lower correlations with the nonrelated GATB factors are presented as evidence for discriminant validity. Correlations between the OASIS-2AS subtests and Iowa Test of Educational Development (ITED) and SRA Achievement Series subtests also show expected patterns of correlations. Vocabulary and General Ability scores have correlations in the .57 to .77 range with the achievement subtests. Vocabulary has its strongest relationship with the Reading achievement subtests. Computation correlates moderately with SRA Math (.44) but higher with ITED Math (.64); correlations with other achievement subtests are in the .31 to .44 range. Spatial Relations shows its strongest correlations with SRA Math and Science subtests (.49 and .46, respectively). As expected, the two perceptual-motor subtests (Word Comparison and Making Marks) share the least in common with achievement subtests, particularly Making Marks which correlates negligibly with all ITED and SRA achievement subtests except for SRA Language ($r = .17$).

Statements that the tests should be used only in the context of stimulating occupational exploration are repeated throughout the manual. The author refrains from saying the tests are predictive of occupational success. However, the lack of claims for prediction do not eliminate the need for evidence of relationship between test performance and occupational criteria. After all, the scores have to be interpreted with respect to some criteria, and the inclusion of job titles grouped according to the "minimum level of aptitude estimated to be needed to perform the work" (p. 30) certainly implies a linkage between test performance and job performance. Although nearly two-thirds of the section on technical information comes under the heading of Validity, only one study used a relevant criterion (academic major in a community college) to examine this relationship. Results partially supported the occupational aptitude groupings. There is a definite need for further supportive documentation that how students perform on these tests is related to occupational criteria; specifically the validity of the occupational aptitude groupings must be examined.

Other studies cited as evidence of construct validity examined test performance in relation to learning styles and decisiveness in selecting a major, and investigated group differences among students with and without learning and emotional disabilities. References for these studies are given in the Examiner's Manual and should be of value to those working with special populations.

The Examiner's Manual contains a significant number of errors. Some readers may be confused by an error on page 13 where scores of 85, 75, 50, and so on are referred to as stanine scores. It is apparent these were intended to be percentile scores. On page 15 of the manual the following appears, "Criterion-related validity includes the subcategories of content- and criterion-related validity." Obviously, this should have read, ". . . the subcategories of concurrent and predictive validity." The title of Table 11 on page 23 claims to present validity coefficients between the OASIS subtests and 15 GATB factors and subtests, when in fact the table presents correlations for 7 GATB factors. Other similar types of confusing presentations in text and tables abound.

The OASIS-2AS appears to have promise as an instrument for assisting adolescents to begin a career search. Reliabilities are acceptably high for exploratory guidance purposes. This test is less time consuming to administer than some established instruments, yet the OASIS-2AS shows evidence for relationship with the GATB scales. However, there is a definite lack of evidence for occupation-specific criterion-related validity. Although there is some comfort in the substantial correlations of these scales with the GATB, it is incumbent upon the test developer to demonstrate the validity of the suggested score interpretations.

Review of the Occupational Aptitude Survey and Interest Schedule, Second Edition—Aptitude Survey by THOMAS E. DINERO, Associate Professor of Evaluation and Measurement, Kent State University, Kent, OH:

The Occupational Aptitude Survey and Interest Schedule, Second Edition—Aptitude Survey (OASIS-2AS) was developed to assist secondary school students in "self-exploration, vocational exploration, and career development" (p. 1) while they are in the early stages of developing career goals. The feedback provided to the students by the instrument includes several aptitude areas selected so that their interpretation stimulates the "process of self-exploration and vocational exploration" (p. 2). The instrument was designed for students in grades 8 through 12.

The authors based the rationale of the profile on Anastasi's use of the term "developed abilities" in an effort to avoid the distinction between aptitude as an "intrinsic, relatively stable" (p. 2) ability and achievement as the effects of learning. They unabashedly credit the General Aptitude Test Battery (GATB) for the structure and development of the OASIS-2AS.

The OASIS-2AS comprises five paper-and-pencil subtests selected to parallel the GATB: Vocabulary, Computation, Word Comparison, Making Marks, and one test which is similar to the Differential Aptitude Test's (DAT) Space Relations and the GATB's Three-Dimensional Space, here called Spatial Relations. A sixth score, General Ability, is based on the raw scores of the Vocabulary and Computation subtests. The tests are timed and take a total of 35 minutes.

An extended section describes how the counselor can determine the standard scores available (percentile ranks and stanines) for the individual students. Information in the manual concerning the norming group indicates that scores on 1,505 8th through 12th grade students in 13 states comprised the initial data set. Quota and representative sampling were used to generate a sample which well matches the demographics of the United States. Norms are presented for the combined male and female samples because there were no statistically significant differences. The scores do not appear to be normally distributed.

Reliability information on the subtests includes Cronbach's alpha (for Vocabulary and Computation), split half (for Spatial Relations, because alphas are "negatively affected" by multifactorial tests), test-retest, and alternate form (Word Comparison and Making Marks) data. All reliabilities are above .70 for a group of 357 students at five grade levels. The authors should be commended for being selective in their use of reliability coefficients, but it is curious that a split half would be considered appropriate for a bifactorial test when an alpha would not. They then present Lord's estimates (Lord & Novick, 1968) of KR 20s for the General Ability test. Presenting these values for general ability (which might indeed by multifactorial) is inconsistent with their assertion that alpha might be affected because alpha and the KR20 are essentially the same. Internal consistency data on word comparison would have been a good addition but probably would have been high given the other information available.

Validity data on the OASIS-2AS appears to have been well conceptualized, but the potential user is warned to study the data before implementing any use. For example, the first five factors resulting from a principal axis factor analysis with varimax rotation accounted for only 73% of the variance. The authors present these results while writing of and discussing a five-factor and two-factor solution.

Item-total point biserials (not biserials) were calculated using a group of Texas students who may or may not have been part of the norming group. Most correlations were between .20 and .60.

Correlations of the separate subtests with their appropriate match on the GATB were evenly spread between .37 on the Manual Dexterity test to .84 on the Verbal. Data are also presented showing moderate validity coefficients with the three subtests of the Iowa Tests of Educational Development.

The OASIS-2AS is highly recommended for the intended, rather modest and useful, purpose of vocational counseling. If used for no other purpose, the tests can prompt a beginning dialogue specifically focusing on the entire profile of five subtest scores. School-based users are encouraged to supplement these data with portfolio style information from the students' school history or teacher-made tests that would add to the content validity of the data set. Researchers, particularly those who are familiar with the GATB, will find this test familiar and should be encouraged to help increase the factorial validity of this promising instrument.

REVIEWER'S REFERENCE

Lord, F. M., & Novick, M. R. (1968). *Statistical theories on mental test scores*. Reading, MA: Addison-Wesley Publishing Co.

[61]

PACE.

Purpose: Developed to identify learning deficits for use in pre-school screening, educational placement, and remediation planning.
Population: Ages 4–6.
Publication Dates: 1986–88.
Scores, 6: Motor Coordination, Sensory Integration, Auditory Memory, Discrimination, Attending/Responding, Social Interaction.
Administration: Individual or group.
Comments: Ratings by parents and teachers.
Authors: Lisa K. Barclay and James R. Barclay.
Publisher: MetriTech, Inc.

a) PACE.
Price Data, 1991: $17 per 50 individual record forms; $180 per software program for scoring (IBM version only) including manual ('88, 50 pages).
Time: Administration time not reported.

a) FAST PACE.
Price Data: $12.95 per 10 group record forms.
Time: (10–15) minutes.
Cross References: See T4:1915 (1 reference).

Review of the PACE by SCOTT SPREAT, Administrator of Clinical Services, The Woods Schools, Langhorne, PA:

The PACE is a third party rating scale that is designed to identify learning skill deficits in young children. It is a 68-item instrument that yields six scale scores. The six scale scores are Motor Coordination, Sensory Integration, Auditory Memory, Discrimination, Attending/Responding, and Social Interaction. The 68 items are rated as Satisfactory, Deficient, or Needs Improvement. Although no direct statements are made about scalability, it would appear that items within each of the six scales are developmentally sequenced, such that the more complex items come toward the end of the scale. The

PACE also includes 10 items for parents, and a brief screening device called FAST PACE is also available.

Administration of the PACE is generally flexible. It can be administered to groups of students or to a single individual. It can be completed at a single session, or the evaluation may be spread over several days. No information is provided on the impact of these varying administration methods.

The PACE offers a computerized data analysis system. Performance scores are entered into the computer, and the system is able to generate both individual and group summary reports. The system is menu driven and easy to use. This same system will also generate prescriptive recommendations for the teacher.

NORMS. The norm group for the PACE consists of 1,285 children, ages 4 to 6. Data were collected from these individuals from 1976 to 1985. Approximately 80% of the norm group is 5 years old, a finding that tends to reflect the admissions policies of most kindergartens. An analysis of the male versus female performance on the PACE led the authors to conclude that a single norm group was satisfactory. Although male-female differences were evident on the PACE, the percentage of score variance attributable to sex was only about 3%. The authors seem justified in the election of a single norm group.

RELIABILITY. The test guide manual reports both test-retest and internal consistency reliability data. No interrater reliabilities were reported, although the administration process and the type of items would seem to invite interrater variation.

Test-retest data were collected on 31 children. The PACE was administered at the start and end of a school year, and the resultant scale scores were compared. A median Pearson product moment correlation of .73 indicated relatively impressive stability given the amount of time between ratings. Test-retest data collected over a shorter interval and without educational or developmental intervention would have been interesting. The calculation of a test-retest coefficient over a significantly shorter period of time would be likely to enhance the reported reliability.

Internal consistency estimates ranged from .47 to .99, with a median alpha coefficient of .78. The first three subscales (Motor Coordination, Sensory Integration, and Auditory Memory) seem particularly weak with respect to internal consistency, whereas the final three (Discrimination, Attending/Responding, and Social Interaction) are stronger. Psychometricians have debated about the criterion for acceptable internal consistency, with some suggesting that scales should have internal consistency in excess of .90 for use with individuals. Clearly, only two of the PACE subscales (Attending/Responding and Social Interaction) meet this lofty criterion. There are, however, mitigating factors that should be considered. The PACE was developed for and normed on a specific group. It is probably quite reasonable to expect this group to be relatively homogeneous with respect to performance on the PACE, and this homogeneity would be likely to force a limitation on the obtained internal consistency coefficient. Given the limited purpose of the PACE and with the provision that the PACE be part of a comprehensive assessment strategy, the obtained reliabilities seem acceptable. Nevertheless, one might suggest that an item analysis might improve the internal consistency of the first three subscales.

VALIDITY. The test manual offers some information on several types of validity. The most thorough work appears to have been done with respect to construct validity. Factor analytic work provided relatively sound support for four of the six subscales. The construction of the remaining subscales (Sensory Integration and Auditory Memory) did not receive appreciable support from the factor analytic research.

Some information is presented on predictive validity. The reported study suggests that the PACE was "highly effective in assessing students' readiness skills and in specifying effective intervention strategies to promote skill development" (p. 35). A second study suggested that the PACE identified training strategies that led to significant increases in performance on the PACE. Although both of these studies are relevant to the validation of the PACE, considerably more information about these studies would have been beneficial. With the information presented in the test manual, it is a bit difficult to evaluate the adequacy of the validational work.

A primary validity question would seem to be the relationship between PACE scores and achievement. The test manual describes a study in which PACE scores were found to be positively related to scores on the SRA achievement series test. These correlations ranged from .27 to .67. Although the sample size was under 70, these findings suggest that PACE ratings are related to achievement.

In addition to the full-length PACE, the test offers a brief screening scale called FAST PACE. FAST PACE consists of 18 of the PACE items. No information is provided on the rationale for selecting these 18 items. The correlations between PACE and FAST PACE scores are acceptable. It was also reported that FAST PACE tends to err in favor of false positives rather than false negatives. That is, FAST PACE would rather incorrectly suggest that

a child has a need than fail to identify a need. This claim was supported in a sample of 391 children. Cross-validational data are presented, but never explained.

The PACE offers prescriptive suggestions as well as evaluative data. A computer program will generate a report containing programming recommendations for students with identified needs. Although the computer-generated prescriptive report is certainly helpful and easy to use, the user is not privy to the decision rules that lead to the specific recommendations, nor is the theoretical model supporting the recommendations ever specified. This reviewer generated several individual prescriptive reports and noted that recommendations tended to incorporate sound teaching strategies such as shaping and task analysis. It was not possible to determine if there was any integration of strengths and needs in making recommendations, or whether each identified need resulted in an independent recommendation. Although there is some controversy over the use of computer-generated test reports, it seems the PACE system would be a useful adjunct to the teaching/assessment process.

The PACE is a brief rating scale that addresses a number of areas that are related to learning, and it seems appropriate for use with kindergarten children. The reliability is generally acceptable; however, improvements in two scales would be appreciated. Additional validational work would be beneficial. The computerized report generator will make this scale an asset for teachers and parents.

Review of the PACE by DONNA WITTMER, Assistant Professor of Education, University of Colorado, Denver, CO:

The PACE, a computer-based instrument for assessing and developing learning skills, covers 12 primary areas of skill development including motor coordination, eye-hand coordination, small muscle coordination, visual-perceptual, rhythm pattern recognition, listening, visual matching, tactile, motor behavior memory, verbal memory, attending/task-order, and social interaction skills. These 12 areas are then presented in terms of six broad scales: Motor Coordination, Sensory Integration, Auditory Memory, Discrimination, Attending/Responding, and Social Interaction. Thus, this assessment evaluates skills that have been found through research to be related to school success. This assessment also taps academic knowledge acquired, such as knowledge of names of colors and shapes, but this is a very small part of the total assessment. Because the assessment emphasizes skills such as matching, visual-perceptual, and motor behavior memory skills, the assessment is less culturally bound than other available measures.

The PACE is inclusive of the primary areas of skill development including social skills. It has a 10-item parent questionnaire. Although very brief, this at least involves parents in the assessment process. To its credit this assessment is not designed to be used to "screen" children out of kindergarten, but rather to determine the needs of the children, so that teachers and parents can plan a more appropriate program for the kindergarten children.

This assessment is recommended for teachers or trained aides to use in the classroom after the child has entered kindergarten. The assessment is easy to administer with few materials required. A short "screening" version, FAST PACE, is available. Many items on the PACE seem as if they would be fun for the child taking the test. Area 11 (attending/task order skills) and Area 12 (social interaction skills) are to be rated based upon generalized observations of the child's behavior over time. This ensures ecological validity concerning these important areas of development. A number of items can be administered to a group of children easing the administration time. However, if a child does not do well, the child should be assessed individually. Also, professionals should exercise care in the administration of this test by making sure that children are familiar with the person administering the test and that testing conditions are as comfortable and familiar as possible.

I would question the basic philosophy of the assessment which, as stated by the authors, is to "meet the need for early identification and remediation of learning skill deficits in kindergarten children." I have concerns with the computer-written report that specifies whether the child was superior, above average, average, below average, or deficient in the six broad skill areas. Is it fair to say that 4-year-olds have "deficits" if they cannot copy a diamond or letters? The computer then generates "strategies for intervention" that focus on the areas of "deficit," giving activities to "remediate" these areas. This general philosophy seems contrary to IDEA (Individuals With Disabilities Education Act) which promotes the assessment of children's strengths and needs as opposed to the identification of "deficits" only. Those professionals who use the computer program should be aware that the assessment is based on a "deficit" model.

The normed samples could have been obtained with greater sophistication. The PACE is advertised to be directed at preschool and kindergarten-age children thus including norms for 4-, 5-, and 6-year-old children. However, only 2–3% of the standardization sample were 4-year-olds, whereas approximately 17% of the total sample of 1,285 children were 6 years old at the time of testing. The remainder of the sample was composed of 5-year-olds. An equal representation of the three age groups seems warranted. The standardization sample taps the south central region of the United States. The authors state that a "number of states are included" (p. 29); however, they do not specify how many states nor how many children in the sample were from these states. Also, the authors state that the sampling includes a "number of children who might be designated as culturally somewhat disadvantaged" (p. 29). What is the definition of "culturally somewhat disadvantaged"? Head Start children seem to have been included in the sample. The ratio of children from each socioeconomic group is not specified. This information is critical to the test users for interpretation of the assessment results.

Validity and reliability issues are addressed. When area scores were analyzed, three main higher-order factors were identified. The first represents a broad dimension of motor-perceptual coordination. The second factor combines the attending/responding area and the social skill area. The third broad factor that emerges was called the auditory-verbal memory factor. Concurrent validity was studied by comparing SRA achievement series test scores for 39 boys and 29 girls to PACE scores for these children tested at the beginning of first grade. Correlations are reported to have ranged between .27 and .67 with a median value for the various scales. There were significant, high correlations between achievement in reading, language, and mathematics, and scores on the attending/responding and social skills scales. There are no predictive validity studies reported. Reliability studies were completed on a group of 31 Head Start children of kindergarten age at the beginning and end of a year. The median pre-post correlation across scales was .73. The median alpha coefficient for the six primary scales is .78 and the overall degree of internal consistency for the system is reported to be high.

In summary, this assessment is useful for determining strengths and needs of children who have entered kindergarten, so that teachers and parents can plan a more developmentally appropriate classroom and program for the child. However, professionals need to exercise caution when using the norms and when using the computer program printouts of intervention strategies that emphasize "deficits" of the child rather than building on strengths and interests that each child has.

[62]
Partner Relationship Inventory (Research Edition).

Purpose: "Designed to assess interactional, emotional, and sexual needs in a relationship and to point to areas of conflict."
Population: Married couples.
Publication Date: 1988.
Acronym: PRI.
Scores, 2: Interactional Needs, Emotional Needs.
Administration: Individual.
Forms, 3: Long Form, Form I (includes 2 alternate forms), Form II (includes 6 alternate forms).
Price Data, 1992: $18 per 25 Long Form test booklets; $15 per 25 self-scorable short form test booklets (select 1A or 1B); $14 per 25 scoring forms (select form); $22 per manual (30 pages); $23 per specimen set.
Time: (10–30) minutes.
Author: Carol Noll Hoskins.
Publisher: Consulting Psychologists Press, Inc.

Review of the Partner Relationship Inventory (Research Edition) by BRADLEY ELISON, Partial Hospitalization Program Team Leader, Virginia Treatment Center for Children, Virginia Commonwealth University, Richmond, VA:

The Partner Relationship Inventory (PRI) is a self-report measure designed to assess interactional and emotional needs in a relationship and to help couples identify areas in which their needs are perceived as being unmet. There are three forms of the PRI: the 80-item Long Form, Forms IA and IB (which are short forms derived from the original 80 items), and Form II (which includes items from the Long Form as well as new items designed to assess sexual needs in a relationship). In addition to the scores on the Interactional and Emotional Needs scales, the Long Form and Form I provide scores for eight categories of needs: agreement in thinking, communication, disagreement in behavior, perception of others feelings, companionship and sharing, emotional satisfaction, security, and recognition. Form II produces a combined Interactional/Emotional Needs score and a Sexual Needs score.

ADMINISTRATION, SCORING, AND INTERPRETATION. The 80 items of the PRI are presented in statement form and respondents are asked to rate each statement on a 4-point scale that includes *definitely feel, feel slightly, cannot decide*, and *definitely do not feel*. The asymmetry of the response options is not well justified in the manual and appears to bias responses in the positive direction. Scoring can be done using the available hand-scoring form, which is easy to understand and use.

The standardization of each form of the PRI is based on small convenience samples and the author appropriately cautions users that the norms are not representative of all couples and are only references for comparison. The author goes on to suggest that users establish local norms and/or interpret results by looking at item-by-item comparisons. No guidelines for the interpretation of individual item differences are provided. The only interpretive information derived from scores on the PRI is an assessment of the need for counseling. Cutoff scores indicating the need for counseling are set at the 70th percentile for the Interactional Needs scale and at the 60th percentile for the Emotional Needs scale. No rationale for these cutoff scores is provided and their derivation from nonrepresentative samples requires they be used with extreme caution.

THEORETICAL BACKGROUND AND DEVELOPMENT. The PRI grew out of a study by Matthews and Mihanovich (1963) that explored the frequency of specific problems in happily and unhappily married couples. Fifty items for the PRI were obtained from the Matthews and Mihanovich study and were classified into the eight categories mentioned above plus Perception of Behavior. Additional items were added to expand the number of items per category to 10. No rationale for the development or selection of items is provided and the process for assigning items to categories is not described. Independent corroboration of item selection and category assignment is not provided. Field testing and factor analysis resulted in one category being dropped as a result of its loading in the factor analysis. No item analysis is reported and apparently no items were dropped or altered as a result of the field test. Form I was derived directly from the Long Form by ranking items according to their mean scores and dividing them into two roughly equal parts. Correlations between Form IA and IB are reported to be .94 for the Interaction Scale and .93 for the Emotional Needs scale.

Form II represents an attempt to incorporate a Sexual Needs scale in the PRI and to develop multiple forms of the inventory. For Form II a total of 31 sexual needs items were added to the 80 items of the Long Form and the resulting 111 items were administered to a sample of 212 subjects. Analysis of the responses was used to develop six alternate forms of Form II. The specifics of the tryout are not provided in the manual although it indicates that many revisions were necessary.

RELIABILITY AND VALIDITY. Reliability and validity data for the PRI are minimal. Much of the data that are available are suspect as they are derived from the same small samples used to field test and norm the instrument. Reliability coefficients for the PRI based on a test-retest comparison are reported to range from .26 to .95. The manual author does not provide a complete listing of the reliability data nor are the scales with the .26 and .95 reliability coefficients identified. Correlations between partner scores are reported for both the morning and evening administrations of the PRI and range from .49 to .58. Split-half reliability coefficients were determined for Forms IA and IB using the Spearman-Brown formula and range from .75 to .92. Although additional reliability data are needed and some of the reliability coefficients are low, the PRI appears to be a reliable instrument.

This reviewer found the statements making up the PRI to be good representations of the constructs they were designed to assess. The only independent validation of the PRI is a study correlating the PRI scales with the Locke Wallace Marital Adjustment Scale. This study produced correlations ranging from -.40 to -.75. The correlations were in the expected direction and are high enough to lend support for the validity of the instrument. An initial factor analysis of the PRI leads credibility to the assignment of the categories to two larger needs scales.

SUMMARY. The PRI seems to have potential as a useful tool in both clinical and research applications. In order for this potential to be realized a substantial amount of research and clarification is needed. The push to develop alternate forms appears to have overshadowed the need for well-planned and executed validation studies. Normative data relevant to a broader range of couple populations are needed and should include different ethnic groups, groups from different socioeconomic classes, and groups of non-married couples. The 4-point response format either should be revised to provide for a full range of negative and positive responses or justified in more detail. Rationale and evidence are also needed to support the cutoff scores used in interpretation of the PRI. Last but not least, the manual must be organized in a manner that helps the user differentiate data relevant to specific forms of the inventory.

REVIEWER'S REFERENCE

Mathews, V. D., & Mihanovich, C. S. (1963). New orientations on marital maladjustment. *Marriage and Family Living, 25,* 300-304.

Review of the Partner Relationship Inventory (Research Edition) by STEPHEN OLEJNIK, Professor

of Educational Psychology, University of Georgia, Athens, GA:

The Partner Relationship Inventory (PRI) is based on research findings first reported in the 1960s, which indicated that perceived unmet interactional and emotional needs are primary sources of conflict among couples. Multiple forms of the inventory are available and they are not gender dependent. A Long Form consists of 80 items with the Interactional Needs scale consisting of five categories (Agreement in Thinking, Communication, Disagreement in Behavior, Perception of the Other's Feelings, and Companionship and Sharing). The Emotional Needs scale consists of three categories (Emotional Satisfaction, Security, and Recognition). Each category contains 10 declarative statements soliciting the perceptions of the respondent's partner. Responses are made on a 4-point scale from *Definitely feel* to *Definitely do not feel.* Items are presented in a random order and to avoid response sets approximately half of the items are phrased in reverse form.

Form I consists of two alternate forms (IA and IB) each having 40 items selected from the Long Form. Finally, Form II was developed to facilitate the repeated measurement of respondents and consists of six alternative forms. Each form contains 33 items and a Sexual Needs scale is provided in addition to the Interactional and Emotional Needs scales.

Scoring of the inventory is easy and can be completed quickly by hand. One disadvantage of the scoring procedure, however, is that responses to the inventory must be transferred twice. First, responses on the inventory itself must be transferred to a scoring form that assigns item point values. The item point values are then recorded on a special grid that groups the items into categories to facilitate summing and the computation of category and total needs scores. Because this is done by hand, chances of recording errors are possible.

Interpretation of the Total Interactional Needs and Emotional Needs to the Long Form is based on the responses from 104 individuals (52 couples). First, second (median), and third quartiles are reported and the author suggests that individuals with scores above the 70th percentile for the Interactional Needs scale and above the 60th percentile for the Emotional Needs scale be considered as candidates for counseling. No rationale is provided for these guidelines nor is an explanation offered for the difference in criteria between scales. Characteristics of the distribution of the couples' discrepancy scores are not reported. Very little information is provided regarding demographics of the participating normative group.

Quartiles are also reported for the 52 couples on Form IA and IB. Interpretation of scores obtained on Form I is not offered. Means and standard deviations on the two Needs scales and the division points for the lower, middle, and upper thirds of each category are reported from a second study based on 336 respondents using Form I. The author suggests the division points be used to identify low, medium, and high conflict levels.

Form II is still under development and no guidance is provided regarding the interpretation of the Sexual Needs scale nor any of the six alternative forms.

Content validity is based on the opinions of two judges. No information is provided on the qualifications of these individuals other than their professional affiliation (educational psychology and marriage counseling). In terms of construct validity, appropriate negative correlations between each of the category scores and a marital adjustment scale are reported. Correlations with the Interactional and Emotional Needs scales, however, are not reported. Two other correlational studies are cited as providing evidence of convergent and divergent validity but no details are provided. Finally, the authors report the intercorrelation matrices for Form IA and Form IB and the results of a factor analysis based on category scores. Factor loadings support the two-factor model and the grouping of the categories. No details are given regarding the complete factor solution and it is not clear whether the solution is based on the Long Form, Form IA, or Form IB. Justification of the grouping of items into the eight categories is not provided. The author does not provide any evidence indicating that individuals having high scores on either of the Needs scales or any of the category scores are experiencing high conflict. $ Reliability for the Long Form is based on the correlations between morning and evening administrations of each category. Individual correlations are not reported but are said to range between .26 and .95. Consistency for the Total Needs scale is not reported. Correlations between partners on the Interactional and Emotional Needs scales are reported for each of the two administrations and range between .49 and .58. The author does not report a measure for internal consistency for the Long Form.

Form IA and Form IB were developed by splitting the Long Form in half. Alternate forms reliability for each category was obtained by correlating the two halves from each administration of the inventory (morning and evening). For morning administration reliability estimates range between .55 and .90 and evening administration reliability estimates range between .68 and .88. The author also reports Spearman-Brown reliability for each administration of each category. Using the Spearman-Brown formula, I could not reproduce the reported values using the alternate forms correlations reported. The usefulness of these values is limited because they predict the reliability of the category scores if the number of items in a category is increased or decreased. A much better estimate of internal consistency could have been provided through coefficient alpha.

The research edition of the Partner Relationship Inventory will require considerably more research before its use can be justified in either a clinical or research setting. Scores on this instrument are virtually meaningless. A much larger and more representative sample of couples is needed. In addition, more evidence is needed to support the belief that high scores on this instrument truly do reflect conflict in a relationship. At best, responses to this inventory might be used by counselors to begin a discussion in a clinical setting. The author does caution users that this is a research edition and not to over interpret the responses. However, the Long Form and Form I have been available for some time and it appears that little new evidence has been gathered to support the validity and reliability of the instrument. Guidance for the interpretation of the responses focuses on the two Needs scales but the reliability and validity estimates provided apply to the category scores. Additional reliability and validity studies are needed for the Needs scales. Alternatively, guidance for the interpretation of the category scores are needed. Finally, the research studies supporting the theory on which the instrument is based were conducted more than 20 years ago. Because society has changed considerably since that time, more recent research is needed to provide current support for the theory.

[63]
Personal Experience Screening Questionnaire.
Purpose: "Designed as a brief screening tool to aid . . . in the identification of teenagers likely to need a drug abuse assessment referral."
Population: Adolescents.
Publication Date: 1991.
Acronym: PESQ.
Scores, 3: Infrequency, Defensiveness, Problem Severity.
Administration: Group.
Price Data, 1993: $70 per complete kit including 25 test forms and manual (30 pages); $29.50 per 25 test forms; $42.50 per manual.
Time: (10) minutes.

Author: Ken C. Winters.
Publisher: Western Psychological Services.

Review of the Personal Experience Screening Questionnaire by STUART N. HART, Associate Professor of Counseling and Educational Psychology, Indiana University-Purdue University at Indianapolis, Indianapolis, IN:

The primary general purpose set for the Personal Experience Screening Questionnaire (PESQ) was "to provide clinicians with a standardized self-report screening tool to assist in the identification of teenagers needing a drug abuse assessment referral" (p. 1). The author intended more specifically to provide a quick screening, standardized, adolescent-specific instrument, sensitive to alcohol and other drug abuse and to response distortion tendencies. To accomplish this the author produced the 40-item PESQ intended for youth 12 to 18 years of age and consisting of three subsections dealing with drug involvement problem severity, psychosocial problems, and personal drug history; and including items to assess faking bad and faking good response tendencies.

The manual for the PESQ is well developed and presents information in a clear and logical manner, which displays the respect of the author for the criteria of the *Standards for Educational and Psychological Testing* (AERA, APA, & NCME, 1985). The PESQ can be easily administered by a properly prepared and supervised technician or clerk and interpretations should be made or closely supervised by an appropriately trained professional. No time limit for completion of the PESQ is set but it is usually completed in approximately 10 minutes. Individual administration is preferred but group administration is indicated to be acceptable and was incorporated in addition to individual administration in the development of normative data. Required test materials include a two-sided PESQ "Auto-Score" form and a pencil. Examinees place their responses on the questionnaire/answer sheet, and the responses transfer to the scoring section on the examinee-inaccessible inside of the form. The instructions and items of the PESQ are at approximately the 4th grade reading level. By having an examinee read the instructions aloud the examiner can determine whether it will be necessary to read the items to the examinee.

The PESQ scores are organized to provide results for three scales labeled Problem Severity, Defensiveness, and Infrequency; and to provide information on two content areas labeled Psychosocial Indicators and Drug Use History. Part I of the PESQ contains 18 items that accumulate to give a global measure of Problem Severity indicating the extent to which the individual is psychologically and behaviorally involved with drugs. The items fall within subcategories exploring frequency of use of drugs under various conditions and behaviors associated with drug use and procurement. Part I also includes the three items of the Infrequency scale, to measure faking bad and dealing with extremely unlikely drug use behavior. All items of Part I are responded to on a 4-point scale (i.e., *never, once or twice, sometimes, often*). Part II of the instrument contains eight items that accumulate to provide information for the content area of Psychosocial Indicators covering "emotional distress, problems with thinking, and physical and sexual abuse" associated with adolescent drug use. Part II also includes the five items of the Defensiveness scale to measure faking-good response tendencies. All items of Part II require yes or no responses. Part III requests information about the respondent's Drug Use History by asking the frequency of use of various drugs during the last 12 months and provides seven response options ranging from never to over 40 times for alcoholic beverages and marijuana or hashish and once or more for a list of hard drugs; and additionally two questions are asked about the time when the person first got high or first used drugs regularly.

Scoring the PESQ is relatively easy, requiring only that simple instructions inside the response form be followed to accumulate totals for the three scales and two content areas. To guide interpretations cutoff scores and ranges are provided for the Problem Severity scale by age and sex subgroupings. Scores above specified points are labeled "red flag" to indicate the examinee may be in need of a referral and that a "more complete and reliable drug abuse assessment" (p. 10) is advised, or "green flag" to indicate a referral is probably not needed. The results for the Infrequency and Defensiveness scales are to be used to modify considerations of profile results, particularly for the Problem Severity scale. Scores above the red flag cutoffs for the faking-bad and faking-good scales suggest that the validity for the rest of the profile is in question and that caution is needed in interpreting results, whereas scores in the green flag range indicate "the profile is probably valid" (p. 10). Information contained in answers to specific questions on the three scales and from the two content areas provides the interpreter with opportunities to derive additional meaning. The author urges the interpreter be knowledgeable regarding drug abuse and interpretation of these tests in order to maximize the validity of the test.

The PESQ was developed through the Chemical Dependency Adolescent Assessment Project

(CHDAAP), which was established in 1982 to develop "assessment tools to aid clinicians in the identification, referral, and treatment of teenagers suspected of drug abuse" (p. 11). The Problem Severity scale of the PESQ was developed by selecting unused items from the pool of items previously used to construct the Personal Involvement With Chemicals scale of the Personal Experience Inventory (PEI), a well-respected CHDAAP instrument meant for the clinical evaluation of drug abuse and treatment needs (see reviews of the PEI in *The Eleventh Mental Measurements Yearbook*; 11:284). These items were part of the set that had a high loading for a general drug abuse severity factor. The specific items selected for the Problem Severity scale of the PESQ met requirements of having Pearson product-moment correlations greater than .50 with the PEI Personal Involvement With Chemicals scale, and less than -.40 with the Marlowe-Crowne Social Desirability scale. The PESQ five faking-good Defensiveness scale items were derived from the Marlowe-Crowne Desirability Scale, whereas the three faking-bad, inattentive, or random responding Infrequency scale items and the content area items were derived from logical analyses of the PEI's psychosocial section and adapted from national survey instruments.

Reliability of the PESQ has been addressed only through internal consistency estimates for the Problem Severity scale thus far. The population sample employed for this purpose included 2,744 subjects from schools ($n = 1,885$), juvenile detention centers ($n = 611$), and drug clinics ($n = 248$). School and juvenile center populations completed questionnaires similar to the PESQ which included the 18 Problem Severity items whereas the drug clinic sample completed 203 items of the original PEI pool. Quite good alpha coefficients ranging from .90–.95 were produced across samples. Internal consistency measures were essentially the same regardless of the nature and length of the larger item pool within which the PESQ items were placed; and across male and female, white and nonwhite subjects. Test-retest reliability, stability over time, clearly needs to be addressed in future research. Although it would be expected to be adequate on the basis of the very good to good test-retest results that have been found for the similar longer scale on the PEI, this is not sufficient evidence.

The content validity of the Problem Severity scale of the PESQ is clearly tied to the content validity of the PEI, which has been judged to be "quite adequate" (Toneatto, 1992). PESQ items were selected from the item pool used to construct the PEI. A "broad spectrum approach" (p. 17) to adolescent use problem severity guided the development of this pool, which included 10 scales produced by "statistical and rational approaches" (p. 17) derived from 24 content categories identified as relevant. A Pearson product-moment correlation of .94 was found for the relationship between the PESQ Problem Severity scale and PEI personal involvement with chemicals section of its problem severity scales. The items of the Defensiveness scale (adapted from the Marlowe-Crowne Social Desirability Scale) and of the Infrequency scale resulted from a review of empirical knowledge and from consultant advice. They appear to have adequate content validity but, as with all the items of the PESQ, the user must determine their relevance for the population and setting to which they will be applied.

The construct validity of the PESQ is also closely tied to the construct validity of the PEI Personal Involvement with Chemicals scale which has been found to best tap the core of its chemical severity section (Tucker, 1992). This fact, added to knowledge of the fairly high and significant correlations between the PEI and related measures (Toneatto, 1992), the high internal consistency found for the PESQ, and the ability of the PESQ to discriminate between those at various levels of drug abuse (see later section), indicates its construct validity is satisfactory.

Criterion validity, of greatest significance in determining the usefulness of a screening device, appears to be strong for the PESQ. The PESQ has been assessed for its criterion validity relative to distinguishing between treatment populations, current diagnoses, and counselor referrals. Individuals with drug treatment histories and with a clinical diagnosis of dependence were found to have significantly higher PESQ Problem Severity scale scores than those with no prior treatment histories and those with abuse but not dependence problems. Problem Severity scale scores for a drug clinic population were found to be significantly higher than those of juvenile offenders, which were in turn found to be significantly higher than those of a normal school population. Individuals from a school clinic sample referred by counselors for further drug abuse evaluations had significantly higher Problem Severity scale scores than those not referred for this purpose. A post hoc analysis of the relationships between the two response bias scales and the Problem Severity items produced correlations similar to those found for the response bias scales and the PEI Personal Involvement With Chemicals scale items.

The "red flag" criterion is inherently a criterion validity issue. It was developed through discriminant analysis applied to the first half of the school clinic sample in a cross validation procedure. The cut-point on the Problem Severity scale of 40T, one standard deviation below the drug clinic sample, was identified as optimal and found to correctly classify 88% of the initial school clinic sample (sensitivity .91, specificity .84) and 87% of the second half of the school clinic sample (sensitivity .88, specificity .85). This cut-point falls 1½ standard deviations above the mean of the school sample and appears to be appropriate for differentiating those who do and do not need a more comprehensive drug abuse evaluation.

The PESQ, in particular its Problem Severity scale, appears to be a well-developed screening device, which should be quite useful for its intended purposes. Its psychometric properties are strong with the exception of the need to establish temporal stability and to clarify the validity and reliability of the area scores. The "red flag" cut-point provides a good guide to decisions about 12–18-year-old individuals who do and do not require more comprehensive evaluations. The practical and research application potentials of the instrument are promising.

REVIEWER'S REFERENCES

American Educational Research Association, American Psychological Association, & National Council on Measurement in Education. (1985). *Standards for educational and psychological testing.* Washington, DC: American Psychological Association.
Toneatto, T. (1992). [Review of the Personal Experience Inventory]. In J. J. Kramer & J. C. Conoley (Eds.), *The eleventh mental measurements yearbook* (pp. 660-661). Lincoln, NE; Buros Institute of Mental Measurements.
Tucker, J. A. (1992). [Review of the Personal Experience Inventory]. In J. J. Kramer & J. C. Conoley (Eds.), *The eleventh mental measurements yearbook* (pp. 661-663). Lincoln, NE; Buros Institute of Mental Measurements.

Review of the Personal Experience Screening Questionnaire by RICHARD W. JOHNSON, Adjunct Professor of Counseling Psychology and Associate Director of Counseling & Consultation Center, University of Wisconsin-Madison, Madison, WI:

The Personal Experience Screening Questionnaire (PESQ) serves as one of three instruments in a comprehensive assessment package created for adolescents suspected of drug abuse. The PESQ, a brief self-report inventory that can be completed in 10 minutes or less, should be administered first as a screening device to determine if a more thorough assessment needs to be undertaken. The other two instruments, the Personal Experience Inventory (PEI; T4:1971 and the Adolescent Diagnostic Interview (ADI; T4:97), are employed if scores on the PESQ suggest that alcohol or other drug abuse may be an issue.

The PESQ provides a broad range of information concerning the nature and the extent of drug use and related matters. It contains 40 items divided into five parts as follows: (*a*) a Problem Severity scale of 18 items with 4-point response options (*never, once or twice, sometimes, often*); (*b*) a Defensiveness scale of 5 items that measures "faking good"; (*c*) an Infrequency scale of 3 items that measures "faking bad" or careless or random responding; (*d*) 8 individual items that assess psychosocial concerns (emotional distress, problems with thinking, and physical and sexual abuse); and (*e*) 6 items that provide a history of drug usage.

In contrast with most drug assessment measures, the PESQ was constructed especially for adolescents. A number of the questions refer specifically to situations that involve teenagers (e.g., skipping school, making excuses to teachers or parents) but not other age groups. It differs from similar instruments by including validity scales to detect either denial or exaggeration of problems, both frequent concerns when assessing drug use by adolescents in institutional settings.

The instrument can be easily hand-scored by opening a seal on the test booklet that separates the answer sheet from a scoring guide inside the test booklet. In the course of using the PESQ with a client, we noted that one of the items on the Defensiveness scale (Item 29) was keyed in the wrong direction on the score sheet. Test users should check this item (one of only five items on the Defensiveness scale) to make sure that it is keyed correctly in their test booklet.

The PESQ has been normed on adolescents 12 to 18 years old in three settings: drug clinic assessment programs, juvenile detention centers, and public schools. The normative samples have been used to set cutoff scores ("red flags") for referral purposes. The cutoff scores vary somewhat depending on the age and sex of the respondents. However, very little information regarding the actual distribution of scores among the samples has been provided in the test manual. It would be helpful to know the means and standard deviations for all scales and the results of item analyses for the different norm groups. Additional normative data for minority groups are also needed.

The Problem Severity scale of the PESQ possesses high interitem consistency (alpha coefficients = .90 to .95) across different settings and types of clients. No attempt has been made to determine the interitem consistency of the Defensiveness or Infrequency scales because of their brevity. Information regarding the test-retest reliabilities for each scale also should be reported.

The PESQ derives much of its validity from studies conducted on the PEI. Factor analytic studies with the PEI revealed one large general factor that accounted for much of the variance in surveys of drug use among adolescents. This factor, severity of drug use, is measured by the Problem Severity scale of the PESQ. Scores on the Problem Severity scale correlate highly with the scale (Personal Involvement with Chemicals scale) on the PEI that measures this factor.

The most crucial question concerning the validity of the PESQ pertains to its effectiveness in detecting those adolescents in need of a comprehensive drug assessment program. Ideally, the instrument should identify those young people at risk for substance abuse at the same time that it rules out the dangers of addiction for others not at risk. In a cross-validation study reported in the test manual, the author successfully used the PESQ to select 88% of those students who needed additional drug assessment based on a variety of criteria (official records, collateral reports, and interview data) while eliminating 85% of those students who did not need such assessment. In other words, it proved to be both highly sensitive (few false negatives) and highly selective (few false positives). These results should be substantiated by research in other settings.

In conclusion, the PESQ presents a number of advantages as an assessment tool. It has been integrated with other drug assessment procedures as part of an ongoing research and treatment program. It is more comprehensive and less easily faked than other inventories designed specifically for adolescents such as the Adolescent Drinking Index (ADI; T4:98) or the Adolescent Alcohol Involvement Scale (AAIS; Mayer & Filstead, 1979). It can be conveniently administered, scored, and interpreted. Although the PESQ can benefit from further study as described above, research conducted thus far indicates that it is highly reliable and valid for the purpose for which it was designed. I recommend it as a screening instrument for assessing drug use among adolescents.

REVIEWER'S REFERENCE

Mayer, J., & Filstead, W. J. (1979). The adolescent alcohol involvement scale: An instrument for measuring adolescents' use and misuse of alcohol. *Journal of Studies on Alcohol, 40*, 291-300.

[64]

Philadelphia Head Injury Questionnaire.

Purpose: Developed for use in gathering the history of individuals with head injuries.
Population: Head trauma patients.
Publication Date: 1991.
Acronym: PHIQ.

Scores: No scores.
Administration: Individual.
Price Data, 1993: $22.50 per complete kit including 100 questionnaires and manual (2 pages).
Time: [20] minutes.
Authors: Lucille M. Curry, Richard G. Ivins, and Thomas L. Gowen.
Publisher: Western Psychological Services.

Review of the Philadelphia Head Injury Questionnaire by MARK ALBANESE, Adjunct Associate Professor of Biostatistics and Educational Statistics and Director, Office of Consultation and Research in Medical Education, The University of Iowa College of Medicine, Iowa City, IA:

The Philadelphia Head Injury Questionnaire (PHIQ) is a brief questionnaire designed to screen patients who have had a head injury for further investigation and making appropriate referrals. The instrument is based upon the developer's "extensive clinical experience in assessing victims of head trauma," (administration and use document, p. 1) and is composed of two pages of straightforward questions about the symptoms and complaints many people have following head injury. The authors recommend that users of the PHIQ have some background knowledge of head injury assessment and indicate that this knowledge is a valuable asset in interpreting the results of the instrument.

The form itself is divided into six sections: Identifying Information, Accident Information, Persistent Symptoms, Cognitive Aspects of Head Injury, Personality Changes, Pertinent Personal/Medical History, and Comments and/or Additional Information. The two-page document on Administration and Use gives the rationale for each of the six sections; however, there are no citations of literature. Individual items use simple language and are mostly in a yes/no format. The questionnaire may be self-administered, completed by a family member/significant other, or administered by an interviewer. The authors indicate that administration by a skilled interviewer generally elicits the most comprehensive and reliable data. The authors further suggest the reliability of the information obtained can also be significantly increased by asking a spouse or close relative to complete the PHIQ with respect to the injured person. The authors state that some patients may respond in a biased manner and that recognition of response biases depends upon clinical judgment and increases with time. Further, the nature of response biases may give important information to the examiner.

177

The instrument is simply an information collection form and there is no scoring mechanism. Interpretation relies strictly on clinical judgment. Consequently, there is no information on validity and reliability; however, the Administration and Use document alludes to administrative methods for increasing the reliability of the data.

The strengths of the PHIQ are its brevity and simplicity. The language used on the form is very straightforward and information collected seems to be appropriate to the intent to serve as a screening instrument.

The weaknesses of the PHIQ are primarily related to validity issues. There is no literature cited to support the validity of the instrument. Further, there are no data provided to support the use of the instrument for any of the applications for which it is recommended. The Administration and Use document indicates the credibility of the PHIQ relies exclusively on the extensive clinical experience of the authors. Curiously, the document provides no information on the authors' affiliation nor level of clinical experience. The only information provided about the authors is their academic degrees, Ph.D. and J.D.

The validity issue is important for two reasons. First, a screening instrument that omits important information or collects data in ways likely to miss information critical to appropriate referral can be very damaging. Patients may be inappropriately comforted that symptoms are not serious or, conversely, needlessly made to be concerned about a nonexistent or overstated problem. The former problem will result in patients failing to receive medical care they need; the latter will lead to unnecessary costs being incurred for followup.

The second validity issue has to do with use of the instrument in medical-legal settings as is recommended by the Administration and Use document. The potential for abuse of such an instrument in the high-stakes world of injury litigation is troubling. Even describing the instrument as simply a screening questionnaire does not disguise the potential for it to be entered as evidence in court. The fact that one of the authors possesses a law degree heightens this possibility. Under these circumstances it is incumbent on the authors to document the appropriateness of the instrument to its recommended use. This clearly has not been done for the PHIQ.

In summary, the PHIQ is a brief and simple questionnaire designed as a screening tool for assessing whether individuals who have received a head injury need further evaluation. No data are provided from the literature or from the authors regarding the instrument's validity or reliability. As a result, it is up to the user to determine whether the PHIQ serves a specific need.

Review of the Philadelphia Head Injury Questionnaire by WILLIAM W. DEARDORFF, Clinical Director, Spine Pain Program, West Coast Spine Institute, Los Angeles, CA:

The Philadelphia Head Injury Questionnaire (PHIQ) was developed to "aid in documenting areas for further investigation and making appropriate referrals" (administration and use document, pg. 1) vis-a-vis clinical findings secondary to head trauma. It is a structured information and history gathering instrument designed to make a preliminary assessment of head injury. Areas of inquiry include identifying information, accident information, persistent symptoms, cognitive aspects of head injury, personality changes, and pertinent personal/medical history. Most questions are presented in a "yes-no" format. The PHIQ can be self-administered, completed by a family member, or in an interview format. The measure is not a neuropsychological instrument as the patient's performance is not directly assessed and there are no norms for comparing response.

The content of the PHIQ "is based upon the authors' extensive clinical experience in assessing victims of head trauma" (administration and use document, p. 1). The test manual is two pages in length and offers no information regarding test development and little information about test interpretation. It asserts that the PHIQ was developed for use by a wide variety of professionals who assess and treat head injuries, including neuropsychologists, neurologists, and attorneys. The manual authors state that users of the PHIQ should have some background knowledge of head injury assessment and that expertise in the use of the PHIQ and reliability will increase with practice. The authors warn that biased responding can occur (over- or underreporting of symptoms) and that recognition of this phenomenon increases with clinical experience.

No information or standardization data on any type of reliability or validity are presented. One must, therefore, assume that such studies have not been done. In addition, no data are presented which support the utility of the PHIQ in assessing symptoms of head injury. There is no indication the questionnaire can help differentiate between clinically significant and nonsignificant neurological dysfunction. Further, no information is available about false negative rates. This is a crucial issue in this patient population.

Until reliability, validity, specificity, and sensitivity studies of the PHIQ are completed, use of this questionnaire cannot be recommended as an aid to assessing head injury symptoms or making referrals.

[65]

Portuguese Speaking Test.

Purpose: "To evaluate the level of oral proficiency in Portuguese attained by American and other English-speaking learners of Portuguese."

Population: College students and adults.

Publication Date: 1988.

Acronym: PST.

Scores: Total score only.

Administration: Individual.

Forms: 3 parallel forms (A, B, C).

Restricted Distribution: Restricted to qualified test supervisors.

Price Data, 1989: $60 per examinee, including use of test booklet, master tape(s), blank cassette for examinee responses, examinee handbook, test manual (28 pages), and score report by publisher (all materials must be returned to publisher after testing).

Foreign Language Edition: Master tape available in 2 versions: Brazilian Portuguese, Lusitanian Portuguese.

Time: (40–50) minutes.

Comments: Examinee's oral responses are recorded on tape and sent to publisher for scoring; test administered by tape recording in language laboratory setting or individually by using 2 tape recorders.

Authors: Charles W. Stansfield and Dorry Kenyon.

Publisher: Center for Applied Linguistics.

Review of the Portuguese Speaking Test by ANDREW D. COHEN, Professor of English as a Second Language and Applied Linguistics, University of Minnesota, Minneapolis, MN:

There has been a recent move to design semidirect tests to facilitate assessment of oral proficiency in cases where there are few trained interviewers to conduct oral interviews. Although the earliest semidirect oral proficiency test, that of English as a foreign language, appeared a decade ago (see Stansfield, Kenyon, Paiva, Doyle, Ulsh, & Cowles, 1990), the Center for Applied Linguistics has just recently begun developing a series of semidirect oral language tests, all using the ACTFL (American Council on the Teaching of Foreign Languages) guidelines and employing visual as well as aural stimuli.

The Portuguese Speaking Test (PST) consists of six sections:

1. *Personal Conversation*, in which the respondent hears 10 questions about family, education, hobbies, etc., in Portuguese, and is to respond to each in order.

2. *Giving Directions*, in which the respondent is shown a map in the test booklet and is instructed to give directions between two points. In this and in all subsequent sections, all instructions are provided in English.

3. *Detailed Description*, in which the respondent is shown a drawing representing a variety of objects and actions, and is instructed to describe the picture in detail.

4. *Picture Sequence*, in which the respondent is instructed to speak in a narrative fashion about two sets of four or five pictures in sequence, each time being called upon to use different tenses in the narration.

5. *Topical Discourse*, in which the respondent is instructed to talk about five topics, each involving specialized content. The topics are read aloud on the tape and are also written in English in the text booklet.

6. *Situations*, in which the respondent hears and reads, in English, five printed descriptions of situations in which a specified audience and communicative task are identified. The task tests the ability to handle interactive situations through simulated role-play—involving the use of appropriate speech acts such as requesting, complaining, apologizing, and giving a formal toast.

Recently, the authors of the test have also developed a complete set of rater training materials. These include a rater training tape that contains examples of at least three examinee responses representing different levels of proficiency, and a rater training manual that describes the typical rhetorical characteristics of performance at different proficiency levels, as well as procedures for deriving the global rating. The ratings the examinee receives are recorded on a scoring sheet, and are then analyzed using the rules in the rater training manual to determine the global rating. These materials may be used independently by ACTFL trained raters. Individuals without prior experience applying the ACTFL Proficiency Guidelines may attend a 2-day workshop to learn to score the test. Raters are also given the manual and the training tape, so that they may retrain themselves prior to actually scoring the test at a later date.

The authors of the test manual conducted a validation study of the PST, and report high interrater reliability (.93 and higher) and high parallel-form reliability (again .93 and higher). Furthermore, when results on the PST were correlated with ratings of performance on a live interview (the Oral Proficiency Interview), the resulting correlations apparently ranged between .90 and .96, depending on the test form and the rater.

In a survey of 30 respondents, a majority (86%) preferred a live interview over the semidirect test.

The authors of the test attribute this rating to the respondents' unfamiliarity with a semidirect test— the perceived unnaturalness of speaking to a machine. However, the high correlations between performance on the live interview and the semidirect test encouraged the test's authors to promote the PST as an important second choice in situations where direct testing is impractical or impossible. One argument raised in favor of a semidirect test is that it eliminates the interviewer effect, for example, variations in the degree of nervousness on the part of the respondent or different interpersonal relations between the respondent and the interviewer (Stansfield et al., 1990).

The first section, Personal Conversation, is intended to help the respondents begin thinking in the target language while being asked questions about their personal life that might come up in a normal conversation. Some of the questions would not, however, come up in a conversation. Instead, they seem to be the traditional types of questions containing linguistic curiosities in their structure in order to test certain verb tenses (e.g., conditionals).

In the second section, Giving Directions, the map in one of the three forms does not have the usual array of streets at right angles to each other. Hence, problems in preparing directions may be based in part on conceptual difficulties in relating to the map rather than on language deficiency.

The third section, Detailed Description, is not communicative in the modern sense of the term. The task seems to test extensively for specialized vocabulary. As with the preceding section, the fourth section, Picture Sequence, also tests for specialized vocabulary with somewhat more emphasis on verb tense.

In the fifth section, Topical Discourse, each of the five topic areas seems to call for more preparation time than the 15 seconds allowed in order to make a truly cohesive and coherent response. Part of the difficulty is due to the fact that the prompt is in English whereas the response is to be in Portuguese. In a truly communicative context, a native would, in fact, give clues to vocabulary in the very asking of the question.

The sixth section, Situations, calls upon the respondent to be creative in the use of linguistically and socially appropriate responses. Bilingual instructions would have been invaluable as several of the situations evolve around some defective item for which a complaint is being lodged and the item reflects low-frequency vocabulary (e.g., "bedroom slippers").

In summary, the aim of the semidirect test is to shorten test time while obtaining a broader sampling of the speaker's interlanguage than an oral interview

would generally do—in a reliable, valid, and efficient manner. The PST would appear to be doing this well. Nevertheless, paying closer attention to item design in future revisions of this test would be advisable—issues such as authenticity in conversational questions, adequacy of time to prepare a response, problems of cognitive ability in map reading, the language of instructions, and the human interest value of the situations.

Whereas performance on the Hebrew version of the semidirect test and the Oral Interview have correlated highly (Shohamy & Stansfield, 1990), the semidirect test was found to have more features of a literary genre and the Oral Interview more features of an oral text (Shohamy, 1991). For example, there was more paraphrasing and self-correction on the semidirect test than on the Oral Interview, and more switches to native language on the Oral Interview.

In addition, the holistic scoring of the semidirect test is problematic. Whereas this instrument provides an array of speaking samples, it uses a single rating instead of multiple ratings of content vocabulary, function, and contextualized use of structure. The same criticism leveled against the Oral Proficiency Interview—that the single scale is too limiting (Bachman, 1988; Lantolf & Frawley, 1988)—can be leveled against the scales used in the semidirect test. The single rating scale lumps together different behaviors in a presumed unidimensional scale of speaking that often does not reflect reality. Hence, the test constructors deserve praise for producing this test, but attention needs to be paid to potential limitations both in this test and in others like it as the semidirect testing effort progresses.

REVIEWER'S REFERENCES

Bachman, L. F. (1988). Problems in examining the validity of the ACTFL Oral Proficiency Interview. *Studies in Second Language Acquisition, 10*(2), 149-164.

Lantolf, J. P., & Frawley, W. (1988). Proficiency: Understanding the construct. *Studies in Second Language Acquisition, 10*(2), 181-195.

Shohamy, E., & Stansfield, C. W. (1990). The Hebrew speaking test: An example of international cooperation in test development and validation. *AILA Review, 7*, 79-90.

Stansfield, C. W., Kenyon, D. M., Paiva, R., Doyle, F., Ulsh, I., & Cowles, M. A. (1990). The development and validation of the Portuguese Speaking Test. *Hispania, 73*, 641-651.

Shohamy, E. (1991). *The validity of concurrent validity: Qualitative validation of the Oral Interview with the Semi-Direct Test.* Paper presented at the 13th Language Testing Research Colloquium, Educational Testing Service, Princeton, NJ.

[66]

Prevocational Assessment Screen.

Purpose: "Designed to assess a student's motor and perceptual abilities in relation to performance requirements within a local vocational training program."

Population: Grades 9–12.
Publication Date: 1985.
Acronym: PAS.
Scores, 16: Time and Error scores for 8 modules: Alphabetizing, Etch A Sketch Maze, Calculating, Small Parts, Pipe Assembly, O Rings, Block Design, Color Sort.
Administration: Individual.
Price Data, 1989: $1,195 per complete kit including manual (50 pages) and computer software for use in scoring and reporting.
Time: (60–65) minutes.
Author: Michele Rosinek.
Publisher: Piney Mountain Press, Inc.

Review of the Prevocational Assessment Screen by STEPHEN L. KOFFLER, Managing Director, Center for Occupational and Professional Assessment, Educational Testing Service, Princeton, NJ:

The Prevocational Assessment Screen (PAS) was designed to assess motor and perceptual abilities of 14- to 18-year-old handicapped students (defined by the PAS manual to be mildly learning disabled, mildly retarded, or mildly emotionally disturbed) or disadvantaged students (defined by the PAS manual to be economically or educationally deprived and functioning at least one grade below grade level) in relation to performance requirements within a local vocational training program. The PAS was initially developed in a special needs evaluation laboratory in the Cobb County, Georgia School System to provide special needs educators with an alternative to the Vocational Rehab/Department of Labor model of assessment.

A stated purpose of the PAS is to give a school's "vocational team an indication of what a student needs to successfully complete the training program in which he or she enrolls" (manual, Appendix B, p. 2). The PAS includes eight hands-on activities, each measuring a different trait, and a computerized scoring and reporting system (for both Apple and IBM). The activities—Alphabetizing, Etch A Sketch Maze, Calculating, Small Parts, Pipe Assembly, O Rings, Block Design, and Color Sort—can be administered in any order and over any time setting required. All materials required, including activities, manual, and computer disks, are included in the PAS package.

OVERALL EVALUATION. Based on the information provided in the manual, the PAS in its current form has little to offer and clearly must be considered as still under development and in need of further research. The PAS manual provides insufficient detail about the PAS development, interpretation, and

other essential information one would expect. The manual itself needs much work in terms of grammar, spelling, punctuation, and English usage.

SCORING. There are two facets for the scoring of each of the PAS activities—the time it takes an examinee to complete the activity and the number of errors made by the examinee. However, there is no error score for the Small Parts activity, and the methods for scoring errors for the Color Sort and O Rings activities are questionable. Percentiles are provided separately for both time and errors. However, the manual instructs the administrators of the PAS to "obtain a combined rarting (*sic*) by adding the time and error percentile for each sample then divide by two" (manual, p. 8). Such a procedure is clearly problematic because percentiles are not on an interval scale and hence cannot be added. In addition, only selected percentile ranks are provided in the manual's norms table which makes that table difficult to use.

NORMS. The PAS norms were determined by "psychometric techniques and by predetermined time studies (MTM-1)" (manual, Appendix B, p. 5). The norms were generated in eight urban, suburban, and rural secondary and postsecondary vocational training schools in Georgia. According to the manual, additional normative data have been collected from different systems throughout the country; however, it is not clear whether the latter data are included in the manual's norms table. Finally, there is no indication provided to suggest that the students in the norm group are representative of a larger population. Thus, the generalizability of the data beyond the selected schools in Georgia may be questionable.

The manual indicates the "validation research samples" are based on 293 students, of which 112 are average students, 121 are handicapped students (ages 14–16, not 14–18), and 61 are disadvantaged students. However, it is not clear (*a*) why the average students were included in the norming group or how "average" is defined, (*b*) whether norms are based on all three groups of students (especially because the one norms table included in the manual has a heading that reads "average high school students"), or (*c*) whether error percentiles are based on empirical data on the MTM-1 study.

VALIDITY. The manual indicates the PAS "can be used in a variety of ways to assess the aptitudes, work behaviors, learning styles and cognitive performances of students pursuing an occupational course of study" (manual, Appendix B, p. 1). However, there is little, if any, validity evidence provided to substantiate this claim. There is also little evidence provided to show the PAS is valid for the special

181

needs and disadvantaged populations for which it is intended.

In general, validity evidence is sparse. The manual indicates that content validity is established via a Vocational Performance Matrix which sets up a direct relationship between the eight traits and the importance of each activity in each vocational training area. However, no evidence is provided to show how the content validity evidence is established nor how the activities are valid measures of the traits.

The norms table divides the percentile distribution into five categories (superior, above average, average, below average, and needs improvement). There is no explanation about how these categories were developed nor of the validity of their use. Finally, the manual reports the results of an MTM-1 predetermined time study that was conducted to provide criterion-related validity evidence. However, there is no indication of what the MTM-1 predetermined time study is nor how its results or the data furnished provide such evidence.

RELIABILITY. Test-retest reliability data are provided for all of the activities except for the Color Sort and Calculating activities. No information is presented to explain the lack of reliability data for those activities. It is also not clear as to what scores are being compared (number of errors, time, or both). Further, the reliability data are based on 50 average students in the norming sample, not the handicapped nor the disadvantaged students.

In summary, the PAS manual states that "from the inception of PAS in 1981, the developers never intended the module to be a highly scientific or predictive testing instrument" (manual, Appendix B, p. 1). Rather, the intent of the PAS is "to provide secondary special needs educators with an informal, uncomplicated method of gathering vocationally relevant information so that when a student is mainstreamed into a regular vocational training program the curriculum can be modified to accommodate the student's special needs" (manual, Appendix B, pp. 1–2). Nevertheless, even informal instruments must satisfy the principles of measurement called for in the *Standards for Educational and Psychological Testing* (AERA, APA, & NCME, 1985). The PAS, in its current form, does not satisfy those principles. Much more research is needed to clarify the validity, reliability, and usefulness of the PAS in vocational settings, especially for its intended special populations. There are too many questions about the PAS that need resolution before it can be recommended for use.

REVIEWER'S REFERENCE

American Educational Research Association, American Psychological Association, & National Council on Measurement in Education.

(1985). *Standards for educational and psychological testing*. Washington, DC: American Psychological Association, Inc.

Review of the Prevocational Assessment Screen by JAMES B. ROUNDS, *Associate Professor of Educational Psychology, University of Illinois at Urbana-Champaign, Champaign, IL:*

The Prevocational Assessment Screen (PAS) is designed to assess motor and perceptual abilities for mildly handicapped and disadvantaged youth. The PAS was developed to assist special needs educators in student placement in a vocational training program and seems to be modeled after the Department of Labor's (1970) General Aptitude Test Battery. Eight abilities are assessed with a single module (test) per ability (in parenthesis): clerical/verbal (Alphabetizing), motor coordination (Etch A Sketch Maze), clerical/numerical (Calculating), finger dexterity (Small Parts), manual dexterity (Pipe Assembly), form perception (O Rings), spatial perception (Block Design), and color perception (Color Sort). Two scores are reported for each ability test: an error score (the number of incorrect items), and a timed score consisting of the amount of time in minutes to complete the test. The actual test materials and the software that includes a scoring program and a local norms development system were not included with the manual and therefore are not reviewed here.

Once subtest time scores are obtained they can be converted into percentile scores based on PAS high school norms or compared to predetermined time criterion values (the average time it would take an average worker to perform the subtest). Five-point scale ratings varying from 1 = *superior* to 5 = *needs improvement* are then assigned separately to the student's percentile scores and the student's time criterion scores for each subtest. These rating scores for the eight abilities can be compared to a vocational performance matrix of ability (performance) requirements by vocational training programs. The PAS provides a vocational performance matrix with instructor ratings, varying from 1 = *critically significant* to 5 = *no significance*, of the eight abilities for 19 vocational training programs (e.g., auto mechanics). By matching the student's abilities with the ability requirements of training programs, it is assumed that recommendations can be offered for areas of remediation.

Conceptually, the PAS system, modeled after Department of Labor referral system, has the potential to link student abilities to vocational curricula. The actual contents of the PAS system, however, are poorly constructed and documented. For example, the PAS high school norms are inadequate. The norms for the eight ability subtests are based on an accidental sample from the state of Georgia of 81 to 136 "average" students, aged 14–18 years, ranging in education levels from 9th to 12th grade. The authors, however, acknowledge limitations of the normative sample and urge users to develop local norms. The manual does not discuss: (*a*) how the cutting scores were determined for the high school percentile norms or the predetermined time criterion values that result in the 5-point ability rating scores, and (*b*) how instructor's ratings were developed for the vocational performance matrix. But the author does caution the user on the applicability of the PAS vocational performance matrix, again urging users to develop local norms.

More problematically, the manual simply does not provide information to support the intended uses of the PAS scores. The author makes several inaccurate claims about the PAS validity. The author asserts that the "Content validity is established via the Vocational Performance Matrix" (manual, Appendix B, p. 8). By no stretch of the imagination is the Vocational Performance Matrix an indicator of the content validity of the PAS. One study, a predetermined time study of the PAS subtests, is cited to support the criterion-related validity. This time motion study, however, does not provide information about what the subtests measure.

The author refers the reader to Appendix B for "a factor analysis" (of what is not indicated). I could not find the "factor analysis" in Appendix B. I then called the Piney Mountain Press and asked for information on the factor analysis. The press sent the technical manual for the Skills Assessment Module (SAM; 1985; T4:2472). In the SAM manual, I found an outline of a "non-technical factor analysis" (p. 10) of 12 SAM subtests (7 of the 8 PAS subtests have the same name as the SAM subtests). The outline contains a table of subtests crossed with the headings of primary, secondary, and tertiary factor; inserted in cells of the table are the labels: perceptual, cognitive, and motor. No further information is given concerning the factor analysis. It is unclear if a factor analysis on PAS time or error scores was performed.

The author recommends one other major use of the PAS subtests. It is claimed the subtests can be used to determine if a student has the ability to learn with practice. It is suggested that users readminister the subtests until the student shows no further improvement in completion times. Because norms for repeated testing and validity information for such a use of PAS subtest scores are not given, users should refrain from using the PAS to assess learning potential.

Similar to the "factor analysis" example discussed above, the manual contains errors that could have been identified through a close reading. The manual, for example, refers the reader to Appendix F for a list of commercially prepared "interest inventories and surveys" (p. 4) and "work samples" (p. 5). There is no Appendix F. (The information is included at the end of Appendix E.) The reader will find statements such as "Consult directions for using the MATRIX on page 00000" (p. 6), "follow the guidelines discussed on pages [blank]" (Appendix B, p. 13), and "See page 6 in manual on READMINISTRATION TECHNIQUES" (p. 7). In this last case, the READMINISTRATION TECHNIQUES are found on page 5 rather than page 6. Numerous typos can be found in the text and on the materials used for scoring and reporting. The quality of the manual reminds me of Thorndike, Cunningham, Thorndike, and Hagen's (1991) observation that "the care that has gone into preparing the test manual is often a good indicator of the care that has been exercised in constructing the test" (p. 151). It is surprising that a manual available since 1985, with so many errors that are easy to correct, has not been revised.

I cannot recommend the PAS: It does not meet the basic standards for a psychological test. I have several suggestions. Teacher evaluations and ratings probably provide the best sources of information on student weaknesses and strengths for specific curriculum areas. If testing needs to be conducted, the Armed Services Vocational Aptitude Battery (ASVAB; U.S. Department of Defense, 1984; T4:196) is recommended. The ASVAB is designed for use in high school vocational guidance programs and provides information to aid in matching student abilities to vocational training programs.

REVIEWER'S REFERENCES

U.S. Department of Labor. (1970). *Manual for the USES General Aptitude Test Battery, Section III: Development*. Washington, DC: Manpower Administration.

U.S. Department of Defense. (1984). *Test manual for the Armed Services Vocational Aptitude Battery* (DOD 1304.12AA). North Chicago, IL: U.S. Military Entrance Processing Command.

Piney Mountain Press. (1985). *Technical manual: Skills Assessment Module*. Cleveland, GA: Piney Mountain Press.

Thorndike, R. M., Cunningham, G. K., Thorndike, R. L., & Hagen, E. P. (1991). *Measurement and evaluation in psychology and education* (5th ed.). New York: Macmillan Publishing Co.

[67]

Primary Test of Cognitive Skills.

Purpose: Designed to "measure verbal, spatial, memory, and conceptual abilities."

Population: Grades K–1.

Publication Date: 1990.

Acronym: PTCS.

Scores, 5: Spatial, Memory, Concepts, Verbal, Total.

Administration: Group.

Price Data: Price information available from publisher for test materials including manual (70 pages), norms book (82 pages), and technical bulletin (23 pages); scoring service available from publisher.

Time: (30) minutes per subtest; (120) minutes total test.

Authors: Janellen Huttenlocher and Susan Cohen Levine.

Publisher: CTB Macmillan/McGraw-Hill.

Review of the Primary Test of Cognitive Skills by SHERRY K. BAIN, Visiting Assistant Professor of Psychology, University of Southern Mississippi, Hattiesburg, MS:

DESCRIPTION. The Primary Test of Cognitive Skills (PTCS) is a group-administered ability test designed for use with kindergartners and first graders. The authors recommend the PTCS be used in screening for problems such as learning disability or developmental delay, and to identify referrals for gifted programming. The authors also state the PTCS can be used for planning instructional programs both for individuals and for groups of children.

TEST MATERIALS, ADMINISTRATION, AND SCORING. Test items are presented in multiple-choice format, with students filling in the circle beneath the correct choice. Administration instructions are clearly written, and the graphic presentation of items is well designed for the age level.

Subtests of the PTCS are untimed. Recommendations are to allow 30 minutes for each of the four subtests and to spread the testing over at least 2 days. The minimum total testing time, not counting needed breaks, would therefore be 2 hours. The test may be administered by the teacher to small groups, with proctors in charge of 10 or fewer kindergartners and 15 or fewer first graders.

The PTCS can be hand scored by the examiner or machine scored by the publisher. Scale scores and standard errors of measurement by subscale are provided by a method based upon Item Response Theory or by a less accurate method based upon the number of correct responses. Percentile ranks based upon age and grade, and stanine scores are also available. Finally, a Cognitive Skills Index provides an age-based standard score ($X = 100$, $SD = 16$), giving an indication of the student's overall performance.

STANDARDIZATION, RELIABILITY, AND VALIDITY. PTCS standardization was carried out on a national sample of 7,562 kindergartners and 8,504 first graders in Fall 1988 and Spring 1989. The authors state that students were selected from public, private, and Catholic schools and represented diverse geographic areas, socioeconomic levels, and ethnic backgrounds. Demographic characteristics of the standardization sample are fairly representative of the U.S. population. A breakdown of means and standard deviations for correct responses by ethnic groups and gender is presented in the Norms Book.

Test-retest reliability is relatively low, but probably not unexpected for a group-administered test. Reliability coefficients range from .50 to .80 ($X = .66$) across the four subscales. Test-retest reliability for the PTCS Cognitive Skills Index is not presented in the Technical Bulletin but would be valuable information to include.

Internal consistency data were obtained, based upon the Kuder-Richardson Formula 20. Coefficients range from .60 to .78 for subscales, and .84 or above for the total test.

Support for predictive validity was obtained by comparing PTCS scores with scores from the California Achievement Test and the Comprehensive Test of Basic Skills. PTCS Total scores, compared to achievement subtests from both batteries, produced coefficients within an adequate range (.36 to .65).

Evidence of construct validity is presented only in intercorrelations among the four subscale areas, but not for the two subtests within each subscale. Factor analytic studies were not reported. For the kindergarten level, subscale intercorrelations ranged from .35 to .54. The Concepts subscale for the kindergartners correlated with both the Spatial and Verbal subscales at .50 or greater, raising the question of subscale specificity. For first graders, subscale intercorrelations ranged from .22 to .44, indicating better subscale specificity.

The PTCS Cognitive Skills Index correlated with PTCS subscale scores within a range of .60 to .80 for kindergartners and first graders. Memory produced the lowest coefficient (.60) when compared to PTCS Cognitive Skills Index for first graders.

Test bias was evaluated through statistical examination of tryout items, based upon recommended methods from Item Response Theory. The authors also stated they followed publisher's guidelines for developing nonbiased tests (guidelines were not presented in the Technical Bulletin), and had tryout items and final items reviewed by three people: the project director and two editorial staff members. A panel of independent experts was not apparently used, and no data were presented on predictive validity for various ethnic groups.

RECOMMENDATIONS. Of the authors' primary recommendations for using the PTCS, several seem questionable. When used as a screening test for learning disability and developmental delay, students' performances may be negatively influenced by PTCS format characteristics (e.g., multiple choice, group administration). Students' specific deficits such as poor fine motor skills or poor receptive language skills could interfere with task performance, giving misleading information. Developmentally based checklists, curriculum-based checklists, and normative-based group achievement tests would be more appropriate as screening instruments for developmentally delayed and learning disabled students. Other components of the CTB Early Childhood System, of which the PTCS is a member, might be appropriate screeners (e.g., The Early School Assessment).

The PTCS authors' recommendation that results of the test can be used for instructional planning for individuals and groups is a claim made by previous ability test authors, but not generally verified by research on Aptitude by Treatment Interaction (see Ysseldyke & Marston, 1990). Among the CTB Early Childhood System components, the Early School Assessment (35) and the Developing Skills Checklist (27) are based upon objectives that are matched to an activities package, the Instructional Activities for Kindergarten and First Grade. The PTCS test items, however, are not apparently matched to instructional objectives and are not actually tied to suggested interventions by publishers. In general, the information purportedly gained from PTCS administration for groups of students does not appear to outweigh the time required to administer the test, considering the lack of evidence that results can translate into instructional planning.

The PTCS may prove useful as a screening instrument for identifying gifted referrals, as the test authors suggested, if district guidelines allow group testing for this purpose. The Technical Bulletin does not present data correlating the PTCS scores with individually administered ability test scores, but local districts may wish to collect data on their own gifted referrals to determine the usefulness of the PTCS for screening this special group.

REVIEWER'S REFERENCE

Ysseldyke, J. E., & Marston, D. (1990). The use of assessment information to plan instructional interventions: A review of the research. In. T. B. Gutkin & C. R. Reynolds (Eds.), *The handbook of school psychology* (2nd ed.; pp. 661-682). New York: John Wiley & Sons.

Review of the Primary Test of Cognitive Skills by LAURA L. B. BARNES, Assistant Professor of Educational Research, and DAVID E. McINTOSH, Assistant Professor of School Psychology, Department of Applied Behavioral Studies, Oklahoma State University, Stillwater, OK:

The Primary Test of Cognitive Skills (PTCS) is a group-administered ability measure for the initial screening of giftedness and developmental delay and for instructional planning in kindergarten and first grade. In conjunction with the California Achievement Tests or the Comprehensive Tests of Basic Skills, the PTCS may be used in the initial screening of learning disabilities. The test is to be administered in paper-and-pencil format with visual and verbal stimuli from a test administrator. Practice exercises are included to familiarize young examinees with the mechanics of paper/pencil testing and with the item formats. The PTCS is one component of the Early Childhood System which includes the Early School Assessment (35), the Developing Skills Checklist (27), and an instructional activities book. Four tests with two subtests each make up the PTCS: Spatial (21 items)—Sequencing and Spatial Integration; Memory (21 items)—Spatial Memory and Associative Memory; Concepts (28 items)—Category and Spatial Concepts; and Verbal (24 items)—Object Naming and Syntax.

The PTCS may be given by teachers, psychologists, and others who have had some formal training in test administration. The practice exercises and test instructions to be read aloud to the children are printed in bold for ease of administration. Specific guidelines for preparing the examiner prior to testing with emphasis on the special concerns of assessing young children are provided in the manual. For all items, the child records his or her answer by darkening circles similar to those on computer-scoring sheets. Pilot studies indicated the children did not have difficulties with this task. Although the tests are generally easy to administer, the format in which the Spatial and Associative Memory subtests are administered may prove difficult in a group situation. For example, exposing the stimulus pictures in a standardized fashion so each child can view the pictures, maintaining each child's attention, and manipulating the stimulus books may be difficult. In addition, the phonetic pronunciation of the Associative Memory pictures would help increase consistency in administration.

Both machine and hand scoring are possible with the PTCS. Specific instructions for machine scoring required by the CTB/McGraw-Hill scoring service are in the manual. An answer key and instructions are provided for hand scoring. When hand scored, the number of correct responses (NCR) on each of the four tests is the basis for obtaining several derived scores from the Norms Book. Although subtests are mentioned in the manual and identified for administration purposes, subtest scores are not used and no norms are given for them. Types of derived scores available are scale scores, percentile ranks by grade and by age, stanines, and a Cognitive Skills Index (CSI). The CSI (total test IQ score) has a mean of 100 and standard deviation of 16. An Anticipated Achievement score may be obtained for comparison with obtained achievement scores.

Although the conversion of number correct scores to derived scores is relatively straightforward when only grade-based information is desired, the process is awkward and confusing if age-based norms are also used. Deriving all of the scores requires a great deal of flipping back and forth between sets of tables, making the process both time consuming and prone to recording errors. National stanines are obtainable from either of two sets of tables—one that provides grade-based norms and the other providing age-based norms. However, on the hand-scoring report form, the column is labeled only NS (national stanine) and none of the materials mention that there are actually two sets of stanine norms. Use of the two sets produce different results. The norms tables are organized and labeled in such a way that errors may easily go undetected.

Another potentially confusing aspect of scoring is that when the tests are machine scored, there is an option for either Item Response Theory (IRT)-based scoring or number correct scoring. Scale scores derived through the IRT-based scoring are a weighted function of examinee ability and item characteristics. Research indicates that in most cases, the IRT-based scoring leads to more accurate ability estimation than does number correct scoring, particularly at extreme ability ranges. The Norms Book contains a table presenting standard errors of measurement based upon both scoring methods where it may seem the IRT-based scores have their greatest relative advantage at the low ability ranges. However, the degree of precision gained through the IRT-based scoring must be weighed against the cost associated with machine scoring (because IRT-based scoring cannot reasonably be done by hand).

Little information is reported regarding the development of the test content other than mentioning that items were developed by national leaders in the study of cognitive development. Once developed, the initial item pool was subjected to rigorous screening, incorporating input from teachers and review panels, and statistical item analysis. Statistical methods guiding test development were based in the three-parameter IRT model. Considerable attention was given to preventing the inclusion of items that exhibited gender and/or ethnic bias in the final form. Both subjective reviews and IRT-based analyses were part of the bias studies. These procedures are fully described in the Technical Bulletin.

The norming sample consisted of 16,066 kindergarten and first grade children from locations throughout the United States with standardization occurring during Fall 1988 and Spring 1989. Sample selection was based upon region, school size, socioeconomic status, and type of community. Reported demographics include gender, ethnicity, and percent enrolled in special education programs. Age norms ranged from 61 to 90 months and have adequate sample sizes except for the 61-month age group which has fewer than 200. Less than 5% of the sample for each grade and norming period was composed of students with identified disabilities. The authors suggest these small numbers may be due to participating schools' exclusion of special program children from routine testing and/or the lack of formal diagnosis. In the latter case, the reported figures may underrepresent the actual percentage of these groups included in the norming sample.

Test score reliabilities were computed using traditional and IRT-based methods. Internal consistency (KR-20) reliabilities for the total scale are .88 (fall, kindergarten), .87 (spring, kindergarten), .86 (fall, first grade), and .84 (spring, first grade). Reliabilities for the four tests range from .60 to .78 (median reliability is .70). Median test-retest reliabilities with a 2-week interval for the individual tests are .64 (fall, kindergarten) and .69 (fall, first grade). In general, Memory had the lowest reported reliabilities. These reliabilities are perhaps better than expected considering this is a group-administered test for very young children; however, the total scale reliabilities should probably be considered too low to form a basis for individual decision making (e.g., achievement/ability discrepancies). Both IRT-based and traditional standard errors of measurement are reported in the Norms Book for each scale score. Regardless of the scoring method, measurement error is most pronounced at the extremes of the score range which may result in inaccurate assessment of low and high functioning children.

As with many group-based ability tests, validity evidence is rather weak. Neither content validity nor a specific content description of the types of abilities measured by each of the PTCS subtests are provided in the Technical Bulletin. This information would increase the interpretability of the scores. For example, the Sequences subtest appears to measure the perception of sequential patterns and nonverbal inductive reasoning, whereas the Spatial Integration subtest appears to measure spatial visualization/reasoning, part-whole relationships, and nonverbal reasoning. The Spatial Memory subtest appears to assess short-term visual recall, visual memory, and nonverbal reasoning. Short-term memory, visual memory, and recognition memory for pictures appeared to be measured by the Associative Memory subtest. The Category Concepts and Spatial Concepts subtests appear to measure nonverbal reasoning and visual attention to detail. Receptive language and short-term auditory memory appear to be measured by the Object Naming subtest, whereas the Syntax subtest appears to measure receptive language, understanding oral directions, short-term auditory memory, and using basic language concepts.

Predictive validity coefficients between the PTCS and the California Achievement Tests (CAT) and the Comprehensive Tests of Basic Skills (CTBS) are reported. The median correlation between individual PTCS tests and CAT Form E Level 11 is .39 (range .19 to .55); with CTBS/4, Level 10 the median correlation is .42 (range .23 to .61). The PTCS Spatial and Verbal tests generally had the highest correlations with the achievement tests; the PTCS Memory test had the lowest. The median PTCS Total score correlation with CAT scores is .54; for the CTBS the median correlation is .58. The magnitudes of these correlations together with low stability reliability seem to provide a rather weak basis for predicting achievement scores. No evidence was presented as to the test's relationship with individual measures of intelligence or with other individual screening measures (e.g., the Peabody Picture Vocabulary Test—Revised [T4:1945] and the Bracken Basic Concept Scale [T4:319]).

Evidence for construct validity is presented solely through tables of intercorrelations. The low to moderate correlations among the tests indicate they measure separate constructs (median $r = .43$ for kindergarten; median $r = .35$ for first grade). However, in the absence of other substantial validity evidence, the interpretation of those constructs is difficult. Correlations between the individual tests and the PTCS Total are lower than desired for an ability screening test; the highest correlation is $r = .80$ (Concepts with Total). One possible explanation is that the tests are assessing abilities that are not considered highly salient measures of intelligence. For example, the Associative Memory subtest appears to measure short-term visual memory skills. These have been shown to correlate only moderately with cognitive ability. Although each test is purported to measure two separate skills, no evidence is presented to indicate they do so. Evidence for the construct validity of the test would be enhanced through a detailed description of the rationale for the test content including a discussion of the theory from which the measured constructs were derived. The authors state that a unique feature of the PTCS is its clear distinction between verbal and nonverbal abilities. A more detailed explanation of this distinction and analyses to support this claim are crucial to interpreting the constructs. Correlations with other ability measures would also provide insight into what constructs are being measured.

The authors state the PTCS was created for the initial screening of learning disabilities and developmental delay. We recommend that such screening decisions be made cautiously because less than 1% of the norming sample included these populations and construct validity of the instrument is questionable.

The PTCS is a new ability test that is designed to be group administered during kindergarten and first grade to screen for giftedness, learning disabilities, and developmental delay. The technical aspects of its development, including item selection and bias reduction procedures, are excellent. Although designed to be as "child friendly" as possible, test performance is likely to be influenced by children's poor attention, misunderstanding of directions, and processing difficulties. The PTCS represents a novel approach to assessing ability and may be useful where an initial group screening is warranted. However, it should not be considered as an alternative to sound individually administered measures. The PTCS should be interpreted solely as a screening measure with predictions related to cognitive ability and future academic progress being made with caution.

[68]

Printing Performance School Readiness Test.

Purpose: Developed to identify preschool children who may be at risk for school failure.

Population: Ages 4-3 to 6-5.

Publication Dates: 1985–90.

Acronym: PPSRT.

Scores: Total score only.

Administration: Individual.

Price Data, 1990: $23 per complete kit including flash cards, 50 response sheets, 50 scoring sheets, and manual ('90, 62 pages); $8.50 per set of flash cards; $12.50 per 200 response sheets; $12.50 per 200 scoring sheets; $8.50 per manual.

Time: (10–15) minutes.
Author: Marvin L. Simner.
Publisher: Phylmar Associates.
Cross References: For a review by Carol Mardell-Czudnowski of an earlier edition, see 10:293.

Review of the Printing Performance School Readiness Test by JERRILYN V. ANDREWS, Assistant for Assessment and Data Collection, Office of School Administration, Montgomery County Public Schools, Rockville, MD:

The Printing Performance School Readiness Test (PPSRT) is designed to aid educators in identifying prekindergarten and kindergarten children who may be at risk of later school failure. Research has indicated that young children who exhibit a large number of "form errors" (i.e., addition, omission, or misalignment of parts of a letter or number) have a higher probability of later school failure than students who make smaller numbers of form errors. The test author should be commended for emphasizing that the PPSRT assesses just one early warning sign and that the test should not be used as the sole means of identifying students who may be at risk of later school failure.

The 1990 revised edition of the PPSRT appears to be identical to the earlier (1985) version; the test and supporting technical information match that reported in an earlier review (10:293). What is new is the abbreviated version of the PPSRT which is intended for preschool students ranging in age from 45 to 57 months. The manual says that the full test has been found to be too long for prekindergarten students. Because the current version of the full test has already been reviewed, this review will focus only on the abbreviated test.

The abbreviated test requires students to copy 18 letter and numbers directly below a sample. The 18 numbers and letters were selected, using item analysis procedures, from the 41 contained on the full test. The scoring procedures are straightforward and identical to those used on the full test. The individually administered test is untimed and the manual says testing takes approximately 3 minutes per child, considerably less than the 10–15 minutes per child needed for the full test. The two response sheets, each with nine letters and numbers, are pictured in the manual; the user is told to enlarge the 1.5 by 2 inch models to 8.5 by 11 inches. This will probably require that most users make their own response sheets rather than photocopy the models.

The manual provides little technical information about the abbreviated PPSRT; the reader is referred to a 1989 article by the test author for this information. That article (Simner, 1989) does provide adequate information except for the description of the sample; for that the reader is referred to yet another article (Simner, 1987). It would be better if the test manual itself contained all the information potential users need to evaluate the test.

According to Simner (1989) the study design closely parallels that used for the full PPSRT. For the abbreviated PPSRT, two samples containing a total of 171 prekindergarten students were tested in the fall of prekindergarten and then followed for the next 3 years. Interrater and test-retest reliabilities were both adequate and consistent with findings from the full PPSRT. Report card grades and standardized achievement test scores were used to assess predictive validity; again results were adequate and in line with the full PPSRT. The recommended cutoff score of 16 correctly identified 70–78% of the true positives and only produced 18–20% false positives. Thus, the results of the study of the abbreviated PPSRT closely follow those of the full PPSRT.

In summary, the PPSRT appears unchanged from the version reviewed earlier. The new, abbreviated PPSRT appears to have adequate technical properties as long as the reader follows the author's advice to use it as just one piece of screening information. Having every child ready for school has been called a national priority and will probably lead to more preschool programs. The abbreviated PPSRT may well provide a quick preliminary screening tool to help identify students who may need additional assistance.

REVIEWER'S REFERENCES

Simner, M. L. (1987). Predictive validity of the Teacher's School Readiness Inventory. *Canadian Journal of School Psychology, 3,* 21-32.

Simner, M. L. (1989). Predictive validity of an abbreviated version of the Printing Performance School Readiness Test. *Journal of School Psychology, 27,* 189-195.

Review of the Printing Performance School Readiness Test by AGNES E. SHINE, Assistant Professor of Educational Psychology, Mississippi State University, Mississippi State, MS:

The Printing Performance School Readiness Test (PPSRT) is an individually administered screening test developed to identify form errors in the printing of young children. Form errors occur in printing when the child adds, deletes, or misaligns parts of a letter or number, which results in a marked distortion. The author states that in young children form errors can be used as a warning sign for potential school failure. The ability to attend to a stimulus and coordinate fine muscle movements (e.g., copying, printing) is generally viewed as a measure or index of a child's maturity level. Designed for young children from age 4 to 6, the PPSRT can be administered in approximately 10–15 minutes. Extensive psychometric training is not necessary and with practice the PPSRT could be administered and interpreted by a variety of professionals such as a classroom teacher or public health nurse.

The test material includes a manual, 41 letter and number cards, response sheets, and an examiner protocol. The cards are exposed one at a time in sequential order. For prekindergarten children the test consists of copying 41 letters and numbers, whereas kindergarten children print the letter or number from memory after a 2- to 3-second exposure.

Norms and cutoff scores are provided for three time periods, late spring of prekindergarten (children 51–63 months), fall of kindergarten (children 57–69 months), and late spring of kindergarten (children 65–77 months). The scoring criteria are well written with visual examples of adequate performance and form errors. When scoring the PPSRT the examiner should note that only the child's first attempt is scored. Tracing over a letter or number is not considered a form error as long as the final reproduction closely resembles the presented stimulus. To help the examiner with scoring, the author provides the examiner with 10 practice scoring exercises.

According to the author the standardization sample consisted of 619 children from public schools in London, Ontario. However, the means and standard deviations for the PPSRT were based on the scores obtained from 859 protocols. Upon careful review of the six samples that comprise the subject pool, it was noted that some of the children were retested and their score included in the norming. This reviewer questions the wisdom of including the scores of subjects who had previous exposure to the test material because such exposure may have distorted the means. Because copying and printing tasks are often found in the curricula of young children, practice or remediation may have occurred between test administrations, possibly lowering the mean number of errors in the standardization sample. The mean number of errors for children tested in the fall of kindergarten was higher than the mean number of errors for children tested in late spring of prekindergarten. The rise in the number of form errors suggests that the tasks are not equivalent (e.g., copying to printing from memory).

The author uses cutoff scores with probabilities to describe the child's performance on the PPSRT. Specifically, children with odds of 10 to 1 would require immediate remediation and children with odds of 1 to 1 should be referred for additional assessment. The cutoff scores were calculated to identify approximately 75% of at-risk children. Standard scores or percentiles based on age may have been easier to use and more meaningful than cutoff scores.

The available reliability and validity data are difficult to understand and evaluate. Little information was provided in the manual concerning reliability studies. The author reports test-retest intervals from 1 month to 8 months. Test-retest reliability coefficients ranged from .73 to .87. It appears that as the number of months between test administrations increased, the reliability decreased. The amount or extent of training involved in achieving interscorer reliability was missing from the manual. Therefore, the meaning of the reported interscorer reliability studies (.97 and .98) was unclear given the lack of information.

Studies of criterion validity involved correlating the PPSRT with standardized achievement tests and school performance. When the PPSRT was correlated with achievement tests (e.g., Wide Range Achievement Test, KeyMath Diagnostic Arithmetic Test) the reported correlation coefficients ranged from .40 to .79. It is troubling to note the manual authors reported a correlation coefficient between the Wide Range Achievement Test (WRAT) and the PPSRT for prekindergarten children because the WRAT was normed on children 5 years of age and older. Correlating the PPSRT with school performance (grades) resulted in correlation coefficients that ranged from .27 to .63. The author indicated that these somewhat low correlations may be due to the removal of the children who failed, thus resulting in a restricted range.

Predictive validity was reported for the three different testing times. The sample was divided into high and low achievers. Thirty percent of the sample whose school achievement was described as "C" level were excluded from the analysis. Classification rates for the poor performance group (true positive) ranged from 71 to 85%, whereas the false positive hit rate ranged from 15 to 21%. Because the PPSRT is a screening device purportedly used to identify children at risk for school failure, it is also important to look at the false negative classification rates (e.g., student who had good test performance but poor school achievement). Using the present cutoff scores, 15 to 29% of the children were misclassified. Although the overall hit rate of the PPSRT may be adequate for a screening measure using the present cutoff scores it may result in overlooking children who may be at risk for school failure. The largest misclassification rates occurred in the prekindergarten sample with the lowest misclassifications rates in the sample tested in the late spring of kindergarten.

The author continually reminds the potential test user that the PPSRT is a screening test and should not be the sole instrument used to determine if a child is at risk for school failure. However, the author suggested the use of the PPSRT may avoid having to use longer, more specialized tests when screening young children. The author suggested that local norms be obtained and explained how this might be accomplished.

In summary, the PPSRT appears to be easy to administer. The test materials are well organized. At times the manual is difficult to read and understand. Sections dealing with reliability and validity data are somewhat confusing to this reviewer. Therefore, it is difficult to evaluate the PPSRT to determine if it is appropriate for the intended specific use. Because the test was normed on children in a specific geographic location, the generalizability of the test is questionable. Due to the limited sample of behaviors measured, clinicians should use the PPSRT with caution when screening young children.

[69]
Problem Experiences Checklist.
Purpose: Developed for use prior to the initial intake interview to identify potential problems for further discussion.
Population: Adolescents, adults.
Publication Date: 1991.
Scores: No scores.
Administration: Individual.
Editions, 2: Adolescent, Adult.
Manual: No manual.
Price Data, 1993: $14.50 per 25 checklists (specify Adult or Adolescent).
Time: [10–15] minutes.
Author: Leigh Silverton.
Publisher: Western Psychological Services.

Review of the Problem Experiences Checklist by MARK H. DANIEL, Senior Scientist, American Guidance Service, Circle Pines, MN:

The Problem Experiences Checklist (PEC) is designed to provide an easy and efficient way for a clinician or counselor to find out what kinds of problems are on a client's mind before the initial interview. The client reads a list of statements of problems, emotions, and potentially stressful circumstances and checks any that currently apply. There are no scores, and the PEC is not intended as a measuring instrument.

There are two versions, surveying similar domains but written differently to be appropriate for their intended age level. The Adult Version has 209 statements grouped into 11 categories, covering interpersonal and family relations; beliefs, emotions, and personal habits; job and financial situation; and stressful events. Each category also includes one or two open-ended "Other problems" items. The Adolescent Version is slightly longer, with 246 statements in 13 categories, but without the open-ended items. In addition to the topics covered by the Adult Version, it includes statements about school, recreation, and neighborhood circumstances.

The statements are concise, direct, and easy to read, and the layout of the forms is spacious and attractive. Clients should have no difficulty completing the checklist in the 10 to 15 minutes estimated by the publisher.

The absence of published documentation on these forms is acceptable considering their function and their lack of psychometric claims. One might, however, wonder how the problem domains were selected. The author has stated in personal communication (L. Silverton, October 21, 1991): "To construct the adult items, I reviewed DSM-III-R categories related to V-code diagnoses or problems not attributable to mental disorders . . . . I included all as categories." Silverton supplemented these categories with others commonly screened in intake interviews, such as self-care, beliefs and goals, and emotions. The Adolescent Version was constructed somewhat differently: "A review of the literature about psychosocial stressors in adolescence in general and more specific problems of adolescents seeking treatment suggested the general categories for the checklists" (L. Silverton, personal communication, October 21, 1991). Perusal of the forms suggests that the author's systematic approach resulted in broad and nonredundant coverage.

SUMMARY. The Problem Experiences Checklist appears to be a useful tool for surveying a client's concerns and learning about the psychosocial stressors in their life. It would complement, rather than substitute for, more clinical assessment devices.

Review of the Problem Experiences Checklist by MICHAEL J. SPORAKOWSKI, Professor of Family and Child Development, Virginia Polytechnic Institute and State University, Blacksburg, VA:

The Problem Experiences Checklist comes in two forms, the Adolescent Version and the Adult Version. Neither arrived on this reviewer's desk with any sort of manual or documentation beyond the checklists themselves. They appear to be a typical checklist approach towards a quick, face valid assessment of issues or problems that are concerning the respondent. It is most likely that this evaluation could be of use to the teacher, guidance counselor, clinical counselor, or therapist who might be working with the respondent as an initial self-appraisal of current functioning and/or difficulties. Because no data are presented with these checklists, they have no possibilities for comparison-to-norm scores for either clinical or research purposes.

Regarding the Adolescent Version, areas covered include: school, opposite-sex concerns, peers, family, goals, crises, emotions, recreation, habits, neighborhood circumstances, life transitions, beliefs and attitudes, and occupational and financial circumstances. The Adult Version covers: marital/relationship, children/parents, financial/legal, sexual/social, bereavement, personal habits, work adjustment, life transitions, beliefs and goals, painful memories, and emotions.

These checklists may be functional as part of an initial intake screening for counseling. They would be infinitely more valuable if descriptions of their construction, development, and use were included with them. If employed, users must develop their own normative bases for making comparisons and evaluating the instruments' psychometric qualities. As a counselor, these instruments might have value in stimulating discussion with some clients or offering quick, surface level insights into client's difficulties before they are actually seen. As a researcher or developer of assessments, the Problem Experiences Checklists offer me little.

[70]
Progressive Achievement Tests of Reading [Revised].

Purpose: Designed to assess the skills and abilities of the students in reading with a view to providing instruction adapted to their present stages of development.
Population: Standards 2–4, Forms 1–2, Forms 3–4 in New Zealand schools (Ages 8–14).
Publication Dates: 1969–91.
Scores, 2: Reading Comprehension, Reading Vocabulary.
Administration: Group.
Levels, 3: Primary, Intermediate, Secondary.
Forms, 2: A, B.
Price Data: Available from publisher.
Time: 55 minutes for Comprehension part, 40 minutes for Vocabulary part.
Comments: Raw scores convert to the Level scores (1–10), age percentile rank, and class percentile rank.

Authors: Neil A. Reid and Warwick B. Elley.
Publisher: New Zealand Council for Educational Research [New Zealand].
Cross References: See T4:2141 (7 references) and T3:1912 (2 references); for a review by Douglas A. Pidgeon, see 8:738 (1 reference); see also T2:1579 (1 reference); for excerpted reviews by Milton L. Clark and J. Elkins, see 7:699.

Review of the Progressive Achievement Tests of Reading [Revised] by HERBERT C. RUDMAN, Professor of Measurement and Quantitative Methods, Department of Counseling, Educational Psychology and Special Education, Michigan State University, East Lansing, MI:

TEST CONTENT. The Progressive Achievement Tests of Reading (PATR), originally published in 1969, were designed to measure reading comprehension and reading vocabulary. This 1991 revision continues to measure just these two facets of the reading process. A test user looking for detailed information about enabling skills such as structural analysis (the ability to decode words by syllables, affixes, and root words), and phonetic analysis of consonants and vowels (the relationships between sounds and letters) will have to look elsewhere.

The original version of the PATR was designed to measure literal as well as inferential comprehension of prose material. According to the authors, a "sizable" sample of teachers in New Zealand determined the reading skills and materials to be included in the tests. These skills and materials were weighted by these teachers as well as by reading specialists from 10 regional committees. It would appear that those opinions have remained stable since 1969; the weightings and types of materials are still reflected in this newest version of the PATR.

The comprehension portion of the tests contains an approximately even distribution of factual and inferential items at each battery level. These items accompany passages 100 to 300 words in length. Although differing definitions of reading comprehension are available, most reading specialists would agree that content for such a test can also be identified by function, for example, paragraph reading, textual reading, functional reading (signs, newspapers, rules and regulations, directions), and recreational reading.

The Progressive Achievement Tests of Reading contain passages that the authors have classified under three rubrics: Narrative, Descriptive, and Expository. These passages are distributed rather evenly across grades and battery levels. Although it is possible that an American reviewer could misinterpret the terms, "narrative," "descriptive," and "expository" as used in New Zealand, a careful reading of the passages still indicates that of a total of 58 passages used across three battery levels, only one is drawn from a news magazine (Secondary Level, Form A, p. 12). When compared to reading materials used in comparable standardized achievement tests reviewed elsewhere in this *Mental Measurements Yearbook* series, The PATR's content more closely resembles textbook material than it does a variety of materials drawn from everyday life.

Any well-constructed test should be a reflection of an instructional theory that can be used to describe an instructional domain. Any critique of a test should be based, in part, on how well that domain has been sampled. The material sent for review does not adequately describe such a theory of reading comprehension. The domain appears to be, by definition, narrowly focused as exemplified by the authors' prefatory acknowledgments and their list of illustrative materials of suitable difficulty level (manual, pp. 2, 21).

The domain of words sampled by the various levels of vocabulary tests is defined as the 10,000 most commonly used words in the English language. The words were apparently drawn from one word list (Wright, 1965). This reviewer regrets that no other rationale for the choice of words to be tested was considered except the total number of common words defined. Because the vocabulary tests are school-related it would make some sense if they came from lists of words likely to be encountered in various school activities. Words do, sometimes, have special meanings in a context of academic disciplines. If the words were classified by content groupings, additional instructional use could be made of the data collected from vocabulary tests. Advances in the physical, biological, and social sciences have introduced into the common vocabulary a number of words which may have been considered specialized when Wright's common core vocabulary list was published in 1965. Surely, these words should have been incorporated into the 1991 revision of the PATR.

The Progressive Achievement Tests of Reading are organized into three battery levels: Primary, Intermediate, and Secondary. The Primary battery is used by students in grades 2, 3, and 4; the Intermediate level in grades 5 and 6; the Secondary battery for grades 7 and 8. Two forms, A and B, are available for measuring both reading comprehension and vocabulary. The New Zealand Educational Research Council (the developers and publishers of the PATR) recommend that Form A be administered in odd-numbered years and Form B in even-numbered years.

The authors use eight overlapping levels (or "parts") to measure Reading Comprehension and Reading Vocabulary content from Standard 2 (grade 2) to Form 4 (grade 8). The Primary battery contains 62 Reading Comprehension items divided into three different starting and ending points. Pupils in grade 2 complete "Part Two" (Items 1–41). Pupils in grade 3 begin with "Part Three" (Items 12–51), and those in grade 4 complete "Part Four" (Items 22–62). A similar scheme is used for Reading Vocabulary (45 items). The number of items across all three battery levels total 107 for Reading Comprehension and 125 for Reading Vocabulary. Each succeeding battery uses some of the same items and reading passages contained in the previous lower battery (Primary, Part 4 ranges from Item 22 to Item 62. Intermediate, Part 5 begins with Item 32 and ends with Item 72).

TECHNICAL ASPECTS. The PATR was constructed with considerable care. New items which were written and older items which were retained from the 1969 version were item analyzed in 44 primary, intermediate, and secondary schools throughout New Zealand. Extensive use was made of teachers and reading specialists throughout the item development phase. Reading vocabulary items were selected and calibrated for difficulty based upon previous renorming and item analyses conducted in 1981 and 1988. In some instances sentences used in 1969 were rewritten when "several" words had changed drastically. Neither the number of words nor the words themselves are identified. The basic source for these words remained the 1965 Wright word list used in the original edition of the PATR.

Conventional item analyses were conducted on the revised tests, and items that met the authors' specifications were incorporated into new item analysis versions for final standardization. Equivalent forms were prepared using the following variables for matching: numbers of items and reading passages, types of passages, readability indices, average difficulty and discrimination levels of the blocks of items related to the passages, and the balance of literal and inferential items. Vocabulary test forms were matched in blocks of five using difficulty and discrimination indices, as well as frequency of occurrence on the Wright list.

The PATR was standardized on a representative sample of 1,000 students at each class level from grade 2 (Standard 2) to grade 8 (Form 4). The total standardization sample consisted of 8,016 students and 180 schools drawn from the 12 education districts in New Zealand. The number of students tested represented 1 in 50 of the total population at each class level.

Care was taken to mitigate item bias, both cultural and statistical bias. Items in both the reading comprehension and vocabulary tests were examined for apparent gender, ethnic, or other types of cultural bias which could be offensive to a subgroup of the New Zealand population. Items that were so identified through a judgmental process were either rewritten or eliminated. Statistical control of bias was established through special studies in schools known to have large student populations consisting of Maori and Pacific Island students. Samples of European and non-European students were matched by grade level, gender, and total test score. Test results were then analyzed for differential item performance. A McNemar Chi-Square Test revealed statistical differences for only two items in both Forms A and B. Those items that showed differences between European and non-European students were reviewed by Maori members of the New Zealand Council for Educational Research and by "specialist Auckland advisers." The differences observed were judged to be "chance statistical fluctuations" and were retained in the test.

Reliability estimates for the reading comprehension test, grades 2–8 all yielded respectably high correlations: .85–.88 (equivalent forms); .88–.92 (split-half); and .87–.94 (KR20). Similar reliability estimates for the vocabulary test across the same grade levels were: .91–.94 (equivalent forms), .92–.95 (split-half), and .92–.96 (KR20).

Validity as discussed in the Teacher's Manual is puzzling. Although the importance of content validity of standardized achievement tests is very well stated the authors then seem to back away from the case they make for validity because it appears to be subjective. In their words they offer such sources of evidence of content validity as, "a detailed and thorough examination of the contents of the test—its structure and emphases, its correspondence with accepted syllabuses, commonly used graded reading series, and other resource materials . . . . This is largely a *subjective process* [emphasis added]" (p. 35). They then express concern that no statistical data can adequately establish content validity. Although one can argue that descriptive statistics dealing with frequencies and proportions can indeed help establish a base that relates the content of an instructional program with the content of the test, that really should be self-evident. However, no such specificity is offered in support of content validity except in the general terms just cited.

Examples are offered of concurrent validity in terms of correlations with other tests in the Progressive Achievement Test Series, as well as correlations with other standardized achievement tests in other English-speaking countries. This is impressive, but hardly necessary to establish a case for achievement test validity. I would have appreciated a more specific description of the sources that defined the domains measured in the reading test.

The greatest asset to the test user the PATR offers is the very practical suggestions for interpretation of the test scores. The caveats offered are sound, the case studies offered are realistic, and the discussions of the contributions and limitations of derived scores are as good as I have seen represented in other interpretive materials.

The Teacher's Manual has several tables of data that deal with item difficulty indices for both forms of the comprehension and vocabulary tests for all grades. Other norm tables consist of percentile rank norms by age and stanine (Forms A and B), and percentile rank norms by class and stanine. The tables are easy to interpret and allow individual as well as group interpretation.

SUMMARY. The reading passages are very interesting and should add pleasure to students who do not always view testing as a pleasurable experience. All told, the New Zealand Council for Educational Research has produced a good test for those programs more concerned with reading comprehension than with the measurement of enabling word study skills.

REVIEWER'S REFERENCE

Wright, C. W. (1965). *An English word count*. Pretoria: National Bureau of Educational and Social Research.

[71]

A Rating Inventory for Screening Kindergartners.
Purpose: Constructed "to assess the likelihood that kindergarten children will require future supplemental educational assistance."
Population: Kindergarten.
Publication Date: 1991.
Acronym: RISK.
Scores: 5 factor scores: School Competence, Task Orientation, Social, Behavior, Motor and ratings in 7 developmental areas: Hearing, Vision, Physical, Intellectual, Emotional, Language, Speech.
Administration: Individual.
Price Data: Not available.
Time: Administration time not reported.
Comments: Ratings by teachers; Apple II or IBM microcomputer necessary for scoring.
Authors: J. Michael Coleman and G. Michael Dover.

Publisher: PRO-ED, Inc.
[The publisher advised in January 1994 that this test is now out of print—Ed.]

Review of A Rating Inventory for Screening Kindergartners by LeADELLE PHELPS, Associate Professor and Director, School Psychology Program, Department of Counseling and Educational Psychology, State University of New York at Buffalo, Buffalo, NY:

A Rating Inventory for Screening Kindergartners (RISK) is a screening instrument designed to identify kindergarten students who may require supplemental special education services. The scale consists of 34 Likert-type rating items (1 = *hardly ever*, 6 = *almost always*) that the classroom teacher completes during the spring of the kindergarten year. There are an additional eight items that require "yes or no" responses to questions dealing with health-related impairments (e.g., Does the child have any obvious hearing problems?), developmental delays (e.g., Does the child have any obvious speech problems?), and psychoeducational risk factors (e.g., Does the child have any obvious intellectual problems?). It would appear that the scale can be completed by teachers in approximately 5 minutes.

The scale is organized into five areas: (*a*) School Competence (12 questions), (*b*) Task Orientation (7 questions), (*c*) Sociability (6 questions), (*d*) Behavior (6 questions), and (*e*) Motor Skills (3 questions). These areas were derived using a principal components factor analysis followed by an orthogonal rotation.

School Competence consists of questions concerning the child's estimated level of intelligence, achievement motivation, academic performance, apparent learning problems, and special instructional needs. Not surprisingly, this area is statistically very robust with an eigenvalue of 14.41 and explained variance of 42.41% (explained variance for the total scale = 69.69%). Task Orientation is less robust but still adds 14.40% to the total explained variance. Task Orientation contains items assessing the likelihood of an attention deficit hyperactivity disorder.

The other three scores (Sociability, Behavior, and Motor) add very little to the explained variance or predictive power of the RISK. For example, the five RISK scores were correlated with the Otis-Lennon School Ability Test and the Stanford Achievement Test (SAT). The School Competence correlations with the SAT ranged from .50 (Reading) to .54 (Math). The correlation between School Competence and the Otis-Lennon was .51. Task Orientation correlations with the SAT ranged from .34–.40 and

.44 with the Otis-Lennon. However, all the correlations among the other three RISK areas and the SAT/Otis-Lennon were in the .16–.25 range. Clearly, Sociability, Behavior, and Motor are not very accurate predictors of school achievement/aptitude. In addition, the five scores are generally highly correlated with one another with a mean correlation of .44. In summary, these statistics suggest that the RISK generally assesses one general factor with the five separate areas providing little distinct data of diagnostic or intervention relevance.

The reliability of the instrument is excellent with the authors reporting an alpha coefficient of .96 for the entire scale. The principal method used by the authors for establishing validity for the instrument was to ascertain if the RISK correctly identified students who later received special education placement. Using a series of discriminant function analyses, the authors determined that 78.7% of the children ultimately requiring resource room services were identified by the RISK. As many children are in need of special individualized assistance that can be offered via regular education placement, using special education placement (i.e., school failure) as the outcome variable is not viewed as efficacious in predicting specific achievement in core academic areas.

The greatest strength/weakness of the RISK (depending on your measurement orientation) resides in the use of teacher ratings. There are no national norms for this scale. Rather, each student's ratings are transformed to z-scores based on the ratings of *each teacher* within *each classroom*. The authors state that employing z-scores eliminates differences between how teachers anchored their ratings. Nevertheless, halo effects and leniency errors are very common pitfalls with rating scales. Having no impartial criteria and/or items that directly assess each youngster's competencies are questionable practices when the stated objective is to identify the "risk population."

In summary, the RISK is a quick and easily administered teacher rating scale. If a school district wishes to rely on such data for identifying children at risk, then this scale appears promising. However, scales that provide direct and objective assessments of children's academic aptitude may be a better alternative.

Review of A Rating Inventory for Screening Kindergartners by GENE SCHWARTING, Project Director of Early Childhood Special Education, Omaha Public Schools, Omaha, NE:

Interest has expanded significantly in recent years in the field of early childhood education, resulting in the development of new assessment techniques and instruments. In addition, concerns have surfaced regarding formal "tests" for this age group. A Rating Inventory for Screening Kindergartners (RISK) is an attempt to address both the interest and the concerns, through development of an informal teacher-based assessment tool to identify kindergartners in need of more formal diagnostic testing and at risk for future failure in school as well as placement into special education.

The RISK protocol consists of four pages containing 34 items on which the teacher assesses children near the end of the kindergarten year on a 6-point scale, along with eight indicators of specific concerns regarding the students. These 34 items are often highly subjective, such as to "estimate this child's intelligence," and reflect an informal review of the general skills found in kindergarten curricula at most schools. Resultant ratings are then converted to a z scale, with a score of less than -1.25 being considered significant. The authors indicate that further evaluation is needed if such scores are obtained in two or more domains, or if a score less than -2.0 is obtained for any one domain. Scores are entered into a computerized, menu-driven data bank; as a result of this process, ongoing local norms for "graduating" kindergartners are developed. The program allows for reporting information on an individual student profile, by class, or by school, with an additional feature allowing the previous year's data to be deleted.

The RISK was initially administered to the entire kindergarten population ($n = 2,306$) in two unidentified school districts selected as socioculturally homogeneous during the years 1980–1983. A follow-up in 1986 found 57% of these children still enrolled, of whom 86% were Caucasian—additional information regarding race, socioeconomic status, or other variables was not provided. At this time, information was also gathered as to placement into special education, Otis-Lennon group IQ scores, and national percentile rank on the Stanford Achievement Test (SAT).

Standardization data found coefficient alpha to be .96 with the correlation between the predictor variables based upon the suggested cutoff scores and later placement into special education to be .74. The School Competence scale accounted for 42% of the variance, followed by Task Orientation, Social, Behavior, and Motor in descending order (not surprisingly, this corresponds to the decreasing order of the number of items of each scale). Predictive validity for the norm group found the instrument to be 94% accurate for identifying children for special education, with a false positive rate of 3% and a false negative rate of 21%. It should be noted the special

education placements predicted do not include speech therapy, and are for the most part (83.5%) in resource classrooms with type and severity of handicapping conditions not indicated. The SAT and Otis-Lennon scores are significantly below average for all groups except those predicted by the RISK to succeed in regular education. However, the correlations between these results and the RISK factor scores are .54 and lower.

In summary, it should be noted that the RISK is an attempt to make subjective information more objective and that the instrument is not so much an assessment tool as a reasonably priced data management system. Whether it is an improvement over informal teacher ratings would appear to be based upon the judgement of the teacher. Certainly, the applicability of the norm group to other schools, the high number of children placed into special education in the norm group schools (17.25%), and the 43% loss of the norm group population prior to the follow-up should also be considered by potential users of the instrument.

[72]

Reid Report.

Purpose: "The Report consists of a customized set of scales and questionnaires which focus on key, business-related employee behaviors. Measures attitudes toward conscientiousness and counterproductivity in the workplace and predicts overall work performance and counterproductive acts (turnover, absenteeism, tardiness, theft and inappropriate substance use)."

Population: Job applicants.

Publication Dates: 1969–92.

Scores: 1 of 4 possible evaluations (Recommended, Qualified, Not Recommended, No Opinion) in 4 parts (Integrity Attitude, Antisocial History, Recent Drug Use, Work History) and overall evaluation.

Administration: Group.

Price Data: Price information available from publisher for test materials including examiner's manual ('89, 39 pages).

Time: (15–60) minutes.

Comments: Overall evaluation established by client organization, based upon specific organizational requirements.

Authors: Reid Psychological Systems, Paul Brooks (manual), and David Arnold (manual).

Publisher: Reid Psychological Systems.

Cross References: See T4:2243 (1 reference); for a review by Stanley L. Brodsky, see 8:658 (3 references); for integrated version of Reid Report/Reid

Survey, see T2:1353 (1 reference) and 7:132 (1 reference).

Review of the Reid Report by GEORGE DOMINO, Professor of Psychology, University of Arizona, Tucson, AZ:

The Reid Report (RR) is said to measure "attitudes toward honesty and integrity" and aims to "predict dishonest acts on the job" (manual, p. 1). The test booklet consists of four parts for a total of 320 items (oddly enough the first item is numbered 101), but it is only Part 1, made up of 80 yes-no items (only 70 are scored) and comprising the Integrity Attitude Inventory, that is scored and for which there is psychometric information available.

The Examiner's Manual is well written and presents considerable reliability and validity data, but does not seem to be written for the psychometrically sophisticated reader. The manual is perhaps more noteworthy for what is absent than what is presented.

There is in the manual no distinction made between the RR in its totality and Part 1, with Part 1 typically labelled as the RR. The manual indicates the RR contains 80 items, but the test booklet contains 83. For this reader there was considerable confusion over how scores are generated. The test information indicates that a four-fold evaluation is given (recommended, qualified, not recommended, no opinion), but most of the manual information indicates a two-fold evaluation (recommended vs. not recommended) with a cutoff score of 49–50. No indication is given how this particular score was selected. Although scores are reported as raw scores, as percentiles, and as probability (that the applicant will commit theft) scores, there is no table or other information that allows the reader to equate raw scores with percentiles. There is a table (Table 16) that equates "percent rank" with probability, but nowhere is there information on how the probability scores were computed, nor their degree of validity. The nature of the table strongly suggests that these probabilities are not empirically based, but were calculated "statistically."

The manual authors recommend the RR be administered only to applicants for positions "in which honesty and integrity are major job requirements" and where "dishonest behavior could cause significant economic, organizational or personal harm" (manual, p. 2). The RR has, however, been administered to over 5 million individuals, and what job descriptions are given suggest that many applicants were for relatively low-level positions such as parking lot attendants, laborers, assemblers, as well as salespersons, stock clerks, and warehouse workers.

The manual indicates that 18 internal consistency studies have been carried out, but Table 1 gives results for 14 samples, and it is not clear how the samples and the studies interface. Five of the coefficients are given as Cronbach's alphas, which is puzzling given the dichotomous nature of the item responses.

These aspects, like the misspelling of psychological on the inside frontispiece of the manual, are minor and only slightly irritating. There are, however, a number of more major and frustrating aspects to the RR. First, there is no discussion of the development of the test other than to indicate the authors. The conclusion is that the test was developed by "fiat" rather than by empirical procedures, and that internal consistency analyses or other item selection procedures were not followed. A few of the items are nearly identical with MMPI-CPI (Minnesota Multiphasic Personality Inventory—Californial Psychological Inventory) items, but no mention of this is made.

Secondly, given the aim of the test, its self-report format, and item transparency, faking is of central concern. The manual indicates that there is "extensive research on its resistance to faking" (p. 4), but what is presented does not support this claim. In one study, 51 college students were instructed to fake good, but the obtained mean was not significantly different from that obtained by a randomly selected group of employment applicants. Only when the two samples were "equated" for college education did a significant (but miniscule) difference appear. Incidentally, no means, standard deviations, or ANOVA results are presented in the manual, and of the 30 references cited only 9 are to publications in the public domain. In two other sets of studies the effects of different attitudes toward test-taking and different instruction conditions are explored. Attitudes are related to RR scores but instructions are not. Finally, one study is presented comparing incarcerated felons with randomly selected job applicants, with none of the felons earning a "recommended" score. The evidence presented on faking is neither convincing nor complete.

Two studies of the factorial structure of the RR are reported, suggesting four separate factors, but there is no evidence given for the separate validity (or lack) of these factors. Despite these results, the manual suggests that "integrity" (not one of the four factors) is what is being measured, and two studies are presented in which RR results are compared to multivariate personality inventories, showing that high scorers on the RR are better adjusted than low scorers. Somehow the leap between integrity and adjustment is made without specifying their equivalence.

Several predictive and concurrent validity studies are reported, most utilizing a self-report criterion. The results indicate substantial correlations between RR scores and self-reported criteria of honesty (those who say they are "honest" on the test say they are "honest" outside of the test), but low to marginal correlations when the criterion is not a self-report.

Cunningham, Trucott, and Wong (1990) studied employed college students in an experimental situation where the students were overpaid for their participation in the study, and could retain or return the overpayment. Those who returned the overpayment scored higher on the RR ($r = .33$). However, scores on the RR also correlated significantly with Mach IV scores ($r = -.34$), with the tendency to impress others ($r = .55$), and with the tendency to deny undesirable qualities ($r = .38$). Note that all these coefficients are greater in magnitude than the criterion one.

In summary, the RR has an impressive potential—it has been administered to over 5 million individuals, has apparently no adverse impact on minorities, and addresses an important issue in the workplace. The available evidence, however, provides more questions than answers, and leaves much to be desired from a psychometric point of view.

REVIWER'S REFERENCE

Cunningham, M. R., Trucott, M., & Wong, D. T. (1990). *An experimental investigation of integrity: Testing the predictive validity of the Reid Report.* Unpublished manuscript.

Review of the Reid Report by KEVIN R. MURPHY, Professor of Psychology, Colorado State University, Fort Collins, CO:

The Reid Report is designed to predict acts of dishonesty in the workplace (e.g., employee theft) on the basis of respondents' attitudes toward theft and dishonesty and their admissions of past misdeeds. Various versions of the inventory have been in use for over 40 years; according to Brodsky (1978), at least 19 revisions were undertaken in the first 30 years of its existence. The current Reid Report includes an 80-item Integrity Attitude Inventory, together with up to three optional supplements designed to assess work history, drug and alcohol abuse, and antisocial history. The Attitude Inventory includes 80 items measuring punitiveness toward self and others and projections of one's own honesty and others' dishonesty (Cunningham & Ash, 1988). The supplements include a variety of items, including many that request direct admissions of previous misdeeds, job dismissals, etc. For example, the antisocial history

supplement inquires about committing and being convicted of a number of crimes and misdemeanors.

Each section of the test leads to one of four evaluations: (*a*) recommended, (*b*) qualified (i.e., recommended with qualifications), (*c*) not recommended, and (*d*) no opinion (e.g., if examinee does not complete the form). The overall evaluation resulting from the test is based on the least favorable recommendation from any part. Furthermore, evaluations of "qualified" on two or more parts lead to an overall evaluation of "not recommended." Test reports typically include the overall evaluation, evaluations on each part, and information about specific admissions made on each of the supplemental parts. Approximately 75% of those who complete the inventory receive evaluations of "recommended."

Percentile ranks are reported for the sections of the test on which an evaluation of "not recommended" is recorded. The examiner's manual reports normative data from a total sample of over 200,000 that links these percentile ranks to the probability of on-the-job theft. It is not clear how these probabilities were derived; given the evidence of differences in theft rates across occupations (Hollinger & Clark, 1983), it is not clear that these results could be generalized, even if we assume that they are approximately correct for at least some occupations.

Evidence of relatively high reliability (internal consistency and test-retest coefficients of appoximately .90 and .70, respectively) and of criterion-related validity, in terms of correlations with theft admissions, inventory shortfalls, and self-reports of time theft and substance abuse is reviewed in the manual. Given the fact the three supplements contain many questions that themselves call for these same admissions, these "validity" coefficients seem conceptually more similar to test-retest reliability coefficients than to independent demonstrations of the predictive power of the test. Nevertheless, they do provide some evidence to support the hypothesis that test scores are related to dishonest behavior.

Correlations between scores on the Reid Report and scores on several personality inventories (e.g., the Minnesota Multiphasic Personality Inventory [MMPI]) are presented as evidence of construct validity (Kochkin, 1987). Because no clear definition of the construct this test is designed to measure is ever presented, this type of evidence is hard to evaluate. It is useful to know that individuals who receive unfavorable recommendations on the Reid Report also show elevated scores on a number of personality and psychopathology scales, but until the construct is more clearly defined, it is difficult to sort supportive evidence from evidence *against* the construct validity of this measure.

In 1991, a task force of the American Psychological Association carried out an evaluation of integrity tests. Although the evaluation was on the whole more positive than negative, the use of categorical scoring systems in integrity testing (e.g., recommended vs. not recommended) was strongly criticized. The scoring system employed by the Reid Report presents a number of potentially serious problems, notably the use of the least favorable of the four possible evaluations as the determinant of the overall evaluation reported for each examinee. Although the test manual warns consumers not to use the Reid Report as the sole basis for hiring decisions, the fact that the test labels a person as "not recommended" if *any* of four scores falls below a cutting point that seems arbitrary does not seem likely to encourage the optimal use of information from the test.

On the whole, the Reid Report is representative of a growing class of tests that are used to make inferences about the trustworthiness of job applicants and incumbents. As the APA task force pointed out, this class of tests shoul d be evaluated according to the same standards as other psychological tests, in which case the Reid Report appears to have demonstrated more than adequate reliability, as well as some evidence (independent of admissions similar to those on the test itself) of criterion-related validity. The scoring system and normative data for the test are both far from optimal, but if the limitations of tests of this type (particularly those that report categorical scores) are kept firmly in mind, this test can provide a potentially useful component of a personnel selection program.

REVIEWER'S REFERENCES

Brodsky, S. L. (1978). [Review of the Reid Report]. In O. K. Buros (Ed.), *Eighth mental measurements yearbook* (pp. 1025-1026). Highland Park, NJ: Gryphon Press.
Hollinger, R. C., & Clark, J. P. (1983). *Theft by employees*. Lexington, MA: Lexington Books.
Kochkin, S. (1987). Personality correlates of a measure of honesty. *Journal of Business and Psychology, 1*, 236-247.
Cunningham, M. R., & Ash, P. (1988). The structure of honesty: Factor analysis of the Reid Report. *Journal of Business and Psychology, 3*, 54-66.
APA Task Force. (1991). *Questionnaires used in the prediction of trustworthiness in pre-employment selection decisions: An A.P.A. Task Force report*. Washington, DC: American Psychological Association.

[73]

Revised BRIGANCE™ Diagnostic Inventory of Early Development.

Purpose: Constructed to "determine the developmental or performance level of the infant or child."
Population: Birth to age 7.
Publication Dates: 1978–91.

Scores: 11 areas: Preambulatory Motor Skills and Behaviors, Gross-Motor Skills and Behaviors, Fine-Motor Skills and Behaviors, Self-Help Skills, Speech and Language Skills, General Knowledge and Comprehension, Social and Emotional Development, Readiness, Basic Reading Skills, Manuscript Writing, Basic Math.
Administration: Individual.
Price Data, 1993: $99 per manual with tests ('91, 298 pages); $19.90 per 10 record books; $189.90 per 100 record books; $9.90 per group record book; $39.95 per classroom testing kit.
Time: [15–20] minutes per child.
Comments: "Criterion-referenced."
Author: Albert H. Brigance.
Publisher: Curriculum Associates, Inc.
Cross References: See T4:2256 (3 references); for reviews of an earlier edition by Stephen J. Bagnato and Elliot L. Gory, see 9:164.

Review of the Revised BRIGANCE™ Diagnostic Inventory of Early Development by C. DALE CARPENTER, Professor of Special Education, Western Carolina University, Cullowhee, NC:

The Revised BRIGANCE Diagnostic Inventory of Early Development (Birth to 7 Years) (IED-R) is a 1991 revision of a 1978 instrument of the same name. The original edition was generally well received (Bagnato, 1985; Gory, 1985; Robinson & Kovacevich, 1985). Noted strengths were that the IED was developmental with norm-referenced and criterion-referenced qualities. It was easy to use and appropriate for normal and delayed children, and it had planning goals. Some weaknesses were a lack of psychometric information such as reliability and validity and lack of a section on social-emotional development. In summary, the IED was considered to be a practical, informal tool to inventory a wide range of skills and needed to be adapted to fit the needs of children with unique needs. The IED lacked supporting technical data.

The Revised BRIGANCE Diagnostic Inventory of Early Development retains most of the original version. Some tests have been omitted such as Ball Bouncing, Rhythm, and Wheel Toys from Gross Motor Skills and Behaviors. Some tests have fewer items, particularly in the section titled Preambulatory Motor Skills and Behaviors, and some have more items such as in the section titled Self-Help Skills. The IED-R, like the original, also has 11 sections, but it includes a new section called Social and Emotional Development. The IED-R combines two sections from the earlier edition, Pre-Speech and Speech and Language Skills, into one section called Speech and Language Skills.

The format for the IED-R is unchanged. It uses the same system of recording for multiple administrations. Each page on the Record Book of the IED-R has administration directions and an objective. Some pages are reproducible for consumable use; some are laminated.

New features exist. A kit of materials needed to administer the IED-R is available from the publisher although they are easy to assemble on one's own. The Class Record Book is particularly helpful to monitor up to 15 children and their skills. A new appendix of developmental skills is available for copying.

CRITIQUE. The changes from the original appear to be improvements. Most items eliminated in the revision were not essential. New items appear helpful. Perhaps that is because systematic efforts were undertaken to elicit feedback from users (A. H. Brigance, personal communication, October, 1991). Tests omitted in the revision do not weaken the instrument.

The addition of the section titled Social and Emotional Development was a response to a perceived weakness in the first edition. There are 122 items in three subsections. This reviewer thinks that these items could be reduced to yield a more efficient but still effective instrument. Perhaps user feedback will effect that change in a future revision.

Technical data to demonstrate reliability and validity which were lacking in the original are still lacking with the IED-R. The instrument relies on popular developmental scales and curriculum materials currently in use (Benner, 1992). Cautions about the rigidity of a certain item at a certain age are present. The lack of supporting psychometric data is a serious flaw. The utility of the instrument may depend on the validity of the reference sources used to develop the items and to place them developmentally.

SUMMARY. Users of the IED who were satisfied will find a more efficient instrument in the IED-R. The IED-R is easy to use with all of the features of the IED and more. A new section on Social and Emotional Development has been added to fill a need. Technical data are not available to support reliability and validity, although updated references have been used to select and sequence items. Although there is now more competition in this area than when the original version was published, the IED-R is a viable tool because of its flexibility and planning utility.

REVIEWER'S REFERENCES

Bagnato, S. J. (1985). [Review of the BRIGANCE Diagnostic Inventory of Early Development]. In. J. V. Mitchell, Jr., (Ed.), The ninth mental measurements yearbook (Vol. 1, pp. 219-220). Lincoln, NE: Buros Institute of Mental Measurements.
Gory, E. L. (1985). [Review of the BRIGANCE Diagnostic Inventory of Early Development]. In. J. V. Mitchell, Jr., (Ed.), The ninth mental measurements yearbook (Vol. 1, pp. 220-221). Lincoln, NE: Buros Institute of Mental Measurements.
Robinson, J. H., & Kovacevich, D. A. (1985). [Review of the BRIGANCE Inventories]. In D. J. Keyser & R. C. Sweetland (Eds.), Test critiques (Vol. III, pp. 79-98). Kansas City: Test Corporation of America.
Benner, S. M. (1992). Assessing young children with special needs: An ecological perspective. White Plains, NY: Longman.

Review of the Revised BRIGANCE™ Diagnostic Inventory of Early Development by DOUGLAS A. PENFIELD, Professor of Education, Graduate School of Education, Rutgers University, New Brunswick, NJ:

The Revised BRIGANCE Diagnostic Inventory of Early Development provides a process for assessing and tracking the developmental skills of children from birth to approximately 7 years of age. It is a norm- and criterion-referenced instrument designed to identify the strengths and weaknesses of the child through the use of skill assessment and a comprehensive record-keeping system. Identified strengths and weaknesses may subsequently be used for diagnostic purposes.

The Inventory is broken into 11 broad skill areas (see above Inventory description). Each broad skill area is further divided into a number of subareas which in turn are linked to basic skills and behaviors useful in assessing area and subarea mastery. For example, under the (G) Social and Emotional Development Skills area, the subareas are labelled (G-1) General Social and Emotional Development, (G-2) Play Skills and Behaviors, and (G-3) Work-Related Skills and Behaviors. The first seven broad skill areas represent skills that are developmental in nature, whereas the last four areas place a greater emphasis on cognitive behavior. Methods used to assess skills include (a) parent interviews, (b) observing the child, (c) asking the child to perform tasks, (d) engaging the child in conversation, and (e) teacher interviews. Examiners are encouraged to use their judgment in determining which skills to evaluate and how to best elicit a child's response. Extensive assessment guidelines are provided for each skill area.

There is an important link between the basic skills being evaluated and the approximate developmental age at which mastery is normally achieved. Skills are sequenced within a subarea according to developmental age. Special efforts have been taken to validate the skill sequencing. Given the chronological age of the child, examiners can use developmental age as an index for choosing an appropriate starting point within a skill subarea. Due to the extensiveness of the Inventory, it is not possible to administer the entire Inventory at one time. Examiners are advised to use their judgment in deciding which areas to evaluate in a single sitting.

The Inventory is contained in a seven-ring binder which is easily manipulated. When administering the Inventory, the examiner and child sit opposite each other with the Inventory placed between them. While the examiner reads the instructions, the child observes the visual material and responds to questions. Each broad skill area is broken down into overall goals and objectives, methods of assessment, assessment directions, required test materials, and the references used to validate the sequencing of skills. Questions are presented along with helpful hints for determining successful mastery. Illustrations and drawings are displayed in a clear, concise fashion.

Record keeping is enhanced by using the Developmental Record Book, an intact booklet which consists of an ordered listing of all basic skills and behaviors. Recommended coding for each skill is (a) not assessed, (b) assessed and set as an objective, (c) introduced but not achieved, and (d) skill has been achieved. Examiners are encouraged to modify the coding to meet their individual needs. Instructions for administering the questions are well documented and succinct. One of the strengths of the Inventory is that little specialized training is required of the examiner. A color-coding system has been developed to highlight the record-keeping and tracking process.

It appears that great care has been taken in selecting and arranging the skills to be evaluated. Even though the skills presented in this Inventory represent only a subset of the potential pool of behaviors that could be evaluated within the birth to age 7 range, they do constitute a broad cross section of the behaviors and skills associated with early childhood development. Each basic skill is regarded as a distinct entity, thus there is no cumulative score associated with a skill area or subarea. It is left to the discretion of the examiner to determine when a sufficient number of questions have been answered correctly to justify area or subarea mastery. No reliability or validity coefficients are presented, however, based on the scope of skills assessed by the Inventory, I am comfortable with the content coverage. Assuming that an examiner believes mastery of the skills in this instrument is indicative of positive growth, the Revised BRIGANCE Diagnostic Inventory of Early Development provides a comprehensive method for identifying the strengths and weaknesses of a child's development up to the age of 7.

[74]

Revised Denver Prescreening Developmental Questionnaire.

Purpose: "To facilitate earlier identification of children whose development may be delayed."
Population: Ages 0–9 months, 9–24 months, 2–4 years, 4–6 years.
Publication Dates: 1975–86.
Acronym: R-PDQ.
Scores: Item scores only.
Administration: Individual.
Levels, 4: Ages 0–9 months, 9–24 months, 2–4 years, 4–6 years.
Manual: No manual.
Price Data, 1994: $12 per 100 questionnaires (specify level).
Time: Administration time not reported.
Comments: Ratings by parents.
Author: William K. Frankenburg.
Publisher: Denver Developmental Materials, Inc.

Review of the Revised Denver Prescreening Developmental Questionnaire by STEPHEN N. AXFORD, School Psychologist, Academy District Twenty, Colorado Springs, CO and Counseling Department Chair, University of Phoenix-Colorado Campus, Aurora, CO:

The Revised Denver Prescreening Developmental Questionnaire (R-PDQ) is specific in purpose and finite in scope. According to its authors, the R-PDQ is the "first step" in a "two-step screening process" (Frankenburg, Fandal, & Thornton, 1987). Citing the American Academy of Pediatrics' "Guideline for Child Health Maintenance," the authors note the initial phase of a developmental (i.e., pediatric) assessment includes parent report in documenting the child's developmental progress, and identification of candidates in need of more in-depth objective assessment. The "second step" thus involves use of the Denver Developmental Screening Test (DDST; 9:311), as conceptualized by the authors.

The R-PDQ is essentially a taxonomic parent survey of child development, similar to the Gesell Child Developmental Age Scale (T4:1034) with regard to content but less comprehensive, as would be expected of a screening instrument designed for determining areas of needed additional assessment. Typically, this type of screening is conducted informally. The R-PDQ affords a simple systematic procedure for gathering developmental screening information. The revision involved extending the age range to include ages birth to 6 years, changing the item-response format (from "yes/no/no opportunity" to "yes/no"), and changing the structure of the test to "make it easier . . . to compare a child's perform-ance with DDST norms" (p. 653; Frankenburg et al., 1987). Regarding the change in answer format, the test developers provide the following rationale:

> The screen's purpose is to determine if a child can or cannot do a task, not to answer *why* a child is unable to do a task (e.g., no opportunity). (p. 655, Frankenburg et al., 1987)

Given the particular purpose of the R-PDQ (i.e., identifying candidates for further assessment), this rationale is legitimate, despite the psychometric ad-vantages of a broader range of response choices.

The R-PDQ does not provide standard scores. Instead, data are reported in terms of "delays" and normalcy. A "delay" is defined as "any item passed by 90% of children at a younger age . . . than the child being screened" (Information Sheet). The authors recommend that if a child has one delay, he/she should be reevaluated with the R-PDQ following a 1-month waiting period, whereupon if the delay continues to manifest, follow-up testing with the DDST should be conducted. If two or more delays are identified, then a DDST screening should be initiated as soon as possible, according to the authors. This procedure, fairly conservative in approach (likely erring on the side of caution), seems satisfac-tory for the purposes of prediagnostic screening, as-suming the standardization sample is reasonably rep-resentative of the general population (an area of needed additional research).

Regarding materials, it is apparent that the R-PDQ developers were careful in insuring readability, meaningful sequence, and ease of scoring. The mate-rials are well organized and should be easy to use for parents and specialists alike. In addition, regarding content, the R-PDQ has considerable face validity. It is noteworthy that the authors contacted 12 pedia-tricians to garner critical feedback before revising the PDQ.

In terms of technical merit, research addressing the R-PDQ's validity and reliability is limited. The authors note their research on the R-PDQ has not focused on validity issues, responding instead to "cli-nician's concerns" pertaining to administration and interpretation. Regardless, it seems appropriate that follow-up research be conducted to ascertain the va-lidity of the revised form. Nevertheless, in identifying concordance for delayed subjects, a hit rate of 96% was obtained between the R-PDQ and DDST re-sults, involving 193 children, 73 of whom had one or more delays identified by the R-PDQ. This lends credibility to the R-PDQ as an effective prescreening instrument for developmental delays.

Regarding reliability, test-retest data collected on 51 children revealed 94% agreement over a 1-week interval. In a separate study involving 71 children, 83% agreement was obtained between teacher and parent ratings, again supporting the reliability of the R-PDQ.

The R-PDQ standardization sample consisted of 1,434 Denver area children recruited from six private pediatric offices ($n = 1,012$), eight urban day care centers ($n = 227$), the University Outpatient Clinic ($n = 109$), and one Head Start center ($n = 86$). Of course, in terms of demographic representation and because of selective as opposed to random sam-pling, it is questionable as to whether interpretive data (i.e., range of scores considered "normal") can be generalized to special populations (i.e., various geographic regions, SES groups, etc.). Regarding SES, however, the authors cite research indicating the standardization results are, indeed, generalizable across SES groups. Nevertheless, ultimately it would be best if normative data representative of national demographics were compiled. Also, if this should occur, it may be useful to develop norms for specific populations (e.g., sex, SES, cultural groups, handi-capped populations, etc.).

As a "prescreening" instrument designed to assess developmental progress for the purpose of determin-ing need for additional assessment, the R-PDQ is satisfactory. It is sufficient in scope, quite readable, very easy to score, economical, and provides reason-able guidelines for interpretation and use. In addi-tion, although additional validation and standardiza-tion is recommended, the R-PDQ appears appropriate for its intended use.

REVIEWER'S REFERENCE

Frankenburg, W. K., Fandal, A. W., & Thornton, S. M. (1987). Revision of Denver Prescreening Developmental Questionnaire. *The Journal of Pediatrics, 110*(4), 653-657.

Review of the Revised Denver Prescreening Develop-mental Questionnaire by WILLIAM B. MICHAEL, Professor of Education and Psychology, University of Southern California, Los Angeles, CA:

Four forms of the Revised Denver Prescreening Developmental Questionnaire (R-PDQ) are in-tended to provide a simplified monitoring and screen-ing of children's development in four domains re-ferred to as Personal Social (PS), Fine Motor-Adaptive (FMA), Language (L), and Gross Motor (GM). These four forms contain items that cover age spans from zero to 9 months (30 items), 9 to 24 months (33 items), 2 to 4 years (25 items), and 4 to 6 years (24 items). Each item portrays an activity of the child to which the observer (typically a parent, teacher, or health care professional) responds with a "yes" or "no" answer.

There is no manual for the four forms. A two-page set of instructions for administration of the scales and for the interpretation of the scores is available.

Apparently, the only source of information regarding the research and field testing underlying the preparation of the R-PDQ appears in an article by Frankenburg, Fandal, and Thornton (1987). Only minimal data are presented regarding validity and reliability issues. In addition, no work has been done to develop scoring norms for the separate functions represented on the test. Before such work would be appropriate, factor analyses studies would be needed.

All instruments that rely on the responses and observations of others are vulnerable to the unreliability of such reports. This test is not immune from this potential source of error. Minimally, there should be a certain amount of standardized training for persons who serve as observers, examiners, or evaluators.

Although the R-PDQ has considerable face validity and intuitive appeal, the lack of adequate instructions for its administration and interpretation, as well as the absence of reliability, validity, and comprehensive normative data, suggests the R-PDQ be used most cautiously, primarily as an experimental or exploratory scale in research. The authors should carry out the necessary psychometric analyses so that this promising-looking scale can be employed in an appropriate and valid manner.

REVIEWER'S REFERENCE

Frankenburg, W. K., Fandal, A. W., & Thornton, S. M. (1987). Revision of Denver Prescreening Developmental Questionnaire. *The Journal of Pediatrics, 110*(4), 653-657.

[75]

Revised Evaluating Acquired Skills in Communication.

Purpose: Constructed to assess communication skills in the areas of semantics, syntax, morphology, and pragmatics.

Population: Children 3 months to 8 years with severe language impairments.

Publication Dates: 1984–91.

Acronym: EASIC.

Scores: Ratings in 10 areas: Labels/Nouns and Pronouns, Verbs and Action Commands, Comprehension of Three-Word Phrases, Affirmation and Negation, Prepositional Location Commands, Comprehension of Singular and Plural, Adjectives and Attributes, Money Concepts, Categorization and Association, Interrogatives.

Administration: Individual.

Price Data, 1994: $79 per complete kit including manual ('91, 54 pages).

Time: Administration time not reported.

Author: Anita Marcott Riley.

Publisher: Communication Skill Builders.

Cross Reference: For reviews by Barry W. Jones and Robert E. Owens, Jr. of an earlier edition, see 10:109.

Review of the Revised Evaluating Acquired Skills in Communication by WILLIAM O. HAYNES, Professor of Communication Disorders, Auburn University, Auburn, AL:

The Revised Evaluating Acquired Skills in Communication (EASIC) is an updated version of the original instrument published in 1984. The inventory is organized in five levels. The first level (Pre-Language Level) deals with prelanguage skills of response to sensory stimulation, object relations, means-end causality, motor imitation, matching, rejection, negation, affirmation, comprehension/use of communicative gestures, social interaction, and nonverbal communicative functions. The second level (Receptive Level I) includes comprehension of nouns, verbs, two-word phrases, prepositions, classification and categorization, adjectives and attributes, and interrogatives. The third level (Expressive Level I) includes many of the same areas as Receptive Level I. Receptive Level II includes nouns/pronouns, verbs, three-word phrases, affirmation, negation, prepositions, singular/plural adjectives, money concepts, categorization, and interrogatives. The Expressive Level II includes all of the Receptive Level II areas plus social interaction, sequencing, sentence structure, and pragmatic analysis. The EASIC provides Individualized Educational Plan (IEP) goals related to the assessment levels and suggested treatment procedures for accomplishing these objectives. In the assessment portion, each student's responses are evaluated qualitatively using six performance categories: spontaneous, cued (using a sign, verbalization, gesture, phonetic cue or open-ended sentence), imitated, manipulated, no response, and wrong. The scoring system depicts whether skills are accomplished, emerging, or not developed.

Reviews of the 1984 version of the EASIC (MMY10:109) criticized the instrument on several grounds. First, the EASIC did not provide thorough guidelines for the examiner to use in selecting the initial level of assessment. It appears the appropriate level could be chosen only after the clinician had significant familiarity with the student or after a rather thorough assessment of abilities had already been accomplished. The revised version of the EA-SIC has not provided any additional guidelines for placement of a student on assessment levels and, therefore, the criticism regarding placing students at a particular level remains a valid concern.

A second complaint was the total absence of psychometric data in support of the reliability and validity of the instrument. Attention to psychometric considerations, even in cases of non-norm-referenced tests, is a basic requirement for any test instrument. It is not optional. The issue of interjudge reliability alone is critical.

Another prior concern about the 1984 version of the EASIC was a lack of bibliographic support for the items on the test. The current version contains a list of 33 references; however, they are never specifically referred to in the manual. The only reference to the bibliography is on page 3 where the manual authors state "The age ranges were compiled from numerous sources containing normative and developmental data (see Bibliography)" (p. 3). This in no way justifies the inclusion or particular ordering of items on the instrument.

An additional criticism of the earlier version of the instrument was that little attention was paid to the areas of semantic relations and communicative functions. The revised EASIC does have a small section on communicative intents and does mention semantic relations in the two- and three-word utterance sections of the Receptive/Expressive Levels I and II. One prior review of the test lamented the EASIC had no provision for coding the student's response mode (e.g., verbal, gestural, signed, augmentative) especially because the instrument purports to be ideally used with significantly involved students (e.g., mentally retarded, autistic). These differing response modes are mentioned in the goals sections of each level (e.g., "The student will verbalize, sign, or use an alternative or augmentative communication system to express the size adjectives" [p. 29]) in the current version of the EASIC.

Finally, the picture stimuli are black and white and may be too abstract for some of the students likely to be tested. This has not changed since the earlier version.

The manual does not provide any case examples or illustrations of how scoring is accomplished and interpreted. Such information would be helpful to novice administrators of the test. The EASIC provides only one page of instructions on administering the tasks included in the instrument. There are no verbatim instructions to read to the student and not enough detail on exactly how to go through the tasks on each level.

In its present form, the EASIC fails to provide essential information regarding a rationale for inclusion of and ordering of items, psychometric adequacy, and detailed instructions for administration and scoring. Overall, the author has not responded to prior reviews of the instrument. Many of the same weaknesses remain in the revised version. The present reviewer would not recommend the EASIC for widespread use in assessment of severely involved students until such time as more research is done to support its reliability and validity.

Review of the Revised Evaluating Acquired Skills in Communication by JOHN H. KRANZLER, Assistant Professor of Education, University of Florida, Gainesville, FL:

The Revised Evaluating Acquired Skills in Communication (R-EASIC) is an individually administered communication skills inventory for children between the ages of 3 months to 8 years with severe language impairments. The R-EASIC was originally developed through work with 200 autistic individuals between the ages of 2 and 26 years. No information regarding their sex, race, ethnicity, or developmental level is reported, however. The test author states that the R-EASIC "provides examiners with a systematic tool for assessing a student's communication skills, a simple format for recording the student's performance, and a correlating means for translating that [*sic*] assessment data into an Individual Education Plan" (manual, p. 1).

MATERIALS. Materials provided for the R-EASIC include stimulus booklets that specify the skill assessed, instructions, and stimulus materials needed for each item. Skill profile sheets are included to summarize performance. They can be used to record the results of as many as five administrations of the R-EASIC. Also provided are a stimulus picture book and supplemental picture cards, each of which consists of black-and-white line drawings of isolated objects or actions. The stimuli in the picture book are presented in a multiple-choice format, typically with three pictures per page, and responses can be either by pointing or by uttering single word responses. The supplemental picture cards can be arranged to measure such functions as matching, sorting, and sequencing. A set of index cards with behavioral objectives (correlating to each inventory item) is included for use in instructional planning. In addition to these materials, administration of the R-EASIC requires that the examiner supply at least 50 additional stimulus items. Fortunately, many of these objects are common to most school classrooms.

TEST DESCRIPTION. The Informal Communication Skills Inventories that compose the R-EASIC are divided into five levels: Pre-Language, Receptive Level I, Expressive Level I, Receptive Level II, and Expressive Level II. The Pre-Language Level measures skills that are prerequisite to meaningful speech. According to the author, this level is primarily used to assess children at Piaget's "Sensory Motor Substage V" (p. 2). The Receptive and Expressive Level I inventories assess emerging comprehension and expression skills. The Level II inventories measure more complex semantic, pragmatic, morphologic, and syntactic receptive and expressive language skills. The items presented in the Informal Communication Skills Inventories are arranged according to skill clusters. There are 9 to 12 of these clusters within each level. Each skill cluster is composed of 1 to 10 items that are arranged according to difficulty (from easy to hard). Information is not presented regarding the procedures used in either test development or item selection; nor is the theoretical rationale for placement of the items at Level I and Level II discussed.

Responses on the R-EASIC are evaluated "qualitatively," that is, in terms of six performance categories. These categories are: spontaneous, cued, imitated, manipulated, no response (or noncompliant), and wrong. Based on the number of responses in each category, the skill clusters are judged to be either "accomplished," "emerging," or "not yet developed." Unfortunately, justification for these scoring criteria is not presented. Behavioral goals and objectives can be selected for instruction of the skills that are judged to be emerging. The author states these behavioral goals and objectives "must be functional and integrated into the student's daily routine" (p. 3). Nevertheless, the majority of them appear to require the drill of isolated communication skills.

A "developmental age chart" is provided to show the age range at which each skill is normally acquired. The test author states that these "age ranges were compiled from numerous sources containing normative and developmental data" (p. 3). These sources are listed in a bibliography. The age ranges presented in this chart are rather general estimates of development, however, and should not be used for diagnostic purposes. It is also important to note that the R-EASIC has not been standardized or normed. No other summary scores, such as standard scores or percentile ranks, are available.

TEST CRITIQUE. Guidelines provided in the R-EASIC manual for administration and scoring are minimal. Even the starting and stopping rules are ultimately left to clinical judgment. It also appears the items on the R-EASIC may be administered in any order and over any number of test sessions. In spite of the fact that some additional instructions are presented for assessing autistic children, the scoring of many items may be highly subjective. In addition, the black-and-white line drawings may be too abstract for some children with severe developmental delays or autism or both. Finally, and most importantly, no information at all regarding the reliability and validity of the R-EASIC is reported.

SUMMARY. The R-EASIC is an individually administered communication skills inventory for young children with severe language impairments. No information regarding the procedures used in test construction or item selection is presented; nor is there any information pertaining to the test's reliability and validity. Although a chart showing the age ranges at which each skill is normally acquired is provided, these age ranges are rough estimates of development and should not be used for diagnosis. Finally, the behavioral goals and objectives that accompany the R-EASIC tend to focus on the drilling of isolated communication skills and not on the more functional aspects of communication.

[76]

Safran Student's Interest Inventory, Third Edition.
Purpose: Developed to identify occupational interests.
Population: Grades 5–9, 9–12.
Publication Dates: 1960–85.
Scores, 7: Economic, Technical, Outdoor, Service, Humane, Artistic, Scientific.
Administration: Group.
Levels, 2: One, Two.
Price Data, 1994: $41.95 per 35 test booklets (select level); $25.45 per student's manual ('85, 8 pages); $22.45 per counsellor's manual ('85, 39 pages); $17.25 per examination kit.
Time: Administration time not reported.
Comments: Self-administered.
Authors: Carl Safran, Douglas W. Feltham, and Edgar N. Wright.
Publisher: Nelson Canada [Canada].
Cross References: For a review by Thomas T. Frantz of an earlier edition, see 7:1035; see also 6:1069 (1 reference).

Review of the Safran Student's Interest Inventory, Third Edition by ALBERT M. BUGAJ, Associate Professor of Psychology, University of Wisconsin–Marinette, Marinette, WI:

The Safran Student's Interest Inventory (SSII) was developed in Canada for use in determining the vocational interests of Canadian students. Previously for high school students, the third edition is also available in a version said to be suitable for grades 5 through 9. As a standard test the SSII is considerably lacking. Although it may provoke thought about career interests, its ability to do so in a valid and reliable manner must be questioned.

The SSII is based on an ipsative approach. Students' interests in an occupational area are compared with interest in each of six other areas, so their "highest raw score in an area indicates their greatest interest at a given time" (p. 6). A student completing the SSII can thus determine the strength of his or her own interest in any of seven areas, as compared to the other areas.

The manual indicates that a "powerful and unique feature" (p. 3) of the inventory is the method used to determine the consistency of the testees' responses. This involves arranging seven activities (one from each interest area examined) in pairs on each of the eight pages of the test. Each item is paired once with every other item. The manual authors assert, "if the student has been consistent, one item will have been chosen over all others (six choices), one over all but one (five choices), etc., to one that has been chosen over no others" (p. 39). If an item is chosen twice on a page, the student has been inconsistent. Given items numbered 1, 2, and 3, for example, an inconsistent testee might choose 1 over 2, 2 over 3, and 3 over 1, a logical impossibility. The manual stresses that approximately one-third of the inventories completed cannot be considered valid on the basis of the consistency check.

Before administrating the SSII, the manual authors suggest preparing the students with included background material. This curriculum is theoretically interesting and is one of the strongest points of the SSII.

Also commendable is the inclusion in the manual of lists of selected occupations found in each interest area examined by the test, and a second list examining pairs of interest areas. These occupational areas are further cross-referenced to other sources of information (the *Canadian Classification and Dictionary of Occupations*, and the Student Guidance Information System).

Despite these strengths of the manual, the test itself is questionable. A primary weakness is the small number of items used in deriving the scores for the seven interest areas examined, a stricture resulting from the consistency check. Although the complete test consists of 168 items, a mere 56 different statements are used, resulting in seven items per scale, each item being related to a different occupation.

Although the authors attempt to defend using such a small sampling of items by saying that activities, not occupations, are the focus of the test, one must question whether seven items per scale is sufficient. One hundred forty-two occupations, often involving a wide range of activities *in* an area are listed in the manual. The Economic area, for example, includes the occupations of lawyer, secretary, banker, and computer analyst, along with 17 others.

Although there may be a rationale for grouping the occupations into sets in occupational handbooks, no empirical basis for organizing them in such a way for standardized testing is apparent. This issue is related to the validity of the test itself, reported in the current manual using data collected with the first (1960) and second (1969) edition of the SSII. Apparently no data using the current edition have been collected, and the data from the earlier studies are sometimes presented in a slipshod manner.

Convergent validity was determined by administering the first edition of the SSII and the Kuder Preference Record to ninth graders. Correlations between scales on the tests ranged from a low of .20 in a first study to a high of .77 in a second. However, the first edition of the SSII contained 35 (not the current 56) items, so comparisons to the first edition cannot be made with certainty.

An attempt at assessing the criterion-related validity of the second edition of the SSII is also reported. Unfortunately, the authors chose to use as subjects "young adults" majoring in four areas at a polytechnic institute and a college, instead of sampling the population for which the second edition was designed. Of the 264 students tested, 31% provided inconsistent forms, which could not be used in the analysis.

The results of the analysis are poorly reported. No breakdown of how many subjects produced "usable" data in each major is reported. Although the authors report the results indicated the students' strongest interest areas corresponded with their chosen major, no statistical data are provided. In short, the validity of the second edition of the SSII is doubtful, and that of the present version is untested.

The reliability of the SSII is equally questionable. In this case, the data reported are based on the brief 1960 version. Based on a sample of high school students, the test-retest reliability of the version was high (.92), although the time between administrations is not reported. Kuder-Richardson reliability was also high. Like the validity data, however, the usefulness of such "old data" based on a previous version of the test is doubtful.

Thus far, all comments regarding technical data have been aimed toward Level II of the SSII, for use with grades 8 through 12. Nothing is reported regarding the reliability and validity of Level I, designed for grades 5 through 9. Ostensibly written at a lower reading level, no test of this assumption is reported, nor are data provided regarding its suitability for students in remedial and special education (a claim made in the publisher's advertisement).

The conception behind the SSII, most notably the consistency check, is interesting. However, too many questions remain about the test to recommend its use. The high number of inconsistently completed forms (about one-third of those administered) seems to result in an overly expensive test. The reliability and validity of the second edition were questionable, and this issue is even more true of the current edition. The low number of items used, and their method of selection, seem indefensible. Rather than select a small number of items to keep administration time brief (a strength, according to the manual), a larger number of items and more thorough testing of validity and reliability might result in a superior test. The SSII might promote discussion between a counselor and a student, but the Strong Interest Inventory (88), the Kuder Occupational Interest Survey (T4:1375), or the Jackson Vocational Interest Survey (T4:1297) should provide a more accurate assessment of interests in guiding students in making career decisions.

Review of the Safran Student's Interest Inventory, Third Edition by CAROLINE MANUELE-ADKINS, Professor, Department of Educational Foundations and Counseling Programs, Hunter College, City University of New York, New York, NY:

The main objective of the Safran Student's Interest Inventory (SSII) is to initiate student's "vocational thinking." To do this students are asked to select their preferred career interests, provide self-ratings of ability in four areas (Academic, Mechanical, Social, and Clerical), and indicate which school subjects they like best and least. The SSII was developed in Canada and is primarily designed for Canadian students. This third edition is tied directly to the *Canadian Classification and Dictionary of Occupations* (CCDO) and the Student Guidance Information Service (SGIS). The third edition also provides two versions of the instrument: Level I (grades 5–9) and Level II (grades 9–12). This edition reflects a concern for including more current occupations and removing any bias against females.

Both levels of the SSII ask students to make forced-choice decisions about a set of preferred activities. This results in raw score totals for seven different interest areas: Economic, Technical, Outdoor, Service, Humane, Artistic, and Scientific. The items are simply stated (e.g., "Fix Airplanes or Design Jewelry" [Level I]; "Teaching Children at School or Growing and Harvesting Crops" [Level II]). They are repeated many times, in paired comparisons, for the purpose of providing a "consistency check." This technique is used to identify consistent and inconsistent interest patterns and is used to determine the validity of an individual's profile. Although this appears to be a measure of consistency, the constant repetition of items produces an inventory that respondents might find boring and uninteresting. The self-ratings of ability portion of the inventory asks respondents to compare themselves to other people and rate their ability in quartiles. This presents several problems in that there is no way of knowing to whom they are comparing themselves or what their definition of ability is. The school subjects interests section is fairly straightforward in that students are provided with a list of subjects and asked to indicate, on a continuum, which ones they like best and least.

Items and scales for the SSII were, according to the manual, selected by first defining them and then checking them against the *Dictionary of Occupational Titles* and the Minnesota Occupational Rating Scale. The criteria for defining the items and selecting them is unclear and no information is provided about item analyses, item scale correlations, or theoretical reasons for their inclusion. Scales for the inventory are also not defined so that the user is left to guess what Economic, Technical, Outdoor, Service, etc., really mean. Given the absence of these definitions the selection of occupations related to these areas or scales (used for students' further exploration) is questionable. It is difficult to ascertain how appropriate they are as examples of each occupational area.

Validity studies for the SSII include determining whether or not the inventory differentiated between students who were in Nursing, Electrical, Creative Arts, or Business Administration courses. According to the manual the results showed that "the test did differentiate among the programs" (p. 39) but there was also considerable overlap of interests in the various areas. The manual provided no technical data for these statements so it is difficult to determine the extent to which the results can be perceived as evidence for the validity of the measure. Two additional validity studies are provided that examine the relationship between the SSII and the Kuder Preference Record. The correlations (calculated on male only samples) range from .20 to .70 for one sample and .51 to .85 for another. The validity studies cited are all from 1960 and 1969. Apparently no further studies have been conducted. The absence of specific validity data, the scarcity of studies, and the lack of recent studies on the current version are important indicators that the user needs to question the validity of this measure.

Reliability data are also provided for earlier versions of the SSII but not for the current one. Internal reliability analyses ranged from .85 to .89. Test-retest reliability for 104 high school students is reported as a median of .92. These are robust reliability figures but we do not know what the relationship is between prior and current versions.

Normative data are also not provided for this version. The manual states that "norms were published for the 1969 edition as counsellors found them helpful in determining relative performance. After seven years of use in Canadian schools, it was found that the ipsative approach was a better method" (p. 39). The author here is suggesting that normative data are not particularly useful and advocates an approach whereby students' interests should be interpreted as "personal interests" and need not be compared to the interests of others. This information is rather confusing to interpret because the author tells us that counselors found the normative data useful. It is important to note that given the lack of normative data the SSII should not be used for research purposes and is recommended only for individual counseling sessions.

To assist counselors with interpreting individual scores on the SSII, examples of student profiles are provided with suggestions to the counselor about the meaning of scores and about what the students' next steps in their exploration should be. These examples are brief but helpful. An interesting aspect is the lesson plans for six sessions that demonstrate how one could conduct group activities to introduce students to the concepts of interests and abilities, administration, interpretation, the inventory, career exploration, and application. This context for preparation and knowledge is frequently ignored by test developers.

In summary, the SSII has some major test development areas that have been ignored. It appears to have no theoretical basis for its construction and no evidence is provided for how items were defined, selected, or grouped for the seven scales. Minimal data in support of validity and reliability are provided but these studies refer to earlier versions. Normative data are also absent. Although the Inventory is easy to read and understand, students, when confronted with so many repetitive items, may become disengaged and fail to respond seriously. There are many interest inventories that are superior to the SSII. These include the Self-Directed Search (for a simple assessment; T4:2414), the Vocational Preference Inventory (T4:1910), versions of the Kuder (47, T4:1375, T4:1376) and the Strong Interest Inventory (88). Although these inventories were not developed in Canada, they would provide results the user could use with more confidence.

[77]

Sales Personality Questionnaire.

Purpose: Developed to assess personality characteristics necessary for sales success.
Population: Sales applicants.
Publication Dates: 1987–90.
Acronym: SPQ.
Scores, 12: Interpersonal (Confidence, Empathy, Persuasive), Administration (Systematic, Conscientious, Forward Planning), Opportunities (Creative, Observant), Energies (Relaxed, Resilient, Results Oriented), Social Desirability.
Administration: Group.
Price Data, 1992: $27.50 per questionnaire booklet; $7.25 per answer sheet with prepaid mail-in Bureau scoring; $6.25 per answer sheet for on-site Optic Scan scoring or handscoring; $31.50 per manual and user's guide ('90, 60 pages); $30 per sample set.
Time: (20–30) minutes.
Author: Saville & Holdsworth Ltd.
Publisher: Saville & Holdsworth Ltd USA, Inc.

Review of the Sales Personality Questionnaire by WAYNE J. CAMARA, Director of Scientific Affairs, American Psychological Association, Washington, DC:

The Sales Personality Questionnaire (SPQ) was developed in the United Kingdom in an attempt to identify the attributes required for success as agents for an insurance company. Five overall constructs, with a total of 12 dimensions, were identified from a job analysis and comprise the scales for the SPQ. The SPQ contains 108 items that can be completed in 20–30 minutes. Applicants or job incumbents are asked to read each item or statement and indicate the degree to which they agree or disagree with each, using a 5-point Likert scale. This instrument is part of the Selling Skills Series (SSS), which includes two aptitude tests, "Using Written Information" and "Reasoning with Data." Together, the publishers note, these instruments have been developed to measure "only skills that are specifically relevant to selling" (manual, p. 1).

The test is designed to measure personality characteristics associated with successful performance in a range of sales occupations. The five constructs and 12 scales are: Interpersonal (Confidence, Empathy, Persuasive), Administration (Systematic, Conscientious, Forward Planning), Opportunities (Creative, Observant), Energies (Relaxed, Resilient, Results Oriented), and Social Desirability (Social Desirability).

Test-retest reliability coefficients are reported for the 12 scales from a sample of 113 college students. Retesting of college students varied from 2 to 4 weeks, producing coefficients that ranged from .73 to .88. Internal consistency (Cronbach's coefficient alpha) ranged from .55 to .82 with the combined normative group of 245 sales staff and sales trainees. In a few cases, the internal consistency is too low to have confidence in the dimension measured. No descriptive data are available on the sample of college students, and what little information is reported on the combined normative sample is contradictory. Specifically, the combined normative sample ($n = 245$) is defined as "all persons in the United States who have taken the SPQ as of August, 1990" (manual, p. 51). Yet, breakouts by race and gender, which each include an unknown category, result in 234 cases and 300 cases, respectively. Interrelationships between the various scales are in some cases higher than would be desirable for independence of measures, yet they make intuitive sense. The combined normative group ($n = 245$) results from two samples, 187 sales manager trainees for a national shoe store chain and 58 sales representatives for manufacturing products. Separate norms are provided for these groups, yet the omission of descriptive information on jobs and samples would seem to prevent the user from selecting the most appropriate norm group.

The greatest weakness of the SPQ is the omission of any attempt to define or identify an underlying structure for the five constructs and 12 scales. The resulting scales were developed solely from a job analysis of sales jobs in one organization. Scales have not been confirmed with factor analytic techniques and there has been no attempt to examine relationships with other personality instruments that include similar scales. One available study ($n = 57$) does illustrate that a couple of scales from the SPQ have moderate correlations with three of the seven scales from the Sales Aptitude Test. However, intercorrelations with similar scales on well-established personality tests are required. The manual authors note that test respondents should be honest and that the questionnaire contains certain distortion or consistency checks. Yet, there is no mention of such items or any type of validity scale anywhere else in the materials or scoring profile.

In addition to content validity evidence from the initial job analysis, the publisher provides brief summaries of three criterion-related validity studies using the SPQ. These studies use supervisory ratings and rankings as criterion measures of job performance and provide mixed and often inconsistent results. For example, when ratings of selling skills are used as a criterion measure one study reports moderate, but significant, correlations with the Observant and Relaxed scales. Another study found manager's ratings of selling skills related to the Persuasive and Results-Oriented scales. In one study of sales assistants only 1 of the 12 scales was moderately correlated to actual individual sales ($r = .25$). Although the test does appear to identify important attributes for sales success and possesses a high degree of face validity, additional scientific evidence of validity with larger samples is required. Available studies are not described adequately and prevent potential users from determining if the positions and samples used would generalize to their situations.

The manual does not comply with the *Standards for Educational and Psychological Testing* (AERA, APA, & NCME, 1985) in providing adequate information on the samples used in developing norm tables and in the validation studies, criterion measures, evidence of differential prediction, the content domain of jobs included in job analyses, and appropriate uses of each test.

The test publisher provides little data that indicate if group differences exist across gender, race, or ethnic groups. Instead, they note that research is underway. The publisher does provide appropriate cautions that test users not rely on the test solely for employment decisions and the need to monitor test use.

The test materials are of sufficient quality. The 66-page test manual is adequate in describing administration and scoring procedures. Chapters on norms, validity, reliability, and profiling provide appropriate explanations of these technical measurement concepts. However, the manual is insufficient for determining how to actually use this instrument in employment settings. The manual also contains a number of typographical errors, which suggest that insufficient effort has been made to develop a quality product.

The SPQ can be administered in three ways: a booklet/answer sheet, booklet/pocket computer medium, or IBM compatible computer administration. Booklet/answer sheet administration requires bureau scoring by the publisher or machine scoring on location. Hand scoring is not available.

Until much more extensive psychometric research is conducted, extreme caution should be exercised when using this instrument in making decisions about individuals. At present, the SPQ does not have adequate evidence to support its use as an off-the-shelf test and should be used only when experts in psychometrics and employment testing are available to conduct appropriate job analyses, and normative and validation studies for an organization. Test users should consider specific scales contained within a number of broad-based personality tests, such as the Hogan Personality Inventory (T4:1169), the Hogan Personnel Selection Series (11:163), the California Psychological Inventory (T4:361), and the Personality Research Form (T4:2000), which may be relevant to certain characteristics required for sales positions. Users should also consider the Sales Professional Assessment Inventory.

REVIEWER'S REFERENCE

American Educational Research Association, American Psychological Association, & National Council on Measurement in Education. (1985). *Standards for educational and psychological testing.* Washington, DC: American Psychological Association, Inc.

Review of the Sales Personality Questionnaire by MI-CHAEL J. ROSZKOWSKI, Director of Marketing Research and Associate Professor of Psychology, The American College, Bryn Mawr, PA:

Information about the Sales Personality Questionnaire (SPQ) is contained in a 66-page Manual & User's Guide, consisting of 10 chapters and two technical appendices. The manual presents detailed instructions about how to administer the questionnaire (including such details as to thank the person for participating). This spiral-bound booklet, which is under a corporate authorship (Saville & Holdsworth, Ltd.), discusses not only the SPQ but also provides a brief overview of fundamental psychometric issues.

Together with two aptitude tests, the SPQ constitutes a battery of tests known as the Selling Skills Series (SSS). The aptitude and the personality tests can be administered independently, but the authors recommend that the tests be used jointly in identifying a person's potential to succeed in a selling role. The 108 items constituting the SPQ are grouped into 12 domains: Confidence, Empathy, Persuasive, Systematic, Conscientious, Forward Planning, Creative, Observant, Relaxed, Resilient, Results Oriented, and Social Desirability. Although the first 11 domains are organized in the manual under more inclusive categories (i.e., Relations with People—Interpersonal; Thinking Style—Administration; Thinking Style—Opportunities; and Feelings and

Emotions—Energies), the only scores derived from this questionnaire are on these 12 domains.

The manual authors describe the characteristics of a "low scorer" and a "high scorer" on each of the 12 domains and point to how each dimension may be important in a particular selling position. Although in general the selection process would favor the high scorer on each of the first 11 dimensions, in some sales positions, note the authors of the manual, the type of position will determine whether it is necessary to be high on a dimension like Resilient. Although high Resilient scorers are said to be good prospects for positions that involve cold calling and a large customer base, individuals with low Resilient scores may be successful in selling positions that require long-term relationships with a relatively few customers. The Social Desirability scale is meant to serve a "lie" detection function, but the manual makes reference to research suggesting that Social Desirability scores are positively related to performance in certain sales positions and, therefore, this scale too may serve a predictive role rather than simply determining whether the candidate is answering the questionnaire truthfully.

The items on the SPQ are answered on a 5-point Likert scale. There are no time limits, and it is reported that it typically takes 20–30 minutes to complete the questionnaire. If after 10 minutes the person has completed fewer than 40 items, the administrator is supposed to urge the test-taker to speed up the pace. Three means of taking the SPQ are possible: paper-and-pencil, Casio pocket calculator, or PC. A profile plotting the respondent's sten scores is the format for presenting the results.

Three norm tables are provided in the manual, each one presenting raw score to sten score conversions. The first table ($N = 245$), called the composite table, is based on the responses of all U.S. residents who had taken the SPQ as of August 1990. The other two tables are specific to the two groups that went into forming this composite, namely (a) 187 manager trainees at a national retail shoe store chain, and (b) 58 sales representatives of manufactured products. Summary descriptive statistics on these groups are reported for race, sex, and age. (The race of the latter group is unknown.) The manual's authors report that the test, originally developed in the United Kingdom, has only recently been introduced to the U.S. and that more extensive norm data are being collected. Users are urged to develop their own local norms and to share their data with the publishers of the test. Registered users are promised updated norms as they become available.

Two studies concerned with the SPQ's reliability are discussed. The first one, based on a sample of college students ($N = 113$), dealt with both the internal consistency and the test-retest reliability of the 12 domains making up this instrument. The average internal consistency reliability, measured using Cronbach's alpha, was .73 (ranging from .55 on Resilient to .84 on Creative). Test-retest reliability (2 to 4 weeks between administrations) was somewhat higher on all 12 scales, ranging from .73 to .88, with an average of .82; four domains had reliability coefficients above .85. The second study, using the 245 subjects who constitute the composite normative sample, explored the scale's internal consistency reliability, also using the Cronbach alpha technique. The average internal consistency was .68, with a low of .55 (Forward Planning) to a high of .82 (Creative).

The evidence generated to support the uniqueness of the 12 domains consists of intercorrelation coefficients between these domains. Although some of these correlations are in the .4 to .5 range, it is argued that none of the intercorrelations are "excessively high." On this basis the conclusion is drawn that each domain is measuring a unique dimension of behavior.

The validity of the SPQ was assessed in four criterion-related studies and one content validity study. Little detail is reported on the content validity study other than to indicate that it occurred in the United Kingdom and was based on a job analysis of the insurance agent role. In the first criterion-related validation effort, the concurrent validity of the SPQ was studied by (a) correlating SPQ scores to job performance ratings on six facets (i.e., dealing with customers, selling skills, administration/processing, organization of work, motivation, and an overall performance appraisal rating); and (b) correlating SPQ scores to rankings on two of these six criteria (selling skills, overall performance). The subjects were insurance agents ($N = 151$) who were rated by two of their managers. The correlations between the two raters were used to correct the criterion for unreliability. The uncorrected and corrected coefficients, which were significant at the .05 level, are reported in a table. Out of the 192 correlations (8 criteria x 12 SPQ domains x 2 raters), 38 (20%) were statistically significant. The uncorrected coefficients ranged from .14 to .32. When corrected for criterion unreliability, they went up slightly, ranging from .18 to .47; of these, 5% were in the teens, 53% were in the .20s, 34% were in the .30s, and 8% were in the .40s. Four of the domains did not correlate to any criterion (Systematic, Creative, Relaxed, Resilient). However, when the two managers' ratings were

averaged, four significant correlations (in the upper teens) were found for the Creative and Relaxed domains.

In the second study, a sample of sales assistants ($N = 121$ to 158) in an electrical products retail outlet were rated by their managers on attendance record, enthusiasm, competitive spirit, and overall performance. Their SPQ scores were related to these ratings as well as to an individual sales figure. Of the 60 correlations, 9 (15%) were statistically significant, and ranged between .18 and .34 (average = .23). These correlations involved only half of the domains. The manual's authors explain the failure to find significant relationships between the other SPQ scores and job performance may be due to the nature of the sales assistant's role.

A sample of retail sales assistants ($N = 105$) served as subjects in the third study, which examined the relationship between SPQ scores and nine measures of job performance (confidence with customers, selling skills, general ability, communication skills, conscientiousness, product knowledge, motivation, team work, and overall job performance) derived from a job analysis. The average rating of two supervisors served as the criterion on each job aspect. Fourteen (13%) of the computed correlations were statistically significant, and involved 8 of the 12 SPQ domains. The statistically significant correlations ranged from .19 to .31 (average = .23). Interestingly, the highest correlation was negative in direction, between team work and Confidence, suggesting that sales assistants with low confidence were better team workers.

The last study discussed under validity deals with correlations between the SPQ and a test of selling principles (Sales Comprehension Test) and a series of tests (called The Sales Aptitude Test) that measure seven factors (i.e., sales judgment, selling interest, personality factors, identification of self with selling occupations, level of aspiration, insight into human nature, awareness of sales approach). The correlations involved SPQ sten scores, Sales Comprehension Test percentile scores, and 5-point risk indices from The Sales Aptitude Test. The subjects, on whom no descriptive data are available (according to the manual), consisted of "nation-wide sales representatives" (p. 65; $N = 57$). The 17 statistically significant correlations derived from this analysis, involving 8 SPQ domains, were in the .22 to .37 range, with an average of .27.

With respect to culture-fair testing, the manual authors suggest that an organization relying on the SPQ for selection purposes conduct a job analysis to determine if the SPQ matches the attributes necessary to perform a particular sales position. In other words, "local" validation is recommended whenever feasible. (The publisher of the SPQ is a consulting organization, which can be engaged for this purpose.) It is reported that three of the scales (Empathy, Resilient, and Social Desirability) show ethnic group differences, and that on five of the scales there are differences between the scores of males and females. However, as is acknowledged in the manual, the differences are relatively small, and the manual authors recommend that users not develop separate norms unless differential validity can be demonstrated.

After a careful consideration of the manual and the evidence contained therein supporting the psychometric integrity of the SPQ, several conclusions seem warranted. To begin with, aside from a few minor typos, the SPQ Manual & Users Guide is very well organized and written in clear, concise language. The presentation of psychometric concepts and not just the results of statistical calculations is an excellent idea, given the possibility that the intended consumers of this product may not be very sophisticated about these matters. The manual's authors do an excellent job of giving the test user an orientation to the fundamentals of psychological measurement.

On the other hand, data available in the manual in support of the uniqueness of each of the 12 domains are not very convincing. In order to demonstrate the nonoverlap of domains, it does not suffice to show that only low to moderate interdomain correlations exist. An item analysis indicating that the items on each domain are more highly correlated with the domain on which they are currently located than with the other domains would be more reassuring. Likewise, a factor analysis could be performed to demonstrate some correspondence between the domains and empirically derived factors. When the test-retest reliability on a scale is higher than its internal consistency, as is the case with the SPQ, it suggests that either the items within a given domain have low correlations with each other, or the number of items within a domain is too small.

Both the internal consistency and the temporal stability of the SPQ are low for an instrument meant for supporting decisions about individuals. Generally, a reliability of .85 or better is expected, but admittedly this level is hard to achieve for scales that measure noncognitive variables. If the item analysis discussed above has not been tried, perhaps relocating some items would help improve reliability.

The reported studies meant to demonstrate that the SPQ measures the intended characteristics resulted in modest validity coefficients, even when corrections for attenuation due to the unreliability in the criterion were made. Although the size of the validity coefficients is troublesome, it has been argued by some that even small correlations may have substantial impact on improving decision making. The number of correlations that were statistically significant is rather disappointing when one considers the large number of correlations that were actually computed. One could argue that a substantial portion of the relationships found to be significant were so by chance alone. It is puzzling that in one of the validity studies correlations were computed on percentile scores, especially in view of the cautions given in the manual about percentiles. The manual's authors note this instrument has been adapted only recently for use in the United States. If there are additional psychometric data on the SPQ based on British samples, I think such information should be included in the next manual so as to permit one to get a more comprehensive understanding of this selection tool.

The currently available norms on the SPQ are based on small samples of convenience and may be unique to a specific position in a particular industry. It is known that not all sales positions require the same skills, as the validation studies on the SPQ also seem to suggest. The expanded norms that are promised should make the instrument more useful from this perspective. I therefore recommend that users of the SPQ demonstrate its validity in their own setting, linking it to a job analysis. If group size permits, local norms should be developed.

[78]
Scale for the Assessment of Positive Symptoms.
Purpose: "Designed to assess positive symptoms, principally those that occur in schizophrenia."
Population: Psychiatric inpatients and outpatients of all ages.
Publication Date: 1984.
Acronym: SAPS.
Scores: 35 behavior ratings within 5 areas: Hallucinations, Delusions, Bizarre Behavior, Positive Formal Thought Disorder, Inappropriate Affect.
Administration: Individual.
Price Data: Available from publisher.
Time: [15–30] minutes.
Comments: Intended to serve as a complementary instrument to the Scale for the Assessment of Negative Symptoms (SANS; T4:2325).
Author: Nancy C. Andreasen.
Publisher: Nancy C. Andreasen.

Cross References: See T4:2326 (24 references).

Review of the Scale for the Assessment of Positive Symptoms by JOHN D. KING, Professor of Special Education and Educational Administration, The University of Texas at Austin, Austin, TX:

DESCRIPTION. The Scale for the Assessment of Positive Symptoms (SAPS), available since 1984, is designed to aid in assessing "positive symptoms, principally those that occur in schizophrenia" (p. 2) by adding specific structure to standard diagnostic interviews. It is intended for use in conjunction with the Scale for Assessment of Negative Symptoms (SANS; T4:2325), which serves a similar purpose for negative symptoms. It is suggested for use in clinical practice as well as in psychopharmacologic research in order to make weekly ratings and chart the subject's response to treatment.

The SAPS contains descriptions of major positive symptom groups, suggested interview probes, and 5-point Likert-type scales for assessing the severity of each symptom. There is also a summary sheet for combining and summarizing results from both the SAPS and the SANS. No information is provided on the development of the scale. Symptoms included and their descriptions are consistent with *DSM-III-R* (American Psychiatric Association, 1987, pp. 189–190) diagnostic criteria. In most cases, the symptom descriptions are more complete than those provided in the *DSM-III-R*.

RELIABILITY AND VALIDITY. Although the instrument has been available since 1984, no information is provided on reliability or validity of the SAPS, nor is the user directed to any relevant research. The lack of any information concerning interrater or repeated measures reliability significantly impairs interpretive confidence for research purposes.

STRENGTHS. Used in conjunction with the SANS, the SAPS can provide a useful adjunct to standard diagnostic interviews. It encourages greater specificity in describing symptom clusters, leading to a more exact and individualized account of each patient. The generally quite good symptom descriptions provided should prove helpful in differentiating similar but distinct symptom types, especially for those who lack formal training in psychiatric diagnosis. Most of the scales are well anchored and should facilitate decision making as to the relative severity of a given symptom.

LIMITATIONS. The Hallucination scales all refer to the relative frequency of "voices" regardless of the type of hallucination involved. This oversight needlessly complicates use of the scale. Anchor points for the Bizarre Behavior scales are vague and invite subjective interpretation of severity. This seems likely to reduce interrater reliability. In a similar vein, the Global Rating for each symptom group lacks a specified relationship to the individual symptoms from which it is derived. Again, this invites an overly subjective use of the scale which is likely to reduce reliability.

The lack of any reliability or validity information makes it difficult to interpret observed changes in scale scores over time. There is no empirically derived way to set reasonable confidence intervals for deciding if they reflect real changes in the patient's condition or merely normal variability associated with imperfect reliability. This shortcoming seriously undermines the usefulness of the SAPS for research purposes as suggested by the author.

SUMMARY. The Scale for the Assessment of Positive Symptoms (SAPS) is a guide for the assessment of positive symptoms, particularly those associated with schizophrenia. Along with its companion instrument, the Scale for the Assessment of Negative Symptoms (SANS), it is designed to augment a standard diagnostic interview to track progress in a clinical setting and as a research tool to monitor the effectiveness of psychopharmacological interventions. It promises to provide a more detailed and quantified picture of a given patient's constellation of symptoms than is ordinarily obtained through interview means alone. However, the lack of information about its psychometric properties reduces its appropriateness as a research instrument. Furthermore, some of the wording used as scale anchor points is at times inconsistent with the symptom being assessed. At other times, the wording is not sufficiently specific such that it invites subjective interpretation of the patient's symptoms.

REVIEWER'S REFERENCE

American Psychiatric Association. (1987). *Diagnostic and statistical manual of mental disorders* (3rd ed., rev.). Washington, DC: Author.

Review of the Scale for the Assessment of Positive Symptoms by SUZANNE KING, Assistant Professor of Psychiatry, McGill University, Montreal, Quebec, CANADA:

The Scale for the Assessment of Positive Symptoms (SAPS) is a 34-item scale used to rate the severity of four positive symptoms of schizophrenia: Hallucinations, Delusions, Bizarre Behavior, and Formal Thought Disorder. Each symptom cluster, or subscale, is evaluated on the basis of a global rating plus between 4 and 12 ratings of specific symptoms.

Symptoms are rated on a 6-point scale ranging from zero, for "none," to 5 for "severe." Each possible rating has a brief definition in terms of severity, frequency, and so on. To summarize the ratings, one may either take the mean of the ratings for all items within a subscale, or use the global rating for each subscale. Similarly, a general rating of the severity of positive symptoms can be computed by taking the average of either all individual items, or of the global ratings for all subscales. A 35th item for inappropriate affect is included in the SAPS although research suggests that it does not fit into either a positive symptom or a negative symptom factor. Although inappropriate affect is a symptom of schizophrenia, the score for this item is not to be added into the total SAPS score.

The "test kit" includes a 20-page manual and a 7-page test protocol for use with the SAPS and with the companion instrument, Scale for Assessment of Negative Symptoms (SANS; T4:2325), by the same author. The manual (dated June 25, 1992) includes a half-page introduction followed by one-paragraph descriptions of each of the four subscales, brief descriptions of each item within subscales, one or two suggested probes for items in three of the four symptom clusters, and objective anchors for each possible rating. There is no discussion in the manual of the development of the test, its psychometric properties, norms, scoring procedures, nor the training required to administer the SAPS appropriately. No references to other sources that may provide such information are included. The manual indicates that ratings are to be made on the basis of information gathered and observations made during the course of a "standard clinical interview," which is not described, and that additional information should be gathered from discussions with significant others familiar with the patient. Although no mention of this is made in the manual, training may be received at the University of Iowa. In addition, video tapes of interviews, along with written commentaries for training purposes and for monitoring interrater reliability, can be obtained from the author.

One must search the psychiatric literature for reports of psychometric properties of the SAPS. Walker, Harvey, and Perlman (1988) report that, from their study of 51 schizophrenic and 21 manic patients, the interrater reliability of symptoms in the SAPS and SANS ranged from .72 to .93 and that the average interrater reliability (Kappa) for SAPS scores was .84 (.82 for the SANS). These authors report internal consistency estimates (Cronbach's alpha) for the SAPS of .65 for schizophrenic patients and .41 for manic patients.

Walker et al. (1988) also lend support for the construct validity of the SAPS. Current theory suggests that positive and negative symptoms ought to be independent of each other in schizophrenia, although perhaps not in other psychotic disorders such as mania. These authors found a nonsignificant correlation of .19 between the total SAPS and SANS scores in their schizophrenic sample. Similar results, suggesting the independence of the SAPS and the SANS, have been found by other authors including Gur et al. (1991). Walker and her colleagues (1988) found a significant correlation of .47 ($p<.05$) between the total scores on the SAPS and SANS for manic patients. In addition, their results suggest that schizophrenic and manic patients differ significantly on two of the four positive symptoms from the SAPS as well as the total SAPS score, and on four of the five negative symptoms from the SANS, as well as on the total negative symptom score. These results support the ability of the SAPS and the SANS to discriminate between diagnostic groups. Gur et al. (1991) support the concurrent validity of the SAPS and SANS by showing significant correlations with the thought disorder and anergia factors (respectively) from the Brief Psychiatric Rating Scale (BPRS).

A strength of the SAPS is its use with the SANS to operationally define three groups of patients with schizophrenia: those with the positive symptom syndrome, those with the negative symptom syndrome, and those with mixed symptoms. Although further study is needed into the validity of the distinction among these three groups, recent research supports the notion that background and clinical characteristics of the groups may differ (Andreasen & Olsen, 1982; Andreasen, Flaum, Swayze, Tyrrell, & Arndt, 1990). These results, if replicated, will have important implications for our understanding of the etiology and course of schizophrenia.

The use of anchors for rating levels represents both a strength and a weakness of the SAPS. Although operational definitions of ratings ought to improve interrater reliability, the definitions used in the SAPS may threaten the assumption of equal intervals, calling into question the appropriateness of many statistical analyses with these data. In addition, although definitions for some items are not mutually exclusive, for other items they are not comprehensive.

The lack of a detailed guide to the clinical interview used to gather information needed to make ratings is an important shortcoming of the SAPS. Although there is seldom a guarantee that any two semistructured interviews will ever be identical, leaving the format and content of the interview completely up to the discretion, and mood, of the interviewer threatens the comparability of scores across subjects and the generalizability of results across studies.

Summary information about the SAPS may be misleading: Although the time needed to administer the SAPS is indicated as "15 to 30 minutes," the description of the positive formal thought disorder subscale states that the "anchor points for these ratings assume that the subject has been interviewed for a total of approximately forty-five minutes. If the interview is shorter, the ratings should be adjusted accordingly" (manual, p. 15).

In summary, the SAPS, along with its companion scale the SANS, is a very detailed measure of positive symptoms which, in the hands of a well-trained interviewer, could have adequate reliability and even validity for research purposes. Both scales appear to have gained acceptance in the psychiatric community. The documentation for the instrument, however, is sufficiently poor that caution is urged before this scale is selected. Competing instruments, such as the UCLA version of the BPRS (Lukoff, Liberman, & Nuechterlein, 1986), which is shorter than the SAPS and for which a new manual should be available by the end of 1993, and the Positive and Negative Symptom Scale (PANSS, Kay, Fiszbein, & Opler, 1987), which is gaining in popularity, may be considered as appropriate alternatives to the SAPS and the SANS.

REVIEWER'S REFERENCES

Andreasen, N. C., & Olsen, S. (1982). Negative v positive schizophrenia. *Archives of General Psychiatry, 39*, 789-794.
Lukoff, D., Liberman, R. P., & Nuechterlein, K. H. (1986). Symptom monitoring in the rehabilitations of schizophrenic patients. *Schizophrenia Bulletin, 12*, 578-602.
Kay, S. R., Fiszbein, A., & Opler, L. A. (1987). The Positive and Negative Syndrome Scale (PANSS) for schizophrenia. *Schizophrenia Bulletin, 13*, 261-276. $PWalker, E. F., Harvey, P. D., & Perlman, D. (1988). The positive/negative symptom distinction in psychoses: A replication and extension of previous findings. *The Journal of Nervous and Mental Disease, 176*, 359-363.
Andreasen, N. C., Flaum, M., Swayze, V. W., Tyrrell, G., & Arndt, S. (1990). Positive and negative symptoms in schizophrenia. *Archives of General Psychiatry, 47*, 615-621.
Gur, R. E., Mozley, P. D., Resnick, S. M., Levick, S., Erwin, R., Saykin, A. J., & Gur, R. C. (1991). Relations among clinical scales in schizophrenia. *American Journal of Psychiatry, 148*, 472-478.

[79]

School Readiness Test.

Purpose: Designed to test the student's readiness for first grade academics.
Population: End of Kindergarten through first 3 weeks of Grade 1.
Publication Dates: 1974–90.
Acronym: SRT.
Scores, 9: Vocabulary, Identifying Letters, Visual Discrimination, Auditory Discrimination, Comprehension and Interpretation, Number Knowledge, Handwriting Ability, Developmental Spelling Ability, Total.
Administration: Group.
Price Data, 1993: $41.60 per 35 test booklets, scoring key, class record sheet, and manual ('90, 26 pages); $4.15 per scoring key; $9.95 per manual; $2.15 per class record sheet; $20 per specimen set.
Time: (90) minutes.
Comments: Subtest scores convert to "OK," "Probably Needs Help," "Definitely Needs Help"; total score converts to "Gifted Ready," "Superior Ready," "Average Ready," "Marginal," "Short Delay," "Long Delay."
Authors: O. F. Anderhalter and Jan Perney.
Publisher: Scholastic Testing Service, Inc.
Cross References: For a review by Thorsten R. Carlson, see 8:808.

Review of the School Readiness Test by ESTHER STAVROU TOUBANOS, School Psychologist, Lawrence Public Schools, Lawrence, NY:

The School Readiness Test (SRT) is a group-administered test designed to provide the classroom teacher with information about students' "readiness for learning" and particularly "factors that might interfere with the learning process." No operational definition of readiness is provided, although the authors describe three uses for the test results:

1. To divide pupils into groups that are *ready* for formal learning, and groups that could use varying amounts of further *readiness experience*.

2. To diagnose the strengths and weaknesses of the individual pupils as related to readiness for formal learning in the different skill areas. . . .

3. To improve and individualize the teaching procedures (manual of directions, p. 24).

A potentially useful feature of this test is the availability of a Spanish version.

In addition to a total readiness score, part scores are provided for eight separate areas: Vocabulary, Identifying Letters, Visual Discrimination, Auditory Discrimination, Comprehension and Interpretation, Number Knowledge, Handwriting Ability, and Developmental Spelling Ability. No rationale is provided for the inclusion of various subtests or why some areas traditionally considered relevant to school success (i.e., expressive language, general knowledge, etc.) are excluded.

Total raw scores can be converted to percentile ranks based on norms for either the end of kindergarten or beginning of first grade. The composition of the norm group, however, is not specified in the manual. Verbal ratings are also provided for the Total Score which indicates readiness level according to six institutional groupings (G/R = Gifted Ready, S/R = Superior Ready, A/R = Average Ready, M = Marginal, S/D = Short Delay, or L/D = Long Delay). It is suggested that subtest or "part" scores be examined for pupils whose total score falls in the Marginal, Short Delay or Long Delay classification. Part scores can also be converted into percentiles as well as stanines and ratings of "ok," "probably needs help," or "definitely needs help."

The School Readiness Test appears to be a refinement of an earlier test by the same name. The Word Recognition subtest is now called Vocabulary, Number Readiness is now Number Knowledge, and a new subtest, Developmental Spelling Ability, was added. Although not considered a revision, this version addresses some of the weaknesses described in an earlier *MMY* review by Carlson (1978). However, some problems still remain, including the failure to provide a conceptualization of the nature of school readiness or to describe the instructional relevance of the test scores.

The SRT is designed to be administered at the end of kindergarten or before the third week of first grade. The authors suggest breaking the testing into two 40-minute sessions, though in trials by this examiner it was difficult to maintain most of the students' attention for even 40 minutes. The directions for administration are specific and clear for the examiner to follow, making it easily administered by the classroom teacher or paraprofessionals with little additional training. However, the directions are very confusing for young children who must attend to too much information at once. In general, most of the subtests involve too much information on one page, making it difficult for the child to focus on each item. Sophisticated linguistic concepts like "top," "left," and "corner" are often used in the task directions. Therefore, students' performances may reflect their understanding of these concepts rather than the purpose for which they are formally being tested.

The Vocabulary subtest is particularly problematic in this respect because the directions involve knowledge of vocabulary that may be as complex as that which is formally being tested. For example, on the sample, the child is first instructed to find the page with a picture of a bird in the top left corner, then to "Look at the pictures in the top row, with the picture of a flower in the corner . . . There are pictures of a plate, a cup and a spoon. Draw a ring like this around the picture of the cup" (manual of directions, p. 5). Therefore, although the child is being tested on identification of a cup, he/she must also be able to identify a bird and a flower. Some other words used to identify the rows to which the child must attend include airplane, telephone, and scissors. In a group-administered test, it may be difficult to monitor students' understanding of the directions. Although the teacher is instructed to walk around during administration of the sample to make sure everyone has understood, this precaution is no longer taken once the test begins. Language is an appropriate and important part of school readiness that must be assessed but not in a manner that may confound the results.

The Handwriting Ability subtest is also problematic in that some of the figures to be reproduced are difficult even for older children and, without item analyses reported, it is difficult to determine whether these or any of the items are useful in discriminating between children. In addition, the amount of space provided in which to reproduce the figures is inadequate for young children. This is a timed subtest and although children are instructed not to spend too much time on any one picture, such instruction needs to be emphasized. Furthermore, more information must be provided regarding the scoring of figures. Additional scoring examples would help make decisions less subjective and arbitrary. Guidelines for what happens if a child copies upper case letters in lower case would also be helpful.

A general problem across subtests is the lack of a rationale for the manner in which behaviors are sampled. For example, Identifying Letters tests the child's knowledge of lower case letters. Why was lower case chosen over the more traditional upper case? Auditory Discrimination does not involve discrimination but rather sound recognition. It is unclear what the Comprehension and Interpretation subtest is measuring. It seems to involve visual discrimination and attention to detail, auditory comprehension, and understanding of relational concepts. Visual discrimination is also a factor on Items 17 and 18 of Number Knowledge, where the child must distinguish a penny from a dime drawn in the same color.

It would be helpful to know the authors' definition of "readiness" because many subtests involve more advanced skills than this reviewer considers necessary for "readiness." Number Knowledge measures actual mastery of advanced numerical skills like recognition of order, fractional parts, measures of time and money, rather than just readiness to learn these skills. Handwriting Ability is described as measuring "readiness for formal instruction in handwriting." It seems that if a child can successfully complete this subtest, he or she already has some handwriting skills.

The usefulness of the Developmental Spelling Ability subtest in "predicting later student performance in reading" is also questionable.

The lack of technical data in the manual is a serious limitation and prevents the user from making meaningful conclusions from the scores. Although percentiles are provided, their relevance is unknown because no information is provided regarding the normative sample. Reliability information is not provided in the manual making it impossible for the reader to determine the usefulness of test results. It remains to be seen whether the results of the test can predict later school difficulties, however, validity cannot even be addressed without adequate reliability data.

In summary, the SRT appears to have been developed with little rationale for selection of domains and items sampled. Without evidence of adequate standardization, reliability, and validity, the SRT should not be used to make diagnostic and/or placement decisions. The authors' claim the results can be used to improve and individualize the teaching procedures is unfounded. Furthermore, no recommendations are provided regarding possible interventions that can be generated from the results other than additional time in readiness activities. Aside from the ease of administration, there appear to be few reasons to use this test over the more superior, Metropolitan Readiness Test (T4:1619).

REVIEWER'S REFERENCE

Carlson, T. R. (1978). [Review of the School Readiness Test.] In O. K. Buros (Ed.), *The eighth mental measurements yearbook* (pp. 1348-1350). Highland Park, NJ: Gryphon Press.

Review of the School Readiness Test by LARRY WEBER, Professor of Education, Virginia Tech, Blacksburg, VA:

The School Readiness Test (SRT) was designed to assist the teacher in gathering information regarding entering students' readiness for learning. It is intended that the test be administered by the classroom teacher at the end of kindergarten or before the third full week of the first grade. Eight separate tests comprise the exam and a score is provided for each, in addition to a total readiness score.

There is no information covering why certain topics were chosen as important elements in determining school readiness. Neither is there sufficient justification for the inclusion of the test items. A priori beliefs about which abilities are consequential for success in first grade seem to have guided the choice of test content.

There are several problems associated with various facets of the SRT, beginning with its directions for administration. It is recommended the exam be administered in two sittings (it is 1 hour and 20 minutes long) but the manual states that it can be given in one sitting—with a rest period. A test of such length is too long, for 5- and 6-year-old children, to be taken in a single time period. Another direction is similarly tentative (i.e., "If possible, students should be seated so that they cannot see each other's work during the testing"). Such statements make one believe that conditions under which the exam is administered may be varied to fit the needs of the situation.

Regarding the examination itself, the test on Vocabulary, which requires students to identify pictures of words said by the examiner, seems flawed. In examples given the student before the test, the examinee is asked to identify specific items like "cup" and "mouse." On the actual examination items several of the terms are obtuse, for example requiring the student to identify a hammer as a "tool," a truck as a "vehicle," a violin as an "instrument," etc. It is hard to imagine that the difficulty indices for many of the items on the vocabulary test would be above the chance level.

Other subtests also contain deficiencies. The Identifying Letters subtest contains only lower case letters. The directions for the Visual Discrimination test seem too brief and complex for young children. The Auditory Discrimination subtest, with the possible exception of the rhyming items, will probably be incomprehensible for many examinees. The time limit, 5 seconds, for marking responses to answers on the Comprehension and Interpretation subtest appears insufficient, as does the time limit for several items in the Number Knowledge subtest, which in addition to containing items about numbers has questions about size, shape, time, money and fractions. The Handwriting and Spelling subtests are straightforward.

The scoring key and directions for scoring are adequate. The raw score for the first seven subtests is simply the number of correct answers for those tests. Each item for the Spelling subtest is scored on a 0–5 scale. The Handwriting subtest scoring scale, although admittedly subjective, contains reasonable guidelines for assisting the examiner in scoring that section of the SRT; and the Spelling subtest directions for scoring are rather comprehensive. The total score on the eight subtests comprises the total readiness score which, when converted to a percentile rank, provides a basis for "verbal ratings" that indicate each examinee's apparent readiness level. There are six verbal ratings: Gifted Ready = 96–99 percentile; Superior Ready = 76–95 percentile; Average

Ready = 40–75 percentile; Marginal = 24–39 percentile; Short Delay = 5–23 percentile; Long Delay = 1–4 percentile.

One of the major faults with the SRT is its deficiency in providing data to support statements made about its value and usefulness. The statements that are made seem to reflect the test coordinators' opinions, and are not based on evidence provided in the test materials. For example, they state that "experience has suggested" that the six classifications (listed above) are useful in designating degrees of readiness. However, the system they use is nothing more than an application of stanine score categories to the verbal classifications. That is Gifted Ready = Stanine 9; Superior Ready = Stanines 7–8; Average Ready = Stanines 5–6; Marginal = Stanine 4; Short Delay = Stanines 2–3; Long Delay = Stanine 1. The manual contains nothing supporting the validity for claims that students whose scores fall into a given category will exhibit the type of verbal rating readiness described for that category.

There are other dangers in using the SRT scores for classifying students. One is the problem of interpreting the verbal ratings literally and assuming examinees possess the attributes or deficiencies of the class in which they are categorized. So care must be taken that the values suggested by the "verbal ratings" are not overemphasized. Moreover, it appears the scores earned by students on the test may be a measure of prior experience. Many of the items seem dependent on more or less formal training with similar material. As is stated in the manual, children who have had little training or assistance at home may earn low readiness ratings, yet progress rapidly once they enter school.

School readiness norm tables, which give percentile ranks for children earning specific raw scores, are provided for kindergarten and grade 1 examinees. Also provided are tables that classify students as "definitely needs help," "probably needs help," or "OK," according to their performance on the eight subtests. No suggestions are made as to the type of help a student needs nor is evidence provided regarding the basis for classifying students. There was no description in the manual of the norming population, other than they were "pupils in the national standardization group" (p. 24).

Another major fault with the SRT is the absence of reliability and validity data. Information about individual items (i.e., item difficulty and item discrimination) was not presented. In general there is a noted deficiency of information regarding the technical measurement characteristics of the test.

Because of the weaknesses described above, it is difficult to recommend the SRT as an instrument to be used for assessing readiness for formal learning in schools. The reasons for inclusion of the various subtests are weak; the classification of students into readiness categories is suspect; and evidence about the technical aspects of the exam (norms, validity, and reliability) is lacking. For those reasons alone the adoption of and use of findings from the SRT could be challenged.

[80]

School Situation Survey.

Purpose: Designed to measure "school-related student stress."

Population: Grades 4–12.

Publication Date: 1989.

Acronym: SSS.

Scores, 7: Sources of Stress (Teacher Interactions, Academic Stress, Peer Interactions, Academic Self-Concept), Manifestations of Stress (Emotional, Behavioral, Physiological).

Administration: Group.

Price Data, 1992: $16 per 25 test booklets/answer sheets; $6 per scoring key; $24 per manual (37 pages); $25 per specimen set.

Time: (10–15) minutes.

Authors: Barbara J. Helms and Robert K. Gable.

Publisher: Consulting Psychologists Press, Inc.

Review of the School Situation Survey by THEODORE COLADARCI, Associate Professor of Education, University of Maine, Orono, ME:

The School Situation Survey (SSS) is a 34-item instrument designed to assess "school-related student stress" in grades 4 through 12. Comprising seven scales, the SSS provides separate scores for four "sources" of stress: Teacher Interactions ("students' perceptions of their teachers' attitudes toward them"), Academic Stress ("situations that relate to academic performance or achievement"), Peer Interactions ("students' social interactions or their perceptions of their classmates' feelings toward them"), and Academic Self-Concept ("students' feelings of self-worth, self-esteem, or self-concept relevant to perceived ability"). The remaining three scales yield scores regarding "manifestations" of stress: Emotional ("feelings such as fear, shyness, and loneliness"), Behavioral ("actions, reactions, or behavior toward others, such as striking out or being hurtful or disrespectful"), and Physiological ("physical reactions or functions such as nausea, tremors, or rapid heart beat").

Students rate each item (e.g., "I feel upset") on a 5-point scale ranging from *never* to *always*. Answer sheets can be hand scored easily with the accompanying acetate overlay, or returned to Consulting Psychologists Press for machine scoring. In either case, a student receives seven scores; a composite score across the seven scales is not provided (nor do the authors recommend that such a score be used).

DOCUMENTATION. The SSS manual is a physically attractive document containing helpful information for SSS users and appraisers alike. However, I found the manual wanting in several respects. First, little attention is devoted to the intended uses, and possible misuses, of the SSS. For example, it would seem that different concerns would surface for practitioners than for researchers, yet the authors say little for either audience.

Second, the overall organization of the manual is awkward at times. Suggested strategies for reducing stress are presented after a section on norms, and information regarding factor analyses is alluded to in the construct validity section—where it belongs—but the reader must refer back to an earlier section on item development to see the specifics.

Finally, the authors' treatment of fundamental aspects of instrumentation (e.g., validity) appears to be intended for readers with a technical background. Although the language of psychometrics and statistics is unavoidable in a users' manual, it serves an important educative purpose when presented well. I fear that some of the authors' language will have the unintended effect of distancing many readers from the information needed to make an informed appraisal of the SSS.

STANDARDIZATION SAMPLE. Norms are based on 7,036 students from grades 3 through 12 in 16 Connecticut and Rhode Island school districts. In two appendices, the authors report means, standard deviations, and ranges for interpreting scores for each of four grade-level clusters: grades 3–5, 6–8, 9, and 10–12. Within each grade level, descriptive statistics are broken down by sex.

The impressive number of students notwithstanding, these norms should be used cautiously. Schools were drawn from rural, suburban, and urban communities, but nothing is said about demographic considerations such as ethnicity and socioeconomic status, both of which would seem relevant to the problem of school-related stress. Consequently, the degree to which these norms are appropriate for any one school district remains an open question.

The authors, furthermore, do not report the number of students who were sampled in each grade. Can we assume the sixth-, seventh-, and eighth-grade students are evenly distributed within the 6–8-grade-level cluster? This ambiguity has implications for how confidently the SSS norms can be employed for a particular grade. (Curiously, the authors do not explain why they included third-grade students in the norming group for a survey designed for grades 4 through 12.)

Finally, we are told that SSS norms can be used "to provide feedback on an individual *or group* [italics added] basis" (p. 7). In fact, because the norms are based on individuals, they cannot be used to form judgments about *groups* of individuals (e.g., students in a particular grade or building). Consequently, the authors' three categories for interpreting scores (low, medium, high), derived from individual-level distributions of scores, are inappropriate for interpreting group data.

RELIABILITY. Internal-consistency coefficients for the seven scales are moderate, ranging from .68 to .80 when based on the entire sample of 7,036 students; similar coefficients are reported within each of the four grade-level clusters. Importantly, a standard error of measurement (SEM) is reported for each coefficient. The SEMs, expressed on the SSS 5-point scale, range from roughly one-third to over one-half of a point (.31 to .58), depending on the scale and grade-level cluster. Combined, these data raise questions about the suitability of the SSS for forming judgments and making decisions about students, particularly at the individual level.

Test-retest reliability was determined over a 3-week period for a sample of seventh- to ninth-grade students ($n = 621$), resulting in coefficients ranging from .61 to .71. The lower value of these coefficients is not surprising insofar as affective characteristics are less stable than cognitive aptitudes or academic achievement. Users nonetheless should realize the implication: Students' perceptions of school-related stress today, as measured by the SSS, might well differ from their perceptions in a few weeks.

We do not know how these 621 students were selected for the test-retest reliability analyses, or why a group of students was designated that cuts across two of the four grade-level clusters. More troubling, however, the authors do not explain why test-retest reliabilities are not reported for students in the remaining grade-level clusters. Can we assume, for example, that comparable coefficients would obtain for the youngest cluster? My sense is that the stress perceptions among students in grades 3 through 5 would be less stable than for older students. In any case, the stability of the SSS remains unestablished for a large segment of the target population.

VALIDITY. The authors invested considerable time and effort in the validation of the SSS.

Content validity. The content-validity question is raised by the authors this way: "To what extent do the items of [the SSS] adequately sample from the intended content domain?" (p. 14). The reader is then referred back to an earlier section on item development, which touches on the authors' procedure for constructing an initial set of 56 items by consulting the literature and talking with groups of students, parents, educators, and specialists. In my view, this discussion falls short of establishing the universe from which these 56 items were drawn. Consequently, it is difficult to determine how well (*a*) each scale samples the domain of items represented by that scale or (*b*) how well the seven SSS scales represent all sources and manifestations of stress.

Construct validity. According to Messick (1989), "construct validity is evaluated by investigating what qualities a test measures, that is, by determining the degree to which certain explanatory concepts or constructs account for performance on the test" (p. 16). The authors approached this task in three ways.

Factor analysis. The initial 56 items were factor analyzed on a sample of 907 students from grades 5, 7, and 9. After some revisions, the instrument was administered to a new sample of 1,111 students (also from grades 5, 7, and 9) and again factor analyzed. From this second set of analyses, 7 of the 14 obtained factors "replicated the original constructs" (pp. 11–12) that earlier had emerged from the literature and the authors' discussions with various groups. It is these seven factors, and their 34 items, that constitute the SSS.

These factors, with the corresponding items and loadings, are clearly presented in the manual. Importantly, factor loadings show a relatively clean separation of the seven factors. And the manner in which the items cluster within each factor makes conceptual sense, as well. For example, each of the three items in the Academic Stress factor pertains to achievement situations in school. Together, these data support the authors' claim that the SSS gets at relatively distinct aspects of students' stress perceptions.

Surprisingly, no factor analyses were conducted on the six remaining grades for which the SSS is intended. Although I have no a priori reason to question the validity of this instrument for these six grades, their absence precludes an adequate appraisal of the construct validity of the SSS. And why did the authors not base their factor analyses on the standardization sample of 7,036 students, rather than the restricted sample of 1,111? After all, the standardization sample provides the basis for the norms and internal-consistency reliability estimates. It would seem that the authors passed up an important opportunity for cross-validation, based on a larger sample, and with all grades represented.

Correlations with the State-Trait Anxiety Inventory for Children. Any instrument, of course, should correlate with existing measures of similar constructs. Consequently, the authors correlated each of the seven SSS scales with the A-Trait scale of the State-Trait Anxiety Inventory for Children (STAIC; Spielberger, Edwards, Lushene, Montuori, & Platzek, 1973), based on the restricted sample of 1,111 students from grades 5, 7, and 9. The obtained correlations range considerably: $rs = .10$ to $.71$, with a median r of $.33$. In general, these correlations provide weak to moderate support for the construct validity of the SSS.

It also would be informative to know whether the SSS scales *fail* to correlate with measures of constructs *dis*similar to school-related student stress. That is, does the SSS demonstrate "discriminant" validity? Correlations with the STAIC, which speak to the "convergent" validity of the SSS, unfortunately provide only half of the story.

Path analysis. To examine further the construct validity of the SSS, the authors tested a series of causal models using the statistical procedure, "path analysis." In three separate models, the four sources of stress (and several other variables) were used to predict each of the three manifestations of stress.

I had considerable difficulty with these analyses. First, the authors do not clearly demonstrate the relevance of path analysis to the question of construct validity. Consequently, the import of these results remains unclear. Second, the logic of the general model rests on tacit—and highly questionable—assumptions regarding causality. For example, academic stress is presented as a *cause* of academic self-concept and academic achievement. In my view, the opposite assertion is equally plausible.

Third, no guidance is offered for interpreting these partial regression coefficients. Nor are we told that R^2—a fundamental summary statistic in path analysis—ranges from .17 to .39 across the three analyses. These modest values, which I derived from available information, would seem to carry important implications for the tenability of the model and, more specifically, the authors' premise that sources of stress have a causal influence on manifestations of stress.

Finally, some of the authors' interpretations are questionable: (*a*) conclusions appear to be made about interactions among variables when, in fact, the statistical analysis did not allow for interactive effects; and (*b*) statements about relations among variables are based on exceedingly low effects.

CONCLUSIONS. The SSS is an easily administered and scored instrument for assessing students' perceptions of sources and manifestations of school-related stress. However, questions remain about the adequacy both of the norms and of the information pertaining to reliability and validity. Consequently, the SSS presently would appear to be more appropriate for researchers than for practitioners, insofar as the former group would be less inclined to use the SSS as a basis for forming judgments or making decisions about students.

REVIEWER'S REFERENCE

Spielberger, C. D., Edwards, C. D., Lushene, R. E., Montuori, J., & Platzek, D. (1973). *Preliminary manual for the State-Trait Anxiety Inventory for Children*. Palo Alto, CA: Consulting Psychologists Press.

Messick, S. (1989). Validity. In R. L. Linn (Ed.), *Educational measurement* (3rd ed.; pp. 13-103). New York: Macmillan Publishing Co.

Review of the School Situation Survey by Le-ADELLE PHELPS, Associate Professor and Director, School Psychology Program, Department of Counseling and Educational Psychology, State University of New York at Buffalo, Buffalo, NY:

The School Situation Survey (SSS) is an instrument designed "to assess students' perceptions of school-related sources and manifestations of stress" (manual, title page). Appropriate for grades 4–12, the survey consists of 34 Likert-type rating items (1 = *never*, 5 = *always*) that students can complete in approximately 10 to 15 minutes. As a screening instrument, the SSS may be useful in identifying youngsters who could benefit from supplemental counseling or mental health services.

The SSS is organized into seven areas: (*a*) Teacher Interactions consisting of six items assessing perceived teacher attitudes towards the student, (*b*) Academic Stress with three items addressing anxiety regarding academic performance, (*c*) Peer Interactions containing six items related to perceived peer attitudes toward the student, (*d*) Academic Self-Concept consisting of four items dealing with academic standing, (*e*) Emotional containing six items assessing stress-related feelings of emotional discomfort, (*f*) Behavioral with six items measuring stress-outcome behaviors, and (*g*) Physiological containing three items indicating physical symptomatology of stress. The first four scales are viewed by the authors as assessing Sources of Stress; the remaining three scales reflect Manifestations of Stress. The seven areas were derived using principal components factor analyses (items for Sources of Stress and Manifestations of Stress were analyzed separately) followed by oblique rotations.

Item selection and the decision to divide the scale into two parts (i.e., Sources of Stress and Manifestations of Stress) was based on a review of the literature and content validity evidence. A pilot form of the scale, containing 56 items was administered to 907 fifth-, seventh-, and ninth-graders. Separate principal components factor analyses followed by oblique rotations were completed for the two areas. Based on the proposed framework and the statistical findings, the authors revised and deleted/added items. The revised form (also 56 items) was administered to a new sample of 1,111 students. The data were again submitted to principal components factor analyses followed by oblique rotations and examined for factors that best replicated the original constructs. Items/factors that did not contribute to a meaningful interpretation were eliminated, resulting in the current 34-item seven-area instrument. The final factor structure of the SSS appears strong with intercorrelations among the seven areas ranging from .01 to .56 ($M = .23$), indicating that the scales are sufficiently independent.

The reliability of the instrument is moderate with the authors reporting alpha coefficients (derived from item-level factor analyses) for the seven areas ranging from .68 to .80. Test-retest data (3-week interval) are acceptable with correlations ranging from .61 to .71. Given that the SSS measures affect, which is quite variable or "personal state dependent" (manual, p. 12), these correlations would be considered supportive of the stability of the instrument.

In addition to the factor analytic procedures used in the development of the instrument, path analyses were completed to provide the user with interpretative information. In addition to the seven SSS scores, five other variables (i.e., gender, grade level, grade-level structure, cognitive ability, and perceived family stress) were included in the path model. The path analyses indicated that (*a*) "males experienced greater behavioral responses to stress, while females experienced more emotional and physiological responses to stress" (p. 17), and (*b*) "the strongest causes of emotional manifestation were academic stress and peer interactions, while the strongest cause of behavioral manifestations was teacher interactions" (p. 19).

Concurrent validity was assessed by correlating the seven SSS scores with the A-Trait scale of the State-Trait Anxiety Inventory for Children (Spielberger, Edwards, Lushene, Montuori, & Platzek, 1973). The correlations illustrate the only weakness with the SSS (as well as similar instruments assessing stress). Is the SSS measuring anxiety, depression, or stress? Discriminant validity is imperative in scales assessing affective issues. Although the SSS is a stress scale that converges in the expected direction, the scale could (and most likely would) also display substantial correlations with other related, yet supposedly distinct, affective constructs such as anxiety and depression. Thus, convergent and discriminant data are needed to support the construct validity of scales such as the SSS.

In summary, the SSS is a solidly constructed instrument that should be strengthened by continued research efforts. It would be particularly useful as a screening device in school systems.

REVIEWER'S REFERENCE

Spielberger, C. D., Edwards, C. D., Lushene, R. E., Montuori, J., & Platzek, D. (1973). *Preliminary manual for the State-Trait Anxiety Inventory for Children.* Palo Alto, CA: Consulting Psychologists Press.

[81]

Screening Assessment for Gifted Elementary Students—Primary.

Purpose: Assesses a child's aptitude and achievment level in order to identify academically gifted students.
Population: Ages 5-0 to 8-11.
Publication Date: 1992.
Acronym: SAGES-P.
Scores, 3: General Information, Reasoning, Total.
Administration: Group.
Price Data, 1992: $74 per complete kit including examiner's manual (40 pages), 25 student response booklets, and 25 profile and summary sheets; $28 per examiner's manual; $39 per 25 student response booklets; $10 per 25 profile and summary sheets.
Time: (30–45) minutes.
Authors: Susan K. Johnsen and Anne L. Corn.
Publisher: PRO-ED, Inc.

Review of the Screening Assessment for Gifted Elementary Students—Primary by LEWIS R. AIKEN, Professor of Psychology, Pepperdine University, Malibu, CA:

This paper-and-pencil instrument, which was designed to identify mental giftedness in children aged 5–8 years, is a downward extension of the original Screening Assessment for Gifted Elementary Students constructed by S. K. Johnsen and A. L. Corn in 1987. The Screening Assessment for Gifted Elementary Students—Primary (SAGES-P) consists of two subtests: Subtest 1: General Information and Subtest 2: Reasoning (Analogies). These two subtests were designed as measures of the achievement and aptitude areas, but not the divergent production area, of mental giftedness. The two subtests, contained in a single Student Booklet, consist of 33 (Subtest 1) and 29 (Subtest 2) five-option items. Two example items are provided for Subtest 1 and four example items for Subtest 2. Each item is identified by number

and by a special picture symbol located next to it. The pictorial, numerical, or alphabetic letter options for each item are placed in large boxes below the question.

As stated in the Examiner's Manual, SAGES-P may be administered either individually or to groups as large as 25 children. The tests is untimed, but requires 30–45 minutes to administer to small groups of primary-school children. Kindergarten children may require two separate testing sessions of 20 minutes each. The subtests should be administered in the order in which they were standardized—first Subtest 1 and then Subtest 2.

Detailed instructions for administration are given in the manual. The teacher or test administrator reads the instructions for each item aloud, making certain the examinees are on the correct item. When testing a group of children, all items in both subtests are administered. When testing one child at a time, testing time may be shortened by determining basal and ceiling ages. In that case, testing on Subtest 1 begins with Item 1 for 5-year-olds, Item 5 for 6-year-olds, Item 10 for 7-year-olds, and Item 14 for 8-year-olds. Testing on Subtest 2 begins at Item 14 for 5-year-olds, Item 3 for 6-year-olds, Item 7 for 7-year-olds, and Item 9 for 8-year-olds. On either subtest, a basal age is established as five items in a row correct, and a ceiling age as four out of five items incorrect.

Scores and other pertinent information about the child and the examiner are recorded on a Profile and Response Form. Separate norms tables for converting raw scores (number correct) to percentile ranks and standard scores are given for "Normal" and "Gifted" groups. These norms are in half-year intervals from age 5 years through 8 years, 11 months. The standard scores have a mean of 10 and a standard deviation of 3. The sum of the standard scores on the two subtests may be converted to percentile rank and quotient scores. Finally, two profiles of the results from testing a child may be constructed—one based on the norms for "Normal" children and another based on "Gifted" children.

Guidelines for interpreting the standard scores and quotients are given on pages 23–24 of the manual. On the basis of these converted scores, a child's performance may be assigned to one of seven categories, ranging from *Very Poor* to *Very Superior*. Other suggestions for diagnostic uses of the SAGES-P, such as interpreting differences between scores on the two subtests and "testing the limits" by probing for answers to items, are also provided.

Information on item development, standardization, reliability, and validity is contained in chapter

4 of the manual. Item construction and selection were clearly based on a sound knowledge of the theoretical and research literature on assessment of the gifted. The SAGES-P was standardized between September, 1990 and June, 1991 on 2,581 normal children and 1,034 gifted children in 19 states. The demographic characteristics of the two samples are specified on pages 30–31 of the manual.

As expected, the median difficulty indexes of the items increase with age level for both normal and gifted groups. Differences between the normal and gifted groups are greater on the Reasoning subtest than on the General Information subtest. For both normal and gifted groups, the median discriminating indexes of the items range from the lower .40s to the mid .60s.

Internal consistency reliability coefficients were computed on 60 randomly selected protocols in the normal group and 60 in the gifted group. These coefficients, for the Reasoning, General Information, and Total test scores in both the gifted and normal groups, are quite respectable. The Cronbach alphas are mostly in the low to middle .90s and none lower than .87.

In a validation study described in the manual, correlations of SAGES-P scores with Wechsler Intelligence Scale for Children—Revised (WISC-R) and Stanford-Binet IQs in samples of 2nd and 3rd grade students ranged from .65 to .74. Other concurrent validity data are found in the significant positive correlations between SAGES-P scores and scores on the Survey of Basic Skills, the Educational Ability Series, the Peabody Individual Achievement Test—Revised, and the Otis-Lennon School Ability Test. Some evidence for the construct validity of SAGES-P is found in the significant positive correlations of the scores with chronological age. It is noteworthy that these correlations are higher for the General Information subtest—a measure of achievement, than for the Reasoning subtest—a measure of aptitude. Perhaps more supportive of the validity of SAGES-P as a measure of mental giftedness is the table of mean raw scores for the four age levels of the normal and gifted groups on the two subtests. Unfortunately, because the standard deviations of the raw scores are not provided in the manual, tests of significance between the "gifted" and "normal" means cannot be conducted to determine which means are significantly different from each other.

The overall impression of this reviewer is that SAGES-P is potentially useful as a measure of general knowledge and mental ability. To determine whether it is more effective than other psychometric measures for identifying giftedness in primary school

children remains to be seen. What is needed to establish its superiority in that respect is a study in which the success of the SAGES-P in differentiating between normal and gifted children is compared with that of other measures of mental ability. More sophisticated statistical methods, including factor analysis an discriminant analysis, might also be helpful in establishing such a claim.

Be that as it may, SAGES-P does boast a theoretical foundation, good standardization, respectable reliability coefficients, and some evidence for validity. The test should also be easy for nonpsychologists to administer, and, by following the suggestions in the Examiner's Manual, useful in diagnosis and placement.

Review of the Screening Assessment for Gifted Elementary Students—Primary by SUSANA URBINA, Associate Professor of Psychology, University of North Florida, Jacksonville, FL:

The Screening Assessment for Gifted Elementary Students—Primary (SAGES-P) is a downward extension of the Screening Assessment for Elementary Students (SAGES), published in 1987. Like its predecessor, SAGES-P aims at assisting in the identification of gifted children. Whereas SAGES was designed for use with children from 7 to 12 years old, SAGES-P is for children aged 5 to 8.

The authors of SAGES-P determined they would assess two areas which they equate, respectively, with achievement and aptitude. The areas they selected make up the two subtests of SAGES-P, namely, General Information and Reasoning.

The General Information subtest consists of 33 multiple-choice questions that are printed on the test booklet *and* read aloud by the examiner. Test takers must reply by selecting the picture, number, word, or letter that represents the best answer out of five choices. About a third of the items deal with numerical or quantitative content; the rest cover an assortment of areas (e.g., facts about animals, properties of objects).

The Reasoning subtest is made up of 28 analogies presented in a pictorial or figural multiple-choice format with five options. In this subtest, examinees are guided only through four sample items and the first test item and are then left to finish the remainder on their own. Considering the abstract nature of the Reasoning subtest and the age of test takers, this does not seem to be a wise course of action.

The directions for administering SAGES-P appear easy to follow when the test is given individually. When used with as many as 25 children, as the manual allows, administration could become problematic. No attempt has been made to establish comparability of individual and group administrations, though due to the use of basal and ceiling levels only in the former, the length of the test can differ significantly depending on administration mode.

Test items are printed in black on a white background. The booklets are plain and unlikely to hold the interest of typical or gifted children of the ages in question for very long.

SCORING. The SAGES-P is scored by a simple count of correct responses; in individual administration, items below the basal are also counted. Once raw subtest scores have been tallied, they can be transformed into percentile ranks and standard scores with a mean of 10 and a standard deviation of 3. An excellent feature of SAGES-P is that it provides normative tables for gifted and normal children at every half-year interval from 5-0 to 8-11. The normal sample consisted of 2,581 children enrolled in regular classrooms with demographic characteristics comparable to those of the school-age population of the United States. The gifted sample consisted of 1,034 children enrolled in gifted classes whose demographic characteristics also resembled those of the school-age population, except for the considerably higher level of education of parents. Both samples were tested from September of 1990 to June of 1991 and were drawn from the same 19 states.

Standard scores on the two subtests are added and the sum is converted to a composite standard score ($M = 100$, $SD = 15$), which in a throwback to obsolete terminology is labeled as a "quotient." The misnaming of the composite score is one of several instances in which the SAGES-P manual is technically inaccurate. For example, the authors state that "standard scores are derived from the properties of the normal probability curve" and refer readers to a table showing the percentages that would fall in various score ranges *if* scores were normally distributed. However, the conversion tables show clearly that for some groups (i.e., the younger normal and older gifted children) score distributions were considerably skewed; this not only renders normal curve percentages inapplicable but also suggests inadequate item difficulty levels for those groups. Test users are also urged in the manual to compare SAGES-P scores to those of other tests, such as the Otis-Lennon School Ability Test (OLSAT; 11:274), by transforming their scores linearly into the same mean and *SD* units used in SAGES-P. This suggestion ignores differences in the content and norms of the tests and falsely implies that comparability is a function of uniformity of score formats.

RELIABILITY. Internal consistency was assessed by the coefficient alpha which was computed on a sample of 120 protocols randomly drawn from the normal and gifted standardization groups. Average alpha coefficients for the subtests, across intellectual classifications and ages, range from .87 to .96. The standard error of measurement is described as an additional "type" of reliability available on the SAGES-P, although it is just another way of expressing data from the alpha coefficients. No evidence of the stability of scores over time is cited. This would be desirable especially in light of the SAGES-P target age.

VALIDITY. In order for a test to show content-related validity, its items must be representative of "some defined universe or domain of content" (AERA, APA, & NCME, 1985, p. 10). "Giftedness" is, by definition, independent of domain and can be demonstrated in a great variety of intellectual, academic, creative, artistic, psychomotor, and interpersonal endeavors. Thus, the notion of content validity is clearly inappropriate when considering a test meant to assist in identifying giftedness. Nevertheless, Johnsen and Corn claim content validity for SAGES-P because "the test's contents are found in the majority of different schools' identification procedures" (p. 32) and because it "conforms to currently used tests" (p. 32) for identifying the gifted.

Data on criterion-related validity consist of correlations between SAGES-P and the Wechsler Intelligence Scale for Children—Revised and Stanford-Binet (unspecified edition), which are both identified as "aptitude" tests. The correlations listed are in the low .70s for the General Information subtest and Total score and in the .60s for the Reasoning subtest. Correlations are also given for all SAGES-P scores and scores on the SRA Survey of Basic Skills, the Education Ability Series, the Peabody Individual Achievement Test—Revised, and the OLSAT. These coefficients range from not significant to .77 and are based on samples apparently gathered on the basis of convenience. All coefficients were corrected for attenuation and for restriction of range; contrary to recommended practice, uncorrected figures are not listed.

For evidence of construct validity, Johnsen and Corn reiterate the findings on concurrent validity, cite correlations between SAGES-P scores and age, and point out that scores of gifted children were substantially higher than those of nongifted children at all ages. Although all these data are compatible with the hypothesis that SAGES-P measures some aspects of intelligence, they do not demonstrate that

SAGES-P can help to discriminate gifted from non-gifted youngsters. In addition, the data are fairly weak (e.g., correlations between Reasoning subtest scores and age are .39 and .46 for the normal and gifted samples, respectively). Moreover, although the means for both subtests are indeed higher for gifted than for normal students, no indication of the significance of those differences or of the overlap in the scores is given. Finally, although emphasis is placed on the distinctions between the SAGES-P subtests, data on their intercorrelations are missing.

OVERVIEW. The SAGES-P cannot be recommended for its intended purpose. Not only is it narrower in focus than the intelligence scales traditionally used to decide who is gifted, but its difficulty range is also insufficient, especially for 8-year-olds. The Wechsler scales (T4:2937, T4:2938, T4:2939, T4:2940, T4:2941), the Stanford Binet Intelligence Scale, Fourth Edition (T4:2853), and even the Slosson Intelligence Test—Revised (84) all provide wider difficulty ranges and greater breadth of coverage than SAGES-P. In addition, the use of an instrument like SAGES-P as a *group test* to make decisions about young children seems indefensible. In fact, the potential for measurement error inherent in using it as a group test should be a deterrent to its being used that way even for research. As an individual test, however, SAGES-P could be of value in a battery for identifying giftedness or as a tool in investigating the nonverbal abilities of young children.

REVIEWER'S REFERENCE

American Educational Research Association, American Psychological Association, & National Council on Measurement in Education. (1985). *Standards for educational and psychological testing.* Washington, DC: American Psychological Association, Inc.

[82]
Screening Instrument for Targeting Educational Risk.

Purpose: Developed to provide a "method by which children with hearing problems (either known or suspected) can be educationally screened."
Population: Students with suspected or known hearing loss.
Publication Date: 1989.
Acronym: S.I.F.T.E.R.
Scores, 5: Academics, Attention, Communication, Class Participation, School Behavior.
Administration: Individual.
Price Data, 1994: $24 per complete kit including 100 screening forms and manual (7 pages); $17 per 100 screening forms; $9 per manual.
Time: Administration time not reported.
Comments: Ratings by teachers.
Author: Karen L. Anderson.

Publisher: PRO-ED, Inc.

Review of the Screening Instrument for Targeting Educational Risk by STEPHEN J. BONEY, Assistant Professor of Communication Disorders, Department of Special Education and Communication Disorders, University of Nebraska-Lincoln, Lincoln, NE:

The Screening Instrument for Targeting Educational Risk (S.I.F.T.E.R.) is a 15-item checklist-format instrument for screening the classroom performance of children who are hearing impaired and mainstreamed in regular education classrooms. The author also suggests the S.I.F.T.E.R. is appropriate for screening the educational performance of children identified through hearing screening programs. Based on national field testing, the S.I.F.T.E.R. is most appropriate for use with elementary-age children with hearing losses up through the moderate degree range. The instrument samples information from five broad areas: Academics, Attention, Communication, Class Participation, and School Behavior. Three questions are proffered in each area. The child's classroom teacher is to rate the student in each area using a 1 to 5 Likert scale. Adjective descriptors (e.g., upper, middle, lower, never, occasionally, frequently) are used as metrics for the middle and endpoint values (e.g., 1, 3, and 5). Teachers mark their ratings on an accompanying standard form. Responses are summed from each content area and entered on a shaded profile grid. Shading on the grid delineates three areas: pass, marginal, and fail. From the grid, a profile is constructed for each child and used to make decisions as to whether further assessment or programming are needed. Sample profiles with suggested follow-up are included in the manual.

Standardization of the S.I.F.T.E.R. was based on data from 530 students with varying degrees of hearing loss and 50 control students. Demographics are given for the students with hearing loss; however, similar information is not available regarding the control subjects. Students in the standardization sample were predominantly Caucasian (92%). Therefore, this instrument may not be appropriate for other racial or ethnic groups. Further, there is no indication of the socioeconomic levels of the students. Validation information presented in the manual is limited. The information presented is primarily descriptive and lacking statistical analysis. The author does, however, indicate that more detailed information regarding the validation process is available upon request.

Interrater reliability was assessed by having two teachers rate the performance of the same 10 students. Reliability coefficients were calculated for each content area and ranged from a low of .33 for class participation to a high of .62 for communication. These values are low and may reflect the use of only a small sample of teachers and students. This area warrants further attention. Reliability may be improved by providing the rater with general guidelines as to criteria that should be used for each of the Likert ratings. Additionally, there are no data concerning intrarater reliability. It would also be useful to determine interrater reliability for students by grade.

To date, the S.I.F.T.E.R. remains virtually the only standardized instrument to screen the classroom performance of mainstreamed hearing-impaired children. The brevity of the instrument along with the cadre of content areas makes it appealing for use in educational settings. Responses to questions are based on the teacher's knowledge and observations of the student. It is not necessary for teachers to supply specific performance information in the various content areas. Simply filling out the instrument may raise the teacher's awareness of potential educational problems the student may be experiencing. Scoring is simple. Professional school personnel other than the classroom teacher (e.g., speech-language, pathologist, audiologist, or teacher of the hearing impaired) are intended to score the instrument. This frees the teacher from an extra time commitment. Interpretation of results is fairly straightforward. The response grid allows the scorer to note quickly areas of difficulty. Examples of various students' S.I.F.T.E.R. profiles are presented in the manual to aid in interpretation.

In summary, the S.I.F.T.E.R. is a simple, quick, and easily scored screening instrument for determining potential classroom problems for mainstreamed hearing-impaired children or those children identified with hearing losses through hearing screening programs. It might also be used for children who experience frequent episodes of otitis media. It should be noted, however, that normative information for this specific population has not been determined. The S.I.F.T.E.R. is most appropriate for use with Caucasian students in grades kindergarten through 5. Results with minority students should be interpreted cautiously. Further, the S.I.F.T.E.R. should be used for those students with hearing losses through the moderate degree range who are primarily served by regular classroom teachers. There are some concerns regarding intertester reliability. In addition, limited validation information is presented in the user's manual. Even with these shortcomings, I would recommend the S.I.F.T.E.R. as part of a screening process to identify potential classroom problems for mainstreamed hearing-impaired children.

Review of the Screening Instrument for Targeting Educational Risk by STEVEN H. LONG, *Assistant Professor of Speech Pathology & Audiology, Ithaca College, Ithaca, NY:*

The Screening Instrument for Targeting Educational Risk (S.I.F.T.E.R.) is a questionnaire about the classroom performance of students with hearing loss. The questionnaire is completed by a student's classroom teacher. Responses are then scored and compared to cutoff values to determine whether further assessment by school personnel is warranted.

TEST MATERIALS. The S.I.F.T.E.R. questionnaire is printed on a single sheet and consists of 15 questions that call for responses on a 5-point rating scale. On the back of the questionnaire informants may write other comments. Information about test development, cutoff scores, and guidelines for interpretation of results are given in a very brief manual.

TEST ADMINISTRATION. Copies of the S.I.F.T.E.R. are distributed to the teachers of hearing-impaired students. The teachers circle the appropriate response to each question and return the form. A scoring grid allows the test user to sum responses in five categories: Academics, Attention, Communication, Class Participation, and School Behavior. By comparing a child's scores in each category to cutoff values, a rating of pass, marginal, or fail is assigned. The ratings profile is then evaluated to determine the most appropriate course of action for each child.

PSYCHOMETRIC ADEQUACY. Content validity for the 15 questions included in the S.I.F.T.E.R. questionnaire was established through logical and statistical analyses. A pilot version of the questionnaire contained 40 questions in seven categories. Based on data gathered from 82 students, the items on the S.I.F.T.E.R. were reduced to their present number. The items not included were ones found to be most discriminating of children with impairments.

The population on which the S.I.F.T.E.R. was standardized consisted of 530 children who had a known hearing loss or had failed a hearing screening. Though the instrument is intended for all children with hearing impairment, the author notes that the standardization group was biased toward Caucasian regular classroom students in kindergarten through grade 5 with faint to moderate losses.

The poorest psychometric feature of the S.I.F.T.E.R. is its interscorer reliability. It was only minimally assessed, with just two teachers each rating the same 10 students. The resulting correlations ranged from .33 to .62 for the five question categories. The author reports the direction of ratings— above or below average—was more highly correlated than the numerical ratings. This suggest that, perhaps, the S.I.F.T.E.R. would have been better designed using a 3-point rather than a 5-point rating scale. As the ratings are assigned by classroom teachers, it is possible that reliability could be improved through inservice training that offered examples of students at each of the rating points. This issue is not discussed by the author of the S.I.F.T.E.R.

SUMMARY. The S.I.F.T.E.R. is a teacher questionnaire designed to assist in the screening of children with known or suspected hearing loss. The content of individual items on the questionnaire was well evaluated. The standardization sample is fairly diverse and its few biases are clearly stated. The instrument's greatest shortcoming is its poor interscorer reliability, which completely undermines its norm-referenced use. Therefore, the only value to be gained from the S.I.F.T.E.R. would be as an adjunct to a more comprehensive evaluation of student performance.

[83]
Slingerland College-Level Screening for the Identification of Language Learning Strengths and Weaknesses.

Purpose: Developed to screen for strengths and weaknesses in language learning.
Population: College or college graduates.
Publication Date: 1991.
Scores, 10: Visual to Kinesthetic-Motor I, Visual to Kinesthetic-Motor II, Visual Perception-Memory, Visual Discrimination, Visual Perception and Memory to Kinesthetic-Motor, Auditory to Visual-Kinesthetic I, Auditory to Visual-Kinesthetic II, Auditory to Visual, Comprehension, Auditory to Kinesthetic.
Administration: Group.
Price Data: Available from publisher.
Time: (45–50) minutes.
Comments: Upward extension of the Slingerland Screening Tests (T4:2478).
Author: Carol Murray.
Publisher: Educators Publishing Service, Inc.
Cross References: See T4:2478 (2 references).

Review of the Slingerland College-Level Screening for the Identification of Language Learning Strengths and Weaknesses by MARY ANNE BUNDA, Professor Educational Leadership, Western Michigan University, Kalamazoo, MI:

This instrument has been developed to be an extension of other Slingerland Screening Tests (i.e., the primary, intermediate, and adult forms). Although some study has been made of the other instruments that use the Slingerland model, this instrument comes with no technical information. The manual suggests that field test information has not yet been collected. Not only are no data available on the reliability and validity of the test, but there are no norms presented. Rather the manual presents two case studies of individual responses to each of the 10 subtests with commentary by the test scorer.

The lack of any technical information on the test makes it impossible to recommend this instrument for any use other than research. The efficacy of other instruments developed within the model developed by Slingerland should not stand as evidence in the case of this instrument. The use of the model in the diagnosis of learning disabilities at other levels was clearly supplemented by additional information from instruments with known reliability and validity. In the case of this instrument, specifically designed for individuals who have attended at least 1 year of higher education, the manual itself acknowledges that the users will have limited objective supplemental data. In one of the cases, the individual provides the scorer with objective information which is used in the diagnosis. In the other, there is a recommendation to use self-report information from the examinee to form a diagnosis. The kinds of supplemental information recommended range from educational quality and opportunity to intelligence and health. However, no attempt has been made in the manual to explain how these factors must be taken into account. In each of the cases, the individual was diagnosed as specific language disabled and a tutor was recommended. Although these recommendations are made, the author points out the test is not called a test and the word disabled is not used in the title. The title of the test is not enough protection for potential examinees.

This test should not be used as a diagnostic device until further study is made of its role in the diagnosis of language disorder in postsecondary adults. Additionally, whether the model of language development and learning ascribed to by the developer warrants it or not, the test should clearly have norms developed. Evidence of the relationship between this test and other measures of both achievement and academic aptitude are definitely in order. At the very least, some evidence of the reliability of the scores which result from a single use of this instrument should be provided. Although the sample of behavior drawn by this instrument is very small, it may provide additional information to a sensitive special educator. A clinical interview may, however, provide the same quality of information.

Review of the Slingerland College-Level Screening for the Identification of Language Learning Strengths and

Weaknesses by THOMAS W. GUYETTE, Assistant Professor of Speech Pathology, University of Illinois at Chicago, Chicago, IL:

The purpose of the Slingerland College-Level Screening for the Identification of Language Learning Strengths and Weaknesses (SCLS) is to identify persons with specific language disabilities. The SCLS is "intended for use with adults who have already graduate from college or for students attending college currently" (p. 4). The SCLS can be administered either to a group or to individuals.

The screening test comes with a teacher's manual, a test booklet, and stimulus materials. The teacher's manual primarily describes the administration and scoring of the test. Scoring and interpretation are also illustrated with two case reports. The test booklet is 10 pages long and can be purchased in packages of 12. The stimulus materials are appropriate in terms of size (for group administration) and professional appearance.

The SCLS is divided into 10 subtests. Subtest I is a "distance copying" test. The student is asked to copy a short paragraph which is posted in the room. Subtest II is a "near point" copying task and involves copying a short outline presented on the test booklet. Both Subtests I and II are timed and the student has 5 minutes to complete each subtest. In Subtest III the student is exposed to a stimulus card for 5 seconds, asked to wait for 5 seconds, and then matches the memory of the stimulus card to stimuli in the test booklet. Subtest IV is a test of visual discrimination which involves matching words. In Subtest V the student is exposed to a stimulus card for 5 seconds, waits for 5 seconds, and then writes or draws what they remember on the stimulus card. In Subtest VI the student listens to dictation, waits for 5 seconds, and then writes down the dictation. In Subtest VII a word is dictated and the student is asked to write down a particular grapheme (either word initial, word final, or vowel) occurring in that word. In Subtests VIII an auditory stimulus is dictated; after a 5-second delay the student is asked to match the auditory memory with a visual symbol. Subtest IX is a comprehension task where the students listen to a paragraph read by the examiner and then write what they remember. There is a 10-minute time limit for this task. In Subtest X the student is asked to write down a word after it is dictated.

The documentation accompanying the test provides the examiner with adequate information to administer and score the test. The description of the subtests is sufficient. Various categories of errors are illustrated including reversals, transpositions, insertions, omissions, inversions, substitutions, and poor

formations. A discussion of self-corrections and other performance factors noted during scoring is present.

There are several significant problems with the SCLS. First, there is insufficient rationale proposed for the content of the test. The manual would be significantly improved by the addition of a section which describes the model of language processing used to derive the 10 subtests.

Second, there are questions concerning the interpretation of test scores. For example, the manual does not indicate when a score is to be considered normal or abnormal. Also, there are no data describing normal test performance and the author states that "no attempt has been made to establish standardized norms" (p. 4). Finally, although the manual states that the test score should be interpreted in relationship to other information such as family history, intelligence, grade-level achievement, and opportunities for learning, the manual does not clearly indicate how this additional information is to be used when interpreting the test results.

Third, the manual lacks information on test reliability. There is no information on the internal consistency of test items, on the reliability of scoring procedures, and on test-retest consistency. The lack of information on consistency of scoring across examiners is a significant omission given the judgement involved in scoring many of the subtests.

Fourth, the manual lacks information on test validity. There are no reports of concurrent, predictive, or construct validity.

In conclusion, the documentation accompanying the test provides the examiner with adequate information to administer and score the test. However, the test has significant weaknesses including: (*a*) insufficient rationale for the content of the test, (*b*) inadequate guidelines for interpretation of test scores, (*c*) no information on normal test performance, (*d*) no information on test reliability and, (*e*) no information on test validity. I would not recommend this test because of the omission of important psychometric information.

[84]

Slosson Intelligence Test [1991 Edition].

Purpose: Designed for use as a "quick estimate of general verbal cognitive ability."

Population: Ages 4-0 and over.

Publication Dates: 1961–91.

Acronym: SIT-R.

Scores: Total score only.

Administration: Individual.

Price Data, 1992: $57 per complete kit including 50 test forms, manual ('91, 45 pages), and norms tables/technical manual ('91, 39 pages); $16 per 50 test forms; $21 per norms tables/technical manual; $23 per manual.

Time: (10–20) minutes.

Authors: Richard L. Slosson, Charles L. Nicholson (revision), and Terry H. Hibpshman (revision).

Publisher: Slosson Educational Publications, Inc.

Cross References: See T4:2482 (43 references); for reviews of an earlier edition by Thomas Oakland and William M. Reynolds, see 9:1142 (11 references); see also T3:2217 (82 references), 8:227 (62 references), and T2:524 (12 references); for reviews by Philip Himelstein and Jane V. Hunt, see 7:424 (31 references).

Review of the Slosson Intelligence Test [1991 Edition] by RANDY W. KAMPHAUS, Associate Professor of Educational Psychology, University of Georgia, Athens, GA:

The expressed purpose of the Slosson Intelligence Test [1991 Edition] (SIT-R) is to serve as "a quick estimate of general verbal cognitive ability" or "index of verbal intelligence" (manual, p. 1). The manual presents appropriate cautions about interpretation of the SIT-R as a screening measure, suggesting at several points that follow-up assessment is necessary to corroborate SIT-R results. The SIT-R may also be used as a second measure of intelligence.

The goals of this test revision were to (a) include a more even distribution of items from various content domains, (b) update the language used in items, (c) provide an updated norm sample, (d) liberalize scoring guidelines to give credit for English or metric measures, and (e) discard the term "Intelligence Quotient (IQ)" in favor of "Total Standard Score (TSS)." The degree to which these changes are advantages or disadvantages and other characteristics of the SIT-R will be addressed next.

The SIT-R has numerous advantages over its progenitor but there remains ample room for improvement. Among the strengths of this version are a more comprehensive manual, updated item pool, better norming, ease of administration and scoring, adequate reliability and concurrent validity data with the Wechsler Intelligence Scale for Children—Revised (WISC-R), and lack of an "IQ" score. Weaknesses in this edition include a lack of detail in the manual, lack of evidence of match of the norming to U.S. Census statistics, dependence on a score classification scheme that may encourage misuse, and dependence on English language fluency.

The SIT-R is extremely easy to administer and score. The use of a small number of verbal item types with a dichotomous item scoring system makes the measure intuitive to use. The SIT-R remains loyal to the original work of Binet (Kamphaus, 1993) by utilizing a variety of item types, ranging from recall of digits to quantitative items, that are ordered by difficulty. This administration format differs from that of the Wechsler tradition of using subtests. The stated administration time of 10 to 30 minutes is likely realistic.

The use of the back of the record form for some drawing items seems ill advised as it invites the older examinee to turn the page over and view his or her own scores. Similarly, although there are some advised starting points for various age groups, these are not marked on the record form. The record form could also benefit from more space to record responses and other examiner notes. The record form, for the most part, is easy to use.

Although the SIT-R manuals, one for administration and scoring and one for norm tables and technical data, contain many important topics they are substandard. The first manual contains only about 10 pages of relevant copy and the second manual 22. The remaining pages of each manual are devoted to norm tables and lists of items. The second manual reports only one concurrent validity study with the WISC-R and one with the WAIS-R (Wechsler Adult Intelligence Scale—Revised). Given that there are currently many alternatives to the WISC-R, studies of the relationship of the SIT-R to the Stanford-Binet Intelligence Scale, Fourth Edition (T4:2553) and the Kaufman Assessment Battery for Children (T4:1343) would seem to be central to such a manual. Information on content validity and the use of item response theory to gauge the distribution of item difficulty is welcome.

The norming of the SIT-R and scaling procedures are poorly described. Because the norm-referenced scores for the SIT-R are offered separately by age group, the representation of the norm sample by age, gender, race/ethnicity, and parental education/occupation should be reported by age group. The sample does significantly underrepresent cultural minorities for the total sample and it would be informative to see if this problem is specific to one or several age groups. The manual does report that "goodness-of-fit" tests were used to test for differences in educational level by age group and that no differences were found. The results of these analyses, however, were not reported.

The scaling procedures are not described adequately enough to determine how the norms were articulated across age groups. There is no indication of the smoothing method used or whether or not one was used to produce reasonable distributions of scores from age to age. Another curiosity is the decision to not offer separate age group norms above age 18. The last entry in the norm table simply reads "18+." According to the reliability data presented on page 7 of the second manual there were 118 cases at ages 35 through 44.9 and 76 cases at age 13. Norms were developed separately for the 12-year-olds but not for the older age group. There may be a very good reason for not showing an appreciation of adult development in the norms but it is not made clear in the manual.

The "Slosson Classification Chart" for the Total Standard Score may encourage misuse of scores. This interpretive chart seems at odds with the cautions against overinterpretation given elsewhere in the manual. Most disconcerting about this table is that it equates low scores with various levels of mental retardation. This classification system suggests that the TSS can be used to diagnose mental retardation or to confirm mental retardation. This chart may lead diagnosticians, or in this case teachers, to make the diagnosis of mental retardation without the assessment of adaptive behavior. The history of mental retardation diagnosis is fraught with problems that have resulted from elevating intelligence tests to preeminence over adaptive behavior measures even though the latter are central to all major diagnostic systems (Kamphaus, 1993). Use of this chart by the diagnostically unsophisticated could lead to the diagnosis of syndromes such as mental retardation and giftedness based solely on intelligence test scores. This is clearly an antiquated practice.

Other dated material is included in the percentile chart where the term "IQ" is used. The use of this term seems incongruous with other parts of the manual where the TSS terminology is favored.

A final concern regarding the SIT-R is its applicability in an increasingly multicultural society. Unlike other new screeners such as the Kaufman Brief Intelligence Test (K-BIT; Kaufman & Kaufman, 1990; 46) the SIT-R may not be used to screen for intellectual problems using less verbal item types. The SIT-R verbal item types are also less practical for the assessment of the undereducated.

In summary, the SIT-R has numerous strengths to recommend its use including a more comprehensive manual than previously included, an updated item pool, improved norming, ease of administration and scoring, adequate reliability and concurrent validity data with the WISC-R, and lack of use of the "IQ" score. Some of the more disconcerting weaknesses include limited evidence of concurrent validity, lack of evidence of a match of the norming to U.S. Census statistics, dependence on a classification system for total scores that may encourage misuse, and excessive dependence on English language fluency. Although the SIT-R is not fatally flawed as a screener there are many good alternatives available with better psychometric properties. Short forms of comprehensive intelligence test batteries can boast larger and better described norming samples that are a better fit to U.S. Census Bureau statistics. The K-BIT possesses strong evidence of concurrent validity and a less verbal screener. The availability of these latter alternatives suggests that for many users of intelligence screeners the SIT-R will have to be supported by a continuing stream of supportive research investigations to become a viable candidate for widespread use. At the time of this review, better alternatives than the SIT-R are readily available.

REVIEWER'S REFERENCES

Kaufman, A. S., & Kaufman, N. L. (1990). Kaufman Brief Intelligence Test. Circle Pines, MN: American Guidance Service.
Kamphaus, R. W. (1993). *Clinical assessment of children's intelligence: A handbook for professional practice*. Boston: Allyn & Bacon.

Review of the Slosson Intelligence Test [1991 Edition] by T. STEUART WATSON, Assistant Professor of Educational Psychology, Mississippi State University, Starkville, MS:

PURPOSE AND RATIONALE. The Slosson Intelligence Test [1991 Edition] (SIT-R) is primarily intended to be a brief screening measure of verbal crystallized intelligence. It is used less frequently to proffer tentative diagnoses and to confirm the results of other tests. The authors caution the SIT-R is measuring only verbal crystallized intelligence and inferences regarding ability in other intellectual domains (e.g., abstract/visual reasoning) are not supported.

Previous editions of the Slosson Intelligence Test were designed using the Stanford-Binet as a theoretical model. The 1991 revision does not model any one test as it purports to combine the components of several intellectual theories into one overarching framework. The theories of intelligence espoused by Wechsler, Thorndike, Hagen, Sattler, Guilford, Cattell, Jensen, and Sternberg are briefly reviewed in the technical manual and serve as the basis for the SIT-R.

TEST CONTENT. The test contains 187 untimed items assessing the cognitive domains of vocabulary, general information, similarities and differences, comprehension, quantitative ability, and auditory memory. More than half of the items from the old Slosson (SIT) remain on this edition. Content validity is said to exist because similar items are found on other major tests of intelligence and the cognitive aptitudes measured have a long and proven history. Item arrangement on the SIT-R represents a significant deviation from the SIT in that items are now arranged in ascending order of difficulty as opposed to by age ranges.

Conceptually, all items except those purportedly measuring auditory memory fall into Cattell's crystallized intelligence domain. Crystallized intelligence is said to be a product of native ability, culture, and life experiences, and reflective of individuals' achievements in their culture.

STANDARDIZATION AND NORMS. The non-random standardization sample of the SIT-R represents a noticeable improvement over that of the SIT. The sample of 1,854 subjects approximates the percentages found in the United States in terms of geographic region, occupational category, educational level, gender, and race. Minorities are underrepresented in the standardization sample as are those living in areas with populations below 5,000 and above 500,000. Most of the data were drawn from subjects residing in areas with a population between 5,000 and 100,000. This section of the technical manual could be improved by presenting stratified data instead of percentages within nominal categories and by indicating the number of subjects tested at each age level.

Despite its vast improvement in the area of standardization, serious questions remain regarding the appropriateness of using this test with persons who score at the extremes of the distribution and with those who evidence various types of handicaps. In addition, the procedure used to select the sample (examiners selecting subjects based on age only and the authors selecting subjects from that pool to match certain demographic characteristics) represents an unorthodox (semi-incidental) means to obtain normative data.

The SIT-R has a mean total standard score (TSS) of 100 and a standard deviation of 16. Raw scores are easily converted to total standard scores by age. Total standard scores may then be converted to standard scores on the Wechsler Scale (presumably the verbal scale, although not specifically stated), College Entrance Examination Board (CEEB), and General Aptitude Test Battery (GATB). One can also derive z scores, T scores, NCEs, stanines, and percentiles from the total standard score. Separate scores are not computed for each of the domains (e.g., vocabulary, comprehension).

A less desirable option is to convert raw scores to Mean Age Equivalents (MAE). The authors state in the technical manual that although MAE scores have "serious theoretical problems and can produce misleading results" (p. 22), they are provided anyway because some educational systems require the use of such scores. A full paragraph in the administration manual is devoted to explaining MAE scores. Doing so, in my opinion, has no virtue and violates the authors' and test publisher's ethical responsibility to provide interpretive data that have a sound theoretical and empirical basis. It also reinforces the continued use and misinterpretation of meaningless test data.

ADMINISTRATION AND SCORING. The age range for the test is 4 years to 18+ years. Administration of the SIT-R is simple and straightforward and requires approximately 10 to 30 minutes. All of the items are presented in a question-and-answer format. Six items require a visual stimulus on the reverse side of the scoring protocol. Basals and ceilings are established by 10 successive correct and incorrect responses, respectively. Responses are scored dichotomously on a one-page protocol. The raw score is computed by adding the highest item in the basal to the number of correct responses after the basal.

RELIABILITY. Kuder-Richardson 20 reliability coefficients by age level range from .88 to .97, indicating a high degree of interitem consistency. Test-retest reliability is reported to be .96, based on a weak sample size of 41 and a one-week administration interval. Split-half reliability, calculated using the Spearman-Brown correction and the Rulon procedure, was .97 for the entire sample.

Overall, the reported reliabilities are sufficient. However, the manual does not explain the reliabilities clearly nor does it give substantial explanations of what they mean for the test consumer. Test-retest reliability could be enhanced by including studies with larger sample sizes and longer administration intervals.

VALIDITY. Concurrent criterion-related validity is based on correlations between the SIT-R total standard score and WAIS-R (Wechsler Adult Intelligence Scale—Revised) and WISC-R (Wechsler Intelligence Scale for Children—Revised) IQs. In a study of 10 subjects, significant correlations were found between TSS and three IQ scores on the WAIS-R. Comparisons with the WISC-R were made utilizing 234 subjects between the ages of 6 and 16. At each of four age levels (6–8, 9–11, 12–14, and 15–16) the TSS correlated significantly with each of the WISC-R IQs.

Clearly, it cannot be said unequivocally that the SIT-R is measuring only verbal crystallized intelligence. Indeed, from the limited validity studies reported, it seems it is measuring a general intelligence factor, or *g*. Many more validity studies should be performed with larger samples and broader populations before even tentative conclusions can be made regarding what this test is actually measuring.

Test bias is a complex and pivotal issue. The authors devote a third of a page to treatment of test bias which does not adequately address the most salient features of this subject. Indeed, it appears from the data tendered, the authors are concluding that the absence of mean raw score differences for ethnicity or gender is sufficient to warrant this judgment. One must also question the appropriateness of analyzing raw scores instead of mean standard scores. When analyzing individual test items using the Rasch model (the most common latent trait model), raw scores are deemed useless for further analysis.

The most portentous information regarding test bias is found in the section on Latent Trait Analysis where discussions on slope and intercept bias and error of estimate are presented. Pairwise comparisons and regression analyses on raw scores did not detect slope or intercept biases for any pair of four ethnic subpopulations or gender.

One disturbing point is the authors' explanation that use of latent trait analysis precludes gaining a representative sample of the population to produce meaningful norms. Despite the assumptions regarding Latent Trait Analysis, there is no substitute for gathering representative data during the normative process when designing a test for use with a variety of populations.

SUMMARY. Overall, the SIT-R is much improved over the original and updated versions. However, a number of problems continue to plague this instrument. The first issue is the selection procedure used to obtain normative data. Subjects were first tested and then chosen for inclusion into the sample based on their demographic characteristics. Noticeably lacking in the data on the normative sample are the numbers of individuals with disabilities tested during standardization. Omitting the percentage of students with various disabilities included in the sample precludes its use with that population, despite the manual's suggestions for testing such individuals.

The second difficulty with the SIT-R is the lack of adequate reliability and validity data. The data that are presented come from studies with meager sample sizes, restricted populations, and do not wholly support the theoretical basis upon which the test was designed.

A third issue concerns the discrepancies between what the authors acknowledge as good practice and what they discuss and recommend in the manuals. Besides use of the Mental Age Equivalent discussed earlier, the authors provide recommendations for testing individuals with handicaps. On the same page, however, they caution that administering the test to subjects not represented in the normative sample "may yield invalid scores and lead to erroneous interpretations" (p. 9).

Like its predecessor, the SIT-R may be used cautiously as a preliminary screening device to crudely estimate overall IQ. If one's goal is to predict IQ on the Wechsler scales, a more valid and reliable procedure is to use the dyads, triads, or quatrads from the Wechslers, for which psychometric properties are more robust.

[85]

Slosson Oral Reading Test [Revised].
Purpose: Designed as a "quick estimate to target word recognition levels for children and adults."
Population: Preschool–adult.
Publication Dates: 1963–90.
Acronym: SORT-R.
Scores: Total score only.
Administration: Individual.
Price Data, 1992: $32 per complete kit; $14 per manual ('90, 38 pages); $16 per 50 score sheets; $7 per bound word lists; $3 per large print word lists.
Special Editions: Large print edition available for individuals with visual handicaps.
Time: (3–5) minutes.
Comments: Grade equivalent (GE) and age equivalent (AE) scores are also available.
Authors: Richard L. Slosson and Charles L. Nicholson.
Publisher: Slosson Educational Publications, Inc.
Cross References: See T4:2483 (16 references); T3:2218 (15 references), T2:1688 (5 references), and 6:844.

Review of the Slosson Oral Reading Test [Revised] by STEVEN R. SHAW, Assistant Professor of Psychology, Illinois State University, Normal, IL, and MARK E. SWERDLIK, Professor of Psychology, Illinois State University, Normal, IL:

The Slosson Oral Reading Test [Revised] (SORT-R) represents a revision of the original Slosson Oral Reading Test published in 1963. The SORT-R is designed to assess a subject's "level of oral word recognition, word calling or reading level" (p. 9). This instrument is not a diagnostic measure nor does it measure all aspects of reading such as word knowledge and comprehension. It is a "quick screening test to determine a student's reading level." The author also suggests the SORT-R may be used to assess a student's progress, determine a student's grade level in reading, and to determine if a student is in need of further diagnostic assessment. However, the primary use of the SORT-R is as a screening instrument.

The test is composed of 200 words arranged in ascending order of difficulty. The words are organized into 10 groups of 20 words each. Each group represented approximate grade levels, ranging from preschool to 9–12 grades. The SORT-R is designed for use with subjects from age 4 and above.

ADMINISTRATION AND SCORING. A basal level is attained when a subject can pronounce all 20 words in a group. A ceiling is reached when none of the 20 words in a group can be pronounced correctly. Subjects are allowed 5 seconds to pronounce a word. The 5-second limit is waived if the subject has a speech defect (e.g., stuttering) or visual impairment. Criteria for determining errors are provided. The correct pronunciations and several examples of incorrect pronunciation are provided. Examiner discretion is advised if the subject has an articulation difficulty or regional accent. The manual indicates that pronunciations of word endings and tenses must be pronounced in order for a word to be scored as correct. However, in a different section of the manual, the author suggests not counting words as errors if the pronunciation only slightly changes the meaning of a word such as sudden for suddenly, or rivers for river.

The test materials are attractive and easy to read for both examiner and examinee. For convenience, basic administration and scoring procedures are printed on each test protocol. Raw scores, grade and age equivalents, percentile rank, standard scores (including t-scores and normal curve equivalents), and confidence levels can also be determined and recorded directly on the protocol. Despite the limitations of grade equivalents, the author stresses the value of this scoring convention. Moreover, the grade equivalents in the tables are approximations and interpolation is required for some ages.

NORMATIVE DATA. The SORT-R was co-normed with the Slosson Intelligence Test. The sample included 1,331 subjects, ranging from preschool to adults. The author suggests the sample represents the U.S. population. However, close inspection reveals that large differences exist between sample and census data on geographic location and occupational status. There were also large differences in the number of subjects at different age levels. The manual author indicates that subjects were included from "special classes ranging from the retarded to gifted, learning disabled and regular" (p. 7). Yet, no data on special populations were provided. There is a list of participating school districts, but no demographic information about them or how they were selected is given. Thus, it is difficult to determine to whom these norms would be applicable.

RELIABILITY. Internal consistency (Spearman-Brown Split Half, Rulon, and Kuder-Richardson) and test-retest stability all yield coefficients above .95. Interestingly, the highest reliabilities were found in the youngest age groups. All reliability data were collected on the standardization sample with no separate reliability studies reported in the manual. The number of subjects in the test-retest study was only 16 and no age data were provided. The high reliability can be attributed to the SORT-R containing a large number of items, a good sampling of test items, and test specificity as only oral reading is being measured. Based on the data reported in the manual, the SORT-R appears to have satisfactory reliability.

CONTENT VALIDITY. The words on the SORT-R are the same as on the SORT. Words were drawn from the Dolch reading list and "other reading lists" (manual, p. 1), tests of reading, and reading lists in textbooks at selected grade levels. All words were reviewed by reading experts, textbook authors, and compared to various curriculum guides. Words were selected to reflect a steady progress in reading difficulty from preschool to high school level. Based on the Slosson norms, each word represents one-half month progress. The author notes that the added length of word lists improves the content validity of the test. However, without knowing the specifics regarding the origin of the word lists one cannot assume this to be true.

CONSTRUCT/CRITERION. The SORT-R has been administered concurrently with several tests of reading recognition and reading comprehension. The Woodcock-Johnson Test of Achievement (WJTA)—Letter Word Identification and the Peabody Individual Achievement Test (PIAT)—Reading Comprehension both correlate over .90 with the SORT-R. Passage Comprehension from the WJTA and Reading Comprehension from the PIAT correlate with the SORT-R .68 and .83, respectively. The subjects used in these validity studies were not described. The criterion instruments used in these studies are outdated forms of tests that have revised versions. No evidence is presented to support the construct of the SORT-R other than correlations with reading tests that have also been criticized for lack of supporting construct validity. The SORT-R is also correlated highly (.87) with the Slosson Intelligence Test—Revised. This may indicate the two tests do not assess independent constructs. In addition, no validity data supporting the uses of the SORT-R proposed by the author are presented.

SUMMARY. The SORT-R should only be used for initial screening or research purposes. It is a quick test that is easy to administer and score. Although the SORT-R has adequate reliability, the test has limited relevance to school-based instruction. The content and construct validity of the SORT-R is questionable. Estimating reading progress during the school year with a test of word calling appears inappropriate. If detailed diagnostic information is required, informal reading inventories or normative instruments such as the Stanford Diagnostic Reading Test (T4:2555), the Gray Oral Reading Test (T4:1084), and/or curriculum-based assessment are better choices than the SORT-R. Thus, the SORT-R fills a very small niche in reading assessment. This niche may be filled better with teacher's judgment of a student's reading ability.

Review of the Slosson Oral Reading Test [Revised] by CAROL E. WESTBY, Senior Research Associate, Training and Technical Assistance Unit, University of New Mexico Medical School, Albuquerque, NM:

The Slosson Oral Reading Test [Revised] (SORT-R) is a restandardization of the Slosson Oral Reading Test that was originally published in 1963. The purpose of the SORT-R is to provide a quick estimate of a person's oral word recognition or "word calling" level. It takes about 3 minutes to give and score. The SORT-R is not intended to be a diagnostic instrument or to measure reading comprehension. The SORT-R consist of 10 lists of 20 words each presented in a spiral-bound book. There are separate lists for preprimer through grade 8 levels and a list for 9th through 12th grade. Words were chosen from a variety of reading lists and textbooks at selected grade levels so that they represent a steady progression of difficulty from the preprimer to high school level. Words were not chosen according to their phonic characteristics, and hence, the SORT-R cannot be used to determine a person's knowledge of grapheme/phoneme relationships. The print size of the lists reflects the print size in school textbooks. The grades K–4 word lists are in 14-point print and the grades 5–12 lists are in 10-point print. A single-page score sheet has all the lists on the front. Scoring is based on total number read correctly. Words are considered read incorrectly if the reader pronounces them incorrectly, takes longer than 5 seconds to read them, changes their form (hides/ hide), or omits reading them. The starting or basal list is the list at which the person reads all words correctly; the ceiling list is the list at which the person does not read any of the words correctly. The back of the score sheet contains the test directions, space

for recording demographic information (name, age, school, examiner), and test results.

The SORT-R has retained the same lists as the original SORT, but contains updated norms as well as new scoring methodologies such as: age and grade equivalencies and standard scores, T-scores, and stanines by age and grade. The standardization sample consisted of 1,331 individuals from preschool to adult from all sections of the United States. Percentages of the SORT-R sample reflect the gender and racial percentages of the total U.S. population. In addition, the educational level of parents of students in the sample matched the percentage of persons at various educational levels in the general U.S. population.

The SORT-R manual authors provide information on construct, content, and concurrent validity and on split-half and test-retest reliability. The large number of words on the SORT-R (200) contributes to both good content validity and reliability. The SORT-R shows high concurrent validity coefficients (correlations $r = .90$) with the letter identification subtest of the Woodcock-Johnson Tests of Achievement and the reading recognition subtest of the Peabody Individual Achievement Test. Split-half reliability and test-retest after 1 week resulted in correlations of .98. The SORT-R provides a valid and highly reliable means for quickly determining a person's word recognition level.

[86]

Social Skills Rating System.

Purpose: Constructed to screen and classify children suspected of having social behavior problems and to assist in the development of appropriate interventions for identified children.

Publication Date: 1990.

Acronym: SSRS.

Administration: Individual.

Price Data, 1993: $97.95 per preschool/elementary levels starter set including 10 copies of each form and level questionnaires, 10 assessment-intervention records, and manual (207 pages); $89.95 per secondary level starter set; $18.95 per 30 questionnaires (select level and form); $27.95 per 30 assessment-intervention records; $30.45 per manual.

Time: (15–25) minutes.

Comments: Ratings by teachers and parents as well as student self-ratings; expanded version of the Teacher Ratings of Social Skills.

Authors: Frank M. Gresham and Stephen N. Elliott.

Publisher: American Guidance Service.

a) PRESCHOOL.

Population: Ages 3-0 to 4-11.

Scores, 2: Social Skills, Problem Behaviors.
Forms, 2: Parent, Teacher.
b) ELEMENTARY.
Population: Grades K–6.
Scores, 3: Social Skills, Problem Behaviors (Parent and Teacher forms only), Academic Competence (Teacher form only).
Forms, 3: Student, Parent, Teacher.
c) SECONDARY.
Population: Grades 7–12.
Scores, 3: Same as for *b* above.
Forms, 3: Same as for *b* above.
Cross References: See T4:2502 (4 references).

Review of the Social Skills Rating System by KATHRYN M. BENES, Licensed Psychologist, Lincoln, NE:

The Social Skills Rating System (SSRS) is a standardized, norm-referenced instrument designed to provide professionals with a means to screen and classify student social behavior in educational and family settings. Moreover, the SSRS facilitates the development of intervention strategies for youth from preschool through grade 12 who may experience difficulty because of social skills or performance deficits.

Although the SSRS was developed to broadly assess social skills, it not only samples the social skills domain, but the domains of academic competence and problem behavior as well. The authors indicate that information from these additional domains is critical in determining factors that contribute to social skills problems. Moreover, the additional information is necessary in order to develop treatment strategies.

The SSRS manual provides a clear and detailed description of the overall goals and objectives of the SSRS. The authors have developed a user friendly guide for professionals wanting to assess and plan interventions for students with social skills or performance deficits. Much of what is presented here can be found in more thorough detail in the SSRS manual.

CONTENT. The SSRS offers three methods of evaluating student social behavior: (*a*) Parent Form, (*b*) Teacher Form, and (*c*) Student Form. In addition, the parent and teacher versions of the SSRS are divided into three developmental levels: preschool, kindergarten through sixth grade, and seventh through twelfth grades. Because of the reading level, the student version is available for youth who are capable of reading at a third grade level.

The SSRS Parent Form is completed by the student's mother and/or father, or guardian. The number of items on the Parent Form range from 49

(Preschool Level) to 55 (Elementary Level). Items ask the parent to rate the frequency of a specified behavior (e.g., "Attempts household tasks before asking for help") on a 3-point scale (0, Never; 1, Sometimes; 2, Very Often). In addition, the parent is asked to rate the importance of the behavior (0, Not Important; 1, Important; 2, Critical).

The Parent Form yields four Social Skills Subscale raw scores (i.e., Cooperation, Assertive, Responsibility, and Self-Control) as well as a Social Skills Scale total raw score. In addition, two Problem Behaviors Subscale raw scores (i.e., Externalizing and Internalizing) are derived from the responses on each of the three levels of the Parent Form and a third Problem Behavior Subscale raw score is included for the Elementary Level form. A total Problem Behaviors raw score is also included. The Social Skills Scale and Problem Behaviors Scale raw score totals are then converted into Standard Scores (mean = 100; standard deviation = 15).

The Teacher Form is completed by the student's teacher or other school personnel who has had exposure to the student's classroom behavior for at least 2 months. The number of items on the Teacher Form ranges from 40 (Preschool Level) to 57 (Elementary Level). Similar to the Parent Form, the teacher is requested to respond to items (e.g., "Finishes classroom assignments within time limits") using the same 3-point frequency and importance scales.

The Teacher Form responses are collapsed into three Social Skills Subscale raw scores (i.e., Cooperation, Assertion, and Self-Control). These three raw scores compose the Social Skills Scale total raw score. Similar to the Parent Form, the Teacher Form also has two Problem Behaviors Subscale raw scores (i.e., Externalizing and Internalizing) that are combined to yield a total Problem Behavior raw score. As with the Parent Form, the Social Skills Scale and Problem Behaviors Scale raw score totals are then converted into Standard Scores (mean = 100; standard deviation = 15). In addition to the Social Skills and Problem Behavior Scales, the Teacher Form also includes an Academic Competence Scale at the Elementary and Secondary Level. This section of the SSRS consists of nine items (e.g., "In *mathematics*, how does this child compare with other students?") that are rated on a 5-point scale (Lowest 10%; Next Lowest 20%; Middle 40%; Next Highest 20%; Highest 10%). These ratings are also converted into standard scores.

There are two Student Forms (Elementary, grades 3–6; Secondary, grades 7–12) that are self-ratings. The response format of the Secondary Level form is similar to that of the Parent and Teacher Forms;

however, the Elementary Level form requests frequency of behavior only. The Student Forms also differ from the Parent Form in that instead of the Responsibility Subscale being measured, an Empathy Subscale is included. In addition, the Problem Behaviors Scale is absent from the Student Forms.

The final component of the SSRS is the Assessment-Intervention Record (AIR). The AIR is an eight-page form that serves to integrate the information obtained from the Parent, Teacher, and Student Forms. The AIR provides an effective means for analysis of student strengths and weaknesses and for prioritizing areas of concern in regard to student social skills. But more importantly, the AIR functions to facilitate the critical link between assessment and intervention.

STANDARDIZATION SAMPLE. The authors describe their sampling procedure in detail in the SSRS manual. They indicate that the SSRS was developed over the course of a 5-year period. The SSRS emerged from a prior research instrument, the Teacher Ratings of Social Skills (TROSS).

The SSRS standardization sample included 4,170 self-ratings of children and youth, 1,027 parents, and 259 teachers. Approximately the same number of male and female students, representing "sufficient" numbers from each grade level were sampled. The student sample included regular education students, as well as self-contained special education and mainstreamed special education students. The special education students represented in the standardization sample included youth identified as Mentally Handicapped, Learning Disabled, Behaviorally Disordered, and "Other."

Ethnic and racial representation in the SSRS standardization sample included a slight overrepresentation of Whites and Blacks, and a slight underrepresentation of Hispanics. Minority students made up approximately 27% of the normative sample, although the authors report that the U.S. population consists of about 31% ethnic and racial minorities.

The standardization sample was drawn from 18 states in the Northeast, North Central, South, and Western regions of the United States. The sample also represented individuals from urban, suburban, and rural communities.

RELIABILITY AND VALIDITY. The authors addressed the psychometric properties of the SSRS in great detail. They report coefficient alpha, the correlational index of internal consistency, for all forms ranged from .83 to .94 in regard to the Social Skills Scale, from .73 to .88 for the Problem Behavior Scale, and .95 for Academic Competence. These coefficients represent a high level of homogeneity among items.

Test-retest reliabilities were computed using the Elementary standardization sample for a 4-week period. Correlations for teacher ratings were .85 for the Social Skills scale, .84 for the Problem Behavior scale, and .93 for Academic Competence. Correlations for parent ratings were .87 for the Social Skills scale and .65 for the Problem Behavior scale. Finally, test-retest correlations for the self-ratings of students for the Social Skills scale was .68. Although the reliability coefficient for student self-reports was lower than the coefficients from parent or teacher forms, they nonetheless suggest adequate stability of the SSRS for all three forms.

The authors also addressed interrater reliability and standard error of measurement. As they point out, one would not expect high agreement on a measure such as the SSRS, therefore the utility of interrater reliability is somewhat limited. For a more detailed description of the standard error of measurement for the SSRS for the various scales and forms, the reader is referred to Appendix E of the SSRS manual.

In regard to validity, the authors addressed content, social, criterion-related, and construct validity. Gresham and Elliott (SSRS manual) demonstrated content validity by indicating the SSRS items were developed based on extensive empirical research. They also provided evidence for social validity by referring to prior research and the use of the Importance Rating Scale for each item.

The authors dedicated much of the validity section in the manual to criterion-related and construct validity. They cited a number of studies where the SSRS correlated highly with other somewhat similar measures (e.g., Social Behavior Assessment, Stephens, 1978; Harter Teacher Rating Scale, Harter, 1985; Piers-Harris Children's Self-Concept Scale, Piers, 1984; and the Child Behavior Checklist, Achenbach & Edelbrock, 1983, 1986, 1987). The results of the construct validity studies of the SSRS suggest "strong evidence in support of the construct validity of the Social Skills Rating System" (manual, p. 142).

CONCLUSION. Gresham and Elliott, the authors of the SSRS, have provided a psychometrically sound means of measuring the perceived social skills of youth from preschool to secondary school. The manual and forms are written and designed to make administration and scoring convenient. In addition, the items are written in behavioral terms so the rater does not have to use a high level of inference in order to respond. The use of the multirater system provides critical information regarding the student's self-evaluation of his/her behaviors as well as how significant others perceive the student's behavior at home and school. The most noteworthy factor of the SSRS, however, is the Assessment-Intervention Record (AIR). The AIR provides a format to integrate social skills assessment information and link the assessment to planned intervention strategies. By including this simple eight-page form, the authors assist professionals in making the important connection between assessment and intervention.

REVIEWER'S REFERENCES

Stephens, T. (1978). *Social skills in the classroom*. Columbus, OH: Cedars Press.
Achenbach, T., & Edelbrock, C. (1983). *Manual for the Child Behavior Checklist and revised Child Behavior Profile*. Burlington, VT: University of Vermont Department of Psychiatry.
Piers, E. V. (1984). *Piers-Harris Children's Self-Concept Scale* (revised manual). Los Angeles: Western Psychological Services.
Harter, S. (1985). *Manual for the Self-Perception Profile for Children*. Denver, CO: University of Denver.
Achenbach, T., & Edelbrock, C. (1986). *Manual for the Teacher's Report Form and teacher version of the Child Behavior Profile*. Burlington, VT: University of Vermont Department of Psychiatry.
Achenbach, T., & Edelbrock, C. (1987). *Manual for the Youth Self-Report form and profile*. Burlington, VT: University of Vermont Department of Psychiatry.

Review of the Social Skills Rating System by MICHAEL FURLONG, Associate Professor, and MITCHELL KARNO, Doctoral Student, Graduate School of Education, University of California, Santa Barbara, Santa Barbara, CA:

A distinguishing feature of the Social Skills Rating System (SSRS) is a multirater approach involving teachers, parents, and students as well as the integration of assessment results with intervention planning. Social skills items assessing the domains of Cooperation (all forms), Assertion (all forms), Self-Control (all forms), Responsibility (Parent Form only), and Empathy (Student Form only) are rated for frequency and importance to success in the child's specific classroom (Teacher Form) or the child's development (Parent Form). A Problem Behavior subscale is rated by teachers and parents that taps Externalizing, Internalizing, and Hyperactive behaviors. The Teacher Form also includes a very general Academic Competence subscale.

The SSRS actually is a set of eight related rating scales: two preschool versions (parent and teacher), three elementary school versions (parent, teacher, and student [grades 3–6]), and three secondary school versions (parent, teacher, and student). The eight versions contain 34–57 items derived from existing social skills training programs and other social skills rating scales. The eight versions have an average of just 37% of the items in common (range = 33% to 42% by pairs). The manual contains comparatively

little discussion of the Preschool Form; it was not included in the national standardization and normative data are available only for the tryout sample. The Preschool Form should be considered experimental because it requires additional validity evaluation as well as appropriate norms.

The SSRS was originally designed to be a "brief selection/screening measure" (Clark, Gresham, & Elliott, 1985, p. 348) that provided an alternative to the Social Behavior Assessment Inventory, a comprehensive social skills check list. Yet, the various forms of the rating scale take about 15–20 minutes to complete, which is too time consuming for general screening purposes. The SSRS will more typically be used as a post-referral assessment, such as part of a child study team process, or in a comprehensive evaluation.

This instrument is designed to be used with normal and mildly handicapped students for whom social skills deficits might limit academic performance. It does not replace other social skills and adaptive behavior instruments used with students who have more severe disabilities or special social skills needs associated with sensory impairment.

A testament to the fine detail provided in the protocols and the associate summary sheet is that it is possible to complete accurately all scoring and documentation procedures without referring to the manual for directions. However, educational personnel who have limited assessment and psychometric knowledge will find the interpretation procedures a challenge to understand.

RELIABILITY. The Teacher version was the first to be developed and is clearly psychometrically the soundest of the eight SSRS scales. Ninety-two percent of the alpha coefficients from the three Teacher Forms are .80 or higher, with 45.8% .90 or higher. In contrast, only 44% of the alpha coefficients from the three Parent Forms are .80 or higher, and only 20% of the alpha coefficients from the two Student Forms are that high (manual, p. 109). Users should have a very satisfactory degree of confidence in the Teacher Forms and a moderate level of confidence in the Parent Forms. The two Student Forms should be used with some caution. Only the Total Score of the Student Form has adequate reliability—the social skills subscales are not reliable enough to warrant individual interpretation.

VALIDITY. The manual includes an impressive array of data that systematically examine the SSRS's content, social, criterion-related, and construct validity. Criterion-related validity studies are reported for the elementary versions but not for the secondary versions. The construct validity of the Teacher and

Parent versions are supported by moderate to high loading on factor analyses using the normative sample. In contrast, the Elementary Student Form contains 10 subscale items with factor loadings below .30. All but one of these items are on the Cooperation and Assertion subscales, suggesting that they should be interpreted independently with caution.

With respect to predictive validity, the authors suggest in the manual and elsewhere (Gresham & Elliott, 1989a; 1989b) that the SSRS can be used to identify students who have social skills deficits that require special education services. How such a system is to be established is not well articulated. Educational agencies that might carry out such a public policy should first carefully evaluate the reliability and validity of the SSRS scores used to assist in making such eligibility decisions.

NORMING. At first glance, the size of the standardization sample is very impressive, but each user should closely examine the normative sample to decide if it is valid for their use. Ratings were obtained from 4,170 students in grades 3–12, 922 parents, and 259 teachers (88% female) who completed ratings for 1,335 students. The 4,170 students were roughly representative of the U.S. population but the sample underrepresented rural communities, the Northeast and West regions of the country, and Hispanic children. In the West region all the students were from the intermountain states with no students sampled from the West coast. This undoubtedly is partially responsible for the underrepresentation of Hispanic children. This sample characteristic is particularly critical in some regions of the country, such as California, where Hispanic students are the majority in many school districts. SSRS users in specific regions of the country may need to develop local norms and validate its use with specific minority populations.

Yoked ratings (parent, teacher, and student ratings of the same child) were obtained for only 837 children: 352 teacher-parent-student ratings of upper elementary children (grades 3–6); 157 teacher-parent-student ratings of secondary children (grades 7–12); and 328 teacher-parent ratings of early elementary children (grades K–2; no student ratings available). Thus, the Parent and Teacher norms for the early elementary, upper elementary, and secondary groups considered separately are based on less than 1,100 ratings, which are not representative of the U.S. population. More than three-fourths of the teacher ratings were obtained from the South and North Central regions of the country. The secondary school norms are based on ratings provided by just 51 teachers. In a laudable attempt to develop norms

for children with disabilities, special education teachers were over sampled, but this resulted in just 57% of the teachers working in regular classrooms. Because the teacher rating scale is the most psychometrically sound, it is unfortunate that the sample on which the norms for this portion of the test are based is composed of so few and so unrepresentative a group of teachers. In addition, the parent sample contained proportionately too few parents with less than high school education; caution should be taken when the SSRS is used with parents from a low SES background.

SCALING. A peculiar aspect of the SSRS is that normative data for the various subscales in each version are not provided. Instead, subscale raw scores and global scores are classified in terms of Behavior Levels: "Fewer," "Average," or "More." "Fewer" refers to fewer social skills than was common in the norming sample and so on. The scale is reversed for the Problem Behavior subscale so here "More" refers to more social problems than in the norm sample. These classifications were created by placing all scores within one standard deviation of the mean (85–115 range) into the "Average" category, scores below 85 into the "Fewer" category, and scores above 115 into the "More" category. The authors correctly suggest that the "Behavior Levels" should be used for screening and program development purposes only. Standard scores and *SEm* values are provided for the global scores, but not for the subscales. This information is needed to use the SSRS properly. Note, however, that this information can be estimated by using the means and standard deviations for the various subscales on pages 121–123 of the manual.

The authors indicate that, "Since each item on the Social Skills and Problem Behaviors Scales represents a specific behavior, the words 'Fewer,' 'Average,' and 'More' can be directly interpreted as referring to amounts, or frequencies, of behavior" (p. 48). The reader is cautioned that when interpreting the Behavior Levels it is possible to obtain nearly identical raw scores that do not reflect a similar incidence of social skills. Because the items are each rated for frequency (0 = never; 1 = sometimes; 2 = very often), identical raw scores can be obtained with different combinations of specific items and the comparative frequency of the items. To avoid misinterpretation of the Behavior Levels it is necessary to consider simultaneously both the number of social skills exhibited by each child and the frequency with which they occur. Furthermore, the items included in the rating scales do not represent discrete social skills but are broad skills within each domain.

The authors suggest that if just one social skills subscale is below average ("Fewer") across parent, teacher, or student ratings, then an analysis of specific Social Skill Performance Deficits (skills rated as important for success and occurring infrequently) and Social Skills Acquisition Deficits (skills rated as important for success and not occurring at all) is completed. This ultimately means that each item is scrutinized to see if it reflects a social skills deficit or strength. Given the fact the SSRS is likely to be used most commonly in situations when a student is referred because of social skills related concerns, it is likely that across raters at least one subscale will fall in the problem areas defined by the "Behavior Levels." It would have been useful for the publisher to provide information concerning the frequency of the "Fewer" rating within and across the parent, teacher, and student forms. If the incidence of at least one "Fewer" rating is common in the norm sample, then it raises questions about the utility of providing the "Behavior Levels" at all. The value of the "Behavior Levels" classification procedure without supportive norming information is not clear to these reviewers. The authors acknowledge that the Behavior Levels "are very general descriptors that have limited utility" (manual, p. 50).

UNIQUE CHARACTERISTICS. The strength of the SSRS as an assessment system lies in the attempt to link assessment findings with program planning and implementation. Users of the SSRS will appreciate the careful work the authors have done to present a model of social skills program planning that modifies the approach for responding to Acquisition Deficits, Performance Deficits, and Social Skills Strengths in the presence or absence of interfering behavior problems. The model presented is behavioral so users must be comfortable with the use of operant, social learning, and cognitive-behavioral intervention strategies.

Useful materials also have been developed to support appropriate scoring, interpretation, and prevention/intervention planning. A user-friendly computer scoring program (American Guidance Service, 1992) is available. Those choosing to use the computer program will find that they do not need to use the Assessment-Intervention Record Form because the program produces all the information that it contains. The authors have also compiled a structured intervention program that teaches 43 social skills within the five domains measured by the SSRS (Elliott & Gresham, 1991). In addition, Cartledge and Kleefeld (1991) have developed a program for preschool children.

RESEARCH APPLICATION. Given the negatively skewed distribution of the global and subscale scores, outcome studies may be influenced by a ceiling effect. For example, raw scores of 0–19 on the Teacher Form for elementary girls fall below the 2nd percentile. At the other end of the distribution, the top two percentiles are associated with raw scores of 59 and 60. The SSRS produces a better estimate of social skill deficits than well-developed social skills. This general principle applies to the Problem Behavior Scale as well—standard scores below 85 are unavailable. Researchers interested in evaluating the impact of an intervention beyond a broadly defined "normal" range should use another instrument, such as the Child Behavior Check List (Achenbach, 1983; T4:433). In addition, researchers should cautiously use the two Student Forms subscales to evaluate intervention effectiveness because of low reliabilities.

SUMMARY. The authors of the SSRS have articulated an excellent, comprehensive model of social skills assessment/intervention. As discussed in the manual and elsewhere (Elliott, Sheridan, & Gresham, 1989), the assessment of social skills requires a "multimethod" approach that encompasses rating scales, behavioral observations, and interviews. When a rating scale is used as part of such an assessment, the SSRS is recommended for it is currently the most comprehensive one available. Users attending to the cautions cited above will find it to be a valuable program planning guide and secondarily an assessment tool. It should prove to be even more valuable as future revisions address some of the limitations discussed above.

REVIEWERS' REFERENCES

Achenbach, T., & Edelbrock, C. (1983). *Manual for the Child Behavior Checklist and revised Child Behavior Profile*. Burlington, VT: University of Vermont Department of Psychiatry.

Clark, L., Gresham, F. M., & Elliott, S. N. (1985). Development and validation of a social skills assessment measure: The TROSS-C. *Journal of Psychoeducational Assessment, 4*, 347-356.

Elliott, S. N., Sheridan, S. M., & Gresham, F. M. (1989a). Scientific practitioner—Assessing and treating social skills deficits: A case study for the scientist practitioner. *Journal of School Psychology, 27*, 197-222.

Gresham, F. M., & Elliott, S. N. (1989a). Social skills assessment technology for LD students. *Learning Disability Quarterly, 12*, 141-152.

Gresham, F. M., & Elliott, S. N. (1989b). Social skills deficits as a primary learning disability. *Journal of Learning Disabilities, 22*, 120-124.

American Guidance Service. (1991). *ASSIST for the SSRS* [computer software]. Circle Pines, MN: American Guidance Service.

Cartledge, G., & Kleefeld, J. (1991). *Taking part: Introducing social skills to children*. Circle Pines, MN: American Guidance Service.

Elliott, S. N., & Gresham, F. M. (1991). *Social skills intervention guide*. Circle Pines, MN: American Guidance Service.

[87]

Stress Impact Scale.

Purpose: Designed "to assess the perception . . . and impact of potentially stressful events and conditions."

Population: Ages 8-3 to 19-6.
Publication Date: 1990.
Acronym: SIS.
Scores, 3: Stress Occurrence, Stress Impact, Stress Impact Differential.
Administration: Group.
Price Data: Not available.
Time: Administration time not reported.
Authors: Jerry B. Hutton and Timothy G. Roberts.
Publisher: PRO-ED, Inc.
[The publisher advised in January 1994 that this test is now out of print.—Ed.]

Review of the Stress Impact Scale by ROBERT J. DRUMMOND, Professor of Counselor Education, University of North Florida, Jacksonville, FL:

The Stress Impact Scale (SIS) is a 70-item self-appraisal instrument designed to measure the occurrence and impact of potentially stressful events and conditions of children and youth between the ages of 8 and 20. Students are asked to mark "yes" or "no" to whether the event had happened and then if they checked "yes," circle whether the event still bothers them "none," "some," or "a lot." The SIS yields three stress quotients: the Stress Occurrence Quotient, Stress Impact Quotient, and the Stress Impact Differential Quotient. The instrument is based upon the assumption that 8- to 20-year-olds can make reliable and valid reports about their life circumstances, and that the subjective judgment of the impact of events yields useful information. The items represent events and conditions that could happen in the lives of this group in school, at home, or in the community and represent dimensions of academic performance and behavior, social isolation and objectives, mobility, disturbed relationships, and the like.

The authors report criterion-referenced, construct, and item validity. The authors present studies comparing the SIS with the Children's Manifest Anxiety Scale, Children's Life Events Inventory, and Piers-Harris Self-Concept Scale—Revised. The coefficients tend to be significant and in the predicted direction. The cluster analysis of the items tends to support the scale and item validity of the instrument.

The SIS appears to have excellent reliability. Alpha coefficients are reported by age, grade, ethnicity, race, gender, and the like. The coefficients range from .80 to .92. Test-retest coefficients on the Occurrence and Impact scales by grade were equally as high and ranged from .83 to .93 across different grade levels. The authors report the alpha coefficients and standard errors of measurement for the scales by age, grade, ethnicity, gender, and residency. One set of norms is presented for the total age group. The characteristics of the standardization group are well described. Some questions that might help counselors in using the test are not clarified in the manual (e.g., are there differences in scores due to gender, grade, age, or ethnic/cultural group?). Also, does the SIS provide a limited snapshot of a student with problems? How does response set and social desirability affect how a student responds on the instrument? Would one of the problem checklists be equally effective and provide additional information?

Illustrative case studies are presented with suggestions for interventions that might be used. The manual provides an excellent summary of research and interventions dealing with stress.

Overall the SIS appears to be a psychometrically sound instrument and a potentially useful tool for child psychologists and school counselors.

Review of the Stress Impact Scale by SCOTT MEIER, Associate Professor, Counseling and Educational Psychology, State University of New York at Buffalo, Buffalo, NY:

The Stress Impact Scale (SIS) is a 70-item self-report scale designed to assess stressful life events for children and adolescents. The SIS produces two major scores: (a) Stress Occurrence, the total number of stressful events endorsed by the respondent; and (b) Stress Impact, a sum of ratings of the degree to which the respondent is "bothered" by the endorsed stressful events.

The authors developed items for the scale by reviewing the stress literature, interviewing distressed students, and examining related scales. The process resulted in items with apparent validity and a reading level appropriate for the intended population. The item analyses, however, contain several unusual or questionable procedures. First, the test developers administered the scale to a group of subjects and retained items if they correlated (with an uncorrected Pearson r) with the total score above .20. Second, the developers examined scale stability by calculating alpha coefficients across levels of age, grade, ethnicity, race, gender, and urban/rural residency; confirmatory factor analyses would be a preferable procedure. Third, the developers conducted cluster analyses instead of factor analyses to determine the underlying structure of the SIS.

SIS norms appear to be adequate and representative across levels of gender, urban/rural residency, race, ethnicity, parent education level, parent occupation, and national geographic area. Reliability levels also appear adequate to good, with scale alphas consistently above .85 and test-retest reliability at .90 over a 2-week period.

Although convergent validity data are presented, no information is offered for discriminant or predictive validity. Consequently, the SIS's chief weakness, like most other measures of negative affect, is construct validity. The Stress Occurrence and Stress Impact scores are highly intercorrelated ($r = .86$), suggesting they are interchangeable. Individual items which correlate most highly with a scale total (e.g., "Caught doing something wrong," [p. 18], "Teacher yelling at me" [p. 17]) appear to be tapping a conduct disorder or behavioral problems factor, although the test developers' cluster analysis classified these items into a grouping the developers labeled "Conditions/Hassles."

Interestingly, the manual does contain evidence for discriminant validity that is, apparently, unrecognized by the test developers. Correlations between the SIS scales are highest with another measure of children's stressful life events (rs around .70), next highest with an anxiety measure (around .55), and lowest with a self-concept measure (about -.34). This rank order of correlations magnitude provides validity support in that the SIS correlates most highly with measures of similar constructs and less so with different constructs.

Perhaps because of these construct validity questions, self-report scales like the SIS typically are not accompanied by evidence that they can predict behavior or performance. Although the SIS developers present a reference to the contrary, little evidence exists in the stress literature that demonstrates a consistent relation between stress and performance (e.g., Meier, 1991).

The stress-performance link is poorly understood and may be nonlinear. The next steps for the SIS developers, then, are to (a) examine the discriminant validity of the SIS, that is, does the scale measure stress or a conduct disorder factor; and (b) determine whether the SIS can predict performance measures such as grades, school attendance, or teacher/parent ratings of behavioral problems.

Scales like the SIS can probably best be conceived as global measures of such negative affective states as stress, depression, and anxiety. As such, most of these self-report scales, if developed with some attention to psychometric properties, are probably interchangeable for most users' purposes. Users who wish to screen children and adolescents for stress and behavioral problems may wish to use the SIS for that purpose.

REVIEWER'S REFERENCE

Meier, S. T. (1991). Tests of the construct validity of occupational stress measures with college students: Failure to support discriminant validity. *Journal of Counseling Psychology, 38*, 91-97.

[88]

Strong Interest Inventory [Fourth Edition].
Purpose: Designed to "inquire about a respondent's interest in a wide range of occupations."
Population: Ages 16 and over.
Publication Dates: 1927–85.
Acronym: SVIB-SCII.
Scores, 264: 6 General Occupational Themes: Realistic, Investigative, Artistic, Social, Enterprising, Conventional; 23 Basic Interest Scales: Adventure, Agriculture, Art, Athletics, Business Management, Domestic Arts, Law/Politics, Mathematics, Mechanical Activities, Medical Science, Medical Service, Merchandising, Military Activities, Music/Dramatics, Nature, Office Practices, Public Speaking, Religious Activities, Sales, Science, Social Service, Teaching, Writing; 207 General Occupational Themes: Accountant (female, male), Advertising Executive (f, m), Agribusiness Manager (m), Air Force Enlisted Personnel (f, m), Air Force Officer (f, m), Architect (f, m), Army Enlisted Personnel (f, m), Army Officer (f, m), Art Teacher (f, m), Commercial Artist (f, m), Fine Artist (f, m), Athletic Trainer (f, m), Banker (f, m), Beautician (f, m), Biologist (f, m), Broadcaster (f, m), Bus Driver (f, m), Business Education Teacher (f, m), Buyer (f, m), Carpenter (f, m), Chamber of Commerce Executive (f, m), Chef (f, m), Chemist (f, m), Chiropractor (f, m), College Professor (f, m), Computer Programmer (f, m), Credit Manager (f, m), Dental Assistant (f), Dental Hygienist (f), Dentist (f, m), Dietitian (f, m), Elected Public Official (f, m), Electrician (f, m), Elementary Teacher (f, m), Emergency Medical Technician (f, m), Engineer (f, m), English Teacher (f, m), Executive Housekeeper (f, m), Farmer (f, m), Flight Attendant (f, m), Florist (f, m), Food Service Manager (f, m), Foreign Language Teacher (f, m), Forester (f, m), Funeral Director (f, m), Geographer (f, m), Geologist (f, m), Guidance Counselor (f, m), Home Economics Teacher (f), Horticultural Worker (f, m), Interior Decorator (f, m), IRS Agent (f, m), Investments Manager (f, m), Lawyer (f, m), Librarian (f, m), Life Insurance Agent (f, m), Marine Corps Enlisted Personnel (f, m), Marketing Executive (f, m), Mathematician (f, m), Mathematics Teacher (f, m), Medical Illustrator (f, m), Medical Technician (f, m), Medical Technologist (f, m), Minister (f, m), Musician (f, m), Navy Enlisted Personnel (f, m), Navy Officer (f, m), Nurse LPN (f, m), Nurse RN (f, m), Nursing Home Administrator (f, m), Occupational Therapist (f, m), Optician (f, m), Optometrist (f, m), Personnel Director (f, m), Pharmacist (f, m), Photographer (f, m), Physical Education Teacher (f, m), Physical

Therapist (f, m), Physician (f, m), Physicist (f, m), Police Officer (f, m), Psychologist (f, m), Public Administrator (f, m), Public Relations Director (f, m), Purchasing Agent (f, m), Radiologic Technologist (f, m), Realtor (f, m), Recreation Leader (f, m), Reporter (f, m), Research & Development Manager (f, m), Respiratory Therapist (f, m), Restaurant Manager (f, m), School Administrator (f, m), Science Teacher (f, m), Secretary (f), Social Science Teacher (f, m), Social Worker (f, m), Sociologist (f, m), Special Education Teacher (f, m), Speech Pathologist (f, m), Store Manager (f, m), Systems Analyst (f, m), Travel Agent (f, m), Veterinarian (f, m), Vocational Agriculture Teacher (f, m), YWCA Director (f), YMCA Director (m); 2 Special Scales: Academic Comfort, Introversion-Extroversion; 26 Administrative Indexes: Total Response, Infrequent Response, Response Percentages (Like, Indifferent, Dislike) for each of the 7 inventory sections (Occupations, School Subjects, Activities, Leisure Activities, Types of People, Preference Between Two Activities, Characteristics) plus Total for all parts.

Administration: Group.

Price Data, 1992: $13 per 25 test booklets; $18 per 25 Spanish test booklets; $18 per Strong user's guide ('84, 92 pages); $23 per manual ('85, 189 pages); $9 per specimen prepaid scoring packet; $54 per 10 prepaid expendable test booklets; $53 per 10 prepaid profile answer sheets; $85 per 10 prepaid interpretive expendable test booklets; $84 per prepaid interpretive answer sheets; $13 per 50 not prepaid answer sheets; $3.50 per 10 profile reports; $5.75 per 10 interpretive reports; $6 per 10 expanded interpretive reports; $5 per 10 topical reports.

Foreign Language Editions: Available in Spanish (Form T325S), French Canadian (Form T325FC), and Hebrew (T325H) translations, and the wording has been adapted for use in Great Britain (Form T325B).

Time: (20–30) minutes.

Comments: Separate machine-scored answer sheets may be used; test cannot be scored locally.

Authors: Edward K. Strong, Jr. (original inventory), David P. Campbell (test and manual revision), and Jo-Ida C. Hansen (manual).

Publisher: Consulting Psychologists Press, Inc.

Cross References: See T4:2581 (64 references); for reviews by Wilbur L. Layton and Bert W. Westbook, see 9:1195 (17 references); see also T3:2318 (99 references); for reviews by John O. Crites, Robert H. Dolliver, Patricia W. Lunneborg, and excerpted reviews by Richard W. Johnson, David P. Campbell, and Jean C. Steinhauer, see 8:1023 (289 references, these references are for SVIB-M, SBIV-W, and SCII). For references on the Strong Vocational Interest Blank For Men, see T2:2212 (133 references); for reviews by Martin R. Katz and Charles J. Krauskopf and excerpted reviews by David P. Campbell and John W. M. Rothney, see 7:1036 (485 references); for reviews by Alexander W. Astin and Edward J. Furst, see 6:1070 (189 references); see also 5:868 (153 references); for reviews by Edward S. Bordin and Elmer D. Hinckley, see 4:747 (98 references): see also 3:647 (102 references); for reviews by Harold D. Carter, John G. Darley, and N. W. Morton, see 2:1680 (71 references); for a review by John G. Darley, see 1:1178. For references on the Strong Vocational Interest Blank For Women, see T2:2213 (30 references); for reviews by Dorothy M. Clendenen and Barbara A. Kirk, see 7:1037 (92 references); see also 6:1071 (12 references) and 5:869 (19 references); for a review by Gwendolen Schneidler Dickson, see 3:649 (38 references); for a review by Ruth Strang, see 2:1681 (10 references); for a review by John G. Darley, see 1:1179.

Review of the Strong Interest Inventory [Fourth Edition] by JOHN CHRISTIAN BUSCH, Associate Professor of Education, University of North Carolina at Greensboro, Greensboro, NC:

The Strong Interest Inventory (SVIB-SCII) "compares a person's interests with the interests of people happily employed in a wide variety of occupations. It is a measure of interests, not of aptitude or intelligence" (Specimen Brochure, p. 1). The Strong has been used by counselors for about 60 years and reviews have appeared in at least seven previous editions of the *Mental Measurements Yearbook*. The inventory has a long and venerable history of use, in part because its authors have responded to changes during that period.

One of the marks of a professionally maintained testing instrument is a willingness to continually evaluate and revise. The Strong is a wonderful example of this standard. Major changes have occurred during the past 25 years and the following revisions have been made for the 1985 version. Seventeen new vocational-technical occupational groups have been sampled (actually 34 paired male and female scales). Six newly emerging professional occupations (12 scales) have been added. Old occupational norms have been updated. Additional male and female parallel occupational scales have been developed so that currently only five scales are not paired by gender. Sixteen smaller criterion group samples were increased in size. New Men-in-General (MIG) and Women-in-General (WIG) reference samples were constructed to better reflect societal changes. These revisions increase confidence that test results will be relevant for the 1990s.

Since the last MMY review, a fourth edition of the Manual for the SVIB-SCII, a Specimen Brochure, and an updated profile have been published. The manual is a comprehensive description of the purpose and development of three types of Strong scales, the evidence marshaled in support of claims for valid and reliable measurement, and recommendations for interpretation and use. The manual is so extensive, I would choose it for examination in a measurement course.

The Strong is especially good in presenting information to clients in a clear and understandable form; the profile sheet efficiently integrates information from the three types of scales. Numeric, graphical, and verbal score summaries, the arrangement of scores, and statements of appropriate test use in the profile increase the likelihood of appropriate interpretation. The authors emphasize the need for the counselor and the client to integrate test results with other sources of information and to consider carefully discrepant test outcomes. The meaning of each of the scales is completely described and information regarding interpretation of the scales is summarized in the User's Guide for the SVIB-SCII (Hansen, 1984) and the manual. Administrative scales are used to guard against misinterpretation; and the possibility of client-manipulated test results is also discussed. Overall, the interpretive information is outstanding.

A large number of research studies have been conducted on the Strong during the past 30 years. In some instances the number of studies cited in the technical manual seems sparse even allowing that the manual cannot provide a comprehensive review. For example, the evidence regarding racial differences consists of two studies, both of which utilized the pre-1974 version of the Strong. The User's Guide does cite a few additional studies; however, the manual should be the primary source for summary of relevant information regarding the integrity of the scale. Given the extensive research base of the Strong, the authors might consider including a selected bibliographic listing of key studies organized by important issue in the manual. In general, the manual reports a balanced set of studies in support of the claims made for validity and reliability.

Sampling of occupations was an immense project that involved a total of 40,197 individuals in 162 occupations in 1981 and more than satisfies the *Standards for Educational and Psychological Testing* (AERA, APA, & NCME, 1985), which require detailed description of the validation sample. A list of reasonable selection criteria for occupational groups (satisfaction and success in the occupation, minimal experience, etc.) is provided in the manual. The list contains descriptions of the 207 occupational samples that include the sampling frames used, the size of the sample, the year data were collected, the mean age, years of education, and years of experience; no information summarizing variability of those characteristics or racial composition of the sample is provided.

The authors of the manual appear to be somewhat defensive with regard to the occupational samples. This is shown in statements such as, "Percent return, then, has practically nothing to do with the quality of the final sample. A low rate of return does not necessarily project a poor sample, nor does a 100-percent response rate guarantee a useful sample" (p. 52) and "In any case sampling issues often have been overemphasized; the crucial issue is not the sampling method, but the characteristics of the final sample" (p. 52). I believe most reviewers would be realistic in evaluating sampling procedures because the Strong does have knotty problems in identifying sampling frames and obtaining responses. Adequate sampling procedures do not guarantee adequate results; however, procedures which follow accepted traditions for inquiry do make adequate results more *likely*. In the absence of knowledge of population parameters, we must depend on an evaluation of the adequacy of sampling procedures. Response rates for each of the occupational samples should be published.

Some occupational groups consist of subspecialties that are potentially quite different from each other. For example, the Psychologist Occupational Group includes experimental, clinical, counseling, developmental, school, industrial, and other subspecialties. Interest inventories should address the fact that a particular client may show varying patterns of similarity to different subspecialties within an occupation or profession. Because the Strong provides information based on three types of scales, the client will have the opportunity to examine scores on the Basic Interest and Occupational Themes scales as possible approaches to differentiating between interest in, for example, experimental versus clinical psychology.

There is a separate chapter in the manual discussing gender issues. The authors conclude that substantial gender differences exist even when men and women in the same occupation have been compared. They conclude "separate scales and separate norms are necessary, but we must be certain they are used as a means of expanding options, not of limiting them" (p. 86). Occupational Scales are scored on both male and female scales. Although this practice complicates interpretation, the authors wish "to encourage both men and women to consider occupations heretofore dominated by the other sex" (p. 86).

A variety of evidence supports claims that the Strong measures consistently. Although standard deviations and reliability coefficients are provided, standard errors of measurement would be helpful. Some of the Basic Interest Scales are short (at least one consists of five items); exact lengths of those scales should be reported.

Concepts of vocational interest on the Strong were initially defined only in empirical terms, but since 1974 they have been linked to Holland's theory of occupational interests. This theoretical grounding helps in understanding and defining the construct and it provides a theoretical structure to guide and direct inquiry regarding the construct.

Evidence in support of validity claims is organized separately for the three types of Strong scales. Various sources of evidence are cited: analyses of item content, concurrent and predictive validity studies, confirmation of theoretically predicted patterns of intercorrelations between Strong subscales, and factor analytic studies. Concurrent validity evidence for the Occupational Scales is based on the degree of overlap of scores for a particular occupational sample and the General Reference sample; there appears to be a reasonable degree of group separation on the 207 scales. Percent overlap has been approximated by the Tilton Index which assumes a normal distribution. It is unclear why exact solutions are not reported given modern computational capabilities.

The predictive validity evidence for the Occupational Scales examines the relationship between scores and occupational status at some future time and is provided in the form of "hit" rates. Studies conducted on the current (post 1974) SVIB-SCII and reported in the manual include just a few studies in which the criterion was occupational choice or choice of college major. Enough time has passed that we would hope that additional summaries of long-term predictive validity studies would be cited.

The Strong more than satisfies the standards for tests and testing that have been set by the profession. As a vocational counseling instrument, it is among the very best and this reviewer recommends it without reservation.

REVIEWER'S REFERENCE

American Educational Research Association, American Psychological Association, and National Council on Measurement in Education. (1985). *Standards for educational and psychological testing.* Washington, DC: American Psychological Association, Inc.

Review of the Strong Interest Inventory [Fourth Edition] by BLAINE R. WORTHEN, Professor and Chair, Research and Evaluation Methodology Program, Department of Psychology, and PERRY SAILOR, Research Associate, Department of Psychology, Utah State University, Logan, UT:

In the *Ninth Mental Measurements Yearbook* review of the 1981 revision of the Strong Vocational Interest Blank (SVIB), the Strong-Campbell Interest Inventory (SCII), Layton (1985) concluded that it was the foremost interest inventory and was "better than ever" (p. 1480), and Westbrook (1985) called it "probably the best interest inventory available" (p. 1483). Since then, the 1985 revision has been completed, which incorporates normative and profile changes that make this venerable instrument even better, though not yet without flaw.

Test content and use.

The SCII, which can be administered to individuals or groups, measures interests by asking each person to: (*a*) respond "like," "indifferent," or "dislike" to 131 occupations, 36 school subjects, 90 activities (39 of which are ways of spending leisure time), and 24 "types of people"; (*b*) state, for each of 30 paired activities or occupations, which one they prefer; and (*c*) rate how well each of 14 characteristics describes them. The machine-scorable responses are then compared to norms consisting of expressions of interests of persons in a wide variety of occupations who are contented in their jobs. The results, reported on profile sheets, present scores on 6 General Occupational Themes, 23 Basic Interest Scales, and 207 Occupational Scales. Interpretive advice is intended primarily to aid respondents in making occupational choices or curricular decisions, and two other scales—Academic Comfort and Introversion-Extroversion—are offered as counseling tools.

The current edition of the SCII includes the inventory booklet (Strong, Campbell, & Hansen, 1985), a user's guide (Hansen, 1984), a manual (Hansen & Campbell, 1985), and several types of answer sheets, scoring profiles, and descriptive and interpretive aids.

Practical considerations.

The SCII takes an average of 25–35 minutes to complete. Administration requires no special training and can be done by any qualified psychologist, counselor, or personnel worker. In the Specimen Brochure, the authors point out the profile is largely self-explanatory, but "its scores, and patterns of scores, should be interpreted for the respondent by the counselor—after thorough study of the User's Guide and the Manual, and perhaps after participation in one of the regional workshops on the Strong" (p. 3).

The reviewers cannot comment on the workshops but agree that the manual and user's guide should be mastered to make maximum use of the information to be gained from the SCII.

Special commendation should be given to the manual and the user's guide. The manual is the primary technical, psychometric resource for the SCII and contains invaluable information on the rationales underlying scale construction; item statistics; scale norms, reliability, validity, and interpretation; and detailed information on criterion samples. The manual also provides extensive information concerning the processes and criteria used in constructing the Occupational Scales, the Basic Interest Scales, and the General Occupational Theme Scales.

The user's guide overlaps the manual to some degree but is more oriented to the needs of professional practitioners who use the test with clients. It includes very useful information on guidelines for the use of the SCII, pretest orientation, pre-interpretation preparation, using the codes in interpretation, using the SCII with adults, and career-counseling and SCII interpretation sequences. Also included in the user's guide is a discussion of interpretation of the Special Scales and Administrative Indexes (including rules of thumb for checking profile validity), testing special populations and people from other cultures, and interpretation of depressed, flat, and elevated profiles. It is difficult to imagine a better guide for the counselor or other user.

INTERPRETATION. Extensive attention has been given to helping counselors and clients interpret scale scores and patterns of scores; indeed, this is one of the strong points of the SCII. Several areas of difficulty in interpreting scale scores and patterns are noted in both the manual and user's guide. Apparent inconsistencies between the Basic Interest and Occupational Scales, where obviously related pairs of scales (e.g., Art and Fine Artist, Mathematics and Mathematician) yield highly contrasting scores, are discussed. Such inconsistencies are viewed by the SCII developers as assets that aid interpretation by forcing clients and counselors to understand the meaning of the scales and thus to interpret the scales properly. The ability to make correct interpretations of such inconsistencies is hindered somewhat, however, by the fact that the exact item makeup of these scales is not disclosed. The manual's authors state that item information for the Basic Interest Scales and General Occupational Themes may be found in earlier editions of the manual or in other sources cited, but that information was not available in the current materials. Composition of the Occupational Scales has never been released because the test publisher uses test-scoring income to support the research that has gone into improving and updating the inventory through its successive revisions. But the net effect is to leave the counselor who is faced with interpreting a profile that is high on "Marketing Executive" but low on "Sales" wishing to see the precise scale items on which both those scores are based.

The empirically derived "Special Scales," Academic Comfort and Introversion-Extroversion, are handled similarly to the Occupational Scales: The process of constructing them is described at length, there is extensive reliability and validity information provided, but scale construction—even the numbers of items—is not disclosed. Several career counselors have mentioned to the reviewers that interpreting the Academic Comfort Scale can be uncomfortable in the absence of such information about scale items.

Revisions in the 1985 Edition to remove gender inequity.

The SCII's roots go back to 1927, when E. K. Strong first published the SVIB. Beginning with the first SCII in 1974, and continuing through publication of subsequent revisions in 1981 and 1985, Strong's successors, David Campbell and Jo-Ida Hansen, have led successful efforts to: Merge Strong's Men's and Women's forms into a single form; incorporate a theoretical scheme (Holland's hexagonal model of career types) into the inventory's basically empirical framework; expand the number of Occupational Scales, especially in nonprofessional and vocational/technical occupations; and update the norming samples and match them by gender.

The extensive research that culminated in the 1985 revision was largely a result of the women's movement, which focused attention not only on inequities in the job market but also inequities in the SCII's use of separate Occupational Scales and norms for men and women. The developers responded to these concerns with an active program of research on men's and women's measured interests that has served as the foundation for a sex-equalization process that continued for 15 years, "with each revision representing a fairer, more balanced instrument" (manual, p. v). The results have been impressive, leading to development of new normative samples ("Women-in-General" and "Men-in-General") for use in constructing the Occupational Scales and in renorming the Basic Interest Scales and General Occupational Themes. The 1985 revision also increased the number of occupations on which female-normed and male-normed scales could be matched for the same occupations. Of the 106 occupations represented, 101 now have matching scales for females and males.

The manual authors argue persuasively that *equal* treatment is not the same as *identical* treatment, that women and men differ considerably in their responses to about one-third of the inventory items, that these differences remain even among people in the same occupations, and that "Empirical scales constructed on the basis of same-sex criterion and reference samples work better (are more valid) than scales based on opposite-sex samples" (p. 86). The developers also emphasize that sex differences "should in no way be used to discriminate against or repress any individual of either sex . . . . separate scales and separate norms are necessary, but we must be certain that they are used as a means of expanding options, not of limiting them" (p. 86).

Other major revisions in the 1985 SCII.

Although the instrument's 325 items have not changed since 1974 (except for wording on seven items related to religious activities, to make them more generic and less specifically Christian), the profiles and manual have been revised extensively in areas unrelated to sex equity. Other major changes for the 1985 edition include:

1. Expansion of the Occupational Criterion Samples. For the 1981 profile, according to the Specimen Brochure, the development team embarked on "the largest testing program of employed adults in history" (p. 3). For the current edition, they expanded it still further, testing 142,610 people to get 48,238 sample members.

2. Extension of the Occupational Scales to reduce the overemphasis on professional occupations. This effort produced 34 new scales (male and female scales for 17 vocational-technical and nonprofessional occupations).

3. Addition of scales for newly emerging professional occupations. Twelve of these scales (six occupations) have been added.

4. Increase in overall number and breadth of Occupational Scales. In all, there are now 207 Occupational Scales, representing 106 occupations, of which 32% have mean educational levels of less than 16 years or do not require a college degree.

5. Upgrading and renorming the older Occupational Scales. All 207 scales are now reasonably current, being based on Occupation Criterion Samples collected since 1974.

Technical considerations.

Norming of the SCII has been a huge undertaking extended across many years, and notwithstanding concerns discussed in a later section, the SCII is clearly one of the best-normed instruments in print.

RELIABILITY. Scores on the SCII are highly reliable. Median test-retest correlations for the 1985

Occupational Scales over 2 weeks, 30 days, and 3 years were .92, .89, and .87, respectively; means were also quite stable for all intervals. Median test-retest correlations for the Basic Interest Scales, for the same sample and time periods, were .91, .88, and .82, respectively. The median coefficient alpha was .92 for males and .91 for females. For the General Occupational Themes, they were .91, .86, and .81, respectively. The median coefficient alpha was .90 for both males and females.

The numbers of items for the Occupational Scales range from 28 to 71. The stated goal is to have around 60 items, and most scales approach this. It appears the General Occupational Theme Scales contain 20 items each, but the manual is not completely clear in this regard. The Basic Interest Scales range in length from 5 to 24 items, with a median length of 11 items. This may be too short for optimum stability, although the test-retest correlations are quite high nonetheless. Layton (1985) expressed concern that changing responses on only two or three items on such short scales could alter standard scores and interpretations, a potential problem that remains.

VALIDITY. Several types of validity evidence are offered for the SCII, combining to make its use generally well validated for the purposes for which it is intended.

Concurrent validity of the Occupational Scales is the power to discriminate between people currently in different occupations. Two relevant types of validity information are (*a*) contrasts between Occupational Samples and the Men-in-General or Women-in-General reference samples, and (*b*) mean scores of occupations on each other's scales. The former is measured by mean differences between samples expressed in standard deviation units (or, conversely, in the degree of overlap between the score distribution of the groups). The median overlap for both the women's and men's scales is 36%, which corresponds to 1.83 standard deviations (*SD*s) difference in means. The range is from 13% overlap (3.03 *SD*s) to 53% overlap (1.26 *SD*s). The range in overlaps indicates the Occupational Scales vary considerably in their validities. The authors say that scales with the highest validities (lowest overlaps) are usually those for occupations that are "tightly defined and quite distinct from most other occupations" (manual, p. 72).

Mean scores of occupations on the remaining Occupational Scales are not reported because of the huge number of means that would result (207 samples on 207 scales equals 42,849 means). According to information in the manual, mean scores for the various occupations on a given Occupational Scale tend to be normally distributed around the General Reference Sample mean, with a range of three to four standard deviations.

Predictive validity of the Occupational Scales is the power to distinguish between persons who will later enter different occupations (while recognizing that "final vocational choice" is an imperfect criterion, because not everyone enters occupations for which they are well suited). Several studies conducted with the earlier SVIB are presented in the manual with a conclusion that "between one-half and two-thirds of all college students enter occupations that are predictable from their earlier scores" (p. 74). One predictive validity study conducted with the 1974 SCII is reported, using college students and a span of $3^1/_2$ years; results were in line with the earlier SVIB studies.

The manual authors assert that content validity of the Basic Interest Scales is supported by procedures used in constructing them, where the emphasis was on pulling together related items. For example, the Science scale contains the items "Astronomer," "Biologist," "Chemist," and "Working in a research laboratory."

Lists of occupational groups scoring either very high or very low on the various Basic Interest Scales are given as evidence for concurrent validity, with the conclusion that "The patterns of high- and low-scoring occupations demonstrate that scores on these scales are substantially related to the occupations that people pursue" (p. 40). The reviewers concur with this assessment.

The manual authors claim that predictive validity of the Basic Interest Scales is good because "there is considerable agreement between the scores earned by students and their eventual occupations" (p. 40), but give no data, because "the nature of the scales does not permit detailed predictions, (so) there is no way of tallying 'hits' and 'misses'" (p. 40).

Construct validity of the General Occupational Themes is supported by theme intercorrelations, which are generally in line with Holland's hexagonal model; that is, the strongest correlations tend to occur between adjacent themes, the weakest between opposites, when points on the hexagon are labeled, in succession, Investigative, Artistic, Social, Enterprising, Conventional, and Realistic. For example, the Investigative scale correlates .60 with the adjacent Realistic, but .13 with the directly opposite Enterprising. This overall pattern is not as consistent as might be desired, however. In fact, the Social scale correlates lower with the adjacent Artistic (.22) than with the directly opposite Realistic (.26) and nearly opposite Conventional (.39) scales.

Construct validity for the General Occupational Themes is also supported by the correlations between them and the same-named scales on the Vocational Preference Inventory (T4:2910) (median = .765).

Issues and concerns.

Despite the general excellence of the SCII and its ancillary materials, there are still two areas where there is room for improvement or cause for concern. Although neither of these should deter career counselors, school psychologists, or other qualified persons from using the SCII, the following items suggest caution for the user and/or need for further refinement by the developer.

1. Prior criticisms about failure to report response rates in data collected on the Occupational Scales are dismissed in the manual on two grounds: "First, in some cases the figure is not available . . . . Second, the return rate is a meaningless number" (p. 52). Arguments that response rates may result largely from the quality of the sampling frame are cogent, but the argument that representativeness of the sample is peripheral to whether or not the sample is valid seems strained at best. For an occupational scale to have predictive validity, the sample selected to represent the particular occupation must have one additional characteristic beyond the criteria of "experience, success, and satisfaction" (manual, p. 52) in that occupation. The sample must also be *representative of* the broad spectrum of those in that occupation, not only of one small slice of it. The issue is that of possible bias due to volunteer responding, a bias that is uncontrolled if potentially important differences between those who respond and those who do not are ignored. Borg and Gall (1989) have identified many empirically demonstrated differences between volunteers and nonvolunteers, many of which may interact with interest patterns. If "1,000 forms are sent to entertainers featured in nightclub advertisements and only 100 are returned" (manual, p. 52), is it possible that these 100 may be more successful than nonrespondents and, therefore, their scores may be different, as Westbrook (1985) suggests? Or might the 100 be those who are compulsive about details, most inclined to respond to authority, or highest in Academic Comfort, but not necessarily most satisfied, successful, or experienced as entertainers? If so, then they may not represent entertainers well, and many persons who use the SCII for career advice could be led away from an entertainment career (in which they might have been happy and successful) by use of an SCII norm group from which volunteer bias had excluded important, relevant, nonvolunteer segments of the occupation's population. Admittedly, obtaining high response rates (to control volunteer

bias) and conducting nonresponse bias checks (to assess whether respondents and nonrespondents in the sample are similar) are formidable tasks, but difficulty does not excuse the developers of responsibility, and these reviewers feel that such steps are important to assure the validity of the SCII Occupational Scales for their intended purposes. Omitting such efforts and asserting that response rates are meaningless numbers and that self-selection (and therefore sampling bias) may actually be advantageous is unfortunate in an instrument for which development, in so many ways, represents a psychometric standard for instrument development and validation.

2. One part of the "Pre-test Orientation" section of the user's guide is troubling. In it, users are told that "at a minimum, the respondents should be told that: . . . . In general, people respond 'Like' to about one-third of the items, 'Dislike' to about a third, and 'Indifferent' to about a third" (p. 6). This information is not emphasized strongly and is not printed anywhere on the test booklet itself. It seems likely that many test-takers—especially those who are administered the test by mail—never receive this information. Although it obviously is impossible to administer all tests under exactly identical testing conditions, the situation should be made as standard as possible, especially for something as basic as instructions for responding. This seems to introduce an unnecessary source of variation in testing conditions. It is even more disconcerting when one considers that the Occupational Samples—the norming groups—were tested by mail. It is not reported whether they were told anything about the typical distribution of responses. Although the desire to increase variability and avoid the interpretive challenges of flat profiles is understandable, risking loss of standardization is a high price to pay.

SUMMARY. The SCII is a quick, easily taken, easily administered instrument of proven usefulness and psychometric soundness. Its norms are quite up-to-date and avoid sex inequity and other major concerns. The manual and user's guide are outstanding. With the 1985 revision, the SCII is better than ever, and is recommended by the present reviewers as by far the best available interest inventory, notwithstanding the few needed improvements cited herein.

REVIEWERS' REFERENCES

Hansen, J. C. (1984). *User's guide for the SVIB-SCII.* Stanford, CA: Stanford University Press.

Hansen, J. C., & Campbell, D. P. (1985). *Manual for the SVIB-SCII.* Stanford, CA: Stanford University Press.

Layton, W. L. (1985). [Review of the Strong-Campbell Interest Inventory]. In J. V. Mitchell, Jr. (Ed.), *The ninth mental measurements yearbook* (Vol. 2, pp. 1480-1481). Lincoln, NE: The Buros Institute of Mental Measurements.

Strong, E. K., Campbell, D. P., & Hansen, J. C. (1985). Strong-Campbell Interest Inventory of the Strong Vocational Interest Blank. Stanford, CA: Stanford University Press.

Westbrook, B. W. (1985). [Review of the Strong-Campbell Interest Inventory]. In J. V. Mitchell, Jr. (Ed.), *The ninth mental measurements yearbook* (Vol. 2, pp. 1481-1483). Lincoln, NE: The Buros Institute of Mental Measurements.

Borg, W. R., & Gall, M. D. (1989). *Educational research: An introduction* (5th ed.). New York: Longman.

[89]

Student Talent and Risk Profile.

Purpose: To identify talented students as well as students "at-risk" for counseling, guidance, and special teaching strategies.
Population: Grades 5–12.
Publication Date: 1990.
Acronym: STAR Profile.
Scores, 7: Academic Performance, Creativity, Artistic Potential, Leadership, Emotional Maturity, Educational Orientation, At Risk.
Administration: Group.
Price Data, 1990: $40 per 35 test booklets; $.05 per NCS answer sheet; $8 per manual (21 pages); $10 per specimen set; scoring service offered by publisher ($160 minimum charge plus $1.60 or less per subject over 100).
Time: (60–65) minutes.
Comments: Revision of Biographical Inventory Form U.
Author: The Institute for Behavioral Research in Creativity.
Publisher: The Institute for Behavioral Research in Creativity.
Cross References: For reviews by Christopher Borman and Courtland C. Lee of Biographical Inventory Form U, see 9:150.

Review of the Student Talent and Risk Profile by BARBARA KERR, Professor of Psychology in Education, Arizona State University, Tempe, AZ:

The Student Talent and Risk Profile (STAR) was developed to assist teachers in the identification of students who may benefit from gifted education programs and students who may be at risk for educational problems. It is based on the Biographical Inventory Form U (9:150), a well-known measure of a variety of constructs related to creativity, leadership, and outstanding performance. Additional items were added recently to yield measures of emotional maturity and at-risk status. It is a 150-item multiple-choice instrument that includes questions about childhood activities and experiences, attitudes and interests, value preferences, and other self-descriptions. The test can be scored only by the Institute for Behavioral

Research in Creativity. Each of the seven scales of the Student Talent and Risk Profile was developed on a different group, or combination of norm groups. Therefore, validity will be considered for each scale as well as for the test as a whole.

VALIDITY. The Academic Performance Scale was developed with college freshmen but was normed on 10,000 North Carolina high school students. Significant correlations have been obtained between Academic Performance and achievement and I.Q. measures.

The Creativity Scale was developed on a group of NASA scientists and engineers, yielding cross validities in the .40s, and was rewritten for use with students. It has approximately .30 correlation with artistic potential scores.

The Artistic Potential Scale was developed in a study of high school students attending the Interlochen Arts Academy and regular high school students; it differentiated arts from non-arts students and correlated from .40 to .50 with measures of artistic performance.

The Leadership scale was developed on a combination of the above groups. A validity study with North Carolina Governor's School students identified as high in leadership ability showed this scale successfully differentiated between identified leadership students and regular high school students, with cross validities of approximately .70.

The Emotional Maturity Scale was developed to identify at-risk students in junior high school in Utah. No studies were done of relationships with independent criteria. Items were selected through item-test correlations.

The Educational Orientation Scale was developed in a study of high school dropouts to differentiate these from other students. Items were added to show positive attitudes toward school and college aspirations. A recent study showed inconsistent correlations with teacher ratings and activities ratings in school.

The At-Risk Scale is a measure that combines Emotional Maturity and Educational Orientation; it is intended to indicate not only risk of dropping out but also for emotional or substance abuse problems. A recent study failed to show consistent correlations with teacher ratings and activities ratings in school.

Overall, the scales derived from original Form U of the Biographical Inventory remain promising as predictors of outstanding performance in academics, creative activities, artistic endeavors, and leadership. However, the newer scales intended to identify at-risk status clearly need work. There is not enough evidence to support their validity for prediction of emotional maturity, educational orientation, or at-risk status. Rather than relying on item to test correlations, the authors must perform the same kind of painstaking studies they undertook for the development of the other scales.

One concern is the items are quite transparent. Even a young student would be able to guess the import of a great many of them. Students may be able to answer the items in the way in which they wish to be perceived by their teachers or test administrators. A social desirability scale or correction should be included.

RELIABILITY. Unfortunately, reliability estimates for the scales of the STAR Profile were derived only from measures of coefficient alpha, a measure of internal consistency. The coefficient alpha reliability estimates for the scales were fairly impressive, with several in the high .80s. The reliability estimates increased with age, with alphas for grade 10–12 samples being 3 to 7 points higher than those for grade 4–6 samples.

There were apparently no studies done of alternate form or test-retest reliability; therefore, it is unknown what the effects of practice or repeated administrations of this test might be on scores. This is an unfortunate oversight.

USEFULNESS. As stated above, this instrument may be useful for identifying talented students, but is not ready to be used to identify at-risk students. An instrument is sorely needed that can identify talented, at-risk students, that is, those students who have great potential for excellent performance in school but are at risk for social, behavioral, or emotional problems. It is hoped that with further research this instrument could be refined to be able to perform this task.

Another utility concern is the scoring procedure. Because the test can be scored only by the publisher, the test user must consider whether the inconvenience and delay incurred by the use of the test is outweighed by the benefits to be derived by the results. In the case of the STAR Profile, the best use of the instrument is probably as a part of a battery of achievement, intelligence, and personality tests. The user may be unwilling to use the test if this additional inconvenience is not justified by the quantity and quality of the information to be gained. Ideally, this test should be hand scorable and even more reasonably priced; that would make the test immediately attractive to users who want some helpful and potentially intriguing information about a particular student.

Review of the Student Talent and Risk Profile by JOHN W. SHEPARD, Associate Professor of Counselor Education, The University of Toledo, Toledo, OH:

The stated purpose of the Student Talent and Risk Profile (STAR Profile [SP]) is to make for an easier identification of "talented" and "at-risk" students. The present measure is an expanded version of the 1976 Biographical Inventory Form U (9:150). The SP is divided into seven subtest-like categories assessing student performance in: Academic Performance, Creativity, Artistic Potential, Leadership, Emotional Maturity, Educational Orientation, and At Risk status. A Talent Identification Feedback Report is computer generated to assist educators in identifying and advising/counseling talented and/or at-risk students. The instrument is normed for 5th–12th graders.

Inventory results are derived from student responses to a 150-item multiple-choice questionnaire. SP items require students to make self-reported judgements regarding personal and scholastic traits as well as demographic/biographical data. Student performance on each of the seven categories is reported by a percentile comparison with their norm age group. Scores falling in the "top" 25th percentile of any category are starred for significance and easy identification. Although there is no set time limit for taking the SP it would probably require about 60 minutes to complete. Inventory pricing is affected by group size. The cost to simultaneously assess more than 500 students would approximate $2.50 per testee. The cost for 100 students would be approximately $2.80 per student.

It is difficult to validate the SP authors' claims regarding its statistical qualities and overall effectiveness. Very little substantive information is given in the inventory's manual as to reliability, norming, or validity. Much of the manual is dedicated to describing the SP's history. Norming data are scattered throughout the manual and provide a very sketchy description of how norms were gathered. Five of the scales are normed on a 1979 multiaged group and two are normed on a 1990 group of 6th graders. Three tables provide sufficient data as to sample sizes' internal reliability, interscale correlations, means, and standard deviations. Sample sizes appear large enough but are generally restricted to samples in one state. Five of the scale's norms are based on a 1979 sample. Internal scale reliability is satisfactory (.77 to .91) but no test-retest coefficients are reported.

Only one contemporary concurrent validity study, contrasting the inventory's "academic performance" scale with SAT (Scholastic Aptitude Test) scores and teacher ratings of study habits, was cited. Correlations of .59 and .64 were reported, respectively. No data regarding predictive validity were given despite claims to the contrary. Content validity was developed from numerous studies and refinements to past versions of the instrument. The instrument's 5th grade reading level may be too high for many elementary and junior high students. Some questions appeared ambiguous and others could prove embarrassing for students to answer truthfully. Very little assistance is given to the manual's reader regarding how to followup with a student who is identified as talented and/or gifted.

In summary, the SP could indeed provide useful data to educators who wish to identify and assist talented and/or gifted students. The measure is cost and time effective and quite easy to interpret. However, much work must be done in assessing and describing the instrument's reliability and validity. The dated and limited restricted norm group also makes one question whether results can be generalized to urban, rural, and/or suburban populations throughout the nation.

[90]

Substance Abuse Subtle Screening Inventory.
Purpose: To "identify alcohol and drug dependent individuals and differentiate them from social users and general psychiatric clients."
Population: Ages 12–18, adults.
Publication Dates: 1983–90.
Acronym: SASSI.
Administration: Group.
Levels, 2: Adult, Adolescent.
Price Data, 1993: $75 per starter kit; $45 per 25 tests and profiles; $10 per scoring key; $55 per manual ('85, 242 pages); volume discounts available.
Time: [10–15] minutes.
Author: Glenn A. Miller.
Publisher: The SASSI Institute.

a) ADULT FORM.
Scores, 8: Obvious Attributes, Subtle Attributes, Defensiveness, Defensive Abuser vs. Defensive Non-Abuser, Alcohol vs. Drug, Codependency, Face Valid-Alcohol, Face Valid-Other Drug.
b) ADOLESCENT FORM.
Scores, 8: Obvious Attributes, Subtle Attributes, Defensiveness, Defensive Abuser vs. Defensive Non-Abuser, Correctional, Random Answering Pattern, Face Valid Alcohol, Face Valid Other Drug.
Cross References: See T4:2623 (1 reference).

Review of the Substance Abuse Subtle Screening Inventory by BARBARA KERR, Professor of Psychology in Education, Arizona State University, Tempe, AZ:

The Substance Abuse Subtle Screening Inventory (SASSI) is an interesting attempt to deal with the tendency of substance abusers to deny or obscure their substance abuse. It is based on the assumption that self-report responses that do not include substance use in their content may serve as indicators of substance abuse. Most substance abuse screening measures have obvious items concerning the use of alcohol and drug use; substance abusers who deny their condition or for a variety of reasons wish to hide their substance abuse will usually "fake good" on these scales. Therefore, substance abuse screening inventories that do not take this response set into account are not likely to be effective. Mental health centers, university student health centers, and court-ordered substance abuse centers have a great need for this kind of scale, and have greeted the development of the SASSI with enthusiasm (Creager, 1989).

DEVELOPMENT OF THE SASSI. The SASSI is a single-page, paper-and-pencil questionnaire. On one side are 52 True-False questions that seem to be unrelated to chemical abuse. On the other side are the Risk Prediction Scales which allow clients to self-report on the 12 alcohol-related and 14 drug-related items. The test in intended to be readable at the fifth grade level and can also be administered orally. It takes from 10 to 15 minutes for clients to complete both tests. The SASSI can be hand scored in about 1 minute.

The items on the SASSI are empirically derived. Most other current substance abuse screening instruments are rationally constructed, based on theoretical formulations of the symptoms of alcoholism. This scale is composed predominantly of items from other empirically derived scales and new items. Items were borrowed from the Minnesota Multiphasic Personality Inventory (MMPI; 9:715), the Psychological Screening Inventory (PSI; 9:1015; Lanyon, 1973), the Michigan Alcoholism Screening Test (Selzer, 1971), and many other sources that promised to yield items which differentiated between abusers and nonabusers. The subtle items related to a wide variety of behaviors related to health, social interaction, emotional states, preferences, needs, interests, and values. Non-subtle items are asked directly about substance abuse and its usual consequences.

Approximately 1,000 items were administered to close to 300 people in the course of the validation studies. Discriminant analyses were used to develop the major subscales. The subscales are as follows:

The Obvious Attributes Scale (OAT) is intended to measure the openness or the willingness of the client to admit to symptoms or problems related to substance abuse. A high score on this scale means that there are similarities between the client's personal style and the personal style of chemically dependent people.

The Subtle Attributes Scale (SAT) score is probably the most important scale, because it is very resistant to faking. It measures a personal predisposition to develop a dependency on drugs or alcohol. High scores means that the client is similar biologically or in personal style to chemically dependent people.

The Denial (DEN) scale was created to identify the client's defensiveness to test taking, but high scores can result from unconscious denial or deliberate attempts to conceal. Both high and low scores indicate problems: High scores are associated with excessive denial and low scores with feelings of worthlessness and deficiency.

The Defensive Abuser vs. Defensive Non-Abuser Scale (DEN) is used with the Denial Scale score in determining whether a person is in fact an abuser or whether their responses are those of a defensive non-abuser.

The Alcohol vs. Drug Scale (ALD) is intended to show whether the client prefers alcohol or other drugs. Although this is not a strong scale, usually a high score indicates alcohol preference and a low score indicates drug preference.

The Family vs. Controls Scale (FAM) is meant to be a preliminary measure of codependency. It is a weak scale at this point; it is meant to show how similar the test taker is to family members of alcohol and drug abusers.

The second part of the SASSI is made up of two previously developed scales, the Face Valid Alcohol scale (originally the Risk Prediction Scale for alcohol) and the Face Valid Drug Scale (originally the Risk Prediction Scale for drugs [SASSI manual, Appendix B, p. 18, Copper & Robinson, in press]).

Scoring and interpretation of the SASSI involves attention to the elevation and slope of the scales as well as using a variety of decision rules that lead to the classification of abuser or nonabuser. An example of such a rule is: If either of the following two conditions is met, classify as chemical abuser:

1. Obvious Attributes (OAT) or Subtle Attributes (SAT) T-score is above 70.

2. Obvious Attributes and Subtle Attributes T scores are both above 60.

VALIDITY. In the validation section of the manual, the author shows that the SASSI and the RPS measures each did better in identifying low defensive late stage abusers already involved in a residential detoxification program than the more defensive early stage abusers. It is important, therefore, to specify the population on which validity testing takes place. The combination of the SASSI and the RPS was most effective with all populations: The combination identified 90% of the residential detoxification sample, 80% of defensive early stage abusers in a family oriented intensive outpatient program, and 90% of nonabusers who were also codependents. The independent contribution of the SASSI was most important with individuals who were defensive early stage abusers. The subscales were shown to each contribute independently to the decision rules. The Subtle Attributes (SAT) scale did a good job of identifying defensiveness and the Denial (DEN) scale in identifying distortions. The Family (FAM) scale was not successful in identifying codependency.

A later study found the SASSI to be useful in identifying subtle substance abusers among rehabilitation clients in Texas; 87% of the cases already classified as substance abusers by the rehabilitation agency were identified by the SASSI. Also, 32.7% of clients who had not been previously identified as substance abusers by the agency, and about whom counselors were not aware, were classified as such by the SASSI (DiNitto & Schwab, 1991). A dissertation by Kilkunas (1988), using only the SASSI without the Face Valid Scales, still found reasonably good prediction, with the SASSI identifying 94% of controls, 78% of Alcoholics, 71% of Drug Addicts, and 96% of codependents (Creager, 1989).

The SASSI has high concurrent validity with the MacAndrew (1965) subscale of the MMPI (.87), although the use of some of these items and some very similar ones certainly contributes to the high concurrent validity.

RELIABILITY. The internal consistency of most of the subscales of the SASSI is quite low. Because of the discriminant analysis method of construction, each subscale except the RPSA, RPSD, and PAL5 is made up of heterogeneous items rather than items related to a unitary construct. Internal consistency analyses were performed for Detox patients, Outpatients, and Probation groups. Coefficient alpha ranges are reported as follows: OAT, .61–.73; SAT, .25–.49; DEN, .57–.68; DAN, .56–.82; ALD, .44–.49; FAM, .16–.60; RPSA, .90–.92; RPSD, .93–.96; PAL5, .78–.80.

The only study of test-retest reliability which has been performed was one in which the SASSI was used without the Face Valid Scales. Kilkunas (1988) tested 24 subjects on a 4- to 6-week interval and found moderate to good test-retest reliability. The reliability coefficients were reported as follows: OAT, .87; SAT, .91; DEN, .86; DAN, .91; ALD, .78; FAM, .76.

It was puzzling that the author, who obviously put tremendous thought and care into the validation of the SASSI, gave so little attention to reliability. Because of the inconsistent nature of responding of many substance abusers to psychological instruments, and because of the importance of decisions made based on the SASSI, more emphasis on its reliability should be given in future research. All indications so far are the instrument is a reliable one.

CLINICAL USEFULNESS. The SASSI is almost as good as its promotion claims it to be. It seems to have been responsibly developed, and it is clearly created with the practitioner in mind. Its ease of administration and scoring, its clear decision rules and suggestions for interpretation, and the informative and carefully written manual all make it very attractive to mental health providers who have difficult and important decisions to make about treatment.

The SASSI fits its population as well; it does seem to accurately identify those who are denying or obscuring their substance abuse, particularly among less advanced stage abusers. One quibble is that although it is supposed to be at the fifth grade reading level, it looks as though it actually would require a higher reading level, probably seventh or eighth grade.

There may be ethical issues which will require exploration if the SASSI becomes widespread in its use. It must never become the psychological equivalent of the Breathalyzer test; legal decisions about the label substance abuser must be made on the basis of interview material, this and other instruments, and on evidence of actual behavior.

REVIEWER'S REFERENCES

MacAndrew, C. (1965). The differentiation of male alcoholic outpatients from nonalcoholic psychiatric outpatients by means of the MMPI. *Quarterly Journal of Studies on Alcohol, 26,* 238-246.

Selzer, M. L. (1971). The Michigan Alcoholism Screening Test: The quest for a new diagnostic instrument. *American Journal of Psychiatry, 127,* 1653-1658.

Lanyon, R. I. (1973). Psychological Screening Inventory: Manual. Goshen, NY: Research Psychologists Press.

Kilkunas, W. (1988). [Title unavailable]. Unpublished doctoral dissertation. Muncie, IN: Ball State University.

Creager, C. (1989, July/August). SASSI test breaks through denial. *Professional Counselor,* p. 81-84.

DiNitto, D. M., & Schwab, A. J. (1991). *Substance abuse factors which interfere with entry or reentry into employment.* Report for Texas Rehabilitation Commission. Austin, TX: University of Texas at Austin School of Social Work.

Copper, S., & Robinson, D. A. (in press). Cross-validation of the Substance Abuse Subtle Screening Inventory on a college population. *American Journal of College Health.*

Review of the Substance Abuse Subtle Screening Inventory by NICHOLAS A. VACC, Professor and Chairperson, Department of Counselor Education, University of North Carolina at Greensboro, Greensboro, NC:

The Substance Abuse Subtle Screening Inventory (SASSI) consists of two separate questionnaires included in one response form. On one side of the response form is the SASSI, which is a one-page paper-and-pencil questionnaire containing 52 true and false questions designed to assess chemical abuse in an unobtrusive way; items appear unrelated to chemical abuse and, therefore, make them less threatening to the respondent. On the opposite side of the response form is the Risk Prediction Scales (RPS), which was designed to predict the degree of risk of abusing alcohol and other drugs. The RPS, which comes in two forms, was developed by Linda A. Morton (1978) in conjunction with the Department of Mental Health, Division of Addiction Services, State of Indiana. It consists of 26 items designed to assess the level of substance-abuse risk (i.e., non-users minimally at risk, non-problematic users minimally at risk, non-users moderately at risk, non-problematic users moderately at risk, problematic users substantially at risk, and dysfunctional users totally at risk). Use of the RPS enhances the value of the SASSI.

The SASSI was developed to assess chemical dependency by being insulated to the respondent's level of honesty or faking. The author reports the instrument is independent of age, education, and socioeconomic status. The instrument provides information concerning five scales (i.e., Obvious Attributes [OAT], which is designed to differentiate substance abusers who have admitted problems from non-abusers; Subtle Attributes [SAT], which is intended to differentiate substance abusers from non-substance abusers regardless of the respondent's degree of honesty; Denial [DEN], which is designed to identify those substance abusers who are denying their behavior; Personal-Family [FAM], which distinguishes between substance abusers and non-abusers who live with dependency (co-dependency); and Alcohol/Drug Preference [ALD], which is designed to differentiate alcohol abusers from those with a poly-drug abuse pattern). The SASSI takes about 10–15 minutes to complete and can be scored in 5–10 minutes.

A single form of the SASSI is available for both men and women and is designed for respondents 18 years of age through adulthood. Also available is an adolescent form of the SASSI designed for use with children ages 12–18. The adolescent form, which is a more recent development by the test author, appears, like the adult form, to be nonthreatening and is designed for screening adolescents who may be chemically dependent. Other materials related to this instrument that are available through the SASSI Institute are an instructional videotape that provides information concerning the administration, scoring, development, philosophy, and validity data of the SASSI; training workshops (for a fee) that provide participants with the SASSI feedback system to include how the SASSI can be used to assist clients to establish goals and conduct therapeutic interventions; a computer-disk form of the SASSI designed for IBM-compatible computers; and a telephone consultation service provided by the staff at the SASSI Institute. A toll-free number is provided for this free consultation service concerning profile interpretation and program development using the SASSI.

In consulting practitioners, it appears that the computer-assisted scoring disk for IBM or compatible computers is the method of choice. The computer-scoring procedure is easy to learn and operate; clear instructions are available for using the SASSI computer version. The examinee answers the questions by typing the appropriate letter on the keyboard, and the next question appears automatically. After completing the assessment, examinees are asked whether they would like to review their answers. The computer-assisted scoring disk, which requires a password by the practitioner, enhances the scoring process and provides a visual display of the profile on the screen as well as a printed copy of the profile and results. Both the paper-and-pencil and computer versions of the SASSI are user friendly for respondents.

The SASSI's primary purpose as identified by the author is to serve as an objective screening tool to differentiate substance abusers from non-abusers. However, in addition to screening, the SASSI is frequently used by practitioners as a clinical instrument when counseling individuals and families. Yet, the SASSI's value within counseling programs has not been empirically documented. The manual provides a section on clinical interpretation of the SASSI for practitioners, but it also includes a disclaimer that such use has not been validated through empirical research. To be addressed are such questions as how valuable are the subscales in developing treatment plans?

The author reports through informal correspondence accompanying the reviewer's manual, that test/retest reliability was reported for 24 subjects as .87 (OAT), .91 (SAT), .86 (DEN), .78 (ALD), and .76 (FAM) for the adult form. Overall reliability averages appear to be acceptable (G. Miller, personal communication, August 1990). Considerable validity testing is provided in the manual. Unfortunately, adequate description concerning representativeness of the populations involved in the reported validity data is not provided. Notably absent is empirical information concerning the chronological age, social economic status, and ethnic background of the samples. Also, woefully inadequate are some of the cell-sizes of the subsamples reported for the validity and normative information provided. For example, the intensive outpatient program samples of family chemical abusers had *N*s as small as 3 for the male subgroup, 11 for the female subgroup, and 7 for the male family non-chemical abusers subgroup.

The SASSI manual is somewhat confusing and difficult to use. Practitioners have recommended that it is advisable to take the SASSI training workshop with a representative in order to properly understand how to score and interpret the instruments to achieve maximum benefit. This recommendation applies to both the paper-and-pencil and computer version printouts (C. Woods, personal communication, May 2, 1992).

In summary, considering the reasonable cost of approximately $2 a test, the computer version of the SASSI is the instrument of choice as a quick screening instrument in the area of substance abuse. Because it is widely used by individuals involved with the substance-abuse field, including Alcohol Safety Action Programs, the SASSI psychometric properties should meet or exceed professional norms. The information reported in the manual is less than reassuring that this has been achieved. Although the manual appears comprehensive and thorough on quick inspection, it is poorly developed; it does not provide adequate information and the reader has to "dig" in an attempt to judge the value of the instrument. The author should consider developing a technical manual addressing the *Standards for Educational and Psychological Testing* (AERA, APA, & NCME, 1985) and a separate test user's manual written for the practitioner.

Such information as sample descriptions to include ethnic background, chronological age, socioeconomic status, and/or educational level, and a reported reading level index of the two forms would be helpful additions to the manual. Also, the small number of cases used in the development of some of the scales, and the absence of current samples (some samples are pre-1977) are of concern. A more current data base for normative analysis is needed. For an instrument that is often used, additional data need to be systematically collected for the purpose of addressing psychometric issues.

The cost, short testing time, and ease of use by test takers are compelling reasons for the instrument's use. I would use the computer-assisted version and the paper-and-pencil version of the SASSI, but the former version would be my first choice. Additionally, I would suggest prospective users attend a SASSI Institute workshop to better prepare themselves for using the instruments.

REVIEWER'S REFERENCE

American Educational Research Association, American Psychological Association, & National Council on Measurement in Education. (1985). *Standards for educational and psychological testing*. Washington, DC: American Psychological Association, Inc.

[91]

Survey of Work Values, Revised, Form U.
Purpose: Constructed to identify attitudes toward work.
Population: Employees.
Publication Dates: 1975–76.
Scores, 6: Social Status, Activity Preference, Upward Striving, Attitude Toward Earnings, Pride in Work, Job Involvement.
Administration: Group.
Manual: No manual.
Price Data, 1992: $21 per 100 test booklets; $5 per 100 answer sheets; $5 per 100 hand-scoring sheets; general instructions, free.
Time: [15] minutes.
Authors: Bowling Green State University.
Publisher: Bowling Green State University.
Cross References: See T4:2665 (1 reference).

Review of the Survey of Work Values, Revised, Form U by JULIE A. ALLISON, Assistant Professor of Psychology, Pittsburg State University, Pittsburg, KS:

The Survey of Work Values, Revised, Form U (SWV, Form U) is designed to assess several different aspects of the secularized Protestant Ethic. The scale is based on a conceptualization that includes both intrinsic aspects of work: Pride in Work, Job Involvement, and Activity Preference, and extrinsic aspects of work: Attitude toward Earnings, and Social Status of the job. Additionally, one dimension was included that measures aspects of both internality and externality: Upward Striving. These six components are each represented by nine items in the SWV, resulting in a 54-item scale. Respondents are asked to indicate their degree of agreement or disagreement with each statement on a 5-point Likert scale.

Inclusion of the items for each subscale was based on the method of reallocation. Individuals from both industrial and academic settings were asked to place items under the most relevant category of the category labels provided. Retention of any item was based on the perceived relevancy of the item to the category

253

label: Items with a 70% allocation rate to a single category and no more than 20% allocation to any second category were retained.

Reliability measures for each of the subscales were computed from both a sample of industrial workers and a sample of government workers. The reliability figures reported ranged from .53 to .66. Although these figures are relatively low, they are justifiable in light of the small number of items per subscale and a wide range of item means within each subscale.

The authors provide partial support for construct validity: The reallocation procedure was successful, internal consistency is adequate, and the SWV scores successfully discriminated among various occupational groups and correlated with background characteristics of employed and disadvantaged persons. However, evidence for both convergent validity and discriminant validity is lacking and is needed to finalize an overall evaluation of the construct validity. For example, the relationship of the SWV with other tests, such as the Work Values Inventory (Super, 1970; T4:2998) which has excellent psychometric foundations (but focuses more generally on the concept of values) should be documented.

Although the 1979 normative data for the SWV needs to be updated, the SWV could be useful for both academicians and employers interested in the conceptualization and assessment of the Protestant Ethic. Past use of the scale has included evaluation of orientation programs and identification of differences between supervisors and employees. Assistance in the selection of workers is also a potential use of the SWV.

REVIEWER'S REFERENCE

Super, D. E. (1970). Work Values Inventory. Chicago: Riverside Publishing Co.

Review of the Survey of Work Values, Revised, Form U by H. JOHN BERNARDIN, University Research Professor, and DONNA K. COOKE, Assistant Professor, College of Business, Florida Atlantic University, Boca Raton, FL:

The Survey of Work Values (SWV) is designed to measure a person's general opinions about work and is based on Weber's concept of Protestant Ethic (Weber, 1958). The focus of the instrument and the underlying theory is on work values rather than attitudes toward a specific job, a respondent's career, or a particular organization. Consequently, work values are hypothesized to be less a function of the immediate work circumstances and more a function of relatively stable, personal factors. The utility of the SWV lies in the belief that these work values are more enduring than specific attitudes such as

organizational commitment and job satisfaction (cf., Morrow, 1983).

For the current version of the SWV, the gender-neutral Form U, respondents are instructed to place a check mark on a 5-point Likert scale to indicate degree of agreement or disagreement with 54 statements. The survey is separate from the answer sheet, allowing for its reuse. One weakness is that the only norms currently available are from student samples. A manual would be very helpful to interested researchers because articles oftentimes do not reference the SWV in their titles or abstracts, thus, detailed study of the instrument's characteristics is difficult.

The scales operationalize six secular or nonreligious aspects of Protestant Ethic: Pride in Work, Activity Preference, Job Involvement, Social Status of Job, Attitude toward Earnings, and Upward Striving. The first three dimensions represent the intrinsic value of work or the opinion that work is valued for its own sake. Social Status of Job and Attitude toward Earnings are dimensions of the extrinsic value of work, that is, work is valued as a means to other ends. Upward Striving is not classified as either an intrinsic or extrinsic dimension.

The scale was developed through a painstaking process. Faculty and graduate students developed 91 items for the subscales. Fifty-eight glass-manufacturing workers were given these items and the definitions of seven categories and one "other" and told to assign the items to corresponding categories. The criteria for acceptance were at least 70% placement into a single category and no more than 20% placement into a second. The surviving items along with some additions were again successively judged by two samples of undergraduates using the same criteria. Industrial and nonindustrial groups were used to improve the likelihood that the final items would be generalizable. Small samples of the same industrial and undergraduate groups (46 and 45, respectively) assigned scale values to the items presented in their categories by associating them with five hypothetical workers. This step rests on the assumption that the raters had stereotypical impressions of the hypothetical workers. Because one would strongly expect high levels of stereotyping about fictitious people, the fact that different samples were used is of debatable utility. Both samples were equally unfamiliar with the hypothetical workers. Although the correlation of both sets of scale values was .94 ($N = 67$), it should be noted that the sample size reported for this correlation is lower than the already small combined sample of 91 who did the scaling. A larger sample size would have been preferable. Presenting the items by category may have enhanced these correlations.

Four hundred and ninety-five employees from the same glass manufacturing company completed the 67 items using a 6-point agreement scale. The items were in mixed order. An item was retained if it correlated highly within its subscale, contributed to the scale's alpha, increased the subscale value range, and had low scale value variability. Form U uses the more customary 5-point scale and it is expected that the change should result in increased scale reliability.

Principal components analysis resulted in six factors which accounted for 36% of total variance. The first factor comprised mainly items from the intrinsic dimensions (Pride in Work, Activity Preference, and Job Involvement). Social Status of Job, Attitude toward Earnings, and Upward Striving loaded separately. Despite not loading on a common factor, Social Status of Job and Attitude toward Earnings are said to be on the extrinsic dimension. Their subscale intercorrelation is a very modest .27. Two other factors, Conventional Ethic and Organization-Man Ethic were also identified in the original study (Wollack, Goodale, Wijting, & Smith, 1971) but are not included in Form U. Factor loadings seem to indicate two orthogonal axes, one of which could be labeled "extrinsic" and one of which could be labeled "intrinsic." The data do indicate that a bipolar, intrinsic-extrinsic scale is inappropriate.

Despite claims by DeMeuse (1985) that the SWV is a frequently used instrument, our literature search revealed very few studies. One of the authors of the instrument reported that an unpublished Master's thesis conducted at Wayne State University revealed that the "attitudes toward earning" subscale was negatively correlated with bank teller errors and performance appraisals. No other subscale was significantly correlated with the criteria under study (P. C. Smith, personal communication, January 9, 1992).

One weakness of the SWV is its low subscale reliabilities. Although they are expected to improve with the use of the 5-point rather than the 6-point agreement scale, they are still low, with alphas reported in the .53 to .66 range across two large samples. The test-retest reliabilities over a 1-month period are more respectable, ranging from .65 to .76. For a scale for which the main selling point is that it assesses stable work attitudes, such low reliabilities are problematic, although they can be explained by the differences in difficulty levels for the items comprising each subscale. They cast doubt on the construct validity of the SWV. Compared to related, and relatively stable concepts such as the various forms of commitment whose alphas typically range in the .80s and .90s

with fewer items, the SWV does not fare well. Increasing the number of items for each subscale would most certainly improve internal consistency.

The SWV has been related to a number of demographic variables including race, sex, and education. According to the letter addressed to prospective test users, the SWV-U is being validated for selection purposes. It will be interesting to see if its use is likely to result in any adverse impact, or is confounded by social desirability. Scoring transparency could certainly be a problem in real selection situations. It remains to be seen if the assessed work values change over time as circumstances such as income and career stage change. Judging from the items (e.g., "A good job is a well paying job"), it is very likely that one's opinion could be a function of the immediate work situation and not largely a function of an enduring orientation towards work. As for the utility for researchers, the SWV is lengthy compared to other measures of Protestant Ethic (54 items to Mirels & Garrett's [1971] 19 items). Some of the items themselves are long and time and space considerations may sway surveyors away from the SWV.

In summary, the SWV-U was a very carefully developed operationalization of an important set of employee attitudes which appears to have great potential for use. However, many psychometric questions persist. Since the original work in 1971, the field has become more crowded with shorter questionnaires that purport to measure not only Protestant Ethic but similar stable attitudes. The need for a test manual updating the documentation, low subscale reliabilities, possible confounding with social desirability, insufficient evidence of temporal stability 20 years after the publication of the original study, and the length of the survey make it difficult for us to recommend its use. Although the research certainly started out on the right foot, the authors of the instrument should present a stronger case to potential users.

REVIEWER'S REFERENCES

Weber, M. (1958). *The Protestant Ethic and the spirit of capitalism* (T. Parsons, Trans.). New York: Scribner.

Mirels, H. L., & Garrett, J. B. (1971). The Protestant Ethic as a personality variable. *Journal of Consulting and Clinical Psychology, 36,* 40-44.

Wollack, S., Goodale, J. G., Wijting, J. P., & Smith, P. C. (1971). Development of the Survey of Work Values. *Journal of Applied Psychology, 55,* 331-338.

Morrow, P. C. (1983). Concept redundancy in organizational research: The case of work commitment. *Academy of Management Review, 8,* 486-500.

DeMeuse, K. P. (1985). A compendium of frequently used measures in industrial/organizational psychology. *The Industrial Psychologist, 23,* 53-59.

[92]

Teacher Evaluation Scale.

Purpose: "Evaluates characteristics of teacher behavior which lead to success in the educational environment."

Population: Teachers.

Publication Date: 1986.

Acronym: TES.

Scores, 4: Management of Student Behavior, Professionally Related, Instructional, Total.

Administration: Individual.

Price Data, 1992: $50 per complete kit including 50 Option 1, 2 or 3 rating forms, 50 classroom observation forms, technical manual (35 pages), and Professional Improvement Manual (53 pages); $20 per 50 Option 1, 2 or 3 rating forms; $10 per 50 classroom evaluation forms, $10 per technical manual; $10 per Professional Improvement Manual.

Time: Administration time not reported.

Comments: Manual title is The Professional Improvement Manual; ratings by administrator.

Authors: Stephen B. McCarney and Kathy K. Cummins (The Professional Improvement Manual).

Publisher: Hawthorne Educational Services, Inc.

Review of the Teacher Evaluation Scale by GREGORY J. MARCHANT, Associate Professor of Educational Psychology, Ball State University, Muncie, IN:

The Teacher Evaluation Scale (TES) is an evaluation instrument designed to identify teachers' performances relative to behaviors defined as effective and representative of standard professional behaviors. Teaching practices are rated on a 1 to 5 Likert-type scale indicating the frequency of the practice as demonstrated by the teacher. This rating is made by an informed observer, usually the teacher's principal. The TES includes a technical manual; a "Classroom Observation Form," which serves as an observational worksheet; a "Teacher Evaluation Scale," which allows for rating 35 items across the three areas of management of student behavior, professionally related, and instructional; along with a rating summary and a profile. A professional improvement manual is available. Teaching practices relevant to each of the scale's items are included in the manual.

The scale was developed as a means of evaluating "those characteristics of teacher behavior which lead to success in the educational environment" (manual, p. 4). An early version of the instrument was created by reviewing teacher evaluation instruments from school systems in 20 states. The total number of items on the instrument was reduced from 42 to 35 based on the comments of 30 administrators who reviewed the initial item list. An underlying basis for the scale was universal teaching principles drawn from effective teaching research with particular emphasis placed on characteristics identified by Kounin (1970).

Although the scale ratings are based on observations of teacher performance, the instrument is not a low-inference observational record. There are no specific guidelines concerning the nature of observations or for the number or duration of observations. The author does emphasize the need to gather evidence when an administrator has no knowledge of the teacher's performance on a particular item.

The author provides a good review of the psychometric properties of the instrument including the results of normative standardization data, principal components analysis, item and scale analyses, reliability coefficients, and validity estimates. The good-sized normative sample of 2,212 teachers from nine states appears to be fairly representative geographically and demographically of U.S. teachers. Four standardization tables are presented based on grade level (elementary teachers, and intermediate and secondary teachers grouped together), and for each of these categories divided into two groups based on more than or less than 3 years of experience. The author does not provide the rationale nor statistical test results suggesting the specific groupings.

Although the author identifies three distinct subscales for the TES, there is little statistical evidence to support the distinctions. Interpretation of a scree plot of eigen values suggests one strong factor. All of the items cross load on more than one factor (when considering loadings greater than .30). All but one of the items load (>.30) on the first factor with 21 of the 35 items having their highest loading on the first factor. Fourteen of the items are included in subscales on which they do not have the highest loading. All of the subscales are highly correlated ($r>.85$).

The instrument demonstrated good reliability with high internal consistency within the subscales (item/total $r>.61$), reliability of subscales to the total instrument (KR-20 coefficients $\geq .95$), test-retest on the whole scale ($r = .96, p<.01$), and interrater reliability ($r = .92, p<.01$). The high reliability is not surprising considering the nature of the instrument and ways in which the reliability was assessed. As suggested by the factor analysis, the instrument seems to be consistently measuring one thing. That one thing is not based on discrete observations of data, but rather an accumulation of information. Therefore, the fact that a total of 14 administrators rated one or more teachers in a similar manner after a period of one month is not surprising. The credibility of the interrater reliability is also hindered by the relationship of the raters (principals and their assistant principals).

The validity of the subscales comes into question for reasons related to previously mentioned analyses; however, the instrument on the whole does appear to be a valid measure of effective teaching practices as defined by teacher evaluation documents and administrators. Principals have demonstrated relatively strong support for research-based effective teaching behaviors (Marchant, 1992); however, they do not have a history of accurate judgements of effective teaching (Medley & Coker, 1987). Medley and Coker (1987) concluded that principals may not be good observers or that they may hold inadequate models of effective teaching. It is unlikely that the TES would do much to improve either of these possibilities. The instrument does not provide direction that would facilitate accurate observations of teaching behaviors and it provides a model of effective teaching defined primarily by the consensus of administrators. At this writing the search for generic or general effective teaching behaviors has all but come to an end. Currently there is an emphasis on situation-specific and content-specific pedagogy that suggests the need to consider the context in the evaluation of effective teaching. A decontextualized generic evaluation instrument would seem to run counter to this approach to understanding and improving instruction.

In summary, the TES provides a means for administrators to document their perceptions of a teacher's performance relative to a general set of accepted teaching practices. The TES should not be considered an objective measure of differentiated effective teaching behaviors.

REVIEWER'S REFERENCES

Kounin, J. (1970). *Discipline and group management in classrooms.* New York: Holt, Rinehart, & Winston.

Medley, D. M., & Coker, H. (1987). The accuracy of principals' judgments of teacher performance. *Journal of Educational Research, 80*(4), 242-247.

Marchant, G. J. (1992). Attitudes toward research-based effective teaching behaviors. *Journal of Instructional Psychology, 19*, 119-126.

Review of the Teacher Evaluation Scale by TERRY M. WILDMAN, Professor of Curriculum and Instruction, Virginia Polytechnic Institute, Blacksburg, VA:

The Teacher Evaluation Scale (TES) was designed to assist school administrators in the identification and documentation of teacher behaviors that lead to success in elementary, intermediate, and secondary classrooms. The scale is composed of 35 items, organized around the general categories of managing student behavior, instruction, and professionalism. The items are written in the form of a performance statement (e.g., "reinforces/rewards appropriate social and academic behavior") the administrator must rate on a 5-point scale ranging from *does not demonstrate* to *demonstrates consistently.* Each item is written to include, parenthetically, two or three brief examples of actions which would satisfy the performance expectations measured by that item.

The TES includes an easy-to-read technical manual, a two-page classroom observation form, a four-page teacher rating booklet, and a 53-page Professional Improvement Manual. The Professional Improvement Manual provides a laundry list of brief suggestions to improve teaching or professional behavior for each of the 35 items, and is designed to be used by the administrator and teacher in developing a plan for professional improvement. The potential utility of the manual seems limited considering no conceptual basis for teaching suggestions is given or discussed.

The items themselves were culled from examination of the evaluation procedures used by approximately 20 school systems across the United States. The authors suggest the items selected are in general accord with the process-product research on effective teaching, and thus are likely to be positively correlated with teacher success. Regardless of research relevance, the performance statements included in this scale will likely be very familiar to administrators and teachers who have even modest experience in schools.

The administration directions suggest the rating form for a teacher can be completed in about 15 minutes. The rating form can be completed, however, only after administrators are confident they can rate the teachers' typical performance across all 35 items. This may involve many observations over a period of time. The authors also suggest the TES provides for an objective performance assessment because the items are behaviorally stated. My own reading is that the user of this scale will actually be making relatively high-inference judgments. The items are stated in very general terms (e.g., follows school system's policies and procedures) and the rater must decide what behaviors apply and the extent to which the behaviors are in teachers' day-to-day repertoires.

Once the rating is completed, which involves assigning a score of 1–5 to each of the 35 items, the rater uses a set of conversion tables to derive a standard score ($M = 10$; $SD = 3$) for the three subscales, and an overall "quotient" score ($M = 100$; $SD = 15$). These standard score derivations are based upon norms generated from a standardization sample of

2,212 teachers, representing elementary and intermediate/secondary assignments, and low and high experience levels.

Overall, the TES appears to have been carefully constructed and based upon a broad review of existing teacher performance assessment procedures. In terms of content validity, this instrument probably represents fairly the performance areas considered most important across diverse school systems during the 1970s and early 1980s. Reliabilities for the three subscales are provided and are above .90. Norms are provided for a national sample of teachers, but I do not see how they will be of much benefit given (*a*) the small sample of teachers in some grade level-experience categories, and (*b*) the primary intended use of the scale for professional development purposes at the local level.

One major problem I see with this scale in terms of current use is that it does not relate very well to the present knowledge base on teaching and teacher performance. Examples of performance areas that current users will miss in the TES include emphasis on collaboration, teaming, reflective practice, teaching approaches based on cognitive-constructivist theory, and integrated curriculum practices, to name just a few areas of current interest. Further, although the technical manual claims the items are closely tied to the 1970s process-product research, I do not find any useful mechanism in this performance assessment system to relate the individual items even to the older research base.

In summary, the author contends that the TES provides a standard evaluation system that will contribute to improved service delivery. This assertion seems to hinge on the proposition that success in teaching is a matter of displaying appropriate behaviors that have been identified as important through practice or research. I am frankly skeptical of this approach, and concerned that the fragmentation of teaching into 35 behavior categories, or even 50 or 100, risks diverting attention from the rich understandings that teachers are constructing for themselves regarding their work. The dominant focus on discrete behaviors seem overly technical, highly susceptible to bureaucratic manipulation, and insensitive to the rich metaphors that teachers use conceptually to define themselves and their work. If we can put these concerns aside, the TES does provide a well-organized way to direct evaluators' and teachers' attention to a general set of performance expectations.

[93]
Teacher's School Readiness Inventory.
Purpose: Constructed to screen for children who are at risk for school failure.

Population: Pre-kindergarten to kindergarten children.
Publication Dates: 1986–88.
Acronym: TSRI.
Scores: Total score only.
Administration: Individual.
Price Data, 1991: $12.50 per 200 rating forms; $7.50 per manual ('88, 44 pages); $11.50 per specimen set.
Time: (2–3) minutes.
Comments: Ratings by teachers.
Author: Marvin L. Simner.
Publisher: Phylmar Associates.

Review of the Teacher's School Readiness Inventory by THEODORE COLADARCI, Associate Professor of Education, University of Maine, Orono, ME:

The Teacher's School Readiness Inventory (TSRI), developed by Marvin L. Simner of the University of Western Ontario, is a five-item teacher rating scale designed to help prekindergarten and kindergarten teachers "make proper referral decisions" (scoring manual, p. 2) for children who are "at risk for school failure" (p. 12). Using a 5-point Likert-type scale, a teacher rates each child on distractibility, attention span, and memory span; verbal fluency; interest and participation; letter-identification skills; and printing skills. These five ratings are then summed to form a total score (the only score Simner recommends for decision making). Children receiving a TSRI total score at or below the established cutoff point are considered to be academically at-risk and, in turn, are referred either for additional testing or for immediate remediation, depending on the child's score.

DOCUMENTATION. The TSRI manual is quite impressive, especially in light of this instrument's brevity. Simner offers a clear and generally comprehensive treatment of the essential aspects of his instrument: (*a*) item development, (*b*) administration and use, (*c*) definitions and rating criteria, and (*d*) reliability and validity. In short, the author does a commendable job providing readers with the necessary information to evaluate the TSRI.

Importantly, Simner also repeatedly reminds the reader of the need to be cautious and circumspect when making judgments about any student's at-risk status. At one point, he proffers the following caveat:

We do *not* recommend using the TSRI as the sole means of identifying children who are at risk for school failure. Instead, we believe that it would be far more appropriate to employ the TSRI as the first stage in a two-stage early identification program. (scoring manual, p. 12)

Curiously, this admonition seemingly applies only to children falling at or just below the cutoff point, who, Simner correctly recommends, should undergo additional testing with such instruments as the Metropolitan Readiness Assessment Program or the McCarthy Scales of Children's Abilities. In contrast, teachers immediately should "refer for assistance" (p. 14) any child with a TSRI total score below 12. Contrary to the caveat above, however, this latter recommendation effectively renders the TSRI "the sole means" of identifying at-risk children—at least for this subset of children. In my view, additional testing would be necessary for *any* student flagged by a five-item rating scale.

STANDARDIZATION SAMPLE. All reliability and validity analyses were based on March data (1983–1984) from 581 prekindergarten and kindergarten children—two samples of each—and their 38 teachers from 22 public elementary schools in lower- and middle-income areas of London, Ontario. The relevance of this norming group for districts involving other curricula, grading practices, demographic groups, or geographic regions remains to be established. For this reason, particularly cogent is Simner's recommendation that users establish local norms—a process requiring at least 3 years—before using the TSRI for making referral decisions.

RELIABILITY. Interrater reliability was established by having seven pairs of raters independently rate children in their respective classes, which resulted in a reliability coefficient of .86 for the TSRI total score. The reader is told that .86 is "within the range generally considered acceptable for tests that are to be used solely for screening purposes" (pp. 18–19), and Salvia and Ysseldyke (1985) are cited as support. In fact, Salvia and Ysseldyke argue for a minimum reliability of .90 where a test is to inform "important educational decisions, such as tracking and placement in a special class" (Salvia & Ysseldyke, 1991, p. 142). It seems to me that the TSRI *is* used for important educational decisions, insofar as children with TSRI scores below 12 are singled out, not for further (and more sensitive) assessment, but for immediate "assistance." In my view, this consideration calls into question the adequacy of the TSRI reliability, particularly for children having TSRI scores below 12. (The absence of a reported standard error of measurement merely compounds the problem.)

VALIDITY. As Salvia and Ysseldyke (1991) state, "Since decisions made on the basis of readiness tests are so important, *the validity of the tests is crucial*" (p. 471; italics added). For this reason, I cover the TSRI validity information in some detail.

Content validity. The five items that make up the TSRI represent important aspects of school readiness. However, Simner provides no rationale for restricting the TSRI to *these* five items, other than a passing reference to supporting research. Rather than refer readers to a publication in which this rationale appears, Simner should bring the thrust of that argument directly into the TSRI manual.

Concurrent validity. The TSRI total score shows a strong relationship with the child's June "class standing," a mark provided by the teacher using a 12-point scale from D- to A+. For prekindergarten and kindergarten children alike, correlations between TSRI and class standing range from the mid-.70s to mid-.80s. As the author acknowledges, however, these correlations are difficult to interpret insofar as the same teachers provided both ratings. These values doubtless would be smaller had Simner secured independent ratings (Hoge & Coladarci, 1989).

Concurrent validity coefficients also were obtained between the TSRI and two standardized tests. Among prekindergarten children, the TSRI correlates .71 with the Developmental Tasks for Kindergarten Readiness and .69 with the Wide Range Achievement Test (WRAT); for kindergarten children, the TSRI correlates about .79 with the WRAT. These values suggest an acceptable level of concurrent validity, given these two criteria.

Predictive validity. Laudably, Simner attempted to secure longitudinal data on these 581 children through the second grade in order to assess predictive validity, "the most important type of validity for a readiness test" (Salvia & Ysseldyke, 1991, p. 488). For example, teacher marks in reading, written composition, and mathematics were obtained for many of these children at the end of their first- and second-grade years. Not surprisingly, correlations between teacher marks and the TSRI total score are slightly higher (a) when based on the earlier, first-grade criteria; and (b) when based on kindergarten children, irrespective of when criterion information was obtained. In any case, the correlations are modest, ranging from .39 to .62. Further, interpretation is rendered somewhat problematic by student attrition: Roughly 25% of the 581 TSRI children had moved before completing the first grade. For the second grade, the number grew to almost one half.

Simner also correlated the TSRI with the Woodcock Reading Mastery Test and the KeyMath Diagnostic Arithmetic Test, which were administered in the first grade. Correlations range from .52 to .58 for prekindergarten children and .57 to .65 for kindergarten children. As with the correlations involving teacher marks, these coefficients should be interpreted cautiously because of student attrition in the first grade, and also because roughly 20% of those children who *were* present were not tested.

Classification analyses. Does the TSRI permit accurate classification of children? To be sure, this is the most important question for a screening test. Using the most recent information available, Simner placed children in the "poor performance" category if they had not been promoted to the next grade or if they were assigned "to a slower or junior section of the next grade" (p. 24). These children generally received teacher marks in the *D* range. In contrast, the "good performance" category was reserved for children who later received overall-performance ratings of *B*- or higher. Simner then established the TSRI cutoff score that correctly identified at least 85% of the children in the poor-performance category (13 and 15 for the prekindergarten and kindergarten level, respectively).

In his Tables 3 and 4, Simner clearly reports these data for each of the four samples. For example, we see that 86% to 88% of poor-performance children had earlier received TSRI total scores at or below the cutoff point ("true positives") and 88% to 96% of the good-performance children had fallen above the TSRI cutoff point ("true negatives"). In assessment argot, the TSRI thus demonstrates both "sensitivity" and "specificity."

It follows, of course, that high "hit rates" also are obtained: 88% to 94% of children later demonstrating either "poor" or "good" performance in school had earlier received a TSRI total score consistent with their performance category. From these data, Simner concludes that "the overall predictive validity of the TSRI not only equals but often exceeds the predictive validity achieved by the majority of psychometric screening devices in use today" (p. 25).

This conclusion, however, must be tempered by at least four considerations. First, claims regarding TSRI validity would be strengthened considerably if these results were replicated, both with additional samples and from other sites. (One independent study, also from the Ontario region, was presented in an endnote and reported favorable, albeit less positive, findings.)

Second, because of student attrition, criterion information for some students was taken from first grade, kindergarten, or even prekindergarten. As Simner warns the reader, had second-grade data been obtained for all 581 children in the four TSRI samples, the validity results "might have been somewhat different" (p. 24). *How* different, of course, is not known.

Third, the high hit rates reported by Simner reflect, in part, his definition of "good performance" (*B*- or higher). But if the TSRI is designed to flag children who are "at risk for school failure" (p. 12), then one would expect that children falling above the cutoff score would *not fail.* That is, these children later should receive teacher marks of *C*- or higher. Calculations based on the comparison of *this* group and Simner's poor-performance group yields hit rates of 71% to 88% across the four samples, which are lower than the figures reported in the manual. Curiously, Simner uses the relaxed definition of success (*C*- or higher) for classification analyses he reports elsewhere (Simner, 1987)—contrary to the methodology appearing in the TSRI manual.

Fourth, and most troubling, *one half* of all children identified by the TSRI as academically at risk actually went on to earn teacher marks in the *C* range or higher. This large percentage of "false positives" is not surprising in view of the modest correlations between TSRI and teacher marks (.39 to .62). If these data are generalizable, then one out of every two children who are flagged by the TSRI will be flagged unnecessarily.

CONCLUSIONS. The TSRI is a brief, inexpensive, and easily administered instrument for making referral decisions about prekindergarten and kindergarten children who are academically at risk. In school districts that do not regularly screen this population with more in-depth testing, the TSRI might be regarded as an attractive device for quickly identifying children for further assessment (once local norms have been established). Contrary to the recommendation of the author, however, decisions regarding "assistance"—whatever this term may suggest to the prospective user—should not be based solely on a one-page, five-item rating scale.

REVIEWER'S REFERENCES

Simner, M. L. (1987). Predictive validity of the Teacher's School Readiness Inventory. *Canadian Journal of School Psychology, 3,* 21-32.

Hoge, R. D., & Coladarci, T. (1989). Teacher-based judgments of academic achievement: A review of literature. *Review of Educational Research, 59,* 297-313.

Salvia, J., & Ysseldyke, J. E. (1991). *Assessment* (5th ed.). Boston: Houghton Mifflin.

Review of the Teacher's School Readiness Inventory by BETH DOLL, *Assistant Professor of School Psychology, University of Colorado at Denver, Denver, CO:*

The Teacher's School Readiness Inventory (TSRI) is a rating form intended to assist preschool and kindergarten teachers in identifying students at risk for school failure in later grades. The purpose of the inventory is to provide more accurate estimates of school readiness than global teacher ratings, using a format that is briefer and so more practical than other kindergarten screening inventories.

The TSRI is a five-item measure, every item of which has shown a meaningfully strong relationship to later school performance in previous research. After working with a student for a minimum of 2 to 3 months, teachers complete the inventory by rating a student on a scale of 1 to 5 for each item. Every item is a composite of several discrete characteristics. For example, the first item incorporates teacher judgements about the degree to which a student fidgets, is inattentive, and has poor memory for details. Raters are instructed to consider both the number of item characteristics a child has difficulty with as well as the degree of difficulty a child experiences when assigning a rating on an item. The end points of each rating scale are loosely described with descriptors such as *highly distractible* or *very good attention span*. To assist in the rating, the manual provides teachers with a one-to-five-paragraph descriptor of each item. However, the ultimate decision about when a student evidences a 2 instead of a 4 for any item is up to the discretion of the individual teacher. Despite this apparent laxity in item values, the TSRI manual reports cross-rater reliabilities of a respectable .86 in an early reliability study (Simner, 1987). If these results can be duplicated in subsequent research, the scoring format of the TSRI may prove to be adequate.

Ratings are summed across the five items for a total range of scores from 5 to 25. Total scores are then interpreted using both cutoff points, below which a student is considered to be at risk for subsequent school failure, and probability scores, representing the likelihood that a student with that score will experience subsequent school failure. The manual provides cutoff points and probability scores based on an unrepresentative sample of 581 public school children in Ontario, as well as instructions for developing local cutoff scores for the inventory. The instructions for gathering local norms are clearly written and accompanied by illustrations explaining their analysis; the process requires comparing kindergarten and prekindergarten TSRI scores to students' end-of-the-year teacher ratings in first and second grades. As it is described, local norming is an ambitious one requiring a period of 2 to 3 years to complete. Most users are likely to use the provided cutoffs instead.

The TSRI manual suggests setting cutoff scores such that 85% of the children who subsequently experience school failure are identified; in the Ontario sample, this cutoff also identified false positives (children who were rated low on the TSRI but subsequently performed adequately in school) at a rate of 10%. Probability scores were then computed by determining the proportion of kindergarten students with each TSRI score who experienced school failure in first or second grade. The probability scores were computed using those students who clearly experienced failure in subsequent grades (with end-of-the-year grades of D or lower) and with those who were clearly successful (with end-of-the-year grades of B or higher); students whose school success was less clear were eliminated from the probabilities computations. As a result, the probabilities are somewhat distorted, overrepresenting the likelihood that a child with low ratings will experience difficulty and underrepresenting the likelihood that a child with a high rating will. It may not be possible to derive probability scores that are not misleading without identifying a more precise criterion variable than teacher grades from which to derive the scores.

The validity of the TSRI has been rigorously tested by the scale's author using the Ontario samples. Rating scores on the measure were compared 1, 2, and 3 years later to teacher grades, and to standardized measures of academic skills such as the Woodcock Reading Mastery Test, the KeyMath Diagnostic Arithmetic Test, the Developmental Tasks for Kindergarten Readiness, and the Wide Range Achievement Test. Despite the brevity of the scale, ratings showed respectable correlations ranging from .52 to .67 with standardized measures administered 1 year later, and ranging from .47 to .64 with teacher grades or promotion rankings made 1 year later. Moreover, within this sample, the scale was able to identify nearly 90% of the Ontario students who subsequently had learning difficulties; over 80% of the students declared to be at risk using the TSRI did experience learning difficulties in subsequent grades. This degree of validity is strikingly strong for a five-item scale.

The TSRI is a promising kindergarten screening inventory that may be both effective and practical. However, despite its strong reliability and validity in the Ontario samples, the fact that it has been evaluated only relative to a single community cannot be overlooked. The TSRI can be used only as the author recommends—with the development of local norms and decision points, and with demonstration of ample reliability and validity in the alternative populations where it is being used. These restrictions may limit the utility of the inventory for many users.

REVIEWER'S REFERENCE

Simner, M. L. (1987). Predictive validity of the Teacher's School Readiness Inventory. *Canadian Journal of School Psychology*, 3, 21-32.

[94]
Team Effectiveness Survey.

Purpose: Designed to assess process issues associated with team dynamics.
Population: Team members.
Publication Dates: 1968–86.
Acronym: TES.
Scores: 4 scores for each team member: Exposure, Feedback, Defensive, Supportive, plus Total Team Effectiveness score.
Administration: Group.
Price Data, 1991: $6.95 per test booklet/manual.
Time: Administration time not reported.
Author: Jay Hall.
Publisher: Teleometrics International.
Cross References: For a review by William G. Mollenkopf, see 8:1055.

Review of the Team Effectiveness Survey by GREGORY H. DOBBINS, Associate Professor of Management, The University of Tennessee at Knoxville, Knoxville, TN:

The Team Effectiveness Survey (TES) is designed to assess process issues that affect team effectiveness. It is based upon the assumption that team effectiveness will improve as team members understand more about their own interactional tendencies and discuss these tendencies with team members. Hence, it is an instrument designed primarily for organizational development purposes.

The TES provides individual and team scores for exposure (the tendency to engage in open expressions of one's own feelings and knowledge) and feedback (the tendency to solicit information from others about their feelings and knowledge). These dimensions are proposed to influence the effectiveness of communication and problem solving. Based upon Exposure and Feedback scores, four types of individuals and/or groups can be identified: Type A—low feedback and low exposure; Type B—high feedback and low exposure; Type C—low feedback and high exposure; and Type D—high feedback and high exposure. Hall (the test author) argues that Type D groups are creative and have high levels of interpersonal trust and support. The performance of the other groups (Types A, B, and C) is restricted because information flow and the open exchange of ideas are prevented.

The TES also assesses supportive and defensive climates. Hall argues that if an individual's Defensive climate score is higher than his or her Supportive climate score, then the individual may have a constraining effect on the team and foster feelings of insecurity, vulnerability, and lack of trust among members. If the individual's Supportive climate score is higher than his or her Defensive climate score, it indicates that the individual helps the team work effectively and encourages feelings of well-being and warmth.

Both individual and team scores are calculated with the TES. Thus, each team member will have a score on the four dimensions (Exposure, Feedback, Defensive climate, and Supportive climate) and a group average for each dimension. These scores are used to discuss interactional and process problems in the group.

ADMINISTRATION AND SCORING PROCEDURES. The TES could probably be completed in less than 30 minutes. However, it may take an additional hour to score. Group members are asked to rate each other on 20 behaviors. After making ratings, each group member distributes his or her ratings to all other group members. Each group member then transcribes how they were rated by all other group members on a tally sheet. Team members then add the 10 items that assess exposure and the 10 items that assess feedback. This is done separately for ratings made by each team member. Thus, in a group that contains nine team members, each team member will hand calculate nine sets of scores (i.e., how they were rated by Person A, Person B, and so forth plus self-ratings).

Scoring the climate measures suffers from similar problems. It requires each team member to add the five items that form the Defensiveness and Supportive scales. In addition, team members are asked to calculate average scores for each scale. Once again, these calculations will be time consuming and cumbersome for team members. In addition, without careful instructions and guidance, some individuals will probably miscalculate their scores.

The scoring procedure should be computerized in future revisions of the TES. In addition to reducing the time commitments of team members, better feedback could be provided by a computerized scoring system (e.g., medians and ranges could be calculated for each group, organizational means could be determined, and normative data could be accumulated by the publisher).

PSYCHOMETRIC PROPERTIES. The psychometric characteristics of the TES are unknown at this time. In fact, it fails to meet almost every technical standard put forth in the *Standards for Educational and Psychological Testing* (AERA, APA, & NCME, 1985). The reliabilities of the scales are not presented. There is no discussion of the manner in which the scales were constructed. At a minimum, the author should calculate coefficient alphas for the scales on the TES.

Furthermore, criterion-related validity studies have not been conducted. Clearly, the correlation between TES scales and team effectiveness should be determined. Finally, normative data are not available for the TES.

I am also concerned with the construct validity of the instrument. For example, the instrument proposes that exposure and feedback are independent constructs. Although the two constructs may be theoretically independent, the instrument may be assessing nothing more than social potency. I would not be surprised to find that individuals who actively participate in groups receive higher scores on both Feedback and Exposure than individuals who do not actively participate in groups. These findings would reflect opportunity for exhibiting behaviors, instead of actual feedback and exposure tendencies. In addition, the scales could be contaminated by friendship bias and all the other problems with peer ratings.

SUMMARY. The TES may prove to be a psychometrically sound instrument and have a positive effect on organizational effectiveness. At the present time, however, it should be used cautiously. Not only is there no evidence to indicate that it assesses the constructs that it purports to measure, but its use could actually cause friction and conflict in some work teams, especially if discussions of TES findings are not skillfully guided by facilitators.

As more and more organizations move to teams, it will be important for the testing industry to design instruments that assess team functioning accurately. The TES may be very valuable in this effort. Hence, Teleometrics International should make an intense effort to validate the TES. Furthermore, personnel managers and organizational consultants should demand evidence of sound psychometric properties before adopting instruments such as the TES. Such actions would send a strong message to publishers of organizational development instruments and force these instruments to meet the same standards as other psychological tests and inventories.

REVIEWER'S REFERENCE

American Educational Research Association, American Psychological Association, & National Council on Measurement in Education. (1985). *Standards for educational and psychological testing.* Washington, DC: American Psychological Association, Inc.

Review of the Team Effectiveness Survey by HARRISON G. GOUGH, Professor of Psychology, Emeritus, University of California, Berkeley, Berkeley, CA:

The Team Effectiveness Survey (TES) is not so much a test as a training and self-study device for working with teams or small groups. The materials envisage up to 10 persons in the team, plus the self. Each member rates self, and all other members, on 20 bipolar items, using a 10-point scale graduated for how consistently the defined behavior occurs. The 20 items are grouped into two broad categories: *Exposure*, or the degree to which open and candid expression of own feelings, attitudes, and strategies for dealing with others are disclosed; and *Feedback*, or the degree to which the feelings, opinions, and goals of others are elicited and respected. An example of an "exposure" item is "Is openly affectionate toward other members that he or she likes. (As opposed to being inhibited, restrained, or acting embarrassed.)" An example of a "feedback" item is "Presses for additional information when other members are apparently not leveling. (As opposed to letting the matter drop or changing the subject.)"

Five of the items are also classified as indicating defensiveness, and five as indicating supportiveness. Averaging of the ratings received from others on these two clusters will show whether the individual functions more within a "defensive climate" or a "supportive climate." Team averages can also be computed from the Defensive and Supportive vectors.

The Exposure and Feedback averaged scores for self, and for self described by others on the team, are plotted along two axes from which a four-fold classification is derived: The Arena (reported by both self and others), the Blindspot (reported by others but not by self), the Facade (reported by self but not by others), and the Unknown (reported by neither self or others). The larger the area covered by the Arena, the more effective the individual member, and the more effective the team.

Although all of the above is plausible enough if offered as hypotheses to be confirmed, no evidence whatsoever is given as to the empirical validity of the scores and inferences as indicators of either team or individual effectiveness. Among the other things absent from the manual are (*a*) correlations among the 20 items and their factor structure; (*b*) single-trial or test-retest reliability data for the four major scores and two additional scores; (*c*) norms for the scales, and for frequencies in the four categories; (*d*) gender differences on scales and items; (*e*) relationships of the scales to other tests that assess interpersonal style in groups, and group climates, such as FIRO-B (Schutz, 1958) and the Moos Social Climate Scales (Moos, 1976); (*f*) information on the vulnerability of the TES to willful manipulation and faking; and (*g*) references to published research on the instrument.

Under the guidance of a proficient and well-trained psychologist, the TES could furnish raw material, as it were, of possible utility for self-study and group discussions. However, as an assessment tool capable of providing valid, meaningful, and reliable information it must as of now be deemed unacceptable.

REVIEWER'S REFERENCES

Schutz, W. C. (1958). *FIRO: A three-dimensional theory of interpersonal behavior*. New York: Rinehart.

Moos, R. H. (1976). *The human context: Environmental determinants of behavior*. New York: Wiley.

[95]

Test of Early Language Development, Second Edition.

Purpose: Designed to measure the early development of oral language in the areas of receptive and expressive language, syntax, and semantics.

Population: Ages 2-0 to 7-11.

Publication Dates: 1981–91.

Acronym: TELD-2.

Scores: Total score only.

Administration: Individual.

Price Data, 1994: $109 per complete kit; $29 per 25 Form A Profile Record Forms; $29 per 25 Form B Profile Record Forms; $26 per picture book; $29 per Examiner's Manual ('91, 74 pages).

Time: (20) minutes.

Authors: Wayne P. Hresko, D. Kim Reid, and Donald D. Hammill.

Publisher: PRO-ED, Inc.

Cross References: See T4:2749 (6 reference); for reviews of an earlier edition by Janice Arnold Dole and Elizabeth M. Prather, see 9:1250 (1 reference).

Review of the Test of Early Language Development, Second Edition by JAVAID KAISER, Associate Professor of Education, Virginia Polytechnic Institute & State University, Blacksburg, VA:

The primary purpose of the Test of Early Language Development, Second Edition (TELD-2) is to screen children for language deficiency. The test is designed for normal children of ages 2-0 through 7-11 but can be administered to special populations after making proper adjustments in administering the test and establishing separate norms. The TELD-2 is administered individually without time limits and is available in two parallel forms: Form A and Form B. Each form contains 68 items. The test is well grounded in theory and measures form and content of language development. The syntax, morphology, and semantics are measured in receptive as well as expressive modes. Phonology that was measured in the first edition of the Test of Early Language Development (TELD) has been deleted from this second edition.

The TELD-2 is very easy to administer and score. It comes with explicit item-by-item instructions. A shortened version of these instructions is printed directly on the Record form for experienced examiners. The Picture Book accompanying the test is well organized and is easy to use. Additional objects needed to administer certain items are completely specified. The testing time is efficiently reduced by identifying different entry points on the tests for different age groups. Examples explaining basals and ceilings have minimized the probability of making scoring errors.

Items are scored correct (1) or incorrect (0). The sum of item scores is called the raw score. Knowing the chronological age of the child (without rounding days to the next month), the raw score can be converted into language quotient (LQ), normal curve equivalent (NCE), or age equivalent scores by using tables given in the manual. The authors have also provided a conversion table to convert the language quotient of the child into percentile rank, z-score, T-score, or stanine with little interpolation. The ranges of LQ and NCE scores have been labeled from "very poor" to "very superior" to make the interpretation of test scores easier. The authors are to be commended for emphasizing the proper role of test scores in the process of clinical diagnosis and for discouraging users from using age equivalent scores. Normal curve equivalent scores should also be avoided whenever possible, because authors have smoothed the curve on visual inspection.

Although the normative sample of 1,329 children was selected from multiple sites, the selection of sites was arbitrary and was determined where friends and colleagues of the authors or past users of the TELD resided. The description of sampling procedure (p. 44) further suggests that the selection of children at individual sites was not under the control of authors and may have included children who had or were suspected of language deficiency. In addition, normative groups for various age levels were small and ranged from 178 to 268 children. Although the authors have included adjacent age groups to produce more stable norms, the representativeness of normative groups is still questionable.

The content validity of the test has been established adequately. The criteria for the final selection of items included item validity as expressed by 22 professional experts, item difficulty, item-total correlation, and item bias. Only items that were free of gender and racial bias were included in the test.

The test has excellent internal consistency for all age levels. The coefficient alpha ranged from .91 to .97 with a median value of .97. Test-retest and equivalent-form reliability (.97 to .98) is available for children of ages 6-5 to 7-5 and is based on small sample size ($N = 55$). The same estimates for other age levels are not reported. The evidence produced in support of criterion-related validity is also questionable. The use of the TELD as a criterion measure of the TELD-2 is inappropriate because the TELD-2 is an extension of the TELD and included items from its first edition. Moreover, the sample size is very small ($N = 55$) and included children of only upper age levels (6-0 to 7-5). The correlation of TELD-2 scores with The Test of Language Development-2, Receptive Expressive Emergent Language, Preschool Language Scale, and Peabody Picture Vocabulary Test, though statistically significant, had only 16%–36% variance in common. Again, these correlations are based on very small sample sizes ($N = 30$ to 45) and did not cover all age levels for which the TELD-2 was developed.

The construct validity of the TELD-2 has been demonstrated through its correlation with intelligence and other cognitive measures. Here again, one encounters the same problem of small sample sizes ($N = 15$ to 55) and lack of representation for all age levels. Although authors claimed that TELD-2 was successful in differentiating various levels of language impairment in the state of Texas, the correct classification rate of the TELD-2 when administered to children with normal and mild language impairment is not known.

SUMMARY. The authors should be commended for developing a test in a difficult area like language development. The test is content valid and internally consistent but lacks evidence in support of its construct validity. Test administration, scoring, and interpretation of test scores is easy. The manual is well written except Chapter 4 where authors have caused confusion by introducing the performance statistics of the TELD.

Review of the Test of Early Language Development, Second Edition by DAVID A. SHAPIRO, Associate Professor of Communication Disorders, Department of Human Services, College of Education and Psychology, Western Carolina University, Cullowhee, NC:

The Test of Early Language Development, Second Edition (TELD-2) is designed to measure early oral language abilities. Results from the TELD-2 can be compared with relative strengths and weaknesses in cognitive aptitude and early academic achievement. The authors appropriately cautioned that "the test results should be treated as hypotheses to be investigated further and either validated or invalidated through direct observation, additional testing, or future events" (p. 34). They further indicated that "the TELD-2 was designed to complement rather than replace systematic, naturalistic observation" (p. 2). Within this context, the test lists five purposes. In abbreviated form, they are to: identify students who are significantly below their peers in early language development and may be candidates for intervention, identify strengths and weaknesses of individual students, document students' progress in intervention, aid in directing instruction, and serve as a measurement device in research studies pertaining to academic achievement. These purposes represent a significant expansion of those reported in the original TELD (1981).

The Examiner's Manual is well organized and presents information that is critical to using the TELD-2 and to the assessment process in general. Other materials include a Picture Book and Profile/Record Forms (A and B). The rationale and overview of the TELD-2 are addressed concisely, as is the model upon which the test is based (Bloom & Lahey, 1978). Although the model includes form (phonology, syntax, and morphology; i.e., the structural components of language), content (semantics; i.e., knowledge of objects, relations among objects, and relations among events), and use (pragmatics; i.e., appropriateness of the language to specific contexts and communicative purposes), the TELD-2 addresses form (syntax and morphology only) and content only. The authors highlighted significant changes in the TELD-2 including expanding the test range for children aged 2-0 to 7-11 years, increasing the number of items on two alternate forms to 68 items each, shortening item directions and scoring instructions, and expanding the norm tables to include normal curve equivalent (NCE) scores.

Administration and scoring procedures are clear. The TELD-2 is administered to individuals in approximately 15 to 40 minutes. No time limits are imposed and the test may be administered in more than one session if necessary. All responses are recorded as either correct (1 point) or incorrect (0 points) on the Profile/Record Form, summed to form the TELD-2 total raw score, and then converted into a language quotient (LQ). Testing begins with the item corresponding to the child's chronological age. Preliminary items require direct observation or parental report. Later items require children to repeat words and sentences, answer questions, and respond to instructions with and without accompanying pictures and other materials presented by the examiner.

The basal and ceiling are established by determining that point at which the child passes or misses, respectively, five consecutive items. Useful examples for establishing basals and ceilings are provided in the manual. All pictures used as stimuli are contained within a conveniently organized Picture Book. Turning the book one way enables presentation of the Form A pictures. Turning the opposite way presents Form B pictures. A few additional and easily accessible materials are required for administration and are specified in the manual. Administration instructions are followed immediately by scoring directions that include examples of correct responses. Every attempt has been made to simplify the scoring and reduce the amount of inferential judgments required of the examiner.

During an administration and scoring pilot implemented by this reviewer, several concerns arose. For example, the earliest items are scored on the bases of either observed language behavior or parent/caregiver report. Although the authors have established a precedent for parental reporting in assessment (p. 39), the reliability between the child's language behaviors observed by the examiner and those inferred by parental report for the TELD-2 should be verified. Further, the picture stimuli are typically presented neatly and without distraction. However, several items seem potentially confounded by the child's visual discrimination ability. For example, it is not clear in Picture 2 (Form A, Item 24) if the car is part of the "day" picture or an individual picture itself. Other items seem confounded by the structure of the verbal instructions and/or the visual stimuli. For example, Item 30 (Form A) directs "Show me the ball that is bigger" and "Show me the house that is smaller." The contrastives (bigger/smaller) imply a comparison between two units. Picture 8, however, provides three units each for balls and houses. Either a comparison of only two units or use of superlatives (biggest/smallest) would be more appropriate. Assessing knowledge of prepositions, Item 36 (Form A, Picture 10) directs "Show me the rope going around the tree." Because there is no ongoing action, deleting "going" in the instruction would be more linguistically correct and would provide a more direct comparison (around vs. not around/at the base of). Assessing knowledge of same and different, Item 49 (Form A, Picture 21) directs the examiner to point to a cluster of blocks and say "These toys are the same." A careful look at the blocks reveals that they are not the same (i.e., identical). Similar questions are raised regarding test items on Form B. Item 21 (Form B, Picture 3) assesses knowledge of big/little and directs the child to "Show me the big bear. Show me the little bear." This wording implies a comparison between two units, whereas Picture 3 has three bears. Changing the wording or picturing only two bears would be more appropriate. Both Items 42 and 46 seem culturally/linguistically biased in the response expectation. Item 42 requires familiarity with television and asks "What's your favorite TV show?" Many children in mountain communities do not get television reception; others cannot afford television. Yet the response must contain a program name or indicate "I don't have one," implying one among others does not surface as the favorite. Item 46 assesses knowledge of morning/afternoon and asks "Do you take a nap in the morning or in the afternoon?" Some children nap in the morning, some afternoon, some neither, some both. Although item selection and content validity will be addressed later, this reviewer experienced difficulty regarding the structure of the verbal instructions and visual stimuli when administering the test. In addition, although examples of correct responses are provided, a longer list of both acceptable and unacceptable responses would facilitate scoring. Responses that did not fit the examples of correct responses in the manual and the Profile/Record Form rendered some scoring subjectivity. Finally, the following concern is of considerable magnitude. The test objectives listed above imply the TELD-2 is a diagnostic measure, one that helps identify language-related strengths and weaknesses, design instruction, and document progress through intervention. However, the method of scoring (1–correct vs. 0–incorrect only) compromises valuable diagnostic information. Some form of verbatim recording would permit an analysis of the errors in order to determine the child's linguistic knowledge and level of cognitive abstraction. For example, several items call for the child to analyze on the basis of causality and/or functionality. Item 34 (Form A) asks "Why does X go to work?" Item 48 (Form A) asks "What do you do with a (pencil, knife, bus, clock)?" Neither the bipolar scoring scale (1 vs. 0) nor the Diagnostic Profile (which quantifies the number of items passed under System [i.e., Receptive and Expressive], and Feature [i.e., Syntax and Semantics]) permits an understanding of the nature of the child's response, rendering the TELD-2 a screening test only.

Explicit directions are provided for completing the Profile/Record Form and for determining and interpreting the raw score, standard scores (language quotient and normal curve equivalent), percentile rank, language age (i.e., age equivalents), and overall rating. However, the data provided on the sample Profile/Record Form, Form A (specifically for the language quotient, normal curve equivalent, and percentile rank, p. 30) do not agree with that provided in the appropriate tables in Appendix A (pp. 60–64). The individual scores are discussed in terms of their proper use and interpretation. The language quotient has a mean of 100 and a standard deviation of 15, thus enabling comparison with other standard scores across other instruments. The normal curve equivalent has a mean of 50 and a standard deviation of 21.06, providing an exact match between NCEs and percentile ranks of 1 and 99, thus having the same range and midpoints. The authors advised against using age equivalent scores (language age) whenever possible, reviewed significant cautions in interpreting test results, and reminded test users that the TELD-2 results "augmented by additional test findings, direct observation, and knowledge acquired from secondary sources, will eventually result in proper diagnosis and program" (p. 32). Furthermore, the TELD-2 "should be used as the first level of assessment" (p. 37). If a child demonstrates reduced early language skills on the TELD-2, "his or her abilities in this area should be more thoroughly investigated either by using specific language ability measures, or through language sampling, diagnostic observation, or other clinical language methods" (p. 37).

The authors provided a thorough review of item development, item analysis, standardization procedures, normative information, reliability, and validity. The original TELD (1981) items formed the basis of the TELD-2. The procedures to design a set of additional items to broaden the range of language abilities sampled were described adequately. Items were analyzed on the basis of discriminating power (i.e., by using the point biserial correlation technique where each item is correlated with the total raw score) and item difficulty (i.e., by determining proportions of examinees who get each item correct and incorrect). Some items with difficulties below 15% and above 85% were retained in order to account for both the lower and upper age ranges and language potentials. Although the authors reported having paid particular attention to eliminating bias on the bases of ethnicity and sex, several individual items may be problematic as noted earlier.

The TELD-2 was standardized on a sample of 1,329 children at varied settings from 30 states. The characteristics of the subjects seem to represent a national sample on the bases of gender, urban/rural residence, race, geographic region, parental occupation, ethnicity, and age. The rationale for using the four kinds of normative scores is clearly presented.

Reliability estimates were obtained using the techniques of coefficient alpha, test-retest, and alternative forms. These estimates focus on two types of reliability (internal consistency and stability) and two sources of test error (content sampling and time sampling). All coefficient alphas exceeded the established criterion of .90. Standard errors of measurement associated with the coefficient alphas for Forms A and B were sufficiently small. These data indicate that both forms have sufficient internal consistency. A Rasch analysis, where both forms were analyzed at two levels with a one-parameter item response modal analysis, was conducted as another method for determining internal consistency. Results indicate that there appears to be good measurement of a single dimension of the material covered. Estimates of test error were determined by time sampling including immediate and delayed test-retest with alternate forms and delayed test-retest with the same form. The coefficients that resulted indicated sufficient temporal stability and consistency of response to the different forms.

Evidence is reported for content validity, criterion validity (concurrent only), and construct validity. Content validity was supported by detailed reporting of procedures for test construction, item development, and item analysis; data regarding discriminating power; and the relationship of the items to the theoretical construct. Concurrent validity was established by correlating the TELD-2, Form A and B, with the total score of the original TELD on 55 children (language ability not specified) ranging in age from 6-0 to 7-5 years. Although this procedure was unfortunately limited to the older age range and on a relatively small sample, the correlations are high (.96 and .97). Additional evidence of concurrent validity was reported by correlating the TELD-2 raw scores for both forms with those of two selected criterion tests on a sample of 45 language-normal children between the ages of 5 and 6 years, and two other criterion tests on 30 children (language ability not specified) between 4 and 5 years old. Again representing a relatively small sample within limited age ranges, correlation coefficients, reportedly significant beyond the .01 level, ranged from .47 to .66. These data, within the limitations noted, reflect adequate evidence of concurrent validity. Construct validity was supported by delineating a core of assumptions that underlie the test and hypotheses generated by these assumptions, and by presenting data to verify these hypotheses. Specific premises that were addressed included the relationship of the TELD-2 to chronological age and experience, intelligence, academic and school-related ability, and group differentiation. Although coverage could have been more complete and precise, these data provide some evidence of construct validity. This reviewer concurs with the authors that "Further data gathered from varied samples of children throughout the country would add significantly to assumptions pertaining to the test's usefulness" (p. 52).

In summary, the TELD-2 presents a useful measure of expressive and receptive language abilities in the areas of semantics and syntax of children aged 2-0 to 7-11 years. The Examiner's Manual, Picture Book, and Profile/Record Forms are well organized. Although the bipolar method of scoring is intended to simplify the scoring process, some subjectivity exists regarding interpreting correct versus incorrect responses. Furthermore, the method of scoring diminishes the diagnostic value of the language-related data collected, thus rendering the test a screening tool only. Taking seriously the authors' caution that results gained from the TELD-2 must be supplemented by other formal and informal measures of language including conversational language analysis, this test should prove helpful as a preliminary component of an assessment plan.

REVIEWER'S REFERENCE

Bloom, L., & Lahey, M. (1978). *Language development and language disorders*. New York: John Wiley and Sons.

[96]
Test of Early Reading Ability—Deaf or Hard of Hearing.

Purpose: Designed to measure "children's ability to attribute meaning to printed symbols, their knowledge of the alphabet and its functions, and their knowledge of the conventions of print."

Population: Deaf and hard of hearing children ages 3-0 to 13-11.

Publication Date: 1991.

Acronym: TERA-D/HH.

Scores: Total score only.

Administration: Individual.

Forms, 2: A, B.

Price Data, 1994: $124 per complete kit including picture book, 25 Form A and 25 Form B profile/examiner record forms, and manual (49 pages); $41 per picture book; $29 per 25 profile/examiner record forms (select Form A or B); $29 per manual.

Time: (20–30) minutes.

Comments: Adaptation of the Test of Early Reading Ability-2 (T4:2751).

Authors: D. Kim Reid, Wayne P. Hresko, Donald D. Hammill, and Susal Wiltshire.

Publisher: PRO-ED, Inc.

Review of the Test of Early Reading Ability—Deaf or Hard of Hearing (TERA-D/HH) by BARBARA

A. ROTHLISBERG, Associate Professor of Educational Psychology and School Psychology 1 Program Director, Ball State University, Muncie, IN:

Early reading behavior or emergent literacy has become an area of increasing interest given education's growing concern for early identification and intervention with children experiencing special educational needs. Acknowledging that interest, Reid, Hresko, Hammill, and Wiltshire have introduced the Test of Early Reading Ability—Deaf or Hard of Hearing (TERA-D/HH), a specialized version of the earlier Test of Early Reading Ability (2nd edition; TERA-2; T4:2751). The TERA-D/HH is designed for 3- to 13-year-old children with moderate to profound degrees of hearing loss. It can be adapted for administration using simultaneous communication or American Sign Language (ASL).

Recognizing that learning to read may be especially problematic for the auditorily challenged child, the TERA-D/HH seeks to pick out key components of early print experiences and assess children's relative competence in deriving meaning from such print symbols. Three aspects of early reading behavior are specifically addressed: constructing meaning from print, knowledge of the alphabet, and understanding print conventions. Construction of meaning encompasses a child's ability to "read" frequently encountered signs, logos, and words; relate words to one another; and understand the contextual nature of written discourse. Alphabet knowledge is defined as letter and word decoding (either orally or through sign). Finally, assessment of print conventions looks at the child's awareness of text orientation and organization (i.e., book handling, the spatial orientation of print on a page, and ability to uncover textual or print errors). The authors propose that deaf or hard-of-hearing children go through the same stages of early literacy behaviors as their hearing counterparts albeit at a different rate—hence the norms for 3- to 13-year-olds. Therefore, the intent of the TERA-D/HH includes the charting of progress in reading and the identification of children who may differ significantly from the norm in their early reading development.

The authors present a convincing rationale for their view of early reading behaviors. Linked to the literature on emergent literacy, the argument that hearing-impaired children experience print in a similar fashion to hearing children is logically made. The unknown element is in the way auditorily challenged children interpret the visual references associated with oral language. However, the TERA-D/HH evidently seeks to put children's print knowledge in a common context and identify the relative acquisition of understanding both within the auditorily challenged population and between this group and hearing children (through comparison with the TERA-2).

The administrative structure of the TERA-D/HH appears to be straightforward with specific instructions given for each item; however, examiners must have general training in assessment and interpretation as well as be proficient in the communication method employed by the student. This could include ASL, manual English, total communication, and/or finger spelling. The basic testing package includes the two forms—A and B—of the instrument printed in a back-to-back item booklet. Each form consists of 44 items scored as correct or incorrect. One point is awarded for each correct response with total raw score then converted into a percentile, T score, standard score (reading quotient), Normal Curve Equivalent, and/or stanine. Basal and ceiling levels are used to shorten testing time. Children 3 to 5-5 (years-months) begin with Item 1, those 5-6 to 7-5 start at Item 10, and still older students begin at Item 25. Questions are asked in ascending order until five consecutive errors are obtained (ceiling). If, in establishing a ceiling, the examinee has not obtained five consecutive *correct* responses, the examiner would then proceed to test backward from the starting point until five consecutive responses are correct or Item 1 is reached. Examples of scoring variations are provided in the manual.

Items representing the three early reading constructs (e.g., knowledge of alphabet, constructing meaning, understanding print conventions) are interspersed throughout the test although questions relating to knowledge of alphabet tend to occur earlier in the item sequence. To insure optimal performance, any item can be repeated or reworded if the concept being tested appears unclear. Attention is paid to the familiarity of particular print components. That is, several items require that the examiner select regionally appropriate logos or labels so that the questions take advantage of the child's actual experiences with print. Item instructions specify if portions of an item must be signed or presented in a prescribed way (i.e., finger spelled). Item stimuli are presented simply in a black-and-white format which may limit examinee interest in the testing situation.

The student record form is complete and easy to follow. In addition to the expected sections for scoring and listings of score conversions, this form includes a sheet which allows the examiner to picture the student's "Instructional Target Zone" by examining item performance in the three components of early reading to identify the types of concepts that

might be profitably taught. This may be especially useful with early elementary-aged students because the breadth of items increases at this point.

The design of the TERA-D/HH Forms A and B appears to be adequate. Preliminary item content and categorization (as an early reading construct) were reviewed by a panel of experts to judge item quality and relevance. Items then were field tested to determine those with the best discriminating power and difficulty level. However, a limited set of items seem to be geared for the youngest age levels (under 6).

Once items had been selected, the TERA-D/HH was normed on 1,146 deaf and hard-of-hearing children dispersed across 29 states and the District of Columbia. Given the variations in this population (i.e., ethnicity, degree of hearing loss, method of teaching, etc.) the sampling seemed to be adequate. Number of cases per age level differed across the sample with the smallest number of cases occurring at the extremes (e.g., 76 children at 3 years, 71 cases at 13 years). No information was provided as to the distribution of cases (i.e., mean age of testing in years and months) within each year level or on the actual distribution of performance obtained at each age (i.e., degree of skewness).

Reliability estimates of the TERA-D/HH were established through the use of coefficient alpha and alternate form test-retest procedures. Coefficient alphas were computed for the entire standardization sample and averaged .95 for Form A and .94 for Form B suggesting a high degree of item homogeneity and the interrelation among components of early reading. Thus, although knowledge of meaning, the alphabet, and print conventions are portrayed as different constructs, they exhibited a high level of association. Alternate form test-retest reliability was conducted over a 2-week period on a limited sample of 25, 6- to 9-year-olds. The obtained correlation coefficient between Form A and B from this sample was .83. No reliability information on preschool-aged groups was included.

Evidence of test validity seemed to be the most problematic for the TERA-D/HH. Although the concept of content-related evidence of validity is aided by the use of experts to identify and structure the items used, the real test of this content is in the relation of the test to reading itself. The test items are supposed to indicate the acquisition of skills necessary and related to early reading. The number of items representing each component of early reading was not stated explicitly but can be gleaned from the pupil record form with its "Instructional Target Zone." For instance, of the 44 items on Form A,

16 were devoted to construction of meaning, 13 to knowledge of the alphabet, and 15 to knowledge of print conventions. Unfortunately, the evidence provided in support of criterion-related validity was extremely weak and basically unrelated to non-test behavior. Instead of correlating responses on the TERA-D/HH to other reading situations to determine the TERA-D/HH's relevance to instruction, only correlations relating the TERA-D/HH to the TERA-2 for a sample of eleven 7- to 9-year-olds are noted in the manual. Intuitively, this type of analysis seems better associated to preliminary evidence of construct validity (i.e., the relation of this new test to the preexisting measure purported to assess the same concepts) than it does to concurrent or criterion-related utility. Indeed, no confirmation that TERA-D/HH test scores relate to other reading measures or behaviors was provided.

Arguments for construct validity were uniformly based on small samples of older subjects. For instance, 15 students diagnosed with learning disabilities (LD) were distinguished from 13 diagnosed as mentally retarded (MR). The manual states that the average scores for the LD students were "markedly different" from the MR students; however, the small samples used may not have allowed for significant differences to be obtained.

Perhaps the bit of evidence most damaging to the TERA-D/HH utility as a measure of early reading skill is related to the tabled information (Table 4.6) in the manual on the standardization sample's mean raw score performance on the TERA-D/HH; standard deviations were not offered. According to this information the mean raw score of 3-year-olds was 1.3 (Form A) and 2.2 (Form B), of 4-year-olds was 3.5 (Form A) and 4.3 (Form B), and of 5-year-olds was 10.2 (Form A) and 10.7 (Form B). Recognizing the potential delay in acquisition of print concepts as a contributing factor, it is nevertheless sobering to see the potential lack of skill differentiation at the very ages where identification of early reading needs would seem most beneficial. For instance, what assistance can the TERA-D/HH provide to the instructional planning of a deaf 4-year, 2-month-old whose raw score on Form A was 2 but placed her at the 55th percentile? Certainly, basing the child's "reading" ability on such a limited sample of behavior may gravely misrepresent her capabilities. The TERA-D/HH did not appear to have the necessary number of simple items to establish a reasonable "floor" for analysis. Diagnosis or remedial planning based on such limited samples of items probably will not improve instructional practice for the very young.

At this point, the TERA-D/HH would be better treated as a research instrument than as an approved diagnostic tool—especially with preschoolers. The severe limitations on reliability and validity information raise serious questions regarding the measure's actual capacity to provide more than a gross and limited overview of deaf and hard-of-hearing children's recognition of print. Although the TERA-D/HH is an intriguing attempt to address a necessary assessment need, until supporting documentation can firm up the TERA-D/HH's claims of reliability and validity this instrument should not take the place of existing evaluation procedures related to early reading behavior.

Review of the Test of Early Reading Ability—Deaf or Hard of Hearing by ESTHER STAVROU TOU-BANOS, School Psychologist, Lawrence Public Schools, Lawrence, NY:

The Test of Early Reading Ability—Deaf or Hard of Hearing (TERA-D/HH) is a special edition of the Test of Early Reading Ability (TERA-2; T4:2751) designed for students with sensory hearing loss. It is intended to assess early reading behaviors through three constructs: (*a*) the child's ability to attribute meaning to printed symbols, (*b*) knowledge of the alphabet and its functions, and (*c*) knowledge of the conventions employed in reading and writing English. The TERA-D/HH is not considered a readiness test but rather a measure of early literacy behaviors which "gradually evolve into standard reading and writing." The stated purposes for the TERA-D/HH are to identify students who are significantly different from peers in the early development of reading, to document a student's progress in learning to read, to serve as a measure in research projects, and to suggest instructional practices. The rationale used for the development of the test and its items is clearly stated in the manual and incorporates both theory and research.

The TERA-2 and TERA-D/HH assess the same constructs but differ in that items incompatible with sign were replaced and the wording of some directions was changed to facilitate sign interpretation. Because deaf and hard-of-hearing children generally take longer in learning to read, the upper age range was extended beyond age 9 to age 13-11. A broader age range is desirable because children with hearing loss tend to display a great deal of variability in rates and patterns of language development. The authors suggest comparing the results of TERA-D/HH with TERA-2 norms to estimate how well a deaf or hard-of-hearing student is progressing in comparison to hearing peers; however, it has not clearly been established the two tests are comparable.

The TERA-D/HH was designed to be used with simultaneous communication or American Sign Language (ASL). The authors suggest using the TERA-2 for students who rely heavily or exclusively on oral/aural communication. Examiners using the TERA-D/HH must be proficient in the administration and interpretation of assessment data as well as the use of various manual communication methods. The use of a certified interpreter is also acceptable, providing standardization is maintained. Comprehensive information is provided regarding administration conditions and procedures. Because parts of the TERA-D/HH assess students' awareness of logos and other forms of environmental print that may differ regionally, the TERA-D/HH was standardized using local variations by including examiner-made items. This unique feature could potentially cause difficulties in standardization if examiners are given too much leeway. However, specific instructions for selecting and field testing logos are provided to minimize differences among examiners.

Administration instructions and scoring criteria are conveniently contained on the record form and most responses are easily scored as either right or wrong. The basal and ceiling rules are somewhat problematic in that it is possible for a child to fail many items before attaining the basal of five consecutive correct answers, and still have them counted as correct. As a result, even though it is common for children with hearing loss to perform inconsistently, these inconsistencies within the test are ignored. This also causes practical problems in that children can reach a ceiling without having established a basal and the examiner must awkwardly move from difficult items to much easier items.

Raw scores for the total test can be converted into percentile ranks, normal curve equivalents, and reading quotients. It was surprising and refreshing to note the authors resist the temptation to include age/grade equivalents and provide a strong argument for this decision. Instructional target zones intended to pinpoint areas for direct instruction are provided. Although instructional target zones are a potential useful feature, the procedure for determining the instructional target zone is confusing and requires access to the child's mental age or conversion of an IQ using the ratio method. Considering many of the arguments against the use of the mental age, this procedure is not recommended.

The technical section of the manual is comprehensive. Technical data are also provided on the record

form, although it is questionable whether this is necessary, particularly if it adds to the expense of the already costly record forms. Nevertheless, if this information is to be included on the record form, it should at least be consistent with what is stated in the manual. This is not the case.

Test items were selected based on the research literature in emergent reading behaviors, systematic observation of print available in preschooler's environments, and the literature on literacy acquisition of the deaf and hard of hearing. They were then examined by a panel of experts in both reading and hearing impairment to determine their appropriateness for inclusion. Items were validated statistically through examination of item difficulties, and item discrimination indices calculated using the point biserial correlation method. The criterion for inclusion of an item was a "conservative" .30 index of discrimination. This fairly low criterion was, according to the authors, followed "for the most part." Median item discrimination indices tended to be higher on Form A than Form B, particularly at ages 3 and 10 where the differences between the two forms are very large. This leads one to wonder if the two forms are really equivalent at these ages. Table 4.1 in the manual is difficult to interpret (at least for this reviewer) but appears to be displaying the median difficulty values for the total number of items by age. Based on this table, it appears that items of a wide variety of difficulties were included, with median values ranging from .06 to .93, depending on age and test form.

The standardization group included 1,146 children, stratified based on sex, race, ethnicity, geographic region, urban/rural residence, degree of hearing loss, and age of onset of hearing loss. All students used their customary aids during norming. Inspection of the demographic characteristics of the standardization group indicate the inclusion of children with moderate (41–70 db), severe (71–90 db), and profound (91 and above) hearing loss. The degrees of hearing loss are inconsistent with what is described in the introductory chapter, which categorizes the moderate group as having a loss of 41–62 db and severe, 63–90 db.

The percentages in the normative sample closely approximate the national percentages of deaf and hard of hearing for each variable except ethnicity, where Hispanics are underrepresented. No information is provide on how the normative group compares to the nation in their primary method of teaching. The majority of the sample used sign and speech. Because a large percentage of those with moderate hearing losses are often multiply handicapped, with associated conditions such as epilepsy, cerebral palsy, brain damage, learning disabilities, and visual impairment, it would be helpful to have information on the presence of other handicapping conditions in the normative sample.

According to the PRO-ED catalog, normative data are provided at every 6-month interval from 3-0 to 13-11. However, this is inconsistent from the norm tables which provide only 1-year intervals for age 3 and from ages 8 to 13-11. One-year intervals may be too long at age 3. The 1-year interval may not permit enough sensitivity to rapid developmental changes at this age.

Reliabilities are reported in terms of internal consistency and test-retest using alternate forms. Depending on age, coefficient alphas range from .93 to .97 ($M = .95$) for Form A and from .87 to .97 ($M = .94$) for Form B indicating strong internal consistency except for age 3. Test-retest reliabilities were calculated based on a limited sample of 25 students between the ages of 6 and 9 who were given the two alternate forms after a 2-week interval. They were inconsistently reported as .87 on the record form and .88 in the manual and are not useful for children outside the age range of 6 to 9. Given the small size of the sample, it would have been helpful to provide a description of the subjects. For the reading quotients, the mean standard errors of measurement associated with coefficient alpha were 3 (Form A) and 4 (Form B). Because the TERA-D/HH is meant to be used to measure student progress through the use of alternate forms, it would be important to report the standard errors for test-retest reliabilities. In addition, evidence of interrater reliability would be important because there may be variability among examiners in sign interpretation that could affect performance.

The authors provide arguments for content validity based on the method of item selection. Criterion-related validity was demonstrated in terms of fairly high correlations between both forms of the TERA-D/HH and their respective forms of the TERA-2. However, these correlations were based on a small group of 11 subjects, ages 7 to 9, with moderate to severe hearing loss. Support for construct validity is based on high correlations between raw score and chronological age. A low negative correlation between TERA-D/HH scores and degree of hearing loss was also reported. The TERA-D/HH correlated moderately with the Wechsler Intelligence Scale for Children—Revised (WISC-R) (.78 and .77 for Forms A and B respectively). The scores of a group of 15 learning disabled and 13 mentally retarded

subjects were examined and both groups earned mean scores within the expected range.

In summary, there are few psychological and educational tests specifically normed for hearing-impaired children, and although PL 94-142 mandates appropriate assessment practices with handicapped children, practitioners are forced to conduct assessments using tests without adequate norms for the hearing impaired. Because the TERA-D/HH is the only individually administered test of its kind normed on the hearing impaired, its development is important. Its actual value is yet to be determined, however. Studies are needed to show that testing and successful intervention are linked.

The authors of the TERA-D/HH provide a comprehensive and informative manual, despite some inconsistencies. The test materials themselves, however, are dull and uninteresting for young children. The availability of two forms is helpful in documenting student progress but further evidence needs to be provided as to whether the two forms are truly equivalent. In addition, there appear to be serious floor and ceiling effects for children at the lower and upper age ranges of the test. For example, on Form A it is not possible for a 3-year-old to earn a score lower than 89 even if every item is failed. If the child gets just two items correct, he or she earns a score of 109, placing that child in the high average range. Similar ceiling effects are noted. Given the authors' goal of identifying children who are delayed or gifted, this is a serious limitation.

The authors appropriately recommend supplementing test results with observational information. In addition, because variable performance is the rule rather than the exception for children with hearing loss, one needs to use multiple instruments in assessments. Users of the TERA-D/HH may also want to supplement the results with those from criterion-referenced tests.

[97]
The Time-Sample Behavioral Checklist.
Purpose: Developed to measure the level and nature of functioning of adult residential patients and also used to document how and where residents and staff spend their time.
Population: Adults in residential treatment settings.
Publication Date: 1987.
Acronym: TSBC.
Scores: 7 categories: Location, Position, Awake-Asleep, Facial Expression, Social Orientation, Concurrent Activities, Crazy Behavior combined in a variety of ways to produce 9 higher-order scores:

Appropriate Behavior (Interpersonal Interaction, Instrumental Activity, Self-Maintenance, Individual Entertainment, Total), Inappropriate Behavior (Bizarre Motor Behavior, Bizarre Facial & Verbal, Hostile-Belligerence, Total).

Administration: Individual.

Price Data, 1991: $18.95 per manual/checklist (286 pages).

Time: 10 2-second observations.

Comments: Should be used in conjunction with the Staff-Resident Interaction Chronograph.

Authors: Gordon L. Paul, Mark H. Licht, Marco J. Mariotto, Christopher T. Power, and Kathryn L. Engel.

Publisher: Research Press.

Cross References: See T4:2840 (1 reference).

Review of The Time-Sample Behavioral Checklist by CYNTHIA ANN DRUVA-ROUSH, Assistant Director, Evaluation and Examination Service, The University of Iowa, Iowa City, IA:

The Time-Sample Behavioral Checklist (TSBC) is a "standardized direct observational coding (DOC) instrument that employs technician-level observers to collect objective data" (manual, p. xv). The TSBC, originally designed for client assessment, "was extended to clinical staff to provide ongoing assessment of how and where staff spend their time as well as for monitoring some less stable personal-social characteristics" (p. 4).

Measurement is based on a series of observations. Observational rounds are made hourly over a week's period. During a single round, several individuals are measured, each for a 2-second period. In each single 2-second observation, the presence or absence of 69 behavioral codes are recorded on the TSBC response sheet. The time and activity are also recorded for each observation. "*Occasions sampling* follows the specified hourly time-sampling schedules to cover all days of the week and all times of the day when clientele are scheduled to be awake, with stratification over all behavior settings ('activities') proportionate to their occurrence in the treatment program" (p. 4). At least a full week of hourly time-sampling is needed to attach an appropriate interpretation.

Behavior descriptions listed in diagnostic manuals, abnormal psychology and psychiatry texts, and items in psychiatric rating scales were supplemented by "free-field" diary samples in several treatment units to arrive at the characteristics coded. Code scores are calculated by adding the observed frequency across multiple observations and dividing the total frequency for each code by the number of opportunities for occurrence. The 69 codes are then combined into various higher-order indexes. In addition, a Stereotypy/Variability set of scores is composed of a Location Index (relative amount of movement among geographic areas), a Position Index (range of physical positions), a Social Orientation Index (range of classes of people with whom clients spend their time), Concurrent Activities Index, Facial Expression Index, and Crazy Behavior Index.

The most recent normative study involved 1,205 clients obtained from 35 treatment units in 17 facilities covering both urban and rural locales. The normative sample ranged in age from 18 to 99 years. An examination of score distributions across a relatively wide range of values indicated that discriminations among both individuals and groups may be made. All indexes except Instrumental Activity and Self-Maintenance showed significant discriminations among treatment units.

An examination of repeated assessment across time indicates that the TSBC Indexes based on one-day summaries are not representative and could not substitute for full-week summaries within any of the subgroups of a multi-institutional sample (alcohol and acute units, chronic and mixed units, mentally retarded units, and community facilities).

A study was then made of stability of scores for various subgroups of patients in a longer week-to-week analysis. Highest correlation coefficients were reported for the chronic client subgroups. Clients within a structured environment reported higher stability coefficients (.28–.95) than those in an unstructured environment (.14–.85). (Hostile Belligerence scores indicated .00 stability in both environments.)

The average intraclass replicability over all client weekly TSBC Indexes and Codes exceeded $r = .97$. Interobserver replicabilities for client TSBC scores based on one-day observations had a median $r = .97$ for all higher order indices and a median $r = .94$ for individual code scores. Users are warned that some care should be taken in use of the TSBC with geriatrics and/or profoundly mentally retarded as decisions based on summary scores from the usual minimum of 10 observations as interobserver replicability coefficients fall below $r = .80$. More than 10 observations should then be employed as a basis for summaries that are intended for testing rather than for generating hypotheses.

The discriminant and convergent interrelationships among the higher-order TSBC rate scores provide evidence for the intended interpretation of both total indexes, all inappropriate component indexes, and two appropriate component indexes (Interpersonal Interaction and Individual Entertainment).

Limitations on intended interpretations were suggested for both the Instrumental Activities and Self-Maintenance indexes. The interrelationships among the Stereotypy/Variability indexes provided empirical support for interpreting both the Concurrent Activities and Crazy Behavior indexes only.

The convergent/discriminant relationships between TSBC indexes and other direct observational coding systems, as well as interviews, ward rating scales, and questionnaires were examined across various subgroups of institutional units. All component indexes except for Instrumental Activity and Self-Maintenance were supported. Of the six Stereotypy/Variability indexes, only Concurrent Activities and Crazy Behavior demonstrated convergent/discriminant relationships.

Comparisons were made of means for various demographic characteristics. No evidence of sex bias was suggested for any score. "The failure of any TSBC score to demonstrate consistent age differences across all subgroups in the normative samples provides evidence against the existence of systematic age bias" (p. 175). The pattern of convergent and discriminant differences among racial groups and socioeconomic status groups is apparently consistent with the literature assessing behavior among mental patients. Blacks and lower class patients score lower on appropriate behavior and higher on inappropriate behavior. No attempt is made to study a possible interaction of the two factors. The test developers caution that TSBC indexes for racial minorities should not be used as predictors nor employed with norm-referenced interpretations without extensive additional investigation of cultural norms in local circumstances.

The Standards for Educational and Psychological Testing (AERA, APA, & NCME, 1985) state that with clinical testing, establishing a high level of criterion-related validity is of great importance. These standards further state that when validity is appraised by comparing the level of agreement between test results and clinical diagnosis, the diagnostic terms or categories employed should be carefully defined, and the method by which a diagnosis was made should be specified. In response to this requirement, TSBC researchers attempt to compare only broad diagnostic disability groups. Groups were formed by combining institutional diagnoses into broad graded categories on the basis of overall severity and pervasiveness of disability (alcohol and drug abuse, neurotic and lesser disorders, major affective psychoses, organic brain syndromes, schizophrenic psychoses, and mentally retarded). No examination is made of the source of these diagnoses. Comparisons are then made between these relatively broad groups by comparing means and overlap of confidence intervals on the higher-order indexes. Further analyses were made for degrees of retardation and paranoia. All but the Social Orientation Stereotypy/Variability Index score could be interpreted as more general indicants of behavior.

Evidence collected previous to the most recent edition of the user manual had demonstrated the ability of the TSBC indexes to predict which clients achieved successful discharges and the level of client functioning in the community up to 18 months later (rs in the .60s and .70s). Score means for the various indexes were compared between groups that were successful for 30 days in not returning to equally restrictive mental or correctional facilities. All major indexes, except Self-Maintenance and Instrumental Activity, and Concurrent Activities and Crazy Behavior Stereotypy/Variability Indexes displayed significant differences in score means between successful and unsuccessful release clientele. A study was then made as to what combination of the indexes would successfully discriminate between those who were successfully released and those who were not. This decision was based on maximizing the decision success similar to a loss function approach, although no method was clearly described. The best discrimination resulted from a combination of cutoffs that consider levels of the Total Appropriate Behavior, Interpersonal Interaction jointly with levels of the Concurrent Activities Stereotypy/Variability Index. The 95.9% success rate for independent discharges within 2 weeks of meeting TSBC readiness guidelines and 97.8% success rate for community placements within 4 weeks of meeting TSBC readiness guidelines displays further predictive validity.

In summary, the TSBC is an instrument requiring immense training of the observer called to record behaviors. The high level of replicability recorded over time and between observers is testimony, however, that observers can be suitably trained. The researchers are to be commended in their exhaustive examination of reliability and validity for each of their higher order indexes. Precautions for use of their instrument and its interpretation are clearly given. Strong evidence for all higher order indexes except for the Instrumental Activities and Self-Maintenance is clearly provided. The Stereotypy/Variability indices do not stand well under close examination. My one recommendation is that an editor be found for their user's manual. Reading through paragraph-long sentences was both frustrating and a deterrent from examining their very thorough research process.

REVIEWER'S REFERENCE

American Educational Research Association, American Psychological Association, & National Council on Measurement in Education.

(1985). *Standards for educational and psychological testing.* Washington, DC: American Psychological Association, Inc.

Review of The Time-Sample Behavioral Checklist by SUSAN L. CROWLEY, Assistant Professor, and BLAINE R. WORTHEN, Professor and Chair, Research and Evaluation Methodology Program, Department of Psychology, Utah State University, Logan, UT:

The Time-Sample Behavioral Checklist (TSBC) is a standardized direct observational coding (DOC) instrument for multiple-occasion use in residential treatment facilities for mentally ill or mentally retarded adults. The authors state that the TSBC is intended to provide all the objective information and documentation needed on client functioning to (*a*) support a variety of "rational" decisions regarding client care (e.g., placement and disposition, problem identification, and description), and (*b*) answer specific research questions. Additionally, the TSBC assesses where clients and staff spend their time. It is intended to be used in concert with the Staff-Resident Interaction Chronograph (SRIC) as an entire assessment protocol. However, the authors state that the TSBC can be used alone for more "limited purposes."

The technical manual for the TSBC is Volume 2 of the five-volume *Assessment in Residential Treatment Settings* series. However, continuous references to other volumes reveal that much pertinent information about the TSBC is contained in those other volumes, which is frustrating for the reader. For instance, norm-referenced interpretation information is in Volume 4, the rationale for construction and data on cost-effectiveness is contained in Volume 1, and Volume 5 contains crucial information regarding the implementation of the system. Scattering such crucial information across four volumes is a major impediment to those attempting to understand the TSBC.

Data for the TSBC are collected by trained technician-level observers using discrete 2-second observations taken on a stratified time-sampling schedule during each hour that residents are scheduled to be awake. The authors suggest a minimum of 10 observations to gain an accurate picture of a client's functioning. However, they also caution against interpreting data from a limited number of observations, urging a full-week summary (50–100 observations) for most TSBC uses.

The TSBC has seven categories, including 69 behavioral codes and 3 control codes. TSBC computer program provides four types of summary scores: detailed code scores, category stereotypy/variability scores, and higher-order functioning scores at both intermediate and global levels. Calculation of summary scores is straightforward, often depending on simple averages.

The administration and coding manual for the TSBC (in Volume 2 of the series) is commendably thorough and detailed. Observational rules and procedures are outlined in meticulous and sometimes excessive detail (e.g., suggestions for clothing and makeup observers should wear). Code definitions are clearly organized and explicit, providing (*a*) a description of the behavior being coded, and (*b*) both typical and rare/difficult examples. Descriptions and codes are described in behavioral terms, minimizing the need for inference. The one glaring exception to this is the "crazy behavior" category. Although some of the codes in this category can be viewed as "crazy" (e.g., incoherent speech), others clearly cannot (e.g., crying, swearing). Further, "crazy" is both imprecise and value-laden, and a less emotionally laden term, perhaps "maladaptive" would be better.

The origin of the items comprising the TSBC is not well described. A multidisciplinary group of 10 professionals participated in the development. The authors state that after a "pilot test with trained observers, the coding system was standardized" (p. 2.3), but how (or whether) these test results were used in selecting and/or modifying the final pool of items is not specified.

The authors do an excellent job of describing the TSBC summary scores and identifying what each score can and cannot do, repeatedly identifying confidence intervals and the amount of change necessary for statistical significance. Limitations and cautions in data interpretation are emphasized, including cautions against overinterpretation and making dispositional attributions. The authors carefully critique the data throughout the volume, identifying which recommended interpretations are supported by sufficient data.

TECHNICAL INFORMATION. Reliability, validity, and normative data are based on nearly 19 years of research by the authors. The manual summarizes previously published information but is focused more on new information from a multi-institutional generalizability/feasibility study. The selection of data collection sites is clearly described and the authors have collected TSBC data on an impressively diverse sample varying in degree of chronicity, type of facility, and type of client (psychiatric, mentally retarded, and "normal" hospitalized). The only serious weakness of the sample is the omission of private residential facilities.

The authors claim the TSBC can also be used to identify where staff spend their time; however, the technical information presented is focused primarily on the scores collected on clients. The practical significance of collecting staff information is mentioned only briefly. Consequently, staff uses of the TSBC are distracting. Perhaps these data would become more relevant when the instrument is employed as part of the broader TSBC/SRIC system.

NORMATIVE INFORMATION. The normative sample includes 1,205 clients on whom TSBC data were collected. Characteristics of the entire normative sample of 1,205 clients are presented in tabular form, along with characteristics of subsamples representing the primary types of residential settings. The authors attempted to collect data on the broadest range of treatment settings and clients to demonstrate the feasibility of using the TSBC in these diverse facilities (except for private residential centers). The authors recommend using separate norms for the two major facility types (public and community). Although the authors present data suggesting their sample is generally representative of gender and racial characteristics of the population at large, they acknowledge specific limitations, such as the underrepresentation of some ethnic groups.

RELIABILITY. The reliability of TSBC codes and scores depends primarily on interobserver replicability. Training of observers is reviewed and issues of observer reactivity, drift, bias, and decay are addressed. In all cases, the replicability coefficients were high, usually $r>.90$. Standard errors of measurement and standard errors of differences between two scores are also presented within each major facility grouping.

The authors apply generalizability theory to TSBC data, although rather half-heartedly. Variance components for Clients, Observers, and the Residual are presented for the total sample and public and community facilities. Unfortunately, the authors go no further in evaluating the replicability of the data within the framework of generalizability theory or contrasting it with the results of applied classical test score theory.

VALIDITY. The authors address validity issues for the TSBC in a variety of ways, including: internal relationships among codes and indexes, differential stability and sensitivity to change, discrimination among groups differing on clinically relevant characteristics, concurrent information from other assessment tools, and predictive relationships with other performance and outcome measures. Generally, the validity evidence presented for the TSBC is impressive and supports the intended uses of the instrument. There are few areas of weakness. Where a score does not perform as well as would be desired, the authors

call this to the reader's attention, identifying the limitation in a forthright manner.

In all cases, the authors do an excellent job of presenting the data, supporting interpretive suggestions, identifying limitations, and presenting plausible alternative hypotheses. Within each validity section, the TSBC score/code is presented and data reviewed in a systematic and thorough manner. The level of detail presented is probably excessive for most readers, however. Acknowledging this, the authors include summary sections with references to specific sections in the text. For ease in understanding, tables follow a similar format across chapters. Although clearly presented, the authors chose to omit nonsignificant correlations from the tables. It would have been better to leave these correlations in for comparative purposes, especially considering the limitations of statistical significance testing.

SUMMARY. The TSBC is a direct-observation coding system for use in adult residential treatment facilities. The authors have made a valuable contribution by providing a way to assess change, improvement, and specify strengths and weaknesses in a residential population. Additionally, TSBC data can be used for program evaluation, group comparisons, and numerous research questions. In reality, the TSBC is a research and assessment protocol rather than merely an assessment tool.

The authors present an abundance of evidence attesting to the sound psychometric properties of TSBC data. The most frustrating aspect of this instrument is that one must root through several volumes to obtain all the information necessary to use it intelligently.

Whether this instrument will ever be widely used is still a question. The authors make a convincing argument regarding the cost effectiveness of implementing the TSBC (and SRIC), but they acknowledge that there are significant tangible and intangible startup costs. Because many residential facilities are plagued by tight budgets and nearsighted administrators, the adoption of the TSBC may be limited.

[98]

Voc-Tech Quick Screener.

Purpose: Designed to identify job interests.

Population: Non-college bound high school students and adults.

Publication Dates: 1984–90.

Acronym: VTQS.

Scores, 14: Administrative Support/Clerical, Agriculture/Animals and Forestry, Construction Trades, Design/Graphics and Communication, Food/Beverage Services, Health Services, Health Technicians,

Industrial Production Trades, Marketing/Sales, Mechanical/Craftsmanship Trades, Personal Services, Protective Services, Science/Engineering Technicians, Transportation/Equipment Operators.
Administration: Group.
Price Data, 1990: $.50 per folder/questionnaire; $89.95 per microcomputer software package (Apple or IBM).
Time: (20–25) minutes.
Authors: Robert Kauk and Robert Robinett.
Publisher: CFKR Career Materials, Inc.

Review of the Voc-Tech Quick Screener by ALBERT M. BUGAJ, Associate Professor of Psychology, University of Wisconsin—Marinette, Marinette, WI:

The Voc-Tech Quick Screener (VTQS) is ostensibly designed to assess the job interests of non-college-bound high school students and adults. However, the screener is only "quick" in the sense that upon its completion it supposedly identifies the occupations in which the test taker is most interested. It then encourages them to seek further information about those occupations through such tasks as visiting career information centers, training sites, and people already "on-the-job." Given the nature of the test, the information seeker might be better served going to those sources first, and not bother taking the VTQS.

On the first page of the test, the testee is asked to rate (on a 3-point scale) how interested he or she is in finding a job that would match one of six personality traits (doer, thinker, creator, helper, persuader, organizer). Three activities (working with data, people, and things) are similarly rated. No concern is apparently taken by the authors of the VTQS that these ratings might be affected by social desirability.

The next three pages involve matching the previous characteristics with 14 "vocational-technical occupational clusters." This task is performed by matching the self-ratings to profiles for the 14 clusters constructed by the authors. For example, a person interested in construction trades, would, in part, have a high interest in occupations requiring people to be doers, a moderate interest in being a thinker, and a low interest in being a creator. When the testee's self-rating of a trait or activity matches that for the profile, a point is earned (5 points for key characteristics).

The explanation in the user's guide of how the point values were assigned to each of the characteristics in the profiles is cryptic. However, the reader is assured they are based on "a rational judgemental procedure," using "expert" data, "rather than strictly quantitative data" (p. 2). Hence, the point values seem qualitative in nature, and have not been empirically tested.

The 14 cluster groups of occupations are equally non-empirical in nature. According to the user's guide they "ally closely with the 12 clusters (work groups) used in the GUIDE TO OCCUPATIONAL EXPLORATION, U.S. Dept. of Labor", (p. 3) although the correspondence is not direct, and exceptions were made. Two clusters were added because the authors felt they were significant enough to warrant distinct groups, whereas another grouping was split in two.

Each cluster typically contains over a dozen disparate occupations. The transportation/equipment operators cluster, for example, ranges from air traffic controller to taxi driver. No attention is paid to the varying degrees of training or education which may be needed in the various occupations. Further, no empirical data justifying these groups are provided. Although the Department of Labor may group various occupations together, this does not mean they form a construct for use on an interest inventory.

Once the testee's interests are matched to these profiles, he or she is instructed to complete the final portion of the VTQS, given the name "the Occuputer." Here, the test taker lists the three fields receiving the highest number of points, and then rates (on 5-point scales) his or her interests in gaining the skills and completing the studies needed, chances of success, and interest in jobs related to the fields (information to aid in each task is provided). Points earned are again summed, and the high score indicates the field in which the testee has the greatest interest. Again, no concern for social desirability or other problems inherent in self-ratings is noted.

Finally, the test taker is asked to review lists of related jobs in the preferred cluster, and write the three he or she would like best. No quantitative ratings are made at this point. The testee is then directed to seek further information from the previously mentioned sources (e.g., career centers) about those occupations.

Little data are provided about reliability and validity of the VTQS. The user's guide reports an 88% correlation of preferred job clusters (not individual jobs selected) over a 2-week period. However, the number and age of the students is not reported.

It is also stated that a "large sampling of junior and senior high school students and adults" (p. 3) reported the reading level and directions are understandable, and found the test interesting and motivational. One assumes this means the students were motivated to seek other sources of information, after taking the VTQS (this point is unclear in the user's guide). However, it should be noted that no measure of whether the students were motivated to seek information *prior to* taking the survey is reported. Without such knowledge (or a matched group not taking the VTQS for comparison) its effect on motivation cannot be known with certainty.

The user's guide authors further indicate that over 90% of 1,000 students (ages not reported) indicated they were highly satisfied with the objectives and results of the test. Unfortunately, it is not said whether this judgement was made soon after taking the test, or once the subjects had entered an occupation on its basis and found it satisfying. Whether the test led them to consider new occupations, or simply confirmed previously made decisions is not stated. No measures of convergent validity are reported.

The use of the VTQS cannot be recommended, and it cannot begin to compare with a test like the Strong Interest Inventory (88). It is most likely susceptible to a high social desirability bias. The major constructs (the occupational clusters) have no empirical basis. Reliability and validity data, as provided in the manual, are insufficient. Because the students are instructed to seek other, major sources of information which should aid greatly in making a career decision, students might be better off seeking out these resources without the use of the VTQS.

Review of the Voc-Tech Quick Screener by DEL EBERHARDT, Program Administrator, Greenwich Public Schools, Greenwich, CT:

The Voc-Tech Quick Screener (VTQS) was, according to the authors, designed and field tested "to meet a specific career interest assessment: to provide means for valid and reliable personal assessment of job interests and to relate that assessment to specific jobs in 'vocational technical' clusters—often referred to as the 'high tech' area of work" (p. 1, user's guide). To meet this need the VTQS is available in a printed as well as a computerized format. It is suggested that the printed form will require about 20 minutes to complete and the computerized version will require only 5–10 minutes. This review is based on the printed version of the VTQS.

The printed version consists of two documents. The response document is a six-page fan-fold document that compresses an impressive amount of print and information into these few pages. In fact, there is so much material here that the reader is apt to become confused. Page 1 of the response document provides the student with a brief statement of the purpose of the VTQS, a description of the steps required to complete the project, and a scale for rating their occupational interests.

The student then rates him/her self on each of six qualities of a job. The terms doer, thinker, creator, helper, persuader, and organizer are used and very brief definitions of each are provided. The authors acknowledge these variables were worded and coded to "inter-correlate" with the Holland-RIASEC types.

Finally, the student does a self-rating in terms of the traditional DATA, PEOPLE, THINGS categories. Following the completion of the rating on nine variables, the student begins transferring these ratings onto four pages of the form. These categories resemble the basic interest scales and the occupational scales of the Strong Interest Inventory. However, in contrast to the Strong, the student does no personal ratings on these categories. The student is led to understand that despite the terms "quick" and "screener" in the title, they can draw conclusions about careers. Like so many assessment devices that are termed "screening" devices, there is a real danger that the client may draw conclusions that are not warranted based on the limited number of variables considered. The omission of mention of abilities, especially in an area referred to as "high tech" seems worth noting and should serve as a note of caution to the user of the VTQS.

The second document provided for the printed form of the VTQS is a user's guide. It is a very brief four-page document that is intended to be an instructional guide to the printed and computerized versions of the VTQS. This user's guide contains a one-paragraph "forward," a section on the rationale of the instrument, and a section on the design of the instrument. Other sections review the construction of the variables and the results of field testing. The user of the VTQS will be somewhat concerned about the limited material in the user's guide. The target audience for the instrument is not specified, but it seems reasonable to assume that high school juniors and seniors might constitute the primary audience. Although the reading difficulty level of the instrument is not reported in reference to any of the standard techniques for determining readability, the authors report the VTQS is sufficiently "easy to enable over 90% of upper level high school students and adults" (p. 4) to complete the instrument.

For the professional accustomed to test manuals that provide psychometric information consistent with the AERA/APA/NCME *Standards for Educational and Psychological Testing* (1985), the VTQS user's guide will be a major disappointment. For example, in reference to field testing (norming?) the authors mention using a "large" sample of junior and senior high school students and adults. However, there is no mention of the nature of this sample in terms of geography, SES, or any of the other aspects of a norming sample one has come to expect from test publishers. This reviewer found one mention of reliability in the user's guide. The authors report "test-retest" of the VTQS given in a 2-week duration that "there was an 88% correlation of preferred job clusters" (p. 2). The authors made no reference to validity studies of the VTQS. In summary, this reviewer would suggest that the professional looking for career assessment instruments consider other instruments before using the VTQS. Certainly the Strong Interest Inventory (88) and Holland's Self-Directed Search (T4:2414) would provide better techniques. The VTQS may best serve as an educational device. It might help high school students gain new information about the technical occupations under the careful guidance of a teacher or guidance counselor. It is not recommended for serious career guidance.

REVIEWER'S REFERENCE

American Educational Research Association, American Psychological Association, & National Council on Measurement in Education. (1985). *Standards for educational and psychological testing*. Washington, DC: American Psychological Association, Inc.

[99]
Vocational Interest Inventory and Exploration Survey.

Purpose: Designed to "assess a student's interest in school based training programs" and provide "information about the training area."
Population: Vocational education students.
Publication Date: 1991.
Scores: 15 vocational training interest areas: Auto Mechanics/Transportation, Business and Office, Construction, Cosmetology, Drafting, Electro-Mechanics, Electronics, Food Service, Graphic Arts, Health Occupations, Horticulture/Agriculture, Marketing, Metals, Occupational Home Economics, Technology Education.
Administration: Individual or group.
Price Data, 1991: $495 per set.
Time: (15–20) minutes.
Authors: Nancy L. Scott and Charles Gilbreath.
Publisher: Piney Mountain Press, Inc.

Review of the Vocational Interest Inventory and Exploration Survey by LARRY COCHRAN, Professor of Counseling Psychology, Faculty of Education, The University of British Columbia, Vancouver, B.C., Canada:

The Vocational Interest Inventory and Exploration Survey (VOC-TIES) is not so much a test as a test-like intervention to help prospective students to decide upon a vocational training program. It is composed of an audio-visual presentation (slides and prerecorded narration) in which 15 vocational training programs are described. After each program is described, the student is asked whether he or she "would be interested in vocational training" in that area. To respond, the student marks on an answer sheet either yes, maybe, or no. As optional forms of administration, the test administrator can read the program descriptions or stop the audio-visual presentation after each description to discuss the area, answer questions, and encourage comments. The 15 training programs include automobile mechanics, office work, construction, cosmetology, drafting, mechanical equipment repair, electronics, food service, graphic arts, health, horticulture and agriculture, marketing and distribution, metals, occupational home economics, and technician. As a vocational intervention, the VOC-TIES is intended to provide information to assist students in making more informed decisions about training programs and careers. Program descriptions introduce the general nature of an area of work, indicate some criteria for selection, specify training requirements, and provide examples of jobs that training would qualify one to pursue. Generally, the program descriptions seem clear and informative, introducing a wide range of programs in a short amount of time. The VOC-TIES is unusual in the sense that most interest tests were designed to assess a pattern of interests and to relate those interests to possible occupations. The VOC-TIES stresses an institutional perspective, attempting to inform individuals of and gauge interest in training programs likely to be offered by vocational training institutes.

Ordinarily, however, when one has designed a program, it is then evaluated through research to sharpen statements of purpose, and investigate what it does and does not do. Currently, there is no evidence the VOC-TIES is an effective intervention. There is no evidence that prospective students learn enough to make an informed decision, that the information is adequate (for example, why were salary ranges not mentioned?), or that it stimulates exploration, and so on. There is no information regarding the soundness of program construction and its effectiveness.

As a test of training interest, the VOC-TIES does not meet any standard of test construction. There were no reported reliabilities, no evidence of validity, no norm groups, and no technical information of any kind in the manual. It was assumed that a *yes* response would indicate a high level of interest, a *maybe* response would indicate the need for exploration, and a *no* response would indicate lack of interest with no need for exploration.

The VOC-TIES might fill a potential need of community colleges and vocational training institutes. Although it seems like a worthwhile intervention to try out, it has not yet earned credibility. As a test, it lacks substance and ought not to be regarded as such without further evidence. In summary, the VOC-TIES is an untried intervention and test that will require much more grounding to be used with confidence.

Review of the Vocational Interest Inventory and Exploration Survey by KEVIN R. MURPHY, Professor of Psychology, Colorado State University, Fort Collins, CO:

The Vocational Interest Inventory and Exploration Survey is not an interest inventory in the usual sense of the term. It consists of a series of descriptions, presented via videotape or narrated slides, of 15 areas or clusters of training found at most U.S. vocational training schools. It provides students with information about the content of each cluster, about vocational criteria and training requirements, and with examples of the types of jobs that might be pursued after receiving training in each cluster. Following the presentation of information about these training clusters, subjects are simply asked if they are interested in each (response categories are "yes," "maybe," and "no"). These answers, it is hoped, with help direct vocational counselors in providing additional information about training and careers to examinees.

The manual that describes this inventory provides no data that can be used to evaluate this rather simple instrument. However, given the controversy over expressed versus inventoried interests, this inventory cannot be accepted as a simpler substitute for more elaborate measures. In my opinion, vocational interest measurement represents one of the success stories of applied psychology, and a number of exemplary measurement instruments exist (e.g., the Jackson Vocational Interest Survey [T4:1297] and the Strong Interest Inventory [88]). This inventory does not seem to fill a well-defined need, nor does it stand up to the same level of psychometric scrutiny as do several other alternatives.

To the authors' credit, the idea of presenting information about vocational training opportunities as part of the process of interest assessment is a very reasonable one. However, simply asking examinees whether or not they are interested in an area that has just been described to them is not likely to provide as much information about career and training interests as could be obtained from a psychometrically sophisticated inventory.

[100]

Vocational Interest, Experience and Skill Assessment (VIESA), Canadian Edition.

Purpose: Designed to stimulate career exploration. '
Population: Grades 8–10, 11–adults.
Publication Dates: 1985.
Acronym: VIESA, Canadian Edition.
Scores: Scores for Interests, Skills, and Experiences in 4 areas: People, Data, Things, Ideas.
Administration: Group or individual..
Levels, 2: 1, 2.
Price Data, 1994: $57.45 per 25 guide books and job family charts (specify level); $17.45 per examination kit level 1 & 2; $18.95 per user's handbook (61 pages).
Time: (40–45) minutes.
Comments: Self-scored inventory of career-related interests, experiences, skills and values, with supporting materials for counselors; adapted from VIESA, Second Edition, U.S. Edition (1984).
Author: ACT Career Planning Services.
Publisher: Nelson Canada.
Cross References: For information for VIESA, 2nd Edition, see 9:1338; for a review by Charles J. Krauskopf of an earlier edition, see 8:1025.

Review of the Vocational Interest, Experience, and Skill Assessment (VIESA), Canadian Edition by DAVID J. BATESON, Associate Professor of Mathematics and Science Education and the Educational Measurement Research Group, University of B.C., Vancouver, B.C., Canada:

Authors of the Users Handbook state the Vocational Interest, Experience, and Skill Assessment (VIESA) is designed to stimulate and facilitate self/career explorations. The primary goals are to help counselees: (*a*) expand self-awareness, (*b*) develop career awareness, (*c*) identify relevant career options, and (*d*) begin exploring and evaluating their career options. Counselors are encouraged to be thoroughly familiar with the handbook and the counselee materials. The need for thorough counselor familiarity with all the materials, and also with the Canadian Classification and Dictionary of Occupations (CCDO) and other job classification systems such as the Holland and Roe typologies, cannot be understated and it seems essential to the successful use of the VIESA. As a self-administered and self-scored tool, which it claims to be, the VIESA can be very confusing; counselees must be provided continuous guidance and supervision as they work through the document.

Based on data from the 1977 scoring accuracy study, only infrequent errors were reported when examinees transcribe and summarize at various places in the instrument. Small measurement errors for the instrument are also reported. None of these errors have a great effect individually, but when taken together, and when one considers the decision consequences on individuals of such instruments, the effect can be quite serious. Reliability statistics provided do not appear adequate given that results of the VIESA apply only to individuals and not to groups. If the instrument leads to individual decision making regarding career choices, issues of reliability are very serious and require serious attention.

A study undertaken by F. M. Gault and H. H. Meyers (1987) showed that subjects using the instrument believed they had learned more about career decision making and most found that they were able to identify previously uncontemplated career options. However, the study also found that peer counselors tended to prefer the Self-Directed Search (SDS; T4:2414) to the VIESA.

It would seem that the instrument is probably much better suited to be a teaching and learning tool, or a framework for a guidance program or course, than an assessment instrument. If it were to be used in conjunction with a computer-based career information system such as CHOICES, the Student Guidance Information System (SGIS), or the Career Factory (Bridges, 1987), its potential would be greatly enhanced. The opportunities for counselees to explore their interests, their skills, and their career possibilities are considerable with these materials; they can be extremely valuable. However, used with insufficient guidance, the results of the VIESA could be totally misleading for some individuals.

In summary, as an assessment instrument, the VIESA appears confusing and of insufficient reliability for the serious individual decisions that might be made. However, as a teaching tool, the VIESA has much to commend it.

REVIEWER'S REFERENCE

Bridges, M. (1987). Resources to find and evaluate counseling software. *Career Planning and Adult Development Journal, 3*(2), 34-42.

Gault, F. M., & Meyers. H. H. (1987). A comparison of two career planning inventories. *The Career Development Quarterly, 35*(4), 332-336.

Review of the Vocational Interest, Experience, and Skill Assessment (VIESA), Canadian Edition by BRENDA H. LOYD, *Professor of Education, University of Virginia, Charlottesville, VA:*

The Vocational Interest, Experience, and Skill Assessment (VIESA) is a career planning inventory that assesses perceptions of career-related interests, experiences, skills, and values. The instrument's main purposes are to expand self-awareness, to develop career awareness, and to begin to identify, evaluate, and explore career options. The assessment is designed to be used by eighth grade students through adults and may be used individually, in small groups, and in instructional settings. The instrument may be self-administered and self-scored or may be administered under the supervision of a counselor.$PThe instrument includes eight units. An introductory unit explains the purpose of the assessment and introduces the key concepts PEOPLE, DATA, THINGS, and IDEAS as ways of understanding different kinds of jobs. The second unit presents an interest inventory divided into four sections corresponding to the four key concepts. For each of the four sections, examinees indicate which activities they would like to do or not like to do and score their results. The third unit asks the examinee to focus on identifying his/her best skills by choosing among sets of three choices under each main concept. In the fourth unit, a trial job choice is selected. Building upon this foundation, the individual examines a World-of-Work map in Unit 5 and identifies job possibilities that appear to be most consistent with his/her interests, skills, and trial job choice. In Unit 6 the individual is given tips about selecting job possibilities from available resources based in part on the results of the assessment, but is encouraged also to seek out experiences and opportunities in clear contrast to those which the assessment might suggest, in order to broaden the experience upon which decisions will be made. Unit 7 focuses on job values, to help identify the relative importance of security, availability, pay, etc. to the individual and to relate these values to the identified job possibilities. The final section of the student booklet is an "experience" inventory, which purports to compare the individual with other students in terms of the amount of their experience with PEOPLE, DATA, THINGS, and IDEAS in the world of work.

VALIDITY AND RELIABILITY. Validity and reliability information have been collected since the original form of the instrument was constructed in 1976, and interest profiles for more than 40,000 persons in 352 educational and occupational groupings have been examined and reviewed. One caution in interpreting the reliability and validity evidence is that the data supporting the instrument were gathered from examinees in the United States. In evaluating the Canadian edition, it must be considered that although many, if not most, of the findings may generalize to the Canadian population, additional information supporting this generalization would be a helpful addition to the supporting documentation for the instrument.

Content and construct validity of the VIESA is supported by the clear structure underlying each section of the instrument. The two bipolar dimensions of Data/Ideas and Things/People form the basis for the interests, experiences, and skills sections, as well as the organization of the work map and the listings of jobs. The Dimensions were identified by analyzing all occupations listed in the *Dictionary of Occupational Titles* (DOT) from the U.S. Department of Labor and were supported by analyzing interest scores of over 110,000 people in the U.S. This basic information on occupations was organized into 23–25 job families, then into six job clusters that relate directly to the World-of-Work map. The information has been restructured from general to specific within the assessment instrument so that an examinee begins at the general level of the map and then proceeds through job clusters and families to specific occupational titles. Conversion of U.S. Department of Labor occupational titles to appropriate Canadian titles was accomplished by comparing the similarity of the work performed and the vocational preparation required of the U.S. DOT occupations and the occupations listed in the *Canadian Classification and Dictionary of Occupations*.

Construct validity of the assessment is also supported by evaluating the two bipolar dimensions and the interest structure represented by Holland's theory, as well as the interest structure represented by Roe's interest types. Supporting evidence suggests that the Holland's hexagonal and Roe's octagonal interest structure can be summarized on the Data/Ideas and Things/People dimensions.

In addition to the question of the validity of underlying dimensions, special consideration was given to producing an interest inventory that did not limit men and women in their consideration of job possibilities due to possible early differences between male and female interests or societal expectations. An attempt was made to select items that measure the dimensions but minimize sex differences at the item level. Several reported validity studies suggest that the use of sex-balanced items has been successful in minimizing sex differences (i.e., in minimizing the situations in which one set of career options is suggested to males and another set to females).

Evidence of reliability includes reports of several studies of scoring accuracy. The self-scored instrument requires examinees to follow fairly straightforward instructions on how to sum responses, determine the difference between scores, and graph the

intersection of scores on a grid (on the World-of-Work map). Among high school students, 8% to 14% of those sampled made errors in scoring or mapping the results onto the correct regions of the map. These results suggest some of the limitations of self-scoring, and also suggest the value of having a counselor or teacher available to assist in scoring or to check the work of examinees.

SUMMARY. The VIESA is a well-developed and clearly presented interest assessment that seems appropriate for use with high school students and adults. The intent of the assessment is to give a wideband approach to developing career awareness; thus it encourages examinees to consider many types of careers. The intent is not to help examinees make fine choices among a few occupations, but to facilitate exploration and evaluation of possibilities. This suggests that the instrument would have its most appropriate use as part of a more comprehensive approach to career development, either as part of an instructional program or as one of many sources of information in a counseling situation.

[101]
Woodcock-Johnson Psycho-Educational Battery—Revised.
Purpose: Designed to measure "cognitive abilities, scholastic aptitudes, and achievement."
Population: Ages 2–90.
Publication Dates: 1977–91.
Acronym: WJ-R.
Administration: Individual.
Parts, 2: Cognitive, Achievement.
Price Data, 1992: $475 per complete WJ-R kit (Cognitive and Form A Achievement); $29.95 per technical manual ('91, 367 pages); $195 per computer scoring system (select Apple or IBM).
Comments: Aptitude/Achievement discrepancies can be calculated using actual norms when the Cognitive and Achievement Sections have been administered; 1977 edition still available; the Early Development Scale for Preschool Children is composed of fewer tests.
Authors: Richard W. Woodcock (examiner's manuals and test books), M. Bonner Johnson (test books), Nancy Mather (examiner's manuals), Kevin S. McGrew (technical manual), and Judy K. Werder (technical manual).
Publisher: The Riverside Publishing Company.
a) TESTS OF ACHIEVEMENT.
Scores: 9 Standard Battery test scores: Letter-Word Identification, Passage Comprehension, Calculation, Applied Problems, Dictation, Writing Samples, Science, Social Studies, Humanities

plus 5 Standard Battery cluster scores derived from combinations of the above test scores: Broad Reading, Broad Mathematics, Broad Written Language, Broad Knowledge, Skills and the Ability to Calculate Intra-Achievement Discrepancies, and 9 Supplemental Battery test scores: Word Attack, Reading Vocabulary, Quantitative Concepts, Proofing, Writing Fluency, Punctuation & Capitalization, Spelling, Usage, Handwriting plus 6 Supplemental Battery Cluster scores derived from combinations of scores from the Standard Battery and Supplemental Battery: Basic Reading Skills, Reading Comprehension, Basic Mathematics Skills, Mathematics Reasoning, Basic Writing Skills, Written Expression.

Forms, 2: A, B.

Price Data: $195 per complete kit including Standard and Supplemental test books, 25 test records, 25 subject response books, examiner's manual ('89, 230 pages), and norms tables ('89, 275 pages) (select Form A or B); $32 per set of 25 test records and 25 subject response books (select Form A or B).

Time: (50–60) minutes for the Standard Battery; additional administration time for the Supplemental Battery not reported.

Comments: Tests may be administered separately.

b) TESTS OF COGNITIVE ABILITY.

Scores: 7 Standard Battery test scores plus 1 cluster score: Memory for Names, Memory for Sentences, Visual Matching, Incomplete Words, Visual Closure, Picture Vocabulary, Analysis-Synthesis, Broad Cognitive Ability (Standard or Early Development) and 14 Supplemental Battery test scores: Visual-Auditory Learning, Memory for Words, Cross Out, Sound Blending, Picture Recognition, Oral Vocabulary, Concept Formation, Delayed Recall (Memory for Names, Visual-Auditory Learning), Numbers Reversed, Sound Patterns, Spatial Relations, Listening Comprehension, Verbal Analogies plus 14 Supplemental Battery cluster scores derived from combinations of scores from the Standard Battery and Supplemental Battery: Broad Cognitive Ability-Extended Scale, Cognitive Factor (Long-Term Retrieval, Short-Term Memory, Processing Speed, Auditory Processing, Visual Processing, Comprehension-Knowledge, Fluid Reasoning), Scholastic Aptitude (Reading, Mathematics, Written Language, Knowledge), Oral Language (Oral Language, Oral Language Aptitude), and Ability to Calculate Intracognitive Discrepancies.

Price Data: $330 per complete kit including Standard and Supplemental test books, 25 test records, audiocassettes, examiner's manual ('89, 204 pages), and norms tables ('89, 297 pages); $195 per complete Standard kit; $180 per Supplemental expansion including test book, 25 test records, audiocassette, examiner's manual, and norms tables (to be used only in conjunction with the Standard Battery); $32 per 25 Standard and Supplemental test records; $25 per 25 Standard test records.

Time: (30–40) minutes for the Standard Battery; an additional 40 minutes required to administer the Supplemental Battery.

Cross References: See T4:2973 (90 references); for reviews of the 1977 edition by Jack A. Cummings and Alan S. Kaufman, see 9:1387 (6 references); see also T3:2639 (3 references).

Review of the Woodcock-Johnson Psycho-Educational Battery—Revised by JACK A. CUMMINGS, Chair, Department of Counseling and Educational Psychology, Indiana University, Bloomington, IN:

The Woodcock-Johnson Psycho-Educational Battery—Revised (WJ-R) was designed to sample various cognitive and academic achievement abilities for individuals ranging in age from 2 through 95 years. The 1989/1990 revision of the original 1977 version of the Woodcock-Johnson Psycho-Educational Battery (Woodcock & Johnson, 1977) reflects the wisdom of a distinguished group of consultants and advisors (among whom were Jack B. Carroll, H. Carl Haywood, John L. Horn, and Kevin McGrew). Unlike revisions in the tradition of the Wechsler Scales, the authors of the WJ-R did not follow the market-preserving formula of retaining 80% of the original items with very minor adjustments to the structure of the scale. In contrast, Woodcock and Johnson made substantive changes, especially to the revised Tests of Cognitive Ability. The most significant criticism of the 1977 Tests of Cognitive Ability was the lack of a theoretical framework for the user to interpret an individual's cognitive functioning.

The WJ-R is not intended to be administered in its entirety, but rather in a selective fashion. For instance, on both the cognitive and achievement sections of the battery, there are a reduced set of subtests that comprise the "standard battery" and additional subtests for supplemental testing. Thus, the examiner has the option of using the standard battery, and then using referral information and additional subtests to test hypotheses generated in the initial phase of testing.

This review will provide an overview of the WJ-R and address issues associated with the quality of the normative sample, test administration, reliability, validity, and interpretation. Finally, comments will be offered on the relative merit of the battery when compared to other available measures.

The 1989/1990 revision of the Woodcock-Johnson used the Horn-Cattell model of intellectual processing (Horn, 1976, 1985, 1988; Horn & Cattell, 1966) as the foundation for selecting and organizing cognitive subtests. Ten new subtests were added to the Tests of Cognitive Ability. From the Horn-Cattell model, seven broad abilities are assessed by the WJ-R: Fluid Reasoning, Gf; Comprehension-Knowledge, Gc; Visual Processing, Gv; Auditory Processing, Ga; Processing Speed, Gs; Long-Term Retrieval, Glr; and Short-Term Memory, Gsm. This factorial model of the Tests of Cognitive Ability was derived following analyses of the 1977 normative sample for the 12 subtests of the Woodcock-Johnson Tests of Cognitive Ability and the first 25% of the normative sample for the 1989/1990 revision of the scale. Appropriately, no adjustments were made in the model following the collection of the remaining 75% of the sample.

The standard battery of the WJ-R Tests of Cognitive Ability is composed of seven subtests, each representing one of the Horn-Cattell abilities. The first level of the supplemental cognitive battery consists of seven subtests, again with each assessing one of the seven Horn-Cattell abilities. Further assessment of Long-Term Retrieval, Short-Term Memory, and Fluid Reasoning is possible with subtests 15–21.

The WJ-R Tests of Achievement include a Standard Battery and Supplemental Battery. Two parallel forms (A & B) are available for the nine subtests that comprise the Standard Battery. Five achievement clusters may be interpreted from the Standard Battery: Broad Reading, Broad Mathematics, Broad Written Language, Broad Knowledge, and Skills. Five supplemental subtests may be administered to provide a more in-depth understanding of a child's abilities in reading, mathematics, and written language.

NORMATIVE SAMPLE. The normative sample included 6,359 individuals from "over 100 geographically diverse U.S. communities" (WJ-R Tests of Academic Achievement examiner's manual, p. 93). Normative tables are available for the following groups: age 2.0 through 90+ years. The inclusion of college students is an important addition as a potential normative comparison group. With the advent of greater sensitivity to college students with learning disabilities, the WJ-R may be used to assess their cognitive and academic functioning. Comparison of the demographic characteristics of the sample to the U.S. population reveals a close match. This means that the WJ-R sample faithfully represents the U.S. population as described by the 1980 census distribution. Frequently, racial and ethnic minorities are undersampled for test norms. This is not the case, and to the contrary there is slight oversampling of racial/ethnic minorities. All normative data were collected from September 1986 to August 1988. A continuous-year procedure for normative testing was employed, rather than testing to create separate fall and spring norms.

ADMINISTRATION. Incorporated in the examiner's manual are suggested activities to acquaint the new examiner with appropriate administration and scoring practices. Checklists of learning activities, sample protocols, pronunciation tape, and scoring exercises will undoubtedly increase the likelihood of accurate administration and scoring. Accurate administration of the WJ-R is facilitated by the design of the examiner's pages in easel kit (e.g., spoken directions are highlighted in bold blue print, answer keys list appropriate probes for borderline responses, and warnings against common administration or scoring errors are included). Although the easel format simplifies administration for the examiner, there is an inherent liability. The repetitive page flipping does not sustain some young children's interest as well as when manipulable tasks are interspersed with verbal subtests. Thus, the examiner must be extra sensitive to the child's need to take breaks.

RELIABILITY. The internal consistency reliability coefficients for the WJ-R fall in the mid .90s for the major clusters on the Cognitive and Achievement scales. The split-half method corrected by the Spearman-Brown formula was used to estimate internal consistency, except on timed subtests where test-retest stabilities were appropriately substituted. Reliabilities for the subtests on the Standard and Supplemental Cognitive Batteries ranged from the mid .70s to low .90s, with most falling in the .80s. These estimates compare favorably to other available cognitive measures.

The internal consistency reliabilities for the subtests on the Achievement scale were slightly higher, most falling in the high .80s and low .90s. The exception among the Achievement subtests was the Writing Fluency subtests, which had a median coefficient of $r = .76$. Compared to other measures of achievement the pattern of reliabilities is similar. Likewise, a review of test-retest reliabilities presented in the technical manual indicates adequate stability of the major cluster and composite scores. Hence, the WJ-R should be judged favorably with respect to reliability as indicated by internal consistency and stability estimates.

Although included in the technical manual, information on the test-retest stability of the Woodcock-Johnson clusters and subtests was not presented in the examiner's manuals. These data would have been appropriate to include in the examiner's manuals because interpretation of the practice effect is necessary in situations where retesting takes place (e.g., second opinion cases). Because differential practice effects have been observed for the Wechsler scales, information on mean standard score gains would provide insight for these interpretations.

VALIDITY. Content, concurrent, and construct validation efforts for the battery are discussed in the technical manual and in briefer versions in the examiner's manuals. Although the coverage of various validation approaches is generally very comprehensive for the WJ-R, the content validation efforts are covered in a superficial manner. It is stated that expert opinion was used in the process of selecting items. Whether individuals who would bring alternative racial/ethnic perspectives to the scrutiny of items were included in the content validation process is not stated.

Concurrent validity was investigated across different age levels and with different anchor measures. For instance, at the age 9 level, comparisons were made with scores on the Kaufman Assessment Battery for Children, the Stanford-Binet Intelligence Test, Fourth Revision, and the Wechsler Intelligence Scale for Children—Revised. The respective validity coefficients for the Broad Cognitive Ability standard scores were .46, .53, and .52. The authors of the examiner's manuals note the reported correlations may slightly underestimate the true correlations for the general population due to the standard deviations of the samples being smaller than 15. Data are also provided on samples of children age 3 and age 17, with independent measures including the Boehm Test of Basic Concepts, Bracken Basic Concept Scale, Peabody Picture Vocabulary Test—Revised, and the Wechsler Adult Intelligence Scale—Revised. When the Broad Cognitive Ability standard score is compared to composite indices for the other scales the coefficients were observed to be in the high .50s to mid .60s. When all 14 subtests of the Extended Battery were included the coefficients were larger (i.e., mid .60s to low .70s), indicating a slightly large degree of shared variance between the Woodcock-Johnson Tests of Cognitive Ability and the anchor measures.

To assess the concurrent validity of the Tests of Achievement, the BASIS, the Kaufman Test of Educational Achievement, the Peabody Individual Achievement Test, and the Wide Range Achievement Test—Revised were administered to samples of children ages 9 and 17. The pattern of intercorrelations among the scales provides further support for the domains as they are labeled.

A surprising omission from the technical manual is any information on standard scores obtained from the revised Woodcock-Johnson and compared to other measures. This omission is curious, especially given the controversy surrounding mean score differences on the 1977 version of the battery (Cummings & Moscato, 1984a, 1984b; Thompson & Brassard, 1984; Woodcock, 1984). Information on the comparison of mean scores for the WJ-R with the original 1977 version of the Woodcock-Johnson and with other anchor measures of cognitive ability and measures of achievement would have provided a context for interpretation of any differences noted when comparing old scores to WJ-R scores in the situation of a 3-year re-evaluation.

McGrew, Werder, and Woodcock provide an erudite discussion of the construct validity of the Tests of Cognitive Ability in the WJ-R Technical Manual. Confirmatory and exploratory factor analyses across age levels (grades K–3; grades 4–7; grades 8–12; young adult, <age 40; middle adult, 40–59; older adult, >age 60) are reported and provide evidence of the fidelity of the Horn-Cattell model in the Tests of Cognitive Ability. Only at the older adult age level did the Goodness-of-Fit Indices (GFI) and root-mean-square residuals (rmr) reveal a slightly weaker match of the Horn-Cattell (Gf-Gc) model to the test. Additionally, the authors of the technical manual tested the Woodcock-Johnson against alternative models: first-order "g," nonverbal-verbal dichotomy, and hierarchical "g." These analyses again revealed that the Horn-Cattell model was superior, especially when compared to the first-order "g" and verbal/nonverbal models.

INTERPRETATION. The Broad Cognitive Ability standard score provides a "broad-based measure of intellectual ability" (WJ-R Tests of Cognitive Ability examiner's manual, p. 25) and consists of the seven subtest scores from the standard scale. The extended scale Broad Cognitive Ability score may be obtained from the 14 subtests of the standard and extended scales. In addition to the Horn-Cattell abilities, the cognitive subtests may be grouped to form four scholastic aptitude clusters: Reading, Mathematics, Written Language, and Knowledge. These clusters are recommended for use in determining aptitude/

achievement discrepancies. The aptitude clusters may be used to predict achievement. For instance, four cognitive subtests (Memory for Sentences, Visual Matching, Sound Blending, Oral Vocabulary) are weighted to obtain a Reading Aptitude score. It should be noted the aptitude clusters correlate with their representative achievement domains in the .70s. Two more clusters may also be generated from combinations of the cognitive subtests: Oral Language and Oral Language Aptitude. The subtests that compose the Oral Language cluster include tasks associated with receptive language (listening comprehension) and mixed receptive and expressive language tasks. The Oral Language Aptitude cluster includes nonlanguage tasks, and may be used as a measure of nonverbal ability.

Multiple figures are included in the examiner's manual to assist the examiner in conceptualizing the skills assessed by the various subtests. The tables have the skills arranged on continua, delineating less to more complex tasks. The figure that describes the Writing subtest will illustrate this point. At the bottom of the figure is the less complex motoric output component of producing legible handwriting; next is writing production of isolated units as in spelling single words; and at the highest level is connected discourse such as recognizing usage errors in text and at a higher level in producing writing samples. These figures may assist the examiner conceptualize and interpret an individual's results.

To say there are many options when selecting derived scores would be an understatement. The options include: age equivalents, grade equivalents, Relative Mastery Indices (which was labeled the Relative Performance Index, RPI, on the 1977 version of the Woodcock-Johnson), percentile ranks, extended percentile ranks, standard scores, and extended standard scores. Woodcock and Mather (authors of the examiner's manuals) appropriately caution the user not to calculate all the possible scores. Rather they recommend the user recognize the strengths and weaknesses of the various scores and select the scores that have the greatest likelihood of effectively communicating the individual's test results. To this end there is a lucid discussion of the advantages and disadvantages of the various derived scores included in the section of the manuals on test interpretation.

Unlike other batteries, the authors of the Woodcock-Johnson have incorporated tables for evaluating an individual's aptitude/achievement discrepancy. Although authors of other cognitive measures (Stanford-Binet Intelligence Scale, Fourth Revision; T4:2553; Wechsler Intelligence Scale for Children, Third Edition, T4:2939) suggest their measure is appropriate for assessing children with learning disabilities, no specific guidelines are provided or referenced.

CONCLUSION. The WJ-R Battery represents a significant contribution to norm-referenced psychoeducational assessment. The test authors selected a factor analytic model on cognitive functioning with an impressive empirical foundation. The Horn-Cattell model served as the framework for constructing the WJ-R Tests of Cognitive Ability. The data from the standardization sample provided evidence for the fidelity of the WJ-R with the Horn-Cattell model. Likewise, the inclusion of supplemental tests is a positive feature of the battery.

The Woodcock-Johnson Tests of Achievement are unlike most available achievement measures for two reasons. First, the results of a single subtest are not used to estimate skills in a broad domain. For example, the Wide Range Achievement Test—Revised (10:389) has a single subtest, "Reading," that involves only letter and word recognition. In contrast, the Woodcock-Johnson Reading cluster is based on letter-word recognition and on a modified cloze approach to reading comprehension. Second, the Woodcock-Johnson differs from other survey measures of achievement in that supplemental subtests are available. For example, if an examiner administers the two standard reading subtests and wishes to learn more about the individual's reading skills, a word attack subtest and a reading vocabulary subtest may be used. There are a total of five supplemental subtests for the domains of reading, mathematics, and written language.

In conclusion, the WJ-R merits the attention of all who are engaged in norm-referenced psychoeducational assessment. The standardization sample is representative. The cognitive portion of the battery is based on a theoretically sound model of intellectual functioning. The achievement section of the battery is designed to assess multiple facets of important academic skills. And finally, ample research has been conducted on the 1977 and new revised version of the battery.

REVIEWER'S REFERENCES

Horn, J. L., & Cattell, R. B. (1966). Refinement and test of the theory of fluid and crystallized intelligence. *Journal of Educational Psychology*, 57, 253-270.
Horn, J. L. (1976). Human abilities: A review of research and theory in the early 1970s. *Annual Review of Psychology*, 27, 437-485.
Woodcock, R. W., & Johnson, M. B. (1977). Woodcock-Johnson Psycho-Educational Battery. Allen, TX: DLM Teaching Resources.
Cummings, J. A., & Moscato, E. M. (1984a). Research on the Woodcock-Johnson Psycho-Educational Battery: Implications for practice and future investigations. *School Psychology Review*, 13, 33-40.

Cummings, J. A., & Moscato, E. M. (1984b). Reply to Thompson and Brassard. *School Psychology Review, 13*, 45-48.

Thompson, P. L., & Brassard, M. R. (1984). Cummings and Moscato soft on Woodcock-Johnson. *School Psychology Review, 13*, 41-44.

Woodcock, R. W. (1984). A response to some questions raised about the Woodcock-Johnson I. The mean score discrepancy issue. *School Psychology Review, 13*, 342-354.

Horn, J. L. (1985). Remodeling old models of intelligence. In B. B. Wolman (Ed.), *Handbook of intelligence* (pp. 267-300). New York: John Wiley & Sons.

Horn, J. L. (1988). Cognitive diversity: A framework of learning. In P. L. Ackerman, R. J. Sternberg, & R. Glaser (Eds.), *Learning and individual differences* (pp. 61-116). New York: W. H. Freeman.

Review of the Woodcock-Johnson Psycho-Educational Battery—Revised by STEVEN W. LEE, Associate Professor of Educational Psychology and Research, University of Kansas, Lawrence, KS, and ELAINE FLORY STEFANY, Certified School Psychologist, Lyons, KS:

The Woodcock-Johnson Psycho-Educational Battery—Revised (WJ-R) is a comprehensive measure of abilities and achievement spanning broad age ranges. The revised edition was normed on 6,359 subjects and represents a significant revision and expansion of the 1977 edition. The norming procedures are excellent and include the following randomly stratified variables: census region, community size, sex, race, origin, funding of college/university, type of college/university, education of adults, occupational status of adults, and occupation of adults in the labor force. Studies are cited which support the appropriateness of the WJ-R for special groups including learning disabled, mentally retarded, and gifted.

The authors state the test development measurement procedures are designed to ensure high technical quality and the *Standards for Educational and Psychological Testing* (American Educational Research Association, American Psychological Association, & National Council on Measurement in Education, 1985) were taken into account in developing the instrument. A review of the manuals supports this assertion.

Extensive information is provided in the test manuals. A spiral-bound examiner's manual and an additional book of norms tables accompany each of the two main sections, that is a measure of abilities (WJ-R COG) and a measure of achievement (WJ-R ACH). The examiner's manuals describe the underlying theory, test development, administration and scoring, interpretation, and reliability and validity studies. A 350-page technical manual covers both test sections and includes an appendix with additional supporting data and bibliographies.

The technical manual includes a section on theories of intelligence, with emphasis upon the Horn-Cattell Gf-Gc (fluid and crystallized abilities) theory of intellectual processing on which the WJ-R COG is based. Factor analytic support is provided for seven broad intellectual abilities, including Long-Term Retrieval, Short-Term Memory, Processing Speed, Auditory Processing, Visual Processing, Comprehension-Knowledge, and Fluid Reasoning. Evidence is provided that two of the cognitive subtests measure each of the seven broad abilities.

Detailed instructions for administration, including practice exercises and cautions, are given in the manuals. Specific wording for each item is color-coded on the reverse side of each page of the flip easel as it is shown to the subject. Some COG subtests are administered on audiotape to insure uniformity of presentation.

The authors describe the instrument as a tool kit intended for use in selective diagnostic testing. Each of the two main sections includes a standard and a supplemental battery bound in separate easels. Two forms of the achievement test (A and B) allow for more frequent retesting. However, no data regarding Form A and B equivalence are cited in the manual. Detailed statistics are given for finding significant discrepancies, both within the cognitive and achievement sections as well as ability/achievement discrepancies. The norming of the COG and ACH sections on the same sample reduces measurement error in finding discrepancies.

Subtest reliabilities are very good. Split-half procedures corrected for test length were used for all except the three timed subtests, on which test-retest correlations were used. Reliability coefficients are reported for all COG and ACH standard and supplementary subtests across age ranges. Forty-nine of the 55 median reliabilities reported are at the .80 level or higher. Standard errors of measurement are reported with reliabilities.

Many validity studies covering wide age ranges from preschool to adulthood are cited. These studies provide a broad variety of content, criterion-related, and construct validity evidence supporting the WJ-R. Besides the typical criterion-related validity information, extensive evidence is provided from confirmatory factor analytic studies.

A range of interpretive information is available for each subtest and cluster of subtests. The manual outlines the types of scores available with their levels of interpretation. After obtaining the raw score, grade and age level equivalents are available on the test blank without resorting to the norms tables. Also available on the test page is the W score, or Rasch Ability Score. Criterion-referenced statistics available in the norms tables include Rasch Difference Scores, Relative Mastery Indexes, Developmental Level

Band (WJ-R COG), and Instructional Ranges (WJ-R ACH). Norm-referenced statistics available include standard scores with a mean of 100 and standard deviation of 15, T-scores, NCEs, standard score discrepancies, and percentile ranks with discrepancies.

Overall, the WJ-R represents an outstanding contribution to the field of cognitive and achievement testing. Psychometric properties are exceptional. Some of its most notable advantages include the solid grounding in theory, the broad age range, the norming of the cognitive and achievement sections on the same sample to provide for more reliable comparisons, the usefulness for selective diagnostic assessment, and the broad variety of statistical data that may be obtained.

Any disadvantages of the WJ-R are fundamentally practical rather than technical. In order to be used effectively, the test necessitates a reorientation in philosophy and practice for evaluators and consumers accustomed to global measures of cognitive ability. Careful study and practice are essential before using the instrument. Otherwise, examiners might develop a routine subtest battery and fail to utilize its rich diagnostic potential. Because of the large amount of test materials (four stand-up easel books plus manuals), itinerant evaluators may find it a challenge to have appropriate sections of the test available for diagnostic testing when needed. Computer scoring is recommended, as hand scoring may become tedious and prone to error because of the large number of norms tables. Also, without computer scoring there may be a tendency for evaluators to obtain only the age and grade equivalent scores on the test form instead of taking advantage of the various statistics available.

Nevertheless, the advantages of the WJ-R far outweigh any disadvantages. The instrument represents a significant advancement in the field of cognitive and achievement testing, and it is this reviewer's hope that it will receive the attention and use that it deserves.

REVIEWER'S REFERENCE

American Educational Research Association, American Psychological Association, & National Council on Measurement in Education. (1985). *Standards for educational and psychological testing*. Washington, DC: American Psychological Association, Inc.

CONTRIBUTING TEST REVIEWERS

LEWIS R. AIKEN, Professor of Psychology, Pepperdine University, Malibu, CA

MARK ALBANESE, Adjunct Associate Professor of Biostatistics and Educational Statistics and Director, Office of Consultation and Research in Medical Education, The University of Iowa College of Medicine, Iowa City, IA

SARAH J. ALLEN, Assistant Professor of School Psychology and Counseling, University of Cincinnati, Cincinnati, OH

JULIE A. ALLISON, Assistant Professor of Psychology, Pittsburg State University, Pittsburg, KS

JOHN O. ANDERSON, Associate Professor, Faculty of Education, University of Victoria, Victoria, British Columbia, Canada

JERRILYN V. ANDREWS, Assistant for Assessment and Data Collection, Office of School Administration, Montgomery County Public Schools, Rockville, MD

F. MARION ASCHE, Professor of Education, Virginia Polytechnic Institute and State University, Blacksburg, VA

PHILIP ASH, Director, Ash, Blackstone and Cates, Blacksburg, VA

STEPHEN N. AXFORD, School Psychologist, Academy District Twenty, Colorado Springs, CO and Counseling Department Chair, University of Phoenix-Colorado Campus, Aurora, CO

SHERRY K. BAIN, Visiting Assistant Professor of Psychology, University of Southern Mississippi, Hattiesburg, MS

JANET BALDWIN, Assistant Director, GED Testing Program, Washington, DC

DEBORAH L. BANDALOS, Assistant Professor of Educational Psychology, University of Nebraska-Lincoln, Lincoln, NE

LAURA L. B. BARNES, Assistant Professor of Educational Research, Department of Applied Behavioral Studies, Oklahoma State University, Stillwater, OK

DAVID W. BARNETT, Professor of School Psychology, University of Cincinnati, Cincinnati, OH

RITA M. BARNETT, Teacher, Oak Hills Local School District, Cincinnati, OH

DAVID J. BATESON, Associate Professor of Mathematics and Science Education and the Educational Measurement Research Group, University of B.C., Vancouver, British Columbia, Canada

KATHRYN M. BENES, Licensed Psychologist, Lincoln, NE

RONALD A. BERK, Professor, School of Nursing, The Johns Hopkins University, Baltimore, MD

H. JOHN BERNARDIN, University Research Professor, College of Business, Florida Atlantic University, Boca Raton, FL

JEAN-JACQUES BERNIER, Full Professor, Department of Measurement and Evaluation, University Laval, Quebec, Quebec, Canada

LYNN S. BLISS, Professor of Communication Disorders and Sciences, Wayne State University, Detroit, MI

SONYA BLIXT, Professor of Evaluation and Measurement, Kent State University, Kent, OH

LISA A. BLOOM, Assistant Professor of Special Education, Western Carolina University, Cullowhee, NC

DAVID L. BOLTON, Assistant Professor for Education, West Chester University, West Chester, PA

STEPHEN J. BONEY, Assistant Professor of Communication Disorders, Department of Special Education and Communication Disorders, University of Nebraska-Lincoln, Lincoln, NE

J. DAVID BOYLE, Professor and Chairman, Department of Music Education and Music Therapy, School of Music, University of Miami, Coral Gables, FL

RIC BROWN, Acting Director, University Grants and Research Office, California State University, Fresno, Fresno, CA

ALBERT M. BUGAJ, Associate Professor of Psychology, University of Wisconsin—Marinette, Marinette, WI

MARY ANNE BUNDA, Professor Educational Leadership, Western Michigan University, Kalamazoo, MI

JOHN CHRISTIAN BUSCH, Associate Professor of Education, University of North Carolina at Greensboro, Greensboro, NC

WAYNE J. CAMARA, Director of Scientific Affairs, American Psychological Association, Washington, DC

KAREN T. CAREY, Associate Professor of Psychology, California State University, Fresno, Fresno, CA

C. DALE CARPENTER, Professor of Special Education, Western Carolina University, Cullowhee, NC

ELAINE CLARK, Associate Professor of Educational Psychology, University of Utah, Salt Lake City, UT

LARRY COCHRAN, Professor of Counseling Psychology, Faculty of Education, The University of British Columbia, Vancouver, British Columbia, Canada

ANDREW D. COHEN, Professor of English as a Second Language and Applied Linguistics, University of Minnesota, Minneapolis, MN

THEODORE COLADARCI, Associate Professor of Education, University of Maine, Orono, ME

JUDITH CONGER, Professor of Psychology and Director of Clinical Training, Purdue University, West Lafayette, IN

DONNA K. COOKE, Assistant Professor, College of Business, Florida Atlantic University, Boca Raton, FL

ALICE J. CORKILL, Assistant Professor of Counseling and Educational Psychology, University of Nevada, Las Vegas, NV

MERITH COSDEN, Associate Professor, Counseling/Clinical/School Psychology, Department of Education, University of California, Santa Barbara, CA

KEVIN D. CREHAN, Associate Professor of Educational Psychology, University of Nevada, Las Vegas, Las Vegas, NV

LAWRENCE H. CROSS, Associate Professor of Educational Research and Measurement, Virginia Polytechnic Institute and State University, Blacksburg, VA

SUSAN L. CROWLEY, Assistant Professor, Department of Psychology, Utah State University, Logan, UT

JACK A. CUMMINGS, Chair, Department of Counseling and Educational Psychology, Indiana University, Bloomington, IN

LARRY G. DANIEL, Associate Professor of Educational Leadership and Research, University of Southern Mississippi, Hattiesburg, MS

MARK H. DANIEL, Senior Scientist, American Guidance Service, Circle Pines, MN

WILLIAM W. DEARDORFF, Clinical Director, Spine Pain Program, West Coast Spine Institute, Los Angeles, CA

THOMAS E. DINERO, Associate Professor of Evaluation and Measurement, Kent State University, Kent, OH

GREGORY H. DOBBINS, Associate Professor of Management, The University of Tennessee at Knoxville, Knoxville, TN

BETH DOLL, Assistant Professor of School Psychology, University of Colorado at Denver, Denver, CO

GEORGE DOMINO, Professor of Psychology, University of Arizona, Tucson, AZ

E. THOMAS DOWD, Professor and Director of Counseling Psychology, Kent State University, Kent, OH

PENELOPE W. DRALLE, Associate Professor of Psychiatry, Louisiana State University School of Medicine, Department of Psychiatry and Psychology, New Orleans, LA

ROBERT J. DRUMMOND, Professor of Counselor Education, University of North Florida, Jacksonville, FL

CYNTHIA ANN DRUVA-ROUSH, Assistant Director, Evaluation and Examination Service, The University of Iowa, Iowa City, IA

DEL EBERHARDT, Program Administrator, Greenwich Public Schools, Greenwich, CT

ALLEN JACK EDWARDS, Professor of Psychology, Southwest Missouri State University, Springfield, MO

BRADLEY ELISON, Partial Hospitalization Program Team Leader, Virginia Treatment Center for Children, Virginia Commonwealth University, Richmond, VA

CLAIRE B. ERNHART, Professor of Psychiatry, Case Western Reserve University and MetroHealth Medical Center, Cleveland, OH

JENNIFER J. FAGER, Assistant Professor of Education, College of Education and Counseling, South Dakota State University, Brookings, SD

DOREEN WARD FAIRBANK, Adjunct Assistant Professor of Psychology, Meredith College, Raleigh, NC

NORMAN FREDMAN, Professor and Coordinator, Counselor Education Program, Queens College, City University of New York, Flushing, NY

MICHAEL FURLONG, Associate Professor, Graduate School of Education, University of California, Santa Barbara, Santa Barbara, CA

JERRY S. GILMER, Assistant Research Scientist, College of Medicine, The University of Iowa, Iowa City, IA

BERT A. GOLDMAN, Professor of Education, University of North Carolina at Greensboro, Greensboro, NC

HARRISON G. GOUGH, Professor of Psychology, Emeritus, University of California, Berkeley, Berkeley, CA

KATHY E. GREEN, Associate Professor of Education, University of Denver, Denver, CO

ROBERT M. GUION, Distinguished University Professor Emeritus, Bowling Green State University, Bowling Green, OH

ARLEN R. GULLICKSON, Professor, Western Michigan University, Kalamazoo, MI

THOMAS W. GUYETTE, Assistant Professor of Speech Pathology, University of Illinois at Chicago, Chicago, IL

STUART N. HART, Associate Professor of Counseling and Educational Psychology, Indiana University-Purdue University at Indianapolis, Indianapolis, IN

JOHN HATTIE, Professor of Education, The University of Western Australia, Nedlands, Australia

WILLIAM O. HAYNES, Professor of Communication Disorders, Auburn University, Auburn, AL

MARTINE HÉBERT, Assistant Professor, Department of Measurement and Evaluation, University Laval, Quebec, Quebec, Canada

CHARLES HOUSTON, Director of Planning and Research, Virginia Western Community College, Roanoke, VA

STEPHEN H. IVENS, Executive Director, DRP Services, Touchstone Applied Science Associates, Brewster, NY

RICHARD W. JOHNSON, Adjunct Professor of Counseling Psychology and Associate Director of Counseling & Consultation Center, University of Wisconsin-Madison, Madison, WI

JAMES A. JONES, Doctoral Candidate and Graduate Assistant in Evaluation and Measurement, Kent State University, Kent, OH

JAVAID KAISER, Associate Professor of Education, Virginia Polytechnic Institute & State University, Blacksburg, VA

RANDY W. KAMPHAUS, Associate Professor of Educational Psychology, University of Georgia, Athens, GA

MITCHELL KARNO, Doctoral Student, Graduate School of Education, University of California, Santa Barbara, Santa Barbara, CA

KATHRYN W. KENNEY, Director, Kenney Associates, Certified Speech-Language Pathologists, Gilbert, AZ

BARBARA KERR, Professor of Psychology in Education, Arizona State University, Tempe, AZ

JOHN D. KING, Professor of Special Education and Educational Administration, The University of Texas at Austin, Austin, TX

SUZANNE KING, Assistant Professor of Psychiatry, McGill University, Montreal, Quebec, Canada

STEPHEN L. KOFFLER, Managing Director, Center for Occupational and Professional Assessment, Educational Testing Service, Princeton, NJ

JOHN H. KRANZLER, Assistant Professor of Education, University of Florida, Gainesville, FL

S. DAVID KRISKA, Personnel Psychologist, City of Columbus, Columbus, OH

STEVEN W. LEE, Associate Professor of Educational Psychology and Research, University of Kansas, Lawrence, KS,

SUE M. LEGG, Associate Director, Office of Instructional Resources, University of Florida, Gainesville, FL

IRVIN J. LEHMANN, Professor of Measurement, Michigan State University, East Lansing, MI

STEVEN H. LONG, Assistant Professor of Speech Pathology & Audiology, Ithaca College, Ithaca, NY

BRENDA H. LOYD, Professor of Education, University of Virginia, Charlottesville, VA

CAROLINE MANUELLE-ADKINS, Professor, Department of Educational Foundations and Counseling Programs, Hunter College, City University of New York, New York, NY

GREGROY J. MARCHANT, Associate Professor of Educational Psychology, Ball State University, Muncie, IN

SUZANNE MARKEL-FOX, Post Doctoral Fellow, Center for Mental Health Policies and Services Research, University of Pennsylvania, Philadelphia, PA

KEVIN J. MCCARTHY, Department of Psychiatry and Psychology, Louisiana State University School of Medicine, New Orleans, LA

DAVID E. MCINTOSH, Assistant Professor of School Psychology, Department of Applied Behavioral Studies, Oklahoma State University, Stillwater, OK

ROBERT F. MCMORRIS, Professor of Educational Psychology and Statistics, State University of New York at Albany, Albany, NY

SHARON MCNEELY, Associate Professor of Educational Foundations, Northeastern Illinois University, Chicago, IL

SCOTT MEIER, Associate Professor, Counseling and Educational Psychology, State University of New York at Buffalo, Buffalo, NY

WILLIAM B. MICHAEL, Professor of Education and Psychology, University of Southern California, Los Angeles, CA

M. DAVID MILLER, Associate Professor of Foundations of Education, University of Florida, Gainesville, FL

GALE M. MORRISON, Associate Professor of Education, Graduate School of Education, University of California, Santa Barbara, CA

KEVIN R. MURPHY, Professor of Psychology, Colorado State University, Fort Collins, CO

PHILIP NAGY, Associate Professor of Measurement, Evaluation, and Computer Applications, The Ontario Institute for Studies in Education, Toronto, Ontario, Canada

LOIS NICHOLS, Teacher of Gifted and Talented, Oak Hills Local School District, Cincinnati, OH

STEPHEN OLEJNIK, Professor of Educational Psychology, University of Georgia, Athens, GA

D. JOE OLMI, Assistant Professor of School Psychology, Department of Psychology, University of Southern Mississippi, Hattiesburg, MS

DOUGLAS A. PENFIELD, Professor of Education, Graduate School of Education, Rutgers University, New Brunswick, NJ

LEADELLE PHELPS, Associate Professor and Director, School Psychology Program, Department of Counseling and Educational Psychology, State University of New York at Buffalo, Buffalo, NY

MARK POPE, President, Career Decisions, San Francisco, CA

RUDOLF E. RADOCY, Professor of Music Education and Music Therapy, University of Kansas, Lawrence, KS

MICHAEL J. ROSZKOWSKI, Director of Marketing Research and Associate Professor of Psychology, The American College, Bryn Mawr, PA

BARBARA A. ROTHLISBERG, Associate Professor of Psychology in Educational Psychology and School Psychology I Program Director, Ball State University, Muncie, IN

JAMES B. ROUNDS, Associate Professor of Educational Psychology, University of Illinois at Urbana-Champaign, Champaign, IL

HERBERT C. RUDMAN, Professor of Measurement and Quantitative Methods, Department of Counseling, Educational Psychology and Special Education, Michigan State University, East Lansing, MI

JOHN RUST, Senior Lecturer in Psychometrics, Goldsmith's College, University of London, London, England

DARRELL L. SABERS, Professor of Educational Psychology, University of Arizona, Tucson, AZ

PERRY SAILOR, Research Associate, Department of Psychology, Utah State University, Logan, UT

DALE P. SCANNELL, Professor of Education, University of Maryland at College Park, College Park, MD

STEVEN SCHINKE, Professor, Columbia University School of Social Work, New York, NY

GREGORY SCHRAW, Assistant Professor of Educational Psychology, University of Nebraska-Lincoln, Lincoln, NE

GENE SCHWARTING, Project Director of Early Childhood Special Education, Omaha Public Schools, Omaha, NE

DAVID A. SHAPIRO, Associate Professor of Communication Disorders, Department of Human Services, College of Education and Psychology, Western Carolina University, Cullowhee, NC

STEVEN R. SHAW, Assistant Professor of Psychology, Illinois State University, Normal, IL

JOHN W. SHEPARD, Associate Professor of Counselor Education, The University of Toledo, Toledo, OH

AGNES E. SHINE, Assistant Professor of Educational Psychology, Mississippi State University, Mississippi State, MS

JEFFREY K. SMITH, Professor of Educational Psychology, Graduate School of Education, Rutgers, the State University, New Brunswick, NJ

MICHAEL J. SPORAKOWSKI, Professor of Family and Child Development, Virginia Polytechnic Institute and State University, Blacksburg, VA

SCOTT SPREAT, Administrator of Clinical Services, The Woods Schools, Langhorne, PA

ELAINE FLORY STEFANY, Certified School Psychologist, Lyons, KS

HARLAN J. STIENTJES, School Psychologist, Grant Wood Area Education Agency, Cedar Rapids, IA

CHRISTINE F. STRAUSS, Graduate Assistant in Evaluation and Measurement, Kent State University, Kent, OH

DONNA L. SUNDRE, Associate Assessment Specialist/Assistant Professor of Psychology, James Madison University, Harrisonburg, VA

MARK E. SWERDLIK, Professor of Psychology, Illinois State University, Normal, IL

CATHY TELZROW, Psychologist and Director, Educational Assessment Project, Cuyahoga Special Education Service Center, Cleveland, OH

DONALD THOMPSON, Professor of Counseling Psychology, School of Education, The University of Connecticut, Storrs, CT

GEORGE C. THORNTON III, Professor of Psychology, Colorado State University, Ft. Collins, CO

GERALD TINDAL, Associate Professor of Special Education, University of Oregon, Eugene, OR

ESTHER STAVROU TOUBANOS, School Psychologist, Lawrence Public Schools, Lawrence, NY

LAWRENCE J. TURTON, Professor of Speech-Language Pathology, Indiana University of Pennsylvania, Indiana, PA

SUSANA URBINA, Associate Professor of Psychology, University of North Florida, Jacksonville, FL

NICHOLAS A. VACC, Professor and Chairperson, Department of Counselor Education, University of North Carolina at Greensboro, Greensboro, NC

T. STEUART WATSON, Assistant Professor of Educational Psychology, Mississippi State University, Starkville, MS

LARRY WEBER, Professor of Education, Virginia Tech, Blacksburg, VA

ELLEN WEISSINGER, Associate Professor of Educational Psychology, University of Nebraska-Lincoln, Lincoln, NE

BERT W. WESTBROOK, Professor of Psychology, North Carolina State University, Raleigh, NC

CAROL E. WESTBY, Senior Research Associate, Training and Technical Assistance Unit, University of New Mexico Medical School, Albuquerque, NM

TERRY M. WILDMAN, Professor of Curriculum and Instruction, Virginia Polytechnic Institute, Blacksburg, VA

ROBERT T. WILLIAMS, Professor of Occupational and Educational Studies, Colorado State University, Fort Collins, CO

DONNA WITTMER, Assistant Professor of Education, University of Colorado-Denver, Denver, CO

BLAINE R. WORTHEN, Professor and Chair, Research and Evaluation Methodology Program, Department of Psychology, Utah State University, Logan, UT

TAMELA YELLAND, Psychologist, Veterans Administration, Anaheim Vet Center, Anaheim, CA

JOHN W. YOUNG, Assistant Professor of Educational Statistics and Measurement, Rutgers University, New Brunswick, NJ

JAMES E. YSSELDYKE, Director, National Center on Educational Outcomes, University of Minnesota, Minneapolis, MN

INDEX OF TITLES

This title index lists all the tests included in The Supplement to the Eleventh Mental Measurements Yearbook. *Citations are to test entry numbers, not to pages—e.g., 54 refers to test 54 and not page 54. (Test numbers along with test titles are indicated in the running heads at the top of each page, and page numbers, used only in the Table of Contents but not in the indexes, appear at the bottom of each page.) Superseded titles are listed with cross references to current titles, and alternative titles are also cross referenced.*

INDEX OF ACRONYMS

This Index of Acronyms refers the reader to the appropriate test in The Supplement to the Eleventh Mental Measurements Yearbook. *In some cases tests are better known by their acronyms than by their full titles, and this index can be of substantial help to the person who knows the former but not the latter. Acronyms are only listed if the author or publisher has made substantial use of the acronym in referring to the test, or if the test is widely known by the acronym. A few acronyms are also registered trademarks (e.g., SAT); where this is known to us, only the test with the registered trademark is referenced. There is some danger in the overuse of acronyms, but this index, like all other indexes in this work, is provided to make the task of identifying a test as easy as possible. All numbers refer to test numbers, not page numbers.*

ACO: Assessment of Conceptual Organization (ACO): Improving Writing, Thinking, and Reading Skills, 5
AMI: Athletic Motivation Inventory, 6
AUI: Alcohol Use Inventory, 4

BBTOP: Bankson-Bernthal Test of Phonology, 8
BDIS: Behavior Disorders Identification Scale, 11
BES-2: Behavior Evaluation Scale—2, 12
BPI: Basic Personality Inventory, 9
BRI: Basic Reading Inventory, Fifth Edition, 10
BRP-2: Behavior Rating Profile, Second Edition, 13

CAAS: Children's Attention and Adjustment Survey, 21
CAT: Children's Articulation Test, 20
CBI: Career Beliefs Inventory, 19
CCAT: Canadian Cognitive Abilities Test, Form 7, 17
CCQ: Chronicle Career Quest™, 23
CCTST: California Critical Thinking Skills Test, 15
CISE: Children's Inventory of Self-Esteem, 22
CLI: Campbell Leadership Index, 16

DAB-2: Diagnostic Achievement Battery, Second Edition, 30

DAP:SPED: Draw A Person: Screening Procedure for Emotional Disturbance, 33
DAR: Diagnostic Assessments of Reading, 31
DAT: Dental Admission Test, 25
DFTT: Digital Finger Tapping Test, 32
DIAL-R: Developmental Indicators for the Assessment of Learning—Revised/AGS Edition, 28
DPP: Dropout Prediction & Prevention, 34
DSC: Developing Skills Checklist, 27
DTLA-A: Detroit Tests of Learning Aptitude—Adult, 26

EASIC: Revised Evaluating Acquired Skills in Communication, 75
EDI: Eating Disorder Inventory-2, 36
ESA: Early School Assessment, 35

FES: Family Environment Scale, Second Edition, 41

K-BIT: Kaufman Brief Intelligence Test, 46

LAW R/W: Language Assessment Scales, Reading and Writing, 48
LBAII: Leader Behavior Analysis II, 49

297

CLASSIFIED SUBJECT INDEX

The Classified Subject Index classifies all tests included in The Supplement to the Eleventh Mental Measurements Yearbook into 16 major categories: Achievement, Behavior Assessment, Developmental, Education, English, Fine Arts, Foreign Languages, Intelligence and Scholastic Aptitude, Miscellaneous, Neuropsychological, Personality, Reading, Sensory Motor, Social Studies, Speech and Hearing, and Vocations. Each category appears in alphabetical order and tests are ordered alphabetically within each category. Each test entry includes test title (first letter capitalized), population for which the test is intended (lower case), and the test entry number in The Supplement to the Eleventh Mental Measurements Yearbook. All numbers refer to test entry numbers, not to page numbers. Brief suggestions for the use of this index are presented in the introduction.

ACHIEVEMENT

BEHAVIOR ASSESSMENT

DEVELOPMENTAL

EDUCATION

ENGLISH

FINE ARTS

FOREIGN LANGUAGES

INTELLIGENCE AND SCHOLASTIC APTITUDE

ACER Advanced Test B90: New Zealand Edition, college students and adults, see 1

ACER Test of Reasoning Ability, educational years 9–11 in Australian school system, see 2

California Critical Thinking Skills Test, college and adult, see 15

Canadian Cognitive Abilities Test, Form 7, grades K–2, 3–12, see 17

Detroit Tests of Learning Aptitude—Adult, ages 16-0 and over, see 26

Henmon-Nelson Ability Test, Canadian Edition, grades 3–6, 6–9, 9–12, see 44

Kaufman Brief Intelligence Test, ages 4–90, see 46

Learning Efficiency Test-II (1992 Revision), ages 5–75, see 50

Memory Assessment Scales, ages 18 and over, see 55

Primary Test of Cognitive Skills, grades K–1, see 67

Screening Assessment for Gifted Elementary Students—Primary, ages 5-0 to 8-11, see 81

Slosson Intelligence Test [1991 Edition], ages 4-0 and over, see 84

Woodcock-Johnson Psycho-Educational Battery—Revised, ages 2–90, see 101

MISCELLANEOUS

Family Environment Scale, Second Edition, family members, see 41

Life Experiences Checklist, adults, see 54

Personal Experience Screening Questionnaire, adolescents, see 63

The Time-Sample Behavioral Checklist, adults in residential treatment settings, see 97

NEUROPSYCHOLOGICAL

Digital Finger Tapping Test, individuals with potential cortical damage or impairment, see 32

Philadelphia Head Injury Questionnaire, head trauma patients, see 64

PERSONALITY

Alcohol Use Inventory, adults and adolescents 16 years of age and over, see 4

Athletic Motivation Inventory, male and female athletes ages 13 and older and coaches, see 6

Basic Personality Inventory, ages 12 and over, see 9

Campbell Leadership Index, leaders, see 16

Career Beliefs Inventory, junior high school and over, see 19

Children's Inventory of Self-Esteem, ages 5–12, see 22

Draw A Person: Screening Procedure for Emotional Disturbance, ages 6–17, see 33

Eating Disorder Inventory-2, ages 12 and over, see 36

Executive Profile Survey, prospective executives, see 40

Learning Style Profile, see 52

The Leisure Diagnostic Battery, ages 9–18, adult, see 53

Menstrual Distress Questionnaire, women who experience strong to severe premenstrual or menstrual distress, see 56

Meyer-Kendall Assessment Survey, business employees and job applicants, see 57

The Mother-Child Relationship Evaluation, 1980 Edition, mothers, see 58

Partner Relationship Inventory (Research Edition), married couples, see 62

READING

SENSORY-MOTOR

SOCIAL STUDIES

SPEECH AND HEARING

VOCATIONS

PUBLISHERS DIRECTORY AND INDEX

This directory and index give the addresses and test entry numbers of all publishers represented in The Supplement to the Eleventh Mental Measurements Yearbook. *Please note that all numbers in this index refer to test entry numbers, not page numbers. Publishers are an important source of information about catalogs, specimen sets, price changes, test revisions, and many other matters.*

Institute of Athletic Motivation, 1 Lagoon Drive—Suite 141, Redwood Shores, CA 94065: 6

Kendall/Hunt Publishing Company, 4050 Westmark Drive, P.O. Box 1840, Dubuque, IA 52004-1840: 10

MAT, Boston University, School of Music, 855 Commonwealth Ave., Boston, MA 02215: 59

MetriTech, Inc., 111 N. Market Street, Champaign, IL 61820: 61

Modern Curriculum Press, Customer Service Department, 13900 Prospect Road, Cleveland, OH 44136: 29

National Association of Secondary School Principals, P.O. Box 3250, 1904 Association Drive, Reston, VA 22091-1598: 52

NCS Assessments, P.O. Box 1416, Minneapolis, MN 55440: 4, 16

Nelson Canada, 1120 Birchmount Road, Scarborough, Ontario M1K 5G4, Canada: 17, 44, 76, 100

New Zealand Council for Educational Research, Education House West, 178-182 Willis Street, P.O. Box 3237, Wellington, New Zealand: 1, 70

NFER-Nelson Publishing Co., Ltd., Darville House, 2 Oxford Road East, Windsor, Berkshire SL4 1DF, England: 7, 54

Phylmar Associates, Educational Publishers and Consultants, 191 Iroquois Avenue, London, Ontario N6C 2K9, Canada: 68, 93

Piney Mountain Press, Inc., P.O. Box 333, Cleveland, GA 30528: 66, 99

PRO-ED, Inc., 8700 Shoal Creek Blvd., Austin, TX 78758-6897: 13, 26, 30, 33, 60, 71, 81, 82, 87, 95, 96

Psychological Assessment Resources, Inc., P.O. Box 998, Odessa, FL 33556-0998: 36, 55

Reid Psychological Systems, 200 South Michigan Avenue, Sutie 900, Chicago, IL 6060402401: 72

Research for Better Schools, Inc., 444 North Third Street, Philadelphia, PA 19123-4107: 5

Research Press, Dept. G., Box 9177, Champaign, IL 61826: 97

Richardson, Bellows, Henry & Co., Inc., 1140 Connecticut Ave., N.W., Washington, DC 20036: 18

The Riverside Publishing Co., 8420 Bryn Mawr Avenue, Chicago, IL 60631: 8, 24, 31, 38, 101

The SASSI Institute, P.O. Box 5069, Bloomington, IN 47407: 90

Saville & Holdsworth Ltd USA, Inc., 575 Boylston Street, Boston, MA 02116: 77

Scholastic Testing Service, Inc., 480 Meyer Road, Bensenville, IL 60106-1617: 79

Sigma Assessment Systems, Inc., Research Psychologists Press Division, 1110 Military St., P.O. Box 610984, Port Huron, MI 48061-0984: 9

Slosson Educational Publications, Inc., P.O. Box 280, East Aurora, NY 14052-0280: 84, 85

Teleometrics International, 1755 Woodstead Court, The Woodlands, TX 77380: 94

Therapy Skill Builders, 3830 E. Bellevue, P.O. Box 42050, Tucson, AZ 85733: 39

United/DOK Publishers, P.O. Box 1099, Buffalo, NY 14224: 37, 42

University of Washington Press, P.O. Box 50096, 4045 Brooklyn Avenue NE, Seattle, WA 98145-5096: 51

Western Psychological Services, 12031 Wilshire Blvd., Los Angeles, CA 90025-1251: 32, 56, 57, 58, 63, 64, 69

Wonderlic Personnel Test, Inc., 1509 N. Milwaukee Avenue, Libertyville, IL 60048-1380: 43

INDEX OF NAMES

This analytical index indicates whether a citation refers to authorship of a test, a test review, or a reference for a specific test. Numbers refer to test entries, not to pages. The abbreviations and numbers following the names may be interpreted as follows: "test, 73" indicates authorship of test 73; "rev, 86" indicates authorship of a review of test 86; "ref, 13r" indicates a reference (unnumbered) in one of the "Reviewer's References" sections for test 13. Names mentioned in cross references are also indexed.

Abidin, R. R.: ref, 58r
Achenbach, T.: ref, 86r
Achenbach, T. M.: ref, 21r
ACT Career Planning Services: test, 100
Adelman, H. S.: ref, 3r
Ager, A.: test, 54
Aiken, L. R.: rev, 81
Albanese, M.: rev, 64
Allen, S. J.: rev, 13
Allison, J. A.: rev, 41, 91
American Educational Research Association: ref, 34r, 39r, 43r, 63r, 66r, 77r, 81r, 88r, 90r, 94r, 97r, 98r, 101r
American Guidance Service: ref, 86r
American Psychiatric Association: ref, 21r, 36r, 78r
American Psychological Association: ref, 34r, 39r, 43r, 63r, 66r, 77r, 81r, 88r, 90r, 94r, 97r, 98r, 101r
Anastasi, A.: rev, 44; ref, 43r
Anderhalter, O. F.: test, 79
Anderson, J.: ref, 46r
Anderson, J. O.: rev, 17, 44
Anderson, K. L.: test, 82
Andreasen, N. C.: test, 78; ref, 78r
Andrews, J. V.: rev, 10, 68
Angoff, W. H.: ref, 46r
APA Task Force: ref, 72r
Arndt, S.: ref, 78r
Arnold, D.: test, 72

Asche, F. M.: rev, 18, 45
Ash, P.: rev, 36; ref, 72r
Astin, A. W.: rev, 88
Atwater, L. E.: ref, 49r
Australian Council for Educational Research: test, 1
Axford, S. N.: rev, 74

Bachman, L. F.: ref, 65r
Bacon, E. H.: ref, 13r
Bagnato, S. J.: rev, 73; ref, 73r
Bain, S. K.: rev, 67
Baldwin, J.: rev, 25
Balla, D. A.: ref, 3r
Bandalos, D. L.: rev, 5
Bankson, N.: test, 8
Bankson, N. W.: ref, 8r
Barclay, J. R.: test, 61
Barclay, L. K.: test, 61
Bardos, A. N.: test, 33
Barnes, L. L. B.: rev, 60, 67
Barnett, D. W.: rev, 3, 28, 42; ref, 3r
Barnett, R. M.: rev, 42
Bateson, D. J.: rev, 44, 100
Beery, K. E.: test, 29
Bell, J. E.: rev, 58; ref, 58r
Benes, K. M.: rev, 86
Benner, S. M.: ref, 73r

307

SCORE INDEX

This Score Index lists all the scores, in alphabetical order, for all the tests included in The Supplement to the Eleventh Mental Measurements Yearbook. Because test scores can be regarded as operational definitions of the variable measured, sometimes the scores provide better leads to what a test actually measures than the test title or other available information. The Score Index is very detailed, and the reader should keep in mind that a given variable (or concept) of interest may be defined in several different ways. Thus the reader should look up these several possible alternative definitions before drawing final conclusions about whether tests measuring a particular variable of interest can be located in the 11MMY-S. If the kind of score sought is located in a particular test or tests, the reader should then read the test descriptive information carefully to determine whether the test(s) in which the score is found is (are) consistent with reader purpose. Used wisely, the Score Index can be another useful resource in locating the right score in the right test. As usual, all numbers in the index are test numbers, not page numbers.